D0207471

A HISTORY OF
JAPANESE LITERATURE

VOLUME ONE
The Archaic and
Ancient Ages

A History of
Japanese Literature

VOLUME ONE
THE ARCHAIC AND
ANCIENT AGES

By Jin'ichi Konishi

TRANSLATED BY
Aileen Gatten AND
Nicholas Teele

EDITED BY
Earl Miner

PRINCETON UNIVERSITY PRESS

Published by Princeton University Press, 41 William Street,
Princeton, New Jersey 08540
In the United Kingdom: Princeton University Press,
Guildford, Surrey

ISBN 0-691-06592-6 (clothbound). 10146-9 (limited paperback edition)

Publication of this book has been aided by a grant from
The Andrew W. Mellon Foundation

The publisher and author wish to thank
the Japan Foundation for its support

This book has been composed in Linotron Sabon

Printed in the United States of America by
Princeton University Press
Princeton, New Jersey

TO THE MEMORY OF

Sir George Sansom

CONTENTS

LIST OF TABLES AND ILLUSTRATIONS

TABLES

MAP

FRONTISPIECE

A young lady under a flowering tree (8th century screen painting).
Known as "The Lady with the Feathered Robe," although
the feathers have disappeared. In the Shōsōin (Royal Household
Museum, Nara). By courtesy of the Royal Household and
Kōdansha publishers, Japan

FIGURES

Figures 3, 4, 7, and 8 by courtesy of Kōdansha publishers, Japan

AUTHOR'S PREFACE

This first volume of *A History of Japanese Literature* initiates a planned series of five. It deals with the Archaic and Ancient Ages, and subsequent volumes will follow—with exceptions that must be mentioned—in chronological order. Because this account of Japanese literature is comparative and because it defines Japanese literature to include Ainu and Ryukyuan literature, discussions of the "ancient" periods of Japanese, Chinese, Korean, Ainu, and Ryukyuan literatures refer to *conceptual* elements. In other words, what is ancient in Chinese literature is taken to predate what is ancient in Japanese, and what is ancient in Japanese predates what is ancient in Ainu and Ryukyuan. For comparative and conceptual purposes, a volume on ancient Japanese literature must therefore refer to different years of Western reckoning for each of the literatures discussed. This is explained in detail in the General Introduction, but it is also a matter of sufficient importance to require explicit mention here.

In this and subsequent volumes chronology will also be violated for interpretive and comparative purposes. In this volume such violation is relatively small, amounting to little more than comparison of the poetry of the *Man'yōshū* (interpreted in terms of the age in which it was written) with some modern interpretations (based on modern criteria). Since some of the modern interpreters of the *Man'yōshū* were themselves poets who wrote with the poetry of that collection as an ideal, it has seemed necessary to clarify the difference between their understanding and the actual historical and poetic nature of the *Man'yōshū*. This should pose no problems for readers of this volume, although examples in later volumes may prove to be more radical.

These departures from chronology literally considered owe something in my thought to T. S. Eliot's ideas as expressed in his essay "Tradition and the Individual Talent." Of course, he did not have Asian literature in mind, and his ideas have required considerable adaptation to be useful for my purposes.

In order to avoid possible misunderstandings, it has seemed best to make clear matters that might possibly confuse readers. If I dwell on them here, the chief reason is that this is the first volume.

As the Contents show, the main account of the Archaic and the Ancient Ages is here divided into four parts, consisting in all of eleven chapters. The aim is to recover as much as is now feasible from long-distant times and to present it in intelligible order guided by the historical principles introduced at the outset. Although this work is obviously a history, it has often seemed necessary not merely to relate and describe but also to analyze and evaluate. In such instances, my criteria will be explicit.

To save space, I have adopted two means of annotation. In the text there are parenthetical references—by author's name, date of work, and volume or page numbers—to works cited in the Bibliography at the end. By such means I can cite my indebtedness to others and direct readers who desire to explore a specific matter without unduly cluttering the page. On the other hand, more explanatory matters are handled in footnotes.

Further matters of importance are referred to in the dedication, my Acknowledgments, and the Editor's Foreword.

J. K.

The Library of Congress
Washington, D.C.

May 1982

AUTHOR'S ACKNOWLEDGMENTS

I would like to offer my heartfelt thanks above all to the late George Sansom, who effected the scholarly bond between Earl Miner and myself. If Sir George had not generously invited me to Stanford University in 1957, this work would probably never have come into being.

The considerable and still undisclosed efforts made at that time by Professor Donald Keene in connection with my visit to Stanford are also the object of my unforgettable gratitude. I have, in fact, benefited twofold from Professor Keene, in that he also gave me the direct motivation for writing this work.

During my two years at Stanford, I learned a great deal from Earl about literary criticism. This, together with what he taught me in later years, plays a vital role in this work. Yet I would hardly have been able to comprehend Earl's instruction without the presence, at that time, of Robert H. Brower, then at Stanford. It is thanks to Bob that I was able, despite my poor English, to master difficult critical theories over a relatively short time.

Those years at Stanford, blessed by good friends, were the finest of my life. There was further cause for gratitude in the warmth and cordiality given by Professor John D. Goheen to my family and me, as well as in the kindness of the late Professors Arthur F. and Mary C. Wright, of Professor Thomas C. Smith, and of Professor Nobutaka Ike. The gracious academic life I enjoyed through their good offices became an important if indirect impetus in the writing of this work.

Since then I have visited the United States six times. Each time my desire has grown stronger to publish a work in English on Japanese literature. Spurred on by Professor Keene, I decided to write the volumes of this envisioned history, and in 1980 I was able to conduct a short period of research at Princeton University. My objective was to examine research materials not available in Japan. This first volume, in particular, is considerably based on data obtained at Princeton. I am greatly indebted here to Earl and to Marius Jansen, another close friend since 1957, as well as to many other people.

In addition, on a short visit to the University of Michigan I obtained the kind cooperation of Mr. Masaei Saitō and other officials of the Graduate Library. Needless to say, Bob Brower administered to my every convenience.

During six months of 1982 I have been in the United States as a resident member of the Council of Scholars at the Library of Congress. To me there is no greater delight than the opportunity to utilize freely the manifold resources of this, the largest library in the world. I must express my sincere gratitude for the kindness shown me there, especially by the Librarian of the Congress, Dr. Daniel J. Boorstin, and by Dr. Warren M. Tsuneishi, Dr. James H. Hutson, and Mr. Hisao Matsumoto.

Chinese culture exerted an enormous influence on early Japanese literature. In addition to this direct impact, a Koreanized version of Chinese culture, communicated to Japan via Korea, also made fundamental contributions to Japanese literature. This is an area in which I have been strongly interested. Yet despite the geographical proximity of Japan to Korea, the books necessary to carry out Korean studies in Japan are, regrettably, exceedingly scarce. Through the kindness of Professor Kim Chi-gyu and his colleagues at Korea University I obtained considerable source materials, but certainly not enough to suffice. The Korean collection at the Library of Congress is, however, like its Chinese collection, extraordinarily fine: my concerns were resolved at a single stroke.

My heartfelt thanks are also due to Professor Peter H. Lee of the University of Hawaii for his assistance in Korean and other linguistic matters; to Professor Shuen-fu Lin of the University of Michigan for his fine-tuning of Chinese; to Drs. Key P. Yang and Sung Yoon Cho of the Library of Congress for their generous cooperation on the question of the romanization of Korean; and to Professor Kang Tong-jin of the University of Tsukuba.

Funds for the English translation of this work were provided by the Japanese Ministry of Education. Assistance was also provided by the Japan Foundation and the Japan-U.S. Friendship Commission for research activities. Without this material assistance provided by both the Japanese and United States government agencies, publication of this work would have been nearly impossible.

I would like also to state my warm thanks to the Executive Office of the Shōsōin for giving its permission to publish, as the frontispiece to this volume, a photograph of the Torige Tachi Onna (picture of a standing woman, her robe decorated with feathers), and also for their loan of its photographic negatives.

J. K.

EDITOR'S FOREWORD

The chronological range of Japanese literature is somewhat greater than that of English literature. The main differences are of other kinds: what is assumed of authorship, the grounds of value, genres practiced and their patterns of emergence, philosophical assumptions, and various human, cultural emphases. In terms of these differences and in terms of a determination to write a volume a year of his *History of Japanese Literature*, our author has undertaken a heroic task. His readers will wish to know something about him, about features of the enterprise, and perhaps about those of us involved in putting this version into English.

The title page gives the names. "Jin'ichi Konishi" specifies the author, although with his surname after his given name, in a fashion opposite to that of all other Japanese names in this and succeeding volumes. "Konishi Jin'ichi" is a name familiar in Japan and the United States, the name of one who has written extensively on Japanese literature from its earliest stages, who is known as a haiku poet, and who has been involved with the stage as writer and actor. Professor Konishi became known to some of us when, in 1956, Donald Keene wrote that he had read a brief book by Konishi, *Nihon Bungakushi* which, Keene said, stood out for quality from other histories of Japanese literature. If that earlier work had been translated it would bear the same English title as this work, although for reasons given in the preface to that book and made explicit in this *History*, Professor Konishi prefers to designate his subject as *Nihon Bungeishi*. "Bungei" emphasizes Japanese literature rather than its study. In this, he shows awareness of changes in the meaning of "literature" in English as well as in Japanese.

That earlier brief book went through numerous reprintings before its publisher went out of business. Many of us discovered that it offered what Professor Keene said it did—an account brief, lucid, and independent in view. The lucidity and independence of mind will certainly be found in this work thirty years later, but the brevity has given way to a plan for five volumes, each far longer than the earlier work. It is not irrelevant that Konishi and Keene have long been good friends and that, at mature stages in their careers, both have turned to writing their personal and different versions of the history of Japanese literature.

It bears remarking that many years have passed since full-scale histories of a European or of an American literature have been written with success. After one fashion or another, accounts of groups of poets or novelists or dramatists have been written in English, and accounts of historical subjects have certainly appeared in French and German. It is also true that Marxist students of literature have maintained a faith in what they like to term the concrete reality of history, including that of literature. But the dominant critical schools of Western European and American literary study have been clearly inimical to full literary histories. We have had biography. Perhaps in some readers' minds biography has been a substitute for the so-called classical realistic novel now so hard to find. It seems yet more likely that students of Western literature do not possess the heroic faith necessary to produce a full-scale history of English, French, or American literature.

It is also noteworthy that just as literary history seems so feasible in Japan, and just as distinguished biographies appear in English (on Diderot or Proust, for example), in Japan there have been few biographies such as we conceive of them. There is no dearth of Japanese books with a writer's name as title: Konishi's own *Sōgi* names the great writer of Japanese linked poetry (renga). But it and similarly titled books do not offer what we think of as biography. Our attention to the so-to-speak isolated, integral individual is one thing. The Japanese attention to the persons of writers in a historical continuum is another.

Many features of this present history are exceptional, beginning with the Japanese title. It and other matters are discussed in the General Introduction, a major section of this volume. Those unfamiliar with other histories of Japanese literature can scarcely guess what an extraordinary thing it is for one to begin with inquiry into the meaning of "history," "Japanese," and "literature." Or for an author to consider radically the problem of periodizing. For that matter, those of us who have read histories of Western national literature will find it difficult to recall other raising of these hard questions. My own knowledge of these matters is very imperfect, but it does seem to me that to find a Japanese precedent for the French preoccupation with a discourse on method one must go back to Motoori Norinaga (1730-1801). It may be no more than an accident that Norinaga and Konishi are from Ise, that cradle of independent-minded scholars.

This history is unusual in other respects. It is not surprising that it deals with Sino-Japanese literary relations. Konishi has written extensively on the Chinese presence in Japanese literature in various articles and books, no doubt most significantly in his edition and study, *Bunkyō Hifuron Kō*, two volumes presenting a particularly important and difficult work by one of the greatest Japanese thinkers, Kūkai (774-835). It was this that won Konishi the coveted Japan Academy Prize for literature at an extraordinarily young age. In addition, he pays unprecedented attention to Ainu and Ryukyuan writers as well as to achievements by those Korean writers who, in the period covered in this volume, were tutors of important Japanese writers.

The author's lucidity has always been a hallmark of his work. (Comments on our tampering with his sentences will be given later.) Like any language, Japanese can be written clearly or obscurely. No doubt clarity is as much a rhetorical stance as is the far easier obfuscation. But the choice of the former over the latter signals a respect for readers that is not epidemic today. One of the English poets whom Konishi likes, T. S. Eliot, seems to me to have expressed the aim of our author's style in a phrase (from the *Four Quartets*): "to purify the language of the tribe." Where purity and clarity fail in this history, the responsibility does not lie with the author but with us who have endeavored to put his ideas into English.

Yet the most remarkable feature of this history seems to me its daring candor. Konishi is wholly responsible in acknowledging what he takes from others. And he also makes clear in a mild or calm demeanor his disagreements with received wisdom, reassuring platitudes, and comfortable truisms. I once telephoned him from Princeton to Tokyo to ask if such-and-such were not the Mahāyāna theory of time. His answer was, "I think you have got it directly wrong" (Gyaku da to omou). This candor is a sign of true friendship. It will also cause tongues to wag when the five volumes of this work appear at once in Japan. As that sentence shows, this history is unusual in the likelihood of one or two volumes of the English version appearing before the original Japanese.

The title page shows that this volume has been translated by two people versed in early Japanese literature. It remains to say what parts each has rendered and what we have done with the original. Aileen Gatten has translated chapters one through seven, and Nicholas Teele what precedes and follows. I have taken it to be my duty as editor to impose a consistency of method and of style in both the ordinary and—so far as possible—the editorial senses. I have yielded to the translators in various ways. To give one example: for translations of Japanese, I have regularized to Gatten's format rather than follow my own notions. We have provided additional information, both in square brackets in the text and, more frequently, in similar brackets in the notes, where "Trans." or "Ed." indicates responsibility. It is in the nature of the case that we should have needed to add more material as explanation than what we needed to cut as of little use to readers of the translation. The cuts, where substantive, have been noted.

My aims as editor have been as modest as is my task. The first is that already mentioned, consistency. (We now have a style sheet.) And I have taken it as first desideratum the conveying of an old friend's thought in something like the American language of today. To that end I have tampered with his syntax, often radically, as also with the work of the translators when, in my judgment, it was too close to the Japanese. I have reduced the length of hundreds of sentences. Those who know

Konishi's early *Bungakushi* and compare it with the Japanese version of this when it is published will discover that although his lucidity is all that I have said it is, the syntax of his writing in the original of this *History* is far more complex. He has told me that his earlier history was written especially for the benefit of that generation of young people whose education was deficient because of the upheavals and deprivations of the Second World War. Here he has allowed himself a syntactic complexity befitting the ambitious, complex nature of his ideas after a full career of study. The readers of this volume in English will be mature people. But complex if lucid Japanese is a very different article from its English counterpart. I have decided that preserving the original lucidity required numerous breakups of sentences, rearrangements, and departures. Or rather I doubted the possibility of ensuring natural English counterparts to the author's Japanese in word-by-word and clause-by-clause equivalence.

We offer romanized versions of quotations only for Japanese verse. Chinese is difficult to understand when romanized, and few readers would benefit from Ainu or Ryukyuan. Of course we do include romanized versions of Chinese, Korean, Ainu, and Ryukyuan (as well as Japanese) names, titles, and various technical terms. Something must be said of the systems used. The Ainu and the Ryukyuan have been supplied by the author, and I do not know what system he may have used. Japanese is represented in a version of the Hepburn system. An apostrophe is used to indicate where a syllable break occurs when there is some possibility of misreading: Jin'ichi (not Ji'nichi) Konishi. The language is modernized from Old Japanese: Hitomaro, not Fitomaro; Gemmei, not Genmei; shōgatsu, not shaugwatsu, etc. Chinese is romanized according to the Wade-Giles system as being easier for those without knowledge of Chinese. That is, with the help of Professor Shuen-fu Lin of the University of Michigan, we have used the present American version of the Wade-Giles practice. We are very grateful to Professor Lin. Korean is presented in the McCune-Reischauer system with assistance to me from Professor Peter H. Lee. I hope that this has got most things right. But I lack knowledge to verify the Ainu and Ryukyuan words.

Japanese and other non-English words are presented without quotation marks or italics when the words would be so handled in English. This yields a cleaner page, and it is difficult to believe that anyone will mistake for English any word in the other languages used here. By the same token, capitals and italics are used for Japanese and other romanized words and titles if they would be for English equivalents, although normally a translated title is given.

Many important terms have been left in the original language, albeit romanized. They are usually introduced, if not defined, on first appearance. Entries in the index will include notice of pages where a given term is described or introduced. No doubt it is initially hard to digest, and even to pronounce, terms such as "setsuwa" and "chōka"; "hyangga" and "sasŏl sijo"; "fu" and "shih." But in fact these terms are understood only in context and by examples. "Chōka" means "long poem(s)," but the longest extant example is 149 lines. "Fu" is sometimes translated "rhapsody" and sometimes "rhyme prose." We sometimes use "rhapsody" but more often "fu," since there is really no other word to designate the object. Other matters of usage are indicated in notes.

I have moments of sudden fright when recalling that for each name, quotation, date, and fact there have been a minimum of three people involved (the author, the translator, the editor) before the much-scribbled manuscript went to the typist. We have all done the best we could in the time available.

My editorial work (revising, retranslating, editing for the typists, checking with the author, and reediting retyped versions) was done for the most part while a fellow at the Woodrow Wilson International Center for Scholars, in the old Smithsonian Institution Building, or "Castle." (By a happy coincidence, Professor Konishi spent three overlapping months in the Council of Scholars at the Library of Congress.) I thank the Wilson Center for generously supplied facilities. Colleagues at its Kennan Center assisted me several times in Russian matters. The typing was supervised by Eloise Doane and performed, on word processors, by Donna Watson and Ann Smith, both of whom I thank heartily. The support, the collegial atmosphere, and the intellectual exchange of the Wilson Center put me very much in its debt.

I am deeply grateful to William Hively for his intelligent, careful copyediting of this volume, with all its complexities somehow handled without fuss; as also to Tam Curry, who skillfully saw this book through proof. And I want to record that most of the figures were drawn by Allison Fulz, an architecture major at Princeton.

Finally, I wish to thank R. Miriam Brokaw, Associate Director and Editor of Princeton University Press, for her strong furthering of this important enterprise: the first volume of a full-scale history of Japanese literature by one of its greatest students.

If a mere editor had a right to a dedication, mine would be to Aileen Gatten, Peter H. Lee, and Shuen-fu Lin.

The Wilson Center
Washington, D.C.
Spring, 1982

The Translators and the Editor

Aileen Gatten is Research Associate at the Center for Japanese Studies at the University of Michigan. Born in California, she received her Ph.D. from Michigan for a dissertation on the *Genji Monogatari*. She is author of several essays, chiefly related to the work on which she wrote her dissertation. As this is written, she is busy translating the second volume of this *History* and working on further studies of *The Tale of Genji*.

Nicholas Teele has spent many years in Japan, where he presently teaches comparative language and literature at the University of Tsukuba. He has also taught at Korea University in Seoul. He received his Ph.D. from the University of Texas, Austin, in 1978, with a dissertation on love poetry in the *Kokinshū*. His publications have chiefly concerned Heian literature, although he also has a strong interest in the earlier literature dealt with in this volume.

Earl Miner is Townsend Martin, Class of 1917, Professor of English and Comparative Literature at Princeton University. He has known the author of this *History* since 1957 when engaged in studying waka with Robert H. Brower. He has held teaching appointments at Williams College and UCLA before Princeton, as well as visiting teaching duties at Kyoto and Osaka Universities, Oxford, and Columbia. He has written chiefly on seventeeth-century English literature, classical Japanese literature, and comparative poetics.

A HISTORY OF
JAPANESE LITERATURE

VOLUME ONE
The Archaic and
Ancient Ages

GENERAL INTRODUCTION

AIMS AND METHODS

"A History of Japanese Literature." The meaning of the phrase may be thought self-explanatory. In truth the question of meaning has seldom been raised in earlier histories of the subject. None of this is to suggest that answers are self-evidently true or simple.

First of all, we must consider what we mean by Japan. If the area making up the Japanese archipelago is taken to constitute Japan, there are great problems in systematically describing as one's object both the literature that existed and the literature that exists in that geographical entity. Ainu literature came into being in that area. But because there was no connection between the yukar, the important representative of Ainu literature, and that of the Yamato people, it is not inevitable that Ainu literature be included.[1] The basic reasons for lack of contact are the fundamentally different characteristics of the Ainu language and Japanese. It is also important that Ainu society was based on a hunting and gathering method of food supply, whereas Yamato society was based on farming. Ainu literature is a priceless cultural asset in itself, and unlike the usual histories of Japanese literature mine will include it. Doing so requires recognition of the differences between Ainu and Yamato literature, and my method will therefore be comparative, contrastive, not involving a single mixed entity.

There is also Ryukyuan literature. The Ryukyu language is very closely connected to Japanese: it is certainly not a foreign language.[2] Yet it is altogether impossible to account for Ryukyu and Yamato literature as parts of a single temporal sequence. To explain: in the Ryukyus of about the twelfth century there were azi, patriarchs who ruled agricultural settlements, although the spread of iron tools led to a revolution in farming during the thirteenth and fourteenth centuries. Thus the equivalent of the Archaic Age in Japan, the Ryukyuan archaic culture, stretches on to the mid-thirteenth century, when the islands became separated into small kingdoms, further on to the time of the "Three Mountains," yet further to the consolidation of rule in the period of the Kingdom, and continues through the invasion by the Satsuma han [domain] from Kyu-

[1] In the Ryukyus, the term "yamatonyu" refers to people from the Japanese main isles. The naming comes from the older name for those isles. The definition of "Yamato" used here will be given subsequently.

[2] One influential theory posits a relation between Ryukyuan and Yamato Japanese as common dialects (Hattori, 1968, 1-14). This cannot be taken conclusively, although there is certainly some fraternity between them. The Ryukyu language also has fraternity with Malay and Polynesian, although the nature of the relation is not clear.

shu. Because Japan was then well on in its Middle Ages, one can see the enormous chronological disparity between Ryukyuan and Yamato literatures. Moreover, the development of Ryukyuan genres is not necessarily the same as what took place to the north. It is most difficult to consider both the Ryukyuan and the Japanese literatures in a single cultural circumference. For these reasons, in the ensuing history of *Japanese* literature, Ryukyuan literature will be taken up, not as a practice shared in a given year or century with Yamato-Japanese literature, but rather at points at which it has equivalence in literary qualities with the literature of the Yamato. In considering Ryukyuan literature comparatively rather than in terms of influence, my decision implies comparing the Ryukyuan *Umuru Suosi*, a collection of songs transcribed in the fifteenth century, alongside the Yamato songs of the *Kojiki* and *Nihon Shoki* recorded in the eighth century.

A further major issue for Yamato literature concerns Chinese-language poetry and prose written in Japan. For Japanese, composing verse or prose in Chinese of course involves using a foreign language. Foreign language or not, the thought and the feelings expressed in these works derive from Japanese authors. And the setting, the materials for the works, came from a nature and society basically Japanese. So it becomes necessary to include Japanese poetry and prose written in Chinese in a history of Japanese literature. No doubt a Chinese intellectual reading Japanese composition in Chinese would fail to understand it correctly without notes and explanation. To the Chinese as (differently) to the Japanese, Japan's poetry and prose in Chinese can only be work in a foreign language. In France, from the beginning of the fifth through about the middle of the eleventh century, and in England from the seventh through the ninth century [and later], many literary works were composed in Latin. If these were excluded from the histories of French and English literature, in what literary history could they be included? Furthermore, the Japanese sometimes regard poetry and prose in Chinese as available styles of writing. As we shall see, there is no adequate reason for excluding this body of work; on the other hand there is also no reason to identify writing in Chinese with the Yamato tradition.

An important reverse case also exists. We must consider carefully the situation where something is written in Japanese although the contents are foreign: translations. There is of course an original from which the translations grow independent, and if sentences now in Japanese impress or entertain the cultured reader, there is good reason to include them in a history of *Japanese* literature. There are, on the one hand, famous translations: for example, Hasegawa Futabatei's *Aibiki* (1896), a partial translation of a work by Turgenev; Mori Ōgai's *Sokkyō Shijin* (1902), a rendering of Hans Christian Andersen's *Improvisations*; and Ueda Bin's

Kaichōon (1905), Japanese versions of fifty-seven poems originally in Provençal, French, German, English, and Italian. We must put in the same category as these the mass-produced translations of this century. Whether cultivated or popular, translations are part of my subject, because the heart of literary study is literariness, which is to say that the work moves and pleases the reader, effects that are derived from a work's structure and texture.[3] To be sure, with translations the structure is mainly provided by the original author, and the texture mainly by the translator. Yet structure and texture are separated only with difficulty, and the responsibility for arousing impressions and entertaining must be allotted to both the author and the translator. And since translations have had an active, positive reception in Japan, I think that there is really no reason to exclude them from a history of Japanese literature.

We must also consider the word "literature" (bungei) in this history of Japanese literature. What kinds of things fall within its scope? Some things will obviously be included: such poetic kinds as waka or haiku, and such narrative kinds as monogatari [prose narrative written in the past tense] or otogizōshi [popular stories of the Middle Ages]. But what of yet other kinds? There are histories, factual accounts (jitsuroku), discourses (ronsho), and sermons. Do they qualify for a literary history? To be sure there are *some* nikki [prose narrative written in the present tense], kikō (travel accounts), and zuihitsu (prose miscellanies) that are hard to include as literature. What are the standards, however? For example, by its factual, historical, plain Chinese nature, Fujiwara Teika's *Meigetsuki* is not a literary nikki. Yet in reading it we are deeply moved by the sections treating the death of his father, Shunzei, whereas many nikki in Japanese, nikki that the usual histories of Japanese literature discuss, are hardly interesting at all. What standards are being followed? What answers do we have? Again, what about travel accounts such as Jūbutsu's *Daijingū Sankeiki*, Kōun's *Kōun Kikō*, Gyoko's *Ise Kikō*, and Gyōe's *Zenkōji Kikō*? Do they have features qualifying them for a literary history? If not, what do they lack that is possessed by other travel accounts—like Ichijō Kanera's *Fujikawa no Ki* and Sōgi's *Tsukushi no Michi no Ki*—to justify inclusion of these others in so-called histories of literature (bungakushi)? Or take various miscellaneous prose compositions such as Ichijō Kanera's *Tōzai Zuihitsu*, Ban Kokei's *Kanden Kōhitsu*, and Ōta Nampo's *Ichiwa Ichigen*. All too many have little flavor, and one may

---

[3] [In the original, the author often quotes the Japanese and puts the English in parentheses. Since he often does so for explanatory purposes or for nuance, the technique may be remarked this once on its first appearance. We have not always followed his emphasis and have sometimes added our own: e.g., material added to the main text by a translator or the editor is set forth in brackets to distinguish it from that supplied by the author.—Ed.]

well wonder whether miscellanies belong in any history of Japanese literature.

These several questions require me to clarify distinctions between conventional genres and what I call literature (bungei). Both the English word "literature" and the French "littérature" originally meant "the knowledge or study of writing," but they gradually came to refer to "literary productions in general."[4] In Japan, however, the translation of the European terms as "bungaku" gave rise to the meaning of *study*. Its objects included not only poetry, prose, novels, and drama, species that are intentionally aesthetic, but also biographies, letters, discourses, and reportage, other species that are essentially unaesthetic in nature. The inclusion of so much derives from what Edo kokugakusha [scholars of national learning] agreed on as the subject of their study. The same conception, now termed "bungaku," was maintained, almost without opposition, from the Meiji Restoration in 1868 onward. It may be natural for numerous works in unaesthetic genres to be included in many of those books I might call "the usual history of Japanese literature," "histories of Japanese literature heretofore," or "so-called histories of Japanese literature." I do not reject out of hand those "histories of Japanese literature" (bungakushi). I would find the inclusion desirable—providing there were some means of connoting the unaesthetic nature of certain genres and a way of setting everything forth in a coherent, connected account. But I have decided to limit *this* history of Japanese literature by taking as my object of study works possessing literariness (bungeisei). For unless I set such limits, it will be extremely difficult to present a coherent account after the Middle Ages.

Works with that literariness as their object—that is, belles-lettres—and the concept of bungei were characterized in the strong claim accompanying the nineteenth-century expression "l'art pour l'art." Consequently, works historically prior to that newer conception were not meant to possess pure literariness. In the Archaic and Ancient Ages, this is seen in extremity: in the Archaic Age, literature was not distinguished from history, politics, religion, etc. To a large degree, this mingling of kinds of knowledge was inherited by the Ancient Age. On the other hand, with the Middle Ages we see the rise of other kinds such as monogatari, nikki, and travel accounts.

None of this requires that a history of literature be restricted to the

---

[4] René Wellek reports the opposition of Lane Cooper of Cornell University to the designation of the department he headed as "Comparative Literature," holding that it should be "The Comparative Study of Literature." This must be due to a desire to limit the meaning of the English word "literature" to (literary) things that have been written down. The *Oxford English Dictionary* dates the usage in that sense from 1812. But the conception must have been brought from France toward the end of the eighteenth century (Wellek, 1965, 3-4).

nineteenth century and later. It does require that scholars deal analytically with the Archaic and Ancient Ages, during which times the concept of literature was mixed with other subjects. The *Kojiki* serves as an example. Obviously it was not compiled for art's sake. But there is also no reason to exclude it from a history of literature (bungei), providing we include only the artistic aspects of the *Kojiki* in the literary history.

Heretofore it has been common in Japanese literary study to take into account only the viewpoint of the author. This assumption is illustrated when the rightness of a given interpretation of a work is judged by the "intention of the author." Yet literariness involves feelings and interest, and these are aroused in the audience, whose point of view is necessary to our grasping the concept of literariness. As the Rezeptionsästhetik critics have emphasized, the meaning of a work is not necessarily limited to the intention of its author, and in fact is completed by the participation of its audience.[5] In identifying literariness for the purposes of a history of literature, then, the identifiers are those making the study, and what is identified cannot be limited to the intention of the author. For example, I shall include Dōgen's *Shōbō Genzō* in this history of Japanese literature, although that violates the author's intention. For Dōgen roundly declared that "prose style [bumpitsu] and poetry [shika] are not to be discussed; in no respect are they a match for the morality opposing them" (*Zuimonki*, 2:341). Had he heard that someone had decided to analyze his style for literary ends, he probably would have protested, "That should not be discussed!" I shall disregard that objection, however.

Another aspect of the meaning of "literature" (bungei) must be clarified. Not only things set in writing but also those transmitted orally can be regarded as literature. Of course the word "literature" comes from the Latin "littera," which means both "letter" and "written things." This no doubt has led people deliberately to specify only written things as literature. Yet there is no reason to limit the signs of communication to letters or characters, since oral signs represent equally well. When oral communication is quickly achieved, its ephemeral nature may be of little concern. Written symbols are, however, superior when the time required exceeds a certain amount. Oral communication is over so quickly that the retention of information necessarily depends on memory, and it is not easy to be certain about information so preserved over a long period of time. It is, then, quite reasonable to give works published in written

---

[5] Various critical schools influenced by the Russian Formalists have held that without the participation of the reader, the meaning of a work is incomplete. See Hans Robert Jauss, *Literaturgeschichte als Povokation* (Frankfurt: Suhrkamp Verlag, 1970), Wolfgang Iser, *Der Implizite Leser* (Munich: Fink Verlag, 1972), and *Der Akt des Lesens* (ibid., 1976). (Fokkema and Kunne-Ibsch, 1977, 136-64.) [The later use of "literariness" or "bungeisei" may suggest a connection with Russian Formalism, but it is in fact a characteristic usage by the author.—Ed.]

characters prime concern. But the instability of oral transmission is no reason to deny that it may convey things characterized by literariness. This is easily understood, and detailed argument is unnecessary.

The last concept requiring consideration is the word "history" in my title. History is usually understood to account for reality in chronological sequence, and that is not wrong. At least one cannot deny that there are many histories of the kind. Mere chronology is not enough for scholarly history, however. Scholarship does proceed with investigation and observation. More than that, its fundamental character requires rules of method that comprehend an entire range of phenomena, and correct observation of the phenomena in light of the rules. So employed, a scholarly literary history will investigate and observe; yet if it fails to inquire—by its principles of method—into an entire body of historical phenomena, its existence is not easily justified. When historical phenomena are illuminated by rules of method, then for the first time it is possible to give a thoroughly logical account.

To be sure, the relative importance of observation as opposed to the institution of rules differs from field to field and from age to age. For example, in contrast to biology, modern physics shows a tendency to inquire into laws before investigating facts, whereas for biology the investigation of facts must come first. Biology contrasts with physics by setting the homogeneity of facts as its object of investigation, taking individual characteristics more as its end, with the usual method involving the inference of laws from data accumulated by previous investigation of various phenomena. The differences between these two sciences amount to no more than a tendency, one that became marked only in the twentieth century. In earlier periods thesis-making in physics did not necessarily precede observation.

In literary research, the object of study is decidedly more directed to particular instances and, in common with biology, has as its guiding principle the observation of certain phenomena. When Edo national study (kokugaku) was resuscitated as modern literary study in Japan, the paradigm used was that of nineteenth-century science, so that it was natural for literary scholars at the time to be concerned with the accumulation of data. The goal lay in as large and exact an accumulation as possible. The problem is that Japanese literary history of this factual kind has continued to rule into the present.

In the second half of the twentieth century, biological research also rose from the molecular to the quantum level; it has grown ever clearer that its aim is to systematize phenomena with individual characteristics, using rules that characterize all biology. This is not to say that systematic regularity is the one and only aim, or that it is the single right way of thinking. We can think, however, that the central feature of science is the attempt to go beyond data that can be directly observed by the senses and to grasp "principles" from a world that cannot be directly experienced.[6] It should not be thought that the value of the new method relies solely on its being new or scientific. For literary study as well, it is natural that people should come to aim at comprehending the "principles" of the whole and not simply seek to accumulate data. This is not to deprecate the accumulation of data, but rather to hold that the accumulation must be ordered in light of the "principles" of the whole. In the process the principles first formulated will no doubt be modified. That is, in practice the principles of science are first regarded as hypotheses, and science can only be the process of correcting hypotheses according to the observation of data. A properly scholarly history of Japanese literature must of necessity possess hypotheses in this sense.

The history of Japanese literature that I have set before me can be said to begin with as much accumulated data about literary matters as is feasible today and, from such information, to issue in the systematic delineation of the special qualities of Japanese literature. I have done exceeding little myself in the accumulation of such data. Since in the main I have relied on the work of my predecessors, my own work can be said to begin at the point of making hypotheses about the special characteristics of Japanese literature. Although the hypotheses will, in turn, be tested for their congruence with the literary data, the data necessary to that elaboration will be those that help clarify the aesthetic nature of Japanese literature. Without hypotheses to provide a large frame for the whole, with no aim beyond stringing facts in chronological order as a history—why, then the more data the better. To the extent that data alone matter, questions of part versus part or of magnitude do not enter, for if one only compiles by obtaining all one can, the account is fully achieved without distortion. But the account of Japanese literature that follows differs. The literary phenomena of Japan will be arranged, ordered by unifying principles. The first step will be the presentation of hypotheses about the special nature of Japanese literature. On their bases the range of evidence will be reexamined. To that end, it seems best to fix our concern on the aesthetic nature of the works involved, an aim which, however modest, is appropriate here.

JAPANESE LITERATURE DEFINED

Japanese literature has properties inherently Japanese and others transformed through contact with the cultures of foreign countries. Both are

---

[6] [For "principles" here and subsequently in this section, the author quotes the character for "kotowari," "ri."—Ed.]

joined to form "the special characteristics of Japanese literature." From its earliest stage of development, Japanese literature has been influenced by foreign cultures: the writing system, needless to say, also techniques of expression, and even patterns of thought and of conceptualizing are so pervaded with foreign elements that it is impossible to think of properties of Japanese literature without attention to the foreign. All the same, the inherent Japanese properties, rather than vanishing, have retained vitality throughout each age. If there were periods when foreign characteristics were prominent, soon the inherent Japanese qualities revived—a phenomenon that can be observed from numerous vantage points. Alternatively, we may posit historically certain periods when the inherent properties dominate and others when foreign ones do, holding that neither exclusively inherent nor exclusively foreign qualities can be determined to exist as literary phenomena. If, however, the spectrum described is examined as an opposition between Japanese and foreign properties, a certain degree of qualitative analysis becomes feasible. The essential thing is contrast with the culture that directly influenced Japanese culture, namely Chinese during the Ancient and Middle Ages and Western during the Modern. And in considering more fundamental elements, a yet wider, or "world," perspective is more effective in numerous ways.

Special Characteristics

To identify the most fundamental characteristics of Japanese literature, it seems best to try to set it in contrast with the "world" as background. Considering the present state of such study and my personal limitations, the reader will plainly see that it is impossible to presume inquiry into every area and every ethnic group. All that can be done is to create a semblance of the contrastive world on the basis of available information. This should not cause difficulty: the purpose of postulating a world with characteristics designed for contrast is the desire for hypotheses with which to describe the special characteristics of Japanese literature. Should future research and investigation show the need for revision of some parts of this work, it may be thought sufficient to modify part by part as occasion requires.

In considering general qualities of Japanese literature in contrast to that other literary "world," we recognize first of all, if only as a matter of external form, Japanese brevity. For poetry, the haiku with its fixed form of seventeen syllables may well be the shortest poetic form in the world. The fact that it and the tanka, with its thirty-one syllables, still flourish at the present time after so many centuries means nothing less than that brevity is one of the most important properties of Japanese literature. In the Ancient Age, the chōka, or long poem, flourished. But even the longest of them, Kakinomoto Hitomaro's "Elegy on the Death of Prince Takechi" (*Man'yōshū*, 2:199) is only 149 lines long. This is no match in length for the *Iliad* or the *Odyssey*, nor does it compare with either the literature of the Ainu or of the Ryukyus. And even the chōka declined steadily after Hitomaro, losing its vitality by the end of the ninth century. There was a later attempt to revive the long poem for one kind of chanson (kayō) in versions such as the fast-song (sōga) and banquet poem (enkyoku). It was a brief affair. Among the fast-songs there were none that remained impressive to readers of later ages. In twentieth-century Japan, the kinds still practiced are limited to those not greatly different in length from tanka and haiku.

Perhaps there is an exception to this rule in the poetry and prose of nō libretti (yōkyoku). It is possible to think of these as works of considerable length and to find famous plays that impress modern theatergoers. This view is one, however, ignoring the theater in favor of reading a text, taking the poetry and prose of nō as poetic literature. But the prose simply cannot be taken as poetry. Also, if nō had been deliberately written as long poems, they would probably not have reached their present length. Their scripts were originally libretti supported by the actors' performance. Because there is a musical interest added by the chorus and musicians, the script can be sustained with enjoyment, even though the prose and poetry are rather long. Simple reading aloud would not enable a Japanese listener to sustain enjoyment for so long a time.

Perhaps there are those who would rebut this by arguing that there must have been stories of a considerable length in the Archaic and the Ancient Ages. The argument would show that although such stories are no longer extant, there are in the *Kojiki* and *Nihon Shoki* myths and certain legends related to the royal line. [If "royal" is obscure, see ch. 7, n. 24.] One would presume that these stories were recited by a group like the kataribe [an office or rank of reciters] before being set down in writing, and that some were of great length. But even if those supposed long poems existed, they were not long *literary* works as we conceive them. The stories we have tell about the activity of the royal line from the age of the gods in order to bring about favorable occurrences for Yamato and its people—stories supported by faith in kotodama [see below, Part Two]. And in all this, history, literature, politics, and religion were absorbed into one. The fusion of historical, political, and religious qualities supported the length of the stories, corresponding to the support of performance and music for nō. That is why, to the degree that literariness advanced, kotodama weakened, for literary culture involved narration in conditions making sustained length difficult. For reasons of this kind we can understand the difficulty in cultivating lengthy prose plots.

It is easy to imagine a counterclaim: that there are in Japanese such very lengthy prose works as Murasaki Shikibu's *Genji Monogatari (The Tale of Genji)* [fifty-four chapters, early eleventh century] and Kyokutei Bakin's *Nansō Satomi Hakkenden (The Story of the Eight Virtuous Heroes)* [ninety-eight chapters, 1814-42]. Although it is true that the *Genji* is long by the standard of Western novels, in content it is not more than a collection of stories of short or middle length, with none of the structure that gives life to a novel. Western novels are structured so that each part carries out some task for a pertinent degree of the whole, an arrangement that makes effective use of length. The absence of this structure in the *Genji* is clearly shown by Arthur Waley's translation. In spite of the fact that a whole chapter, "Suzumushi" ["Bell-Crickets"], has been all but entirely left out, the story line advances without obstacle and in fact the omission smoothes the shift from the chapter before, "Yokobue" ["The Flute"], to that after, "Yūgiri."[7] As for Bakin's *Eight Virtuous Heroes*, certainly one can find to a certain extent a method of unfolding and advancing the story, but it is a linked chain of many small plots gathered together. The omission of any one of the small plots does the whole no fatal injury. Japanese authors are weak in structural powers that effectively articulate the development and progress of a work into great length, but they show an amazing genius in ways of linking short segments, as in Ihara Saikaku's *Kōshoku Ichidai Otoko (One Man Who Devoted His Life to Love)*. Here again, the outward form shows that brevity is clearly the first special characteristic running through the whole of Japanese literature.

The second major characteristic is that, in numerous respects, there are not stark oppositions. I shall enumerate for convenience' sake:

1. the lack of an opponent and systematic oppositions;
2. the lack of distinction between the human and the natural;
3. the nonexistence of class barriers in literary kinds;
4. the tendency to harmonize the individual with the group;
5. the relation of mutual dependence between author and audience.

Although there are numerous other instances of the weakness of confrontational elements, these five are representative.

Let us begin with an examination of what, in more or less external terms, is the lack of opposition in the organization of Japanese literary works. In nō the waki or deuteragonist is not the opponent of the shite or protagonist. In fact it has long been a central organizational point about nō that the shite alone is the center of attention (Nogami, 1930, 1-41). Although particularly obvious in nō, the same thing can be ob-

---

[7] Waley's *Tale of Genji* retains one small part of "Suzumushi" (Waley, *The Tale of Genji*).

served in jōruri [puppet and other popular performance] and kabuki [popular actors' theatre]. The various supporting actors are, as a general rule, nothing more than assistants who enhance the main actor, with whom they do not share responsibility for enhancing the main themes of the work. In the West, it is normal for there to be an antagonist who does share the duty of acting out the issues by opposing the main actor or protagonist. However, what is called the "supporting actor" in Japan is simply a byplayer, not an antagonist. So far is this the case that I have had to invent for this book a term, "taiyaku," for that antagonist so familiar to Western readers. This situation can also be seen in monogatari and ukiyozōshi [stories of present-day life] like Saikaku's. To a slight degree, in the third section of *The Tale of Genji* Prince Niou shows features of being an antagonist to the main character, Kaoru. But this is very much an exception (the work is exceptional in some other features as well). Usually the organization is such that the main character shoulders the main theme, and therefore the story line lacks the articulated organization of Western novels. Japanese stories tend to flow easily, with description accompanying the actions of the protagonist. This is true also with modern so-called "I" novels (shishōsetsu; watakushishōsetsu).

There are also more internal matters. Given the close relation between the human and the natural in Japanese literature, no conceptual barrier between them is felt to exist. This has been pointed out some time ago (Ōnishi, 1943, 129-74). As I see it, Japanese literature has been imbued from its beginnings both with the primitive disposition of Japanese mental states and with the homogeneous nature of child and mother during infancy.[8] In addition, because the human is not cut off from the natural in Japanese literature, discrete descriptions of nature did not develop, as they did in the West. The fact that the Japanese did not feel much opposition to nature does not mean that they were always on relaxed terms with it. We can find in the songs (kayō) of the *Kojiki* and *Nihon Shoki* phrases such as "yutsu matsubaki" (*Kojiki, Song,* 57) and "itsu kashigamoto" (*Nihon Shoki, Song,* 92). Both "yutsu" and "itsu" indicate a sense of reverence filled with sacredness, showing an attitude of awe toward nature.[9] In the Ancient Age, nature held for the Japanese an intimate depth and solemnity arousing awe, and it was not something that could be separated from humanity. When later a Chinese-like rational spirit predominated, there began to be a gap between the human

[8] In what psychologists term primitive mentality, the three characteristics are as follows: a complex, in which perception and symbol are not differentiated; nebulousness, in which the part is not separated from the whole; and emotionality, in which impulse figures strongly.

[9] In ancient Japan, the prefixes "yu" and "i" were widely used, showing feelings of awe. For people at that time, because plants seemed so importantly natural, they were to be revered (Tsuchida, 1962, 236).

and the natural; this is found in what I shall be terming "ga" [high, elegant] literature. Now, when the rationalism of the Western world seems even more appealing, the very Japanese sense of life appears to have altered, with the old sense of the relation between the human and the natural almost lost. Still, in what I shall be terming "zoku" [lower, popular or vulgar] literature, this sense of nature has remained alive from the primitive period forward, and in some deeper stratum of their minds the Japanese of the twentieth century are not altogether separated from nature.

My third point concerns the fact that class distinctions have never extended to literary practice in Japan. In the Ancient Age, men from outlying regions who were drafted for service as frontier guards (saki-mori) tried to express their thought in the same waka [Japanese poetry] used at court, even if the guards might do so falteringly and in dialect. The officers and men of the army of the Kamakura bakufu became disheartened in conducting the siege of Chihaya Castle in 1331. So they called a renga master from the capital for a renga [ga-level linked poetry] match (renga awase) of ten thousand stanzas, enjoying the poetic competition with fine tea and leisurely critical discussion (*Taiheiki*, 7:127). Waka and renga were not literature possessed solely by the nobility. A number of kyōgen [comic nō interludes] concern the enthusiasm of common people for renga, and there is other evidence to show that the plays reflect their times.

Another important feature is the possibility of a given kind to ascend in estimation. Renga, which began in trivial wordplay, rose before long to the status of a noble, ga literature. As haikai no renga [ga-zoku-level linked poetry] emerged to take the former low position of renga, fondness for it led to its being accepted by the warrior class. Later still such lower haikai kinds as senryū [satiric haikai] also rose in estimation. Moreover, with the help of female entertainers (yūjo) and reciters (kugutsu), the nobility developed a love for certain kinds of popular song. These were influenced by Buddhist balladry. But they developed on their own into present-style songs (imayō), which were in turn replaced later on during the Middle Ages by short songs (shōka). Yet again, certain kinds of acting such as sarugaku had once been no more than vulgar farce. But when imbued with art as sarugaku no nō under the Ashikaga shogunate, it came to have the mysterious elegance and beauty (yūgen) of the flower of art (hana) as its end. The place of the now risen nō was then occupied by kyōgen, which rose in their turn. The phenomena of ascending can only have been possible because in literary matters there was no firm separation between classes. It is difficult therefore to believe that in modern Japan the new shōsetsu [usually rendered "novel"] emerged as a result of class conflict between the common people and the privileged.

Our fourth concern is with the individual and the group, between whom there was no radical distinction. Individual Japanese usually take to one group or another, leaving very little room for opposition.[10] Authors form groups composed solely of persons who think and feel in similar ways in writing and enjoying their works. The writers and their groups alike are convinced that only the creations of their particular group are attractive. If an individualistic person creates a new style, that author does not act alone but instead institutes a group of like-minded people, and the new group goes on self-sufficiently writing and appreciating what its members write. The opposition or conflict that does occur is therefore between one group and another rather than between an individual and the group belonged to. Whether in waka, in haikai, or in any other kind of artistic accomplishment, there is no development without the formation of groups or schools. This is true still. There are said to be over eight hundred tanka and as many haiku schools. It should be noted that there are almost no poets of either kind who do not belong to one such society. An individual is usually permeated by the thoughts and attitudes common to the group and approaches the group's leader, the sensei, with loyalty and devotion. Since Romanticism in the West, it must be impossible to conceive that the creation of fine work could be premised on attitudes restricted to the group to which one belongs.

Finally, when a work circulates within a certain group, there is no reason for opposition between the author and the audience. Because group attitudes are prerequisite for both artistic creation and reception, the members use codes that are held in common, and it becomes possible to use a kind of shorthand expression. When, however, a writer addresses other groups with their differing attitudes, the writing is best if extended and detailed: what is called redundancy in information theory becomes much more important. If, within a group, there are numerous codes that work highly effectively, then redundancy will not only be unnecessary but will be considered a defect. In cases involving a single group, and among writings similar in nature, the briefer one will be openly held to excel: another reason for prizing brevity. Moreover, it is far less important for the author to tell all than to provide an "expressive-affective" form of expression which, to a certain extent, depends on the understanding

[10] Even in modern Japanese society, it is usual for the individual to be incorporated in some group, and in it the individual does not attempt to express private opinions. This is also reflected in national elections, in which one votes according to the will of the group one belongs to, so that no matter what bait reform parties might have offered to voters in terms of their policies, the conservative party has gone on winning. Those who leave the group organization of their home towns to work in larger cities have been shown to have abstained from voting in large measure: "Organization Voting and Movement Voting," *Asahi Shimbun*, 12 January 1980.

of the recipient.[11] Of course in the modern West (this can be traced back to Homer) the attitude underlying expression is usually author-centered, expressive. By contrast, Japanese literature has perhaps never abandoned its affective-expressive attitude. In speaking about expression in haikai, Bashō taught that "it lies in not telling all of every crook and quarter." As part of this, when Kyorai was impressed by a certain stanza, he said, "it is in really not finishing what you say." As Bashō said in partial correction, "After finishing speaking, there should be something left" (*Kyorai Shō, Senshihyō*, 20-21).

To move now to another set of characteristics of Japanese literature, there are its emotionality and implicitness of tone.[12] It is not that Japan has lacked intellectuality. Far from it. In the Middle Ages waka, which provided the index of literary tone, was decidedly intellectual. In the style of poetry established by the compilers of the *Kokinshū*, one did not simply express feelings directly, but rather through the refraction of reason [ko-towari, ri]. Poets relied on assumed characteristics of things, expressing the emotional nature of the material indirectly with an intellectual skill that became characteristic. That intellectual style was in fact borrowed from China, although Ki no Tsurayuki (the central figure in establishing the *Kokinshū* style) aimed in his later years at direct expression of feeling without the earlier prominence of rationality. Fujiwara Shunzei, who asserted that the *Kokinshū* should be esteemed as the basis of poetry, also tended to the emotional in his poetry. His son Teika, who in his youth advocated an intellectuality of a kind that would have interested Tsurayuki and his group, also inclined toward more direct emotional expression in his later years. Facts such as these show that an intellectual tone comes, at some juncture, to be felt not fully in accord with inherent Japanese response.

The sole Western poetry for which the modern Japanese possess understanding and sympathy is probably the Romantic, and for even that the Japanese have been slow to grow familiar with its concealed intel-

---

[11] Western literature has had an expressive emphasis since Greece and Rome. In contrast to this, Japanese literature is affective-expressive: see Miner, 1978-79.

[12] It is difficult to explain my special usage [of naikōsei] adequately. The "yin principle" is easy enough to turn to, but such are the manifold complexities stretching out from the concepts of yin-yang thought that the exact meaning is hard to convey. The passive [shō-kyoku—negativism or conservativism in the dictionary] may express some features of the idea, but I fear that many other features in my concept would thereby be lost. English "implicitness" being fairly close to what I have in mind, I have ventured to use "naikōsei" [usually defined by dictionaries as "introversion," etc.], although it is inadequate. I have had the suggestion (from Ulrich Mammitsch) of the German "beredtes Schweigen" (meaningful or expressive silence). When that phrase works, it is fine, but since it does not always do so, I am left with my usage. [We have had to weigh various English words, rather lamely deciding on polar terms: implictness/explicitness and introverted/extroverted according to context.—Ed.]

lectual features. It is even truer that, for English Metaphysical poetry—no matter how much T. S. Eliot praised it—the Japanese have found enjoyment impossible. That Montaigne's *Essais* should be considered literature does not seem natural to the Japanese.

This emotional attitude should, in principle, justify the expression of any kind of feeling. In reality, however, the Japanese emphasis has been on implicit, introverted emotions. If one replaces "introverted" with "negative," then by contrast the explicit, extroverted emotions are positive. The proof that the distinction has validity can be shown first of all by the absence of epic poetry in Yamato literature. The querulous assertion that Japan has an epic poetry is a mistake: its nonexistence is a characteristic of the literature. Many peoples have had epic poetry in the formative period of their literature. Beginning with the *Gilgamesh* of the people of Sumer, composed several thousand years ago, from the *Iliad* and *Odyssey* of Homer, to the *Mahābhārata* of ancient India, and to the *Beowulf* of England or the *Shanamah* of Persia, numerous epics obviously exist.[13] Even in the twentieth century, epic poems have been recited in such parts of the Soviet Union as Kirghiz, Uzbek, and Kazakh—as also in such countries as Yugoslavia, Armenia, Albania, and Bulgaria.[14] In Japan as well, heroic poems such as the yukar have flourished among the Ainu. In spite of all that, Yamato literature has no epic poetry. The lack of intent to write epics is of obvious importance in Yamato literature. But, and this returns us to issues of tone, we may contend yet more seriously that in their affection for introverted emotions the Yamato people found no appeal in aggressive extroverted positiveness. The hero of an epic poem is decidedly active, one who boldly stands and faces troubles, no matter how great.

The same complex of reasons no doubt explains why tragedy did not develop in Japan. Because we Japanese are accustomed to translating "tragedy" as "higeki," we have taken it to mean, simply, "sorrowful drama." But "tragedy" derives from the Greek "tragōdia," which comes from the "tragōdis" [literally, "goat-song"] of the chorus dressed in costumes of weird half-men, half-beasts. Aristotle said that it was better when a plot took the hero from happiness to unhappiness. But he also recognized "tragōdia" in which the plot moved from unhappiness to happiness: for example, Aeschylus' *Prometheus Unbound* and Euripides' *Iphigeneia.*[15] In modern Western literature, the central conception of

[13] The date of the composition of the *Gilgamesh* is unknown. The Sumerian civilization prospered from six to four millennia ago, and a Gilgamesh is named fifth king of the second dynasty; but the dynasty is perhaps mythical (Doi, 1960, 294).

[14] Marfa Kruykova wrote an epic during the Russian Revolution under Lenin (Bowra, 1952, 116-17). Such facts would seem to show a kind of epic activity within the Soviet sphere.

[15] Following the explanation by Matsura Kaichi, *Shigaku* (Iwanami Bunko, 136-37).

tragedy has a hero who directly moves our better inclinations, who confronts a very serious and severe destiny. The issue: will that figure be engulfed in it because of some irresistible chain of events? Or, although the protagonist sets out to act, exerting the very soul, depending on such action in opposition to the world, will the person inevitably and unavoidably meet with mental and physical destruction?[16] Here lies the central conception of tragedy. Superior physically, intellectually, or virtuously to the run of humanity, the tragic figure has a nobility that purifies our souls even when, with all those abilities, it is necessary to stand bravely and confront destructive circumstances in which there is no chance for success. Accordingly, we take from tragedy feelings of purity and nobility. It is not a miserable sadness.

Even prior to the misconception of translating "tragedy" as "higeki" there was, we must recognize, a Japanese mentality that would accept such translation without suspicion, a lasting mentality in which the "sadness" (the "hi" of "higeki") of bitterness, grief, misery, etc. was one easily inclined to compassion. Because of that, tragedy could be understood only as "sorrowful, sad drama." This fundamental disposition of the Japanese probably explains why tragedy did not develop. Only a few works exist for which the word "tragedy" seems proper. One is the nō *Kagekiyo*. Even in this there are elements that cannot be included properly in a Western conception of the tragic. In jōruri and kabuki, many characters confront a severe and menacing world. On facing such a state of affairs, however, the protagonist in Japanese theater lacks the solemn resolution to gamble personal ruin on the resolution of the problem. Instead, he grieves over the inevitable fate, flies to the happiness of the next world, and abandons solutions in the actual world. This tendency indicates why the general tone of Japanese literature has the introverted character mentioned.

Much the same can be observed in other literary contexts. There is, for example, the nō. Although laughing is considered vulgar, base—and so is almost never seen in a performance—weeping can be seen on the stage all the time. Of the roughly two hundred plays in the current repertoire of nō, the sole one in which laughter is heard is performed only once every several decades—the unpopular *Sanshō*. Kyōgen, which has laughing as its reason for being, is normally assigned a status a level lower than nō, and on various points it is treated as if it were beneath nō. (An opinion with which I disagree.) For example, in the dressing room, the kyōgen actor, who may be senior to, and far excel, his coun-

---

[16] Tragedy must be defined as presenting a situation in which there is "grave suffering" on the part of the protagonist, and not as something consisting of pathos or pity (Mandel, 1961, 88-95).

terparts in nō, will be given a seat lower than even the youngest, inexperienced nō actor. This is not a private matter. It reflects the difference in quality judged to exist between laughing and weeping. In waka as well a great volume of tears has been shed. So large is the number of such poems that the ordinary Westerner cannot help but have a strange sensation. Waka dealing with love are expected to treat the painful, sad thoughts of yearning rather than joy. Before the modern age, joyous love is so rare in poetry that the only examples that come to mind are poems by Fujiwara Kamatari (*Man'yōshū*, 2:95) and Shiki no Ōji (ibid., 4:513).

Kobayashi Hideo has distinguished "the movement of bristling muscles" with "the gleam of the sun and the sweat of men and horses" as essential elements for the *Heike Monogatari (The Tale of the Heike)*.[17] But if we use his comments as a touchstone to this military tale, we see they are relevant only to parts. The transitions from one political incident to another, along with episodes in the plot related to them, are far more numerous. Moreover, it cannot be denied that the principal feature running through the whole work is the elegiac tone over the downfall of the Heike. When all is said, the keynote to this work is "that opening statement of pathos in the imayō style."[18] Given this emphasis, there is nothing discordant about the sorrowful chapters devoted to women: "Giō," "Kotoku," "Kosaishō," "Yokobue," etc.

In nō, special emphasis is given to stories in which the effective beauty of the mood centers on a woman. All agree that the most nō-like of nō are those in which the dance of a young woman is the most significant feature—namely in the third category of plays.[19] Although an actor may be praised for a wonderfully artistic performance of *Kumasaka* or *Kuruma Tengu*, that is not his highest joy. But when he is told that his performance was brilliant as the woman in *Izutsu* or *Nonomiya*, he will rejoice from his heart. In considering the characteristic tone of Japanese literature, one must not overlook the belief that womanly grace constitutes the pinnacle of beauty.

Compared to brawny muscles and the sweat of horses and men, the quality of a graceful woman's dance is clearly implicit. The expressed grace of that dance is not entirely introverted. Set beside the "old woman" pieces—*Sekidera Komachi, Obasute, Higaki*, etc.—in which the grace has outwardly disappeared and the acting is not obvious, the third class of plays still has some explicit extroverted elements. The fact that the

[17] Kobayashi Hideo, *Heike Monogatari*, "Mujō to Yū Koto," p. 25. As Kobayashi himself says, "Such things [sweat, etc.] are not written about at all, but. . . ."

[18] Ibid., p. 27.

[19] [The third of five conventionally distinguished groups of plays, this is also known as wig pieces (kazuramono), because the male actor of course needs a wig to play the part. —Ed.]

"old woman" plays are known as the secret essence of the art reveals how unarguably esteemed is the implicit, introverted tone. The lonely desolation of sabi, the gloomy distress of wabi, the shiver of hie—these are prized as artistic qualities of very high beauty and surely have a conception in common. Music confirms this, for in it the low note points to sharp judgment; and "astringency" (shibusa), which is far from ideal to our sense of physical taste, is felt to designate one kind of true beauty.

Japanese Literature as Part of Asian Literature

To examine the special characteristics of Japanese literature in greater detail, we must proceed contrastively within the context of Asia. By Asia is meant East Asia, particularly China and Korea as well as Japan. Although there are many points where Japan has had some kind of relation with India, the major influence has been limited to Buddhism. Indian literature was not directly known in Japan, and Buddhism itself was so changed by Chinese culture, being transmitted to Japan in Chinese translation, that Indian literature is not appropriate for comparison with Japanese. Because Indian literature is Aryan, for any contrastive analysis with Japanese literature the Indian is rather part of "the world."

To begin as before with externals, both Chinese and Korean literature may be termed middle length. That is, although their external forms are not as brief as Japanese, neither are they as lengthy as those of the West. The shortest form of Chinese poetry is the chüeh-chü, with its four lines in five or seven characters. For all its brevity, it may convey twice the content of a tanka and four times that of a haiku. In some cases, what is contained in one line of a chüeh-chü may correspond to an entire tanka. Comparison is easy with those tanka that have one or more Chinese verses for their topics (kudai waka).[20]

Warblers chatter about the end of spring.

Uguisu wa	It is warblers,
Suginishi haru o	Grieving, grieving on that the spring
Oshimitsutsu	Has come to an end,
Naku koe ōki	Whose multitudes of song
Koro ni zo arikeru.	Lament the season now no more.

(*Senzaikaku*, 41, 519)

[20] [The object of kudai waka is to present a Japanese version—in revision, expansion, contraction—of an esteemed line or couplet from Chinese. Other topics (dai) might tell the circumstances of composition, be counterparts of English titles, or be set topics such as "Love in the Winter." In what immediately follows, the Chinese verses are represented by italicized translations, and the Japanese by transliterations and translations.—Ed.]

The only thing that has been added is "oshimitsutsu" (grieving). The more usual proportion, however, is probably that two lines of a chüeh-chü correspond to one tanka. For example:

Falling leaves sound like rain;
The white moonlight looks like frost.

Koe bakari	Their sound, theirs alone,
Ko no ha no ame wa	The tree leaves that sound like rain
Furusato no	At my native home,
Niwa no migaki mo	Where also on the garden wall
Tsuki no hatsushimo.	Shines the moon's first frost.

(*Shūi Gusō*, "Ingai," 3236)

A couplet of seven-character Chinese lines will often hold more than can be included in one tanka.

The lamp turned back that we can enjoy the midnight moon,
We tread fallen blossoms, sharing regret for the
spring of our youth.

Ariake no	For the moon that melts
Tsuki ni somukuru	In the morning sky we turn
Tomoshibi no	The lamp against the wall
Kage ni utsurou	That we may look upon the flowers
Hana o miru kana.	Fading in the fading light.

(*Shūgyoku*, 4:4385)

The chüeh-chü is the shortest form of Chinese poetry, being four lines long. A Chinese poem may sometimes run to two hundred lines, as in Tu Fu's "Composing My Thoughts on an Autumn Day at the Office of K'uei-chou" (*Toshi*, 19:1394) and in Po Chü-i's "Reply to a Poem of Dreaming about an Excursion on a Spring Day" (*Hakushi*, 12:1919). But these are very much exceptions, and normally it can be thought that a fifty-line poem is rather long. So if two hundred lines is not especially long next to an epic, it is long in Chinese terms which, like Japanese, exclude epic. These considerations lead me to consider Chinese forms as of middle length.

Because as much as eighty percent of extant Korean literature was poetry written in Chinese, up to the Kabo Kyŏngjang (1894 Reform), it is also of middle length. In indigenous Korean poetry, the standard form from about the seventh through the tenth century was the hyangga, whose lines consist of certain clusters of syllables. A hyangga would have lines of given clusters of syllables as a longer first part, followed by a briefer hugu of a differing syllable cluster. The sijo, which developed in the fourteenth century, runs to about forty-six syllables, and so is slightly longer than the tanka. Without the hugu, the short form of the hyangga is slightly longer than the haiku. In addition to those two, a form called the kasa arose in the fifteenth century and continues to be practiced. This has two lines or parts in 4 + 4 + 4 + 4 and a third that runs from 3 + 6 to 11 + 4 + 4. For the sijo, the middle line or unit may be multiplied at the discretion of the poet. This principle of expansibility resembles that of the chōka, in which the 5 + 7 units can be repeated to some length—with a final seven-syllable line giving a decisive ending. By a similar multiplication, kasa may run to more than a hundred lines, but there are no epics and no poems extending over thousands of lines.[21] In sum, like Chinese poetry, Korean is of middle length although a bit closer to the brevity of Japanese.

There is difficulty in taking syllables as equivalents in all three Asian languages. In Chinese poetry, one character represents one syllable and usually one word, whereas in Japanese and Korean more than two syllables are commonly needed to make a word. Between those last two languages, judgment by syllable count may be fruitful. It will therefore be clear enough, for all the rude approximation by syllable count, that Japanese poetry tends to be briefer than either Korean or Chinese. The thirty-one syllable tanka had been established as a standard form by the Ancient Age. When the Japanese later came to adopt Chinese poetry, they therefore customarily cut off from the original a section comparable in semantic scope to a tanka. This can be illustrated by recalling the kudai waka given above. The Chinese couplet quoted earlier is from a famous lü-shih (regulated verse) by Po Chü-i, "During the Spring, Lu Chou-liang and I Stayed Together at Hua-yang Temple" (*Hakushi*, 13:1932). The whole poem follows.

> When not punctilious by nature, one enjoys the pleasures of
>   intimacy,
> And one's secluded dwelling is suitable for visits from a neighbor.
> The lamp turned back that we can enjoy the midnight moon,
> We tread fallen blossoms, sharing regret for the spring of our youth.
> My Almond Retreat is a countrified place, but it well suits one who
>   is ill,

---

[21] Among kasa, there are works like Hanyang Kŏsa's *Song of Hanyang* (1844), which is over 1,800 lines long. This is simply made up of lines of 3 + 4 syllables, and as a genre it would seem more akin to Japanese zuihitsu. Kim Tong-uk, 1974, 159-61; English translation, 134-37.

Whereas the pavilions of the literati demean officials, not easing
  poverty.
Going the way of letters like you, sir, still haggard in grief—
I wonder, for what kind of person does the mist on the Han River
  wait?

As will be evident, two lines have been taken from eight as a topic for
kudai waka, a flourishing practice during the Middle Ages. Because of
the parallelism in Chinese poetry, and particularly in regulated verse,
Japanese poets normally drew on antithetical parallel couplets. This is
clear from the evidence of the selections in the *Wakan Rōei Shū* and the
Shinsen Rōei Shū, where nearly all the Chinese selections are such couplets.

This Chinese absorption in units of parallel couplets requires attention.
For parallelism to exist, the couplets must consist of lines at once independent of each other semantically and yet related in syntactic expression.
Without a caesura or cut between the two lines, meaningful parallelism
is not feasible. This holds for Chinese poetry in which the lines consist
of the same number of syllables, whether five or seven. In waka as well
it is possible to have couplets made of units equal in their number of
syllables, although matters are a bit tight with the tanka, whose five lines
vary between five and seven in syllable count: $5 + 7 + 5 + 7 + 7$. In
waka generally, a line of five and a line of seven syllables may be joined
into a unit that can be repeated a certain number of times, with a final
seven-syllable line added to conclude: $N(5 + 7) + 7$ is the basic pattern.
So the tanka is simply the special case of $N = 2$. In chōka, with the $N(5
+ 7)$ section so extended, there is no special hindrance to the use of
parallelism. At its zenith, in the works of Hitomaro, the chōka flourished
with numerous examples of brilliant parallelism. In tanka, the use of
parallelism in the $2(5 + 7)$ lines leaves the last (seven-syllable) line a
waif, and it is difficult to integrate the poem. In the face of such difficulties,
it was impossible to obtain chōka-like parallelism of the Chinese kind in
the tanka $(5 + 7) + (5 + 7) + 7$. Instead tanka came to be divided
quite differently: $(5 + 7 + 5) + (7 + 7)$, with a break between the
three upper and two lower lines within the integral whole. This technique
was referred to as sankugire (third-line break). The inequality of sev-
enteen- and fourteen-line units precludes the kind of parallelism found
in Chinese poetry. Nonetheless, the sankugire has been the basic cause
giving rise to that parallel organization which, as said earlier, must consist
of units at once independent of each other semantically yet related in
syntactic expression, with a cut between them.

The principle of cuts or breaks between lines of a Chinese poem extends
to gaps between words. For in Chinese each monosyllable can have its

own meaning, something very rare in Japanese, which uses inflections for adjectives and verbs along with particles to inflect nouns and for other functions. To a Japanese view at least, Chinese with its separated, non-inflected character-syllables consists of highly separable units. If Japanese is sequential, continuous, Chinese is digital, discontinuous—characteristics also reflected in the poetry written in those languages. So if waka and haiku expression can be compared to the sound of a violin, Chinese poetry resembles that of a piano.[22] There are not a few examples of waka and haiku which, for all their fundamental sequential character, have a somewhat discontinuous nature. That is because their poets have had a deep understanding of Chinese poetry and have been able to impart some discontinuity to their poetry.

The perhaps more than eighty percent of extant Korean poetry written in Chinese of course has the Chinese characteristics of antithetical parallelism and discontinuity. In indigenous Korean poetry, however—in hyangga and sijo—one sees little parallelism, and the breaks are not conspicuous. In both Japan and Korea, then, the essential character of linguistic expression is not discontinuous. Discontinuity of the Chinese kind did not infiltrate the indigenous poetry, probably because those Korean poems that were thought ga—elegant, refined in nature—are all in Chinese. Surely the result was that, in composing poetry in Korean, the poets were little inclined to confront Chinese poetry in its ga terms. Why else should the non-Chinese poetry of Korea be less than a fifth of the total?

We should now inquire into a second point raised earlier, the degree to which subjective opposition is incorporated into literature. Both Chinese and Korean literature are about midway between Japanese and Western literature in this respect, although indigenous Korean genres more closely resemble Japanese literature in this respect as well.

In the articulation of individual works, neither Chinese nor Korean literature is much given to the use of opposition, in this respect being at one with Japanese. Let us take as an example something Chinese to compare with nō. That would be the Yüan Dynasty tsa-chü, where only the main actors—the male role (cheng-sheng) and the female role (cheng-tan)—sing: the other actors are limited to prose. Because the essential lines of a play are those sung, it is clear that the organization of the tsa-chü shares much with the shite-alone principle of nō. The fact that, as in Japan, tragedy did not come into existence in China implies the same reason, lack of an antagonist. As in Japan, there is "sad drama," but tragedy is not to be found. In the Yüan tsa-chü, *Tou O Yüan (The False*

---

[22] This is a generalized comparison. For just as in Japan the waka of the *Shinkokinshū* period are more broken than those of the *Kokinshū*, and haiku more broken still, in China tz'u are more continuous than shih (Yoshikawa, 1952, 75-95).

Accusation of Tou O), the story concerns the wretched life of the heroine. The first part is especially gruesome. The opening derives, however, not from a willed decision by Tou O herself but from a fate that could not be avoided.[23] Having been ensnared by gangsters, Tou O is arrested on suspicion of killing her father-in-law. The action reaches an extreme pitch when not only she but her aged mother-in-law are tortured. In order to save the old woman, Tou O confesses to the crime and is executed. In this scene not one drop of blood gushing from her decapitation falls on the ground. Instead, the blood flies into the air, dyeing the flag at the execution site. Because of Tou O's just anger, snow falls, although it is the Sixth Month, and poor harvests follow for three years. This kind of action certainly reaches the limits of wretchedness. But it does not produce tragedy, in which the protagonist actively confronts fate through personal will, bravely electing or daring a determined destruction. The lack of opposition and its results in Chinese drama will be found in other genres, and the same holds for Korean literature.

In another respect, Chinese literature has a fundamental sense of opposition in the relation presumed between the human and the natural. One tangible manifestation is the scarcity, from ancient times, of Chinese poems that deal with nature *as* nature, although it must be recognized that this refers to the northern, Han line of people. In agriculturally dependent ancient China, people encountered nature throughout actual life, and yet almost no poems are to be found on the beauty of nature. Poets were given instead to lyric expression of personal feeling. Of the 305 poems in the *Shih Ching (The Book of Songs)* , nature appears only as a metaphorical image of personal affairs. It is no exaggeration to say that natural topics are highly limited: "A Mushroom" (ko-chün), "Eastern Mountains" (tung-shan), "Bulrushes" (chien-chia), and "To Have No Sheep" (wu-yang).

It is not entirely true that the Han Dynasty fu [rhyme-prose or rhapsody] lacks description of the beauty of nature, but most examples treat nature artificially. Any real sensitivity to nature is highly limited. In contrast to that, the Ch'u people of the south did appreciate nature, and not a few poems in the *Ch'u Tz'u (The Songs of the South)* deal with natural myths or with fragrant grasses and trees. In the Six Dynasties period the capital was moved south, and with the reclusive thinking of Taoism reinvigorated there came to be many poems on mountains, rivers,

[23] Wang Kuo-wei claims that "among the works of a most tragic nature are, for instance, Kuan Han-ch'ing's *Tou O Yüan [The False Accusation of Tou O]* and Chi Chün-hsiang's *Chao-shih Ku-erh [The Orphan of Chao]*. Although in these plays there appear wicked people who meddle with the fate of the protagonist, the very action of throwing oneself into the jaws of a terrible death derives from the protagonist's own will. These plays are by no means inferior to the greatest tragedies in the world" (Wang Kuo-wei, 1915, 125).

fields, and gardens (Aoki, 1935a, 552-91). The mainstream of the whole of Chinese literature is Confucian, however. Hsieh Ling-yün (385-433), who opened up a new phase of poems on natural scenery, had benefited from a knowledge of Indian culture. So far was contact with a foreign culture necessary for many features of the Chinese appreciation of nature, which is of little relative importance.[24] The poetic fusion of natural scenery and human feeling in China reaches its highest peak with Tu Fu. To be as remarkable as he, however, is to attain complete realization through the utmost exertion. And conversely, the necessity for exercising such talent to fuse natural scenery and human feeling shows that in Chinese poetry the human and the natural are deemed separate.

It is more difficult to judge the degree of separation between the natural and the human in Korean literature. So much of the indigenous poetry has been lost. Only twenty-five hyangga remain, only some forty-two yŏyo (ballads and poems from the late Koryŏ period), about 3,500 sijo from the seven or eight centuries of the Koryŏ period and the Yi Dynasty, and not more than several hundred of the longer sasŏl sijo. Obviously, the data are not altogether adequate. To judge by what there is, Korean poetry takes human affairs as its chief subject, and few poems deal with nature itself. The yŏyo, "Tongdong," is a wŏllyŏng'che concerned with the sequence of events and landscapes through the year.[25] And this subject is continued in the modern "Sach'in ka."[26] By comparison, Chinese poems composed on seasonal topics include "Seventh Month" (Ch'i-yüeh) from *The Book of Songs* and "A Seasonal Tale" (Chi-chieh Ko), a long folk song of the modern Miao people (a south China mountain people).[27] But the central theme of the Korean "Tongdong" is love for a woman, and that of "Sach'in ka" concerns the reminiscence of one's parents. The events of the seasons and the scenery are only vehicles to emphasize the main theme. By contrast, in the kasa written among the scholarly intellectuals from the fifteenth through the nineteenth centuries there are a number of poems such as "The Song of Myŏnang Pavilion" (Myŏna-

[24] Depiction of natural details can be found in fu by Sung Yü (290-22 B.C.) and to some extent in the Han period. But their use is not concerned with natural beauty, being simply lists of various natural conditions. Hsieh Ling-yün (385-433) was the first to write of the beauties of nature "with heartfelt praise" (Obi, 1962, 290-305).

[25] Wŏllyŏngch'e or calendrical-style poetry first presents the main subject, and then goes through each month of the year from the first, dealing with activities, conventions, and scenery associated with each month, and ends with a prayer for the happiness of the speaker's lover and his longing for her (Kim Sa-yŏp, 1973, 213-214).

[26] Sach'in ka make up one kind of Korean folk song. It is treated as one kind of poetry that emerged during the period of Confucian rationalism (Chŏyŏ, 117-25).

[27] *Chi-chieh Ko* is a 518-line poem handed down by the Miao, a South China mountain people living in the Ch'ing River basin in Kweichow province. It has been recorded by the Kweichow People's Literary Production Group: *People's Literature* (People's Literature Press, October 1960), pp. 43-53.

ngjŏng ka) in which natural scenery becomes an evident subject (Kim Tong-uk, 1974, 156-57). On balance, the relation between the natural and the human seems more intimate than in China.

Our next criterion involves the relation between social class and writing in various genres. The Chinese strongly held, from the Han Dynasty on, that worthy literature could be composed only by a group that was thoroughly versed in the classics, and whose ideas of life were shaped by the classical spirit: the literati class, in other words. When a new genre was devised by a nonliteratus, it was regarded either as worthless literature or as something other than literature. The literati were not supposed to have anything to do with romances or other worthless genres. Of course, dissolute or unsuccessful literati did in fact write plebeian pieces. When they did, however, the author's name was not given with the work—so demonstrating the gulf between the genre and a literatus' social position. And no literatus was permitted to enjoy such works in public. Moreover, the highly valued kinds of writing were solely restricted to the literati in the bureaucracy, who held social responsibility for politics and morality. The lower classes—who held no political responsibility and could not rise to the administrative levels of government—could not be active in literary creation.[28] By the end of the Sung, merchants and landowners begin to appear in poetic circles (Yoshikawa, 1962, 223-33). But by comparison with Japan, this is a far later phenomenon. Until the beginning of the literary revolution of 1917, the sense remained in China that the literati held responsibility for maintaining the valued species of literature.

The same held in Korea, but not in Japan. The Japanese did feel that only writing based on classical precedent was proper to literature, and that those of good standing should not publicly acknowledge their connection with other kinds of writing. This conception was brought from China in the Ancient Age and was strongly held in the Middle Ages. So in contrast to waka, renga, haikai, etc., where the author's name is specified with the work, monogatari [tales or prose narratives] and wabun nikki [diaries or personal accounts in Japanese, also thought part of literature] did not mention the name of the author even if widely known. This reflects the Chinese attitude. For all that, in a manner strikingly different from China, the royal anthologies include poems written by people who did not belong to the upper social strata. Among poets included in the *Kokinshū*, for example, there are at least fourteen low-ranking courtiers, namely those below the sixth court rank—and among them are three of its editors, Ki no Tomonori, Ōshikōchi Mitsune, and

[28] See Yoshikawa, 1948, preface, 2-13, and Saeki, 1970b, 220-21. In the Yi Dynasty, Korean officials were more systematically organized than in China at the time (Kim Sa-yŏp, 1973, 419).

Mibu no Tadamine. It is thought that for form's sake some poets of lower rank were included among the "anonymous" (Yomibito shirazu). Moreover, twenty-three female poets were included, among them at least one woman of pleasure (8:387), possibilities unthinkable in China. For other evidence there is *The Tale of Genji*: although it had originally been thought little better than something to interest women, by the end of the twelfth century it had become a central classic for waka. Fujiwara Shunzei, the highest authority in poetic circles, declared that "writing poems without having looked at the *Genji* is an unforgettable crime" (*Roppyakuban Utaawase*, "Fuyu," 1:505). In China, members of the highest nobility such as Ichijō Kanera (1408-81) and Sanjōnishi Sanetaka (1455-1537) would never have lectured, like them, on a woman's prose narrative as something of high cultural value.

We now consider the degree of opposition between the individual and the group. Such opposition in China was striking during certain periods, but on the whole it has not been extreme. The Six Dynasties provides a representative example of a period when the individual was not conspicuous. Without memorizing the poems of the time, no one could distinguish among authors when their names were concealed on the page.

> Yü Hsin's style is fresh and clear;
> Pao Chao's thought splendid and free.
>
> *(Toshi*, 1:1102)

More precisely, although it is possible to make critical distinctions between the poetic styles of Yü Hsin and Pao Chao, that would require the accumulation of long years' familiarity with the work of both poets and the minutest investigation of distinct features. They could never be distinguished with ordinary study. Beginning with the mid-T'ang, however, poems appeared with distinctive personal features. One hardly confuses the poetic styles of poets like Li Po, Tu Fu, Han Yü, or Po Chü-i. By the Sung Dynasty, there was a conception of a poet's relation to a master— of whom this or that poet was a disciple (Yoshikawa, 1962, 127-28). This could even involve entanglement in political controversy like that between the Yüan-yu and Shao-shu parties. Although this may seem a reversion to the group, poets in the groups were not impeded from displaying their individuality. There were those of "Su's Gate," disciples of Su Tung-p'o like Huang T'ing-chien, Ch'en Shih-tao, Ch'in Kuan, Chang Lai, Ch'ao Pu-chih, Wen T'ung, and Mi Fei. Each has his own special characteristics. The styles of Ch'en Shih-tao and Huang T'ing-chien are especially distinct. We can compare this with the more homogeneous Japanese groups. Teika's included Shunzei's daughter, Nijō In Sanuki, Impunmon'in no Taifu, etc. Kyōgoku Tamekane's group included Fushimi

In, Gofushimi In, Hanazono In, Eifuku (or Yōfuku) Mon'in, Yūgi Mon'in, Shōsammi Tameko, and others. Neither group was as individualistic as those within "Su's Gate." By comparison with the recent West, however, it is difficult to conclude that poets of either nation emphasized individuality.

We are also concerned with the relationship between author and audience. As we have seen, Japanese poets have always shown a strong tendency to constitute groups. Valued literature was that which included the writer and the reader in the same sphere, for reasons resembling those of the Chinese. So far as the Chinese social conception was understood by the Japanese, it supported their belief that the writer and audience shared a common world. There is no difference between Japan and China in result. To say it again, when a Chinese poet drew on earlier works to write in a classical style, the literature produced had value by definition. In order to write in that fashion, however, special training was necessary from one's earliest years, something not feasible for everyone, and poetry based on the classics required of the reader a similar familiarity with them. Any need for verbosity was eliminated by the shared literary code.

This conception of the common world of author and audience also guaranteed poetic value, so that writing which lacked the classical elements was thought of little value. Works by the literati used the shared knowledge of classics in discussing the grand principles of government, morality, and etiquette, more precisely those of *The Six Principles of Government.*[29] The prose of lower officials lacking classical training consisted, by contrast, of the documents of ordinary bureaucratic business. In the same fashion, music that divided society into performers and audience was not valued as real art, but was regarded as the work of artisans like carpenters. Valued, true music entailed the kind of accomplishment that the literati could wholeheartedly share as performer or audience in small, select groups. This included, for example, such instruments as the zither (ch'in). So also painting. The concept of true literature or art, based on the shared knowledge of artist and audience, was also held in Korea.

Our third comparative subject is tone. In contrast to Japanese literature, which is emotional and implicit or introverted, Chinese is volitional, intellectual, and extroverted, with a strong tendency to esteem the past. The tone of Korean literature is generally close to that of Chinese, although there are not a few examples of the emotional and implicit.

Since ancient times Chinese poetry has been taken to "state the will

---

[29] In the "Lun-wen" section of Wei Wen-t'i's *T'ien Lun*, there is: "I believe that literature [wen-chang] is a necessary great achievement for governing a state, a glorious thing that will endure immortally" (*Wen Hsüan*, 52:1128).

or intentions."[30] The only Western counterpart must be the lyric. In Japanese, "jojōshi" (the dictionary counterpart of "lyric" or "a lyric") is taken to suggest (in its "jō") "feeling," "emotions." Such a conception does not altogether fit Chinese poetry. Of course when the human heart is the subject, feelings and emotions will naturally be explored. But for Chinese poetry it is not enough to consider the emotionally affective— the morally affective is also of great consequence. To poets who were scholar-officials, the greatest, the grandest theme was social improvement. For that end, poetry is zealous, intentional in tone, with the important thematic end criticism of government. Tu Fu's lengthy poem, "A Lyric Poem of Five Hundred Words, Composed on the Way to Feng-hsiang from the Capital" (*Toshi*, 4:1133), is not so much a travel poem as one with clear political criticism as its main theme.[31] This political criticism is obvious even in Po Chü-i's *Ch'in-chung Yin (Songs of Ch'in)* and his *Hsin Yüeh-fu (New Ballads)*. In Japan there has never been a preoccupation with political criticism in waka: poetry has been simply lyrical, and only the lyrical (as described) has flourished. We have seen that during the Middle Ages poets might isolate two lines from a Chinese poem that appealed to them or offered an attractive poetic topic (kudai waka). The lines selected were consistently lyrical or descriptive, even if the original poem might have been concerned with political criticism. This holds for prose works as well. Although Bakin's *Eight Virtuous Heroes* dangles morality before us, that is mere pose and is not radical enough to control the tone.

Another characteristic distinguishing Chinese literature is its intellectual emphasis. With their proneness to draw on empirical fact, the Chinese have made less of the imaginative or fleeting. This contrasts with the Western aspiration to a unity of empiricism and imagination. The relative poverty of mythology in China may be a manifestation of this.[32] Chinese intellectuality may well be the main reason that epic poetry did not develop there (Bowra, 1952, 12-14). As intellect rises in poetry, individual peculiarities and opinions tend to become more prominent, group thoughts and feelings more restricted. It is for other reasons than those prevailing

[30] In the general preface to the *Mao Shih*, we read: "Shih [poetry] is the destination to which chih [will or intention] goes. When it is in the mind we call it chih, and when it is expressed as words as we call it shih [poetry]." Apparently, a nearly identical pronunciation of the two words in ancient Chinese was taken to show that poetry and authorial intention were practically the same.

[31] For the critical nature of this poem, see *To Ho Shiki*, vol. 1 (Yoshikawa, 1950, 269-92).

[32] Yoshikawa, 1944, 247-76. The paucity of Chinese myths applies to the Han people, and does not necessarily pertain to the non-Han peoples to the south and southwest (Itō Seiji, 1970, 61-62).

among the Chinese that epic poetry also cannot be found in Yamato poetry and in Korean literature.[33] In China, intellectuality gained prominence as the result of two millennia of ideological leadership by Confucianism. Confucius "did not talk about 'extraordinary things, feats of strength, disorder, and spiritual beings' " (*Analects*, Bk. 7, v. 20, trans. Legge; cf. Waley's, p. 127). Confucians held no faith in a world that cannot be sensed or felt. This attitude expresses the spirit of the Han people. Or a large part of it. But that very mistrust seemed necessary in view of a strong trend toward belief in the uncanny and divine, a tendency too strong to be disregarded. From the Six Dynasties stories treating the fearsome, through the late Ming and early Ch'ing, there flows an undercurrent of many, varied kinds of works concerned with the divine, the immortal, the strange, and the frightening. These include *Hsi-yu Chi (The Journey to the West)* and some less familiar works such as the Northern Sung *San-sui P'ing-yao Chuan, Feng-shen Yen-i, Nü-hsien Wai-shih*, and *Liao-chai Chih-i*. This evidence suggests that the fearsome and the supernatural, with their Taoist connections, did not lose their hold on the common people during two thousand years or more. But Confucian intellectuality prevented these elements from becoming the main current of thought.

The tone of Korean literature is, by contrast, similar to that of Japan, largely emotional. Volitional and intellectual attitudes can easily be discerned in Korean literature—that is, in literature of the kinds Koreans borrowed from China and wrote in Chinese. Native Korean literature is more strongly emotional. From the Three Kingdoms period forward there is an abundance of myths and stories, and in the Koryŏ period as well there is no lack of stories turning on the fearsome or supernatural. Here is testimony that Korean literature is not inherently given to intellectualism. With the Yi Dynasty, stories are less often set down, an inevitable consequence of the peculiar circumstances of Korean society at the time. Buddhism had been the main ideology through the Koryŏ period. But from the Yi Dynasty the Chu Hsi school of Neoconfucianism dominated politics, banishing Buddhism and Taoism from the center of society. It follows that Yi literature should be marked by the same tone as Chinese. It is, although in comparison with the prose and poetry of China, Korean literature is weaker in the volitional. Poems like Hŏ Kyun's, critical of society, can easily be found (Kim Tong-uk, 1974, 134-37). But the dominant line is generally lyrical and descriptive. Some literary species originating in China were unlikely drinking companions of the Korean mil-

[33] Yi Ka-wŏn has mentioned the *Tongmyŏngwang P'yŏn* as an important example of epic (1961, 132-34). But his sense of epic differs from that used here. Apart from this poem, Korean literature offers no other poem extroverted in tone.

itary and scholarly aristocracy. In spite of their low merit on the Confucian scale, however, there are nearly six hundred of these old Korean prose tales of supposedly inferior nature. Among them are Hŏ Kyun's *Hong Kiltong Chŏn* and Kim Man-jung's *Kuun Mong*. That they, if only as the prime examples, could be placed among works of the aristocracy shows that the treatment of popular literature in Korea was not necessarily the same as in China.

Next to tone or attitude in Chinese literature is the question of the larger interplay of the explicit or extroverted and the implicit or introverted. In *The Book of Songs*, there is more sorrow than joy, but there is no loss of expectation that good human intentions will bring prosperity. (Although, properly speaking, the poems of this collection have no titles, the later, conventional ones will be used in this volume.) On the other hand, from the end of the Han through the Six Dynasties, human existence was taken to be inherently feeble, and the keynote of these periods became the pathetic feeling that one could do nothing in the face of fate. Although in the T'ang period the recovery of ancient optimism was held as an article of faith, the sense of the hopelessness of life was not lost. In the Sung period, human life was taken to have not merely its portion of suffering but to contain happiness as well. There would be occasions for sadness, but if one saw deeply enough there would be grounds for asking whether a given incident was truly sorrowful. This way of thought was well conveyed by Su Tung-p'o (Yoshikawa, 1962, 34-39), and it was an attitude carried on to the Yüan and Ming Dynasties.

Although the grounds for appreciating beauty did differ in the outstanding periods of Chinese literature, the implicit and explicit elements seem in basic complementary balance. In the prose and poetry of the Six Dynasties, the works of linguistic craftsmanship embellished with magnificent lines represent a Chinese explicitness of tone, whereas the simplicity and monochromatic tendency of Sung prose and poetry offer a good example of the implicit in Chinese literature. In terms as it were of quantity, the explicit predominates. That is because for the most part the implicit, the introverted, was bound up with the thought of either Lao Tzu and Chuang Tzu or with Buddhism. And in a Chinese society controlled by Confucian thought, the implicit was no match for the explicit. The balance of the two elements in Korea is that of China: in large measure they are found together. If one considers just the poetry and prose written in Chinese during the Yi Dynasty, there will be found more of the implicit. In that respect, Korea is closer to Japan than to China. In native Korean genres it is generally difficult to specify the attitude.

The most basic element in Chinese literary thought is no doubt its classicism, which continued with little change for over twenty centuries. For both Japan and Korea as well this was the most valuable legacy in the heritage. On such common ground, the three East Asian countries should be distinguished from the rest of the world. To begin with, the spirit of the Han people, although sensitive enough to unity, is even more sensitive to disunity. Their hostile interpretation of disunified matters must imply an effort to realize perfection in things available to present experience, whose worth is established by the valued past. To hold that perfection exists in the past means, for writing, that literature with precedents is the most beautiful (Yoshikawa, 1944, 10-18). As a consequence, writers had to memorize an enormous number of works, and their only appropriate audience was composed of people sharing their knowledge. This classicism led the poet and audience to share values. Both Japan and Korea inherited this assumption, although in the case of Korea those persons sharing the prized culture were limited to the yangban, the military and scholarly aristocracy. In Japan, by contrast, tanka and haiku societies of socially mixed membership have survived and flourished into the twentieth century.

Japan is overly enthusiastic in its reception of foreign cultures and demands more of itself than of them (Yoshikawa, 1960, 159-67). It applied the Chinese standard of precedented language in extreme fashion. During the thirteenth century Teika stipulated that the vocabulary of waka "must not exceed that of the first three royal collections [sandaishū]" (*Eika Taigai*, 114). The total number of poems in those first three collections does not exceed 3,888 (in the Teika manuscript), and many, many words are of course repeated. It is therefore demonstrably impossible that all waka of the present and future could manage with the vocabulary of the first three collections. Teika's preceding words, "as for what *should* be . . ." (naru beku wa) are therefore a proviso that must be explained as a hope. In accepting the Chinese idea that literature with precedents is most beautiful, the Japanese went compulsively further to hold that for waka "precedent" might be strictly limited to the sandaishū.

It is possible to criticize Tu Fu's poetry by saying that every single word has some poetic source. An example can always be found *somewhere* in classical or semiclassical writing, but such a notion of "source" is overwide. In waka, Japan's native poetry, the classicism is founded in Japanese attitudes themselves. In Korean literature as well the classicism taken from China is remarkable, but it is limited to composition in Chinese and so does not apply to native Korean kinds like the sijo. Because the absorption of Chinese classicism is the most remarkable fact of Japanese literature, it has been necessary to use the basic coordinates of distinct periods in the three literatures. The absorption itself will be discussed subsequently.

Yamato Literature and Non-Yamato Literature

As I have stated earlier, my history of Japanese literature is based on a definition of it as that of the Yamato people. It is now necessary to define the Yamato line: as the *peoples* who formed and developed the culture represented by Yayoi-style pottery and the literature of their descendants; their *works* produced in both modern Japanese and its older versions; and the *audience* for their work. In other words, Ainu literature cannot be discussed as of the same kind as Yamato literature. It is supposed that, even in Japan's ancient period, the Ainu peoples inhabited the northern part of the Japanese archipelago. But in spite of sharing the same regional climate, they produced a distinct literature. This is probably due to the differing bases of the societies, one being founded on hunting and gathering, the other on cultivation. It is sometimes held that climate influences the character of literature: for example, that poetry in the style of the *Man'yōshū* arose because the area around Asuka was bright and open, and that the *Kokinshū* and *Shinkokinshū* styles were born because the Heian capital was girt by somber mountains. These threadbare explanations continue, but in the end they are just theories without scientific basis. Because climate will influence modes of production regionally, it should indirectly influence the formation of culture. It is unthinkable, however, that the cultural pattern should have a map-like correspondence to climate. Much less can climate be held to influence directly the expressive forms literature takes on.

In contrast to Ainu literature, that of the Ryukyus—of which the Okinawan archipelago is the center—cannot be called non-Yamato. The prime reason is that although it is difficult at present to account exactly for the origins of the Ryukyuan language, it shares much with Yamato-line Japanese.[34] If suitably transliterated, the text of an umuru can be understood with no special difficulty by people on mainland Japan. If overstatement be allowed, one can say that the Ryukyuan language is a Japanese dialect with great differences from the standard version. Moreover, from the seventeenth century on, Ryukyuan literature, at least on the main island of Okinawa, developed while the islanders were in contact

---

[34] According to the methodology of historical linguistics, it has been calculated, on the basis of a comparison between the dialect of Kyoto and that of the Okinawan capital, that Japanese and Ryukyuan separated from a common ancestor some fourteen and a half to seventeen centuries before the middle of the twentieth century (Hattori, 1959, 82-83). But historical linguistics clarifies linguistic matters only among languages in which a common source can be known, and it is not clear by what means Ryukyuan is related to Yamato Japanese.

with the mainland. Good examples exist in the appearance of nakafu poetry, the result of the union of ryūka, and kumiūduri dance (*Shūsin Kaneiri*, etc.).[35] Of course we should not regard this as a strict Yamato literature. Also, in the more distant islands, Yaima and Myāku, there is another remarkable literature whose qualities differ from those both of the Yamato line and from the literature of the Okinawa Islands or the Amami Islands—probably because of the great differences in the conditions and periods of development in relation to the Japanese homeland.

As will be clear from what follows in this Introduction, it is initially possible, in terms of periodizing, to set umuru lyrics against the songs of the *Kojiki* and *Nihon Shoki* and to treat them as part of the Yamato line; but when it comes to the nature and development of genres, it is difficult to establish clear equivalence with the literature of the main Japanese islands. Finally, in terms of literary awareness, the minimal Ryukyuan absorption of Chinese literature contrasts markedly with the situation on the mainland. Because Yamato literature came into being when a highly valued Chinese model held sway, the Six Dynasties style was reborn in the [Japanese] *Kokinshū* style, which was the standard of waka composition for a thousand years. To read and write Chinese poetry and prose were thought yet higher cultural activities. It is hard to discern such an inclination toward Chinese literature in the Ryukyus. In sum, Ryukyu literature is related to the Yamato line, although in being different to some extent it may properly be called semi- or quasi-Yamato.

Once again we must find contrastive bases, for our task is now to compare Ainu and Ryukyuan literature with that of the Yamato line. Our purposes will be served in part by the criteria of external form and tone. And if the subjective opposition of individual versus group is no longer of contrastive utility, poetic mode and imagery are useful and will therefore be added.

For contrastive purposes, then, the external form of Ainu literature has length as its special characteristic. Ainu literature consists of two general classes: ballads that are set to music and pieces that are recited. Among the ballads are "Upopo," a festival song; "Ihumke," a lullaby; "Rimse-shinotcha," a dance song; "Iyohaiochish," a song of pathos; "Yaitkatekar," a song of deep love; "Yaishamane," a lyric; "Chip-o-hau," a boat song, "Tusu-shinotcha," an oracular song; etc. (Kubodera, 1956, 40). Some of the ballads are short. But because the Ainu conceive that everyday affairs should be detailed at length for poetic recitation, long pieces are logically more feasible than short. The yukar, which is central to Ainu literature, contains many works that seem abnormally

[35] In the nakafu, the first lines are in Yamato form: 7 + 5, 7 + 7, or 5 + 5, whereas the later lines are in ryūka form, 8 + 6 (Ikemiya, 1976, 362-63).

long by Japanese standards.[36] Among the yukar there are various kinds of works, as Figure 1 shows (ibid., 198). Although the titles of the yukar in the narrow sense (poems from Iburi, Hidaka) have names different from those in the yukar in the wide sense, such as "Sakorpe" (from Tokachi, Kushiro, Kitami), "Hau" (from Hidaka, etc.), "Hauki" (from Sakhalin), "Yaierap" (from Iburi, Oshima), the methods of recitation and the contents are so nearly alike that only the name of the hero and his place of birth may differ (Kubodera, 1956, 150-51). At the shortest, these yukar are 2,000 or 3,000 lines long, and the longest reach a few tens of thousands of lines.[37] Nothing of comparable length is preserved in either the literature of China and Korea or of the Yamato line.

In the mat-yukar (epics about women), the heroines are characters such as Princess Shinutapka, Princess Osatam, Princess Murai, and Princess Ruppetom. In the oina there is the male god Okikurmi, as in the kamui-yukar the main characters are such animal gods as the sparrow, crane, crow, woodpecker—and thundergod. In each the texts are long. But in the yukar of human heroism, many *very* long works are found.

Nothing in Ryukyuan literature compares with the length of the oina or the various yukar, even if "Ryukyuan" conceals considerable differences from one region to the next. Archaeological study has shown remarkable differences between the central group of southern islands (the Amami archipelago and the Okinawan archipelago) and the group of southernmost islands (the Yaima archipelago and the Myāku archipel-

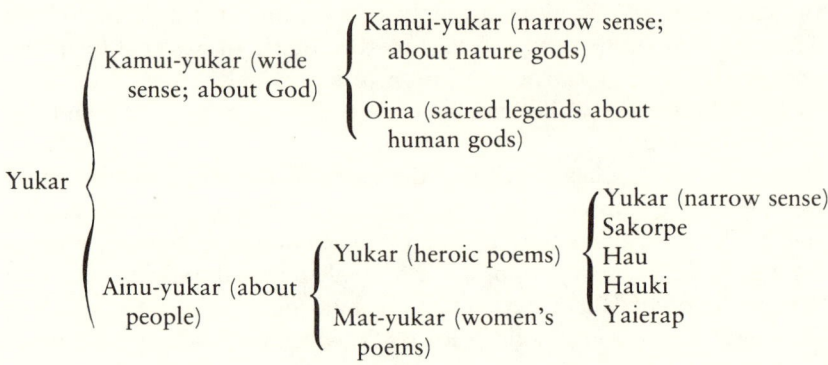

FIGURE 1. Ainu Yukar

---

[36] In Ainu the word is yukar or yūkar, derived from Sakhalin Ainu, and means "singing" (Chiri Mashiho, 1953, 160). In what follows I reserve the term for the heroic oral poetry of the Ainu.

[37] The story of the demon with the poison hook (naukepkorpkur) by Kotanpira of Hidaka is said to be more than 31,000 lines long (Kubodera, 1956, 156-57).

NORTHERN REGION	KYUSHU — Kagoshima — Tanegashima — Yaku — Tokara Islands	ŌSHIMA
CENTRAL REGION	Kikai — Amami Ōshima — Tokunoshima — Okierabu — Yoron	AMAMI
	Iheya — Izena — Ie — Okinawa–Main Island — Naha — Kume — Kerama Islands	OKINAWA
SOUTHERN REGION	Irabu — Myāko — Minna — Tarama	MYĀKO
	Isigaki — Taketome — Hatoma — Kurushima — Iromote — Hateruma — Yunaguni — Taipei — TAIWAN	YAIMA

RYUKYU ARCHIPELAGO

ago).[38] The accompanying map will make geographical distinctions feasible.

Of these areas only the Okinawan has produced literature sharing qualities with the Yamato line. For example, the umuru may be thought the representative of all Ryukyuan literature, but the umuru of the so-called umuru poetic form is limited to the Okinawan archipelago (Ono, 1977a, 22).[39] As to their length, among the 1,248 poems extant there are 24 that are between fifty-one and seventy lines long, and there is only one poem each of seventy-one, seventy-five, and ninety-three lines. There are preserved, however, from the main island of Okinawa and from its peripheral islands, many kwēna and umui that are much longer than the umuru.[40] Although longer works are representative of the southern group of islands, and although the umuru cannot be termed representative of the entire Ryukyus, it does have unique importance as a product of the ancient towns at the center of the kingdom. Among the umuru is the ryūka (Ryukyuan poem), which stopped growing in length during the latter half of the sixteenth century and the first half of the next and settled into the fixed form of 8 + 8 + 8 + 6 syllables. And from the eighteenth century to the nineteenth (when the main island of Okinawa was conquered), it was transmitted to the Amami Islands, thereby exerting a decidedly late influence on the south (Ono, 1977a, 218). This spread did not lead in practice to the development of longer forms. To the contrary, it made the ryūka shorter. It shares, then, with Yamato literature the characteristic of brevity, even if that does not hold true for all Ryukyuan literature.

To the south, namely in the Yaima and Myāku Islands, longer works are characteristic. This does not mean that longer ballads outnumber middle-length or short ones, but rather that there is no small number of

[38] The linguistic demarcation between the Okinawa archipelago and the Myāku archipelago is the contrastive "wa" of the central and "ba" of the southern areas, a distinction confirmed by archaeological evidence (Murayama-Kokubu, 1979, 202-18).

[39] According to Ono (1977, 131-41) in *Umuru Suosi*, after the lines running in a sequential section and indicated by an initial "mata" (again) character, there are repetitions that are indicated by an "ichi" (one) character. If one uses the sign "ichi" rather than reprint a line, the line totals in the *Umuru Suosi* would be markedly smaller. [Since the functions of "mata" and "ichi" are hypothetical and since Ono's explanation—which is no doubt right—seems so remote from the meanings of "again" and "one," we omit these signs but retain the author's note and other references to honor this obscure feature of the poetry.—Ed.]

[40] For example, the *Ōyumi no Uina* from Sakimotobu Village has 67 lines; the "Takeneshiinu Umui" of Zamami Village Asa consists of 85 lines; "Nakazato Magiri Kwainya" of Nakamakiri Hika Village is 63 lines; and the "Hika Mura Ame Kotsu no Toki Dosho Hai Kuinya Tsuji nite Kwainya" of Nakazato Mahiri Higa Village runs to 71 lines (a kwainya praying for rain on the village). This shows that the Kume Island songs tend to be a little longer than those of the main islands of Okinawa. For example, the umuru on building a castle for the Lord of Ishkigo at Gushikawa Village is 71 lines long.

longer ballads and that they are of good quality. Nor does the presence
of longer poems imply any lack of inclination toward brevity, but instead
that the subjects treated by the main line of southern poems were such
that adequate expression required somewhat greater length. Some poems
may be mentioned to give an idea of the lengths employed. There is
"Paifuta Funtaka Yungutu," preserved from Kurushima in the Yaima
archipelago, which is 495 lines long.[41] There is a poem sung by women,
"Aziyamanu Pyāshi," from Karimata, the main island of the Myāku,
which is 291 lines long.[42] And from Ikima, also in the Myāku group,
there is "Fuyiaranu Āgu," which is 201 lines long.[43] Among traditional
Ryukyuan works, similar and analogous pieces have names differing from
region to region, and there are definite distinctions feasible in terms of

TABLE 1
CLASSIFICATION OF RYUKYUAN LITERATURE

	AMAMI	OKINAWA	MYĀKU	YAIMA
Oracles	kutsi	misisiru otakabi	kamfutsi	kamfutsi
Prayers	tahabwe	nudatigutu tirukugutsi	nigari kazaingutsi	nigaifutsi
Incantations	umuri madzinyoi	tiruru majinaigutu	tābi majinaigutu	kazarifutsi dzinmunu
Ritual songs	umuri	kwēna umui	fusa pyāshi nīri	yātakabi amaguitizi umishagu ayō
Communal songs	nagari yētu yungutu	umuru	āgu kuichā-āgu	siraba yunta yungutu
Popular songs	uta shimawta	uta (ryūka)	kuichā taugami shunkani	uta (fushi-uta) tubarāma sunkami

[41] Transcribed by Kishaba Eijun from Takegoshi Kenra, Nishiharu Akata, etc. (Kishaba, 1937, 376-401). "Paifuta" is the name of a village, "Funtaka" of a man.

[42] See *Nan'yō-Myāku*, 92-97. In the Myāku Islands, "tābi" are sung solely by women, "nēli" by men, "pyashi" by both.

[43] Ibid., 247-51: an āgu in which a shamaness prays for a fruitful year at the time when the millet ripens in the Eighth Month.

contents. In general, however, Table 1 sets forth an acceptable classification.[44]

These numerous kinds of poems show a tendency to brevity on the main island of Okinawa that is exceptional. Lengthier works are characteristic for the Ryukyus at large, although there may be no small number of short and middle-length poems. More accurately, of course, this is longness by comparison with Yamato literature, since the poems are of middling length by comparison with Ainu poetry—never above five hundred lines. Of course poems recited or sung cannot be compared solely on the basis of their numbers of lines. But at least there is no doubt that the tendency toward long works in the Ryukyus is not as strong as in Ainu literature.

The degree of individualism or subjectivism also provides a basis for comparison of Yamato, Ryukyuan, and Ainu literatures. Ryukyuan literature differs little from the Yamato in this respect, but in Ainu literature there is scarcely any stress on individualism at all. Until at least the middle of the twentieth century, the speech and conduct of the main characters in kamui-yukar and oina were patterned, it is said, on the uniform life of the Ainu people (Kindaichi, 1923, 306). There was no margin for individual thoughts and feelings, and naturally no awareness that an author should create individualized language and personalities. In comparative historical terms, this is because Ainu literature has not had, until the twentieth century, its Middle or Recent Ages. It has simply maintained its Ancient Age in undiluted primitivism. For this reason it is not proper to compare it with the whole of Yamato-line literature. If comparison is to be made, it should probably be limited to the ancient segment of Yamato literature. Even that raises problems, since a Hitomaro created chōka of which we could say, "How like Hitomaro this is!" Or again, Yamanoe Okura inclined so much toward individualism that he might enter his own name: "Okura shall take his leave now" (Levy, 1981, 186). And Ōtomo Yakamochi wrote on his activities certain tanka that more or less constituted a private diary. In contrast to this degree of individualism in the Ancient Age of Yamato literature—which itself does not show remarkable subjective opposition by comparison with Western literature—the distinction between author and audience in Ainu literature is very weak. The reason for this no doubt lies in the protracted "ancient" character of Ainu writing.

In Okinawa, on the other hand, or at least on the main island, the tendency to individualism was realized relatively quickly. The appearance

---

[44] The classifications are not the same in all areas. Songs with the same characteristics may have different names area by area, while those different in nature may have the same name. This classification has been based on Hokama (1979, 158), with the genres being based on Ono's interpretation (1977a, 80).

of ryūka about the sixteenth century meant not only a shift to greater brevity but also an advance in individualism. Poets' names are known: King Shōin, Prince Gushichā, Azi Mutubu, Akami Wēkata, Hwisicha Chōbin, Tasatu Chōchoku, Unna Nabi, the pleasure woman Yusiya, etc. The fact of known authorship necessarily implies that the writers were aware of a distinct person involved with each poem, as something leading one to think, "This is my own work," or "That must be by a certain somebody." Of course there is no necessary, direct connection between this personality of creation and *works* distinctive in literary individuality. Seen by the eyes of an outsider, these Okinawan poems resemble in style and kind many waka of the *Kokinshū* period. In other words, we can identify common elements of conception and expression.[45]

> Oh, Katsurin Island,
> How I would like to go there,
> But at the mouth of the Wanyamazonu,
> The tide may fly up and kick me.

> Oh, Uhudananu,
> I would like to be your bride,
> But that is a path ahead
> Whose ways are too rocky.

> Although it is hard to pass
> Over ways that are too rocky,
> Would it not be wonderful still,
> If you were Uhudananu's wife!

> Much as I wish to become a bride
> On distant Ichi Island,
> There are countless problems getting water
> Out of the Inna River.

> I want so to visit my beloveds
> In Mazyatu and Manaka villages,
> But the floor of the Sirasi forest
> Is too densely overgrown.

Here are five poems (*Ryūka*, 850, 476, 477, 871, 2443) sharing the conception that obstacles prevent one from doing what is desired (or at least pretending so). Waka of the *Kokinshū* period, the least individualistic in Yamato-line literature, and the ryūka, the most individualistic

---

[45] The poems are given by Misato Chōkei (1966, 123-27) and are collected in the *Ryūka Zenshū*.

of Ryukyuan literature, show about the same level of individualism. By comparison with Ainu poems, however, these ryūka seem decidedly personalized. Throughout Ryukyuan literature, longer and shorter poems alike, individualism is pretty well concealed within the group. Still, as the use of authors' names shows, authors of all classes are treated alike, whether they be royalty, high officials, aristocrats, common people, women, or even prostitutes. The same holds for the royal waka collections.

Ainu and Ryukyuan poetry also contrast in their modal features. Narrative is obviously the standard mode for the yukar, that principal genre of Ainu literature. Narrative implies a relation of phenomena and events in accumulating order, something closely tied to the lengthiness characteristic of the varieties of yukar. In contrast to the sprawling nature of yukar, the middle-length nature of poems like "Upopo" and "Rimse-Sinotcha" leads description to play the dominant role, a mode in which poets alternate places and affairs. Even in these poems, however, an element of narrative coordinates the sequence of events. These features will be clear in the chant of an Ainu workman from Sakhalin, which will serve even if less than perfect in its brevity.

> Until now
> In a secret grove
> There stood
> The great tree's spirit—
> Because it was cut down,
> For two days' time,
> For three days' time,
> Its feelings were heavy—
> But now already
> It has come out to a bright place,
> Its spirits buoyant once again.
> Oh, people!
>
> (Chiri Mashiho, 1955, 92-94)

Things are different in the Ryukyus. To begin with, there is greater variety. In the poems of the Okinawan and Amami archipelagoes, description and lyricism dominate, whereas narrative is not uncommon in the Yaima and Myāku Islands. In the poetry of the north, an individual's feelings are expressed in lyricism, giving a deep impression of a single, completed unit. Lengthy descriptions are not so effective for presenting an impression at once deep and integral. So it is quite logical in lyric terms that the uta [songs sung or chanted or written], which are said to be representative of the ryūka of the main island of Okinawa, are always short.[46] By comparison with Yamato poetry, this is notable for combining narrative and descriptive modes. But *by comparison*, the poetry written to the south is narrative, even if so often descriptive. Like the yukar of the Ainu, it is narrative-descriptive in mode. Most umuru are not lyrical.[47] Yet they resemble neither the yukar nor heroic poetry. Here is one example (*Umuru*, 14:986).

> Chibana comes
> With the graceful features of a lord;
> Chibana comes,
> Beautiful is the mouth of our lord.
> His headband
> Lightly twisted on him.
> His white silk robes
> Worn in many layers;
> How many times has not the sash
> Been wound about and tightened?
> His great sword
> He has hung at his side,
> His hip sword
> He has firmly thrust forth;
> His goat-leather boots
> Are pulled up neatly.
> The pack-horse master,
> The groom, Kotara,
> Puts a yellow gold saddle
> On the pure white horse;
> At the front of the saddle
> He paints a picture of the sun;
> At the back of the saddle
> He paints a picture of the moon.[48]

This is a useful example of the narrative-descriptive mode: many matters are joined with appealing phrases, and the sympathetic longing for the lord is not presented from the point of view of a lyric speaker. The audience follows the piling up of phrases with their numerous details, feeling first of all the gloriousness of their lord.

[46] There are some rather long ryūka, but only 14 longer poems out of a total of about 3,000 are known so far (Hokama, 1976, 184).

[47] Lyrical umuru exist (see *Umuru Suosi*, 12:730 and 14:996), but they are relatively rare.

[48] [In this poem, each odd-numbered line has a "mata" character before it—see n. 39, above. Henceforth we omit both the signs and mention of them.—Ed.]

To that Ryukyuan audience, the following could not possibly seem satisfactory.

Shirogane no	At his side a sword
Menuki no tachi o	Wrought with silver hilt-studs,
Sagekakite	He promenades
Nara no miyako o	Through Nara, our capital:
Neru wa taga ko zo	Whose is this strolling lad?
Neru wa taga ko zo.	Whose is this strolling lad?

(*Kagura*, 21)

This reveals the very different awareness of the Yamato-line audience. In the Ryukyuan poem many actions take place around the lord without any advance in time. Without the passing of time, there is a limit to the number of actions feasible, since the setting remains changeless. Put quantitatively, in this descriptive-narrative mode it is impossible to attain lengths of thousands or tens of thousands of lines. For if the poem on Chibana does possess narrative, it must be distinguished from the narrative-descriptive literature to the south, where in fact narrative dominates. Although not characteristic of all Ryukyuan literature, the highly narrative literature of the south has elements quite distinct from the qualities of Yamato literature, a difference remarked on earlier in other terms.

From Kuru Island in the south there is "Paifuta Funtaka Yungutu," in which the main character, Funtaka, wakes in the morning, sharpens his ax, hews a boat, slips it into the sea, is seen off by the islanders, navigates the tidal currents, procures precious gems at Myāku Island, returns to his own island, turns toward the gods, and boasts of his exploits. With its well-connected episodes the poem extends to 495 lines. There is almost no straightforward narrative like this in either the Okinawan or Amami Islands to the north, and of course none at all in waka.

The imagistic qualities of these three traditions also provide contrast. Given that Ainu literature is fundamentally narrative in mode, one naturally finds numerous actions—but very little imagery. And what there is can hardly be termed elaborate. For example, in the 6,964-line "Pon Oina" (a legend), there are but sixty-six distinct images.[49] Consider the following imagistic figures.

[49] Following Kindaichi's analysis. Examples not mentioned in the text are given hereafter with the number assigned by Kindaichi. Numbers in parentheses indicate that the same figure is repeated in the parenthetically identified poems: 783 (4059, 5053, 5547), 1387, 1388, 1391, 1401, 1485, 1491, 1492, 1508 (3498, 4000), 1578 (4072, 4787, 5186), 1761 (1806, 5155), 1762, 1857 (3517, 3977), 2172 (5396), 2176 (6673), 2342, 2346, 2449 (2706), 2583, 2597, 2672, 2673, 2716, 2725, 2878 (4594), 3108, 3115, 3123, 3307, 3315,

Similes. "Sword rays, / Jewel's glow, / Like the shining of the mid-day sun, / A full house, Radiant with sunbeams"(68).

Metaphors. "The ripping of two strands of kelp [i.e., cloth], / The ripping of three strands of kelp" (1488, 1489).

Simile. [Flat nose] "Like the palm of the hand" (3313).

Simile. "[I] come in swaying like the wind" (3787).[50]

Metaphor. [Younger sister] "digs up our graves / [i.e., where there are nine dead and one lives, she] Has come to find me" (4661).

Simile. "[The god] comes flying like a bird" (6668).

Both the number and the variety of images are small, in contrast to the Ryukyuan "yungtu" that will be described later. Their use and their simplicity are equally striking, in remarkable contrast to the complex, minute Homeric similes. For example, here is a simile from the *Iliad*, 4:275-82.

As from his watching place a goatherd watches a cloud move
on its way over the sea before the drive of the west wind;
far away though he be he watches it, blacker than pitch is,
moving across the sea and piling the storm before it,
and as he sees it he shivers and drives his flocks to a cavern;
so about the two Aiantes moved the battalions,
close-compacted of strong and god-supported young fighters,
black, and jagged with spear and shield, to the terror of battle.[51]

In the structure of the simile, complex phenomena are compared with other complex phenomena, revealing the literary temper of a people with an advanced culture. In the Ainu poem, the conceptual gap between the vehicle and tenor, or signifier and signified, is not so great. All is a readily understood comparison of the sun's rays to the gleam of jewels or swords, comparison of the nose to the flat of the hand (another part of a human body), or, when speaking of the flight of a god, the comparison using a bird as the vehicle.

In umuru as well, the images are restricted in number and variety.

3343, 3363, 3450, 3455, 3474, 3616, 3719, 3782, 3853, 3972, 5760, 6147, 6902. Dead metaphors have been excluded.

[50] The distinction between similes and metaphors is not one introduced by Kindaichi but is based on the original Ainu text. In the original, "ne," "kune," "shikobayar," and "korrach" designate similes. These examples would be taken as similes in Kindaichi's analysis, but in the original the "omausuyere" requires that they be taken as metaphors. Also, even if "ne" is used—for example, "kamui shiri-ne" (in the beautiful manner of a god, 4551)—because the god is speaking of himself, the expression is not considered a figure at all.

[51] [Trans. Richmond Lattimore. The episode is part of that at which "the two Aiantes" (or two Ajaxes)—Aias, son of Telemon, and the lesser Aias, son of Oileus—lead to the front the military forces of the Achaeans (or Greeks).—Ed.]

Comparison with the oina or yukar involves a problem of contrasting unequal units, since the umuru do not extend beyond short or middle-length pieces. The ballads of the Yamato-line *Chronicles* [*Kojiki* and *Nihon Shoki*] are somewhat closer in length and content, however, and we can therefore set beside an umuru a piece from the *Nihon Shoki*. First the umuru.

> Great Lord, cloud-like coursing the sky,
> Known even in distant great lands,
> Victorious in conquest, oh, return!
> Like a cloud descended to earth,
> Lead, Great Lord,
> The troops from the capital settlement,
> The army of the king.
> Attack the wood gate with your full force,
> Attack the iron gate with your full force;
> Take the wooden gate by storm,
> Take the iron gate by storm;
> Drive them to their sacred lair—
> Defeat, kill a hundred foes,
> Defeat, kill seventy more!

> > (*Umuru*, 10:519)

And now a poem from the *Nihon Shoki*.

Kamukaze no	By the Sea of Ise
Ise no umi no	Where divine winds blow
Ōishi ni ya	A periwinkle snail,
Ihai motorou	A periwinkle snail
Shitadami no	Creeps round and round
Shitadami no	A great rock, oh!
Ago yo	My lads!
Ago yo	My lads!
Shitadami no	Like periwinkle snails
Ihai motoori	We shall creep round and round,
Uchiteshi yaman	Then smite our enemy dead,
Uchiteshi yaman.	Then smite our enemy dead!

(*NSK, Song*, 8)

Both are songs to lift morale in battle. The Yamato song of the Kume clan (*Kumeuta*) not only incorporates in its expression the situation and appearance with "creep round and round," but also introduces the figure of the periwinkle snail and the scene where it crawls, on the great rock. By contrast, the umuru offers rather abstract descriptions in its urgings to attack. The initial images of the clouds are not used in the combat that is at the center of the poem, and the pleas to the young lord serve as nothing more than decorative instructions. The mere 218 poems in the *Chronicles* have far more variety of imagery than do all the 1,248 umuru.

The situation is very different with the ballads of the southern area of the Ryukyus. In the Kuru Island poem mentioned earlier, "Paifuta Funtaka Yungutu," there are twenty-eight examples of imagistic figures.[52] There are kinds like the following, classified as before.

Similes. "Like the cough / Of a nonagenarian, / A grand old man, / Like the cough / Of an octogenarian, / A grand aged man / Coughing on and on— / That is how it was!"(96-101)

Similes. [Similes for people seeing others off] "In the bright spring time, / In the youth of summer, / The crabs crawl down, / Come down to the sea, / Just like that, / Like the black hills clustered together, / That is how it was" (164, 168, 169).

Similes. [The spray of surf] "Like silver waves lighting up the moon, / Like golden waves lighting up the sun" (263-64; 311).[53]

Simile. [An island receding in the distance] "Like inserting / A bamboo tube / In the mouth of the sake server / Of the wood-worker, / Until it disappears, / Since that is how it is" (340-46).

Similes. [Using precious stones and pearls] "Like pulling in / Morning glories strung along the shore / [and putting them in the boat] Like taking handfuls of sand on the shore / [filling up the boat] Taking up handfuls, / Handfuls that I put in"(404-9).

Metaphors. [In apology for verbally slighting the gods] "You trepangs that are manako / From whose edges / Grow thin hairs / Like garlic roots in sandy soil: / Rushing up the sandy shore, / Dancing along, / I see you" (469-76).

Simile. [With an apology for a rudeness] "Like an octopus caught / At the year's greatest ebb-tide, / Hands clasped together, / I offer my apologies" (483-86).

[52] Based on the translation in *Yachōsan Koyō* (Kishaba, 1970, 2:235-68); another, slightly shorter version appears in *Nantō Kayō Taisei* (Yachōsan section, 147-49). Examples not mentioned can be found in the original Ryukyuan in Kamita Sōei's *Ryūkyū Bungaku Hassō Ron*, pp. 544-73, as follows: 75-76, 78-79, 87, 89, 120-21, 122, 219-23, 275-77, 278, 295-98, 299-300, 317-18, 319, 413-14, 416-17, 446, 487.

[53] From the translation, this appears to be a simile. But Kishaba's translation is a free one. The original text is, "Tski yu tirashi / pyū ma tirashi." Fairly directly rendered, this means, "lighting up the moon, lighting up the sun." This meaning is, "radiant, shone on by the moon and sun," so that the original must be taken as a metaphor.

The twenty-eight examples of this kind in the 495 lines of the poem represent a comparatively high frequency by comparison with but sixty-six instances in the 6,964 lines of the Ainu "Pon Oina." Although the signifiers and signifieds are sometimes too close in nature (as is markedly the case with a cough referring to a cough, 96-101, above), there is usually a marked separation, as in comparing a no longer visible island to a tube that has disappeared into the sake pot, or the clasping of hands in apology to the caught octopus. By criteria of the range of imagery in Yamato literature, these are successful images, and this southern Ryukyuan literature has a richer and more active imagery than that of the poetry written to the north.

Tone or attitude provides our last category of comparison. The yukar, the most markedly Ainu-like in the Ainu corpus, is conspicuous for its explicit, extroverted tone. The motive is to express as much as possible to others rather than to keep matters within. This leads to a wealth of description, and in the presentation of one fact or thing descriptions of the same kind are piled one on another. For example:

> Long ago now,
> Long since in the past,
> The country-making great god
> First came to make a village,
> And about to make a country
> Came to this human land—
> Descended from the heavens,
> Came to make a country,
> Came to make a village
> And now has finished off the village,
> Has finished off the country.
>
> (*Shin'yō, 495*)

What a Yamato audience would think stiffly rigid expressions here are beautiful by Ainu standards. Similarly, to those with a taste for the variety and complex patterns in the design of Jōmon pottery, the severer lines of Yayoi pottery and the ware of the [Korean] Yi Dynasty may be lovely but will be thought lacking something. But to one prizing as limitlessly interesting the brevity of haiku, the heavy repetition of the Ainu poem just given seems persistent, overwrought.

To Ainu taste beauty lies in what is contrary to the so-called designless (mumon) writing of waka and renga. With the Ainu "Pon Oina" mentioned earlier, the princely goddess who narrates must lead off with details of her own birth and upbringing before getting to her tale—the heroism of the god of Nishihama, developer of the whole area from heaven to the underworld. Although the hero is called a god, the world described is not that of the immortals, but a condition of life virtually identical with the everyday life of the Ainu. There is an elder-sister goddess busy at sewing, a baby younger-sister goddess playing by the hearth, and all in a house where the ancient family wealth is hoarded just below the ridgepole of the roof. Tired of playing, the prankish goddess scatters ashes about, and some fly to the bosom of the elder-sister goddess. She teaches the younger-sister goddess how to sew. When the younger-sister goddess frets and cries because she is unable to sew well, the elder-sister goddess skillfully calms her down and puts her to sleep in a bed beneath the clothes-drying pole. The next morning, the elder sister devotes her energies to cooking for the elder-brother god, who sits in silence except for mealtimes. . . . Some 268 lines are consumed in this relation (*Yūkara*, 51-66). Although the events are merely matters of daily life, to the Ainu they acquire great beauty when they can be piled in large accumulations of homely incidents.

The tone turns heroic when the character's actions are shown with the same explicitness. The god who is the main character of "Pon Oina" is no human hero, and in his war with an enemy god he flies into the sky, causing vibrations strong enough to crumble heaven; he tears apart and scatters the defending enemy as if they were bits of food in soup; he mows down, sends flying over the side of a cliff, armed warriors compared to a colony of ants; and in the aftermath the human villages and countryside are nearly demolished, rocking uneasily like cradles. The god of Nishihama, victorious in that battle, finally descends to the underworld to do battle with an army of demons. There innumerable mounds wriggle up, ugly ghosts with hair like knitting bags appear and in the ensuing attack shoot poisoned arrows that are compared to hail and snow. The god grows faint from the poison. His body slouches as though it is a stand to hang kettles on. Yet, near collapse as he is, he makes it back to his own mountain and there recovers his strength. To Ainu people of the twentieth century as well as earlier, this heroic figure can only be the source of those articles of faith necessary for one's life. The Yamato hero may be a heroic figure but tends to wander in tearful misfortune, and in fact rather than exert heroism is likely to place highest value on what is reclusive. To such an extent are the extroversion of Ainu literature and the introversion of Yamato literature distinct.

Similarly striking divergence appears in the differing Ryukyuan literatures. Heroic figures do not make much of an appearance in the umuru of the main island of Okinawa to the north. Instead there are the young nobles on white horses with golden saddles—like the lord Chibana whom we observed earlier (*Umuru*, 14:986). Instead of involving high feats of bravery by which the enemy is crushed with brute strength, the battle scenes in umuru—and there are not many to the north—are of this kind:

> Scarlet Koshirai
> The famed Koshirai,
> Devised my plan:
> Attack fiercely and win fame;
> At sacred Ichi Forest,
> At holy Ai Forest,
> Putting on gold helmets,
> Wearing gold plates of armor;
> Holding a stout shield of stretched cowhide,
> Grasping lacquered arms,
> Fiercely attack the castle's board gate,
> Fiercely attack the castle's gold gate.
>
> (*Umuru*, 21:1446)

The commander boasting about his resplendent armor and weapons seeks victory in skillful planning.[54] There is no sense of the heroic collision of horses and men. Even in relating events in the war against the Satsuma invaders the battle scene comes to this:

> Grabbing their arms and throwing them down,
> Grabbing their legs and throwing them down,
> Shaving them into raw fish of the offing,
> Shaving them into raw fish of the coast.
>
> (*Umuru*, 3:93)

There is nothing here of the epic tone.

There are, however, a few ballads extant from the Yaima and Myāku Islands to the south that have something of the heroic. There is a poem about Nakazuni Tuyumya's subjugation of Untura, head of the Yuna Island kingdom (part of Yaima) about 1522, on the order of the Ryukyu kingdom. This is an āgu entitled "Āgu of the Invasion of Yuna Kingdom by Nakazuni Tuyumya."[55] What follows is from the second half of the poem.

---

[54] "Akenokoshirai" or "Scarlet Koshirai" is a shamaness. Are we to imagine her as a narrator reciting the actions of the military commander? If so, it is proof of Origuchi Shinobu's theory of the confusion of person in such narration. "Ichi Forest" and "Ai Forest" are shrines for prayer within the Ue castle on Kume Island.

[55] The texts in *Myāku Shiden* (*Nan'yō-Myāku*, 298-99) and *Myāku Shima Kyūko* (*Nan'yō-Myāku*, 408-9) differ slightly in wording and lineation. I have relied on the former, using my own transliteration and translation into Japanese.

Selecting those skilled in war, skilled in fighting;
Galloping to greater Yaima Mountain, to lower Yaima Mountain,
Galloping to the land of Yuna Island,
The place where the war was fought—
Like the dance of the dragonfly, the dance of the butterfly;
When a hundred of the advance guard are mowed down, mowed
   down,
When a hundred of the rear camp are mowed down, mowed down;
At the last island of Yuna country, Untura
Turns, stands, and turns in his gallop;
Surapiru kicks out his foot as a threat,
Tuyumya thrusts out his belly as a threat;
(Untura) "Come on, Tuyumya! Come show what you can do!"
(Surapiru) "So? See how you like my sword, Dziganimaru!"
The voice is heard, but what is heard comes too late,
And Untura is cut down, falling like a giant tree—
Favored in war, the victors pacify the island with their glory.

This tone does not appear in the poems of the Okinawan or Amami Islands to the north. The battle scenes in the two umuru mentioned earlier (21:1446, 3:93), like the battle scene of the handsome lord Chibana discussed earlier (10:519), are distinctly rare examples. Furthermore, their representation is tenuous, lacking the concreteness of the āgu on Nakazuni Tuyumya Surapiru. We must conclude that the heroic tone is found only in the poetry of the southern part of Okinawa, and to the extent that this tone differs from that of Yamato poetry, we recognize it as one of the important characteristics of Ryukyuan literature. And yet even as we grant this contrast with Yamato literature, if we judge the Ryukyuan poems by the standard of the extroverted attitude of Ainu literature, we realize that although the Ryukyuan does have the heroic tone, it does not have the requisite mass, and that in short the poems cannot be judged genuine epics.[56]

It seems necessary to define genuine heroic poetry as that possessing a combination of the external formal property of considerable length, the modal property of extended narrative, and the tonal property of an active, extroverted, or explicit attitude. The definition provides us with means for judging whether an individual work is a heroic poem. It is no guarantee that epics will actually appear in a tradition, nor does it guar-

[56] The fact that the āgu on Nakazuni Tuyumya is not an epic can be demonstrated from its brevity: in its entirety 52 lines. In the Ainu yukar *The Song of Sorrel*, the account of the battle of Menashima Village alone runs to 743 lines (5628-6370), and the comparatively brief account of the strife at Towisara Village goes for 150 lines (6528-6678), providing a fair basis for comparison (Kindaichi, 1931, vol. 2).

antee that a given work will be truly great. But it is fully clear that the application of the definition to Yamato literature reveals the absence of a heroic poetry. And that is, as we have been seeing, one of the particularly distinctive features of Japanese literature. In spite of this fact's having been pointed out long ago (Tsuda, 1947, 17-18), there are not a few people who have continued to propound the existence of a heroic Yamato poetry. That this is a serious error about a fundamental characteristic of Yamato literature and the fact that Ainu literature does have a genuine heroic poetry are the precise grounds for counting the Ainu as non-Yamato art. To close this discussion, although Ryukyuan literature does not have a proper heroic poetry, in the poems we have seen there is a residual, symptomatic element that possesses a tone and a mood held in common with epic. The absence of the epic form with the presence of the heroic tone are the grounds for deciding that this literature is in general but quasi-Yamato.

The Method of Periodizing

Equivalences of Periods and Cultural Regions

For Japanese literature, the periods used in this history will be the Ancient Age, the Middle Ages, and the Modern Age. These are the three major, gross divisions, and other times will be distinguished. For example, as has already been shown, prior to the Ancient Age I distinguish an Archaic Age, a time for which we have evidence of archaeological and other kinds and from which certain verbal creations were bequeathed orally for transcription in the Ancient Age. It will be necessary to divide further that long period I have termed the Middle Ages, and the question to be asked is the principle for such divisions. One method is to punctuate the linear flow of time at certain junctures by using chosen criteria, and another is to punctuate by changes in the location or nature of government. The second principle is the one most frequently used, so that subdivisions of the Middle Ages are taken to correspond to changes in the seat of government:

Period of Time	Center of Power
Early Middle Ages (chūko)	Heiankyō (Kyoto)
High Middle Ages (chūsei)	Kamakura, Muromachi
Late Middle Ages or Recent Age (kinsei)	Edo

And this leaves, after 1867, the Modern Age (kindai) with Tokyo the capital.

This method of division is only a convenience, and there are many places where it does not fit the actual historical situation of *literature*. It may be appropriate to think of a temporal flow as something straight and singular in movement, but the temporal order that makes history is not singular. This becomes apparent as soon as we consider what may be termed the pace of a culture. Because of various factors and limits, cultures do not progress at the same rate in every area. For example, in A.D. 57 it was recorded that the King of Nu ("Nu Kuo Wang") presented tribute to Emperor Kuang-wu of the Later Han Dynasty. China had by then achieved a considerable literature, whereas Japan was still in its Archaic Age, when literature, history, government, and religion were undifferentiated. That is, in the same historical year when Japan was still in its Archaic Age, China was in the latter stages of its Ancient Age. For general Asian literary history, the differing time vectors of both Japan and China must be considered.

Similar discrepancies exist in other instances. In the fifteenth century, the Ryukyus were in their Ancient Age: the umuru, which reflect the Ryukyuan culture of that time, correspond to the Japanese poems included in the *Chronicles* set down in writing in the eighth century from earlier oral tradition. The same may hold true within Japan itself. While the people in the Early Middle Ages were composing waka in new styles at the capital, in remoter provinces other people were no doubt composing pieces much like the songs in the *Chronicles*. Highly cultured social classes develop a sensitive, changing literature unmatched by social classes weak in culture. This is to say that even in substituting social classes for countries in accounting for literary change, the discrepancies will be similar. So if we include both national areas and social classes in the single cultural world, the passage of time becomes a function of the speed of cultural change manifested in a plurality of these vectors.

As this implies, we can express linear temporal flow in terms of more than one vector. Here we have in axis t a representation of time, and in axis xyz a representation of the cultural world, so determining a four-dimensional system of time-space coordinates. On those grounds, "temporality" t and "spatiality" xyz are in parity, and it is clearly inappropriate to represent, by means of a temporal coordinate alone, *historical* time. (The figure does represent the four-dimensional world in two-dimensional terms.) Although historical periods must be classifed by attending to all coincident vectors, any description of them in syntax cannot avoid being linear. For that reason, the ensuing history will use periods based on the highest cultural world, with attention also to the other cultural worlds. The writings by people highly developed in culture will sensitively reflect the movements of their society, easily introducing innovation, whereas people with a low stage of cultural development show

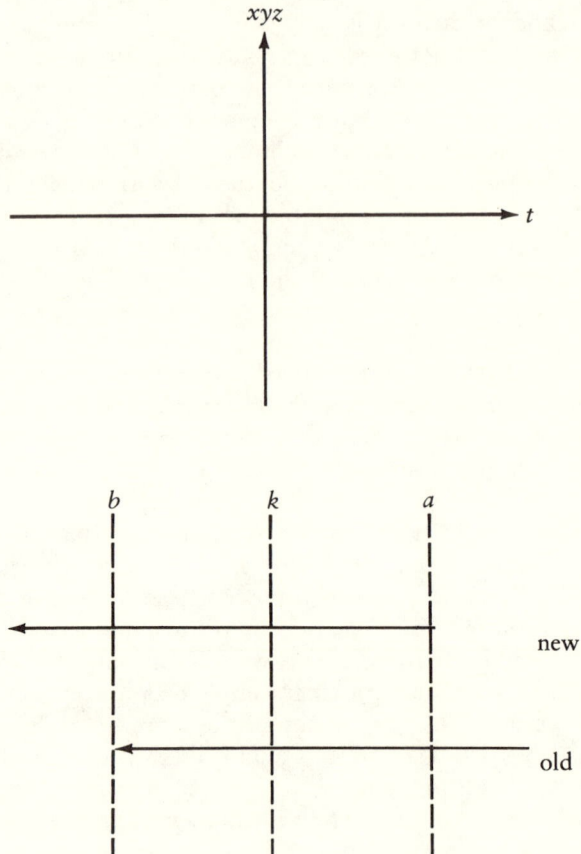

small change. This comparative matter probably holds for other factors as well. That is, when geographical and social factors are added together in the cultural world, the flow of time becomes a function of the tempo of the culture, and therefore a number of different vectors are involved.

Even after periods have been worked out by careful attention to these matters, it is difficult to isolate moments when there are clear boundaries to temporal units. This is so because literary phenomena do not all change to new forms at a single occasion. Particularly in an advanced cultural world, new movements are often born while traditional styles of writing are still vigorous, producing literary works that can be historically placed at the end of one period or at the beginning of the next. Circumstances like this are very common.

In the next diagram an older kind of literary practice is shown to have been active until the point indicated by dotted line *b*, whereas the new practice had already begun at the point indicated by dotted line *a*, and the space between *a* and *b* corresponds to the period of coexistence of old with new. Neither *a* nor *b* provides a clear point of cutoff. If, however, we say that at some point the old period changes to the new, we may be permitted to take some event that shows the clear imprint of the transition, indicating that transition symbolically by dotted line *k*. For example, the *Kokinshū* style in waka, which seems the essence of the Middle Ages, first took shape about the ninth century. Meanwhile, ancient practice in waka continued till the end of the tenth century, the transition continuing from the ancient to the early medieval period, over a time of a century and a half. Yet if we choose an occasion within that span to separate symbolically (as with *k* above) the Ancient Age from the Middle Ages, it may be the compiling of the *Kokinshū*, ca. 905-20. Appropriately enough, the collection contains poetry in both the ancient and new, medieval style. Symbolic line *k* thus expresses the durational development from *a* to *b* in one-dimensional terms.

The event chosen for this symbolic division may be of any kind. My selection of a literary event—the compiling of the first of the royal collections—is founded on the assumption that in principle we should use literary evidence to explain the development of literary phenomena. In the past, it has been usual to determine literary periods on the basis of such political events as moving the capital to Heiankyō (Kyoto) or establishing the Kamakura bakufu (shogunate). This view holds that literary periods, too, are born from social movements, and is based on the premise that social events determine literary events. But the linkage is not direct, and causal connections between literary phenomena and social movements are normally established after the literary phenomena are well over. Nor is it possible to limit the development of literary phenomena to the status of reflections of social change. If literary historians believe that literary periods must conform with those of political history—"the Heian period" or "the Edo period"—then their own credibility is in question. The reason that such divisions have continued to be used is simply the ease bred by habit. And *that* is the chief reason they are difficult to discard.

If these are the bases for classifying literary periods, what should be the particular standards for them in a history of Japanese literature? I shall now consider qualitative changes in Japanese literature in a world context and later I shall attempt to use the divisions discussed here. My rationale for the comparative procedure is that peculiar or individual characteristics intersect those held in common. That is, by placing Japanese literature within the spatial coordinates of the world, its characteristic qualities can be distinguished from those of the various other countries, East or West. At the same time, common characteristics will be revealed, along with yet other characteristics that are thought of as original Japanese propensities but that can be seen on analysis to contain many un-Japanese elements derived from foreign impact. A remarkable feature of Japanese culture is that it has advanced by ready reception of foreign cultures, and unless this is borne in mind, little else will be clear.

The principle is, then, that we distinguish the qualities of Japanese culture by considering its relation to foreign cultures. We first discover the existence of a culture that evolved only on the Japanese archipelago, that is, with no known connections with outside cultures. Next, that preexisting culture altered in relation to what was accepted from China and became a new culture. Finally there has been a further transmutation involving Western culture. A period defined on the basis of one of these three series of events is, then, not a one-dimensional segment of time but rather a four-dimensional cultural world containing the attributes of time and space. More specifically, this is the classification:

First period:	When only indigenous Japanese culture existed.
Second period:	When that culture accepted elements of Chinese culture.
Third period:	When another change occurred with the acceptance of Western culture.

Chinese culture is taken to include the Buddhist culture that was received from India by way of China. Western culture refers to recent times, especially from the nineteenth century and following, and does not include anything of the Western Renaissance or earlier.

In Japan's first period there was no differentiation of literature, politics, history, religion, etc., and a large number of other primitive features remained. This I have called the Archaic Age (senko jidai). Because in the third period Japanese culture was transformed by modern Western culture, that is Japan's Modern Age. In the long stretch between the Archaic and the Modern Ages, further division is necessary. That is because even if the "same" Chinese culture was the basic influence throughout, in one subdivision features of the Archaic Age remain distinguishable in numerous areas, not yet transformed into *literary* existence; and in another subdivision literary awareness has been created in leading genres by the acceptance of Chinese culture. I shall call the former division the Ancient Age (kodai) and the latter the Middle Ages (chūsei).

In both the Ancient and the Middle Ages, a further degree of distinction is no doubt necessary. For in the Ancient Age it is possible to distinguish one time when literature was not yet thought independent of history and other kinds of thought, and another when people were aware of literature as literature. I shall term the former the first stage of the Ancient Age, and the latter the second. During the Middle Ages we can distinguish a succession of subperiods by using as criteria literary awareness resolvable to certain key concepts: fūryū (aristocratic beauty), michi (artistic vocation), and jōri (reason and feeling). These three subdivisions of the Middle Ages are necessary to account for successive changes within the Chinese culture being accepted: Six Dynasties culture, T'ang Dynasty culture, and Sung Dynasty culture. These subdivisions distinguished in the Ancient and Middle Ages do not have a one-to-one correspondence with the Six Dynasties, the T'ang Dynasty, or the Sung Dynasty, because the subdivisions also involve elements derived from purely Japanese circumstances.

To summarize matters to this point, we can periodize the history of Japanese literature, revising the three large divisions made earlier into four.

Archaic Age:	Only indigenous Japanese culture exists; literature, history, politics, religion are undifferentiated.
Ancient Age:	Primitive elements remain while changes occur during the acceptance of Chinese culture. *Stage one*: Literature is not thought independent of history, politics, religion, etc. *Stage two*: An awareness of literary expression emerges.
Middle Ages:	In the main genres, literary awareness undergoes change with the acceptance of Chinese culture. *Stage one* (Early): Fūryū ideology. *Stage two* (High): Michi ideology. *Stage three* (Late): Jōri ideology.
Modern Age:	Different changes occur with the acceptance of Western culture.

These divisions are not complete, but even if further division is possible the ones given are basic.

This manner of periodizing is a way of interpreting, not a chopping of temporal development into however many bits and lengths. As was said earlier, the indices of time periods are no more than symbolic points. In reality there are no points where periods can be cut apart, for even though we stick on the label "medieval," somewhat of the "ancient" remains in what we have labeled, and similarly the last phases of the ancient contain the first of the medieval. Accounting for these matters would require transitional stages overlapping any periods distinguished. But because so doing would render unclear the basic division according to symbolic points, one must place specific transitional literary phenomena in one period or the next. Historians would also have difficulty in constructing any descriptive account without assistance from that kind of time represented by calendar years or without other useful conceptual designations. That is, one says "the ninth century," "the tenth century"; "the era of government by cloistered sovereigns," "early Kamakura," "late Meiji," etc. In so doing we use time segments, unidimensional intervals of physical time as convenient supplements. These intervals must be distinguished from the concept of a period when we attempt to account for the development of literary phenomena.

Indices of Periodizing

We have observed the inadequacy of literary periodizing that employs political concepts like the Heian or the Edo regimes. But what kind of index should be used? Desiring indices expressive of ideology, I have chosen ga (the refined, the high) and zoku (the popular, the low), terms requiring more than dictionary definition.

We seem unable to exist without searching for something eternal. Although our need is not necessarily obvious in everyday situations, in even our quotidian thought there are hidden aspirations not merely of a passing moment. When they are brushed by some unusual opportunity, the prospect of the endlessly desired shines through a rift in our clouds. We will not exist eternally, life is decidedly limited, and existence seems ever less secure. Realizing the transience of our state, we aim intensely for something eternal, and by our aim are joined with it. But our aspirations are not likely to be realized, and when they are directed to immortality, their expression bears fruit in the guise of religion, art, science, etc. Or one may say that by the mediation of religion, art, or science we join with the eternal.

In actuality, our longing for the eternal has in practice, like the north and south poles, two focuses. One may be termed consummation and the other infinity.[57] In artistic terms, at the pole of consummation there flowers something so highly refined that it can be made no finer than it is. By contrast, at the pole of the infinite one must wager for progress through uncertainty without knowing how to proceed. The former ideology is the one I designate as ga, and the latter as zoku.

---

[57] The idea of resolving, in the arts, classicism and romanticism respectively into consummation (Vollendung) and infinity (Unendlichkeit) comes from Strich (1924, 1-15). The classic and the romantic in Western literature are, however, not necessarily compatible with the development of Japanese literature, and the application of that classicism or of that romanticism to the infinity perceived in Japanese literature invites misunderstanding. I have postulated instead the concepts of "ga" and "zoku." In this I am indebted to Strich's thesis, but I have suggested a pattern that is different in practice. Strich's thesis is very abstract, groundless, and incorrect in application; it has been radically criticized for the too sweeping nature of its thesis concerning infinity (Ōnishi, 1960, 89-90). In these pages I attempt to deal with that criticism by introducing the ideology of zoku.

Because writing denominated ga is, by definition, fully formed, examples of writing short of that state are considered inferior. It follows that when people conceive of a fully consummated literature, they will assign the same beauty to writings similar in kind. The status of such a work is consonant with earlier works of its kind that had reached that consummate state, and the new is appreciated for representing an attitude correct in practice. Already existing writings establish the criteria. Because formal waka are those precedented in language and in the way they are read, poets who happen to disregard the precedents meet trouble. That was the fate of Sone no Yoshitada, "a fellow of lunatic sensations."[58]

The standard of ga also applies to the audience, which must possess requisite knowledge. If one cannot discern what configuration a particular example of writing aspires to, or if one is ignorant of the kind of precedents on which it is based, one is not capable of understanding its beauty. The audience appreciative of ga writings must have a wide, deep knowledge of the precedents on which the works are based. Just as it is impossible for those who do not know such things to produce and appreciate such works, it is also necessary for the audience to belong to the cultural group of the poet. For that reason, it has been historically true of ga literature in Japan that its *audiences* were composed only of those who could participate also in the *creation* of the type of literature involved (Konishi, 1953c, 30-37). The fine texture of such works cannot be understood by those of unrefined sensibility, of inadequate training in the decorous, exquisite, delicate, and profound.

Zoku writings, by contrast, belong to a world without precedents, a world without fixed form. They may come with a strange roughness; with a simple, intimate gentleness; with unsettling darkness; with frivolous originality; or with raw urgency. Zoku writing may take on any of these features, being unacquainted with any settled place. It is an artistic world in which we may discover jewel-like brilliance, and not a little rubbish. In fact it is the rubbish that is usually thought of as zoku. Anyone told, "Your taste is zoku!" will certainly take it as severe criticism. The negative does not characterize the whole of that world, however. Exuberant health, youthful and fresh purity, freedom of expression, and more are its positive qualities. This is the zoku to which Bashō refers: "You should enlighten your mind to the heights and then return to the low [zoku]."[59] In Chinese usages as well, zoku (Ch. su) did not have a bad meaning from the start, since it originally designated styles widely

---

[58] So wrote Fujiwara Kiyosuke (1104-77) in his *Fukurozōshi*. [Kiyosuke was a learned but hidebound critic; Yoshitada a sometimes awkward but original poet. Disagreement was inevitable.—Ed.]

[59] "Takaku kokoro o satorite zoku ni kaeru beshi" (*Sanzōshi*, "Aka" [red vol.], 101; Nose, 1948, 45).

found in society (Yoshikawa, 1942, 241-45). Certainly there is in zoku a readiness to descend to vulgarity, but it should not be thought that zoku amounts to no more than that. Ga writing as well often becomes corrupt. Yet if the two are compared, zoku is far less stable and may easily degenerate.

In using these connotations of ga and zoku as indices for periodizing, there will be points in their application to actual literary phenomena for which their power as descriptive terms proves inadequate. To explain: once ga writing has set a norm, it may come to be thought that what has taken root in ga may float in the zoku world; bit by bit this in-between kind comes to occupy a larger and larger domain in which it is impossible to distinguish between ga and zoku. Long ago, the classification of such writing was "haikai." Although with such precedent it would be quite proper to use "haikai" as a third term or index in periodizing, the word later came into general use for a specific kind of poetry. Because of that, and therefore possible confusion over my usage, I wish to introduce a new expression, ga-zoku. This does not designate a class of expression compounding ga and zoku. To repeat the terms of the earlier waterplant metaphor, it is rather something with its roots in ga and floating in zoku. Or, while being clearly recognized as ga, it has set foot squarely in the zoku world. Or, ga-zoku has one foot in ga and another in zoku, and even if there are some changes of emphasis according to which leg bears the moving body, leg ga and leg zoku move along as one. "Haikaika" [more properly, hikai no uta, irregular waka], "haikai no renga," and other kinds belong to this class of expression.[60]

How, then, can we relate these three classes of expression to periodizing? First of all, the identification of the primitive or Archaic Age with zoku surely requires no explanation. Once entered into the Ancient Age, Japanese culture altered with its active acceptance of elements of Chinese culture. And although several centuries were required to effect full change, as far as Japan was concerned that continental culture was ga itself. To the backward country that Japan was, Chinese culture was nothing other

---

[60] Although in China, fei-hsieh, the counterpart of "haikai," refers to that which is not serious, in Japan "haikaika" (haikai waka) refers to poems in which the expression is separated from ga. That earlier sense became merged with another of the humorous, and at the beginning of the Edo period haikai no renga was usually taken to be humorous. Bashō countered that idea, and there consequently were haikai stanzas and sequences that were not humorous. In earlier writing, I used "haikai" as the tertium quid of ga and zoku (Konishi, 1951d, 4-7), and later as an index of periodizing in literary history (1953i, 5-6). However, from various concerns mentioned in this section, I have decided to replace it with "ga-zoku." [Haikaika, properly hikaika, is a designation appearing as early as Book 19 in the *Kokinshū* (ca. 905-20). Haikai (no) renga, or more simply haikai, designates the kind of poetry written by Bashō and Buson, who also wrote a kind of prose designated "haibun." It is anachronistic to speak of them as haiku poets, although since "haiku" is an abbreviation for "haikai no ku," it too fits the author's terms of reference.—Ed.]

than consummate. The Japanese decided that there was no way for their culture to advance except by faithfully dedicating themselves to the pursuit of what that other offered. In spite of the awareness, there was no corresponding sudden change in the kinds of writing familiar in the narratives (katarigoto) and songs (utaimono) still present from the Archaic Age. Beginning with the *Jūshichijō Kempō*, 604 (*Constitution in Seventeen Articles*), many prose writings in Chinese appeared. Crown Prince Ōtomo and Prince Nagaya frequently composed poems in Chinese with the aim of establishing a ga culture in Japan. The result was, however, a taking-on of merely the externals of Chinese-style ga, while the conceptions remained unchanged from the Archaic Age. There is also the splendid, delicate parallelism of Hitomaro's chōka, which we think adapts features of the Chinese shih and fu. But the conceptions of his works are expressed directly in his own thoughts and feelings, and there is no attempt—such as the *Kokinshū* poets made—to revise them to fit an already existing idea of expression.

In consequence, during the Ancient Age the fundamental ideology of writing in Japanese was zoku. Differences can be distinguished between earlier and later phases. In the first stage of the Ancient Age, there remained no distinction between literature and religion; both narratives and songs drew on kotodama, the concept of words as incantatory and divine, so that poets not only transmitted meaning but imparted a sense of the supernatural.[61] The lively belief in kotodama during the first stage did not become extinct in the second. It lingered through the Middle Ages and it exists in dormant condition today. But its swift weakening occurred in the second stage, and it could only have been the new awareness of literature as literature in this stage that relegated kotodama to a now separate realm of religion.

What Japanese in the Ancient Age thought of as "literature" was of course a literature like that of China. In order to replicate in Japan the Chinese cultural map, it was thought essential to have what was called "karazae" (genius, talent for matters Chinese). The important authors in the second stage—Ōtomo Tabito, Yamanoe Okura, Ōtomo Yakamochi, and on to Kūkai and Sugawara Michizane—all attained a high level of karazae in composing poetry and prose in Chinese. The second stage of the Ancient Age may well be termed the period of karazae.

The realm of ga was thoroughly established in the Middle Ages, although it remains possible to distinguish a number of stages with different conditions. The cultured Chinese who formulated the original nature of ga ["ya" in Chinese; "miyabi" in fully Japanese reading] held an arresting

---

[61] [On the idea of the kotodama, cf. what Western anthropologists term the "mana" of words; and see at large Part Two of this volume.—Ed.]

formulation of an ideal life. In public they would be Confucian, in private lead Taoist spiritual lives. This attitude appeared in the latter stage of the Ancient Age. And as the separation of literature from politics was completed in the Middle Ages, cultured Japanese men were publicly Confucian, with their private lives suggesting a sensitivity to Taoism. Along with a tendency to think of literature in terms more Taoist than Confucian came a concept of life touched with Taoist-like feelings that was termed "fūryū." The conception of fūryū involved the drive to create the beautiful by realizing to the highest degree ideals typified by music, poetry, banqueting, and amours. No work surpasses *The Tale of Genji* in offering so definitive and composite an example of fūryū. At an ideal stage of achievement, this idealized "beautiful" was called "en." The use of a word of Chinese derivation, "en," to designate this ideal shows that there were matters that could not be expressed in native Japanese. In practice the ideal was derived from the conception of ideal beauty existing in China from the Six Dynasties and on into the T'ang Dynasty. It is for this reason that the Early Middle Ages was previously termed the period of fūryū.

The fūryū life could not be realized without an economic base to support it. The Midō Kampaku, Fujiwara Michinaga, represented the apex of fūryū, which began to weaken in the twelfth century and died out after the thirteenth. A beauty now lost to reality is yet more beautiful, however, and the courses of the banquets, the relations with women— and the Radiant Genji at the center—was to people of the thirteenth century a world that they could but draw with the colors of their thoughts. It was therefore finer and deeper in its loveliness than any actual beauty. Under these circumstances, ideal beauty was sought after in the fūryū world of the tenth and eleventh centuries; from the thirteenth century and after, the earlier world became "classical." People in the Early Middle Ages located their classics in Chinese culture, but people in the High Middle Ages discovered classics in Japan. In waka the *Kokinshū*, in monogatari the *Genji*—these were classics without question. There came into being pseudoclassicism that prized works whose writing was as close as possible to that of the idealized past; and also neoclassicism that urged living writers to create a splendid beauty founded on classics but also derived from one's very self. These mark the High Middle Ages. We also observe that, in music as well as poetry and prose, groups divided into specialties with a sense of artistic inheritance according to the concept of "ie," of family. This was connected to the "endonkai" of Tendai Buddhism as the Japanese created the ideology of michi.[62] Michi—vo-

[62] [Endonkai were the precepts for enlightenment set forth by Saichō, founder of Tendai Buddhism in Japan.—Trans.]

cation, cultivation of a way of life that would lead to Buddhist enlightenment—was the central ideal aspired to by writers of the High Middle Ages. The beauty they sought had qualities derived from Sung aesthetic ideals: the simple (p'u), the rough (cho), and the withered and bland (k'u-tan). Other terms were born. There was that chill (hie) which retained the rosy glow of the "en" (Ch. yen) of the T'ang. There was stillness and attenuation (sabi) and suffering (wabi), in both of which magnificence was not openly shown. The terms testify to the desire for a new kind of beauty, even going to the limits of logic with destruction (ha), in which expression as such was denied and a separate aesthetic world opened to surpass intellect and sensitivity.

One of the most important features of Sung culture was the radical pursuit of this-wordly reason (Ch. li; J. ri). Among the versions of this reason was the metaphysical one practically schematized and methodized by Sung Confucianists and mainly made known in Japan by Zen priests. There also entered a zeal for rationalizing every kind of matter and a kind of moral logic that was termed "duty" (Ch. i-li; J. giri). At the same time, the rapid development of printing techniques enlarged the literary audience, which in turn meant that individual feeling, ninjō, became an important subject of literature, often leading to contradictions because of its incompatibility with duty. The opposition between duty and human feeling, giri and ninjō, is a distinctive feature of the Late Middle Ages. The belief that the two incompatibles could properly co-exist was concisely termed "jōri" (reason and feeling, affective reason)—a theme that runs throughout this third stage.[63] Inasmuch as ninjō, by its very nature, involves an aiming for freedom, it should properly be assigned to the zoku world. By similarly easy logic, because giri had already existed as an accepted norm, it should be included in the ga world. When it consorts with the zoku world seeking to keep vital the rationality of ga, it becomes part of that ideology earlier termed ga-zoku. Of course both ga and zoku literary kinds existed in the Late Middle Ages, but the leading literature was of the ga-zoku kind. The particular characteristics of beauty in this period—stylishness (sui, iki), worldly connoisseurship (tsū), and similar ideals—could only have arisen from the ga-zoku.[64]

It has been mentioned that during this period the Japanese drew heavily on Sung culture. That was not all, however. The earlier T'ang and the later Ming and Ch'ing cultures were included in the broad levies of the

---

[63] At one time, I used the term "ninjō" to characterize the leading ideology of the Late Middle Ages (Konishi, 1975, 15-17), but I now wish to use "jōri," for reasons given in the text. ["Jōri" is a typical Japanese compound-abbreviation, using (nin-jō and gi-ri) "jō" + "ri."—Ed.]

[64] ["Sui" and "iki" are differing readings of the same character, the former being an earlier, Kyoto-Osaka term, the latter an Edo one. Both imply thorough knowledge of what is stylish, particularly in the pleasure quarters.—Ed.]

time. But it was the *terms* of Sung culture that determined the use made of earlier or later Chinese civilization, so that, for example, although T'ang culture remained more or less what it had always been, it was now adapted in new ways. There is no escaping the fact that throughout the Late Middle Ages literary development was equated with the acceptance of Chinese culture, and in that sense it is possible to consider both the Ancient and the Middle Ages as a single period. It is scarcely necessary to say that the swift development of the Modern Age from the second half of the nineteenth century forward is a period marked by the acceptance of Western culture.

That acceptance of the West's offerings poses a considerable problem. The change in direction not only ended three centuries of national isolation but also meant a shift from the adaptation of Chinese to the adaptation of Western culture. This in turn meant redefining culture to accommodate natural science and technology, which Japan seized as energetically as possible in an urgent desire to close the gap between her and the West. The aim implied that the Western culture adapted was that of the nineteenth century. Japan had no use for Western classical, medieval, or early modern culture. The phase of modern Western culture beginning with the seventeenth century seems to have been brought to its last stage in the nineteenth, and with the dawn of the twentieth century Western culture took on different characteristics. Because Japan swiftly absorbed only the tail end of the modern West, the fruits of this enterprise are not equivalent to the whole of the Modern Age of the West. Here lies a remarkable difference from the situation found during the acceptance of Chinese culture.

The differences between twentieth-century Western culture and its earlier modern phases can be symbolically represented by the advocacy of the quantum theory in physics (1900) and the setting out of the theory of relativity (1905). Following the formation of the quantum theory into quantum mechanics (ca. 1930) and the explosion of the atom bomb (1945) in accordance with the theory of relativity, the nature of these new characteristics becomes clear. The conceptualizing differs from that of classical or Newtonian mechanics in that the subject of the new study presumes a reality not directly apprehensible by the senses. Equivalent trends have arisen in the arts. In the so-called avant-garde fine arts and music, and in literature as well, books have appeared with elements of meaning obscure in thought and feeling. This kind of writing has not yet, nor will it probably soon have, a single established style of expression. Japan's modern period also possesses works of these kinds—which is rather like being at the tail end of the first stage of the contemporary and the head end of the Modern Age: the fundamental personality remains difficult to define. In consequence and provisionally, without making much distinction between the reception of Western culture at the end of the earlier, modern period and at the first stage of the present—we have no choice but to call this Japanese period the Modern Age. A full definition will probably be possible in the twenty-first century.

We have been seeing that Japanese literature has always developed through some correspondence with the continuum of foreign culture. It must be understood, however, that connections with Chinese culture were continuously made about 350 years after the actual events in China, as the following (Table 2) shows. (See also the Chronological Table at the end of this volume.)

Take 730, the date of the Baikaen, or Ōtomo Tabito's thirty-two poems on plum blossoms at his banquet in Dazaifu [the government's southern headquarters, in present Kyushu], which was used to symbolize the division between the two stages of the Ancient Age. Its prototype, the Lan-t'ing Banquet, took place in 353, or 378 years before. Again, when Emperor Chien-wen of the Former Liang Dynasty was crown prince and Hsü Ling compiled the *Yü-t'ai Hsin-yung (New Songs from the Jade Terrace)*, his work was done between 547 and 549—just over 350 years before the *Kokinshū* was compiled in 905-20. Further, the *Shinkokinshū*, compiled ca. 1205, has at its center the style of ethereal beauty (yōen) that is close to the style represented by Wen T'ing-yün, who died ca. 870, about 335 years earlier. Another example still: as mentioned, the improvement of printing techniques and diffusion of printing was a characteristic of the Late Middle Ages. It can be symbolized by the Keichō Royal Printer (Chokuban) instituted in 1597. Although it is difficult to define an equivalent symbolic event in China, the printery may correspond to the commercial printing centered in Hangchow following the invention of movable wooden type and especially by the Ch'ens of Lin-an.[65] This reached its height around the middle of the thirteenth century, a time difference of about 350 years. In such fashion can one follow the development of Japanese culture and its points of equivalence with Chinese culture to the end of the Middle Ages.

The 350-year time lag we observe can only mean that there was a fundamental temporal disparity in intellectual matters between Japan and China. Of course travel conditions imposed limitations, and information was not transmitted from China with the speed it is at present. But if those were the only difficulties, the time lapse should have narrowed in later periods. Because the same gap persisted for about 1,300 years,

---

[65] For detailed information, see Nakayama Kyūshirō, *Sekai Insatsu Tsūshi*, 2:579-80. [The Chinese invented movable wooden type at an early time, but the existence of sophisticated wood-block printing and the lack of need for large editions prevented widespread use for a lengthy period. For somewhat similar reasons, Japanese did not take to movable type quickly when it was brought to Japan by Jesuit missionaries.—Ed.]

TABLE 2
EVENTS IN CHINESE AND JAPANESE HISTORY

China		Japan		
End of Later Han Dynasty		Han		
Rise of Wei Kingdom	220			
		Early Six Dyn.		Archaic Age
Lan-t'ing Banquet	353			
Liu Sung Dyn. rises	420	Later Six Dyn.		
Yü-t'ai Hsin-yung	547?			
Sui Dyn. rises	581	Sui		
End of Ch'en Dyn.	588			
			604	Ancient Age, 1st stage *Constitution in 17 Art.*
End of Sui Dyn., Early T'ang Dyn.	618	T'ang		
			730	Tabito's Waka Banquet Ancient Age, 2nd stage
Wen T'ing dead	870?			
			905	*Kokinshū* comp.
Later Liang Dyn. rises	907	Five Dyn.		
End of T'ang Dyn.				
End of Later Chou Dyn., rise of Sung Dyn.	960	Northern Sung		
Southern Sung Dyn.	1127	Southern Sung		Early Middle Ages
			1205	*Shinkokinshū* comp.
Rise of Yüan Dyn.	1275			
End of Sung Dyn.	1279	Yüan		
End of Yüan Dyn., rise of Ming Dyn.	1368	Ming		High Middle Ages
			1597	Keichō Chokuban (Royal Printer)
End of Ming Dyn.	1616			
Rise of Ch'ing Dyn.	1661			Late Middle Ages
		Modern period	1885	Tsubouchi Shōyō, *Shōsetsu Shinzui* (*Essence of the Novel*) published
End of Ch'ing Dyn.	1912			

it was not travel conditions but ways of thinking that so separated Japan and China that a period of about three and a half centuries was required to bridge the separation.

This kind of intellectual delay is not necessarily limited to relationships long ago with other countries. It is generally observable as the interval between what is culturally central and what is peripheral. For example, here are the dates of publication of some important modern works involving haiku.

January 1897: The haiku magazine *Hototogisu* appears.
January 1899: Masaoka Shiki's *Haikai Taiyō* published.
December 1899: Shiki's *Haijin Buson* published.
December 1900: Takahama Kyoshi's *Sunkōshū* and *Kangyokushū* published.
May 1901: Shiki's *Shunka Shūtō* published.
December 1902: Kawahigashi Hekigodō's *Haiku Shohō* published.

Looking at this record, one has the impression of a haiku reform in full bloom at the turn of the century. Haiku reform can only be dated between twenty or twenty-five years later, however. Considered in terms of the whole nation, the haiku world at the end of the nineteenth century was unquestionably dominated by the Tsukinami school with its traditional stanza style carried over from Edo times. There is no mistaking that haiku reform was very much a step-by-step process.

In similar fashion, we can imagine an important event that occurred during the seventeenth [Japanese] embassy to the T'ang court (Seventh Month, 838, to the twenty-sixth of the Third Month of 839). The momentous news was that the poems of Po Chü-i were on everybody's lips— from aristocrats to women and those of low rank—as the most fashionable and important poetry. Now, it is a fact that the embassy necessarily knew of the reputation of Po.[66] All the same, the Japanese visitors could not possibly have understood the qualities of writing in his poems or why he was so widely and enthusiastically taken up by the people of the T'ang. In order to attain such an understanding, they would have had to have full information about trends in poetry circles at the time and how to place Po's poems among them. So ill informed was the embassy that it did not even get satisfactory information about Li Po or Tu Fu. Even if they had heard someone speak of those poets, they would have lacked information to understand the grounds of their greatness. And even had they been given it, the ability to interpret it was not available

[66] In 838, Po Chü-i was alive (and in his sixties), and his poems were written on walls in the capital of Ch'ang-an; they were sung by royalty, singing-girls, and cowherds; and copies of his poems were widely set down and sold by others. Thus Yüan Chen in the preface to *Po-shih Ch'ang-ch'ing Chi* (824, fourteen years before).

in ninth-century Japan.[67] At that time, Japanese understanding extended to writings of Six Dynasties poets. What did not fit that mold they lacked methods to understand. From the Ancient through the Middle Ages, then, the Japanese were spiritually and culturally in a peripheral position to China, and important new Chinese achievements required a period of about 350 years to gain currency.

On the intellectual frontier as she was, compared with China, Japan required that time lag in order to produce equivalent literary phenomena from the map provided by Chinese culture. It seems that the tempo of Japanese cultural progress was slow, given those three and a half centuries. Yet the Chinese pace was not fast either—both seem to have advanced in the same direction at much the same speed, keeping the time lag constant. On abolishing their policy of national isolation, the Japanese felt an urgent need to follow the map of progress observed in Western culture, and the pace of Japanese cultural change suddenly accelerated. Japan came abreast of Western culture in a decidedly short period, and by the end of the nineteenth century could match, with almost no time lag, the Western pace of progress. To borrow a term from topological mathematics, at this point "catastrophe" occurred in Japan's relation with China, and the temporal-cultural lag evident up to that point disappeared.[68] The result was that Ch'ing literature influenced Japan very little. This "castastrophe" can be considered a fundamental opportunity for modern Japanese literature. Of course it is not true that the Chinese tradition handed down from Edo times ceased to possess vitality. But it has regressed to the periphery of modern Japanese literature. Unfortunately, the eager desire for Western-style progress could not be arrested.

Periods of Asian Literary History

Concepts like the Ancient or Middle Ages just discussed are simply means of investigating the way literary phenomena develop. They provide a method of explanation, and it is obvious that differences in explanation will arise according to the scale the investigator uses. By applying the

[67] The time lag also occurred between China and Korea. Ch'oe Ch'i-wŏn, a great Silla poet, was in T'ang China from 868-85 and should have had contact with the classical revival movement of Han Yü (768-824) and Liu Tsung-yüan (773-819). Yet his prose stayed in the old four-six elegant style of the Six Dynasties (Kim Sa-yŏp, 1973, 100-102). And writing in the classical revival style in Korea begins only in the middle of the twelfth century with Kim Pu-sik. See n. 76, below.

[68] I must point out that even after the beginning of the Meiji era, ties were not wholly severed with previous traditions. In recognition of the continuities from the Edo period, some have attempted reperiodization, a work of which Katō Shūichi's is representative (1980, 223). However, it is obvious that when cultural phenomena enter social turning points they do not sever connections with the past. And if continuities are all that one considers, the possibility of periodizing will be lost.

measure of the ga and zoku standards in the development of Japanese literature, we obtain the kind of historical outline just described. But a given measure is not always effective. The meanings attached to ga and zoku permit one to conceptualize Japanese literary phenomena, but if we view them in the larger context of Asia, we see that they do not suit Chinese literature in the same fashion. For Japan, ga was the actual mapping of Chinese culture. So far is that so that I have used the Japanese acceptance of Chinese culture to define the entirety of the Ancient and Middle Ages. China's own culture developed independently until nearly the twentieth century, however, so that it is impossible to index its literary periods according to its relation with another country.

The Chinese complacently referred to their country as the Middle Kingdom (or Central Glory, using another character). They named the four surrounding ethnic groups (in Asian order) the Eastern, Western, Southern, and Northern Barbarians. Given this haughty attitude, China took up Buddhism as a resource to enrich *its own* culture. Its self-sufficiency was in no danger. Instead, Buddhism changed in China, becoming Sinified. One simple example of this is the rise, from the Indian dhyāna (school of meditation), of the very different Ch'an or Zen school. In short, it is possible to periodize Chinese literature only in accordance with principles inherent in the history of China itself.

The major issue in periodizing Chinese literary history is whether to posit the Sung Dynasty as part of the Middle Ages or as part of the Recent Age. There are various theories about this, all theorists agreeing that there was a major shift between the T'ang and the Sung with the emergence of a new social system (Saeki Tomi, 1970a, 145-47). These theories have been developed on such nonliterary grounds as politics, economics, and general culture. It is normal that new literary phenomena appear somewhat later than new political developments, and a characteristic Sung literature is said to have been established roughly between 1023 and 1064.[69]

During the roughly sixty years from the founding of the Sung Dynasty to what is taken in literature as the true Sung, writers continued in the vein of the late T'ang. Steps were taken toward Sung-style writing by Ou-yang Hsiu (1007-72), with further pursuit by Su Tung-p'o, Wang An-shih, Huang Shang-ku, Yang Wan-li, and Lu Yu. Their poetry reveals an esteem for intellect as well as emotion. Narrative elements also emerged at this time. Their subjects were not limited to what had formerly been supposed to be poetic but included much of everyday life, ranging in

[69] Yoshikawa Kōjirō, in his *Chūgoku Bungakushi* (1974), classifies the Sung and Ming Dynasties in the Recent Age. That is, however, a generalization; more precisely, in matters philosophical and ethical, Recent Age characteristics appear from about the third decade of the twelfth century (Yoshikawa, 1941, 550).

nature from songs of personal lyricism to poems expressing feelings of solidarity with society. In tone or attitude, the poets avoided the expression of sorrow that had been the central concern until then. They observed human life from many vantage points, seriously attending to tranquillity rather than to strong passions (Yoshikawa, 1962, 12-53). These tastes were different from those of the poetry of the preceding millennium and would be the dominant ones for the next millennium. On such grounds, it seems appropriate to place Sung poetry in the Recent Age.

During the Sung, new kinds of writing were added to extant ones. Among them were songs of a fixed type, tz'u, and prose essays, sui-pi.[70] In earlier periods there had been prose pieces in which authors had expressed opinions and feelings about various features of society, but these authors and their audiences had not been numerous among the literati until after the institution of the Sung. The multifacetedness or diversity characteristic of the Sung at its height probably reflected the thought and feeling of the common people. That is because the civil service examination was then being used properly for selecting the kuan, or public officials. Careers in public were no longer limited to the lettered aristocracy, and even those of merchant or landholding families could enter active life as men of letters and officials (Yoshikawa, 1944, 233-39). From early in the Sung, commoner-poets increased in number. Poetry continued, in the minds of all, however, to be something belonging to the scholarly class, so that poets of mercantile or rural backgrounds necessarily had to regard themselves as literati. This widening of the social classes eligible to be thought literati continued in the Yüan and Ming Dynasties.

Another prose kind, the shuo-hua, arose in the variety halls (wa-she) in the capitals of both the Northern and Southern Sung. These prose tales were the origin of hsiao-shuo.[71] That the hua-pen, story collections, began to flourish in the Sung Dynasty also leads to the decision that this dynasty as well as the Yüan, Ming, and Ch'ing make up the Recent Age.[72]

The Middle Ages in China include the span from the Later Han to the first stage of the Northern Sung. There were genres peculiar to it, and elaborate expression was valued. The first *literary* genre to come into

[70] [The Japanese reading is "zuihitsu." Chinese versions tend to be somewhat more compendious than Japanese; at least current Japanese usage is more restrictive and is usually exemplified by works like Kamo no Chōmei's *Hōjōki* (*Account of My Hut*) that seem more literary to Western readers than the vast number of the kind put together in modern Japan as well as in China. For the wider sense, scholars may consult a zuihitsu jiten.—Ed.]

[71] Only the *Ta-t'ang San-tsang Fa-shi Ch'ü Ching Chi* (an early predecessor of the *Hsi-yu Chi, The Journey to the West*) can be determined to have been published in the Sung period, but it is unthinkable that it alone was published.

[72] [Hua-pen (J. wahon) are stories told in colloquial language as if being narrated by a storyteller.—Ed.]

existence must have been the fu.[73] Before the fu there were esteemed kinds of poetry, and in the Ancient Age there were many kinds of writing, naturally varying in skill with the abilities of their practitioners. But in the Ancient Age the splendor of that writing was not taken to be of a belles-lettres kind in which works are assigned their value by their audience. The works were taken instead more as edifying writings functioning as the voice of the people. The first genre in which poets were taken to demonstrate their abilities as private individuals was the fu, and although there were conspicious examples of writing in the genre by Chia I (201-169 B.C.) and Ssu-ma Hsiang-ju (179-117 B.C.?) of the Former Han, it did not flourish till after the beginning of the Later Han. By this time, in addition to the fu there was also poetry, the shih, which was given individual stylistic traits by the last stages of the Later Han. The first important poet was Ts'ao Chih (192-232), one of seven famous men of letters in the Chien-an period (196-220). Then in the second half of the Six Dynasties, in the Liu Sung, the Southern Ch'i, the Liang, and the Ch'en, both the fu and the shih were pursued with what one must call an extraordinary linguistic technology of elaboration. In addition, the number of genres increased. The tendency toward excessive adornment was reflected during the T'ang Dynasty in the strong awareness of *how* something should be expressed as well as *what* should be expressed. There was a revival of more delicate writing in the late T'ang and through the Five Dynasties. During this period from the Later Han to the Northern Sung, writing had acquired the character of belles-lettres, and although its tone underwent a variety of changes, it was fundamentally positive. There was not yet that conservative attitude of the Southern Sung, which prized the quiet and simple life.

The Ancient Age of Korea began much later than did China's. Silla was founded in 57 B.C., Koguryŏ in 37 B.C., and Paekche in 18 B.C., so yielding the Three Kingdoms. For reasons of its proximity, Koguryŏ had readiest access to China, and with the adoption of Chinese characters at an early date it established a flourishing Sinified culture. In 372 Buddhist studies began, and at the same time a national school (J. daigaku) was founded. There students from the aristocracy studied the five Chinese classics, also receiving instruction in a variety of works, whether canonical Chinese ones such as the *Shih Chi (Records of the Historian)*, the *Han Shu (History of the Former Han)*, and the *Wen Hsüan (Selections of*

---

[73] [No one has found an adequate translation or simple explanation for the fu. The usual translations, "rhyme prose" and "rhapsody," do properly suggest a genre with features of Chinese poetry (rhyme, parallelism) and rhetorical aim in an overgoing that is to dazzle the reader. The term was used in Japan, either to designate that kind of writing which was not much to Japanese tastes, or to designate almost whatever the designator chose to, and so in that sense is less explicable even than the Chinese usage.—Ed.]

Refined Literature) or a dictionary like the *Yü-p'ien*. Buddhism was introduced to Paekche in 384, and when it entered Silla in the first half of the fifth century, its priests took over cultural leadership. After unifying the Three Kingdoms in 669, Silla opened its own national school in 682 along the lines of that in Koguryŏ. Sŏl Ch'ong and Ch'oe Ch'i-wŏn were among the most important poets in Chinese. And one after another important writers appeared—Kang Su, Kim Tae-mun, Ch'oe Kwang-yu, Pak In-bŏm, and Ch'oe Sin-ji—all writers with Buddhism at the heart of their work.

With the Unified Silla period, Korean prose and poetry as well as poetry in Chinese reached heights of brilliance. That flowering and the sudden development of the Korean hyangga enable us to divide Korea's Ancient Age into two stages: the first running from the establishment of the national school in Koguryŏ in 372 to the unification by Silla, and the second being the period of Unified Silla.

The Unified Silla was followed by the Koryŏ Dynasty. During this period, Chinese influence remained important for literature, but Korean genres also flourished. This marked development enables us to identify this and much of what follows as the Korean Middle Ages, with the middle of the twelfth century a dividing point within it. In the first part of the Korean Middle Ages, Buddhist ideology played a leading role, and Korea sought to acclimatize the literature of the T'ang. In the second part Buddhism was less important, and Sung literature was energetically studied. Literature in Korean also flourished, the hyangga continuing from the Silla through the first part of the Middle Ages, then disappearing, being replaced by sijo.[74] The range of songs generally known as yŏyo flourished in the Middle Ages, but it is not clear when individual varieties were popular. During the first part of the Middle Ages poetry in Chinese by Koreans was T'ang in inspiration, but it is important that at about the beginning of the twelfth century the *Selections of Refined Literature* was removed from the list of required texts at the national school. This reflected a sensitivity to the classical revival at the height of the Sung and became a leading ideal for Koryŏ poets in the latter half of the century.[75]

---

[74] Important Koryŏ hyangga are in the *Pohyŏn Sipchong Wŏngwangga (Poems on the Ten Vows of Samantabhadra)* by Kyunyŏ (923-73). Since we also have King Yejong's "To Ijang Ka" (composed 1120), we must presume the genre was actively practiced into the twelfth century. The date of origin for sijo is uncertain, but it is clear that it was at its height in the sixteenth century.

[75] It seems that much the most popular—in numbers at least—style of writing in the first half of the twelfth century was that of parallel prose, practiced in Korea since the Silla Dynasty. [Ch. p'ien-wen, J. bembun, bentai, or benreibun is writing in four- and six-character couplets; concerned more with display than with pith, this kind began with the Six Dynasties, so that its practice in the twelfth century is tantamount to classical revival.— Ed.] During the Sung, the *Kao-li T'u-ching*, compiled by Hsü Ching, observed of circum-

The symbolic point separating the two parts of the Middle Ages is the collection, by Kim Pu-sik, of many poems and prose pieces in the style of Su Tung-p'o for inclusion in his *Samguk Sagi* (*History of the Three Kingdoms*, 1145).[76] On such grounds the first and second of Korea's Middle Ages mirror China's, just as do the Japanese Early and High Middle Ages.

The literature of the Yi Dynasty (1392-1910) constitutes, in my view, the Korean Recent Age. As such, it parallels the Recent Age in China, although it approximates what was in Japan the Late Middle Ages. The literature of the Yi Dynasty should be considered the Recent Age because of its close approximation to literary developments in China, something far less true in Japan. The age may be divided into two parts, before and after the Japanese invasions of 1592 and 1597. By continuing to accept Sung culture, the first part of the Korean Recent Age extended the second of the Middle Ages. But there was a drastic difference in the terms of acceptance. Now Buddhism, which had guided Korean culture for a thousand years, was suppressed, and Neoconfucianism, particularly that of the Chu Hsi school, became the propelling force in culture as well as politics. When reason (Ch. li; J. ri) became the guiding principle in politics, its systematizing influence was more strictly applied than in China, and Korean society took on fixed social ranks with the yangban—a bureaucracy made up of the literary and military aristocracy—marked off as an elite class. In ranks beneath were those of lesser valued social or occupational specialties such as the chungin, or middling, and the sangmin, or lower, mostly agricultural people. In spite of various irrational features in this hierarchy, it was a period firmly ordered and stable. Unfortunately, as if the Japanese invasions had not been heavy enough blows, in 1636 Korea was subjected to invasion by the armies of the Ch'ing. Korean social life became uncertain as a result, although there was no corresponding change in the structure of yangban society. The stagnation that resulted could only find expression in escapist pleasure or lament.

In both its first and second parts, the literature of the Yi Dynasty inevitably had close connections with China, being founded on the principle that the only real literature was the prose and poetry of China.

---

stances ca. 1124: "Generally speaking, Koreans make most use of parallel prose, although not as successively as in Confucian documents. Their style of composition resembles the florid one of the late T'ang." The classical revival in Korea took place after the movement of Kim Pu-sik, Im Wan, Kwŏn Chŏk, and Kim Hwang-wŏn (Kim Sa-yŏp, 1973, 173-76).

[76] A somewhat annalistic history, the *Samguk Sagi* occupies a place like that of the *Kojiki* in Japan. It was compiled in 1145, with Kim Pu-sik chief compiler. The work is chosen as a symbolic division point of the Middle Ages because of the extraordinary efforts by Kim Pu-sik, and not necessarily because of the characteristics of the *Samguk Sagi* itself.

There still exist thousands of individual collections of poetry in Chinese by Koreans—ten thousand volumes or more. Meanwhile, as if in a subterranean current below the Chinese, literature in Korean took its course (Kim Tong-uk, 1974, 122). But this must be said: if prose and poetry in Chinese are omitted from a history of Japanese literature, it will be incomplete; if they are excluded from a "history of Korean literature," there will be far less worthy of that name to discuss.

It is true, however, that during the Yi Dynasty there was a considerable development of literature in Korean. The hummin chŏngŭm, or hangul, a syllabic system for representing the Korean language, was invented in 1443 and proclaimed in 1446. This made both the production and reception of literature in Korean much simpler than before. One result was that the sijo, which had been in existence from the Koryŏ Dynasty, was actively practiced in the sixteenth century; and another was the birth of a longer poetic form, the kasa, around the fifteenth century. In the second period of this Yi or Recent Age, the middle-ranking chungin took part in literature as writers and audience. From about the seventeenth century, the sijo came to dominate the work of the lesser branches of the yangban as well as the practice of the chungin. During these years a middle-length song or poem, the sasŏl sijo, appeared.

The birth of p'ansori, chanted narrative, in the eighteenth century also deserves note. This is a kind that employs interpretation by tonal expressions termed yibaek or aniri, with many parts that are chanted as narrative. They might be composed in prose or verse, and the best example is probably *Ch'unhyang Chŏn (The Song of Spring Fragrance)*. Because the authors and reciters of p'ansori were social outcasts later called kwangdae—ranking even below peasants—p'ansori was not considered to be literature.

Toward the end of the nineteenth century, the Recent Ages of China as well as Korea came into contact with the modern West, abruptly taking on modern features. As we have seen, much the same modernizing occurred in Japan, although at a more rapid pace and with greater success. These times before contact with the West constitute what I have been terming the Recent Age for both China and Korea, whereas at a comparable stage Japan can be said to be in its Late Middle Ages—on grounds, for example, that the medieval ideal of vocation (michi) remained strong. In China and Korea alike, the literati were sustained by the national civil service examination. This determined an individual's status. For even if one's father was a high official, a son of limited knowledge could not automatically attain his father's position. He had to pass the national examination (k'o-chü) to secure appointment in the aristocracy. Since the examination was based on the Confucian demand for codified knowledge, the aristocracy was composed solely of those who shared classical ideas and outlook. And that kind of thought drifted further and further from contemporary reality.

In Japan, by contrast, the skills of various specialties were perfected by the idea of michi, vocation. Because a person who could excel in the given vocation was so highly respected, it was possible to rise by excellence to the very top in the succession of the specialty of a given family (ie). Because Japan did not have the Chinese civil service system, and because it maintained outstanding men of talent in a variety of fields, it was able so quickly to take and digest modern Western culture at the end of the nineteenth century. For such reasons, Japan can be said to have skipped the Recent Age of China and Korea. Such relative differences among the Asian literatures treated here can be understood more readily if charted, as in Figure 2.

The quasi-Yamato Ryukyuan literature shifted from medieval to modern just as the Yamato did. What was of the Middle Ages in the Ryukyus was not necessarily of the Middle Ages in Japan, however. Instead, it is better to think of the Ancient and Middle Ages of Yamato literature having a Ryukyuan correspondence in one joint period. As on a day in May in Hokkaido or in New England the plum, the peach, and the cherry bloom at the same time, so did what was separate and protracted in Yamato occur in the same age in the Ryukyus. Developing swiftly during a period of about 270 years, Ryukyuan culture had no one-to-one correspondence with the Yamato periods. In particular I wish to posit that the Ryukyuan Middle Ages had their legacy from primitive times, or in other words that there was no preceding Ancient Age. Common opinion holds that there was an Ancient Age from the time of the Three Mountains period through the Kingdom period and until the invasion by the Satsuma domain. But as far as literature at least is concerned, it is difficult to find evidence. The common view holds the umuru as an ancient form. But an archaic sort of religious incantation is essential to umuru. (The yesa umuru and the yētu umuru are free of the incantatory, but they exist in small numbers.) Songs of religious recitation also dominate the island groups apart from the main island of Okinawa. The tahabwe, kamtutsi, nigaifutsi, etc. give such evidence of archaic features that there really seems no period that can be called the Ancient Age. Popular opinion likes to equate the *Umuru Suosi* with the *Man'yōshū* (Hokama-Niizato, 1972, 529), but that is no more than folk opinion. The Japanese collection [*Man'yōshū*] is one of lyrics in which private sentiments are expressed in a literary tension. By contrast, the *Umuru*, a common product of a single society, represents only phases of attempted advance from religious invocation toward songs with narrative elements and lyrics (ibid., 531).

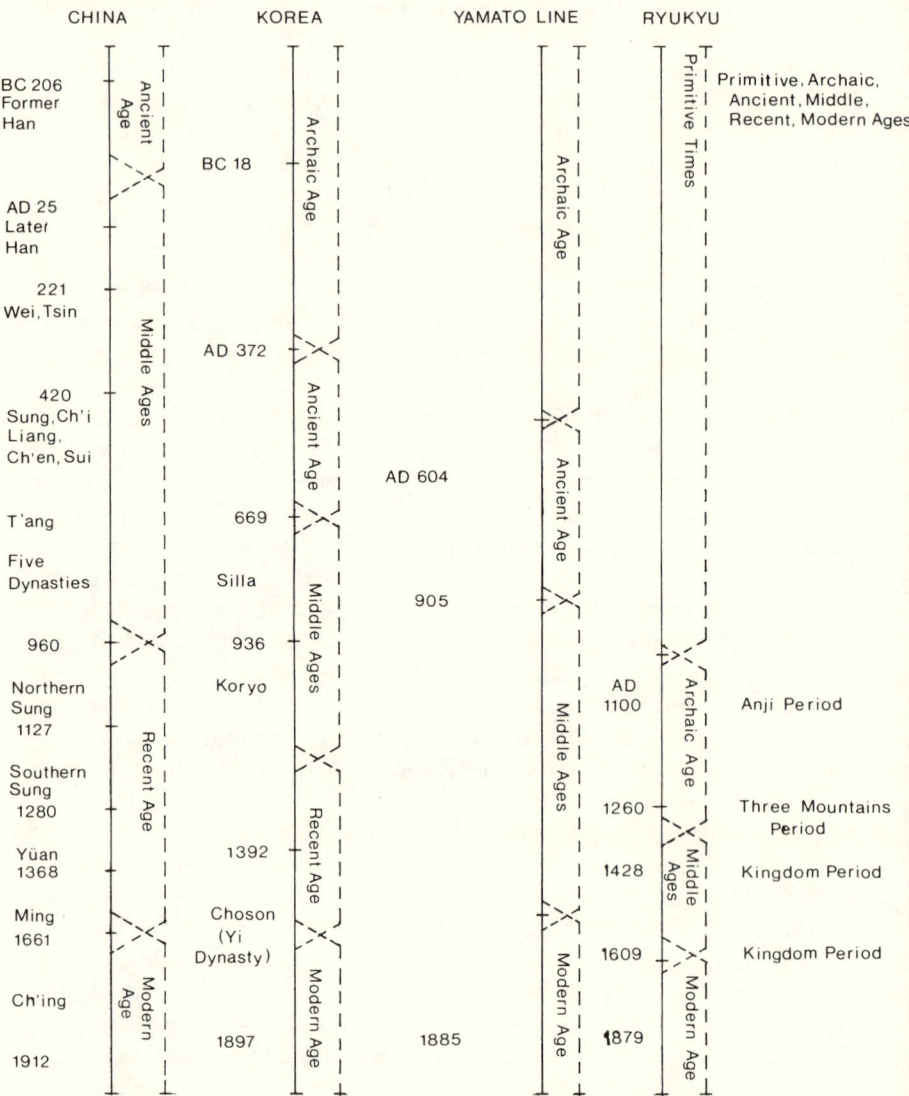

FIGURE 2. Correspondence of Periods in East Asian Literature

Before the process could mature into the literary poetry characteristic of the Ancient Ages in the other traditions, the Satsuma invasion burst upon Okinawa. As a result, on the main island culture progressed from the Archaic Age to the Middle Ages, skipping an Ancient Age. The other Ryukyuan archipelagoes retained more of the archaic and entered into their Middle Ages more slowly than did Okinawa.

PART ONE

The Archaic Age:
From Chaos to
Differentiation

CHAPTER 1

Primeval Chaos

PRELITERARY TIMES

The Archaic Age in Japanese literary history is, as we have seen, that time in which literariness existed only as a part of religion, government, and history. If we consider that such preliterary attributes developed a recognizable quality as literature only well into the Ancient Age, it follows that the acceptance of Chinese culture served as the impetus that brought about an awareness of literature as an individual entity. Or, what is much the same thing, that the "Archaic Age" in Japanese literary history designates the time before native Japanese culture was transformed by contact with Chinese civilization.

Official relations between Japan and China took place as early as A.D. 57, during that period of Chinese history known as the Later Han (A.D. 25-220).[1] Contemporary Japanese society, however, had not yet attained a level sufficient to enable it to partake of Chinese civilization. Fifty years later, in A.D. 107, records show that the Japanese presented further tribute to the Han Empire.[2] Of all the tributary missions to China, one stands out: that sent by Himiko, "Queen of Wa" [Old Japanese "Fimiko"; "Wa" is "Wo" in Chinese], to the Kingdom of Wei in 239. The following year, an embassy from Wei came to Wa and presented the Queen with an edict and seal of state from Emperor Shao.[3] The Chinese language probably served as a limited means of communication between the Wei embassy

[1] "In [A.D. 57], the Land of Nu in Wa offered up tribute and congratulations to the Emperor. The envoys from Nu styled themselves ministers. Their land is in the southernmost region of Wa. A seal of state was bestowed on them by Emperor Kuang-wu." *Gokanjo*, ch. 115, *Waden*, "Record of the Eastern Barbarians." What is acknowledged to be the same gold seal of state was unearthed in Shiganoshima in northern Kyushu in 1789, so verifying the Chinese account.

[2] "In [107], in the reign of Emperor An, the King of Wa presented him with one hundred and sixty slaves, and humbly requested an audience" (ibid.).

[3] "In the Sixth Month of [239], the Queen of Wa sent envoys . . . to Wei. They arrived in the province, and humbly requested an audience with the Emperor to present him their tribute. . . . In [240], by order of the Emperor, Governor-General Kung Ch'ieng sent a mission led by the official T'i Chün to present the Queen with an edict and a sash and seal of state. The Wei mission arrived in Wa and recognized the Queen as the tentative ruler of Wa" (*Gishi Wajinden* "Record of the Eastern Barbarians"). [As in notes 1 and 2, we here alter Chinese specifications of dates by reigns to Western reckoning, correcting the first date here, as the author shows is necessary, citing Wada-Ishihara, 1951, 49.—Ed.]

and their Japanese hosts. Practical matters, evidently transacted through interpreters, must have been barely manageable. The primitive cultural level of Japan in the third century is best represented by the contemporary pottery, called Yayoi after a discovery site in Tokyo. At this stage the Japanese acceptance of Chinese civilization did not go beyond the acquisition of Chinese silk and woolen goods, bronze mirrors, and swords, and admiration for the fine workmanship of these articles.

There need be no doubt, however, that various kinds of songs, at least, were widespread in third-century Japan. According to records made by the Chinese visitors, singing and dancing were performed at funeral ceremonies in the country of Wa:

> When a death takes place, the entombment ceremonies last ten days or more. Prior to the entombment, meat is not eaten, the chief mourner weeps and wails, and other people come to sing, dance, and drink liquor. When the entombment is completed, all the members of the bereaved family go to the river and purify themselves by bathing, much as with our custom of lien-mu.[4]

The practice of singing at funeral ceremonies is also ubiquitous among present-day primitive peoples: should we not then call its existence in third-century Japan axiomatic? A further example, although taken from mythology, is found in the *Kojiki* description of the funeral of the god Ame no Wakahiko:

> Immediately in that place they built a funeral house. They made a wild goose of the river the bearer of the burial offerings; a heron the broom-bearer; a kingfisher the bearer of the food offerings; and a pheasant the weeping woman. Having thus determined the roles of each, [they performed asobi] for eight days and eight nights.[5]

"Asobi" is taken to mean "singing and dancing," because the corresponding narrative in the *Nihon Shoki* is, "they wept and sang for eight days and eight nights" (*NSK*, 61).[6] Furthermore, we have this narrative as an instance of song and dance appearing in nonfunerary circumstances:

[4] Ibid. "Lien-mu" refers to purification by water, performed while wearing mourning of glossed silk, a rite associated with the first anniversary of a death.

[5] [*Kojiki*, ch. 34; see Philippi tr. Abbreviated *KJK* hereafter, the work combines myth and history, prose, and poetry ("*Song*" hereafter), and was set down from oral recitation in 712. We have made alterations of Philippi in his bracketed material and have converted his style of romanizing Old Japanese. This is the place to say that, after much thought, we have decided on the grounds of simplicity to translate "kami" as "god" in the traditional way. There are great differences between what the words are usually taken to mean, as what follows will show: a kami can die, may be the reigning tennō, the spirit of an illustrious dead person, a tree spirit, etc. Like the *Nihon Shoki* (see next note), the *KJK* is often referred to by earlier Japanese as a history of the kamiyo, the Age(s) of the Gods.—Trans., Ed.]

[6] *The Chronicle of Japan*, similar to the *KJK* but composed in Chinese, was compiled in

Another tradition says: "The goddess Izanagi, in giving birth to the Fire God, was burned, and so she passed away. Thus she was laid to rest in the village of Arima in Kumano, in the province of Ki. The local people honor the memory of her divine spirit, and when the trees bloom they offer up flowers to her. They also honor her by playing drums and flutes, carrying banners, singing and dancing" (*NSK*, 13).

This document records an eighth-century festival, but it seems safe to assume that the practice of singing and dancing as an accompaniment to worship existed in the third century or earlier.

Moreover, analogies drawn from research conducted on modern primitives leave no doubt that songs were recited on various occasions, whether as prayers for good harvest, for rain and deliverance from pestilence, or for celebrations of success, marriage, or victory in battle. Unfortunately nothing is known of the style and content of these early songs. C. M. Bowra observes that the Yamana tribe of Tierra del Fuego in South America repeats the following meaningless sounds, regularly and monotonously, in their dances: "Ma-las-ta xai-na-sa ma-las-ta xai-na-sa"; or "Hau-a la-mas ke-te-sa hau-a la-mas ke-te-sa." Similarly meaningless sounds are also recited among the Eskimos, the Veddas of Ceylon, and the Arapaho tribe of American Indians, from which one may conjecture that Japanese primitive song, in its earliest phases, closely resembled those modern examples. The Arapaho also recite intelligible songs, but on quite separate occasions they chant only the following meaningless syllables:

> Ye no wi ci hay
> Yo wi hay
> Wi ci hay
> Yo wi ci no
> Wi ci ni.

Words formed by the combination of a consonant and a vowel, producing an open syllable, are not common in the Arapaho language: it is therefore believed that they were consciously created for purposes of recitation, and that an extremely ancient "song antedating song" has been preserved through ceremonial practices. When song reaches a more advanced level, intelligible words are recited in response to particular conditions. For example, Tulaba, a member of the Kurnai of Australia, recited a song

---

720, and was in former times usually referred to as *Nihongi*, as often still. Hereafter abbreviated to *NSK*. This and the *KJK* will be referred to collectively as *Chronicles.*— Trans.]

which he believed had the power to stop pain, "Show belly moon-to," with much emphasis placed on the word "moon."[7] The weather incantations of the Eskimos include the following, recited when they wish the sky to clear: "The sun up there, up there."

As a rule, such songs do not exceed one line, though there are instances in which the single line is repeated. The same line will be repeated an indefinite number of times if it accompanies a dance. By contrast, when the song exists separately from the dance, subtle variations can be added to the single line. A Southwest African Bushman, for example, recited this song when his tobacco had been carried off by a dog:

> Famine it is,
> Famine it is,
> Famine it is here.[8]

"Here," included for emphasis at the end of the chant, is the sole addition. This variation is identical to the device of simple repetition as far as meaning is concerned, but the emphasis it provides proves to enhance somewhat the conclusion of the song, and to regulate the rhythm of the whole. Once the possibility of alteration is grasped, variations tend to evolve into ever more elaborate forms. The following song is a noteworthy instance of the manner in which the Eskimos express desire for a certain kind of weather:

> Only come, only come,
> Only come, only come,
> I stretch out my hands to them thus,
> Only come, only come.

The variant line, serving to reinforce the main statement, has developed a further function, to elucidate the scene. A Bushman legend about a lion hunter includes this song:

> O my younger brother, *hn*,
> My younger brother's wind feels like this,
> When he seems to have killed a lion.

---

[7] Howitt, 1904, 388. Howitt translates literally from the Kurnai; hence what seems broken English. He quotes Tulaba's report that the miraculously efficacious charm was imparted to him by his dead father in a dream.

[8] Bleek-Lloyd, 1911, 235. [Bowra is cited ch. 2, n. 7.—Ed.]

Once this level has been reached, the next step—the creation of a means of expression based on the expansion of a given subject—is probably inevitable. The Gabon Pygmies of Africa recite a song about a sacred spider called *rri*:

> *Rri*, your threads are well stretched,
> Clever hunter, your threads are well spun,
> *Rri*, you are sure of abundant food,
> Spirit, be kind to me,
> Grant that, like *rri*, my chase is lucky.

> (Trilles, 1931, 147)

The capabilities of the song are ordered—things are this way, things are that—in a conversion of constituents. The structure of the song possesses a train of thought that reveals the sense of the entire song only when the last line has been recited. The length of such songs varies. The aborigines of the Arnhem Land peninsula in northeastern Australia have ritual chants, identical in structure to the Pygmy song above, but which have as many as fifty lines. As a song grows in length, its structure evolves into one of several stanzas, and parallelism also comes into being. Parallelism seems to appear first in dance songs and then to appear in other kinds. This is illustrated by an old woman's song from a Bushman legend:

> The old pot must remain,
> The old pot must remain,
> For I lie in the old hut.
>
> The old soupbrush must remain,
> The old soupbrush must remain,
> For I lie in the old hut.
>
> The old kaross must remain,
> The old kaross must remain,
> For I lie in the old hut.
>
> The old bed must remain,
> The old bed must remain,
> For I lie in the old hut.
>
> The old dish must remain,
> The old dish must remain,
> For I lie in the old hut.

This song is clearly intended for solo recital. If it were used to accompany a dance, the refrain—"For I lie in the old hut"—would be taken up by the chorus of dancers, while the main body of the song—"The old pot must remain," etc.—would be assigned to the soloist, a nondancer. This structure, represented by the main body of the song plus the refrain, is believed to have been taken over by songs intended for solo performance, unaccompanied by dances.

Yet dance songs and songs unaccompanied by dance differ in spite of sharing the structure of a main body and refrain. The dance song has the stanza as its basic unit, and the plain song a single line of verse. In the Bushman song, the main body consists of repetitions of "The old pot must remain," etc. But if subtle variations are introduced, the technique of highly evolved parallelism is likely to be developed within the main structure of the song, and it is for this reason that its prototypes have been shown.

The preceding discussion summarizes Bowra's thesis (Bowra, 1962, 63-79). As his study makes clear, primitive song can be assumed to have passed through the following stages in its evolution [ibid., 88]:

1. The single meaningless line.
2. The single intelligible line, emphasized, when desired, through repetition.
3. An accumulation of several lines. If the lines are somewhat regular, they may form a simple stanza.
4. An accumulation of several stanzas in response to repetitions in a dance. Units of several lines may be collected into even larger units.
5. Accumulations, within the framework of fixed sections or cycles, of unrestricted length, which possess the status of poetry.

Although representing an important theory, these gradations cannot be made to correspond directly to Japanese archaic song. That is because Bowra's theory is based on investigations of "modern primitives." The peoples share several social characteristics: they live by hunting and gathering, have no fixed abode, do not keep livestock as a food resource, and form communities of units no larger than twenty houses or one hundred people. Their culture corresponds to that of the Late Paleolithic Age. The culture of third-century Japan, on the other hand, was that of the late Yayoi period, when ironware had come into fairly wide use. Thus, when the Chinese embassy noted that the Japanese "sing, dance, and drink liquor" in the course of their entombment ceremonies, it may be concluded that the songs recited at that time were somewhat more advanced presentations than the primitive songs we have considered up to now.

The *Chronicles* do contain songs from various historical periods. Several songs, describing events connected with the reigns of the sixth-century Keitai and Kimmei, can serve as examples of obviously late composition. Although it is very difficult to determine the dates of earlier works, regardless of their time of composition, the songs in the *Chronicles* indisputably contain a far higher quality of expression than do the primitive songs cited by Bowra. One must go to some lengths to discover a Japanese song from this period that corresponds to the first stage of Bowra's theory. The Kagura song "Achime Waza" (Rite of Achime) is one such example:

> LEFT: Achime!
> Oh, oh, oh, oh!
> RIGHT: *Oke.*
> Achime!
> Oh, oh, oh, oh!
> LEFT: *Oke.*
> BOTH: Oh, oh, oh!
> RIGHT: *Oke.*
>
> (*Kagura*: 1)

This conforms to Bowra's first-stage song insofar as it is a recitation of meaningless sounds. The "Rite of Achime," however, is thought to be a species of incantation, and should be distinguished as such from rhythmic songs. I cannot find an example which conforms to Bowra's second-stage song, but the responsive verses recited by Izanami and Izanagi fit the form of a third-stage song:

> IZANAMI: Ana niyashi   My, oh lovely,
> E otoko o   What a fine man!
> IZANAGI: Ana niyashi   My, oh lovely,
> E otome o   What a fair maid!
>
> (*JDK*, 178)

Although not easily recognized as a song, these verses were probably accompanied by specially designated rhythms and movements, so constituting a prototype of a genre containing both melody, the basic element of song, and rhythm, the fundamental constituent of dance. An instance of recognizable song is transmitted by the *Kogo Shūi*: when the Sun Goddess emerges from the Heavenly Rock Cave, the assembled gods, seeing the earth again grow light, chant,

Aware	Really!
Ana omoshiro	Ah, how gladdening!
Ana tanoshi	Ah, how delightful!
Ana sayake	Ah, how refreshing!
Oke	*Oke*!

(*Kogo Shūi*, 195)

This song is probably a more or less sophisticated creation by a member of the Imbe clan. Even so, the author doubtless wrote it knowing that, in primitive expression, a stanza is made up of just such simple lines. In other words, we have evidence of the survival of primitive memories. There is also a saibara:

Chikara naki kaeru	Helpless frog,
Chikara naki kaeru	Helpless frog!
Hone naki mimizu	Boneless worm,
Hone naki mimizu.	Boneless worm!

(*Saibara*, 55)

This corresponds in form to Bowra's third-stage song, but its date of composition is relatively late.

A very similar level of expression can be found even today in Ainu incantations. Earthquakes, the Ainu believe, are caused by the movements of a gigantic subterranean fish. When an earthquake occurs, they draw a sword, thrust it into the hearth ashes if indoors, or into the earth if outside, and loudly recite this incantation:

> I've pierced
> Your belly,
> I've pierced
> Your belly!

(Chiri Mashiho, 1960, 11-12)

The form of this chant corresponds to the first half of the saibara "Helpless Frog," and might be better seen as one of Bowra's second-stage songs. "Tusekari Upopo" (The Net Carriers' Song), recited at the Bear Festival in Horobetsu [on the coast near Muroran, Hokkaido], is an example of a song in several stanzas:

> In Ayoro village,
> In the village square,

The god-bear dances
Round and round.

In Karapto village,
In the village square,
The god-bear dances
Round and round.

(Ibid., 82)

This corresponds to one of Bowra's fourth-stage songs. It is, however, extremely rare for an Ainu song to retain primitive characteristics to this extent: the vast majority possess a far more complex structure. Ainu songs as a whole do not conform to the concept of primitive song as discussed in Bowra's theory.

Much the same can be said for Ryukyuan songs, which are considerably more advanced as forms of expression than are Bowra's primitive songs. Only a few Ryukyuan incantations retain primitive elements. One such instance is this incantation, or tahabwe, recited on the main island of Amami during earthquakes to make them stop quickly:

Kyonssika
Kyonssika
Kyonssika.

In Iri Akina, Amagusiku Town, on Tokunoshima, one of the Amami Islands, the same charm is pronounced:

Kyurotika
Kyurotika.

In both cases the meaning of the incantation is unknown (*Nan'yō-Amami*, 123). This may be classified as one of Bowra's first-stage songs. On another part of the main island of Amami, Usinami, Setouti Town, this is chanted when earthquakes strike:

Yurimiti
Yurimiti.

(Ibid., 123)

This means "stop shaking" in Ryukyuan: because it is intelligible, it falls into the category of second-stage songs. Again, the following charm (habuguchi) against poisonous snakes is found in Akina, Tatugu Town, on Amami:

It's pure salt
From the Black Current,
It's pure water
From the river.
I'm a scion
Of Hōji,
I'm a scion
Of Hōji.[9]

(Ibid., 120)

The variations between the first and third lines would classify this as a third-stage song, although its technique is of somewhat higher quality than that found in the songs of that level cited by Bowra. An example of a fourth-stage song appears in a yungtu of Kawahira Village on Isigaki Island, in the Yaima chain of islands:

What's that clanging noise?
What's that banging noise?
It's the rice in the paddy fields
Left me by my father.
It's the rice in the paddy fields
Tilled for the shrine.
Cut it down
And cut it down,
There's still more to cut.
Carry it off
And carry it off,
There's still more to carry.
So much that
The horses' backs are bald,
So much that
The oxen's backs are bald,
So much that
My sisters' heads are bald:
Carry it off
And carry it off,
There's still more to carry.
(Nan'yō-Yaima, 124)

A song about farming can hardly be called primitive. Despite that and the detailed variations throughout, the basic form of the song does belong

[9] Hōji is the ancestor's name; it was related how, as a boy, he saved a habu (a poisonous snake) accompanying him when a mountain fire seemed to cut off all possible escape.

to the fourth stage of Bowra's theory. Actually, it might rather be said that unless one compromises to this extent, primitive vestiges in Ryukyuan songs are not to be found.

It is clear that the songs in the *Chronicles*, as well as the Ainu and Ryukyuan songs cited above as supplementary references, are far more sophisticated modes of expression than the primitive songs defined by Bowra's theory. What rare glimpses of the primitive we do find in early Japanese song may be considered as incidental manifestations of memories, inherited from distant ancestors, which survived deep in the national memory. On the other hand, by applying Bowra's stages of primitive song development to Japanese songs of the Archaic Age, as they survive in Japanese literary history, not only are we made aware of the developmental stages undergone by archaic song but also we are given considerable knowledge of the formative processes of the songs in the *Chronicles*.

No other process of archaic song ranks in importance with repetition and parallelism. The technique of repetition must have originated earlier. One of the Songs of Kume will serve as an example:

Ima wa yo	Now we have you,
Ima wa yo	Now we have you—
Aa shiyao	Hey, you scum!
Ima dani mo	How now,
Ago yo	My lads!
Ima dani mo	How now,
Ago yo.	My lads![10]

(*NSK, Song,* 10)

The form is primitive and, what is more, the date of composition is probably extremely early for these examples. Parallelism is formed when a variation is added to part of a repeated line, and it is an important technique in archaic Japanese song. The following is an example of it in the early stages of development:

Waga kado o	A man strolls
Tosan kōsan	Back and forth
Neru onoko	Before my house.
Yoshi kosaru rashi ya	There's sure to be a reason,
Yoshi kosaru rashi ya	There's sure to be a reason.

[10] [This song was recited by Jimmu Tennō after his elite Kume warriors had lured the enemy to a banquet and then slain them. See Chapter 2.—Trans.]

Yoshi nashi ni	A man strolls
Tosan kōsan	Back and forth
Neru onoko	For no reason at all.
Yoshi kosaru rashi ya	There's sure to be a reason,
Yoshi kosaru rashi ya.	There's sure to be a reason.

(*Saibara*, 13)

"He's loitering about for no reason, because there really is a reason": this is quite an intellectual concept, one which suggests that the date of composition is relatively late. Yet if we look at the song without its refrain, "There's sure to be a reason, / There's sure to be a reason," we have:

> A man strolls
> Back and forth
> Before my house.
> A man strolls
> Back and forth
> For no reason at all.

Now the song appears to be not so late a composition after all. If we think of these six lines—the main body of the song—as the part recited by a soloist, and the refrain, "There's sure to be a reason, / There's sure to be a reason," as the part taken by a chorus, we have a structural prototype corresponding to the level of the Bushman song cited by Bowra, the old woman's song beginning "The old pot must remain . . ."

Here is another song from the *Chronicles*:

Hirakutsuma no	Wild geese eat rice
Tsukureru	From the hilltop fields
Onoeda o	Farmed by
Karigari no kurau	The little hunchback.
Mikari no	Wild geese eat rice
Tawami to	From the hilltop fields
Onoeda o	When you
Karigari no kurau	Neglect to hunt.
Mikoto	Wild geese eat rice
Yowami to	From the hilltop fields
Onoeda o	When your commands
Karigari no kurau.	Have no strength.

(*NSK, Song*, 122)

The repetition of the lines "Wild geese eat rice / From the hilltop fields" suggests that a primitive refrain has been grafted to the form. There is a record of this song having been recited in the sixth year of Saimei's reign (660), and we have good reason to give it credence.[11] But the song has only borrowed the form of a refrain from earlier songs: if the repeated lines, "Wild geese eat rice / From the hilltop fields," are omitted, the remaining lines make no sense at all. The saibara "A Man Strolls" still constitutes an intelligible song even if its refrain is omitted: its date of composition should therefore be considered to antedate the seventh century. "Helpless Frog" (*Saibara*, 55), given above, may also have been originally recited with a refrain.

In Bowra's theory, such refrains may have been created out of a dialogue between the soloist, who sang the main body of the song, and the dancers, who sang the refrain; and the concept of "main body plus refrain" later became a fixed song form, recited by the soloist alone (Bowra, 1962, 78).

The refrain [here designated by the "mata" as opposed to the "ichi," or main part] to a Ryukyuan umuru lends support to Bowra's theory:

Ichi

The Great High Priestess
Sings and dances, possessed by the god:
Then may our King rule the land.

Mata

The Holy Priestess of wide renown—

Mata

She dwells in the shrine of Shuri fortress.

Mata

She dwells in the jewel-like fortress shrine.[12]

(*Umuru*, 1:1)

The significance of the headings "Ichi" and "Mata," written before certain lines of every song found in the *Umuru Suosi*, has not been determined, although Ono Jūrō has advanced a persuasive interpretation: that

[11] This is surely satire on the incompetent behavior of Tsumori Kutsuma, Tsumori the Hunchback, who returned from Paekche three years before (657): it is difficult to imagine the song written under other circumstances.

[12] The position of Great High Priestess (kikoe ōigimi) was the highest priestess position in the Ryukyus, following the establishment of the Ryukyu kingdom. Generally the Queen or a younger princess was appointed. "Sedakako" (Holy Priestess) signifies one possessing abundant spiritual power and is a decorative epithet for "kikoe ōigimi."

the headings are to be treated separately, as a refrain.[13] If we apply this theory to the song and omit those lines identified as refrains, we are left with a poem in two parallel couplets:

> The Great High Priestess (1a)
> The Holy Priestess of wide renown (1b)
> She dwells in the shrine of Shuri Fortress (2a)
> She dwells in the jewel-like fortress shrine (2b)

This represents a doubling of the parallelism in couplet form given above in the saibara "A Man Strolls." The lines marked 1a, 1b, 2a, 2b are each accompanied in the same fashion by the refrain,

> Sings and dances, possessed by the god:
> Then may our King rule the land.

The umuru refrain thus belongs to the same prototype as the saibara refrain "There's sure to be a reason, / There's sure to be a reason," or the refrain to the Bushman song, "For I lie in the old hut." With its marked techniques of repetition and parallelism, archaic Japanese song seems to have passed through these stages in the process of its development.

The Spiritual and the Incantatory

The most prototypical of songs recited by primitive people throughout the world tend to be those linked to spiritual forces. During a storm the Eskimos, for instance, invite its spirit to enter their bodies with this song: "Man outside, please come in, please enter into me," adding to it meaningless sounds, "ai yai ye yi yai ai ye," an indication that this song belongs to the least evolved stage of primitive song (Bowra, 1962, 68). In Japan as well, the song recited before the Heavenly Rock Cave, which preserves the most primitive of Japanese lyric forms, shares certain characteristics with incantatory chants. And we have seen how primitive Ainu and Ryukyuan song forms tend to be connected with incantations or religious rites. Given this, it seems only natural to go one step further and propose

[13] Ono assigns the terms "consecutive section" and "repeated section" to these song parts, but since it is not clear what is consecutive to what, I have substituted the terms "main body" and "refrain," respectively. [The author agrees that we should leave the Okinawan "ichi" and "mata" unrendered in our translation of the song. See also General Introduction, n. 39.] Ono also regards the kwēna, with its parallelism, as the source, and stresses that the rhythm-marking words (hayashikotoba) added to the kwēna developed into the refrain (1977a, 141, 141-43; 1977b, 148-54). There is not necessarily a direct link, however, between this and the fact that the kwēna antedates the umuru.

that the origins of literature lie in charms and incantations, believed to
be divine gifts. This concept was advocated by Origuchi Shinobu (Origuchi, 1924, 63-75).

Origuchi based his theory on parallels drawn between Japanese and
Ryukyuan culture. Comprehensive and multifaceted as his treatise on the
origin of Japanese literature is, we must content ourselves here only with
those of his conclusions which concern the Archaic Age.[14]

1. Powerful clan chieftains, who governed the ancient village communities, also served as religious leaders. High priestesses or shamanesses, chosen from among the chieftains' close relatives to be
brides of the gods, transmitted divine oracles, on the basis of which
the chieftains, as deputies of the gods, controlled their communities.

2. The gods left the Land of Eternity to pay regular visits to the
world of men; there they bequeathed incantations designed to improve human life and labor. The spirits of the deceased also participated in these visits to their descendants' villages. Divine incantations were given in the form of direct commands to local spirits,
commands which the spirits were obliged to obey. The visiting gods
were called "marebito" (those who rarely come, or guests).

3. Divine incantations, uttered by a shamaness while in a state of
trance or possession, represented the thoughts or the deeper awareness of the entire tribe. The content of such incantations ranged from
accounts of a god's own antecedents or the creation of the country
to pronouncements on the growing of food, human destiny, requisite
conditions for receiving the gods (misogi, purification), the eradi-
cation of evil spirits (harae, exorcism), or the origin of the tribe. At
first, incantations existed as independent units, but gradually they
were collected into a single body.

4. Incantations, in their later stages, came to contain both narrated
(ji) and spoken (kotoba) sections. The narrated section, made up
essentially of contents such as those listed above, was well suited
for being told in the third person; but because it was told from the
god's own standpoint—that is, in the first person—narrative per-
sonae were occasionally confused. Narrated sections later came to
be exclusively in the third person, and developed into descriptive
recitations. Since the spoken section consisted of the god's own direct
utterances, it continued to be narrated in the first person. It later

[14] The Origuchi theory appeared over a period of several years and through several
editions of his book, *Kokubungaku no Hassei (The Genesis of Japanese Literature)*, from
the first in 1924 through the fourth in 1927. Since I consider the last three editions as
expansions of the first edition, I shall refer to the whole as if the 1924 theory.

evolved into uta, short lyric passages of concentrated purity, or again into kotowaza, proverbs.

5. The original concept of incantations, as a means of translating past events into reality, was replaced by the idea of recited narratives demonstrating how the past was related to reality. These narratives were passed down from one generation to another by professional storytellers, the kataribe. When a member of the kataribe, having for some reason fallen on hard times, drifted off to another part of the country, his style of recitation would likely have degenerated into one that stressed the entertaining over the traditional. With this straying from the sacred rites, narrative was simultaneously liberated as art.

Origuchi's achievement, appearing at a time when Japanese literary studies were conducted solely by philological methods, introduced anthropological procedures into the field, and so opened up areas of research beyond the reach of documents. We may well call his work great, because most of it remains valid to this day. Since the publication of his theory, and despite the unending series of intense yet vague attacks from philologically minded scholars to which it has been subjected, Origuchi's work continues to attract enthusiastic exponents. The only possible explanation is that the theory contains a great many unshakable truths, although one cannot possibly conclude that everything in the Origuchi theory is true. As long as we remain aware of the boundaries within which anthropological methods can effectively operate, the Origuchi theory retains its validity even today.

The results of Bowra's research in primitive song have been found apposite because of their assumption that cultural characteristics held in common by contemporary primitive societies date back to prehistoric times. Bowra's theory rests on the premise that the present existence—in Africa, South America, Alaska, Australia, Ceylon, and Malaysia—of societies that share a common primitive culture, despite their mutual isolation, is not the result of borrowings or influence from other societies. Conversely, if the culture of another society is, at some stage, intermingled with a primitive culture, then the latter cannot be called identical to its prehistoric antecedent. Archaeology utilizes carbon radioisotopes (C^{14}) to determine the age of excavation finds, and an absolute date is computed from the half-life of radioisotopes, which is in turn caused by the breakdown of radioactive particles. This method of calibration actually rests on the assumption that several basic hypotheses are valid: one such hypothesis is that the finds have never been exposed to carbon from external sources. If external carbon contaminates an object, then no number of half-life calibrations will mesh with its actual date. Similarly, the question of the survival of primitive characteristics within a culture rests on the hypothesis that the observed culture has never been influenced by other societies. Ever since the fifteenth century, however, the Ryukyuans have engaged in considerable intercourse with other countries, so that the hypothetical conditions, by which we can infer that all extant Ryukyuan conventions and songs preserve their ancient form, are not honored. Even from a geographical standpoint the hypothesis is invalid: the island of Yonaguni, for one, is very close to Taiwan, and so it cannot be confidently asserted that it never experienced an influx of Taiwanese culture.

The Yaima Islands in the Ryukyus provide an instance of the gods coming from the Land of Eternity to visit as "marebito." The procedure, which conforms precisely to Origuchi's description, is based on the following conventions. On the first day of every season, a grotesque divinity called Mayunganashi, his body completely concealed beneath a coat and hat of betel-palm fronds, visits each house to pronounce on farming matters and to utter congratulatory formulas (Figure 3). He then leaves

FIGURE 3. Mayunganashi (Okinawa). In this festival, a man disguises himself as a deity from another island far out to sea.

by sea, his form gradually fading in the distance.[15] Origuchi's deduction—that the chieftain-priest had as his associate a close relative, the high shamaness—was probably inspired by the relationship between the King and his Great High Priestess in the Ryukyuan kingdom.[16] Moreover, Origuchi's theory of the content of divine incantations is based in part on Ryukyuan songs. The origin of the country is sung in an umuru (*Umuru*, 10:512), and procedures similar to ritual ablution or purification can be found in umuru, kuti, and tahabwe. The Ryukyuan song corpus does not, however, contain narratives of a god's personal history and antecedents. This feature of Origuchi's theory would seem to be based upon the Ainu kamui-yukar and oina epics. Certainly kamui-yukar and oina suggested to Origuchi his concept of narrative-voice confusion as the result of the first-person recital of material appropriate to third-person narration.[17] Although such comparisons are definitely not, in themselves, devoid of meaning, to conclude that these modern phenomena have not altered since prehistoric times requires adequate proof of numerous basic assumptions.

In comparing the forms of songs recited by primitive peoples throughout the world, we saw that the most unevolved was the single meaningless line, followed by the single line made up of intelligible words. This deduction is methodologically free of difficulties: it is quite reasonable to think that if the Japanese in the Jōmon Period—now represented by its straw rope-patterned pottery—carried out a nomadic existence by hunting and gathering, as modern primitive societies now do, their songs too would have consisted, at some early date, of a single meaningless line. Moreover, it seems sound reasoning to conclude that although primitive songs, in groups of several lines, no longer survived in fifth-century Yamato Japan, they continued to exist deep within the collective memory as remote recollections of ancient times, appearing at random when circumstances required especially primitive songs. The soundness of this conclusion, however, is based on the assumption that Japan in the Jōmon period was not a new culture evolved out of the adoption of elements from other societies, but rather a society whose way of life paralleled that of modern primitives.

[15] A photograph of Mayunganashi appears in *Kami to Kami o Matsuru Mono (Gods and their Worshipers)*; Kobayashi-Ikeda-Kadokawa, 1967, 22). A village youth is chosen to disguise himself as the god; both the boy and those he visits are obliged to believe he is the god.

[16] [See n. 12.—Ed.] Beneath the Great High Priestess were senior shamanesses known as noro, utchigami, nigami, etc. (*Umuru*, 1972, 505). It is supposed that Queens and princesses had served as Great High Priestesses in the Anji period, and the same pattern is assumed to have been in use in Yamato.

[17] Kindaichi (1931, 1:420) reports a discussion with Origuchi in which Origuchi suggested that kamui-yukar and oina are first-person narratives because the shamaness, when possessed by the protagonist-god, reproduced his manner of speaking.

Furthermore, we must reconsider the view that all literary genres derive solely from incantations. To be sure, anthropological research has proved conclusively that the lives of primitive peoples were closely linked to incantatory practices. For that reason, as we have just seen, many of their songs are concerned with gods and spirits.[18] Nevertheless, it cannot possibly be demonstrated that incantations were the one and only source of literature. Among modern primitives, songs dealing with the supernatural coexist with songs of mundane life, although clearly drawn distinctions separate the two categories. Whereas the supernatural, concerned with gods and spirits, are sung in the hope of attaining a state superior to the singer's present one, the mundane, pertaining only to human affairs, deal with the present state in itself. Fundamental differences exist between the two categories, despite some instances of overlapping that render a more strict demarcation difficult. Moreover, while incantations definitely served as a source not only for the brevity, dignity, and symmetry of song but also for the techniques of repetition and parallelism incorporated into and developed by song, song itself nevertheless is believed to have evolved from participation in the rhythm of dance or pantomime by words adjusted to the rhythm (Bowra, 1962, 38-55). That was likely the case for Yamato songs; there are no grounds for stating that the birth of song would have been impossible without the preexistence of incantation. The content of very many modern primitive songs, moreover, is not easily judged incantatory. The following song, for example, is recited by the Bushmen of the southern Kalahari Desert in South Africa (Kirby, 1937, 59):

> The Bushman girl with "peppercorn" head,
> The lice are playing in her hair,
> But she has lovely legs,
> There, away on the dunes, they are "gathering medicine."
> Legs, you lovely legs!
> My mother says that I can have you,
> "Pick the flower while it blooms."[19]

One would be hard put to explain the evolutionary course followed by such a song from its presumed origin in incantation.

---

[18] ["Spirits" is used for "ryō"—malign or benign personalities who reenter the human world. The same Chinese character is also read "tama" or "tamashii"—soul, suggesting the easy gradation from human to spiritual to the divine in Shinto. See n. 5 on "kami."—Ed.]

[19] Kirby says in a footnote that he was unable to find apposite words for the last line, no matter how hard he tried, and so ended by quoting from Robert Herrick's "To the Virgins, to Make Much of Time." [Kirby's song is so far from Herrick's carpe diem lyric that we have altered the last line.—Ed.]

In archaic Japan as well, songs that had sprung from the worship of gods coexisted with those originally composed to depict everyday human life. There can be no reason to deny the existence of the latter any more than the predominance of songs dealing with the spirit world. The reason for this predominance is found in the response of primitive peoples to their environment, which is filled with incomprehensible phenomena. Making no effort to understand the causes of even those events with which, in the course of hunting and gathering, they were well acquainted, they had no choice but to rely on whatever surpassed human understanding. Songs that brought abundance into their lives would likely have been more carefully preserved than those that did not, from which we may conclude that songs concerned with the supernatural world formed the greater part of the corpus of Japanese primitive song. This is not a phenomenon limited to Japan, but a characteristic of all primitive song. What distinguished Japan in this regard is not the predominance of songs addressed to the spiritual world, nor the fact that these songs became the source for all others. Rather, they are remarkable because they have survived, albeit in somewhat attenuated form, through countless generations, down to the present day.

Primitive people frequently found their natural environment a terrifying adversary, one that posed a threat to the security of their food supply and the safety of their dwelling. This awareness survived long past the primitive epoch and into the Archaic Age in Japan, sustained perhaps by distant memories of primitive times. It is just such an awareness that motivates the god Ōkuninushi to pronounce this kotoage (spell) when he creates the Land of Izumo:

> Then he uttered this kotoage:
> "That Land in the Midst of the Reed Plains [Japan] has long lain desolate. All its creatures, down to the very rocks and plants, are fierce and wild. But once I had overpowered them, not a rebellious one remained" (NSK, 1:47).

Humanity has on occasion been confronted by both rocks and vegetation as violent forces. The purpose of the kotoage is to make them cease their violence. The god's use of the pluperfect, "Once I had overpowered them," emphasizes that this will indeed happen and is believed to be a means of coercing the rocks and vegetation. Such kotoage possessed authority because the rocks, trees, and other plants understood language. This is reflected in the words of Amaterasu, the Sun Goddess, as she prepares to send her grandson Ninigi down to govern the Land in the Midst of the Reed Plains:

"And what is more, in that land there are many gods who sparkle like fireflies, as well as wicked gods, noisy as a swarm of summer flies. And even the grasses and trees have the power of speech" (*JDK*, 59).

The gods who sparkle like fireflies and are as noisy as a swarm of summer flies are evidently personifications of natural phenomena that pose threats to humanity. The speaking grasses and trees, in this case, are complaining or protesting, actions human beings would interpret as "violent." Yet as long as the plant world shows its insubordination through language, it can also be confronted with the power of language: the means by which people do so is known as "kotoage."

Kotoage does not refer to the simple act of speech. A review of passages in the *Chronicles* where acts of kotoage are described reveals only instances of words uttered in response to a particular situation and in expectation of a particular result. When, for example, the god Izanagi leaves the Land of the Dead to return to the Land of Himuka, he washes away the defilement of death:

Then he uttered this kotoage: "Upstream the current flows too fast, downstream the current flows too slow," and he purified himself in midstream (*JDK*, 17).

Here the kotoage reveals the inappropriateness of both the upstream and downstream currents and is uttered in order to inform the river that purification is efficacious only in midstream. The river hears this, and thereupon manifests its power in accordance with the kotoage, with the result that Izanagi is able to cleanse himself of his death defilement. This kind of kotoage was probably not pronounced in the manner of ordinary speech but in some kind of special tone, for the same reason that the Kurnai emphasize the word "moon" in chanting their painkilling song.

Change of tone was not accompanied by elaborate rhetoric, although some decoration might have been added if an especially strong response was anticipated. For example: the god Hōri borrows a fishhook from his elder brother, only to have it carried off by a fish. Hōri then goes to the palace of the Sea God in search of the fishhook, by whose good offices it is then restored to him. As Hōri prepares to return to land with the fishhook, the Sea God gives him the following advice:

When you give this fishhook to your brother, tell him, "This fishhook is an obo hook, a susu hook, a madi hook, an uru hook," and give it to him with your hand behind your back (*JDK*, 287).

The "madi" of "madi hook" is derived from (Old Japanese) "madusi," poor, and evidently means that the owner of this fishhook will become

impoverished. "Obo hook," "susu hook," and "uru hook" also undoubtedly possess the power to bring about adverse conditions. When
this verse is recited, the fishhook hears it. It manifests its power as it has
been told to do, and so the elder brother, to whom the fishhook is
returned, is beset by evil. Hōri is cautioned to give the fishhook to his
brother "with your hand behind your back," that is, to turn his back on
his brother and with his hand behind his back pass the fishhook to him.
A probable explanation for this action is that, were Hōri to face the
fishhook after it had received his command, he would be in danger of
inhaling the fishhook's charmed spirit. Repetition of words of similar
meaning, such as is seen in Hōri's charm, is one instance of primitive
embellishment.

A further example of decorative language can be found in a passage
from the *Nihon Shoki*. Ame no Wakahiko is sent from heaven to the
Land in the Midst of the Reed Plains. Eight years pass with no word
from him, and so a pheasant is sent to take stock of the situation. Ame
no Wakahiko kills the pheasant with an arrow, and the arrow thereupon
flies up to heaven. Amaterasu is surprised to see it, because she bestowed
it on Ame no Wakahiko on the day of his departure from heaven.

> Then Amaterasu picked up the arrow and pronounced this spell:
> "If Ame no Wakahiko loosed you with evil intent, he will surely
> meet with misfortune. If he loosed you with good intent, he will
> surely be unhurt." So saying, she cast it back. The arrow fell directly
> to earth and pierced Ame no Wakahiko through the breast. So he
> died on the spot (*NSK*, 67).

If we omit "Ame no Wakahiko" from Amaterasu's speech, we are left
with "If [he] loosed you with evil intent, he will surely meet with misfortune. If he loosed you with good intent, he will surely be unhurt."
This parallelism is more complex in its elaboration than was the repeated
word sequence given in the previous example. The *Nihon Shoki* notes
that Amaterasu "pronounced this spell" (hokite notamawaku). The verb
"hoku" signifies the act of invocation in anticipation of a given result,
be it good or evil. An invocation set to verse was called "hokiuta," a
spell song; and "hokaibito" referred to itinerant beggars whose chief
stock in trade was the recitation of auspicious events.[20]

These terms all stem from the belief that spiritual forces in language

---

[20] In the *Kogo Shūi*, 198, "mihokitama" is interpreted to mean "the uttering of a prayer."
"Hokiuta" is applied to a song by Takeuchi Sukune, in which a wild goose's laying eggs
is hailed as an auspicious event (*KJK, Song*, 72): "This was the first part of a hokiuta"
(*Nintokuki*, 220). Two songs said to have been recited by "hokaibito" appear in the
Man'yōshū (16:3885-86).

cause either lucky or unlucky occurrences. The spiritual forces have a more precise name: "kotodama," or language spirit. The word itself does not appear before the age of the *Man'yōshū*, but the concept definitely existed in the Archaic Age. As the *Man'yōshū* poet Yamanoe Okura wrote,

Kamiyo yori	From the Age of the Gods
Iitsutekuraku	It has been said:
Soramitsu	"The Land of Yamato
Yamato no kuni wa	Seen against the sky
Sumekami no	Is a land where our sovereign's
Itsukushiki kuni	Divine Forebears hold power,
Kotodama no	A land where the kotodama
Sakiou kuni to	Brings us good fortune."
Kataritsugi	So it has been told
Iitsugaikeri	From generation to generation,
Ima no yo no	And in our time
Hito mo kotogoto	Each and every one of us
Ma no mae ni	Witnesses this truth displayed
Mitari shiritari.	Before our very eyes.[21]

(*MYS*, 5:894)

To judge from this poem, the kotodama existed from that remote period when gods were believed to have ruled the land. By the time of the *Man'yōshū*, however, emphasis was placed only on the felicitous aspect of the kotodama. By this shift, the invocation of blessings from the kotodama—in order to assure a bright and prosperous future—seems to have been commonplace:

Shikishima no	The Land of Yamato
Yamato no kuni wa	Of girded islands
Kotodama no	Is a land succored by
Tasukuru kuni zo	The kotodama: then
Masakiku ari koso.	May our future be happy.

This poem is the envoy to the following chōka, or long poem:

[21] ["*MYS*" in the citation refers (as hereafter) to the *Man'yōshū*, the first great collection of Japanese poetry, compiled in the eighth century, citing scroll or book and poem number(s). The author will be discussing the significance of prosodic irregularity in the next chapter.—Ed.]

Ashihara no	Our land, with its nodding ears of rice
Mizuho no kuni wa	In the Midst of the Reed Plains,
Kamu nagara	Our land, heeding the divine command,
Kotoage senu kuni	Does not utter kotoage.
Shikaredomo	And yet for all that
Kotoage zo aga suru	I shall utter a kotoage:
Koto sakiku	"May you be secure,
Masakiku mase to	May you have good fortune," and
Tsutsumi naku	"If you meet with no hindrance,
Sakiku imasaba	If you are blessed by fortune,
Arisonami	Then I pray that I may see you."
Arite mo min to	Waves strike the reefs,
Momoenami	They spread themselves a hundredfold,
Chienami ni shiki	A thousandfold upon the shore:
Kotoage su are wa.	Just so shall I utter my kotoage.

(MYS, 13:3253)

"They say that it is best not to utter kotoage, but I will do so all the same." Given the content of this chōka, one may conclude that its envoy intentionally stresses the felicitous side of the kotodama. If we consult the *Chronicles*, we find occasional transmissions of kotoage scenes, although this would seem to contradict the poet's statement that "Our land, heeding the divine command, / Does not utter kotoage." Yet from the start a kotoage was to be uttered only in response to special circumstances and in anticipation of special results. Under normal conditions it was to be approached with caution.

The reason for such caution is found in the nature of the kotodama: if its formidable power were directed toward the creation of an inauspicious event, it might result in the unleashing of a wholly unanticipated magic force that would sow evil through the world. Moreover, if the kotodama was overworked at its task of bringing about felicitous events, its power ran the risk of debilitation. Whether invoked for good fortune or calamity, then, the kotodama was not to be unleashed frivolously.[22]

[22] Kobayashi-Ikeda-Kadokawa, 1967, 155-58. The concept appears elsewhere in the MYS. For example:

Chiyorozu no	Though ten million
Ikusa naritomo	Warriors threaten,
Kotoage sezu	He will not utter kotoage,
Torite konu beki	But go off to subjugate the horde—
Onoko to so omou.	This man for whom I yearn.

(6:972)

A careless kotoage invited disaster: an example appears in the *Kojiki* story of Prince Yamato Takeru. On his way to subjugate the god of Mount Ibuki, he encounters a white boar in the foothills and utters a kotoage: "That white boar must be the mountain god's messenger in disguise. I need not kill him now, for I shall kill him on my return." Then, as he climbs the mountain, sheets of hail begin to fall, damaging the prince's health and eventually bringing about his death (*KJK*, 2:142). The narrator of the *Kojiki* comments: "That was not the mountain god's messenger who had disguised himself as a white boar, but the mountain god himself. Unaware of this, Prince Yamato Takeru uttered a kotoage, and so he met with misfortune." Prince Yamato Takeru mistook his adversary when he uttered his kotoage: not only was it rendered completely ineffective as a result, but it enraged the mountain god as well, and subjected the prince to harm. Both the auspicious and the calamitous varieties of kotoage were best left unuttered if at all possible:

A Poem Invoking Rainfall

Aga horishi	I prayed for rain:
Ame wa furikinu	Now it has fallen.
Kaku shi araba	If only it continues,
Kotoage sezu tomo	I need not utter kotoage
Toshi wa sakaen.	For a good rice harvest.

(*MYS*, 18:4124)

In other words, if rain had not fallen, the poet would have had to resort to the use of kotoage in his prayers: but happily the rain has fallen, and if it keeps on, there should be a bountiful harvest, and no need for a kotoage.

Although none of the kotoage we have seen qualifies particularly well as a set form, they were, as has been noted, evidently required to be pronounced in a manner different from that of ordinary speech. Or, to look at it another way, if, in the course of everyday conversation, one happened to speak in a manner similar to that used in uttering kotoage, then those words might unleash the power of the kotodama, with unexpected results. This phenomenon is typified by kotowaza, proverbs or,

Akizushima	Dragonfly Islands,
Yamato no kuni wa	The Land of Yamato,
Kamu kara to	True to the gods' ways,
Kotoage senu kuni	Does not utter kotoage:
Shikaredomo. . . .	And yet. . . .
	(from 13:3250)

literally, word charms. Brief in form and accentuated for optimum ease in transmission, kotowaza are in themselves capable of bringing on effects similar to those produced by kotoage. In addition, most kotowaza are based on important legends transmitted from ancient times, and so require great care. A good example is found in the *Kojiki* story of the pheasant sent to report to Amaterasu Ōmikami on Ame no Wakahiko's activities. Killed by his arrow, it fails to return from its mission: "This, then, is the source of our present kotowaza, 'a pheasant-messenger never returns' " (*KJK*, 257). This kotowaza would have given a certain flavor and liveliness to everyday conversation. Behind the kotowaza there is the episode of the pheasant shot down by Ame no Wakahiko. By uttering it, one made it likely that the other participants in the conversation, having been exposed to its kotodama, would never return for another gathering. Those, therefore, who were cognizant of the power inherent in kotodama would ascertain whether its use might be harmful before speaking it.

The derivations of certain kotowaza are given in several episodes in the *Chronicles*. Their purpose, it is thought, was to inform the reader which kotowaza were not to be carelessly employed. Origuchi's view— that incantations evolved into uta and kotowaza—is perceptive in that it points out the incantatory nature of kotowaza. To conclude, however, that all kotowaza originated solely from incantations seems to overstate the case. Because some kotowaza, those with their own legends of provenance, had powerful magical properties, they were to be employed with care. This explains why so many passages in the *Chronicles* are concerned with the origins of those kotowaza.

Wazauta, ancient popular songs, were also thought to be divinely inspired. The "waza" of "wazauta" is synonymous with the "waza" of "kotowaza," and if "kotowaza" is literally a word spell, then "wazauta" is a spell song. Several songs identified as wazauta appear in the *Nihon Shoki*: they were thought to be omens of future events. For instance, in the Tenth Month of 643, the following wazauta was recited:

Iwa no e ni	Atop a rock
Kosaru kome yaku	A little monkey parches rice.
Kome dani mo	Feed him the rice, then,
Tagete tōrase	And let him go,
Kamashishi no oji.	That old man antelope!

(*NSK*, *Song*, 107)

In the Eleventh Month, after Soga no Iruka had attacked the elderly Prince Ohine of Yamashiro [eldest son of Prince Shōtoku], people debated which lines of this uta allegorized which participants and events (*NSK*, 2:199-202), an activity described as "expounding the repercussions brought about by the previously recorded wazauta." The poem was clearly interpreted as a portent of this tragic incident. Other wazauta resemble this example in that they too are seen as omens. They become omens of certain events because the kotodama within these poems is worked to cause the events, an activation signified by the word "waza." The "waza" of "kotowaza" is considered a related term in that it signifies a magical action that will cause a future event. In sum, considerable care had to be exercised in dealing with these waza, because the kotodama they controlled was known to work for evil as well as good fortune.

When other creatures besides human beings have the power of speech, and react to human language, the workings of the kotodama will bring about various phenomena and situations. Rocks, grasses, and trees become conscious beings capable of speech for the simple reason that they possess spiritual natures akin to those of humans. Once it had been established that, "in the Land in the Midst of the Reed Plains, bases of boulders, tree trunks, and leaves of plants also have the power of speech" (*NSK*, 128), all natural phenomena were presumed to possess spiritual natures as well. This concept of a "spiritual nature" presumably resembled that of mana, as it is found throughout Oceania, and may also have shared characteristics of the North American Indian terms "wakan" and "orenda." In other words, Japanese verbal expression in archaic times was inseparable from what has been termed animatism.[23] Animatism can be observed in not a few modern primitive societies, although it also survives among more highly developed groups. "Sedi," a term often encountered in Ryukyuan umuru, signifies the spiritual power of animatism. A similar force was fully active in archaic Japan.

Not itself an especially unusual phenomenon, animatism appears all the more normal in an age when the concept of kotodama flourished. What is extraordinary about Japanese animatism is that it endured over an extremely long period. Even outside the world of letters, the kotodama has managed to survive in Japan down to the twentieth century.[24] In

---

[23] One of the classics of anthropology, Edward B. Tylor's *Primitive Culture*, contains in its eleventh and seventeenth chapters exhaustive research on animism among primitive peoples. In *The Threshold of Religion*, R. R. Marett later postulated a "pre-animistic stage" preceding animism, which he called "animatism." In contrast to animism, in which spirits with human characteristics are believed to be immanent in natural phenomena, animatism is the belief in spiritual powers with nonhuman characteristics (Keesing, 1966, 326, 337-38). [See n. 5, above, on "kami."—Ed.].

[24] In Japan today, when multistory buildings, carefully designed with the most advanced engineering techniques, are built, a Shinto priest is still asked to visit the site to offer prayers during the ceremonies of groundbreaking and completion. If this is not done, the contracting parties will feel uneasy. Also, at weddings one is supposed to avoid the use of certain words: "break off" (kiru), "separate" (hanareru), "leave" (deru), or "grow distant" (tōku

literature, however, the kotodama has (or had) somewhat greater vigor. As will be discussed in later chapters, it was the kotodama that first brought forth the perhaps unique literary techniques of the so-called preface (jo) and the pillow-word (makurakotoba). The advent of the Chinese-inspired ideal of ga (the high, the elegant), however, with its strict limitations on poetry, led to the disappearance of the preface and the degeneration of the pillow-word into a formalistic embellishment. Yet the kotodama survived in much of the vocabulary used by renga (linked poetry), that first manifestation of zoku (the low, the vulgar) literature. Not a few instances occurred of linked poetry using this vocabulary to produce prayers for victory or recovery from illness. When linked poetry eventually ascended into the world of ga it lost much of its incantatory nature, but its spirituality lived on, especially within its seasonal terms. This spirituality was given new life by haikai, which sought to revert to the popular elements of linked poetry, and it survives to this day in modern haiku. It is the result of no mere convention that seasonal terms are a requisite of haiku composition. Those terms represent an opportunity to manifest the spirituality inherent in nature, which, as expressed in the seasonal terms, speaks to the recipients from a level so deep that they themselves remain unaware of its existence. And although they can neither interpret nor explain the language, they understand this spirituality, respond to it, or are moved by it. Those who have encountered such receptivity in themselves must indeed feel that "grasses and trees have the power of speech," even in the twentieth century.[25]

Nō is even more firmly rooted in the spiritual. *Okina (Old Man)*, said to be the least like nō of the nō corpus, clearly evolved from farming rituals performed for good harvests. But spirituality persists even in the more typical nō plays, those belonging to the category of pluralistic specter pieces (fukushiki mugen nō). They evolved from combining the form of the earlier god-play category with worldly rather than spiritual content. As a result, specter pieces center on the correspondence between the spiritual and the mundane. Although spirituality is vested in the shite, or main actor, of a play, it extends as well to the divine nature in blossoms, the moon, the wind in the pines, or snow. The creation of nō plays constructed around just such a central image occurred in the time of Zeami.[26] For example, Zeami's masterpiece, *Izutsu (The Well-Curb)*, is

---

naru). It is even forbidden to speak of monkeys, because the word for monkey, "saru," is a homonym for "leave."

[25] Young Japanese are becoming increasingly ignorant of the names of plants, fishes, and birds. Nature has almost completely disappeared from the cities. The kotodama therefore faces imminent extinction.

[26] The unity of image in nō was first pointed out by Ezra Pound, but it was made known to the Japanese scholarly community by Earl Miner (Miner, 1958, 135-55).

focused in its entirety on the image of the moon. It is only when the spectator strives to experience as reality the autumn moonlight filling the stage that *Izutsu* can be appreciated as the highest art. When the spectator actually perceives the glow—one might call it the elegant purity—of moonlight, then even the plumegrass affixed to the imitation well-curb takes on an eerie freshness, and in its midst the shite's slightest movement communicates Narihira's entire love for the daughter of Aritsune. If, however, the spectator fails to perceive the moonlight, the performers may exert themselves as never before, but the famous *Izutsu* will remain for that spectator an unspeakably tedious and vexatious play. Nō originated in the correspondence between divinities and mortals, and to go further back in time, it is linked to the mythological world. Zeami traces its beginning to the songs and dances performed by the myriad gods gathered before the Heavenly Rock Cave, within which Amaterasu had shut herself in displeasure (*Kaden*, 4:38). Scholars of Japanese literature had dismissed Zeami's statement as a farfetched theory advanced to lend prestige to his art. If we postulate, however, that the origins of nō lie in the correspondence between gods and men, then it follows that Zeami is correct in asserting that it is linked to the world of mythology.

We are capable of rapport with moonlight and plumegrass because an animistic language exists between us and the world of nature. This language differs completely in substance from normal language. If too much normal language intervenes in the expression of animistic beauty, its spirituality will risk debilitation. Over the centuries, Japanese verse has moved toward ever shorter forms, from the chōka to the thirty-one-syllable tanka, and from there to the seventeen-syllable haiku. One reason for this movement may be that wordiness is, if anything, taboo to animistic beauty. Then again, it was known that the kotodama brought on unexpected effects, and that it must not be weakened by overuse; the attitude that kotoage were best left unspoken also figured in the process of abbreviating the Japanese lyric. To those brought up in the tradition of rendering description as minutely as possible—a Western tradition that extends from Greco-Roman times to the twentieth-century psychological novel—the drive to reduce a poem to a mere seventeen syllables may be impossible to understand.[27] It may be equally incomprehensible that highly intelligent people are deeply moved by a seventeen-syllable poem. Nevertheless, haiku does indeed continue to move the Japanese, and more than likely their emotion conceals in its depths an animatistic consciousness dating back to prehistoric times.

Animatism and animism are regarded today as backward attributes of

[27] For a sustained examination of traditional Western aesthetic practice, see Erich Auerbach, *Mimesis* (Princeton: Princeton University Press, 1953).

uncivilized tribes, and this is, of course, undeniable. Yet a literature purged of its animatism or animism cannot be shown to be artistically superior to one which has not been so purged. Certainly, from the nineteenth century there was a rapid development of realism as signified by the honing of ever more precise writing techniques, a literary technology, if you will. This has its regressive as well as its progressive side, especially if one believes that literature is an expression of the human spirit. Although enervated and strictly limited in its manifestations, the kotodama still survives in Japanese literature, a fact which the Japanese themselves would do well to reconsider. As point of departure, I would like to quote from Zeami's theory of the origin of nō, mentioned above:

> Nō is said to have begun in the Age of the Gods, when Amaterasu Ōmikami shut herself within the Heavenly Rock Cave. The earth was thereupon plunged into eternal night. Myriad gods and goddesses assembled at Heavenly Mount Kagu, and to propitiate Amaterasu they performed sacred music and dances, and created humorous entertainments. Then the goddess Ame no Uzume stepped forward. Holding a branch of the sacred tree hung with long paper strips, she lifted her voice in song and, lighting a bonfire, stamped her feet, and sang and danced in divine possession. Her song came faintly to the ear of Amaterasu, who opened the door of the cave a crack. The land again grew light, and the gods and goddesses clearly discerned one another's faces. Thus it is said that the august entertainment performed for Amaterasu was the beginning of nō, etc., etc. Further details will be found in oral traditions.

CHAPTER 2

Toward the Differentiation of Genres

I have been obliged to devise a new name, the Archaic [zenko], for the period under discussion, because I have already defined the Ancient Age as the time during which Japan was transformed by the importation of Chinese culture. The adoption and digestion of Chinese culture was quickly accomplished (at least in those advanced regions that belonged to the Yamato state), and so Japan in the Ancient Age eventually attained a fairly high level of culture. Despite the Yamato genius for rapid responses to foreign cultures, however, the acculturation rate of its society could not have been as high as that of the more modern Japanese. The conditions essential to a ready response had to be present before the response could be made. Several centuries, perhaps, were the necessary preparatory period before such conditions came into being. It is these preparatory centuries preceding the Ancient Age that I have called the Archaic Age. The Archaic was not a primitive epoch but rather a time in which settled, agriculturally based societies became well established, and their level of culture was far higher than that found among modern primitives. The terminus ad quem of the Archaic Age seems to coincide roughly with the end of the Tomb period, to use its archaeological name. It is difficult to assign a precise date to its terminus a quo. Assuming that the culture of the Jōmon period—another archaeological name—was primitive or prearchaic, we cannot automatically conclude that this culture, once it entered the Yayoi period, was transformed into something recognizably archaic. The terminus a quo of the Archaic cannot be assigned to a point earlier than the latter half of the Yayoi period. Let us then tentatively designate, as the point at which the Archaic Age began, the commencement of diplomatic relations (of a sort) with China in the third century.

Primitive characteristics survived in abundance into the Archaic Age, and literature, religion, and history did not as yet exist as separate entities. The Yamato people recited uta then, but this should not be interpreted simply as the recitation of songs, in our sense of the word. Uta served rather as the form in which incantations sometimes anticipated a victory or acted as a necessary code for ceremonial conversations when everyday language would not do. In addition, it was certainly common practice to express oneself, on meeting with unforeseen circumstances, by means of extemporaneous uta. Not until the Ancient Age, however, did such compositions receive social recognition as expressions worthy solely of moving human hearts, that is, as literature. Neither did the various genres have a basis for existence, since in archaic times literature itself did not exist. Both song and prose were regarded as "narrative" (katarigoto), and further subdivision would have been quite beside the point. On the other hand, there did exist material appropriate for later composition of songs and legends. As we shall see, even in the Archaic Age there were two distinct literary impulses, one toward lyric, another toward narrative.

THE COURSE OF LYRIC POETRY

The Works, Their Transmission, and Their Reception

It has been said that in primitive times individual literary production was an impossibility: everything was produced cooperatively within the community. Although correct in a certain sense, this supposition represents a serious misconception. Nearly all primitive songs seem to have been composed by individuals. Among modern primitives as well, songs are composed by skilled individuals within the tribe. Some tribes practice extemporaneous composition, while others ponder the composition of a new song—even if only a few lines long—for several days. When the song has been well polished, it is performed at an appropriate place. No matter how simple the song may be, it is still the product of an individual, not of the Volksgeist or some other nebulous entity. As members of a community that generally numbers few inhabitants, the composers of such songs are nevertheless well aware of the mutual feelings of the community, and because all its members lead the same kind of life, they have common interests and concerns. Accordingly, they do not possess a full sense of the individual. Individual emotions of course exist, but they are expressed as collective emotions. In other words, if I am aware of being happy, then of course everybody else is happy too. To stress that they do not possess a sense of the individual is also to articulate the view that their songs are collective compositions, not individual productions.

When a song is completed, the composer teaches it to others. If a song is associated with sacred rites, it is imparted by a learned elder, but ordinary songs of lesser import are taught by the composer-singer. When a song of three or five lines is completed among the Andaman Islands aborigines, for example, the composer will recite it to his audience and then have them repeat the closing line until he is satisfied with their performance. Finally, the entire song is recited again. The following song was recited by its composer when the dugouts of his hunting party landed on a reef used for foraging by their quarry, the sea turtle:

> Right place, his breakers,
> Therefore I—stop,
> Right place, his breakers;
> He for me hole-pushed,
> He for me hole-pushed.[1]

The closing line was repeated by the other hunters. The process of instruction described above may have given rise to a two-part song structure, in which the main body is first performed solo and the refrain is then taken up by other singers (Bowra, 1962, 41-44).

If we accept that similar systems of primitive song production survived, to a certain extent, into the Japanese Archaic Age, the knowledge so acquired can be applied to the explanation of several problems. The decline or disappearance of simple repetition is one such problem. The kind of simple repetition found in modern primitive song survives only vestigially in songs from the *Chronicles*. This indicates that the *Chronicles* songs, even those from the oldest strata, had already been composed at a level where very few primitive characteristics remained.

I have already given, as examples of the simple repeated lines, the following:

| Ima dani mo | How now, |
| Ago yo. | My lads! |

(*NSK, Song,* 10)

| Onoeda o | Wild geese eat rice |
| Karigari no kurau. | From the hilltop fields. |

(*NSK, Song,* 122)

The song that appears in two versions below offers fuller evidence. Like the first of the preceding quotations, it is one of the Songs of Kume. Since

---

[1] Kurtz, 1922, 109-11. This literal translation from the original has resulted in odd English. "Hole," in the last two lines is, according to Kurtz's note, a translation of "āutboāng": signifying a deliberate, unhurried manner, as though one were digging a hole in the ground.

the differences between the *Kojiki* and *Nihon Shoki* versions are not inconsiderable, both are given for purposes of comparison. The *Kojiki* records the song as:

Kamukaze no	By the Sea of Ise
Ise no umi no	Where divine winds blow
Ōishi ni	A periwinkle snail
Haimotorou	Creeps round
Shitadami no	A great rock.
Ihaimotorou	So shall we creep round and round,
Uchite shi yaman.	Then smite our enemy dead!

(*KJK, Song,* 13)

The longer *Nihon Shoki* version runs:

Kamukaze no	By the Sea of Ise
Ise no umi no	Where divine winds blow
Ōishi ni ya	A periwinkle snail,
Ihaimotorou	*A periwinkle snail*
Shitadami no	Creeps round and round
Shitadami no	A great rock, oh!
Ago yo	My lads!
Ago yo	*My lads!*
Shitadami no	Like periwinkle snails
Ihaimotōri	We shall creep round and round,
Uchite shi yaman	Then smite our enemy dead,
Uchite shi yaman.	*Then smite our enemy dead!*

(*NSK, Song,* 8)

The latter version probably preserves the form of the song as it was actually sung. The italicized lines would, in primitive song, be taken up as a refrain by other participants. We may assume that the *Kojiki* version transmits only the main body of the song. The reverse is true in another of the Songs of Kume: this time, the *Nihon Shoki* transmits only the main body of the song. The *Kojiki* version is as follows:

Osaka no	The great Cavern House
Ōmuroya ni	Of Osaka:
Hito sawa ni	Many men
Kiiriori	May come inside,
Hito sawa ni	Many men

Iriori tomo	May be inside, but
Mitsumitsushi	We the mighty
Kume no kora ga	Lads of Kume will
Kubutsutsui	Take our round-hilted swords,
Ishitsutsui mochi	Our stone-hilted swords,
Uchite shi yaman	And smite the enemy dead!
Mitsumitsushi	We the mighty
Kume no kora ga	Lads of Kume will
Kubutsutsui	Take our round-hilted swords,
Ishitsutsui mochi	Our stone-hilted swords,
Ima utaba yorashi.	And smite him now, the time is right!

(*KJK, Song*, 10)

The *Nihon Shoki* version is:

Osaka no	The great Cavern House
Ōmuroya ni	Of Osaka:
Hito sawa ni	Many men
Iriori tomo	May be inside,
Hito sawa ni	Many men
Kiiriori tomo	May come inside, but
Mitsumitsushi	We the mighty
Kume no kora ga	Lads of Kume will
Kubutsutsui	Take our round-hilted swords,
Ishitsutsui mochi	Our stone-hilted swords,
Uchite shi yaman.	And smite the enemy dead!

(*NSK, Song*, 9)

The only difference between "Many men may be inside" and "Many men may come inside" is the presence or absence, in the original, of the verb stem "ki," come. If we agree, however, that repetition is signified only by identical lines, then these two lines must constitute parallelism. The lines possess only the minimum qualifications for parallelism, yet they were once acknowledged as such, and were treated as part of the main song, when the *Nihon Shoki* was transmitted. In the *Kojiki* version, the part beginning with "We the mighty" (mitsumitsushi) forms a parallel unit composed of five-line units. The only difference between the two components of the unit appears in the last lines: "And smite the enemy dead" is contrasted with "And smite him now, the time is right!" An important factor in this parallelism is, then, repetition.

A literary form which freely crosses, in this fashion, the boundary between repetition and parallelism may be considered to have retained, to some extent, its primitive characteristics. Moreover, in the first of the Songs of Kume given above, the verses, "A periwinkle snail / Creeps round / A great rock. / So shall we creep round and round" are usually interpreted as, "Like the periwinkle snail creeping round and round, we shall encircle the enemy" (Tsuchihashi's note to *KJK, Song*, 13). As will be demonstrated below, however, the act of creeping in a circle is thought to have had incantatory significance when performed with a song. We may therefore regard this song as a means of activating the kotodama in anticipation of a victory. These two points, when considered together, indicate that the Songs of Kume belong to one of the older strata in the corpus of *Chronicles* songs.

It will not do, however, to conclude that certain songs in the *Chronicles* belong to an ancient stratum simply because primitive traces survive within their structure. At a New Year's banquet given by Suiko in the twentieth year of her reign (A.D. 612), the minister Soga no Umako offered this congratulatory chōka:

Yasumishishi	She who holds sway,
Waga ōkimi no	Our royal lady,
Kakurimasu	Is pleased to dwell within
Ama no yasokage	A grand and splendid palace.
Idetatasu	As she graciously departs,
Misora o mireba	I behold its beauteous roof.
Yorozuyo ni	May her reign flourish thus,
Kaku shi mo gamo	Even to ten thousand years.
Chiyo ni mo	May it flourish thus,
Kaku shi mo gamo	Even to a thousand ages.
Chiyo ni mo	May it flourish thus,
Kaku shi mo gamo	Even to a thousand ages.
Kashikomite	And may I reverently
Tsukaematsuran	Dedicate my services,
Orogamite	And may I respectfully
Tsukaematsuran	Dedicate my services.
Utazuki matsuru.	I humbly present this my poem.

(*NSK, Song*, 102)

The date of this recitation is clear. Not only does it postdate 604, the symbolic dividing line between the Archaic and Ancient Ages, but also the parallelism has become structurally integral to the poem, and the content, a paean to royal virtues, is fairly conceptual. Nevertheless, if we consider the chōka as an orderly development of statements, it indisputably belongs to the corpus of very old song. The device of simple repetition used in the lines "May it flourish thus / Even to a thousand ages" was most likely employed as a response to a memory surviving deep within the collective awareness. With its charge to bring still more prosperity to a royal line dating from the Age of the Gods, the kotodama would be strengthened by repetition. Having taken into consideration an exception of this sort, we would be wise to conclude that songs with simple repetitive lines, or lines which come extremely close to simple repetition, retain elements of a tradition of primitive song, and that the composition dates of songs possessing these characteristics belong in the oldest strata within that ancient corpus of songs in the *Chronicles*.

If we assume that modes of composition, conveyed by primitive songs, survived to a certain extent into the Archaic Age, then we will become aware of the presence, in several songs in the *Chronicles*, of what might be called a sense of immediacy or confrontation. "The great Cavern House of Osaka" (*KJK, Song*, 10), quoted above, appears in the *Kojiki* in the following context. Jimmu Tennō devises a stratagem to subjugate the Tsuchigumo tribe: he invites the Tsuchigumo warriors to a banquet, having previously arranged with his cooks that they are to carry swords and, when they hear "The great Cavern House of Osaka" sung, are to strike at the enemy. The cooks hear the song; they "drew their swords and struck them dead all at once" (*KJK*, 2:65). Not one of the many Tsuchigumo men listening to the lyrics of this song had the slightest suspicion that his murder was being plotted—a highly unlikely situation. Many scholars thus believe that this song, within the corpus of Jimmu legends, was the fabrication of a storyteller. This scholarly interpretation is certainly a logical one, and it will doubtless gain the sympathy of our contemporaries. Logic, however, has nothing to do with whether the song conforms to the realities of the work and its reception in the Archaic Age. Consider the Andaman Islands aborigine song cited above, chanted during sea-turtle hunts: if, while the men calmly recited their repetitious song, the turtles had sensed danger and fled, then, because the hunt had been unsuccessful, we might conclude that the aborigines' singing too was a superfluous act. Yet their hunting customs were not invented, but verified in a field research report.

Primitive people are accustomed from infancy to singing. Because song is a constant factor in their lives, they are capable of expressing themselves in song even when confronted with unexpected situations. Umbara, a member of the Wurunjerri aborigines of Australia, was riding with others in a small boat on his way to a gathering when his party happened to run into strong winds. Umbara's song testifies that it was composed while the boat tossed like a leaf, in the midst of cascades of spray, and that its composer, unlike his companions, was not the sort of fellow to receive his songs from dreams:

> Capsizing me, striking me,
> The wind blows-hard, the sea long-stretched,
> Between striking, hard hitting, striking me,
> Dashing-up me, striking.[2]

For primitive people, song is the means most capable of apposite expression in time of crisis. Moreover, a primitive mind would perceive as untidy the issuing of a command like "There ought to be sea turtles near where the surf is breaking, so everyone approach carefully." The hunters' spirits converge upon the sea turtles' location by means of songs chanted in unison, songs with many repeated lines. To express it in the Japanese manner, this is an instance of the kotodama in action and implies an expectation that, thanks to the song, the men will succeed in catching sea turtles. The song signaling the attack on the Tsuchigumo warriors undoubtedly possessed a similar significance: it served to focus the spirits of Jimmu's men, and brought about the success of their coup de main through the activation of the kotodama. Since the Tsuchigumo tribe, of course, spoke only its own dialect, its members would not have understood the contents, even of that daring song, without the help of an interpreter. They would have thought it only natural, then, for singing to take place on this occasion.

Let us consider a few more uta recited in perilous situations. When Prince Oshikuma's rebellion against the government of Jingū Tennō was suppressed by her armies, the prince committed suicide by drowning. The uta he recited to his general, Isachi Sukune, prior to his suicide, is given below. The text differs between the *Kojiki* and *Nihon Shoki*.[3] *Kojiki* version:

Iza agi	Come now, my friend!
Furukuma ga	Sooner than suffer grievous wounds
Itate owazu wa	At Furukuma's hands,
Niodori no	Let us like little grebes

[2] Howitt, 1904, 422-23. Umbara reportedly recited his song while surrounded by people. Howitt, who did not fully understand the last two lines, later asked about their meaning. Umbara said they were intended to mean: "Between the strong wind and the heavy waves of the unending sea I was nearly upset." Once again a literal translation yields unnatural English.

[3] [In the *KJK* version, Furukuma is Jingū's general. In the *NSK* version, the "Minister of the Center" is Takeuchi Sukune.—Trans.]

| Ōmi no umi ni | Dive beneath the waters of |
| Kazuki sena wa. | The Sea of Ōmi. |

(*KJK, Song,* 38)

Nihon Shoki version:

Iza agi	Come now, my friend,
Isachi Sukune	Isachi Sukune!
Tamakiwaru	Sooner than suffer grievous wounds
Uchi no aso ga	From the round-hilted sword of
Kubutsuchi no	The Minister of the Center,
Itate owazu wa	His soul bound by birth and death,
Niodori no	Let us like little grebes
Kazuki sena.	Dive beneath the waters.

(*NSK, Song,* 29)

One can only imagine that the transmission of these uta was based on the memories of someone who happened to be there at the time. How could the prince take the time to recite an uta under such pressing circumstances, and how could his attendant possibly remember it? It is, perhaps, doubts of this sort that have given rise to the view that these uta appeared in a dramatizing of the Prince Oshikuma incident, produced by a member of the losing side to demonstrate his fealty to Jingū (Kobayashi Shigemi, 1967, 6-13). This assumption, made in order to explain logically the presence of unnatural elements within a tense situation, is not unjustifiable in itself. Songs accompanied by dramatic pantomime were undoubtedly performed in the Archaic Age. What seems artificial to us moderns, however, could have been natural to a society which still retained some primitive characteristics. Our contemporaries will be convinced by rationalistic explanations, but it is impossible to ensure that the accounts will concur with the facts as they existed long, long ago. Assuming that kinds of primitive composition persisted into archaic times, we may believe without difficulty that Prince Oshikuma recited a poem prior to diving into the water, and that his poem was memorized and transmitted by someone who had heard the prince recite it.

But what are we to do with the following uta? Prince Ōyamamori, in defiance of Ōjin Tennō's dying wish, plotted a coup d'état to seize the throne. Another prince, Uji no Waki Iratsuko, having learned of the plot, enticed Prince Ōyamamori into a boat. When they came to the deepest part of the river, Uji no Waki Iratsuko tipped the boat, sending Prince

Ōyamamori into the water. As the latter was carried off by the current, he recited this uta.

Kojiki version:

Chihayaburu	Charmed and furious it is,
Uji no watari ni	The ford of the Uji River—
Saotori ni	May a swift and skilled
Hayaken hito shi	Oarsman
Waga moko ni kon.	Come here to my rescue!

(*KJK, Song*, 50)

Nihon Shoki version:

Chihayahito	Charmed and furious one,
Uji no watari ni	The ford of the Uji River—
Saotori ni	May a swift and skilled
Hayaken hito shi	Oarsman
Waga moko ni kon.	Come here to my rescue!

(*NSK, Song*, 42)

Soldiers lying in wait on the riverbanks threatened the prince with drawn bows, however, and the prince, unable to reach land, finally weakened and drowned.

Is it physiologically possible for a man in the process of being swept away by the current to recite a poem instead of crying for help? Umbara, the Wurunjerri aborigine, probably could have recited his song while swimming. His sole means of creation at the time he composed "Capsizing me . . ." was recitation. On the other hand, we cannot be sure to what extent primitive characteristics remained in a prince reared in a fairly advanced civilization. We were not present at the event, and thus have no grounds on which to acknowledge the incident as fact. Yet, even if we assume that his uta was a later creation, it was nonetheless acceptable to an ancient audience simply because the recitation of an uta under such circumstances did not appear artificial. Our modern perception is that events within a drama are, after all, fabrications suited for drama, and thus even the artificial is acceptable if abstracted from reality. But this is based on our power to separate the rational from the affective, whereas people living in a still partially primitive age would accept as fact whatever was told or recited to them. Certainly the act of reciting a poem while being washed away was very unlikely to be rejected as unrealistic.

Although probably differing in method from the recitative of opera, conversation in song also seems to have been commonplace among people of the Archaic Age, playing a principal role in expressing one's emotions in an unusual situation. If, as was illustrated above, circumstances of imminent danger figured among the unusual, so too did formal, courteous exchanges of information. One example of the latter is an exchange between Nintoku Tennō and one of his attendants. Nintoku dearly loved a court lady, Kuwata Kugahime, but because he also feared his consort's jealousy, he decided to marry off the lady. This was the brief uta he recited to his attendants:

Minasokou	Who will look after
Omi no otome o	This our handmaid
Tare yashinawan.	Of sea-deep attractions?

(*NSK, Song,* 44)

Thereupon one Hayamachi, who came from the province of Harima, stepped forward and recited—

Mikashio	I, Hayamachi of Harima,
Harima Hayamachi	Where flood tides overflow the shores,
Iwakudasu	Trembling with awe—
Kashikoku to mo	As at the downhill plunge of mighty rocks—
Are yashinawan.	Do undertake the lady's care.

(*NSK, Song,* 45)

Kugahime was thus bestowed upon him. This is not the only instance of a poetic dialogue involving Nintoku Tennō. Several are to be found in the *Chronicles*. This probably reflects an extensive use of song on formal occasions in fifth-century Yamato.

The use of a special mode of expression in formal circumstances is also found among the Ainu. Their special mode, however, is not the Japanese uta but metric verse recited in a declamatory style. The following poem was recited by a resident of the village of Nitushi in Hidaka Prefecture on the occasion of his meeting with one Wakarpa, from the village of Shiun Kotu in Saru (Kindaichi, 1931, 1:128-30).

> The village may be marshy,
> The land may be marshy,
> But this village of Saru, exalted above all,
> The source of humanity,

Has been told of from age to age,
In ancient tales of the Father of gods,
Our Great God, of whom tradition speaks:
Here man grew and prospered.
Of all villages it is the most venerable,
This village where the gods reside.
Venerable one, come from
The heart of your village,
Let me offer you
My heartfelt felicitations
And my adoration.

Wakarpa's response is also recorded: it is, one could say, couched in equally flowery language. Again, when a conference between people of two villages takes place, the best orator from each village faces his rival and censures the other's misdeeds in chanted verse (sa-kor itak). The orators draw on mythology and history in their exchange of elegant rhetoric, and the event may last all night, or even several days. When one of the orators runs out of arguments or is overcome by mental or physical fatigue, he is declared the loser. He pays an indemnity (ashimpe) and the contest is over. Farewell addresses (iyoitak-kote) at funerals are likewise declaimed in orderly metric verse (Kubodera, 1956, 6-7).

These situations, found among the Ainu, may correspond to those of Yamato Japan in the fifth century, with the difference that, where irregular uta were employed by the Yamato people, the Ainu instead use set prosody.[4] Modern-day primitive tribes do not have long poems, much less set prosodies. If we postulate that Japanese song, from the Jōmon period through the middle of the Yayoi period, was identical in form to modern primitive song, then Yamato song would consequently represent a direct linkage between primitive and archaic song, with no interposition of lengthy songs or set prosody. It is true that lengthy songs did not grow to maturity in Yamato, but it is simply not the case that there was no set prosody: the prototype of the norito texts [ritual prayers] existed in the Archaic Age. The problem lies in the fact that the Yamato Japanese did not use set prosody in the same kinds of situations in which the Ainu now use it. Instead, when formalities necessitated a nonprose statement, the Japanese consistently used either short or medium-length uta. It is not entirely clear why they did so; but the practice may have been connected to an awareness that short texts were more capable of facilitating the emergence of kotodama.

---

[4] [The "set prosody" of Japanese poetry was the alternation of five- and seven-syllable lines (see the next section of this chapter). Here the contrast also includes prose.—Ed.]

In discussing the production and reception of primitive song, one more important phenomenon should be noted: songs and chants are generally accompanied by body movements. This is universally true for modern primitive song. Might it not also apply to the songs of archaic Japan? The *Kojiki* records that when Prince Yamato Takeru dies, his consorts and children crawl around a rice field near his tomb, weeping and chanting (*Song*, 34-37):

Nazuki no ta no	Wild yam vines
Inagara ni	Creep round and round
Inagara ni	The rice stalks,
Haimotorou	The rice stalks,
Tokorozura.	In the nearby field.

The prince's spirit turns into a white bird: it soars into the sky, and flies off in the direction of the seashore. His consorts and children pursue it through a field of bamboo grass and cut their feet on the sharp stubble. They recite:

Asaji no hara	In the field of bamboo grass
Koshi nazumu	Walking is hard, our backs ache.
Sora wa yukazu	We cannot fly into the sky,
Ashi yo yuku na.	But must walk on, step by step.

Still chasing the bird, they run into the sea, reciting:

Umiga yukeba	On the sea floor
Koshi nazumu	Walking is hard, our backs ache.
Ōkawara no	As water plants sway
Uegusa	In the deep riverbed,
Umiga wa	So we lurch in the sea
Isayou.	And cannot progress.

Again, when the white bird descends to rest its wings on a rocky beach, they recite:

Hamatsuchidori	The beach plover
Hama yo wa yukazu	Cannot follow the sandy shore,
Isozutau.	But goes from reef to reef.

The *Kojiki* adds that these uta are recited at royal funerals (*KJK*, 2:143-44). One view has it that the four uta contain no signs of bitterness or sorrow, and when read independently of their prose contexts appear to be children's songs, used in games in the fields or at the seashore (Takagi Ichinosuke, 1941, 187-202). Further elaborations of this theory include one explanation that the four uta were originally popular love songs and riddle songs later put to a different use, and another that the four uta are incantations, associated with agricultural festivals, that were later transformed into dirges.[5] By following the logic of this approach we are obliged to conceive of these uta as if they were independent entities, first composed as folk songs, later absorbed into narrative, and finally evolving into uta devoid of their original significance. But is this indeed the case?

Prehistoric songs, as well as those from the ages that followed, have been transmitted in their original forms over an astonishingly long period precisely because the composer of the song, as its chief reciter, taught the song to others, and because certain songs were always recited on specific occasions. When there is no writing system, songs cannot be preserved in their original form unless these practices are carried out. The circumstances under which a song was used may have changed, for instance from fishing to hunting, but it is quite unthinkable to postulate that a love song would be put to use as a dirge. Primitive people are extremely conservative. The chief reciter would not take it upon himself to devise different circumstances for the use of his song, when such decisions require community agreement in order to be realized. If we postulate that some such conservatism survived into the Archaic Age in Japan, then an uta that has been transmitted as a dirge should also be interpreted as a dirge.[6] Let us now turn to the four uta given above. Their content, it will be noted, reflects actions performed by the consorts and their children. "Weeping, they crawled round and round the rice field adjoining that place, and recited the following uta . . ." refers to actions that are matched by "the wild yam vines . . ." (34), and the same is also true for the other three uta.

Similar correspondence between actions and verse is a phenomenon noteworthy in modern primitive song. Members of the Semang tribe of Malaysia act out their mythology at religious celebrations. The perform-

[5] Tsuchihashi Yutaka thinks the first and second uta are love songs from the folk tradition, the third a parody of the first two, and the fourth a riddle song. He concludes that they were derived from utagaki—dancing and singing parties held in fields and marketplaces (1972, 148-63). Yoshii Iwao hypothesizes that the asobibe, court officers charged with administering songs, became concerned chiefly with funeral ceremonies: thus, charms originally recited for abundant harvest were transmuted into funerary songs (1958, 52-62).

[6] Takagi was evidently inspired by the *Lesser Preface* to *The Book of Songs*, in which Chu Hsi (1130-1200) interprets the poems separately from their introductions. Yet Chu Hsi's interpretation (that the introductions were added by later scholars of the classics) has no application to songs inserted into narrative. Masuda Katsumi expresses misgivings, on grounds similar to mine, about theories that attempt to separate the kamugatariuta (*KJK, Song* 2-5, quoted below; Masuda Katsumi, 1972, 86-87).

ers sing of the Chenoi—imaginary sacred animals who work for the benefit of mankind—while running (Schebesta, 1957, S. 230).

> They hang down, hang down, the long garlands from the brow.
> The young man runs, the children run,
> The voice of the nightingale sounds, the nightingale on the gopal,
> White and dappled.
> They hang down, hang down, the long and scattered rain clouds,
> They drift, the unmarried man runs, the maiden runs,
> The married man runs, the old man runs,
> The garlands drift and turn,
> The young man runs, the maiden runs, the young man runs.[7]

The performers wear wreaths of flowers, and sing as they run wildly and merrily in circles. In other words, the performers make themselves one with the Chenoi, in order to share in their work, the building of a paradise on earth. We can infer from the words "They crawled round and round the rice field" that similar performances of song and matching actions also existed in archaic Japan. Some believe that the act of crawling in a circle, like the Semang's act of running in a circle, accompanied some kind of incantation.

The significance of the incantation is unclear; but the lines "A periwinkle snail / Creeps round a great rock. / So shall we creep round and round" (*KJK, Song*, 13), from one of the Songs of Kume given above, may also have been accompanied by the act of crawling in a circle. In this connection, excavations of the Himezuka tumulus in Shibayama, Chiba Prefecture, have yielded, among the clay haniwa figures, one in a crawling or swimming posture, placed next to a haniwa playing the zither (Figure 4).[8] These two were separate from and higher than the other haniwa, looking down on the rest. This arrangement suggests that the former group was assigned a special function. Masuda Seiichi infers that the act of "crawling round and round" at a funeral had occult significance, and that the act is here represented by a haniwa figure. He also regards Prince Yamato Takeru's funerary uta and the actions performed by Izanagi at the death of Izanami—"Then he crawled around her pillow, and he crawled around the foot of her bed, weeping" (*KJK*, 1:189)—as the transmission of a crawling ritual once performed at funerals (Masuda Seiichi, 1976, 131-37). This interpretation is completely acceptable. The second and third uta sung by the consorts and children were probably

[7] [Trans. C. M. Bowra, *Primitive Song* (New York: Mentor Books, 1962), p. 222.—Trans.]

[8] The haniwa figures are from the Shibayama Haniwa museum collection. Photographs of them appear at the beginning of Masuda Seiichi, 1976.

FIGURE 4. Haniwa (clay image) of a Mourning Man (latter half of the 6th century). Discovered in the Himezuka tumulus and presently in the Shibayama Haniwa Museum, Chiba Prefecture.

performed while walking bent at the waist, and the fourth while walking in a bird-like zigzag. Definite meanings are not easily assigned to each action. Taken as a whole, however, they are believed to have been an occult means of helping the soul of the deceased return to his body. Thus the words "Creeps round and round," from one of the Songs of Kume (*KJK, Song*, 13), are also to be interpreted as referring to a funerary ritual. While several men enacted the burial of their defeated enemy, others would have encircled them and loudly chanted, "Then smite our enemy dead!"

Some consider it odd that such uta, associated with funerals though they are, contain no expressions of grief or bitterness. It must be said that this approach is excessively influenced by modern preconceptions. The view that the object considered should be represented solely by what is expressed in a work does not apply to the Archaic Age. When a song is accompanied by actions, they often supplement information not stated in the text. Primitive song contains instances of yet greater reliance being placed upon actions than upon text. Mragula, an Australian Wolgal tribesman who was known as a composer of songs, once crossed a river at flood stage in a small boat. He described his experience in the following song (Howitt, 1904, 423-24):

> Quickly talking to-his-mate,
> Looking-about,
> Now paddling his-side.

Howitt's translation does not make sense, because it is a literal translation from the Wolgal language. Even if it were put into correct English, however, we would still not understand its meaning. When Mragula recited this song, he punctuated it with pantomimic gestures, so that Howitt, seeing his actions, understood the song to mean this: just as Mragula had pushed out his boat prior to rowing across the current, the bottom began to leak; he tried to stop the water from coming in, to no avail; he rowed back to the riverbank, plugged up the leak with mud, rowed off once more, and crossed successfully. The Wolgals' low intellect, when compared with that of their neighbors, the Kurnai aborigines, is thought to account for their greater use of gestures. Uta with the words "Creeping round" may not have relied quite so heavily on expressive gestures. Nevertheless the entire meaning of a work need not be stated in the text. In any event, primitive characteristics seem to survive to a considerable degree within the funerary uta sung for Prince Yamato Takeru.

Song performance approaches pantomime in direct proportion to the preponderance of actions over text, but it does not always, as a result, approach drama. In order to develop into drama, a song must have a lengthy text and, moreover, must be structured to follow a time sequence. We might note, in this respect, the kamugatariuta.[9] The context of one is as follows. Yachihoko no Ōkuninushi, the God of Eight Thousand Halberds, feeling harassed by the jealousy of his chief consort Suseribime, declares that he will leave Izumo for Yamato. I have no way of knowing whether Suseribime quarreled with him over his pretty Yamato wife, but in any case Ōkuninushi is thrown into confusion. He stands sheepishly with one hand on his horse's saddle and one foot in the stirrup. Then he recites:

Nubatama no	Black as lily seeds,
Kuroki mikeshi o	This handsome robe
Matsubusa ni	Carefully chosen
Toriyosoi	For my array—

[9] ["Songs Telling about the Gods," four uta (*KJK, Song*, 2-5). The "gatari" (katari) of the term suggests a narrative element. The speakers are Yachihoko no Ōkuninushi, here called the God of Eight Thousand Halberds; Nunakawahime, his Yamato wife; and Suseribime, his chief consort. All but the last uta end with the words, "This was transmitted / By word of mouth" (Koto no katarigoto / Ko oba), and we have italicized the formula.—Trans., Ed.]

Okitsutori	Like a waterbird that,
Muna miru toki	Breast-preening,
Ha tataki mo	Beats its wings, so I wave my sleeves:
Kore wa fusawazu	This robe will not do;
Hetsunami	Faster than waves receding from shore,
So ni nuki ute	I strip it off and cast it away.
Sonitori no	Kingfisher-blue,
Aoki mikeshi o	This handsome robe
Matsubusa ni	Carefully chosen
Toriyosoi	For my array—
Okitsutori	Like a waterbird that,
Muna miru toki	Breast-preening,
Ha tataki mo	Beats its wings, so I wave my sleeves:
Ko mo fusawazu	Neither will this robe do;
Hetsunami	Faster than waves receding from shore,
So ni nuki ute	I strip it off and cast it away.
Yamagata ni	Crimson madder, sown in mountain fields,
Makishi atane tsuki	Roots pounded in mortars:
Someki ga shiru ni	In its juice
Shime koromo o	Was dyed this robe,
Matsubusa ni	Carefully chosen
Toriyosoi	For my array.
Okitsutori	Like a waterbird that,
Muna miru toki	Breast-preening,
Hatataki mo	Beats its wings, so I wave my sleeves:
Ko shi yoroshi	This robe will do very well.
Itoko ya no	Oh, my darling
Imo no mikoto	Lady wife,
Muratori no	If as birds gather together
Waga mure inaba	I gathered my suite,
Hiketori no	If as birds are drawn away
Waga hike inaba	I were drawn away from here:
Nakaji to wa	Then you might say,
Na wa iu to mo	"I shall never cry,"
Yamato no	But your head would droop,
Hitomoto susuki	A single stalk of plumegrass
Unakabushi	On the mountain bluff,
Na ga nakasamaku	Your tearful sighs
Asa ame no	A morning drizzle
Kiri ni tatamu zo	Turned to mist.
Wakakusa no	Tender as young grasses
Tsuma no mikoto.	Is my lady wife.

Koto no katarigoto	This was transmitted
mo	
Ko oba.	By word of mouth.

(KJK, Song, 4)

Early in the song, indications appear that its recitation might have been accompanied by actions. They could have taken this form: Ōkuninushi puts on a black robe, straightens up like a waterbird to see his chest, and holds out his wide sleeves for inspection. "I don't like it"—he casts it aside, and changes instead to a blue robe, which he similarly discards. When he is finally satisfied by the madder-red robe, he walks to the gate with his retinue and puts one foot in the stirrup. His consort, who has up to now made a great show of indifference, hangs her head and begins to weep. Now, if in the course of an actual lovers' quarrel the man had leisurely recited such a song, the lady would surely have become enraged. That is why this uta is said by some to be the written record of a stage performance; the text, they explain, acquired its present polish in the course of countless repetitions (Doi, 1977, 18-20). One might reasonably say that Ōkuninushi's uta does not depict a real lovers' quarrel, since the uta is clearly labeled as an ancient narrative by its concluding words, "This was transmitted / By word of mouth." One can be equally sure that the uta was accompanied by actions. On the other hand, it seems less than sound to suppose that the uta originated from verbal descriptions of those actions. If we consider the examples provided by modern primitive societies, we might rather expect that the song and its accompanying actions developed simultaneously. Furthermore, it is irrelevant to assert, in the case of primitive song, that the text becomes polished in the course of repeated performances. A primitive song will never lose the primitiveness of its language, no matter how often it is repeated. The polished style of Ōkuninushi's uta should rather be seen as a reflection of its nonprimitive status, and of the fairly high cultural level attained at the time of its composition.

The Wolgal aborigine Mragula sang, with pantomimic actions, of his own experience. By contrast, Ōkuninushi's uta is an ancient transmission, as is particularly demonstrated by its concluding formula. Similarly, the actions of a given song were apparently the charge of professional entertainers (wazaoki), who performed with the singers. The Chinese characters used in the Nihon Shoki to write wazaoki now signify "actor" (haiyū) to modern Japanese, with the result that the term "wazaoki" tends to be misunderstood to mean the performer of some sort of dramatic action. At best, however, the wazaoki's art would seem to have been on the level of mime. Hōri, who is taught a charm by the Sea God that will raise and quell tempests, uses his new power to persecute his elder brother.[10] The elder brother appeals to Hōri: "If you let me live, my children down to the last generation will not stray beyond your fences, and they will surely serve you as wazaoki." Hōri then stops his incantation, and the wind and waves die down. But, seeing that Hōri is still unmollified, his elder brother,

> ... clad only in a loincloth, kneaded red earth, daubed his palms and face with it, and spoke to his younger brother: "Thus have I sullied my body with paint. I shall forever be your wazaoki." Then he lifted his legs and stamped his feet, and mimed the agony of drowning. When first the tide struck his feet, then he stood on tiptoe. When it reached his knees, then he raised up his legs. When it reached his thighs, then he ran round and round. When it reached his waist, then he held up his hands to his chest. When it reached his neck, then he lifted his hands and waved them in the air. This mime has been transmitted down to the present day (*NSK*, 1:99-100).

The elder god's daubing of red earth on his body is apparently similar in significance to the face-painting practiced by modern primitives.

If we consider that wazaoki may have been present to add their actions to Ōkuninushi's song, the resulting combination would have resembled drama. When Ōkuninushi finishes his song, his weeping consort Suseribime offers him sake. Then she speaks: her lord Ōkuninushi has other ladies here and there. But, she says, because a woman cannot behave so, she has only Ōkuninushi on whom to rely. Don't talk of leaving, she says; instead, tonight—

Ayakaki no	Beneath figured curtains
Fuhaya ga shita ni	Gently swaying,
Mushibusuma	Beneath warm quilts
Nikoya ga shita ni	Soft to the touch,
Takubusuma	Beneath coverlets of
Sayagu ga shita ni	Rustling paper-mulberry,
Awayuki no	You fondle
Wakayaru mune o	My youthful breasts,
Takuzuno no	Yielding as fluffy snow,
Shiroki tadamuki	And caress my arms,
Sodataki	White as paper-mulberry rope.
Tadakimanagari	Our bodies intertwined,
Matamate	We lie pillowed

---

[10] [The brother is otherwise called Homori no Mikoto and is better known (such are the names) as Hikohohodemi no Mikoto.—Ed.]

Tamate sashimaki	Arm on jewel-like arm.
Momonaga ni	Stretch out your legs,
I o shi nase	My lord, and sleep—
Toyomiki tatematsurase	But first partake of this fine sake.

(*KJK, Song,* 5)

And so the matter is amicably settled. Since the content of this two-uta sequence is not without a certain degree of temporal development, the sequence resembles drama. Doi suggests that it was indeed drama, and even supposes that its production involved a raised and covered "inner stage," from which Suseribime speaks, and a lower, open-air "outer stage" for Ōkuninushi (Doi, 1977, 36-59; see Figure 5). This can only be conjectured. The uta are clearly labeled as having been transmitted "by word of mouth," which would indicate that their accompanying pantomime was no more than an accessory.

The problem lies elsewhere. Why, despite the obvious existence of an early, unevolved form of drama, did Japanese drama come into being only at a far later date? This problem is more appropriately studied in the sections on the Ancient and Middle Ages, since it does not actually pertain to the Archaic Age. Because, however, one of the factors in the tardy growth of drama evidently existed as early as the Archaic Age, I would like to raise some features of this question here. The essential elements of mime were present in Greece from its earliest folk songs, and

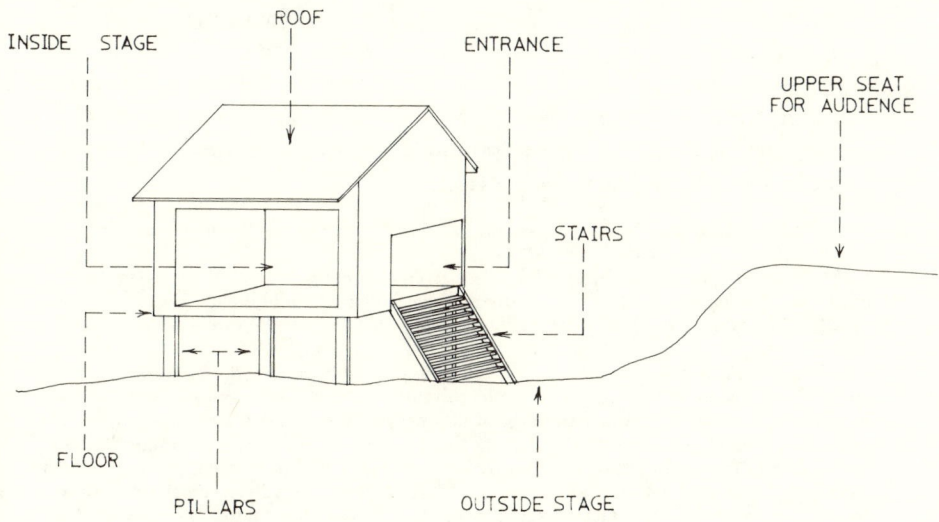

FIGURE 5. Ancient Stage in Doi's Reconstruction

drōmena were performed at several religious festivals.[11] When Dorian song-poetry was united with Ionic speech-poetry, drōmena took the first step toward becoming drama. Thespis, a poet of the sixth century B.C., first made tragōdia into some semblance of drama.[12] He is said to have inserted orations, set in trochaic tetrameter, between intervals in the singing and dancing. As tragōdia came to resemble drama, the composer-poet played the protagonist, a mythological god or hero. Dialogue is not effected with a single player, however: the Greek chorus consisted at this point of two groups, and the leaders of these groups are thought to have responded to the protagonist.[13] They thus become actors in their own right. By the time of Aeschylus, two actors were appearing on stage, and by the time of Sophocles, three (Murray, 1897, 204-8). In archaic Japan, the equivalent of a Greek chorus could not easily perform with a poet in a capacity equal to his. To understand this, we must return to archaic song.

The god Hōri torments his elder brother, who, in return for better treatment, vows that his children and all other descendants will serve as Hōri's wazaoki. The elder brother's vow is an oath of submission, a fact suggesting that the art of the wazaoki was practiced by conquered survivors. Wazaoki performances are mentioned elsewhere in the *Nihon Shoki*: one such instance occurs when the sun goddess Amaterasu hides herself within the Heavenly Rock Cave:

> The goddess Ame no Uzume, distant ancestor of Lady Sarume, thereupon took in her hands a halberd, the hilt of which was wrapped in reeds, stood before the Heavenly Rock Cave, and skillfully played the wazaoki. And she made herself a chaplet of leaves from the sacred trees of Heavenly Mount Kagu, bound back her sleeves with hanging moss, lit a bonfire, pounded on an overturned tub, and spoke in divine ecstasy (*NSK*, 1:32).

[11] "Drōmena," things performed, is closely related to the Greek "drāma" or "performance" (Murray, 1897, 205).

[12] "Tragōdia" was a religious performance given during the festival of Dionysius; it was presented by a man disguised as a creature that was half goat, half human. "Tragos" means "goat." "Tragōdia" originally meant "goat-song" and "tragikos choros" meant "goat-choir."

[13] The chorus, a group of singers and dancers, originally consisted of two groups subsequently designated the "strophe" (the left circuit) and the "antistrophe" (right circuit). In its earliest phase, the chorus consisted of fifty people, and they were the only performers except the playwright. He acted the part of the protagonist, and the supporting roles were performed by two members of the chorus. Thus, in Sophocles' time, the chorus numbered forty-eight. The two actors drawn from the chorus were originally given the role of answering the protagonist, a fact reflected in the Greek word for "actor": "hypocritēs" or "answerer" (Murray, 1897, 207).

In the *Kojiki* version of this story, however, a further action is reported: "She displayed her breasts, and pulled down her skirt band below her private parts" (*KJK*, 1:214). This would seem to have been Ame no Uzume's specialty. When Amaterasu's grandson Ninigi descended to earth to rule as tennō, his advance party of gods discovered a bizarre deity blocking the way. Ame no Uzume was sent out to confront him: "then she displayed her breasts and pulled down her skirt band below her navel," and so initiated a discussion (*NSK*, 1:70). Her role as a performer of such arts is believed to indicate that she occupied an extremely low rank in the divine hierarchy. Her "entertainment" would hardly have been performed by the higher class of gods. Another passage from the *Nihon Shoki* records how Buretsu Tennō paid no heed to the demands of government, and concentrated instead on the following activities: "He was an ardent gourmand who shrugged at the hunger of his people. He gathered dwarf jesters and wazaoki at court, and had them put on lewd performances" (*NSK*, 2:7). In this instance, wazaoki are obviously performers of low status. But they were lowly in the fifth century only because earlier tradition dictated that they were.

If we assume that wazaoki were the surviving remnant of a defeated enemy, or members of the lower classes, then it should also be easy to grasp the transmission process of the Songs of Kume—accompanied perhaps by wazaoki performances—by the warriors of the Kume clan. The Kume apparently lived in the mountains and were hunters, as one of their songs suggests: "In Uda, / On the high ground, / I set a trap for longbills" (*KJK, Song*, 9). To the Yamato people, who farmed on the plain, the Kume were an alien race. When they were subjugated by the Yamato nation, the Kume presented their new masters with their traditional tribal songs, which were eventually designated by the Yamato court as the Songs of Kume (Hayashiya, 1971, 92-96). A similar process was probably applied to the songs and dances of the Hayato and Kuzu tribes. The Hayato were an alien tribe occupying the Ōsumi Islands, off the southern shore of Kyushu, as well as the Satsuma and Hyūga areas in southern Kyushu. They were conquered by the Yamato nation some time in the fifth century. The performance presented by the Hayato at their conquest may eventually have been consolidated into what was later called Hayato dance. The god Honosusori, who pledges submission to his younger brother Hōri, is traditionally the ancestor of the Hayato (*NSK*, 1:65), a tradition due, apparently, to the fact that people remained aware, up to the eighth century, that the losing side performed as wazaoki. The *Nihon Shoki* records that the Kuzu lived in the Yoshino Mountains, ate nuts, berries, and—as a special delicacy—frogs (*NSK*, 1:278). When the Kuzu came to sing before Ōjin Tennō, their preparatory activities were described in this way:

> They brewed sake for His Majesty in their flat mortars, and when they presented the sake to His Majesty, they made a sound like a drumbeat with their mouths, performed their art, and recited this uta (*KJK*, 2:177).

The uta (*KJK, Song*, 48) is then given. The "art" of the Kuzu, like the "waza" of wazaoki, probably signified a kind of mimetic performance. Because the Yamato considered the Kuzu to be "extremely gentle by nature" (*NSK*, 1:278), they were not subjugated by military power. Yet the Kuzu did in fact swear allegiance to the Yamato state, and, perhaps as part of the etiquette of swearing allegiance, they presented the tennō with their traditional songs (Hayashiya, 1960, 92-103).

The presentation, by newly acquired subjects, of waza linked to song may therefore reflect the awareness that such behavior did not pertain to members of the winning or ruling side. In Greece, however, this was not the case. The chorus, in its early phase, was made up of professional participants, even in Athens. Moreover, as the Athenians became more aware of the role of all citizens in the festival of Dionysius, they came to consider service in the chorus both a privilege and a duty, and the professional chorus eventually disappeared. Of course, the amateur chorus did not perform as well as the professionals in song and dance. On the other hand, the spoken part of drama gradually expanded: whereas song occupies two-thirds of Aeschylus' *Supplices* (written before 470 B.C.), five-sixths of Sophocles' *Philoctetes* (performed in 409 B.C.) is spoken.[14] This in turn led to the maturation of the protagonist's role in drama (Murray, 1897, 208-9). If archaic Japan had not formed a tradition of acting as the special province of the conquered and the poor, then drama might well have come into flower far earlier.

If, moreover, Japan had encountered, in its active inception of continental culture, a tradition in which Chinese or Korean nobility and scholars personally performed as actors, then too drama would probably have developed earlier. No such tradition existed in China or Korea, however. Chinese drama did not appear until the thirteenth century, and Korean plays only came into being in the early twentieth century. Korea under

---

[14] A papyrus fragment found in an Egyptian excavation includes a record of a performance of this play (Kure, 1964, 147). The papyrus has sustained some damage in the area of the first line, where the phrase "When [?] was archon" usually appears. But the word ἀρ[χεδημίδου] has been deduced from the surviving text. If this inference is correct, the reference must be to Archedēmidos, who was archon in 463 B.C. The heretofore accepted theory that this play was one of Aeschylus' early works therefore requires revision (Yaginuma Shigetake, personal communication).

the Koryŏ Dynasty had variety shows like the paekchŏng or kwangdae, and during the Yi Dynasty masques and puppet plays were performed. But none bore much resemblance to drama. All were performed by the lowborn, under both dynasties (Kim Tong-uk, 1974, 108, 238-47). Even after Kannami had made nō drama into an art worthy of aristocratic admiration, a critic observed that "nō drama is the business of beggars" (*Gogumaiki*, 7.VI.1378). Similarly, kabuki actors of the Edo period were called "kawara kojiki," riverbed beggars, an allusion to the mendicant actors who performed in dry riverbeds. Korean influence may account in part for this attitude; but it is also grounded in a Japanese tradition that originated in archaic times. There are, to be sure, other causes for the late flowering of Japanese drama. It has nevertheless been necessary to mention here, as one important factor, the absence of a phase like that in Greece when the use of an actor class was rejected in favor of participation by people of social standing.

Old and New Strata

From time to time in this presentation the following kind of statement has been made: "Those songs in the *Chronicles* that belong to the old stratum. . . ." Such statements of course presuppose the existence of a new stratum, and would seem to necessitate a consideration of the transitional stages between the two strata. We may also now inquire into the criteria applied in distinguishing the old stratum from the new.

Archaic songs, with few exceptions, cannot be assigned absolute dates determined from purely objective facts. An absolute date is determined when the facts narrated in the pertinent prose text of the *Chronicles* are highly reliable and when, in addition, the song is closely and inseparably linked to the pertinent prose text. These conditions are interdependent: if only one is operative, there can be no grounds on which to determine a date. Let us consider, for example, two songs connected to the following events in the *Nihon Shoki*. Kena no Ōmi was leader of the Japanese occupation army in Mimana, on the Korean peninsula.[15] He repeatedly failed to govern properly, so that, in the twenty-fourth year of Keitai's reign (A.D. 530), one Mezurako was dispatched to bring Kena back to Japan. On the way back, however, Kena no Ōmi became ill and died on the island of Tajima. His body was taken by boat up the Yodo and Uji Rivers, passing by Hirakata on the way to Ōmi, the home province of the deceased. These events are described in two uta:

[15] [Mimana, or Kaya, was a collective name for several small principalities or territories at the southernmost tip of the Korean peninsula.—Trans.]

Karakuni o	What has Mezurako
Ika ni fu to koso	Come to say
Mezurako kitaru	About Korea?
Mukasakuru	Why has Mezurako
Iki no watari o	Come across the straits of
Mezurako kitaru.	Distant Iki?

(*NSK, Song,* 99)

Hirakata yu	Out of Hirakata,
Fue fukinoboru	A flute plays as we row upstream.
Ōmi no ya	It is Kena,
Kena no wakugo i	The young lord of Ōmi,
Fue fukinoboru.	Whose flute plays as we row upstream.

(*NSK, Song,* 98)

The *Nihon Shoki* grows more reliable as it moves into the sixth century, and so we may accept the above events as factual. The subject matter of the songs centers on the prose account, exactly as it was told, so eliminating the possibility that already extant songs were later adapted and introduced into the text. Moreover, since the songs could hardly have been written after the public memory of these events had faded, the time of their composition should be designated as no later than the end of the sixth century, a period not far removed from that of the events themselves.

When philological evidence is present, as in the above examples, an estimated date of composition may not be greatly in error. But the time range must be widened considerably in cases where the estimate is based on archaeological investigation. It will be recalled that one of the dirges sung for Prince Yamato Takeru, quoted earlier, corresponds to movements suggested by a haniwa figure which was excavated from a tumulus. We may therefore conclude that when the Himezuka tumulus was constructed in the latter half of the sixth century, songs like that dirge, accompanied by the action of "crawling round," were recited in eastern Japan.[16] This is not necessarily in conformance, however, with the date of composition for the individual song which is the dirge for Yamato Takeru. Some ceremonial songs are transmitted in their original form over considerable periods of time. It is possible that the dirge may antedate considerably the construction of the Himezuka tumulus. Archaeologists divide the Tumulus period into seven stages—four former and three latter—and place them in a chronology of units of roughly fifty

[16] The Tumulus period is divided into the Former (subdivided into four stages) and the Latter (three stages). The style of the Himezuka tumulus belongs to the Latter Period, Stage 2, corresponding to the latter half of the sixth century (personal communication from Masuda Seiichi).

years. A similar chronology cannot possibly be hoped for in determining the composition dates of individual songs. A range of estimates based on units of roughly one hundred years might form the feasible boundaries within which to consider the composition of the dirge for Yamato Takeru.

When an absolute date cannot be determined, we can only content ourselves with inferring relative dates. Not only are the external form and the content of a song analyzed in calibrating a relative date, but data useful in reinforcing the analysis must also be on hand. In both cases basic assumptions must be established and if the several results indicated by these assumptions do not contradict one another, then the estimate is regarded as highly reliable. The basic assumptions include

A. The age of the external form
   1. Simple repetition temporally precedes parallelism.
   2. A structure consisting of serial lines temporally precedes one made up of compound line units.
   3. Irregular prosody temporally precedes fixed prosody.
   4. Kinds of no definite form temporally precede those of a specific type.
   5. Guide phrases used as single lines temporally precede those consisting of compound lines.[17]
   6. The nonfixed word modified by a single-line guide phrase temporally precedes the fixed word so modified.
B. The age of the content
   1. Vehicle and tenor (or signifier and signified) related by simple metaphor temporally precede those related by complex metaphor.
   2. Basic vocabulary and syntax not evident in later periods temporally precede basic vocabulary and syntax found in later periods.
   3. Narrative containing subject matter no longer discussed in later times temporally precedes narrative for which this is not the case.

By synthesizing these points one arrives at the conclusion that the "expression" of a given song is old (or new), a conclusion not directly connected to the question of composition dates. This is so because the possibility exists that, under special circumstances, a writer might have adopted a consciously antique literary style. Let us next consider some

[17] I have coined the new term, "guide phrase" (dōshi), to distinguish these elements from the latter-day rhetorical devices—called pillow-words (makurakotoba) and prefaces (jo-kotoba). Earlier the phrases were used while the kotodama was still fully activated. That is, the guide phrases (unlike their later rhetorical counterparts) were as yet undifferentiated, and were used monistically as phrases leading to spiritual entelechy (Konishi, 1978, 64-70).

supplementary assumptions which serve to reinforce these analytical criteria:

1. When old song forms appear with new songs forms within the same body of prose narrative, only the new shares the same period of composition as the narrative.
2. When an obviously imitative relationship exists between two songs, the song that was imitated will be considerably separated in time from its copy.

Relative dates are deduced on this basis. If the relative relationship among songs can be consolidated to some extent, then since the sixth-century song corpus, though small, is known to us, we shall consider this group as the new stratum, and shall be able to deduce correlatively the time period of the old stratum.

According to the basic assumptions outlined above, and addressing first of all the question of external form, we may tentatively assign to the new stratum those songs corresponding to the fixed form we call the tanka, or short poem. This process is connected to Basic Assumptions A.3 and A.4. For example:

Yakumo tatsu	Eight-layered clouds rise
Izumo	In the Land of Izumo:
Yaegaki	Eightfold fences
Tsumagomi ni	To enclose my wife,
Yaegaki tsukuru	Eightfold fences shall I build.
Sono yaegaki o.	Hey now! Eightfold fences!

(*KJK, Song,* 1)

Okitsutori	On this isle wild ducks,
Kamo doku shima ni	Birds of the offing, come to flock,
Waga ineshi	Where we slept together:
Imo wa wasureji	I will never forget you, beloved,
Yo no kotogoto ni.	My whole life long.

(*KJK, Song,* 8)

Okitsumo wa	Seaweed in the offing
He ni wa yoredomo	Draws near the strand, but you do not,
Sanedoko mo	Nor will you give me, love,
Atawanu kamo yo	A place to lay my head—
Hamatsuchidori yo.	When even beach plovers have their mates!

(*NSK, Song,* 4)

All three songs appear in stories on the Age of the Gods.[18] But simply because of that context they are not necessarily part of the old stratum. That having been said, however, it need not follow that the composition period be moved forward to the late seventh century, when setsuwa [stories] dealing with the founding of the realm were systematized. As I have noted, songs with an absolute date corresponding to the mid- or late sixth century (such as *KJK, Song*, 98) are so dated because they are in tanka form. Yet, if "Eight-layered clouds rise" (*KJK, Song*, 1) had been written in the fixed tanka form of later times, then its next two lines would be grouped together into a seven-syllable line: "Izumo yae-gaki" (In the Land of Izumo, eightfold fences). "In the Land of Izumo" and "Eightfold fences" are mutually discrete in this song, however. And the guide phrase "Eight-layered clouds rise" invokes only "In the Land of Izumo," since the next line, "Eightfold fences," acts in concert with "Hey now! Eightfold fences!" That is in turn a repetition of "Eightfold fences shall I build." The total number of syllables in this song is thirty-one, as is the case for a prosodically fixed tanka, but the configuration of meaning in the song does not concur with the syllabic articulation of a tanka into the units of 5-7-5-7-7 prosody. It follows that this song, labeled as a member of the new stratum, should be seen as the product of a phase in which the fixed tanka form was still unfamiliar. Moreover, songs with ancient word forms like "Kamo doku shima" (. . . isle where wild ducks / . . . come to flock, *KJK, Song*, 8), or with ancient conjugated forms like "atawanu" (nor will you give me, *NSK, Song*, 4), may, although members of the new stratum, be regarded as representative of an early stage within that stratum, according to Basic Assumption B2.[19]

Here are two other uta composed by Jimmu Tennō's consort, Isuke-yorihime:

Saikawa yo	Beyond the river Sai
Kumo tachiwatari	Clouds rise and spread;
Unebiyama	From Unebi Hill
Ko no ha sayaginu	Comes the rustling of leaves:
Kaze fukan to su.	A storm will blow our way.

(*KJK, Song*, 20)

Unebiyama	The foliage of Unebi Hill
Hiru wa kumo to i	Moved calmly with the clouds today.

---

[18] ["Setsuwa" now first appears in the *History*. The word has a general meaning of "story" or "narrative" or "tale" and a more particular one of "myth" or "legend." Yet other connotations will appear in the second volume. Since it is a standard Japanese literary term, we use it without translating it.—Ed.]

[19] The fact that "doku" is an old form of "zuku" is corroborated by other examples found in *KJK*. [Note abbreviated.—Ed.]

Yū sareba   Now with evening nigh,
Kaze fukan to so   A storm will blow our way—
Ko no ha sayageru.   So say the rustling leaves.

(*KJK, Song*, 21)

These songs are recited, in their prose context, by Isukeyorihime to warn her three sons of imminent danger. They are commonly seen, however, as compositions satirizing the arrival of some great event (Tsuchihashi's note to *KJK, Song*, 20). If we interpret them as satire, their imagery becomes allegorical. Since we postulate allegory as a fairly advanced technique, according to Basic Assumption B1, the uta must be regarded as among the newest of the new stratum. This reading, however, attempts to impose assumptions gained from reading later literature upon still partially primitive songs, and so is unacceptable.[20] People of the Archaic Age interpreted the roiling of clouds and the rustling of leaves in the wind as nothing less than warnings of imminent calamity.[21] The poems are therefore simple statements, not allegories.[22] This being the case, we may conclude that these uta belong, certainly, not with the newest of the new stratum but rather with the older members of that stratum.

The new stratum can be understood to include, then, compositions of relatively early date, although the texts of uta of the new stratum undeniably conform, on the whole, to the tanka form. In terms of numbers, the largest group of the eighty-four songs in the *Chronicles* consists of those with a complete 5-7-5-7-7 syllabic form, altogether sixty-six songs.[23] Another seventeen songs lack only one syllable, and only one (*NSK, Song*, 93) has a supernumerary syllable.[24] Twenty songs accompany passages which postdate the reign of Kimmei in the middle of the sixth century,

[20] The Homeric epics contain, in no small number, narrative sequences that seem illogical to the modern reader. C. M. Bowra observes, "Some of their characteristics are alien to us who are brought up on books, and these have been misjudged and made the basis of elaborate theories of authorship" (1972, 32). A similar attitude is necessary for considering the songs of the *Chronicles*.

[21] Natural phenomena were thought capable of speech, a fact indicated in the earlier quoted remark by Amaterasu (from *NSK*) to her grandson Ninigi: "even the grasses and trees have the power of speech." The relevant passage in the *KJK* says the land "is in an uproar" (*JDK*, 355). Both passages can only signify a threatening situation.

[22] This does not deny the existence of allegorical songs: one example has already been quoted, "Atop a rock" (*NSK, Song*, 107). Twelve songs of such nature appear in the *Chronicles*, all in accounts from the reigns of Kōgyoku, Kōtoku, Saimei, and Tenji—i.e., from the latter half of the seventh century.

[23] Songs appearing in both the *KJK* and *NSK* are counted but once, both here and in what follows. [Note abbreviated.—Ed.]

[24] [In later times, hypometric (jitarazu) lines are not tolerated, whereas hypermetric (jiamari) lines appear with some frequency. The author's point here is that the prevalence of lines with too few syllables over those with too many is a symptom of early date.—Ed.]

and their dates of composition might well be considered to be not greatly removed from the time period described in their respective passages.

Five-line uta having fewer or more than thirty-one syllables are believed to represent a somewhat earlier version of the fixed tanka form. Here are two representative examples:

Ōmae (4)	Come, take shelter with me
Komae Sukune ga	Beneath the overhanging
Kanato kage	Metal-studded gate of
Kaku yorikone (6)	Lord Ōmae Komae,
Ame tachiyamen.	Until the rain has stopped.

(*KJK, Song*, 81)

Mimoro no (4)	You're like a sacred oak tree
Itsukashi ga moto	Growing in the god's abode,
Kashi ga moto	An oak tree—
Yuyushiki kamo (6)	My touch would be blasphemy,
Kashiwara otome.	Shrine maiden of Oak Plain!

(*KJK, Song*, 92)

One syllable is lacking in as many as three of the five lines of these uta, and in two of each of the above. As long as they were recited as songs, however, a one- or two-syllable variance was not a problem: we can infer that archaic songs were sung to fluctuating beats (Tsuchihashi, 1968, 401-3). The lyrics in the *Kinkafu*, a ninth-century songbook, are known to have been sung with the vowels of each syllable drawn out to match a given musical score: this procedure was probably followed in archaic times as well.

The form represented by a regular five- and seven-syllable beat nevertheless became standard, while the contrary irregularities did not survive. I would like to think that this resulted from the tendency, which grew ever stronger, to recite the same text by means of alternate methods. Tonal accents, stress accents, and long-short accents are not prominent features of the Japanese language. Neither do syllables containing more than one consonant exist. As a consequence, meter can be determined only by a regularly rhythmical distribution of sounds. In order to pronounce the words of a song in a comprehensible fashion, their syllables must be made to cohere into a given unit. Since a four-phoneme unit tends to resolve into two phonemes plus two phonemes, and a six-phoneme unit into three plus three, the only unit feasible for syllabic meter is that using a prime number of phonemes. Anything made up of three or fewer phonemes, however, is too small a unit, and a thirteen-phoneme

unit is too large and lacking in cohesive power: we are thus left with
five- and seven-phoneme units as the only remaining prime numbers. It
is for this reason that meter in Japan is based on five- and seven-phoneme
units (Kanda, 1937, 13-26). Syllabic meter, however, is predicated upon
the presence of a regular beat. It therefore follows that the evolution of
a five- and seven-phoneme meter—notwithstanding the archaic practice
of reciting songs to fluctuating beats—can be explained only by the supposition that the same texts were recited to a fairly regular beat under
different circumstances.

One other requisite of the tanka form is that it consist of five lines.
The following are examples of uta in the five-line form which have not
yet evolved a five- and seven-phoneme meter.

Otome no (4)	At my young lady's
Toko no be ni	Bedside
Wa ga okishi	I left behind
Tsuruki no tachi (6)	That sword—
Sono tachi wa ya. (6)	Oh, that sword!

(KJK, Song, 33)

Uma sake (4)	Morning dawns at Miwa,
Miwa no tono no (6)	Famous for delicious sake:
Asa to ni mo	Let us open the shrine portals
Idete yukana (6)	And go out into the day,
Miwa no tono to o.	Opening the shrine portals of Miwa.

(NSK, Song, 16)

In both examples the fifth line is based on the repetition of an earlier
line: if the lines "Oh, that sword!" and "Opening the shrine portals of
Miwa" were temporarily omitted, the overall significance of the uta would
remain. The same can be said for the third line, "An oak tree," of the
uta which begins, "You're like a sacred oak tree" (KJK, Song, 92), and
for the last line of "Eight-layered clouds rise" (KJK, Song, 1), quoted
earlier: "Hey now! Eightfold fences!" We can only conclude that these
uta originally had a four-line form, and that the later five-line form
evolved from the addition of a repeated line, either a simple repetition
or a slight variation.[25]

In fact, only a very small group of songs in four-line form still survives.

[25] Uta in the five-line form that possess a repeated line appear twice in the KJK (Song,
75 and 80) and three times in the NSK (Song, 24, 81, and 98). Uta in five-line form with
slightly altered repetition appear seven times in the KJK (Song, 1, 33, 59, 84, 92, 95, and
110) and three times in the NSK (Song, 16, 17, and 51)—for a total of fifteen songs.

As examples of complete four-line uta we have, in addition to "In the field of bamboo grass" (*KJK, Song*, 35) given earlier, only the following:

Medori no (4)	Medori,
Wa ga ōkimi no	My beloved,
Orosu hata	Who will wear
Ta ga tame rokamo.	The cloth you weave?

(*KJK, Song*, 66)

If, however, we agree not to count simple repetitions as lines, we can consider that the following uta, quoted earlier, possesses a four-line form:

Nazuki no ta no (6)	Wild yam vines
Inagara ni	Creeping round and round
Haimotorou (6)	The rice stalks
Tokorozura.	In the nearby field.

(*KJK, Song*, 34)

Even given this addition, the survival of so few four-line uta does not act to the benefit of my theory that the five-line uta postdates the four-line form. In modern primitive song, however, even-lined texts are the rule, and it is unlikely that songs with odd-numbered lines preceded those with even-numbered lines in Yamato alone. I believe that there are not more four-line uta in the *Chronicles* because few songs survive from the old stratum.

The standard lyric form in Japan became the uta with an odd number of lines, a fact which may be unparalleled in the world. There are, indeed, nine uta in the *Chronicles* with a three-line form.[26] There are, in addition, three that are parts of pairs.[27] This gives a total of twelve. Thus there are many more three-line uta than there are four-line, and yet this does not necessarily mean that the three-line form is the more basic, or that it predates the four-line form. Three-line uta occasionally appear with the notation, "This is a partial uta": this indicates that it was originally one part of a larger whole and that this one part was occasionally recited as an independent piece.[28] The *Kojiki* gives an example of paired parts in their original form in the episode in which Prince Yamato Takeru leaves the East Country for the Land of Kai. On the journey he recites:

[26] Five in the *KJK* (*Song*, 16, 32, 37, 67, and 73) and four in the *NSK* (*Song*, 44, 88, 109, and 121).
[27] Only in the *KJK* (*Song*, 17 and 18, 25 and 26, 105 and 106).
[28] In the *KJK* (*Song*, 22 and 73).

Niibari　　　　　　　　Since leaving Tsukuba
Tsukuba o sugite　　　　Of newly cultivated fields
Ikuyo ka netsuru.　　　How many nights have I passed?

(*KJK, Song,* 25)

An old man in charge of lighting fires replies,

Kaga nabete　　　　　Time goes by:
Yo ni wa kokonoyo　　Of nights we have spent nine nights,
Hi ni wa tōka o.　　　Of days we have spent ten.

(*KJK, Song,* 26)

Since the content of the two uta gains in coherence when read as one six-line work, the exchange may essentially be seen as the equivalent of a six-line uta.

Four uta in the *Chronicles* are written in the six-line form.[29] Uta in the three-line form may represent either a partial or a derivative version of the six-line lyric form. It may be noted here that some of the uta in three-line form which were recited as "partial uta" contain guide phrases. For instance:

Takayuku ya　　　　My cloth will make a fine cloak for
Hayabusawake no　　*Heaven-soaring*
Miosui ga ne.　　　　Hayabusawake.[30]

(*KJK, Song,* 67)

Minasokou　　　　　Who will look after
Omi no otome o　　　This our handmaid
Tare yashinawan.　　*Of sea-deep attractions?*

(*NSK, Song,* 44)

If we temporarily omit as superfluous the guide phrases "heaven-soaring" and "of sea-deep attractions," both uta are then reduced to two lines, and no longer constitute a song.[31] If, however, the latter uta is read as one part of a dialogue, the entire form of which is—

[29] Two in the *KJK* (*Song,* 49 and 65) and two in the *NSK* (*Song,* 80 and 99).

[30] ["Hayabusawake" designates a person: "hayabusa" or falcon relates to the guide phrase of the previous line, "Heaven-soaring"; and "wake" is a court office or rank.— Trans., Ed.]

[31] "Heaven-soaring" (takayuku ya; *KJK, Song,* 67) is not present in the alternate transmissions of the *NSK.* Therefore it is considered likely that a form without the guide phrase once existed.

Omi no otome o	Who will look after
Tare yashinawan	This our handmaid?
Harima Hayamachi	I, Hayamachi of Harima
Are yashinawan.	Do undertake the lady's care—

then the form is identical to the previously cited

Ana niyashi	My, oh lovely,
E otoko o.	What a fine man!
Ana niyashi	My, oh lovely,
E otome o.	What a fair maid!

(*JDK*, 178)

In other words, uta in the three-line form may have come into being not only as "partial uta" taken from uta in six-line form but also as "partial uta" derived from uta in four-line form.

It might also be noted that four six-line uta found in the *Chronicles* contain, with their third and sixth lines, either repetition or parallelism, as in the following examples:

Yata no	Though like the single stalk of
Hitomoto suge wa	Yata sedge,
Hitori oritomo	*I remain alone,*
Ōkimi shi	If Your Majesty agrees,
Yoshi to kikosaba	It will not matter that
Hitori oritomo.	*I remain alone.*

(*KJK, Song*, 65)

Atarashiki	How we shall mourn
Inabe no takumi	Inabe the carpenter!
Kakeshi suminawa	*He drew flawless inking lines—*
Shi ga nakeba	If he is not with us,
Tare ka kaken yo	Who then will draw them?
Atara suminawa.	*We shall miss his inking lines.*[32]

(*NSK, Song*, 80)

If the superfluous third line is omitted, we have a five-line form: this observation has led to the theory that the set tanka form of five lines may have evolved from uta in the six-line form (Ōta, 1966, 137-38). The

[32] [Inabe is about to be executed. The flawless inking lines were made by snapping a taut, ink-soaked line to mark wood for straight sawing, a practice still seen in Japan.—Trans., Ed.]

third line cannot be omitted, however, making it impossible to determine whether the fixed, five-line tanka form is based solely on uta in six-line form. It may be just as reasonable, or perhaps more so, to consider that uta in the four-line form evolved into uta with five lines through the addition of guide phrases and insistent repetition.

At what stage of the Archaic Age, then, did the genre later known as "chōka" (long poems) develop? Songs of considerable length are found in modern primitive societies, and so it would not be at all illogical to suppose that in Yamato as well songs in multiple-line form already existed in the old stratum of the Archaic Age. On the other hand, not very many of the multiple-line songs now surviving in the *Chronicles* actually belong to the old stratum. Let us apply Supplementary Assumption 2, discussed above, to the following two chōka. The first is from the *Kojiki*, the second from the *Nihon Shoki*.

Yachihoko no	The divine Lord of
Kami no mikoto wa	Eight Thousand Halberds
Yashima kuni	Cannot find a fitting bride
Tsuma makikanete	In all the Isles of Yamato.
Tōdōshi	Then, hearing that
Koshi no kuni ni	In the distant
Sakashi me o	Land of Koshi
Ari to kikashite	A clever maiden dwells,
Kuwashi me o	Then, hearing that
Ari to kikoshite	There a lovely maiden dwells,
Sa yobai ni	He sets off
Aritatashi	To pay her court,
Yobai ni	He comes calling
Arikayowase	To court her.
Tachi ga o mo	He does not pause
Imada tokazute	To loosen his sword knots,
Osui o mo	He does not pause
Imada tokaneba	To loosen his cloak.
Otome no	Does the maiden sleep
Nasu ya itato o	Behind that wooden door?
Oshisoburai	As I stand
Waga tatasereba	And as I push against it,
Hikikozurai	And as I stand and
Waga tatasereba	As I pull upon it,
Aoyama ni	A tiger thrush calls
Nue wa nakinu	From verdant hills,
Sanotsutori	Bird of the fields,
Kigishi wa toyomu	A pheasant cries out;

Niwatsutori	Bird of the garden,
Kake wa naku	A rooster crows.
Uretaku mo	How vexing is
Naku naru tori ka	The racket of these birds!
Kono tori mo	If only I could
Uchiyamekosene.	Make them stop!
Ishitau ya	*By the court servant Ama,*
Ama hase tsukai	*Whose fishing forebears plumbed the depths,*
Koto no katarigoto mo	*This was transmitted*
Ko o ba.	*By word of mouth.*[33]

(*KJK, Song, 2*)

Yashima kuni	In all the Isles of Yamato
Tsuma makikanete	I cannot find a fitting bride.
Haru hi no	Then, hearing that
Kasuga no kuni ni	In the Land of Kasuga,
Kuwashi me o	As fair as a spring day,
Ari to kikite	A lovely maiden dwells,
Yoroshi me o	Then, hearing that
Ari to kikite	There a pleasant maiden dwells,
Maki saku	I push open
Hi no itato o	Her door of cypress
Oshihiraki	Grown thick and splendid—
Ware irimashi	And I go inside.
Atodori	Pulling her quilt
Tsuma dorishite	To the foot of the bed,
Makura tori	Pulling her quilt
Tsuma dorishite	To the head of the bed,
Imo ga te o	I nestle
Ware ni makashime	In my beloved's arms,
Waga te o ba	And in my arms
Imo ni makashime	She nestles:
Masakazura	Luxuriant vines,
Tadaki azawari	We embrace, we entwine.
Shishikushiro	As we lie cuddled
Uma ineshi to ni	Like venison on a spit
Niwatsutori	We hear the crow of a rooster,
Kake wa naku nari	Bird of the garden;

[33] [At the line "Waga tatasereba" (As I stand) the narrative voice changes to the first person, the speaker being Eight Thousand Halberds. See ch. 1, n. 17.—Trans., Ed.]

Notsutori	The cry of a pheasant,
Kigishi wa toyomu	Bird of the fields:
Hashi keku mo	Before I can tell you
Imada iwazute	How beautiful you are,
Akenikeri	Day has dawned,
Wagimo.	My beloved.

(*NSK, Song,* 96)

Since the latter chōka (*NSK, Song,* 96) obviously imitates the former (*KJK, Song,* 2), they should date from periods considerably separated in time. Yet the former, putatively composed by the God of Eight Thousand Halberds, together with other kamugatariuta (*KJK, Song,* 2-5), is neither easily nor readily determined as belonging to the old stratum. The reason lies in the parallelism, outstanding both in quantity and quality, found in *Kojiki* songs 2 through 5: this represents a far more advanced technique than that of primitive repetition. The technique of parallelism also appears in modern primitive song, and its high incidence in every kind of Ainu yukar and in the Ryukyuan kwēna suggests that parallelism was used extensively in archaic Yamato. Yet the technique seen in the *Kojiki* chōka is anything but primitive. The image of the ideal wife is depicted by contrasting "a clever maiden" with "a lovely maiden," putting intelligence before beauty; the lover's loosening of his traveling dress opposes "his sword knots" to "his cloak," indicating that his clothing and accessories will be removed in the order of outermost first; "pushing against" the wooden door is contrasted with "pulling upon it," thus manifesting psychological spontaneity in the depiction of a male who, in trying to open a door, first pushes and then pulls. Above all, there is three-part parallelism: "A tiger thrush calls / From verdant hills," "Bird of the fields, / A pheasant cries out," and "Bird of the garden, / A rooster crows." By this technique a situation is created in which the various birdcalls gradually approach the speaker: hills (far) → fields (midpoint) → garden (near). Such subtle craftsmanship should be regarded as a distinguishing feature of the new stratum. The technique of three-part parallelism later becomes fixed in the jō-chū-ge, or three-line form of parallelism. For all that, this chōka also contains the line "He sets off / To pay her court" (Sa yobai ni / Aritatashi), contrasted to "He comes calling / To court her" (Yobai ni / Arikayowase), a structure approaching simple repetition. With this evidence, the chōka is hardly among the newer compositions in the new stratum.

In another of the kamugatariuta, which begins with the lines "Black as lily seeds / This handsome robe" (*KJK, Song,* 4, quoted above), the first half of the uta constitutes a balance of two ten-line units, both of which conclude with "I strip it off and cast it away." The structure of these units is slightly altered to produce the next ten lines, which respond to the first twenty. This form is even more complex. Still, it seems reasonable to conclude that the kamugatariuta, four uta concerning the God of Eight Thousand Halberds (*KJK, Song*, 2-5), belong on the whole to an old level of the new stratum.

What kind of song, then, belongs to the old stratum? As was stated earlier, those songs which have lines of simple repetition or parallelism that closely approaches simple repetition may be tentatively assigned to the old stratum. Examples include two of the Songs of Kume, "At the great Cavern House / Of Osaka" (*KJK, Song*, 10) and "By the Sea of Ise / Where divine winds blow" (*NSK, Song*, 8), as well as the following *Kojiki* song [Mimaki Iribiko is the personal name of Sujin Tennō]:

Kohaya	Alas,
Mimaki Iribiko haya	Mimaki Iribiko, ah!
Mimaki Iribiko haya	Mimaki Iribiko, ah!
Ono ga o o	Someone is plotting
Nusumishisen to	To snatch away your life:
Shiritsuto yo	He wanders past
Iyukitagai	Your back door,
Maetsuto yo	He wanders past
Iyukitagai	Your front door,
Ukakawaku	Watching for his chance,
Shirani to	Yet you heed him not.
Mimaki Iribiko haya.	Mimaki Iribiko, ah!

(*KJK, Song*, 22)

The *Nihon Shoki* version invests this song with the characteristics of the new stratum:

Mimaki Iribiko haya	Mimaki Iribiko, ah!
Ono ga o o	Someone is plotting
Shisen to	To take away your life,
Nusumaku shirani	Yet you heed him not,
Himenasobi su mo.	But dally instead with young ladies.
Aru ni iwaku	*It is also said*
Ōki to yori	From the great palace door
Ukakaite	He watches for his chance
Korosan to	To kill you,

Suraku o shirani	Yet you heed him not,
Himenasobi su mo.	But dally instead with young ladies.[34]

(*NSK, Song*, 18)

Despite the fact that the latter uta and its variant combined have fewer lines than the one *Kojiki* uta, the addition of "But dally instead with young ladies" to the end of both *Nihon Shoki* uta aids in their general comprehensibility—a characteristic, to me, of their relative newness. If, in the first uta (*KJK, Song*, 22), the lines "Watching for his chance, / Yet you heed him not" were followed by a line describing some aspect of Mimaki Iribiko's appearance or conduct, the meaning would be very clear. But in the text as it stands, there is nothing to respond to the "to" [the quotative particle] of the next to last line, thus creating a vacuum in the total significance of the uta. Because still partially primitive songs are usually accompanied by body movements, however, that part of a song which was not recited in archaic times would have been expressed through movement. We would do well to conclude that incomplete expression of meaning is a characteristic of the old stratum.

For further evidence, let us consider the following uta:

Owari ni	On the Cape of Otsu,
Tada ni mukaeru	Right across from
Otsu no saki naru	Owari, there stands a
Hitotsu matsu	Lone pine.
Aseo	All together now!
Hitotsu matsu	Lone pine,
Hito ni ariseba	If you were a man
Tachi hakemashi o	I would gird you with a sword,
Kinu kisemashi o	I would dress you in a robe,
Hitotsu matsu	Lone pine.
Aseo.	All together now!

(*KJK, Song*, 29)

Owari ni	Right across from
Tada ni mukaeru	Owari, there stands a
Hitotsu matsu	Lone pine,
Aware	Oh my!
Hitotsu matsu	Lone pine,
Hito ni ariseba	If you were a man,

[34] [The phrase, italicized in the poem, "Aru ni iwaku" (It is also said) indicates that what follows is a variant of the text just given.—Trans.]

Kinu kisemashi o   I would dress you in a robe,
Tachi hakemashi o.   I would gird you with a sword.

(NSK, Song, 27)

The first uta provides another example of a work from the old stratum. The second has a somewhat newer configuration. Or, to compare two more uta:

Kono miki o   The man who brewed
Kamiken hito wa   This fine sake
Sono tsuzumi   Surely used his great drum
Usu ni tatete   For a brewing vessel.
Utaitsutsu   Did he sing and sing
Kamikere kamo   While it brewed?
Maitsutsu   Did he dance and dance
Kamikere kamo   While it brewed?
Kono miki no   For this fine sake,
Miki no   Fine sake,
Aya ni utadanoshi   Makes us all quite merry!
Sasa.   Good fortune![35]

(KJK, Song, 40)

Kono miki o   The man who brewed
Kamiken hito wa   This fine sake
Sono tsuzumi   Surely used his great drum
Usu ni tatete   For a brewing vessel.
Utaitsutsu   Did he sing and sing
Kamikeme kamo   While it brewed?
Kono miki no   For this fine sake
Aya ni utadanoshi   Makes us all quite merry!
Sasa.   Good fortune!

(NSK, Song, 33)

Here we find that the first version contains some instances of simple repetition, and thus belongs to an older stratum than the other. In ad-

---

[35] [When sake was brewed—and the ancient version seems to have been mash-like or glutinous rather than free flowing—the event was accompanied by singing, dancing, and the beating of drums, as the uta shows. The ceremony would impart joy to the spirit of the sake, improving its quality. And the fine sake thereby produced would in turn give happiness to its drinkers.—Trans., Ed.]

dition, a third version, midway in form between the two given above, is preserved in the ninth-century *Kinkafu* (20).

It is by such means that relative distinctions can be made between old and new strata. It is also possible occasionally to make further distinctions within the old or new strata—between, say, the new level of the old stratum and the old level of the new stratum. For instance, among the pieces grouped together as the Songs of Kume, one—"Now we have you . . ." (*NSK, Song,* 10)—is so constructed that the only components besides simple repetition are rhythm-marking terms (hayashikotoba), probably sung in chorus. Vestiges of primitive song survive here in abundance, and we may thus conclude that this song belongs to the older layer of the old stratum. Again, "At the great Cavern House / Of Osaka" (*KJK, Song,* 10) is made up almost entirely of simple repetition and lines that come close to simple repetition. Since, moreover, the song does not contain any element indicative of a later date of composition, it too may be included within the older-level songs of the old stratum. "Round-hilted" swords are mentioned in the song: the excavation of such swords from a late tumulus has led to the theory that the *Kojiki* song dates from the seventh century or thereafter.[36] The round-hilted swords taken from the tumulus, however, have pommels covered with elaborate metalwork, whereas swords with simple wooden hilts may well have been present in much earlier times. There is, therefore, no reason to consider this song as other than a member of the old layer of the old stratum.

Let us consider one more uta belonging to the Songs of Kume:

Uda no	In Uda,
Takaki ni	On the high ground,
Shigi wana haru	I set a trap for longbills;
Waga matsu ya	I did not catch
Shigi wa sayarazu	The longbills I sought,
Isukuwashi	But caught instead
Kuchira sayaru	A vigorous hawk.
Konami ga	If my old wife
Na kowasaba	Begs me for food,
Tachisoba no	I'll give her just a bit,
Mi no nakeku o	As much as that buckwheat plant
Kokishi hiene	Bears fruit.
Uwanari ga	If my new wife
Na kowasaba	Begs me for food,
Ichisakaki	I'll give her a lot,

---

[36] It has been said that the songs date from the time of Prince Shōtoku or the date of the compiling of the *Chronicles* (Gotō, 1947, 8-11). This dating has been refuted, however, by Mishina Akihide (1970, 338).

Mi no ōkeku o	As much as the ichisakaki tree
Kokida hiene.	Bears fruit.
E—e—e	*E—e—eh!*
Shiya koshiya	Fools, silly fools!
(*Ko wa inogou so.*)	(*This shows enmity.*)
A—a—a	*A—a—ah!*
Shiya koshiya	Fools, silly fools!
(*Ko wa azawarau so*).	(*This shows ridicule.*)[37]

                  (*KJK, Song,* 9)

There is a high incidence of irregular syllabic meter in this song (Basic Assumption A3), and simple repetition is also present in part (Basic Assumption A1); about halfway through the song, however, a complex parallelism develops between "If my old wife / . . . / Bears fruit" (Basic Assumption A2). It may therefore be best to assign this poem to an intermediate level within the old stratum.

Might we not be able to posit, to a degree, some absolute dating to be derived from the old stratum/new stratum approach to the inference of relative dates? We saw earlier that two uta— "What has Mezurako" (*NSK, Song,* 99) and "Out of Hirakata" (*NSK, Song,* 98)—are believed to date from the mid- to late sixth century. The shape of each conforms respectively to the sedōka and tanka set forms.[38] Although they contain simple repetition—"Mezurako / kitaru" (has Mezurako / come) and "fue fukinoboru" (flute plays as we row upstream)—both represent the recitation of an event in time as a specific occurrence, an attitude one can only call far removed from the primitive. Primitive songs are composed by a certain individual for the purpose of singing about a particular event. The content of their texts lacks specificity, however, and events are not depicted as being limited to a single time. Such songs would be repeated in coming ages, whenever occasions arose resembling those described by the songs, and they might be used under considerably different circumstances. By contrast, songs with specificity, those which refer to a single time, may be considered nonprimitive. The fact that such specific depictions appear in sixth-century song is to be seen as a new feature, in comparison with what had come before. Thus the new stratum of archaic song can be made to correspond roughly to the early through the late

---

[37] [The italicized phrases in parentheses are not part of the uta as such but rather comments interpreting the lines preceding the comments. We may presume that in oral delivery the reciter's facial expressions and tone of voice would have rendered the distinctions of mood clear without the need for comments such as we see here.—Trans., Ed.]

[38] [Sedōka are six-line poems: 5, 7, 7; 5, 7, 7, syllables. They are sometimes used for dialogue, each speaker having three lines of the "partial uta" (katauta) referred to earlier.—Ed.]

sixth century, and the old stratum will accordingly encompass the fifth and earlier centuries.

Yet this only serves to equate the new stratum of archaic song with the sixth century, and the old stratum with the fifth and earlier centuries. It does not present any criteria by which to date individual songs. This is because certain songs, which seem definitely to preserve an ancient literary style, may have been composed in the late seventh century, in spite of their antiquated language. Nor can all songs possessing specific depictions be judged works of the sixth century, despite the transmitted circumstances of their composition. For example, Kenzō Tennō, who learned where his father's bones were buried from an old woman, gave her the name Okime and built her a house near his palace. He stretched a rope hung with bells between her house and the palace, so that when Okime, whose legs were weak, attended court, she could walk there by holding on to the rope.[39] When the bells chimed, the tennō knew Okime was coming. This mark of his concern made it possible for Okime to have free access to Kenzō without passing through the many reception rooms. The following uta was recited by the tennō after he had heard the bells and was awaiting Okime:

> Asajihara   Bells chime—
> Osone o sugi   Jingling like the bells on horses
>   Momozutau   Ranging across the fields
> Nute yuraku mo yo   Of bamboo grass, gravelly wastes—
> Okime kurashi mo.   Okime must be coming.

> (*NSK, Song,* 85)

In the end, Okime, quite enfeebled, entreated Kenzō to let her live out her last years in Ōmi, her birthplace, and he reluctantly gave his consent. When they parted, he is said to have presented Okime with this uta.

>   Okime mo yo   Okime, oh,
> Ōmi no Okime   Okime of Ōmi!
>   Asu yori wa   Will the mountains
> Miyamagakurite   Hide you from my sight
> Miezu kamo aran.   Tomorrow and thereafter?

> (*NSK, Song,* 86)

In the former uta, "Asajihara / Osone o sugi" (Fields / Of bamboo grass, gravelly wastes) is a guide phrase for "momozutau" (Ranging

---

[39] The quotation is from the *NSK* (*Kenzōki,* 400-406). The same story appears in the *KJK.*

across). Other lines—"Ranging across the fields / Of bamboo grass, gravelly wastes"—form in turn the guide phrase for "Bells." Guide phrases thus make up a complex unit, an indication, according to Basic Assumption A2, that the uta is not of great antiquity. In addition, the last three lines of the second uta are poignantly lyrical, even evoking the language of waka. Although the stories of the tennō and Okime are narrated as events of the late fifth century, we can deduce that they were probably collected, in their present form, in the early seventh century. We cannot be absolutely sure, of course, but the possibility of their being so cannot be denied. When I equated the new stratum of archaic song with the sixth century, and sought to base this equation on a specificity of expression, I did so only in order to draw attention to the most distinctive feature of sixth-century song: this does not mean that all songs with specific depictions are determined to belong to the sixth century.

A similar approach is involved for a terminus a quo for the old stratum. We saw that the old stratum of archaic song corresponds to the fifth century or before. The problem, however, lies in the "before." The dirge for Prince Yamato Takeru belongs, as we have already seen, to an old level within the old stratum. But how far back does this old level go? Could the dirge have been composed as early as the third century? There are no definite answers to these questions. No direct connection need exist between the composition dates of an individual song and the concept of old and new strata. And yet, as I have stated, the expression "creeps round" in Yamato Takeru's dirge can be interpreted, by means of the haniwa figure excavated from the Himezuka tumulus, so as to arrive at a definite terminus ad quem, the early sixth century. Because etiquette-related customs such as funeral ceremonies tend, in culturally backward times or societies, to be preserved for a longer period than we might expect, it is quite possible that the dirge for Yamato Takeru was composed as early as the fourth century. The early sixth century has been determined to be the terminus ad quem for the song, however. Hence, if we assume a range of one hundred years for the composition date, the terminus a quo will be equivalent to the mid-fifth century. As we shall see below, the reign of Yamato Takeru's father, Keikō Tennō, evidently belongs in the early fourth century. Therefore, if we assume again that one hundred years is the necessary time period within which contemporary Yamato military incursions into the outlying regions would have been transformed into a body of stories about the deeds of a hero named Prince Yamato Takeru, then the terminus a quo for the composition date of his dirge will be the mid-fifth century.[40]

---

[40] [Dates of composition ought not to be confused with sovereigns' lives and dates. The first tennō now thought "historical," Kimmei (r. 539-71), is twenty-ninth in the traditional royal line. Jimmu, mentioned next by the author, is the first of that line, traditionally

Similarly, the military expedition which provided the subject matter for the songs related to Jimmu Tennō is believed to have taken place in the mid-third century. If, as before, we allow a range of one hundred years for this event to evolve into setsuwa, then the tentative terminus a quo for their composition will be the late fourth century. Since the Jimmu songs do not differ greatly in literary form from the Prince Yamato Takeru songs, however, a more reasonable terminus a quo might be in the vicinity of the early fifth century. The terminus ad quem for the composition of the Jimmu songs should be thought no later than the early sixth century.

THE COURSE OF NARRATIVE

The Works, Their Transmission, and Their Reception

To judge from modern primitive examples, no distinction is made between the composer and the singer of a song at the moment of its creation. Such was also the case, apparently, in archaic Yamato. What, then, were the circumstances under which narrative was composed? Stories are transmitted in the *Chronicles* in no insignificant amount. Because the extant texts are rich in language dating from the introduction of writing, however, few clues remain from which to deduce the state of these works in the Archaic Age. This is not to say that no trace survives. The inferences gathered from what evidence remains are strengthened by authoritative supporting facts. It is these facts which I would first like to discuss.

The Parry-Lord theory, formulated from an inquiry into the nature of Yugoslavian narrative, is of great significance in considering the vital circumstances of setsuwa.[41] We learn from the Parry-Lord theory that the performer of a narrative can be its composer as well, and that we must reject our conception that the role of the performer is simply to recite another's work (or in some cases one's own; Lord, 1960, 13). In other words, performer and composer are only two facets of the same person; composition and performance take place concurrently. The performer composes in the process of reciting before an audience. In order not to bore the audience, he must perform at a considerable speed, an impossible task, it would seem, unless he makes use of already extant texts. This is not the case, however. He can perform at considerable speed

---

reigning 660-585, B.C. which is impossible. In the next paragraph, and in a later chapter, the author provides information from recent historical scholarship that gives some substance to earlier, shadowy figures. But the difficult problems of dating uta in the *Chronicles* are, as he shows, a distinct matter.—Ed.]

[41] The Parry-Lord theory takes its name from two individuals: Milman Parry, a man of genius who met an early death; and Albert B. Lord, who expounded and refined the theory. For Parry's scholarly achievements, see Parry, 1971.

and extemporaneously compose interesting stories as well, because he has amassed innumerable formulas which he binds together in accordance with the place of composition. Parry defines a formula as "a group of words which is regularly employed under the same metrical conditions to express a given essential idea" in a work (Parry, 1930, 80). This represents the true state of oral composition. Such a process took place in the composition of the *Iliad* and the *Odyssey*, a fact deduced from the distributions of formulas within their extant texts (Lord, 1960, 141-97). Homer lived in an age bordering on the period of Greek classical antiquity, with its high civilization, and basic elements of written composition are therefore surely present to a considerable degree in the extant texts. Yet vestiges of oral composition in the extant *Iliad* and *Odyssey* are clearly discernible as a result of textual analysis, which has detected a great many oral formulas. These distinctions show that the Parry-Lord theory may indeed be termed an enduring achievement.

Like the Homeric epics, the *Chronicles* were compiled during a period of rather high literacy, and so the wide variety of setsuwa incorporated into the *Chronicles* was probably transcribed and edited from previously written material. The result is that the extant *Chronicles*, when compared with the epics of Homer, contain scant evidence of oral composition. This is not to say, however, that oral formulas are nonexistent in the setsuwa found in the *Chronicles*. Rather, they appear much as is shown below:

I. She asked him to give her his sword, ten hands long. . . .[42] *She chewed it and chewed it, and when she spat it out her breath spread like mist, giving shape to the gods named* . . . (KJK, 1:204).

He asked her to give him her necklace of jewels. . . . *He chewed it and chewed it, and when he spat it out his breath spread like mist, giving shape to a god named* . . . (ibid.).

He asked her to give him the jewels in the knot of hair on the right side of her head. *He chewed them and chewed them, and when he spat them out his breath spread like mist, giving shape to a god named* . . . (ibid.).

He asked her to give him the jewels entwined in her hair. *He chewed them and chewed them, and when he spat them out his breath spread like mist, giving shape to a god named* . . . (ibid., 205).

He asked her to give him the jewels wrapped round her left wrist. *He chewed them and chewed them, and when he spat them out his breath spread like mist, giving shape to a god named* . . . (ibid.).

He asked her to give him the jewels wrapped round her right wrist.

[42] [I.e., Amaterasu asked Susanoo, her brother. The two deities are the subjects of all the passages in sections I and II.—Trans.]

He chewed them and chewed them, and when he spat them out his breath spread like mist, giving shape to a god named . . . (ibid.).

II. She broke the sword into three pieces, *and with her jewels jingling and clinking she rinsed them and washed them in the Holy Well of Heaven . . .* (ibid., 204).

. . . and with the jewels jingling and clinking he rinsed them and washed them in the Holy Well of Heaven . . . (ibid.).

III. "At the foot of Mount Uka, there you will *make firm on the bottommost rocks the columns of your palace, and thrust its crossbeams high toward the Plain of Heaven,* and there you will dwell" (ibid., 230).[43]

"If she will *make firm on the bottommost rocks the columns of my palace, and thrust its crossbeams high toward the Plain of Heaven . . .*" (ibid., 263).[44]

"He *made firm on the bottommost rocks the columns of his palace, and thrust its crossbeams high toward the Plain of Heaven,* and there he dwelled (ibid., 270).[45]

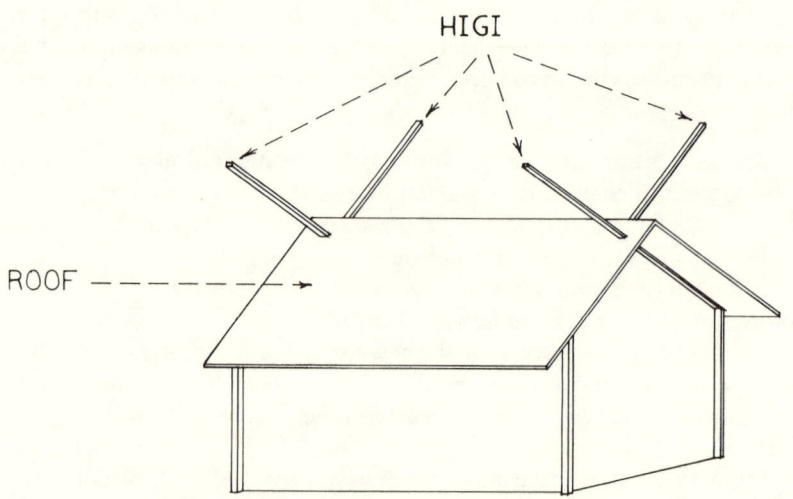

FIGURE 6. Higi of Ancient Palace

[43] [The speaker is Susanoo, addressing his new son-in-law, Ōkuninushi. The "crossbeams" (higi) are part of an early Japanese roof style. The roof beams at the front and back gables cross and continue above the roof, to form an X. The style is preserved in some Shinto shrines, as notably the Great Shrine of Ise. See Figure 6.—Trans.]

[44] [Okuninushi is the speaker, and "she" is Amaterasu. This is part of his abdication speech as ruler of Japan.—Trans.]

[45] ["He" is Amaterasu's grandson Ninigi, come down from heaven to rule Japan.—Trans.]

IV. The voices of the evil gods were *like the buzzing of summer flies, reaching everywhere* . . . (ibid., 201).

The voices of the myriad gods were *like the buzzing of summer flies, reaching everywhere*, and myriad calamities occurred throughout the land (ibid., 209).

V. "The Land of Abundant Reed Plains, of Five Hundred, of One Thousand Autumns of Rice Harvest, *appears to be in a great uproar*" (ibid., 253).[46]

"The Land in the Midst of the Reed Plains *appears to be in a great uproar*" (KJK, 2:55).[47]

In all these cases, only recurrent phrases are considered to be oral formulas. There are instances, however, in which phrases that occur only once are nevertheless assumed to be formulas. The Shinto ritual prayers known as norito are products of a later time. Nevertheless, they contain phrases similar to those appearing only once in the *Chronicles*. For example, the phrase "Kakiwa ni tokiwa ni" (an immutable rock, a solid rock) appears only once in the *Kojiki*, in the section entitled "The Age of the Gods" (Jindaiki):

"... may you, son of the gods in heaven, be forever unchanging, *an immutable rock, a solid rock*, though snow should fall and storms should rage . . ." (KJK, 1:276).[48]

Yet a similar expression appears twelve times in norito, beginning with this passage:

Bless the descendants of the Royal House, that their lives may long continue, *a solid rock, an immutable rock* (Norito, 389).[49]

This may indicate that, in some cases, phrases that were indeed formulas in the Archaic Age were not used more than once in "The Age of the Gods" of the *Kojiki*. A formula which appears three times in that section, "make firm on the bottommost rocks the columns of [one's] palace, and thrust its crossbeams high toward the Plain of Heaven," is used nine times in the norito corpus as well, as fact which lends support to this belief.[50] Moreover, there is another phrase from that section: "Thus were

[46] "The Land . . ." is Japan, the speaker a son of Amaterasu, listening from heaven to the sounds on earth.—Trans.]

[47] [The speaker is one Takakuraji of Kumano, quoting words by Amaterasu and Takamimusubi, who appear to him in a dream and instruct him to take a heavenly sword to Jimmu Tennō.—Trans.]

[48] [The "son" is Ninigi; the speaker is his father-in-law, the mountain god Ōyamatsumi.—Trans.]

[49] See also Norito, 391, 395, 407, 409, 411, 413, 433, 435, 445, 463.

[50] Norito, 389, 395, 405, 407, 411, 425, 437, 441, 453.

their duties determined, and they sang and danced *for eight days and eight nights* (*KJK*, 1:258).[51] This appears, in a somewhat different version, in this norito: "She said, 'I beg you, my beloved, not to look upon me *for seven nights and seven days*' " (*Norito*, 429).

The following pair of passages presents instances of a similar nature. The first is from "The Age of the Gods," the second from a norito.

> "This place . . . *is a land where the morning sun shines straight, a land where the evening sun shines bright.* Therefore this place is the very best place" (*KJK*, 1:270).

> My palace is on *a site where the morning sun shines, a site where the evening sun glimmers*, at Ono in Tachino of Tatsuta . . . (*Norito*, 403).

These facts make it impossible to doubt that oral composition was practiced in the Archaic Age. Yet vestiges of oral formulas in the *Chronicles* are barely discernible, when compared with Homeric epic. Why?

The reasons first to be considered are these: the setsuwa themselves in the "Age of the Gods" section of the *Kojiki* are not numerous. Moreover, roughly thirty percent of these setsuwa are given over to the recitation of divine genealogies. From the very beginning, therefore, fewer scenes demanding the use of formulas were available in the *Chronicles* than in Homeric epic. The names of the gods are enumerated in "The Age of the Gods" from its opening passage: "When heaven and earth were first created, these were the gods then born upon the Plain of Heaven. . . ." Narrative techniques, one might say, are all but useless in such passages. For example [on Izanagi and Izanami]:

> When they had finished the creation of the Land, they created gods. The names of the gods thus created were: the god Ōkotooshio; then the god Iwatsuchibiko was created; then the goddess Iwasuhime was created; then the god Ōtohiwake was created; then the god Ame no Fukinoo was created; then the god Ōyabiko was created; then the god Kazemotsuwake no Oshio was created. Then the Sea God was created. His name was: Ōwatatsumi (*KJK*, 1:183).

Such enumerations of names leave no room for the inclusion of formulas. A further reason to be considered is the introduction of writing at a relatively early stage in the transmission of this setsuwa material, a point that will be discussed in detail below. Suffice it to say here that the extant *Kojiki* is undeniably based in great part on written material that predates the time of the memorizer-reciter, Hieda no Are; and that the archaic setsuwa that appear in this written material originally possessed a form

---

[51] [The rites are for the funeral of Ame no Wakahiko.—Trans.]

appropriate to oral composition, a form that may have been altered to conform to written records at a time when the country was moving toward literacy. This process can be thought to have brought about a sharp decrease in the number of formulas in the *Chronicles*, an effect whose extent we see in the present text.

According to the *Kojiki* preface, written as a memorial to Temmu Tennō, the extant text was compiled by Ō no Yasumaro from the body of *Royal Genealogies* and *Ancient Traditions* which the tennō had commanded Heida no Are to recite.[52] The term "shōshū," translated above as "recite," is interpreted to mean either the memorizing of a written text (Tsuda Saukichi, 1923, 23-24), or the recitation from memory of an oral transmission (Yamada, 1935, 156-64). The former view, which has become quite influential, is represented by the work of Kanda Hideo and Kojima Noriyuki, whose studies are based on exhaustive textual analysis.[53] As Masuda Katsumi's theory demonstrates, however, this does not mean that the latter position has lost its validity.[54] This question still elicits diverse views within the scholarly community, and a definite conclusion has yet to be reached. The following points deserve attention, however:

1. The word "shōshū," as it appears in the Chinese classics and Buddhist scripture, signifies, in effect, recitation from memory: in some cases the activity is based on a written text, but in others it is not. Many instances of recitation are based on written texts, yet this need not hold true for all instances.

2. If we suppose for the moment that Are based her recitation on a written original, then her recitation could only have been a reading. But we cannot imagine that a reading version could involve particular

[52] "There was at that time a royal attendant whose surname was Hieda and whose given name was Are. She was twenty-eight years old, and so intelligent that she could recite whatever she read and memorize whatever she heard. His Majesty thus commanded Are to memorize and recite the royal genealogy and the legends of antiquity" (*KJK*, Preface, 170). [Having memorized so much, she later recited the material for Ō no Yasumaro to set down in writing as the text of the *KJK*.—Trans.]

[53] Kanda, *Kojiki no Kōzō* (*The Structure of the Kojiki*; Kanda, 1959, 18-20), and Kojima, *Jōdai Nihon Bungaku to Chūgoku Bungaku* (*Ancient Japanese Literature and Chinese Literature*; Kojima, 1962, 168-76), share a great deal. They take the same position, which can be expressed in terms of Kanda's analysis, based on usage of Chinese characters. There are three strata: ancient (sixth century), Asuka (first half of the seventh century), and Hakuhō (early eighth century). Kojima sees these strata as designating groups of ancient records that provided material for both of the *Chronicles*. For such reasons I have mentioned their names together.

[54] Masuda maintains that if the transmitted information belonging to the various clans had already been put into writing, then those transmissions which Are was commanded to memorize could not have influenced the clan materials. Are's task is thus interpreted as one of counteracting and regulating the clans' various oral traditions through the remembering and reciting of a single "text" (Masuda Katsumi, 1980, 6-8).

units of phrases in Japanese readings, although without doubt the whole composition was recited and transmitted in Japanese.[55]

3. Yasumaro would have perceived Are's recitation as an oral transmission, whether it was based on written material or not, because Yasumaro heard rather than read Are's material. The task of writing down a recitation is an activity entirely different from the editing and revising of a written text.

4. Contemporary written data were apparently not very substantial. It is doubtful, therefore, whether a quantity equal to or greater than the size of the present *Kojiki* was then in existence. It follows that ancient narratives not based on transmitted written material existed in considerable number, and that it was these oral narratives which Are recited from memory.[56]

In other words, we cannot deny the existence of orally transmitted narratives.

The conclusion so reached is that Are memorized both oral and written legends. The only question remaining is, which body formed the larger part of her recitation? This conclusion is not simply the result of my own reasoning, but one which is borne out by Yasumaro's preface, wherein Are's extraordinary memory is described in this way: "She could recite whatever she read and memorize whatever she heard." "Whatever she read" indicates the existence of a text transmitted in writing, although it does not signify in the least that Are relied solely upon written transmissions: the subsequent phrase, "whatever she heard," indicates a dependence on oral transmissions as well.

The theory maintaining that Are relied only on written transmissions is based, in part, on the idea that Japan in the seventh century already possessed a literate society. In the twenty-eighth year of Suiko Tennō's reign (A.D. 620), for example, the *Tennōki (History of the Royal Family)* and the *Kokuki (History of the State)* were written, as well as the *Hongi (Official History)*, which dealt with the government and the people.[57]

[55] [The logic here depends on the nature of the scheme of writing at the time, the cumbrous man'yōgana in which Chinese characters were sometimes used solely for their appropriated sound values, sometimes for their meaning (a Chinese character pronounced with the Japanese word which meant the same as the Chinese), etc. Reading Japanese and speaking Japanese at the time were, then, very different operations.—Ed.]

[56] The *MYS* uses the word "shōshū" in a context clearly indicative of the absence of any written text: "Lord Imbe Kuromaro dreamt that he composed this love poem and sent it to a friend. Upon waking he found that he could recite it just as he remembered it from his dream" (afternote to *MYS*, 16:3848).

[57] "This year the Crown Prince, on consulting with the Island Minister, decided to compile the *Tennōki*, the *Kokuki*, and the *Hongi*—the last of which tells of the Omi, the Muraji, the Court Miyatsuko and the governing Miyatsuko lords, the one hundred and eighty occupational corporations, and the common people" (*NSK*, 2:159). [The Island Minister, so called by reason of an artificial island constructed in the lake of his estate, was Soga no Umako; Omi, Muraji, and Miyatsuko were court titles for certain offices.—Trans., Ed.]

And in the tenth year of his reign (A.D. 681), Temmu ordered the compilation of the *Teiki (Lives of the Sovereigns)* and of annals that dealt with "various ancient matters."[58] According to this line of thought, the compilation of written histories in the seventh century signified that people no longer bothered with the process of oral transmission. The authority of oral transmission, however, was not automatically invalidated in the gradual course of adopting written records.

The results of research conducted on Micronesian folklore may furnish some useful information in this regard. Prior to the Second World War, research on the folklore of the Micronesian Islands, located between Hawaii and the Philippines, was carried out by a German research agency (Thilenius, 1913-38). In the postwar period, however, American influence brought about rapid modernization. Folk tales came to be serialized in newspapers and magazines, with the result that, by the time William Lessa prepared his collection of folk tales (Lessa, 1961) and Roger Mitchell carried out his research, "ink-stained variants" were on the increase, and the purity of oral transmission had become appreciably marred. Yet the inhabitants of the islands nevertheless were found to value such time-honored practices as the oral delivery of stories by elders of the community.[59] It is hardly unreasonable to suppose that a similar situation existed in seventh-century Yamato. The standard response, even in a society civilized to the point of possessing written records, is to value oral recitation above all. This is supported by the fact that until the eighth century the most typical form of literary reception, even in the case of waka [chiefly court poetry in this context], was auditory.

The practice of hearing works recited as the standard means for receiving important narratives in seventh- and eighth-century Yamato may reflect faith, in archaic and later times, in the kotodama. Although the concept of the kotodama is thought by some not to have emerged before the late seventh or early eighth century (Ōta, 1966, 235), we would nevertheless do well to regard its existence as commencing with the Archaic Age. As mentioned earlier, the fact that the word, "kotodama," does not appear in the Archaic Age is simply explained. The kotodama was so universal a concept in that early age that it need not have been singled out for especial mention. Faith in the kotodama meant that spoken

---

[58] "His Majesty decreed from the great hall of state . . . that a permanent record be made of the lives of the tennō and of various ancient matters as well. Ōshima and Kobito wrote the manuscripts themselves" (*NSK*, 2:357). [Nakatomi Ōshima and Heguri Kobito were high government officials. That they rather than inferiors wrote the documents testifies to the importance of them to the state.—Trans.]

[59] The Micronesian aborigines do not discriminate between myth and legend in their language. Yet young people almost never relate stories classifiable as myths. The reason given is, "They are too important and must be told by the right people." By contrast, telling of local affairs "commemorating outstanding people and events" is open to all (Mitchell, 1972, 40).

language expressed in certain ways would, when pronounced, reach the listener through the medium of breath, and bring about either an auspicious or a calamitous reaction. By the time of Temmu Tennō, a heightened sense of national consciousness led to the belief, apparently, that such reactions also extended to the nation as a whole. The text of the extant *Kojiki*, written for the most part in Chinese, contains occasional passages in the Japanese language, rendered phonetically by means of Chinese characters. These passages serve most frequently to annotate the Chinese text with Japanese readings, but thirty-two instances also indicate the placement of accent marks, as the following case: "The gods then created were named: U-hi-ji-ñi no Kami and next his wife Su-hi-ji-ñi no Kami.[60] (The names of these two deities are to be read phonetically.)"[61] Caution was required to be exercised even in the matter of accentuation, because it was feared that an incorrect pronunciation would lead either to a weakening of the action of the kotodama or to the advent of evil results. Similarly, words expressed in Chinese characters were to be read in Japanese because the kotodama might not function without the use of the Japanese language. The standard manner of reception for the *Kojiki*, then, must have been auditory. In that lies the true nature of the *Kojiki*. In sum, the *Kojiki* is an oral narrative put into writing. It bears no resemblance to a work of history, which relates an account of past facts. A distinction must be made in this respect between the more oral *Kojiki* and the *Nihon Shoki*.[62]

It is commonly acknowledged that, in a society where reading and writing are widespread, a work that is purposely transmitted orally is believed to possess a special value or authority. Of course, narratives not worthy of being written down were also transmitted orally. What kind of narratives, then, were *intentionally* singled out for either oral or written transmission?

Early narrative is commonly divided into myth, legend, and tale.[63] This division is the result of a general application of Bronislaw Malinowski's distinctions among lili'u, lubuwogwo, and kukuanebu in his Trobriand Islands research.[64] It is difficult, however, to classify narratives on the

[60] [In Philippi's transliteration of Old Japanese, these two are represented as U-pidi-ni-nö-kamï and Su-pidi-ni-nö-kamï.—Ed.]

[61] *KJK*, 1:174. One theory has it that the accent marks were not put there by Yasumaro but were added by a later hand (Fujii Nobuo, 1944). I have inclined to this view but so far have been unable to explain why a later scribe would have found it necessary to add accent marks. It is probably best to accept them as the work of Yasumaro.

[62] [The *Chronicles* cover much the same ground. For various reasons, the *Nihon Shoki* was much better known for centuries than the now more highly esteemed *Kojiki*.—Ed.]

[63] [The author's glosses of these English words will be of interest to those who know Japanese: for "myth," shinwa; for "legend," densetsu; and for "tale," minsetsu.—Ed.]

[64] Lili'u are sacred tales substantiating the validity of certain ceremonies and laws. Lubuwogwo are either stories of one's own experience or stories heard from an elder: both

basis of worldwide correspondence, since nationalities vary and cultures differ. Japanese oral narrative contains some works that conform to the tripartite theory and others that do not. It might be appropriately considered collectively as "setsuwa" (folklore).[65] On the other hand, it is true no small amount of Japanese setsuwa—the Creation of Eight Great Islands, the Apparition of the Treasure Sword, the Descent of the Heavenly Grandchild, the Visit to the Sea Palace—has heretofore been subsumed under the generic category of myth. This setsuwa, unlike such tales as "Issun Boshi" (The Thumb-sized Boy) and "Momotarō" (The Peach Boy), was so highly valued that, even in a literate society, the proper treatment was felt to be its intentional preservation as oral narrative. Since it represents, so to speak, weighty oral narrative, it must be distinguished by a special name. I would like to call those stories possessing gods as protagonists and centering on supernatural events deity (jingi) "setsuwa," and to reserve the term "shinwa" (myth) for use in expressing a wider concept. In this sense, deity setsuwa is the representative genre among the weighty narratives, but others, centering on the founding of the realm or a royal succession, might be said to possess a weightiness second only to them.

I have remarked above that thirty percent of the deity setsuwa corpus consists of sections which do not describe the course of events but instead are devoted solely to the enumeration of the names of divinities. These sections, being devoid of plot development, should be strictly distinguished from sections in the narrative mode. Nevertheless, accounts of sixth-century and earlier events frequently contain genealogies written in this format: "Tennō A took as his wife Princess B, and the children born to them were. . . ." This is a clear indication that such genealogical narratives enjoyed an equal status with the factual stories as weighty transmission. Yamato setsuwa does not provide the only instance of genealogical narrative acting as a weighty material. The same is true in other nations, as is seen for example in the Old Testament.

> And Cain knew his wife; and she conceived, and bare Enoch: and he builded a city, and called the name of the city, after the name of his son, Enoch. And unto Enoch was born Irad: and Irad begat Mehujael: and Mehujael begat Methusael: and Methusael begat Lamech. And Lamech took unto him two wives: the name of the one was Adah, and the name of the other Zillah. And Adah bare Jabal: he was the father of such as dwell in tents, and of such as have

---

kinds are held to be true. Kukuanebu are entertaining tales of social interactions and bear no responsibility for veracity (Malinowski, 1926, 30-36).

[65] [Here the author quotes "setsuwa" followed by English "folklore" in parenthesis, using the Japanese term in a special, limited sense.—Ed.]

cattle. And his brother's name was Jubal: he was the father of all such as handle the harp and organ. And Zillah, she also bare Tubalcain, an instructor of every artificer in brass and iron: and the sister of Tubalcain was Naamah ... (Genesis 4:17-22, King James Version).

Sekine Masao regards the biblical genealogies as a literary genre; his interpretation of genealogy as the first workings of the literary spirit among nomadic tribes is very much worth noting (Sekine, 1978, 141-42). One line of thought has it that an uninteresting array of divine and human names was repeated in order to give authority to the royal claim that the sacred sovereign powers of the royal house had remained unbroken throughout history. This is entirely unreasonable. The narration of genealogies instead represents "beautiful language" in societies possessing oral transmissions. Important sections of northern European sagas and Polynesian (New Zealand) folklore also consist of genealogical narrative, perhaps because its manifestation evokes a sense of beauty for the recipient.

As has been said, these "weighty" narratives continued to be transmitted orally even after society became literate, and the process of their transmission is believed to have been deliberate as well as rigorous. Members of illiterate societies have excellent memories, handing down numerous narratives over time periods so extensive as to evoke no less than admiration from the practical viewpoint of a literate society. This was remarked on in ancient Japan: "I have heard that in ancient times, when there was as yet no writing, things were told orally by people high and low, old and young, and they did not forget a single word or deed from the past" (*Kogo Shūi*, 192). The remark is by Imbe Hironari in 807, when literacy had long been established. Yet the actual circumstances of the illiterate period in Japan were surely just as he described them. This view receives strong corroboration from the fact that modern primitives transmit narratives in the manner described by Hironari. For example, among the Maori of Polynesia, one important function of the priests (tofunga) is the preservation of traditions: a priest gathers children in a special building called the whare wananga for rigorous drills, in order to transmit to them genealogies and facts pertaining to past chieftains and family heads. The sole method of instruction is oral. The transmission is conducted with such rigor because, for one, the Maori believe that if the speaker errs in his recitation by one phrase, or even by one word, he will incur the gods' wrath and be visited by death or misfortune. The memorizing of genealogies also proves to have considerable practical value: when a dispute arises over which patriarch shall take the seat of honor or the first portion of food at ceremonial banquets, the deciding factor is to be found in their respective genealogies. Good manners dictate, moreover, that a Maori introduce himself by reciting his genealogy (Ikeda, 1956, 6-12). The drilling to which Maori children are subjected results in their memorizing a quantity of data so large as to seem hardly credible to members of literate societies. One Hawaiian creation legend, for another example, contains a genealogy consisting of the names of six hundred and fifty men and their wives (Beckwith, 1918, 25), and this genealogy is transmitted orally by the storyteller. A further instance is mentioned of a genealogical recitation which spanned the fifty-five generations separating the Creator of the Universe from humanity (Beckwith, 1938, 180-82).

It is unlikely that oral narrative of ancestral lineage and data in third-century Yamato differed in the rigor of its transmission from the circumstances described above. By the fifth century, however, the Yamato state was participating in an exchange of public documents with China. The incidence of exchange was presumably quite small, but in any case such activity confirmed the presence in Yamato of people skilled in expressing intentions through writing. It seems altogether likely that not a few of the literate people took an interest in the weighty oral transmissions of Yamato. Even at this time, as stated above, oral performance was evidently considered the proper means of transmitting weighty narrative, and so its written transmission had probably never taken place. It will be helpful to consider, in this connection, the case of Gaul in the first century B.C. Gaul had no writing system at this time, but the priests (or druids) apparently had a knowledge of the Greek alphabet.[66] Evidence is provided by Julius Caesar, who refers to a note, written in Greek letters, that was sent from the Helvetian encampment. The druids also served as the transmitters of Helvetian narrative, as is seen in this excerpt from the *Gallic Wars* (6:14):

> The druids . . . are said to learn many verses thoroughly there. Thus not a few remain in training for about twenty years. Nor do they think it right to commit these teachings to writing, though for other matters, as in public and private accountings, they use Greek letters. They appear to me to have instituted this for two reasons: they do not wish to have their teachings spread among the common people, nor do they want those who learn to pay too little heed to memory, if they were to rely on writing. And this happens often to many, that through reliance on written records, they slacken their diligence in gaining proficiency and neglect to train their powers of memory.

[66] The Gallic language was written with the Greek alphabet according to Caesar (*The Gallic Wars*, 1:29). This corresponds to the early Japanese practice of using Chinese characters to record the Japanese language. [See n. 55, above.—Ed.]

This also applied to those Yamato intellectuals who possessed the skill of utilizing Chinese characters to record public and private matters. They undoubtedly felt that the more faithful stance to take in transmitting valued narratives was to leave them unwritten.

This awareness is thought to have preserved important narratives within the oral tradition. Once people grew more accustomed to writing, however, their powers of memorizing inevitably declined, despite their awareness that narratives were properly transmitted only by oral means. It was at this point that there appeared people whose function was to transmit by memory matters of importance to the local societies and clans. Before long these people occupied the status of principal practitioners of the art, and came to be known as kataribe, or reciters. This profession is mentioned, probably for the first time, in the record of the twelfth year of Temmu's reign (A.D. 683). On the second day of the Ninth Month, thirty-eight families, up to then members of the miyatsuko court office, were moved into the higher office of muraji, and among them was the "storyteller miyatsuko" (katarai miyatsuko; *NSK*, 2:369). The term "kataribe" does not appear in the passage, but the storytelling "miyatsuko-muraji" is thought to have administered the kataribe. The next earliest reference to the kataribe is found in the *Census Register for the Village of Harube, County of Mihachima, Province of Mino* for the year 702. Under the heading "Family of Inemaro, Senior Official, Kuni courtier" is the entry: "Wife of householder: Yoshime, kataribe. Age forty-one. Principal wife."[67] From the mid-eighth century on, references to the kataribe appear increasingly in the records: several are found, for example, in the *Register of Names for the Great Tax Reduction, Province of Izumo* for the year Tempyō 11 (A.D. 739), or the *Register of Tax Collection, County of Hamana, Province of Tōtōmi* for the year Tempyō 12 (A.D. 740). Kataribe seem to have been particularly numerous in Izumo, which possessed twenty-eight people so named; some have titles like Kataribe no Obito or Kataribe no Kimi, while others are listed simply as kataribe.[68] The term "storyteller of the omi office" also appears in the *Izumo Fudoki (Izumo Topography)*.[69] The kataribe remained in existence into the ninth century and beyond. In chapter seven of the *Engi Shiki*, entitled "The Ceremony of Great Thanksgiving Following the Accession to the Throne,"

[67] *Dai Nihon Komonjo*, 1:5.

[68] "Householder: Kataribe, Obito, Tamaku; family: Kataribe, Obito, Tatsumaro, age 32" (ibid., 2:207). "Householder: Head of the kataribe, Tamaku; family: Kataribe, Sakatsume, age 65" (ibid., 204). "Same (householder): Kataribe, Sarume, age 79" (ibid., 234). The given name in the last example is evidently a conversion into a proper noun of the term "sarume" (*Kogo Shūi*, 197-98), used to designate women who played instruments and danced at court religious ceremonies.

[69] "A daughter of Lord Imaro, Storyteller [katarai no omi], wandered off to this cape, encountered a blue shark, and was killed, so never returning" (*Izumo Fudoki*, 104).

a passage indicates that members of the kataribe were summoned from every part of the country to recite ancient passages from oral narratives before the newly accessed Daigo Tennō: "Kataribe: eight from Mino, two from Tamba, two from Tango, seven from Tajima, three from Inaba, four from Izumo, two from Awaji" (*Engi Shiki*, 151).[70]

From this we ascertain that the kataribe survived to this later time. After the late ninth century, when Japanese society became highly literate, it is difficult to believe that much substantial oral transmission was carried out. By then it was probably limited to the ceremonial recitation of certain texts. This, one might say, was the inevitable fate of the kataribe. Their very origin rested in their specialization in the art of transmission, which was in turn nothing less than the introduction of refinements into the process of oral composition. Whereas the creation and transmission of narrative had originally been a single action, the kataribe manifested themselves as the transmitters of narratives they had not created. Thus nothing but decline was in store for oral transmitters unsupported by living works.[71]

The art of keeping written records made considerable progress in Yamato between the seventh and eighth centuries, although kana, the phonetic syllabary, had not yet been invented. Japanese narratives were not always easily put into writing, when "writing" consisted only of Chinese characters. Paper and writing supplies, moreover, were expensive. It follows that writing and reading were probably limited to those texts deemed of great value. We may assume that "light" stories, those recounted for pleasure, also existed in the Archaic Age. For example, Jitō Tennō, in an uta filled with wordplay, appealed to Shii, an elderly court lady, to recite her stories more often:

Ina to iedo	I used to say, "No, thank you,"
Shiuru Shii no ga	But still Shii insisted on
Shiigatari	Reciting stories willy-nilly—
Kono koro kikazute	Yet, not having heard them lately,
Are koinikeri.	I find I rather miss them![72]

(*MYS*, 3:236)

[70] [The *Engi Shiki* is a compendium of seasonal court ceremonies, official ceremonies, and court etiquette for special occasions. It was partially compiled and presented to Daigo in 927 but completed only in 967.—Trans., Ed.]

[71] According to an account of recitations at court by Fujiwara Kintō (966-1041) in his *Hokuzanshō*, by about the tenth century kataribe were referring to written texts when dealing with older language (Inoue Tatsuo, 1979, 17-18). The strength of memorized recitation seems to have been reaching its end.

[72] According to the *Shinsen Seishi Roku*, there was a Lady Abe Shii and a Lady Nakatomi Shii. They were probably of the same household. It appears that neither was a member of

Lady Shii replied with a courteous riposte:

Ina to iedo	I used to say, "No, thank you,"
Katare katare to	But Her Majesty was pleased to say,
Norase koso	"Recite for me, recite!"
Shii iwamōse	*Then* it was that Shii spoke—
Shiigatari to noru.	Willy-nilly, was that, ma'am?

(*MYS*, 3:237)

This exchange indicates that certain narratives, those composed to while away tedious hours, were recited for the tennō's pleasure, and that these stories seem to have been of sufficient interest for her to order them performed repeatedly: "Recite for me, recite!" This kind of light narrative is thought likely also to have existed in the Archaic Age. Unlike the weighty variety, however, light narratives were not bolstered by a popular feeling of responsibility toward their transmission. Thus they did not become objects of transmission by the kataribe and so eventually disappeared.

Old, Middle, and New Strata

I have postulated (with others) that early narrative is usually ordered chronologically into myth, the earliest manifestation, followed by legend and then by the folk tale. As this division is not always an apposite one, I have decided to group the three categories together as setsuwa. On the other hand, there are indeed many kinds of setsuwa, and it is necessary that appropriate names be given them. If we may agree that "weighty" setsuwa refers to that portion thought to have great significance for a people, and which has been carefully transmitted, and that "light" setsuwa represents that portion which is treated rather less conscientiously, then it is reasonable to conclude that the latter is less easily transmitted than the former. The light will be dealt with haphazardly and without regularity. Moreover, because its content is easily altered, it is difficult to consider the light in terms of old and new strata. The question of old and new strata is, then, limited to weighty setsuwa. Deity setsuwa, defined above, together with narratives about the founding of the realm and the royal succession, therefore comprise the weighty setsuwa of the Yamato state. Since the protagonists of the latter group are members of the royal family, I shall call this group "royal-family setsuwa." During the Archaic

---

the kataribe, and therefore it also seems unsafe to assume that they were descended from the kataribe. The obvious view to take is that old Shii's recitation was not of the weighty kind entrusted to the kataribe.

Age, the only weighty Yamato narratives were those that appeared in deity and royal-family setsuwa.

STORIES OF THE GODS

This category of story will be seen to have, in addition to an old and a new stratum, a middle stratum as well. As I have said, however, the terms "old" and "new" cannot be applied without discriminating among the extant texts. Let us consider, as a representative example of the old stratum, the creation narratives. The narratives of the creation, as they appear in the *Kojiki* and the *Nihon Shoki*, develop chiefly through genealogies of gods. These are divided into three main groups: the lines of Ame no Minakanushi, of Umashi Ashikabi Hikoji, and of Kuni no Tokotachi. Of these, the line which includes the three gods Ame no Minakanushi, Takami Musui, and Kamu Musui differs essentially from the other two lines, in that its members personify an ideal creative force. Opinion is virtually unanimous in proposing that this line therefore represents part of a later extension.[73] As for the remaining two, Kuni no Tokotachi's line, including either twelve (*KJK*) or thirteen (*NSK*) deities, is held by some to be the original divine line (Matsumura, 1955a, 42-48), whereas others claim that the line descended from Umashi Ashikabi Hikoji and Ame no Tokotachi is the oldest of all (Ōbayashi, 1961, 44). Neither assertion is easily proved. Both, however, are in agreement on one point: that these two lines are more ancient than that of Ame no Minakanushi.

It should be emphasized that what is being judged old or new is the ultimate source of the three lines, not the corresponding narrative versions found today in the *Chronicles*. For example, the *Kojiki* description of Kuni no Tokotachi's line is a simple listing of gods' names:

> The gods who then came into being were named Kuni no Tokotachi no Kami, then Toyokumono no Kami. These two gods also came into being as bachelor deities, and they concealed their bodies. The gods who then came into being were named Uijini no Kami, then his wife Suijini no Kami, then Tsunokui no Kami, then his wife Ikukui no Kami, then Ōtonoji no Kami, then his wife Ōtonobe no Kami, then Omodaru no Kami, then his wife Ayakashikone no Kami, then Izanagi no Kami, then his wife Izanami no Kami (*KJK*, 1:173-74).[74]

[73] In 1899 Takahashi Tatsuo indicated that these "three Creator gods" possess the characteristics of heaven- and earth-creating deities (cited in Takagi Toshio, 1925, 1:6). Their unacceptability as early deities has been discussed by Matsumura Takeo (1955a, 35-37) and Ōbayashi Taryō (1961, 47-48), among others.

[74] Textual interlineations, which will be taken up subsequently, have been omitted here.

This narrative method does not differ in the least in the *Kojiki* recitals of Ame no Minakanushi's or Umashi Ashikabi Hikoji's lines: the question of which narrative is old and which new is beside the point.

The Kuni no Tokotachi line is considered old because in it the gradual process of the shaping of the world is suggested by the names of the deities. The form of the story—in which bachelor gods first appear, then married ones are created, and finally, through the marriage of the male Izanagi and the female Izanami, all things come to be created—has much in common with the stories transmitted throughout southern, northern, and eastern Polynesia. A creation setsuwa pattern—describing the very beginning as chaos, from which emerge bachelor divinities, followed by married ones through whom all things are created—passed from central Asia through southern China and spread as far as Polynesia. The legends that most closely resemble Kuni no Tokotachi's genealogy are found in New Zealand, the Society Islands, and the Marquesas in Polynesia (Ōbayashi, 1961, 32). The genealogy which begins with Umashi Ashikabi Hikoji and Ame no Tokotachi is seen as having been created from "something that grew upward" like an ashikabi, that is, like a sprouting reed (*KJK*, 1:173-74). A tradition holding that the land and humankind were created from the earliest plants was widespread from Southeast Asia to Polynesia and Micronesia, and it has been estimated to date back to an ancient culture of early Australoid, plant-cultivating people (Ōbayashi, 1961, 33-37). This is not to say, however, that the Umashi Ashikabi Hikoji line is older than Kuni no Tokotachi's but rather that the legend that is the ultimate source of the former is older than the legend that is the ultimate source of the latter. This matter pertains to the transmission of culture in prehistoric central Asia and Southeast Asia, and poses a problem of so little relevance to Yamato literature that it need not concern Japanese literary history.

The legend that serves as the ultimate source for Ame no Minakanushi's line shares certain characteristics with the tradition of a sky-dwelling Creator known as Tangaloa in Polynesia (Samoa, the Society Islands) and as Tangandawa in Indonesia (Celebes Island). On the other hand, Tengri (or Tangri, Tängära, Tangara, Tagara), a deity worshipped by central Asian nomads whose language belongs to the Altaic family, resembles Ame no Minakanushi more closely in that he is a supreme deity, residing in heaven, and accompanied by subordinate gods. The cult of Tengri is thought to have been introduced into Japan by way of Korea, reaching Polynesia via Indonesia and East Asia (Ōbayashi, 1961, 39-43). These facts do not signify, however, that Ame no Minakanushi's line is part of a later composition. They ought instead to be seen as a reason why the Tengri form of god evolved in Polynesia within a relatively new cultural stratum. In prehistoric Southeast Asia, moreover, various forms of creation stories were already intermingled to some extent. It is difficult to imagine that this intermingling took place in Yamato.

In the creation stories of Sumatra (Nias Island), for example, the following appears: an unmarried goddess, Ina-da Samihara Luwo, born from Chaos, creates the world; the stones of that world split, giving birth to the unmarried goddess Ina-da Samadulo Höse. She gives birth to two pairs of twins, two boys and two girls. The younger son, Lowalangi, rules Heaven, and the elder son, Lautra, rules the underworld. Lowalangi marries Lautra's twin sister, and they become the ancestors of humanity.[75] These motifs correspond extremely well to those in the Kuni no Tokotachi line. In addition to the fundamental motifs, there is an episode that tells of the birth of the first child of Lowalangi and the twin sister of Lautra: the baby's body is smooth and flat like a mollusk's, without arms or legs. The same motif appears in Yamato creation setsuwa, in which the first child born to Izanagi and Izanami is the leech-child. A further episode in the Sumatran folklore tells of the discord that developed between Lowalangi and Lautra, and how Lowalangi threw stones down to earth for nine days. Although considerable variation appears here, the motif of dissension among siblings, leading to violent behavior, applies in this respect to the stories of Amaterasu and her younger brother Susanoo. We may suppose, from these examples, that not only the creation story but a complex of motifs, comprising the birth of the islands by Izanagi and Izanami and the episodes involving Amaterasu, already existed in Indonesia, and that these manifold motifs were evidently introduced into Yamato. The evolution of such motif complexes is a problem for scholars of comparative myth, and cannot be addressed by Japanese literary history.

Yamato creation setsuwa, not their ultimate source, is the appropriate subject of Japanese literary history. This does not mean we should exclude from consideration all studies of ultimate sources, since such investigations provide rather effective supplementary data pertaining to the nature of the setsuwa that were shaped within Yamato. As we saw earlier, deity setsuwa in the *Chronicles* are told in the form of an enumeration of the

---

[75] "In the beginning there was no earth and no world, but Chaos unnamed and unseen. Then this Chaos split and Ina-da Samihara Luwo was born. This goddess caused the world to be created. Then the stones split, and the goddess, the Ancient Mother of all races and gods, arose: Ina-da Samadulo Höse. Although not married, this last named goddess begot four children, two pairs of twins which were born at the same time and married one another. The [younger] son was named Lowalangi and ruled the skies, while the [elder], Lautra, ruled the underworld. Strife arose between these two and Lowalangi threw stones down [upon] the earth for nine days. Lowalangi married a second time, this time the twin sister of his [elder] brother, and this pair became the ancestors of the human race. The second wife gave birth to a child [who] was entirely round, without hands or feet. When the child was [divided] in half, one half was female and the other half male. This couple married and give birth to Hulu, the first person on earth" (Loeb, 1935, 150-51).

names of divinities. Each name is introduced not simply as one part of a genealogy: every one of them suggests the existence of a story deduced, as it were, from the name. Southeast and East Asian transmissions provide supplementary data which are useful in surmising, fairly accurately, the essence of such stories. The names of the gods that appear in the creation folklore of the *Chronicles* have, in this connection, been pointed out by Matsumoto Nobuhiro as "metaphorical expressions of the creation of the universe" (Matsumoto, 1931, 164). It was Ōno Susumu, however, who further systematized Matsumoto's findings by means of a detailed theory. According to Ōno's thesis, Ame no Minakanushi represents centrality, and Takami Musui and Kamu Musui both represent productivity, and as speculative and contemplative divinities they constitute one group. Umashi Ashikabi Hikoji stands for the manifestation of tangible life, and the deity Ame no Tokotachi's name signifies "foundation" (toko) and "standing" (tachi, a manifestation from below to that which is above). In addition, Ōno proposes that a phrase which precedes the appearance of these last two in the texts of the *Chronicles*, "when the islands were like floating oil, drifting like jellyfish," be treated as a god's name, because it is an important concept expressing primeval fluctuation and chaos. These three entities, according to Ōno, form a second group. Furthermore, Ōno divides into two groups the gods who thitherto belonged to Kuni no Tokotachi's line: Toyokumono, "spreading clouds," represents chaos and fluctuation; both "iji" and "ni" in the names Uijini and Suijini signify muddiness, and reflect the fact that they are embodiments of chaos and fluctuation; the configuration of the name Tsunokui, meaning Horn Post, suggests a symbol of growth; and Ikukui, Life Post, is seen as the life force. Further, the *to* of Ōtonoji and Ōtonobe, signifying "gate" (a narrow passage), represents the genitals: the suffixes "ji" (man) and "be" (woman) are then added. The four gods beginning with Omodaru are seen to stand for conversation and enticing behavior between men and women.

A summary of what has been said will be useful.[76]

Group A

1. Ame no Minakanushi (Centrality) [*minaka* = center]
2. Takami Musui (Productivity) [*taka* = (decorative prefix); *musu* = to create; *i* = supernatural power]
3. Kamu Musui (Productivity) [*kamu* = (decorative prefix)]

[76] This is based on the table included in Ōno's discussion (Ōno, 1965, 116), but it is not an exact reproduction. I have taken the indispensable nucleus of his chart and added to it salient details of his theory.

Group B

4. "... like floating oil, drifting ... (Chaos and Fluctuation, treated as a god's name)
5. Umashi Ashikabi Hikoji (Tangible Life) [*ashikabi* = reed shoots, *hikoji* ← *kohiji* = (mud)?]
6. Ame no Tokotachi (Advent of the Foundation) [*toko* = floor; *tatsu* = manifestation of what is above]

Group C

7. Kuni no Tokotachi (Advent of the Foundation)
8. Toyokumono (Chaos and Fluctuation) [*toyo* = (decorative prefix); *kumono* = spreading of clouds]
9. Uijini, Suijini (Muddiness) [*u* = (prefix); *su* = (prefix); iji = ni = mud]
10. Tsunokui, Ikukui (Tangible Life) [*tsuno* = horn = growth; *iku* = manifestation of life; and *kui* = post = growth]

Group D

11. Ōtonoji, Ōtonobe (differentiation of the sexes) [*to* = genitals; *ji* = man; *be* = *me* = woman]
12. Omodaru, Ayakashikone (Conversation) [*omo* = face; *taru* = sufficiency; *aya* = aya (interjection); *kashiko* = obligation; *ne* = (suffix)]
13. Izanagi, Izanami (Enticing Behavior) [*iza* = well now; *na* = *no* = (possessive particle); *gi* = *ki* = man; *mi* = woman]

Ōno's theory resembles Matsumoto's insofar as Ōno considers that the names of the divinities found in his Group B, that is, in what has heretofore been known as the Umashi Ashikabi Hikoji line, and in his Group C, or the first half of Kuni no Tokotachi's line, represent the process by which a foundation takes shape from out of the primeval chaos and fluctuation, and tangible life comes to manifest itself there. Ōno has corroborated this from a linguistic standpoint. What demands notice, though, is that Ōno has put the six deities beginning with Ōtonoji into a separate group, D.

Although paired divinities are found in the first half of Kuni no Tokotachi's line (the two groups of Uijini and Suijini, and Tsunokui and Ikukui), there is no indication of distinctions between male and female. By contrast, in the second half of the line the names Ōtonoji and Ōtonobe contain elements signifying "man" and "woman," and Omodaru, Ayakashikone, Izanagi, and Izanami clearly seem more human, to the degree that they are married, and by comparison with the previous stage of creation formed from Chaos. What is more worthy of note, however, is the fact that the gods' names beginning with Omodaru are based on human behavior. Omodaru, Sufficient Face, signifies regular features, and the name Ayakashikone is made up of "aya," an interjection, and "kashiko," signifying shame or embarrassment, to which is added the suffix "ne," denoting woman. These names are believed to have come into being from a scene much like the following. The god says, "Your face is flawless," to which the goddess replies, "Oh, you're very kind!" Again, the "iza" of Izanagi and Izanami is an invitational interjection, and the syllables "gi" (= "ki") and "mi" in their names correspond to the "ki" of okina (old man) and the "mi" of omina (old woman) respectively. To these has been added the possessive particle "na" (synonymous with "no"). If "iza" is understood to mean an invitation or enticement, it will accord very well with a later episode in which Izanagi and Izanami, in the course of talking together, beget the various countries (Ōno, 1965, 118-19).[77]

We cannot be sure whether the basing of gods' names on setsuwa episodes implies that the setsuwa corresponding to these names existed prior to the formation of the names. We might assume, as one possibility, that though such stories might not have existed as oral narrative, content corresponding to it took shape in the imagination and that these so-to-speak unrelated setsuwa were then transformed into the names of the divinities. The practice of giving names which are not mere signs, but which serve instead to display individual qualities, is also found among modern primitives. In the Mentawai Islands of Sumatra, for instance, people are given names like the following (Loeb, 1935, 189).

Si Ngena-katiri: He who waits on the upper river
Si Telu-malainge: He who is three times beautiful
Si Manjang: An eagle
Si Itjo-tubunia: She who looks at her own body
Si ta-anai-si-ake-nia: She who has no one to give anything
Si Ogo: The flower

[77] The following readings, among others, are found in Suzuki Shigetane's *Nihon Shoki Den (Commentary on the Nihon Shoki)*, vols. 1-3. (1) "Toko" signifies "floor," on which all things came to rest and lived; (2) "kumo" signifies "a gathering of air"; (3) "uijini" refers to the period when the earth was water and mud; (4) "tsunokui" refers to the vigorous sprouting of plants; (5) "chi" signifies the male, and "be" the female, genitals; (6) "omodaru" refers to the regularity of a god's features; and (7) "iza" is a word of invitation between man and woman. This is evidently the basis for Ōno's theory; the originality of his theory, however, resides in the substantiation, through linguistic findings, of Shigetane's readings, and in his reinterpretation of "kashikone" as a goddess's modest reply, as opposed to Shigetane's reading, which held: "She is called Kashikone because she has regular features; she is respected for her majestic beauty. Her name also means the firming (kashiko) of the land's root (ne)" (*Kiden*, 1:204).

Because these are the names of individuals, it is difficult to imagine that each name has its own story recounting its source. Why, we may ask, is a boy named "He who waits on the upper river," and why is a girl named "She who has no one to give anything" appropriate? Evidently an understanding existed between the givers of the name and those who heard it. In the case of gods' names, why is a god called "Your face is flawless," and why is a goddess called "Oh, you're very kind"? Explanations were probably once called for, and so related setsuwa may have accompanied the names in some cases.

The problem does not lie, however, in whether unrelated or related setsuwa form the background for god's names, but rather in the fact that these names are of an extremely temporary nature: they do not possess that permanence which would enable them to be used in all kinds of situations. If the name of the man "He who waits on the upper river" or of the god "Your face is flawless" were introduced into a situation in which the reasons behind the names were not common knowledge, the hearers of these names would not consider them names at all. Such names are given to those gods whom Hermann Usener calls "momentary deities" (Augenblickgötter).[78] When a person, at a certain time and place, momentarily experienced the divine through received impressions, the phenomenon before the eyes became immediately divine in itself, before other phenomena could intervene. The divinity came to be called by the name of the perceived phenomenon. As their intellectual sophistication rose somewhat, people recognized the common features among single, unrelated phenomena, and came to grasp them in terms of "likenesses." At this level, each god in its own specific category or sphere possessed a permanence in individualized right. Usener calls such gods "specialized deities" (Sondergötter; 1896, 280). Although both Ame no Tokotachi and Kuni no Tokotachi are endowed with the characteristic of floor-rising (tokotachi) or the appearance of the earth foundation, a difference exists in the first parts of their names, which signify respectively heaven (ame) and earth (or land, kuni). They will therefore do as examples of specialized deities. More apposite examples, however, are the deities created in somewhat later episodes: the sea god Ōwatatsumi, the river god Hayaakitsuhiko, the mountain god Ōyamatsumi, the field goddess Kayanohime, the fire god Hinoyagihayao, and the wind god Shinatsuhiko, among others (*KJK*, 1:185-86).

When, however, these special qualities are by chance isolated from

[78] Although Usener's theory appeared in the late nineteenth century, Ernst Cassirer recognized its worth and, as a result of his frequent citations of Usener's work, led to its being accepted by modern scholars.

their original circumstances, then that faculty within each name which designates the individual divinity is strengthened. Each name then possesses a personal character, and becomes a proper noun. A god called by such a name is autonomous, capable of acting from its own independent standpoint within a range of diverse categories and domains, pursuing given conduct in the same manner as a human being. These gods, who act without restrictions, are called "personalized deities" (personliche Götter) by Usener (1896, 301-30). Izanagi and Izanami provide a striking illustration of the ideal personalized divinities. To judge from their names, these two probably came into being as "momentary deities." But in the episodes from the Birth of the Islands to Izanagi's journey to the Land of the Dead, they are the subjects of a narrative in which they, like human beings, procreate, become injured and ill, sad, angry, and joyous. They become "personalized deities," possessing, one might say, a physical presence of their own. By contrast, Ame no Minakanushi and the other two creation gods do not have this physical presence. Although they display the special qualities of centrality or productive power, their activities are concerned with a conceptual event, the creation of the universe. To that extent they can be thought gods situated midway between the "specialized deities" and the "personalized deities." As Ernst Cassirer has indicated, creation gods frequently are described as giving form to the gods and the world according to a pattern in which individual things are produced (1925a, 247-48). Even in Amaterasu's case, her identity as a "specialized deity" who rules the domain of Heaven as the Sun Goddess is combined with another facet, that of the "personalized deity," when, in response to Susanoo's behavior, she interrogates him, exchanges oaths with him, and is roused in turn to sympathy, anger, and suspicion by him.

The metamorphosis from instantaneous or specialized to personalized deity may not be easily accomplished, however. This is because of the interventions, between these states, of the phenomenon known as polyonymy (Vielnamigkeit). According to Cassirer, the various attributes integrated within a personalized deity are revealed through aliases as well as through the deity's true name. The Egyptian goddess Isis, for example, is called "myrionyma" (the ten-thousand-named), and the power of Allah is expressed as "one-hundred-named" in the Koran. American aborigines, particularly those of Mexico, worship gods bearing many aliases (Cassirer, 1925b [English version], 281). The same is the case for gods in the *Chronicles*. While Sarudabiko is fishing in the sea at Azaka, his hand becomes caught in a hirabu shell, and he is drowned. When he sinks to the ocean floor, his name is "Bottom-Reaching Spirit"; when bubbles float up to the surface, his name is "Bubble-Making Spirit"; when the bubbles burst, his name is "Bubble-Bursting Spirit" (*KJK*, 1:274). These names indicate his nature as an instantaneous deity. Again, Ōkuninushi's aliases are of six kinds: Ōnamuji, Strong Man of the Reed Plains, Eight Thousand Halberds, Soul of This Very Land, Great Soul of the Land, Possessor of Plenty.[79] Since these aliases are used each in accordance with a particular situation, they are thought to have been given to Ōkuninushi in his role as specialized deity. Ōkuninushi, or Great Lord of the Land, was probably used for his true name because the greatest importance was attached to his character as the principal deity and ruler of the Land of Izumo. When this characteristic alone is especially prominent, his nature as a personalized god is strengthened.

Seen in this fashion, the creation setsuwa, centering chiefly on genealogical records of divine names, are regarded as belonging to the old stratum within the deity setsuwa found in the *Chronicles*. The appearance of no small number of names denoting instantaneous deities evidently indicates that the creation setsuwa date from a period in which the Yamato people did not find these very primitive instantaneous deities unnatural. Furthermore, narrative consisting chiefly of the enumeration of divine names instead of an exposition of events is undoubtedly the product of an era in which the mere mention of a god's name—in the case of instantaneous or specialized deities—was enough to generate a response equal to or approximating that obtained by providing a detailed explanation. This phenomenon is discussed by Cassirer as a "pars pro toto" principle (1925a, 64-65). When divine names existed as living entities, the hearer of the part, i.e., a god's name, immediately and with a magical sensation grasped the significance of the whole divinity. Not only did the part (the name) represent the whole; it was itself the whole. Such facts are highly significant as indicators of the origin of the symbol, which later becomes a basic literary technique. We must therefore take, as an important idea, Ōno's thesis, which examines the names Omodaru and Ayakashikone and imagines that behind them is the conversation "Your face is flawless," "Oh, you're very kind!" and which treats the circumstantial narration "when the islands were like floating oil, drifting like jellyfish" as the equivalent of a divine name.

If we regard as a member of the old stratum that section which centers chiefly on genealogical records of divine names, then an attenuated portion of that section may be considered to be of the new stratum. In the

[79] [The meaning of "Ōnamuji" is uncertain; Philippi speculates "Great Revered One" (p. 546). "Eight Thousand Halberds" (Yachihoko) means one who owns many weapons.—Trans., Ed.]

time when divine names existed as living entities, the act of reciting a god's name signified the summoning of all the power inherent in that divinity, who, when its name was recited, appeared before the supplicant's very eyes (Cassirer, 1925b). In a later age, however, after this sense of immediacy had receded, people realized that they could not expect a god to respond to the point of perceived actions simply through hearing its name pronounced. Supplements, consisting of fairly substantial expositions, therefore became necessary. These supplements form the new stratum. A representative section that belongs to the new stratum might be the story of Hōri's journey to the Sea God's palace (*JDK*, 258-59). Having lost some implement, the protagonist is pressed to return it; he goes to another world, and there he finds it. The transmission of this motif is widespread, from both sides of the North Pacific to the continents and islands of the South Pacific. The legend that comes closest to the story of Hōri, however, is found in the Indonesian islands of Palau, Kei, and Celebes (Minahassa; Matsumoto, 1931, 55-61).[80] A further motif, called the Forbidden Chamber motif, is added to the story of Hōri, however. This motif presents the following pattern (Matsumura, 1955, 764).

1. A man with supernatural properties marries a woman.
2. The marriage takes place on the condition that the husband will not look into his wife's private chamber.
3. Within the forbidden chamber, the wife changes into an animal.
4. Because the husband has transgressed the interdiction, the wife leaves him.

When the story of Hōri is so interpreted, we can only incline to Matsumoto's theory, namely, that the story represents a legend from the area of Indonesia taken to Yamato, probably by way of the Hayato and Ama tribes, and also that the Forbidden Chamber motif was then linked to it (ibid., 689-99.) The problem, however, does not rest in the age of the story's ultimate source, but rather in the relative oldness and newness of the periods in which the Hōri setsuwa now found in the *Chronicles* came into existence.

On reading the Hōri story, one is immediately struck by its extremely orderly structure. Indeed, it is so well ordered that few changes would be required to adapt it from its original form for purposes of presentation, say, on the kabuki stage. The story, moreover, contains the equivalent of the double-plot technique, in which the main story is synthesized with

---

[80] A detailed introduction to the legends of Palau and Minahassa is found in Mishina, 1970, 237-39.

various subplots. If Kawatake Mokuami and his circle had known of this, they might well have slapped their knees with delight at this fountainhead of dramaturgy.[81] In short, the Hōri setsuwa is a synthesis of two motifs: (A) the discovery in a strange land of lost fishing gear; and (B) the collapse of a marriage to a woman from the strange land when the man violates a prohibition. The setsuwa is not simply a combination of the two motifs, however. Its structure is complicated by the inclusion of Motif B within Motif A, and the intertwining of motifs advances the plot of the whole. It is the god Shiotsuchi or Salthammer who holds the key to the structure. As Hōri, griefstricken over the loss of his older brother Hoderi's fishhook, sits on the beach, Salthammer appears and directs him to perform two acts: (1) to go to the palace of the Sea God, and (2) to enlist the aid of the Sea God's daughter. All the events that follow use these suggestions as the momentum for the story to progress.

The direct source or cause of the incident described as Motif A is the loss of the borrowed fishhook. And the result or effect in response to that source is the return of the fishhook. The restoration of the fishhook, however, is realized through the Sea God's efforts on Hōri's behalf, efforts that are due, quite simply, to the counsel he receives from the god Salthammer. The god's advice that Hōri go to the Sea God's palace can be considered an indirect source or connection in that a good result proceeds from it. On the other hand, the suggestion that Hōri enlist the aid of the Sea God's daughter is also an indirect connection, in that it sets in motion the process whereby he obtains the Sea God's cooperation, and at the same time it brings about the marriage with the daughter. Their ensuing marriage then becomes an indirect cause of the catastrophe brought about by Hōri's peeping into the forbidden chamber (effect), thus giving rise to Motif B. The story does not end with the catastrophe, however. The Sea God's daughter, Princess Toyotama, entrusts the child born between her and Hōri to her younger sister, Princess Tamayori, who is left behind on land to act as its nurse. And Toyotama also exchanges uta with Hōri, so their mutual affection does not cease. If we now put this cause-connection-effect relationship into the structure of a kabuki play, it will look like the following diagram.[82]

[81] [Kawatake Mokuami (1816-93) was an innovative Edo kabuki playwright.—Trans.]

[82] This analysis concerns the *KJK* version. Variant versions of Hōri's journey to the Sea God's palace appear as well in the main text of *NSK* and in its variant versions (1-4). Comparision of these with the *KJK* version reveals that all share a compact structure. Because such structural characteristics are believed to date from the time when kataribe became deliberate in refining scripts for performance, it may be appropriate to consider the formation date of the Hōri story a period as late as the seventh century.

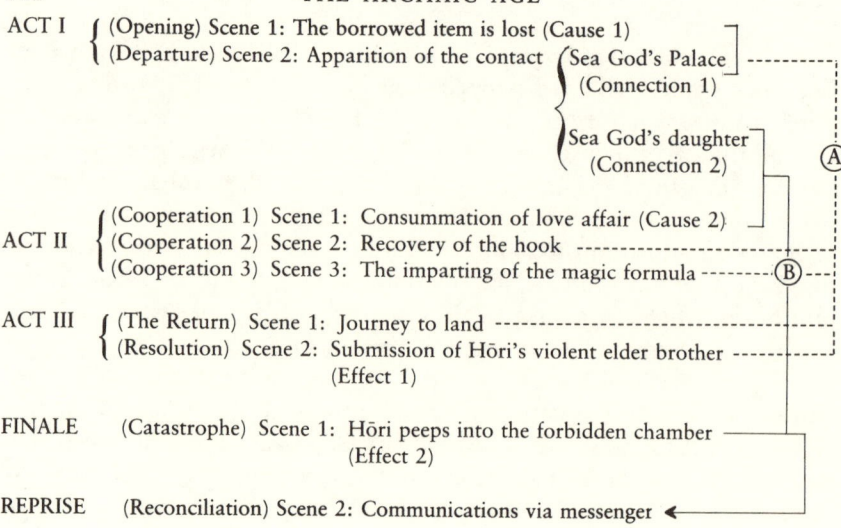

ACT I   { (Opening) Scene 1: The borrowed item is lost (Cause 1)
         (Departure) Scene 2: Apparition of the contact (Sea God's Palace (Connection 1)
                     Sea God's daughter (Connection 2)   (A)

ACT II   { (Cooperation 1) Scene 1: Consummation of love affair (Cause 2)
         (Cooperation 2) Scene 2: Recovery of the hook
         (Cooperation 3) Scene 3: The imparting of the magic formula (B)

ACT III   { (The Return) Scene 1: Journey to land
         (Resolution) Scene 2: Submission of Hōri's violent elder brother
                 (Effect 1)

FINALE   (Catastrophe) Scene 1: Hōri peeps into the forbidden chamber
                   (Effect 2)

REPRISE   (Reconciliation) Scene 2: Communications via messenger ◄

The outline indicates how Cause 1, Connection 1, and Effect 1 in Motif A, and Connection 2, Cause 2, and Effect 2 in Motif B, are skillfully bound together by Act I, Scene 2, in which the god Salthammer appears. Fairly skilled techniques are revealed in this kind of structure. In comparison to the creation episodes, which progress only by means of the enumeration of divine names and the straight narration of successive acts performed by the gods, the newness of the Hōri legend is clearly discernible. Several further points also indicate that this setsuwa belongs to a new stratum.

One is the intrusion of real time. According to Cassirer, stories of gods are founded solely on an individual, isolated matter, and they differ in nature from real time as a physical quantity common to and applicable to all other matters (1925a, 131). By contrast, frequent reference is made to real time in the Hōri setsuwa. For example (*JDK*, 287-89):

And so he lived in that land for three years.

"Though he has lived here for three years, he has never once sighed, and yet last night he gave out one great sigh. What might be the reason?"

"If you do as I have said, your brother will surely become impoverished within three years, because I rule the water."

... among those who estimated a time, one shark seven feet long said, "I can take him there in a day and return the same day."

And so, as he promised, the shark took Hōri to land within the space of one day.

And so Hikohohodemi lived in the palace of Takachiho for five hundred and eighty years.

The "three years" quoted above reflect common experience—three years is the limit of an ordinary man's patience, perhaps, or three years is the estimated time necessary to become poor. They are, then, manifestations of real time, judged according to criteria in common with other natural situations. Again, five hundred and eighty years represent an unrealistically long lifespan. The unit "year," however, is a means of calendrical counting, and is thus real time, held in common with and capable of application by us ordinary mortals. This kind of real time is never found in passages thought to belong to the old stratum.

Another trait characteristic of the new stratum is the fact that genealogies of divinities are all but nonexistent. Throughout the entire Hōri setsuwa, genealogies of the numerous gods encountered so frequently in the creation episodes (among others) disappear entirely from the main story sections. Only after all the events have been settled is a small genealogy appended to the final section (*JDK*, 298). This, presumably, is directly connected to the fact that the gods who appear in the Hōri setsuwa are all personalized deities. A story in which personalized deities behave like human beings was adapted to an audience that was, at that point, finding it more and more difficult to comprehend "momentary" and "specialized" deities, represented solely by their names and as beings bound only to single phenomena or to certain specific abilities. An audience that responded to a well-structured story was gradually becoming incapable of being moved by stories the content of which consisted of the simple enumeration of divine names and genealogies. In consequence, divine genealogies are hardly present in the Hōri setsuwa. This is not to say that momentary and specialized deities no longer existed during the formation period of the Hōri setsuwa. Princess Toyotama commands that a maternity hut, thatched with cormorant feathers, be constructed on the beach at the water's edge. Her labor pains suddenly grow acute, and she enters the hut before it has been completely thatched. She names the son she bears there "Son of the god come from heaven, born before the hut at the water's edge had been completely thatched with cormorant feathers" (Amatsuhiko no Hikonagisatake Ugayafukiaezu no Mikoto; *JDK*, 289). Traces of the momentary deities remain in this name. The god Salthammer, who offers Hōri valuable advice, can be identified from his name as a specialized deity who rules the seaways and tides. His actions, however, are those of a wise old man versed in all things, and in this respect he probably occupies an intermediate position between the personalized and the specialized deity.

What I shall call the middle stratum—not as new as the Hōri setsuwa, and not as old as the creation setsuwa—is represented by the setsuwa group called the Izumo line. One of its episodes, the subjugation of the eight-headed serpent, transmits a version of the Perseus-Andromeda motif. Its ultimate source has been shown to have been South China, by way of Indochina and Indonesia (Ōbayashi, 1961, 177-88). Ultimate sources are, however, not very useful in considering the formation period of these Yamato setsuwa. The differences between the old and new strata might first be studied in light of the relative proportions within each of the name genealogies. In the Izumo line, long passages of divine genealogies appear in three places. When compared to genealogies in the creation folklore episodes, however, the Izumo genealogies are far fewer in number, whereas narrative passages multiply. On the other hand, when the Izumo line is compared to episodes in the Hōri setsuwa, which are confined almost exclusively to the narration of events, the Izumo line is found to possess quite a large amount of divine genealogies. It is, in other words, a transitional work. While part of the middle stratum, it appears to lean toward the old stratum rather than toward the new. This will be deduced from the frequent appearance of what is called a sacred numeral (heilige Zahle).

Real time does not appear in the Izumo line of deity setsuwa. For example, after the gods Ōkuninushi and Sukunabikona have joined in founding the Land of Izumo, Sukunabikona leaves for the Land of Eternity. If this setsuwa belonged to the new stratum, the passage would probably contain a statement like "He stayed there for eight years." Instead, the narrator of this episode does not mention definite numbers, but only states:

> And so from that time the two deities Ōnamuji [or Ōkuninushi] and Sukunabikona worked together to found this Land. But after this the deity Sukunabikona crossed over to the Land of Eternity.

Thus the Izumo line of deity setsuwa is narrated within what Cassirer calls the "mythic conception of time" (mythische Zeitbegriff). When, in this conception of time, temporalities are expressed in numbers, they become sacred numerals in conformance with specific circumstances. Whereas real numbers are no more than quantitatively relative concepts interrelated with, and applicable to, all other matters, sacred numerals are closely linked to the essence of their indicated objects, and each is colored by its own mythic feeling (Cassirer, 1925a, 169-72).

A sacred numeral, in this sense, is expressed in the Izumo line of deity setsuwa by the number eight. Not only is "eight" attached to all kinds of creatures and things—"eight maidens" (yaotome), "the eight-headed serpent" (yamata no orochi), "eight heads and eight tails" (yakashira yao), "eight valleys and eight peaks" (tani yatani o yao), "eight gates" (yatsu no kado), "eight daises" (yatsu no sazuki), "eight-times-brewed sake" (yashioori no sake), "a great house eight ma long" (yatama no ōmuro), "land of eight islands" (yashima no kuni)—but it is also found together with gods' names: Eight-eared Suga (Suga no Yatsumimi), Jinumi of the Eight Islands (Yashima Jinumi), Eight Thousand Halberds (Yachihoko), Princess Eight-tops (Yakamihime), and Mujino of the Eight Islands (Yashima Mujino). The term for Ōkuninushi's brothers, "the Eighty Gods" (yasokami), is also treated as a proper noun. We should pause, therefore, before we dismiss Susanoo's uta, recited as the clouds rise over his newly built palace at Suga, as mere repetition.

Yakumo tatsu	Eight-layered clouds rise
Izumo	In the Land of Izumo:
Yaegaki	Eightfold fences
Tsumagomi ni	To enclose my wife,
Yaegaki tsukuru	Eightfold fences shall I build.
Sono yaegaki o.	Hey now! Eightfold fences!

(*KJK, Song*, 1)

We later readers would do well to note that "eight" is a sacred numeral in the Izumo line of deity setsuwa, and that the appearance of this sacred numeral is a characteristic of the old stratum.

If, within the Izumo line, the concentration of passages with the sacred numeral eight is an important characteristic, that does not mean that the numeral does not appear in episodes of other lines. When Izanagi and Izanami remake and complete Japan, they build a "mansion eight hiro long," and the first countries to which they give birth are the Eight Islands. The "eight thunder gods" grow in the corpse of Izanami; Amaterasu is fond of an "eight-foot curved jewel"; and "eight myriads" of gods gather in the riverbed of Ame no Yasu. Before the god Ninigi descends to earth to rule as tennō, the imprudent Ame no Wakahiko dies tragically, and his kinfolk conduct a funeral spanning "eight days and eight nights." Several examples are found in the Hōri setsuwa as well: the Sea God, preparing to receive the strange and respected god Hōri, readies a seat for him by "spreading eight layers of sea lion pelts, and upon them eight layers of coarse silken sheets."

Not only does the sacred numeral appear proportionately less frequently than in the Izumo-line episodes: yet more strikingly, in those episodes where an opposition between heaven and earth (that is, coordinates based on a vertical conception) is given, actual numerals and actual time appear in addition to the sacred numeral and mythic time. The goddess Izanami's parting words to her husband Izanagi are that she will have one thousand of his countrymen die each day. Izanagi replies that he will then have one thousand five hundred people born every day in his country (*JDK*, 194-95). The resulting difference of five hundred is a numerical value that remains constant whether it is one thousand people subtracted from one thousand five hundred people, or one thousand days subtracted from one thousand five hundred days, or one thousand leagues subtracted from one thousand five hundred leagues. It is a real number. Again, when the god Amenōhi is sent down to earth to negotiate with the local deities so that Ninigi may descend, Amenōhi instead "then curried favor with the god Ōkuninushi, and for three years did not send his report to heaven." When Ame no Wakahiko is sent to investigate, the result is that he "married Princess Shitateru, daughter of the god Ōkuninushi and, in the hope of inheriting his kingdom, did not send his report to heaven for eight years" (*KJK*, 1:256). This "eight years" may contain some significance as a sacred numeral. On the other hand, if we attach importance to the comparison between the former envoy's three years versus the latter's eight, it may be more appropriate to consider it real time. In other words, the story of Ninigi's descent to earth and the episodes that precede it are, like the Izumo line, middle-stratum works; they tend more toward the new stratum than does the Izumo line, however, in that the narrative has been defined in many places by real numbers and time.

STORIES OF THE ROYAL HOUSE

Only an old and new stratum can be distinguished in royal setsuwa, but that distinction is clearer than those made among the strata of the divine. The reason lies in the considerable difference between the rich mythic character of the old stratum of royal setsuwa as opposed to the more predominant annalistic character of its new. Up to now, I have avoided wherever possible the use of the word "myth" (shinwa) and have instead used the term "deity setsuwa" for those stories which have gods as protagonists and center on supernatural events. The use of the term "myth" was deferred until circumstances necessitated the expression of wider concepts. In order to study the old stratum of royal setsuwa, however, it is mandatory that my use of the word "myth" be made clear.

In modern literary criticism the term "myth" is not necessarily used only in its narrow sense, that is, to signify a work which contains gods as protagonists and centers on supernatural events. "Myth" is also widely applied to describe modern phenomena. One might cite, as an extreme example, the "myth of Marilyn Monroe," drawn from the "myth of the perpetual return" (Righter, 1975, 13). It has been remarked that if we go so far as to include such uses of the term, there might well be thousands of ways to interpret present events in the world as myth.[83] We may nevertheless take, as a tentatively reliable definition, Wellek and Warren's view that myth is "any anonymously composed story telling of origins and destinies: the explanations a society offers its young of why the world is and why we do as we do, its pedagogic images of the nature and destiny of man" (Wellek-Warren, 1949, 191). It is not always true that myth is anonymously composed. Consider the case of Marxism and Nazism, two myths that have greatly influenced the twentieth century. It is clear who roughed out their broad concepts, to say nothing of the identities of those rhetoricians who filled in the details. "Anonymously composed" might rather be reconsidered to indicate the absence of a single individual who is indisputably responsible for the veracity of an explanation. Let us consider, for example, the assertion that only one means will bring benefit and happiness to the masses: the continuing struggle waged by a reformed socialist system under the dictatorship of the proletariat, in order inevitably to crush the capitalist system. This is known to be false, although no one can clearly be held responsible for explaining why it is not true. Therefore it is Marxist myth.

The word "myth," and especially its adjectival form "mythical," have from the first implied a hypothetical property. Because of this, the word "myth" was interpreted pejoratively during the European Enlightenment of the seventeenth and eighteenth centuries (Wellek-Warren, 1949, 190-91). We judge the content of myth as fabrication, however, only because our world differs in assumption from that in which myth was created. Those inhabiting the world of myth find its contents to be completely true. Thus the conviction that a myth is true will frequently manifest itself in extreme behavior. The gas chambers of Auschwitz had their basis in the conviction that the Nazi myth was true. Why, then, does truth in World A become fabrication in World B? Because the inhabitants of World B are conscious of the difference between what is explained and what is used to explain it, they will find a matter true only if the correspondence between the two components is correct, and they will find it a fabrication if the correspondence is insufficient. By contrast, in World A no distinction is made between what is explained and what is used to explain it; the images introduced in the explanation are not metaphors or symbols of the matter being explained, but are instead the matter itself (Cassirer, 1925a, 51).

[83] Barthes, making matters yet more complex, adds another definition (Barthes, 1957, 215).

In the sense of what is believed to be true in World A, myth constitutes an important feature of the old stratum of Yamato royal-family setsuwa. The place names which appear in the account of Jimmu Tennō's eastward progress, for instance, are all identifiable with present-day locations. That is, these names are actual, true place names. Also all people who appear in these locations act with the intelligence and feelings of ordinary people. For example, the elder Ukashi brother, unwilling to submit to Jimmu, musters his troops. Since they are not enough to guarantee victory, he feigns surrender. He then builds a reception hall designed to collapse upon and crush the first person who steps inside. The elder Ukashi brother plans to invite Jimmu there and murder him, but the tennō is advised of the plot by the younger Ukashi brother. Jimmu's two generals, Michi no Omi and Ōkume, pursue the elder Ukashi brother with swords, halberds, bows, and arrows, finally driving him into the hall. Thus the elder Ukashi brother is crushed to death by his own trap. This episode (*KJK*, 2:61) has an extremely rational plot, one that World B would perceive as a satisfactory story. That is, the episode transmits facts that pertain to a world congruent with our modern one, and it displays, in substance, a predisposition toward annalistic setsuwa. The account of Jimmu's eastward progess, however, has another facet: supernatural events tend to occur in important scenes. In general, where events removed from reality appear in setsuwa of Jimmu's eastward progress—as when Jimmu and his army, trying to pass through the Hayasui Straits, are piloted by a local god mounted on a tortoise's back (*KJK*, 2:53); or when he and his troops are felled by a noxious vapor in Kumano and later annihilate the evil local gods by the power of a divine sword sent to Jimmu by the gods of heaven (*KJK*, 2:55-58)—we may well say that mythic characteristics inform the narrative to no small degree.

Modern attempts at reinterpreting such mythic stories in conformance with our contemporary mentality could only be extremely annoying to those who lived in the world of Yamato myth. For example, there is that incident when Jimmu and his army come to the Yoshino River and a "man with a tail" emerges from a well. One interpretation has it that since miners and woodcutters tended to sit on rocks, earth, and sand, they wore animal skins over their buttocks to serve as cushions, and that this custom is noticed here.[84] Another man with a tail, who is encountered in the Yoshino mountains, "split great rocks asunder and came out." He is interpreted to be a cave dweller. (See footnote, *Kojiki*, Iwanami Bunko, rev. ed., p. 83.) These readings are little more than a species of euhemerism. In the reality of the mythic world, people with tails actually appear and cleave passageways through boulders with their bare hands.

[84] Headnote, *Kojiki* (*Nihon Koten Zensho*), 2:58.

Attempts to transform the reality of World A to conform to that of World B notwithstanding, a potentially true transformational code might first be effected in a dimension where both World A and World B could be observed on equal ground. This pertains, however, to a dimension separate from that of nineteenth-century rationalism. The thought that one can interpret myth through a process akin to linear transformation in mathematics appears to be an illusion of some magnitude. It is far more vital to recognize that conspicuous mythical characteristics exist in the old stratum of royal setsuwa, and that it is just this fact which differentiated such setsuwa from stories with similar content belonging to the new stratum.

Perhaps the most important myth found in the story of Jimmu's eastward progress is that which states that the reigning house of Yamato is descended from the gods. "Jimmu," a Sinified posthumous name, is of course a later appellation. He first appears as Prince Kamu Yamato Iwarebiko, but this name is used only between the time of his departure from the Land of Himuka and that of his arrival in Kumano. During the ensuing time, which encompasses the events from Jimmu's subjection to extreme hardship in Kumano and his receipt of the divine sword from the deities Amaterasu and Takagi (*KJK*, 2:56) up to his enthronement (ibid., 66), Jimmu is, as Ōta Yoshimaro has indicated, consistently called the "son of the heavenly deities" (Amatsukami no Miko).[85] This can only reflect a conscious effort to stress the descent of Jimmu and his line from the sun goddess Amaterasu—the myth of greatest appeal in Yamato mythology. This is not to say that the myth of the tennōs' divine descent witnessed worldwide dissemination, as did the Marxist myth. Yet it remains of preeminent importance to Japan. Great events, whether the Jinshin War of 672 or the Meiji Restoration of 1868, have been based on the active existence of this myth.[86] Wellek and Warren's definition of myth as "the explanations a society offers its young of why the world is and why we do as we do" is also valid for archaic Yamato myth.

Our model up to now, royal-family setsuwa that are fundamentally predisposed toward annalistic legends but frequently interspersed with myth, corresponds to Book Two of the extant *Kojiki*. But in the accounts of Nintoku and his successors (in other words, once we have reached Book Three of the *Kojiki*) historicity becomes a marked feature, and myth as we know it disappears.[87] Since the difference between the second

[85] Ibid.
[86] [The Jinshin no ran was a war of succession between Kobun Tennō and Prince Ōama following the death of Tenji Tennō. Kōbun was defeated and died in Ōmi. Ōama became Temmu Tennō, and his consort the later Jitō Tennō. The battle is celebrated from the Temmu side by Hitomaro in the longest poem in the *MYS* (2:199-201).—Trans., Ed.]
[87] This has already been noted (Mishina, 1970, 70-76).

and third books is very distinct indeed, it is perhaps permissible, in discussing royal-family setsuwa, to equate the old stratum, in which myth intervenes, with Book Two of the *Kojiki*, and the new stratum, in which myth does not appear, with Book Three. Thus, deity setsuwa are collected into Book One of the *Kojiki*, which is subdivided into old, middle, and new strata. Yet the divine does evidently belong to older strata than those of the royal house. So if we think of the books of the *Kojiki* as units, Book One is seen to correspond to the old stratum, Book Two to the middle stratum, and Book Three to the new stratum.

This means, then, that both viewpoints recognize old, middle, and new strata in the *Kojiki*, although its compiler probably perceived Book One as the old, Book Two as the middle, and Book Three as the new. The division of the narrative into deity and royal setsuwa, and the further subdivision of the former into three strata and the latter into two, can only represent, on the basis of an analysis of mythic characteristics, a formative stage no doubt antecedent to the *Kojiki* compiler's perceptions.

There should be little difficulty in deducing an absolute date for the stories that belong to the new stratum of royal stories. Although Book Three of the *Kojiki* ends with the death of Suiko Tennō in 628, the entries concerning the ten sovereigns from Ninken (traditional; r. 488-98) on down consist solely of genealogies, while setsuwa appear up to and including Kenzō (believed to have reigned in the early sixth century). Thus if we separate, by at least one hundred years, the time period in the *Kojiki* subject matter from its period of composition, we may conclude that the terminus ad quem for the formation of the new stratum of royal setsuwa would fall within the seventh century. In the *Nihon Shoki*, entries resembling setsuwa also appear for Ninken and his successors; these entries, however, are strikingly historicized, and as such do not possess the same properties as the *Kojiki* setsuwa based on the deeds of Nintoku through Kenzō. In other words, because the early sixth century is the latest possible period that could serve as subject matter for royal-house setsuwa, the

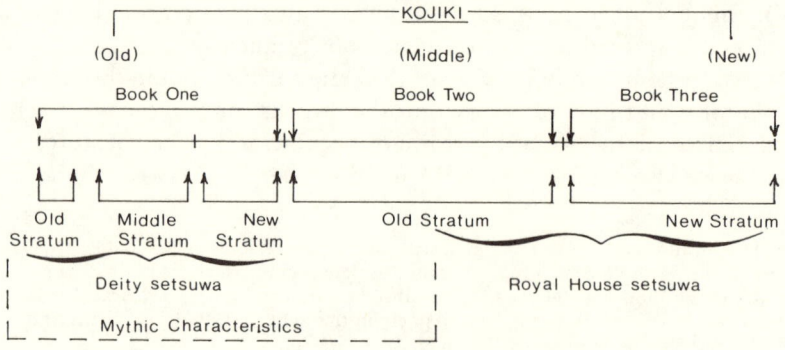

compiler of the *Kojiki*, working in circumstances similar to those which obtained for the *Nihon Shoki* compiler, is thought to have managed with genealogies alone when he composed the accounts of Ninken and his successors. To reject this interpretation is to be left with the hundred-and-forty-year period from the Ninken account through the Suiko account considerably out of balance. If we think Nintoku's reign lasted from 395 to 427, then the terminus a quo of the new stratum will date roughly from the mid-sixth century.[88]

It is more difficult, by contrast, to estimate a terminus a quo for the old stratum of royal setsuwa. One clue would seem to be furnished, however, by the inscription on an iron sword discovered in the Inariyama tumulus in the autumn of 1978. According to Inoue Mitsusada, part of the inscription reads as "Great King Wakatakeru" and is believed to refer to Ōhatsuse no Wakatake no Mikoto, that is, Yūryaku Tennō.[89] Moreover, the name of an eighth-generation ancestor of the putative owner of the sword, Owaka Omi, a nobleman of Yūryaku's time, also appears in the inscription as Owaka's "ancestor Ōbiko." This is thought to have been the same man as the "Prince Ōbiko" who, as one of the generals of the Four Regions, pacified northeast Japan during Sujin's reign (*KJK*, 2:98-99).[90] Because it was the custom for local governors (kuni no miyatsuko) to serve the royal family of Yamato as court attendants, Owaka is postulated to have learned of Prince Ōbiko's expedition to the northeast while in attendance, and to have adopted the prince as the ancestor of his own family (Inoue Mitsusada, 1980, 124-26).

Now, Sujin died, according to the *Nihon Shoki*, in 30 B.C. This artificial date is of course unreliable. The *Kojiki* records the year as falling into the astrological category of the Year of the "Tiger-tsuchinoe." The following years all have the same designation and are relevant to the discussion: 43 B.C.; A.D. 18, 78, 138, 198, 258, and 318.[91] Of course, the most likely years are 258 and 318. In fact, Kanda Hideo has clearly

---

[88] I follow Kanda Hideo's theory (Kanda, 1959, 160).

[89] [Yūryaku is twenty-first sovereign in the traditional list; legendary reign, 456-79. —Trans., Ed.]

[90] [In the tenth year of his reign, Sujin is said to have sent four members of the royal family as generals to the four parts of Japan, to "civilize" and "pacify" the inhabitants. Prince Ōbiko was sent to the Northern Region (Hokurikudō); and the others to the East (Tōkaidō), Kyushu (Saikaidō), and the West Japan Sea (San'indō). Sujin was tenth sovereign in the traditional list, and his legendary reign was 97-30 B.C. Such dates are of course prehistorical for Japan, but the legend probably bears some truth about actions taken later.—Trans., Ed.]

[91] [Dates were specified by combinations of one of the five elements with one of the twelve signs of the Asian zodiac. As Kanda's argument, followed here, shows, the combination of tora-tsuchinoe would recur every sixty years, allowing the historian to keep the sign designation but choose a later cyclic recurrence as date. For a representation of the system, see Takayanagi and Takeuchi, *Kadokawa Nihonshi Jiten*, 2nd ed. [1974; or in English, Miner et al., *The Princeton Companion to Classical Japanese Literature*, Part 7G (forthcoming)—Ed.]

demonstrated that the year of Sujin's death must have been A.D. 258 (Kanda, 1959, 222-23). According to Kanda's theory, Prince Ōbiko went to subdue the northeast region prior, of course, to the death of Sujin in 258, and the year 248 is suggested as the tentative date of the prince's excursion. Yūryaku, on the other hand, is undoubtedly the "King Wu of Wa" who sent an embassy to the Liu Sung Dynasty of China in 478 (*Sōjo Wakokuden*, 86-87). This means, then, that two hundred and thirty years (248-478) separate the events. If we assume the passing of eight generations during this period, the resulting average age of one such generation would be 28.78 years. Kanda's theory is based on the calculation that one generation of tennō at this time would average 27.75 years (1959, 211-12). Since a numerical value somewhat under thirty is not an unreasonable figure for a human generation, we may conclude that both 28.78 years and 27.75 years are within the permissible range of error. Thus the "Ōbiko" of the Inariyama iron sword inscription is identified with the figure of "Prince Ōbiko," who appears within a legend that had become quite firmly fixed around the Yamato royal family by the mid-fourth century. We cannot judge which of Prince Ōbiko's exploits are historical and which fictional, but we may conclude that the activity of regional pacification that served as the basis for these transmissions pertains to the middle of the third century.

The year 248, which we have tentatively fixed as the year of Prince Ōbiko's pacification, corresponds in Chinese history to the last year of Cheng-shih in the Kingdom of Wei, when Himiko, Queen of Wa (Japan), is recorded by Chinese sources to have died.[92] Civil war broke out in Wa upon her death, and the country was only brought under control when Himiko's eldest daughter, Toyo, was made Queen. Yet in 266 Toyo sent an embassy to China. So we must conclude that the disruptive conditions described in the Chinese chronicles, where, in the country of Wa, "they condemned one another to death, and killed over one thousand people at that time" (*Gishi Wajinden*, 83), took place roughly around the year 250. If we were to consider that the powerful figure who came to the thirteen-year-old Toyo's aid at that time and suppressed the insurrection was the man on whom Sujin was modeled, this inference would be extremely reasonable from the point of view of dates. Moreover, prior to Himiko's becoming Queen of Wa, unrest existed in that country: "For years they fought among themselves" (*Gishi Wajinden*, 81). If we are to assume that the powerful figure who brought this situation under control served as the model for the figure of Jimmu, these events would pertain to the early third century. If, on the other hand, we assume that the

[92] Cheng-shih was an era name for Regent Fang of Ch'i (240-48). The notice of Himiko's death is found in the *Pei Shih*, a T'ang history: "Biography 82: Wo," *Pei Shih*, 3135.

situation occurred between the reigns of Emperors Huan and Ling (147-88), as is described in the *Hou Han Shu (History of the Later Han)*—"Between the reigns of Huan and Ling, there was a great civil war in Wa; they fought among themselves, and for years there was no ruler" (*Gokanjo Waden*, 85)—then the unrest prior to Himiko's rule would have occurred in the last half of the second century. As has already been pointed out, however, the entries on the country of Wa in the *History of the Later Han*, though based on the "Wei Chih" (Wei Record) in the *San-kuo Chih (Record of the Three Kingdoms)*, contain many embellished passages, and so it may be more reasonable to assume that the model for the figure of Jimmu was active in the early third century. These events are set forth in Table 3.

The establishment of a stable regime under Queen Toyo applied only to the central regions of the country. It would require a great many years before a consolidated authority, capable of extending its control to the outlying regions, could be established. In the meantime, we may suppose, frequent punitive expeditions were sent to suppress regional uprisings. According to Korean evidence, however, Wa sent a military expedition to Korea in a Year of the Hare-kanoto, attacked Silla, and battled against the forces of Koguryŏ, which had advanced southward to reinforce the army of Silla.[93] We may regard the year mentioned to correspond to A.D.

TABLE 3
REDATING OF EARLY JAPANESE HISTORY

A.D.		
239	First embassy sent by Himiko, Queen of Wa	
243	Second embassy sent by Himiko, Queen of Wa	
258	Death of Sujin Tennō	
266	Embassy sent by Toyo, Queen of Wa	
300	Accession, about this time, of Keikō	
363	Accession of Ōjin	
391	Korean expedition (King Hot'ae's monument)	230 years Eight Generations
395	Accession of Nintoku	
421	Embassy sent by Tsan, King of Wa (Nintoku)	
427	Death of Nintoku	
478	Embassy sent by Wu, King of Wa (Yūryaku)	

[93] "Paekche and Silla were formerly our dependencies and paid us tribute; but Wa, in the year of the Hare-kanoto, crossed the sea [illegible] crushed Paekche [illegible] Silla. They pledged allegiance to Wa" (Inscription, Monument of King Kwanggaet'o). This passage is seen by some scholars, chiefly North Korean, as evidence that the original inscription has been distorted by the tampering of Japanese general staff officers, and theories have therefore been advanced to deny the ascendance of the Wa army (Yi Chin-hŭi, 1972, 60-72). Insofar as one can judge from what survives on the inscription, however, one can only

391 (Kanda, 1959, 162-64). At some time previous to the invasion, a unified power structure had come into being in the Yamato state, which now possessed a military force sufficient to dispatch troops overseas. Since, moreover, it is difficult to imagine that Yamato had been from the first capable of military activity on such a grand scale as battling the united forces of Koguryŏ and Silla, we may conclude that Yamato probably had had previous experience in sending troops to Korea. If we assume that this experience is reflected in the transmission of Jingū Tennō's conquest of Silla, then the year of her son's accession to the throne as Ōjin can be estimated as A.D. 363 (ibid., 161). Therefore the unification of Yamato occurred in the mid-fourth century or slightly earlier. Before this time, the Yamato court evidently sent out repeated punitive expeditions to pacify the outlying regions, and one of these expeditions is believed to have been turned into setsuwa with Prince Yamato Takeru as the protagonist. If this is the case, then we may say that the Kanda theory, in placing the year of Yamato Takeru's father Keikō's accession at around A.D. 300 (ibid., 233-26), demonstrates an extremely valid line of reasoning. To sum up the results of these studies: the old stratum of royal setsuwa utilizes facts from the early third through the mid-fourth centuries as its core.

This period in Yamato, from the early third through the mid-fourth centuries, shares common features in some respects with the ages in which several other nations developed their heroic poetry, although heroic poetry never came into being in Yamato. This notwithstanding, attempts to recognize a heroic period in the history of Japanese literature have been intensely though briefly mounted, and their traces remain to this day.[94] Because the very absence of heroic poetry is one of the great characteristics of Japanese literature, I would like to state my views on the question of why we cannot acknowledge a heroic age in Japan.

The existence of a heroic age in Japanese literature was first advocated by Takagi Ichinosuke. His views were based in some respects on misconceptions, and the several theories which branched out from Takagi's only served to give greater breadth to these misconceptions. Hence the Takagi theory came to nothing before it had begun to bear fruit. The first step of Takagi's theory was to assume that the Songs of Kume (*KJK, Songs*, 9-14, and *NSK, Songs*, 7-14) predated in composition the *Chron-*

---

interpret it as I have indicated. [A note about the debated characters in the Chinese record follows this note in the text, but is omitted here.—Ed.]

[94] Tokumitsu Hisaya has a detailed exposition of the development of the debate over heroic poetry in his *Kojiki no Hihyōteki Kenkyū*. The controversy over a heroic age in Japan ended about 1965. Although somewhat earlier Saigō Nobutsuna used the phrase "heroic age" in the revised edition of his *Nihon Kodai Bungakushi*, in his preface he gives notice that he disclaims the earlier edition. But he does not disclaim the heroic age; in fact, because it is essential to his theory, he even quotes from the previous edition.

icles corpus. With this as his premise, Takagi found that the songs, willful and vigorous expressions centered on combat which, moreover, demonstrated a manner of singing which was closely linked to the singers' lives, differed totally in nature from lyric poetry. He concluded that there existed heroic individuals who served as the subjects around whom such songs were formed, and that it was the heroic age, a transitional period between the primitive age and civilized times, which fostered such figures (Takagi Ichinosuke, 1941, 90-119). His point of departure, the designation of the Songs of Kume as heroic poetry, can be said to be based on a misconception, however. In his inquiry into the nature of heroic poetry, C. M. Bowra bases his conclusions on numerous data beginning with the *Iliad* and the *Odyssey*, ranging from the medieval *Chanson de Roland* and *Nibelungenlied*, and including pieces sung in all parts of the modern world. He indicates that heroic poetry possesses characteristics which can be arranged and summarized as follows (Bowra, 1952, 1-40).

1. Heroic poetry refers to orally composed poetry that narrates the actions of a superior person.
2. This person is a human being who acts, moreover, in the name of honor.
3. His actions are constantly performed through the strength, willpower, and intelligence of a human being. He does not win victory or resolve difficulties solely through magic or other superhuman powers.
4. The story is depicted in the narrative mode, with objective unfolding of events. Unlike the panegyric, which praises, or the lament, which mourns, heroic poetry does not contain subjective elements, nor are there any signs of didacticism.
5. The tone of narration is immediate, vigorous, and marvelous.
6. The external narrative form possesses a rhythm suited to recitation; it is not prose.

In light of these criteria, the Songs of Kume cannot possibly conform to Bowra's fourth point, and are therefore not heroic poetry. The saga presents a similar case: although it meets the criteria through point 5, it does not conform to point 6, and for that reason must be regarded as heroic prose (ibid., 15). Heroic poetry, as a general principle, is either of long or medium length, although this does not mean that scale is always an absolute criterion. The *Manas* of Kirghiz is of immense length, whereas, by contrast, the Russian *Bilina* is only twenty-three lines long (ibid., 330). The narrative mode—that is, the mode in which phenomena and events, or their successive states, are depicted according to chronological order—is essential to heroic poetry, however. One need not be caught up in matters of length: a heroic poem may well be only twenty-three lines long, but if a poem is not a narrative, it cannot be heroic poetry. Some of the Songs of Kume are fairly long: one might mention that song which begins with the lines "In Uda / On the high ground" (*KJK, Song,* 9), for example. Yet the Songs of Kume lack a narrative flow within which phenomena unfold while interacting in a cause-and-effect relationship. No matter how much such pieces are amplified, they cannot possibly mature into medium-length or long poems. The Songs of Kume never possessed the elements necessary for maturation into heroic poetry.

If conditions amenable to the creation of heroic poetry ever existed in Yamato, we would expect to find in some region or stratum poetic fragments which at least resemble heroic poetry. Yet such traces have not been found. This means, as Tsuda Saukichi long ago indicated, that heroic poetry did not exist in Japan, an important fact indicative of the special quality of Japanese literature.[95] Incidentally, it is in light of criterion number 4, above, that heroic poetry can be held not to exist in Japan. This does not necessarily mean, of course, that heroic elements are not to be found in the actions and motives of characters in certain works. Just as Takagi says, heroic actions and intentions are perceived in the Songs of Kume. But this alone cannot make them heroic poetry. In order to be heroic poetry, a work must be conveyed in narrative, and its external form, in turn, must be at least of medium length (or demonstrate the potential to become so). The debate over heroic poetry is ultimately concerned with expression, and the problem undoubtedly pertains to literary history alone. Yet later studies have used Takagi's work as a point of departure in order to discuss heroic poetry as a question of social history, and this has only served to compound the error.

One may endeavor to argue the existence of heroic poetry in Japan, and in the face of the facts to regard as real something that never existed. A debate over heroic poetry was carried out between 1948 and 1963. Based on Takagi's theory, its conclusions may be summarized as follows. The heroic spirit existed in Yamato, but this notwithstanding, heroic poetry came to naught because the society of that time, acting in the interest of a hereditary, despotic royal authority, caused the communal popular spirit of the powerful regional clans to atrophy. This statement amounts in essence to no more than a discourse on the nonexistence of heroic poetry. The problem is that such discourses are to be found together with vigorous claims of the existence of a heroic age in the outlying regions of Yamato. Instead of interesting themselves in the existence or nonexistence of heroic poetry, the writers have from the start concerned themselves with demonstrating the theory that an ancient democratic

---

[95] Tsuda, 1916, 48-49; and, in still clearer form, 1947, 17-19.

system, centering around lesser clans, existed prior to the establishment of the Yamato power structure, and that this democracy was destroyed in the interests of autocratic rule by an enormously powerful clan (the royal house), thus leading to the formation of a class society.[96] In order to demonstrate the existence of this ancient democratic system, proponents compare it to the heroic age of Greece, which corresponds to the heroic poetry of Homer, and they attempt to recognize in Yamato a similar heroic age that served as a transitional period between an age of primitive communal societies and the formation of the ancient state. It would be a fine thing indeed if archaeological or other research findings had formed the bases which corroborated the existence of a transitional period of this nature, a question which is in any case a task for historiography, and not the province of literary history. Yet these scholars have not been able to obtain such data. By discovering heroic actions and intentions within the Songs of Kume, they have used a literary phenomenon as a datum in support of their recognition of a heroic age in Yamato similar to the age Hegel perceived in the background of Greek heroic poetry.

Such views are based on the premise that the existence of a heroic age is a universal phenomenon, because the peoples who formed the various ancient states of the world universally possessed a literary genre akin to heroic poetry. This premise does not accord with the facts. Several nations have no tradition of heroic poetry. For example, there is no heroic poetry in China, Korea, Israel, Africa (Ethiopia, Uganda, and Natal, among others), or the various nations of northern Europe, and for the following reasons (Bowra, 1952, 10-16):

1. Poetry in some countries simply represents a direct narration of the exploits of a specific heroic individual; it lacks sufficient capacity to turn these exploits into a work that maintains a certain distance between the content and the narrator (the case of the various African nations).
2. Because the populations of some countries were highly intelligent, they preferred historical narratives over heroic poetry, and were too serious by nature to be susceptible to fabricated narratives presented as fact (the case of China and Israel).

[96] A period existed in postwar Japan when whatever brandished leftist thought or aligned itself with leftist positions was thought to be "new." The debate over heroic poetry flourished, using this approach: vilification of the royal system and a hasty imposition of Marxist ideology tended to take precedence over calm factual analysis. The "problems" approach of the left—"the practical question is the overthrow of class society" or "the problems produced by the will in the practical process of struggle against state authority"—was quite simply an attempt to drag Takagi's purely academic theory along a specific political route. The fact that the debate came to naught can be traced in many respects to high-handed discussions that preferred ideology to reality.

3. Because of a strong liking for prose, heroic exploits are narrated
   in some countries as sagas (the case of Ireland, among others).

Another view has been put forward about Israel. The family and extended family, or the clan (a slightly larger group), became the unit from
which stories originated, and because questions of government, economics, religion, and culture existed only as family events, a true hero was
not created (Sekine, 1978, 143-45). I wish to posit, as principal factors
in the nondevelopment of heroic poetry in Yamato, a lack of organizational strength in compiling lengthy works, and powerful, durable bonds
to spiritual forces, as seen in the Yamato belief in kotodama. The hero
of a heroic poem acts according to human strengths, will, and intellect,
and if magic or other supernatural powers intervene, the heroic qualities
of a poem will be attenuated and lost (Bowra, 1952, 91-98). These factors
aside, the existence of heroic poetry is definitely not a universal phenomenon. Nor can one say that Yamato poetry ought to have features in
common with Grecian heroic poetry.

If we were to suppose that heroic poetry existed in Yamato, moreover,
it would still be inconsistent with the facts to maintain that a heroic age
like that of ancient Greece was universally present as a backdrop. Spain,
for example, has heroic poetry, but no clearly defined heroic age. Events
of the eleventh century form the subject matter of the representative work
of Spanish heroic poetry, the *Poema del Cid*. But other heroic poems,
known only from surviving fragments, are concerned with facts from a
far earlier period, and so a specific heroic age is not believed to have
existed. The same is true for Yugoslavia, Albania, Russia, and latter-day
Greece. The earliest and latest dates of events that serve as the topics of
their heroic poetry are separated by time periods as great as one thousand
years. Even in cases where a nation has perceived a heroic age like that
of ancient Greece, the composers of its heroic poetry will not have had
a specific historical period in mind as they created their works. The heroic
age was, for them, the age inhabited by the protagonists of their works,
created as a means of joining together numerous subjects and subplots.
The composers of heroic poetry did not happen to have any knowledge
of a precise period (Bowra, 1952, 26-29). The heroic age, then, is nothing
more than a period conceptualized by the composer of a heroic poem as
essential to its composition. If it is as such an object for literary study,
it does not constitute a problem for the study of history. A basic reason
for the ultimately unproductive conclusions drawn from the debate on
the heroic age lies precisely with its advocates. They made no attempt
to study the question from a literary standpoint, but instead proceeded
as if the idea of a "heroic age"—a Marxist revision of Hegel's discourse,

based in turn on Grecian heroic poetry—was universally applicable, thus transforming the matter into a question of social history.

This view, that Hegel's theory, based on Grecian heroic poetry, can also be applied as a matter of course to Yamato, inevitably leads one to insist that the nonexistent is real. The case of the god Susanoo has been advanced as one piece of evidence in favor of this nonexistent heroic age populated with nonexistent heroes. When, after having been driven from heaven because of his simple, passionate, upright, and heroic personality, Susanoo ascends to the High Plain of Heaven, "all the mountains and the rivers resounded, and all the land in the country shook" (*JDK*, 203). One view has interpreted Susanoo, so depicted, as representing the heroic, poetic, and regional in Yamato culture, whereas the sun goddess Amaterasu stands for the state, law, and centrality. The end result of the divinities' opposition and dissension is Amaterasu's judgment, by the authority of the state and the legal system, that Susanoo is a criminal (Saigō, 1951, 40-42). A misunderstanding exists here, however, concerning the nature of the hero. It is wrong to assume that a hero is no more than a man of simple and upright character who performs violent actions. His actions, rather, are performed for the benefit of others, and without concern for any disadvantage or sacrifice he himself might incur. That is, a man becomes a hero only when his acts are seen as meritorious by all others. According to Bowra, even in primitive societies glory does not consist of boasts about one's own actions, but is present rather as respect engendered from working with all one's strength to help one's fellows or family in time of need (Bowra, 1962, 134). Susanoo's behavior on the High Plain of Heaven is an outrage pure and simple, not heroic conduct. Because the passage is narrated in prose, it does not represent proof of the existence of heroic poetry.

When the scene shifts to Izumo and Susanoo destroys the eight-headed serpent, he can be said to act heroically. His actions, however, are performed as if a god within a myth, a fact that must distinguish him from the hero as a human being. Our first view of a human hero in Japanese literature is probably provided by Prince Itsuse, the older brother of Jimmu Tennō. The prince accompanies his brother on his eastward progress and, gravely wounded during the battle at Kusaka, expires after exclaiming, "Am I to die of wounds given me by these lowly wretches?" (*KJK*, 2:54). He is treated by the narrator as having died a glorious death in battle, a reflection of attitudes expressed in a society more advanced than that of the primitive community. A concept of glory is found among modern primitives, but they do not always regard death in battle as glorious. They tend instead to evaluate it on the same level as a failure to make a catch in hunting (Bowra, 1962, 131-32). The fact that Prince Itsuse is perceived to have attained "a glorious death" is thought to reflect the fact that Yamato society had developed to the point of already possessing heroes. Prince Itsuse is very nearly the only clearly heroic figure in evidence, however, and a search for others worthy of a heroic age will not greatly extend this list of one.

Even Prince Yamato Takeru, whom the proponents of the Yamato heroic age have dubbed the representative hero, performs actions which in some respects are not easily accepted as heroic in the same sense as are the actions of Achilles or Hector. This is not to say that Prince Yamato Takeru is unheroic. He attacks the Kumano chieftains by slipping into their banqueting hall disguised as a girl, and then stabs them to death. And he deceives the Izumo chieftain into exchanging his sword for Yamato Takeru's wooden one, then kills him during a fencing match. Both exploits involve the employment of a ruse. In primitive societies, the courage to face danger during a hunt for food is held in high regard, and this courage is expected to be combined with cunning. If a man dies because of foolhardiness, his action is definitely not honorable, because he has brought trouble upon his comrades (Bowra, 1962, 132). Thus the treatment of Prince Yamato Takeru's cunning bravery as a virtue can be said to represent the survival of primitive characteristics. Primitive elements also survive in episodes where the prince encounters extreme danger and performs occult actions to triumph over it. When the Sagami meadow is set afire with Yamato Takeru inside its confines, he saves himself by lighting a counterfire which drives back the original flames. But the flint and steel he uses for his fire have been given to him by his aunt, Princess Yamato, a High Priestess of Ise who is the deputy of Amaterasu, the Sun Goddess. When Yamato Takeru's ship is caught in a storm in the Sea of Hashirimizu (Coursing Water) and cannot progress, his consort Princess Ototachibana sacrifices herself to the waters, and so he escapes danger. Thus, if we are to proclaim Prince Yamato Takeru a hero, we must imagine a heroic age in which primitive elements persist, not a heroic age similar to that of Greece.

We cannot conceive a heroic age which corresponds to the Songs of Kume, because they cannot be called heroic poetry. However (so one might propose), heroic setsuwa typified by the stories of Prince Yamato Takeru do exist, and so a corresponding heroic age ought also to have existed. This is correct. The heroes who appear in the old stratum of royal-house setsuwa differ, however, from the heroes of Greek heroic poetry in that they are more primitive heroes who possess abundant mythic characteristics. It is in this connection that I have stated above, as one cause for the failure of heroic poetry to develop in Yamato, the bond with spiritual power. The old stratum of royal setsuwa is, in fact, less a narrative of heroes fighting on the field of battle than a story of the order of the royal succession.

PART TWO

The Ancient Age:
The Age of Kotodama

CHAPTER 3

The Character of the Ancient Age

KOTODAMA AS AN IDEAL

My definition of the Ancient Age is premised on the acceptance of continental culture by the Japanese. It may therefore seem contradictory if I seek the central idea of ancient times in the indigenous kotodama. Miyabi or courtliness—or, in its Sinified version, ga—was an ideal which arose from the Yamato acceptance of continental culture and was manifested in concrete terms by the principle of fūryū, or elegance.[1] The kotodama flourished, moreover, in the Archaic Age, whereas one notes a certain attenuation in the Ancient Age. If I nevertheless venture to grasp the essential character of the age on the basis of the ideal known as the kotodama, it is because the writers and poets of the age realized that the true nature of Yamato literature lay in the kotodama, and also because fūryū does not take on a tangible character in literary works until the following period, that is, the Early Middle Ages.

As I have noted, the word "kotodama" is not found in the Archaic Age; the first examples appear in the *Man'yōshū*. Yamanoe Okura's uta (*MYS*, 5:894) is one such example. In it Okura sings of Yamato as "A land where the kotodama / Brings us good fortune." This poem was presented to the newly appointed ambassador to the T'ang court, Tajihi Hironari, prior to his departure. Another poem, which celebrates Yamato as the very "land succored by / The kotodama" (*MYS*, 13:3254), contains distinctive language reminiscent of the work of Kakinomoto Hitomaro. The poem forms a set with the preceding chōka (*MYS*, 13:3253), which utilizes sea imagery: "Arisonami / Momoenami / Chienami" (Waves strike the reefs, / They spread themselves a hundredfold, / A thousandfold upon the shore)—an indication that this poem group too may have been presented in farewell to an envoy bound for a foreign post. In both cases, the circumstances of composition would have been linked to foreign travel precisely because the poets perceived that the kotodama was characteristic of the Yamato language alone, and did not exist in foreign tongues. The kotodama was a concept formed from an awakening consciousness of the existence of one's own country in contrast to foreign lands. This

[1] ["Miyabi" is written with the same character as "ga"; or rather is the Japanese as opposed to the Sinified reading (ga). The author here uses the "Japanese" reading to designate an aesthetic ideal, whereas in his usage ga has, with zoku, an ideological function.—Ed.]

formation may have taken place simultaneously with the active period of Hitomaro and his contemporaries, a premise set forth some time ago by Ōta Yoshimaro (1966, 216-35). It is not easily imagined, however, that this awareness came suddenly into being.[2] As Itō Haku has said, the workings of the kotodama, a force in operation long before Hitomaro's and Okura's time, probably became the object of a new awareness. As envoys were dispatched abroad, the kotodama came to be seen as a distinctive characteristic of the Yamato language. The ideal of the kotodama may have been further emphasized by a contemporary perception that the heyday of the kotodama was long past (Itō Haku, 1976c, 13-19). In other words, the kotodama, which had functioned vigorously in the Archaic Age, attenuated in the Ancient Age. But as people directed their consciousness toward foreign matters, the kotodama was rediscovered.

In archaic times the kotodama was alive throughout Yamato, and so people of those times never felt the need for an explicit concept called "the kotodama." All they knew was that the utterance of a kotoage would bring about a result, be it good or evil. It did not occur to them to reflect that this process was caused by spiritual or occult properties hidden within the language. The later, ancient people could distance themselves from the spiritual and occult properties within their language, and were able to observe them as objects. At least, this may be how the concept represented by the word "kotodama" came into being. They were capable of objectifying processes entailing language because their minds functioned somewhat more subtly than did those of their ancestors. And contact with continental culture seems to have influenced indirectly the fostering of this attitude of observation. More importantly, the creation of a concept known as the kotodama led to its idealization, with the result that Yamato literature was given a new, practical-minded direction. People came to realize that the kotodama was the distinguishing feature of Yamato literature only with the passing of that period in which the integrated forces of the kotodama and the act of kotoage had enjoyed their greatest activity. Insofar as the Ancient Age represented the progressive attenuation of an absolute faith in the spiritual power displayed by the kotoage, the people of the age found it necessary to stress their

---

[2] Ōta posits a distinction between the kotoage of the Archaic Age and the kotodama of the Ancient Age. Yet one must consider the emphasis through repetition in a chōka addressed to an ambassador bound for a foreign post, of the words, "I shall utter a kotoage" and "Just so shall I utter my kotoage" (*MYS*, 13:3253), followed by an envoy that tells of "a land succored by / The kotodama" (ibid., 3254). This makes it seem unlikely that in Hitomaro's time the words designated different concepts. The reason why Yamato was called the "land that [does] not utter kotoage" lies in the efficaciousness of kotoage. Because they brought about weighty consequences, either for good or evil, they were to be treated with extreme care.

realization that the kotodama was a feature unique to Yamato literature. This emphasis resulted in assigning a new direction to the works of Yamato literature. Therefore I treat the Ancient Age as the age of the kotodama.

The emergence of the kotodama as a leading idea of the Ancient Age exercised various influences on the development of Yamato literature. The first such influence was the formation of a tradition that dictated waka be composed only in the Yamato language. This tradition proved durable indeed. For roughly thirteen hundred years, up to the time when the waka reform movement of the early twentieth century liberalized waka language to include the use of Sino-Japanese and Western vocabulary, only the Yamato vocabulary was used in the composition of waka. Renga [linked poetry] inherited this tradition: its poets were to use only the Yamato language in their compositions. Linked poetry which employed Sino-Japanese vocabulary was treated as haikai (or haikai no renga), a genre not up to renga. The classic literary style created by the national learning (kokugaku) scholars of the eighteenth century also required the exclusive use of Yamato vocabulary. To them, poetry and prose that employed nothing but Yamato diction constituted a world of ga (miyabi) within Yamato literature. The source of these attitudes was the seventh-century perception of the kotodama.

As we have seen with Itō's help, the kotodama was perceived—on the basis of an awareness of foreign matters—to strengthen the attitude that Yamato literature was to be composed in the Yamato language. Since the kotodama functioned superbly in the Land of Yamato, its literature could be of a quality equal or superior to foreign literature as long as the Yamato works were expressed in the Yamato tongue. If words of foreign provenance were introduced into a Yamato work, not only would the kotodama fail to lodge in that part of the work: it was also evidently thought that the entire piece ran the risk of being deserted by the kotodama.

The complete exclusion of words of foreign origin cannot help but result in the narrowing of expressive boundaries in literature. Waka lost its abundant vitality by the fifteenth century, and regained it only after the modern waka reform had liberalized the rules of diction to include the use of words of foreign provenance. Similarly, when renga lost its vitality in the seventeenth century, considerable advances were made by haikai, which recognized as one of its basic principles the use of Sino-Japanese vocabulary and colloquial diction. Both instances demonstrate the unnaturalness of confining literary expression solely to works written in the Yamato language. Waka nevertheless kept within its boundaries of Yamato vocabulary, simply because waka had, from its earliest stages, a strong tradition of excluding foreign vocabulary.

Because archaic song had always dealt solely with phenomena that occurred within Yamato society, the exclusive use of Yamato diction had sufficed. By the seventh century, however, continental culture had permeated Yamato thinking in many respects. Objects and concepts in considerable number were now expressed more suitably by Chinese vocabulary. Waka nonetheless persisted in its exclusive use of Yamato vocabulary, because the waka tradition had been formed with the kotodama in mind. We know from analyses of parallelism in the chōka of Hitomaro that he was familiar with Chinese tz'u-fu, or prose poetry; and Okura was undoubtedly an expert in the Chinese language. Yet Okura, who wrote splendid Chinese prefaces to his uta, never permitted Chinese vocabulary to invade the poems themselves. Even in uta concerned with such philosophical speculations as the "Destiny of the Four Births" (Shishō no Himetsu) and "Drifting through the Three Worlds" (Sankai Hōryū) (MYS, 5:794, forenote), or in another which is intended to "Point out the Three Norms and then expound the Five Precepts"[3] (MYS, 5:800, forenote), Okura persistently employs Yamato diction as his sole means of poetic expression.

Why, it might be asked, were gifted poets like Hitomaro and Okura incapable of embarking on new poetic ventures like those carried out by Masaoka Shiki and Saitō Mokichi in the nineteenth and twentieth centuries? By the mid-seventh century, prior to Hitomaro's and Okura's active period, the tradition already existed of composing waka in the Yamato tongue alone. Furthermore, people became strongly aware, from the time of Temmu Tennō in the late seventh century, of a Yamato dating back to the Age of the Gods and standing in opposition to foreign lands. Thus no leeway existed in which to experiment with modifications or reforms involving the use of Chinese vocabulary. Hitomaro begins his "Elegy for Crown Prince Kusakabe" with allusions to events from the Age of the Gods:

Ame tsuchi no	When heaven and earth
Hajime no toki	Were made,
Hisakata no	Eight myriad,
Ama no kawara ni	Ten myriad gods
Yaoyorozu	Held divine assembly,

[3] [The Buddhist doctrine of the Four Births maintains that all living things are born in one of four ways: through oviparous or viviparous means, or through generation or metamorphosis. The Three Worlds of Buddhist doctrine are those (from lowest to highest) of Desire, Substance, and Nonsubstance. The Confucian doctrine of the Three Norms concerns relations between lord and vassal, parent and child, and husband and wife. The Confucian Five Precepts are that a father should have reason, a mother mercy, an elder child brotherly or sisterly love, a younger child obedience, and all children filial piety.—Trans. The forenotes are in Chinese, but the poems themselves in pure Japanese.—Ed.]

Chiyorozu kami no	Assembled in the
Kamutsudoi	Far-off
Tsudoi imashite	Heavenly Riverbed.
Kamuhakari	They held divine counsel,
Hakarishi toki ni	Consulted among themselves, and
Amaderasu	The Heaven-Shining
Hirume no mikoto	Goddess of the Sun
Ame o ba	Was chosen to rule
Shirashimesu to	Heaven.
Ashihara no	Our land, with its nodding ears of rice
Mizuho no kuni o. . . .	In the Midst of the Reed Plains. . . .

(*MYS*, 2:167)

When Hitomaro composed this poem he undoubtedly had in mind a perception of Yamato as a land to which the kotodama brought good fortune. Even Okura, in a poem previously cited (*MYS*, 5:894), begins by stating that the kotodama has its roots in the far-distant Age of the Gods: "From the Age of the Gods / It has been said. . . ." The poet's awareness that his Yamato is linked to the divine age underscores the activity of the kotodama. Poems about Yamato, the land to which the kotodama brings good fortune, were to be recited in the Yamato language, a tongue used ever since the Age of the Gods. This realization even seems to have been strengthened in the years following Temmu's reign.

Norito texts also reflect the ancient perception that the kotodama resided only in the Yamato language.[4] Many of the extant norito come from the *Engi Shiki* (composed in 927), but there are clear indications that efforts were made to bring the norito vocabulary as close as possible to the Yamato language spoken in the seventh century. This demonstrates an awareness that the kotodama would not lodge in a work simply because it used Japanese diction: language suitable for inhabitation by the kotodama must attempt to resemble that spoken in the past, in a period closer in time to the Age of the Gods. Evidently the *Engi Shiki* was compiled in an age of enervation for the kotodama, since the utterance of ordinary Japanese diction would not ensure its functioning. With the advent of such times, words of foreign provenance came to be even more strictly excluded from the norito corpus. The tradition has continued to the present day: the norito read by Shinto priests at weddings and groundbreaking ceremonies are composed entirely of seventh-century Yamato diction, with the exception of proper nouns and other necessary vocabulary. This is based on a belief held in common with the waka

[4] The relation between the kotodama and norito has been pointed out by Shiraishi Mitsukuni, 1941, 20-39.

tradition, which refuses to sanction anything but Yamato diction. The source of this belief lies in a faith in the kotodama.

The second phenomenon, which was created as the kotodama evolved into a leading expressive ideal, might be said to be the development of those specialized expressive techniques known as the "pillow-word" (makurakotoba) and the "preface" (jokotoba). I have taken the precaution of stressing that these techniques are *known* by the above names, and have quoted them, because in calling these techniques pillow-word or preface we run the risk of mistakenly assuming that the characteristics usually assigned to the pillow-word and the preface are applicable to poetry of the Ancient Age as well. I have taken this precaution, then, simply to avoid the danger. To avoid the misconception, I have decided to employ a new term, "guide phrase" (dōshi).[5]

Despite the immense amount of research which has been carried out since the Edo period on the subject of the pillow-word and the preface, no one has adequately explained why people of the Ancient Age were moved by the expressions produced by pillow-words and prefaces. If people had not been moved by them, ancient poets would not have made regular and frequent use of them over the centuries. Let us examine one example of literary expression based on pillow-words [guide phrases are italicized]:

Tamamo karu	Passing by Minume
Minume o sugite	*Where they gather fine seagrass—*
Natsukusa no	Our boat draws near to
Noshima ga saki ni	The Cape of Noshima
Fune chikazukinu.	*With its summer growth.*

(*MYS*, 3:250)

If the so-called pillow-words "tamamo karu" (Where they gather fine seagrass) and "natsukusa no" (With its summer growth) are removed from this poem, we are left with, "Passing by Minume / Our boat draws near to / The Cape of Noshima." There is no scope whatsoever within this statement for the evocation of emotion: thus the reason for this poem being counted among Hitomaro's finer works is to be ascribed entirely to the interfusion of "tamamo karu" and "natsukusa no." What manner of function, then, is indicated by "tamamo karu" and "natsukusa no"? Not one satisfactory answer to this question can be found among the

---

[5] With the advent of the Middle Ages, the guide phrase [dōshi] was transformed into a rhetorical device, a change accompanied by change in use befitting the terms known by then: pillow-word (makurakotoba) and the preface (jo, jokotoba). Studies of the subject have hitherto failed to take this transformation into account, maintaining instead a single definition for both the pristine guide phrase and the transformed pillow-word and preface.

superabundance of scholarly theories. None is satisfactory because every theory has heretofore interpreted such expressions as rhetorical techniques. An example of that kind of interpretation would be: "tamamo karu" is added to "Minume" because the place name by itself has no beauty, whereas the "pillow-word" serves to evoke the scene at Minume. If this is the case, however, then why is "natsukusa no" beautiful? The rhetorical approach can hardly furnish an answer. A further example, a poem by Lady Kasa, raises other questions:

Koromode o	You do not know me,
Uchimi no sato ni	A village girl from Uchimi
Aru ware o	Where fullers pound *sleeve-cloth*:
Shirani zo hito wa	That is why you fail to come,
Mate zo kozukeru.	Though I wait for you.

(*MYS*, 4:589)

The usual interpretation—that clothing (koromo) is pounded in the fulling process, and so the so-called pillow-word "koromode o" (sleeve-cloth) uses the "uchi" (pound) of the place name Uchimi as a kind of pivot-word—does not in the least elucidate why these lines arouse interest. Similarly, why were "prefaces" used in such large quantities? How, for example, are we to read the following poem, which possesses a linkage similar in form to "koromode o uchi"? [The preface is that part between slant lines.]

/Masurao ga	/The warrior confronts
Satsuya tabasami	His target, hunting arrow
Tachimukai	At the ready, and he lets it fly:/
Iru/ Matokata wa	The sight of Matokata
Miru ni sayakeshi.	Is refreshing to my eyes.[6]

(*MYS*, 1:61)

[6] Sengaku, in his *Man'yōshū Chūshaku*, quotes a passage now lost from the *Ise Fudoki*, which notes that the composer of the poem is "the sovereign" (identified in an interlineation as Keikō). The slightly different version from the *Ise no Kuni Fudoki* (435) apparently enjoyed wide circulation,

/Masurao no	/The warrior stands before
Satsuya tabasami	His target, hunting arrow
Mukaitachi	At the ready: he lets it fly!/
Iru ya/ Matokata	Oh, Matokata,
Hama no sayakesa.	How refreshing are your shores!

[In both this and the version in the text, the "mato" of Matokata (a coastal village in present Mie Prefecture) is taken to mean "target" as, in the next poem in the text, Takamato is taken to mean "high target."—Trans. Sengaku (1202-ca. 1271) was a Kamakura-era priest known for his treatise on the *Man'yōshū*, otherwise called *Sengaku Sōranjō*.—Ed.]

The objective of this poem is to make the statement, "The sight of Ma-tokata / Is refreshing to my eyes." Yet this affords little scope for the evocation of emotion. Why, then, does it become a good poem with the addition of the preface, "The warrior . . . fly"? This expression was apparently regarded as worthy of arousing interest. It is also used in an elegy by Kasa no Kanamura, dedicated to Prince Shiki (*MYS*, 2:230):

/Azusayumi	/Catalpa bow
Te ni torimochite	Held in his hand,
Masurao no	The warrior,
Satsuya tabasami	Hunting arrow at the ready,
Tachimukau	Confronts his target high/
Takamato/yama ni	On Takamato Mountain
Haruno yaku	The spring slopes
Nobi to miru made	Burn with grass fires:
Moyuru hi o	Is it those I see? I ask
Ika ni to toeba	What are these smoldering flames?
Tamahoko no	A man traveling the
Michi kuru hito no	*Halberd-straight* road
Naku namida. . . .	Answers me in tears. . . .

Again, the usual interpretation is that the purpose of the preface is to evoke the word "target"(mato) from the homonym contained in the place name Takamato. And again, not a single scholarly theory up to now has seemed adequate to explain why this technique should arouse interest. I have presented an explanation of the problem.[7] It includes the following points:

1. Both the "pillow-word" and the "preface" are essentially iden-tical, and differ only in length.
2. Both once imparted the action of the kotodama to the words they modified, so as to create lively expressions.
3. As people gradually lost touch with the kotodama and its action, however, these techniques underwent transformations in their functions which culminated in their being redefined to a rhetorical function.
4. Theories up to now have been unable to offer adequate analyses because they attempted to explain techniques employed during

[7] In his critique of previous studies of the pillow-word and preface, Nakanishi Susumu groups the two as "amalgamating expressions": the pillow-word amalgamates one word (or line) with another, when both components have atmosphere or mood as their basis; the preface amalgamates the descriptive preceding lines and those immediately following by means of opposition, simile, continuity, or transposition (Nakanishi, 1973, 35-37). My approach involves inquiry into the nature of the impetus behind the amalgamation.

the zenith of the kotodama by means of definitions formulated after the kotodama was no longer active.

I have therefore given the name "guide phrase" to these techniques as they existed when the activity of the kotodama was keenly felt. And I have concluded that the terms "pillow-word" and "preface" denote, in earlier critical descriptions, these techniques as they appear in later periods, when they had lost the active power of the kotodama.

If considered in this fashion, the several examples given above can be interpreted from a standpoint other than that heretofore adopted. For instance, the main intent of one of the poems quoted is simply to communicate this statement: "The sight of Matokata / Is refreshing to my eyes." Yet through the agency of the guide phrase, "The warrior confronts / His target, hunting arrow / At the ready, and he lets it fly," the vitality of a dashing hunter is introduced into the place name, Matokata Bay; and the statement made in the last line, "Is refreshing to my eyes," can then summon a response. What joins the guide phrase to the gist of the poem is homonymy: the poet was undoubtedly aware that if the same sound, "mato," was used to signify two separate things—"target" and part of a place name—then the kotodama possessed by the guide phrase could be transmitted into the essence of the poem.

The only medium through which the kotodama could be communicated was the human voice. This attitude is attributable to beliefs dating back to archaic times, and is not to be explained by means of such latter-day rhetorical concepts as the pivot-word (kakekotoba). This guide phrase is employed ironically in the elegy for Prince Shiki: the fires burning brightly on Takamato Mountain, with its stately vitality, turn out on inquiry to be the lights of a funeral procession, an unexpected reversal of meaning. If considered in this sense, the "koromode o" of Lady Kasa's poem can also be seen as a homonymic device that introduces the kotodama into the poem and so imparts vitality to the place name Uchimi. "Koromode o," then, does not differ in any functional respect from the guide phrase, "The warrior confronts / . . . and he lets it fly." This is not to say, however, that the kotodama relied on homonymy alone for its introduction into a poem. It was also feasible as long as an association of ideas was firmly established. Hitomaro's "tamamo karu" and "natsukusa no" are instances of the latter case. The links between the guide phrase and the gist of the poem could be further strengthened through metaphor. The following poem will serve as an illustration.

Awayuki no	By now I should have passed away,
Kenu beki mono o	*A light snow melting,*
Ima made ni	And yet I have dragged out my life

Nagaraenuru wa   Down to this very day,
Imo ni awan to zo.   In hope of making love to you.

(*MYS*, 8:1662)

When the properties of light, quickly melting snow are introduced into
the phrase "should have passed away" (kenu beki), vitality lodges within
the concept of ease in melting or vanishing. The question of whether to
regard "awayuki no" (A light snow melting) as a "pillow-word" or a
metaphor has been a matter of controversy among *Man'yōshū* commentators. This in turn has given rise to various unconvincing viewpoints,
the result of attempts to apply a definition of the latter-day pillow-word
to an ancient poem. If, on the other hand, "Awayuki no" is thought of
as a guide phrase—in the sense I have described—then its linkage to the
gist of the poem can only be metaphorical: there need be no question of
whether it is a pillow-word *or* a metaphor. Since metaphor, however,
has as its medium an intellectual thought process—and insofar as the
original import of the guide phrase lies in its direct introduction of the
kotodama into a poem—we might say that "Awayuki no" belongs to a
later stage of development in the life of the guide phrase. I propose to
examine the nature of the course followed by the guide phrase in the
following pages. Its growth will be discussed in the section on the earlier,
and its decline in the section on the later, Ancient Age.

Awareness of Ga and the Literati's World

"Yamato literature should be composed in the Yamato language." If we
agree that this realization resulted from a perception of "our Yamato"
in contrast to foreign countries, then the Ancient Age in Japan became
the "age of the kotodama" solely in reaction to the Yamato acceptance
of continental culture. The Ancient Age in Japan would most likely not
have evolved as it did without a relationship with the continent. This is
not to say, however, that the acceptance of continental culture worked
exclusively toward furthering ancient Yamato traditions. As continental
culture came increasingly to permeate Yamato society, the ancient kotodama continued its gradual decline, a process which lasted into the
Middle Ages.

The continental culture adopted by Yamato was centered on the ideal
of ga, which held that the only worthy literary acts were those based on
precedent. The spirit of Confucianism is doubtless reflected in this belief.
A thoroughly humanistic philosophy, Confucianism treats everything as
a matter of human responsibility. The underlying doctrine of Confu-

cianism can be represented by the concept of jen. The Chinese character with which the word is written consists of two parts: the left side signifies the human or a single human individual and the right side "two." The combination represents the Confucian belief that the prototype of all acts is found in the bond between human beings. An individual is therefore supposed to make things better through human capacity, not by relying on gods or other supernatural beings. Confucianism also represents a thoroughgoing rationalism. Historical precedents were expected to retain evidence attesting to the goodness of certain acts. And the sole means of making a good life was to follow precedents endorsed as good by many people whose assumptions rested on long years of experience. These precedents were ordered into "proprieties" (Ch. li; J. ri, kotowari) which were to be applied to one's social sphere. Detailed precedents gradually accumulated. There was no special term for precedents as they applied to the literary sphere. Yet the perception of a beautiful expression as one with classical precedents evolved in company with Confucianism: this is the ideal I have called ga.

Confucius studied divination in his later years. Since divination is essentially a form of fortunetelling, its revelations might be expected to come from supernatural beings. But as we know from Confucius' research notes, *Hsi-t'zu*, he tried to redefine divination as a law that governed both alteration in life and society and the order which runs through change. The spirit of rationalism in which he worked can only be called awesome. In the Sung period, these research notes were expanded into the rationalist (li-hsüeh) doctrine of Neoconfucianism formulated by Ch'eng I and Chu Hsi, thus bringing Confucian rationalism to its apex. Yet long before this apex was reached, Confucian rationalism must have created a sensation in seventh-century Yamato. Once rationalism suffused Yamato thought in the ninth century, the kotodama, which had been able to converse with grasses and trees, found itself stripped, at best, of its leading position and obliged to make way for the new ga literature. The transition seems to have occurred with the eighth century.

Confucian rationalism dominated Chinese society for roughly two thousand years, although it was far from being the sole system of thought. The philosophy formulated by Lao Tzu and Chuang Tzu was also present, together with Taoism, a modified version of their thought. Their philosophy was not unlike Confucianism in its scant emphasis on the future and its precept that people should secure the very best life as a prolongation of the present. On the other hand, it demonstrated a marked distrust in the human capacity to realize this goal and, most particularly, in judgments made according to reason. It stressed that reality moved in inconceivable ways, despite the diligence with which one drew inferences from past experience and followed those precedents that were thought to represent the highest good. The amassing of precedents was thought utterly powerless in the face of an eternally changing reality. Yet even a reality in constant flux was ultimately subject to the law of a vast and limitless universe beyond the grasp of human intellect. Lao Tzu gave this law the name of Tao, the Way. Lao Tzu's and Chuang Tzu's system of thought is truly outstanding as metaphysics, but is unsatisfactory in its correspondence to the realities of life. Chuang Tzu's treatise in particular is sharply divergent from reality.

More than the philosophy of Lao Tzu and Chuang Tzu, however, it was the deep roots of Taoism in Chinese folk religions that led it to a still greater inclination toward romanticism. The aim of Taoism became the pursuit of pleasure, thought to be everyone's basic wish. And the very best life so indicated was represented by the extreme idealizing of worldly pleasure. Descriptions of the Taoist paradise, the world of immortals, may provide some understanding of the forms taken by this idealizing. The world is one of eternal youth, where people live very long and pleasant lives. All have the ruddy cheeks of youth, and none experiences physical decline. More marvelous still, no old women are to be found among the female immortals, who consist solely of young beauties. The constituents of that world include fresh colors, opulent perfumes, splendid music and, although they are not singled out for description, one can imagine that the food and drink are superb as well.[8]

In sum, the world of immortals is an idealized extension of the human world. There is no difference whatsoever between the unsurpassed excellence and beauty enjoyed by the immortals and the pleasures of our own world. This is particularly true for the sexual aspects of pleasure. The earthly variety is indistinguishable from that found in the world of the immortals, as is unquestionably manifested by the presence of none but young beauties in the other world. Nevertheless, Taoist discipline demanded that before its practitioners were granted access to the world of immortals, they break away from the trivial pleasures and desires of this world to live the life of a man of nature, one who flees the tumult of the cities and inhabits fields or mountain forests. Those incapable of going to such lengths were at least to reject the idea of living in accordance with earthly morality (or, more precisely, Confucianism). A life in violation of earthly morality was called "madness" (k'uang; J. kyō) by the Taoists. The "mad" attitude toward life is less a Taoist invention than a product of the ideas originally put forth by Lao Tzu and Chuang Tzu: the Seven Sages of the Bamboo Grove are representative "madmen."

Ancient Yamato imported one more culture, that of Buddhism. From

[8] A poetic kind known as "pu-hsü tz'u" (verses on pacing the Void) celebrated the world of the immortals: many were composed between the Liang reign of the Six Dynasties and the T'ang period. I have summarized their descriptions.

the sixth century on, when it was taken up by the Yamato court, Buddhism excited expectations quite out of keeping with a religion intended originally to relieve human suffering. It was expected to function as a novel magic against famine, pestilence, and evil spirits. The *Nihon Shoki* transmits what followed: violent disputes between the proponents of Buddhism and the believers in the ancient gods of Yamato and their occult powers. The eventual triumph enjoyed by the powerful supporters of Buddhism represented nothing less than a grave crisis of faith in the kotodama. The original intent of Buddhism—to relieve suffering through the mastery of one act, the contemplation of mutability—also precipitated an indirect crisis within the ancient Yamato traditions. Yet when all is said and done, the most direct crisis may have been occasioned by the clash of one magic power against another, and the ensuing rout of Yamato beliefs.

In particular, the doctrine of the contemplation of mutability presented a crisis for kotodama literature. This is evident in the rapid decline in the number of elegies recited at the temporary mausoleums (mogari) of the nobility and the royal family, following the general acceptance of the Buddhist practice of cremation (Kanda, 1972, 37-53).[9] As Kanda shows in his study, the practice of cremation was not in itself Buddhist-inspired. It seems to have been suggested by Tibetan or Southeast Asian conventions. The fact that people lost the will to compose elegies is not, however, due solely to the act of cremation, but also in great part to the Buddhist doctrine of mutability, which made its believers fully aware of the break between their world and the land of the dead. The ceremonies held at temporary mausoleums took place in the hope that the soul of the deceased might return to his body. Once it had been concluded that all things return to the Void, however, the elegy, which had heretofore owed its existence to faint hopes that a soul might return, began its gradual transformation into the lament (aishōka), which mourned eternal separation. This alteration reveals the departure of the kotodama from the elegy.

Although Confucianism, Taoism, and Buddhism were all introduced from China, their aims differed greatly. These three systems of belief undoubtedly proved quite bewildering for their Yamato recipients. The Chinese themselves should have been equally bewildered. That did not happen. Instead, Chinese intellectuals harmonized most intelligently these three highly discrepant but preeminent kinds of morality. Attempts to grasp these Three Teachings from a unified standpoint may have begun

[9] [The temporary mausoleums or mogari were part of pre-Buddhist burial custom in Japan. The body of the deceased was first laid out in the mogari, a specially constructed building, so that relatives could recite prayers and attempt to persuade the soul to reenter the body. If the efforts failed, the corpse was buried.—Trans.]

with the *San-tse Lun (An Essay on the Three Philosophies)* of Chou Yung
(d. A.D. 485?) and the *T'ung Yüan (Penetrating to the Source)* of Chang
Jung (444-497), and extended to the *Wen-chung Tzu (Master Wen-chung)*
of Wang T'ung (584-618) and the *San-chiao Lun-heng (An Essay on the
Equilibrium of the Three Teachings)* of Po Chü-i (772-846). As an intellectual matter, the Three Teachings had clearly come to be seen as
representing perfection itself. Of course, insofar as the three possessed
wide discrepancies from the start, however attractive they may have been
as theories, efforts at practical application revealed several points of
conflict. Confucianism, which for nearly two thousand years enjoyed an
assured status as the state orthodoxy, served as doctrine above exception.
Taoism and Buddhism both had their vicissitudes, and both were even
subjected to occasional violent denunciations. A means was devised to
bring about a smooth accord between Confucianism on the one hand,
and Taoism and Buddhism in their less enviable positions on the other.
One's behavior in public life was to accord with Confucian morality,
whereas in private life one was free to nourish body and soul with Taoist
and Buddhist teachings. This was admirably put into practice by one
representative figure, Po Chü-i.

Po Chü-i was the author of the *New Ballads*, fifty poems of ardent
social criticism. He was also a scholar at the Hanlin Academy under the
direct control of the Emperor, and had charge of the preparation of
important government documents. He was, moreover, a capable provincial official, serving as marshal of Chiang-chou, governor of Hangchow,
and governor of Soochow; he rose from the high post of vice-minister
of justice to the even greater eminence of minister of justice. His political
views during this time were rooted in Confucianism, as he himself states
in his "Reply at the Tomb of the Four Wise Men":

> When the Way prevails on earth, show your talent;
> When the Way does not prevail, hide it in the folds of your robe.
> These are the very words of the Sage:
> I learned them from Chung-ni.[10]
>
> (*Hakushi*, 2:1763)

The public servant Po Chü-i was a devout adherent of Confucianism in
both its theoretical and its practical aspects. Yet one certainly is not to
suppose from this that Po Lo-t'ien the private man was equally Confucian.[11] He is famous for calling the zither, poetry, and wine his Three

---

[10] [In the third line "the Sage" and in the fourth "Chung-ni" both refer to Confucius.—
Trans.]
[11] [Po Lo-t'ien (J. Haku Rakuten) is another name for Po Chü-i.—Trans.]

Friends.[12] He had, however, one more Friend: women. When he was sixty-nine, Po suffered a slight walking impairment as the result of a palsy (feng-chi, perhaps a stroke). Realizing that there were limits to his physical strength, he freed his singing-girls, who had been under an obligation to serve him exclusively; but he kept two of them, Fan-su and Hsiao-man. By the following year, however, he had found the voluptuous Hsiao-man a considerable burden, and so, eager to turn her over to a responsible master, he published "A Song of Willow Branches" (*Hakushi*, Go, 17:2388), announcing the availability of this beauty:

> In the spring breeze, the myriad branches of one tree
> Are lovelier than gold, more graceful than silken threads.
> In the western Yung-feng quarter, by a neglected garden,
> She spends her days alone: on whom shall she rely?[13]

Intimacies with such women were, like drinking parties, either proscribed by Confucian morality or, at the very least, frowned upon. Yet in the Taoist scheme of things these activities, as well as those of playing the zither and composing poetry, had a positive value. This was because they represented a miniaturized version of the immortals' way of life. An earthly life replete with agreeable music, splendid writing, ample food and drink, and fascinating beauties may have been insignificant in comparison with the delights enjoyed by the immortals. Yet when a non-immortal patterned himself after these higher beings, the world he created was nevertheless highly desirable. Zither, poetry, wine, and singing-girls were the formative elements of the ideal known as elegance (feng-liu, J. fūryū; Konishi, 1962, 271-78). And the private citizen Po Lo-t'ien continued to enjoy a life of elegance into his old age.

Placed in the same dimension with music, wine, and singing-girls as one of the basic constituents of elegance, poetry refers to verse that expresses personal emotion. It falls within Lo-t'ien's own categories of tranquillity (hsien-shih) and heartache (kan-shang). By Confucian standards such private poetry belonged to a lower dimension, especially when compared with another poetic category, the admonishment (feng-yü), which emphasized social criticism and political principles. Buddhism also took a dim view of such poetry, dismissing it as "frivolous language." It was, to use Po's own expression, no more than "wild words and fancy language" (k'uang-yen ch'i-yü; J. kyōgen kigo).

A basic concept in Buddhism is its view of this world as a place of suffering which is to be transcended. If Confucianism is concerned with

[12] See "Pei-ch'uang San-yu" (Three Friends at the North Window), *Hakushi*, Go, 3:3120.
[13] The circumstances are described in *Yün-ch'i Yu-i*. [The Yung-feng was a pleasure quarter.—Trans.]

the past, and Taoism with the present, then Buddhism may well be said to concern itself with the future. To look at the matter from the Buddhist standpoint, which regards this world in its entirety as suffering, all literature that expresses the various joys, angers, sorrows, and pleasures of this world—not to mention celebrations of zither, poetry, wine, and singing-girls—is "wild words and fancy language." The only worthy prose and poetry are works which sing of the sufferings of this world and one's transcendence of it. Caught up in political realities as a public servant and savoring the elegant life as a private citizen, Po composed works in celebration of these matters. Yet his affirmation that the entire corpus consists of "wild words and fancy language" is qualified by his conviction that even these "wild words" will ultimately become "a factor extolling the Law," because supreme enlightenment is obtained only through the momentum of real-life trivialities.[14] His logic utilizes to the full a basic thesis of Mahāyāna Buddhism, that "worldly passions are one and the same with enlightenment." So glossed, his comments provide an excellent discourse on the concurrence of the Three Teachings. Po Chü-i was not alone in espousing such ideas and their practical application, but rather held them in common with other representative Chinese intellectuals. One might, for example, describe Su Tung-p'o's (1036-1101) approach to the problem in similar terms.

The people of ancient Yamato did not learn the proper application of the Three Teachings—Confucianism in public life, Taoism or Buddhism in private life—through the example of the Chinese poet. This can be said because Ōtomo Tabito (665-731), who demonstrated their proper application in Yamato, died forty-one years before the birth of Po Chü-i. The idea of concurrence among the Three Teachings had, however, been in circulation from the time of the Southern Ch'i Dynasty in the Six Dynasties period and was therefore not suddenly brought into evidence by Po Chü-i, who conveyed an already existing philosophy. My singling out of one Chinese poet is justified only in the sense that he exemplifies the great dexterity with which this concept was put into practice. For their part, Yamato intellectuals probably reproduced, though somewhat clumsily, the Chinese pattern preexisting Po. Tabito's penchant for brandishing Confucian sentiments on public occasions can be seen

---

[14] "I have long cherished one desire, that my deeds on this earth and the faults occasioned by my wild words and fancy language shall be transformed, for worlds to come, into a factor extolling the Law and a link to the preaching of the Buddha's Word. May the myriad Buddhas of the Three Worlds take heed" (Haku Kōzan Shishū). This statement had profound influence on medieval Japanese literature. ["Kyōgen kigo"—"wild words and fancy language"—is an expression that has become part of the Japanese language, amounting also to a term in literary criticism.—Ed.]

in one of his Chinese poems, entitled "On Attending the Royal New Year's Banquet" (*Kaifū*, 44):

Long has His Majesty ruled with lenient heart:
He follows the ancient Way, yet innovates.
His guests, splendid and refined, enter the Four Gates:
A multitude, all versed in the Three Virtues.
On the crumbling riverbanks a snowfall of plum blossoms swirls;
Haze stretches across the early spring skies.
We delight in this banquet by the Sage-King's grace:
As one we celebrate his perfect virtue.[15]

This encomium to the present reign is expressed in Confucian terms, a point that needs no further elucidation. And the *Kaifūsō* contains any number of such Confucian panegyrics, all of which resemble Tabito's poem down to the vocabulary and expressions employed. It was apparently common practice for eighth-century Japanese bureaucrats to adopt a Confucian pose on official occasions, when, for example, they were honored with a royal command to recite a poem at a palace banquet. In other words, this was not an idiosyncracy of Tabito alone. Yet the thirteen "Poems in Praise of Wine" (*MYS*, 3:338-50), made public to his intimate circle by this same Tabito, exhibit a posture akin to Taoism, although it is not known to what extent if any this was intentional. The poems do not celebrate Taoist thought, but their stance—that pleasure in this world is the highest standard—is a Taoist one:

Kono yo ni shi	If only pleasure be mine
Tanoshiku araba	In this world of ours,
Kon yo ni wa	Then let me be reborn
Mushi ni mo tori ni mo	An insect or a bird
Ware wa narinan.	In the world to come.

(*MYS*, 3:348)

Ikeru mono	The fate of
Tsui ni mo shinuru	All that lives
Mono ni areba	Is death:
Ima aru hodo wa	May my allotted span
Tanoshiku o aran.	Be pleasant, then!

(*MYS*, 3:349)

[15] [The "Four Gates" are the palace gates to the four quarters. The "Three Virtues" are the Confucian ones of wisdom, benevolence, and courage.—Trans.]

Tabito also had an understanding of Buddhism, as is clear from his allusion to transmigration, rebirth as a different being in the next world. He did not, however, take a serious view of the next world. And, although he was very likely aware that the prohibition against drinking alcohol was one of the Five Great Commandments within the two-hundred-and-fifty-commandment corpus of Buddhism, we cannot hail him as a champion of Buddhism when he declares:

Iwan sube	Nothing I can say,
Sen sube shirazu	Nothing I can do
Kiwamarite	Will demonstrate
Tōtoki mono wa	The high esteem
Sake ni shi aru rashi.	I feel for wine.[16]

(MYS, 3:342)

Nakanaka ni	If I were not a man,
Hito to arazu wa	Then most of all
Sakatsubo ni	I'd like to be
Nari nite shi kamo	A wine jar,
Sake ni shiminan.	And steep myself in sake.

(MYS, 3:343)

He then introduces the Seven Sages of the Bamboo Grove as the authority behind his vigorous affirmation of wine:

Inishie no	Even the Seven
Nana no sakashiki	Wise Men of
Hitotachi mo	Long ago
Horiseshi mono wa	Craved, it seems,
Sake ni shi aru rashi.	Just one thing: wine.

(MYS, 3:340)

The Seven Sages were, as was noted above, a group of "madmen" who opposed Confucian rationalism. This does not necessarily mean that their aim was to achieve entry into the Taoist world of immortals, but insofar as the philosophy of Lao Tzu and Chuang Tzu was upheld by Taoism, the Seven Sages, together with Tabito the wine jar manqué, can be called

---

[16] [The "sake" of the Japanese is the so-called rice wine. The two terms are used interchangeably in the English version of the following poem, but it should not be assumed that the creature spoken of resembles what we think of as wine, or modern sake for that matter.—Trans., Ed.]

Taoist in the broad sense of the word. Yet at other times Tabito's poetry reveals a sincere conviction that the world is a delusion:

Yo no naka wa	Each time I realize
Munashiki mono to	The transience of
Shiru toki shi	This world,
Iyoyo masumasu	The more, the harder
Kanishikarikeri.	I am struck with sadness.

(*MYS*, 5:793)

These poems show how difficult it is to make sweeping conclusions about Tabito's anti-Buddhist tendencies. Official occasions, more than likely, demanded compositions based solely on Confucianism, whereas either Taoism or Buddhism seems to have been acceptable in private circumstances.

A similar discrimination is found in the works of Tabito's contemporary, Fujiwara Maro (695-737). At official ceremonies like the Festival of Confucius, Maro also assembled the usual Confucian phrases into appropriate verses (*Kaifū*, 97). Yet the Chinese poems he composed at private banquets were not at all Confucian. The reader of the following preface to a Chinese poem (*Kaifū*, 94) could not guess that its author was a dignitary holding the junior third rank and the concurrent offices of war minister and governor of the Left and Right Districts of the capital, a wielder of power who was to become the patriarch of the capital branch of the Fujiwara clan. In fact the reader could only mistake Maro for an unworldly sort who looked askance at politics:

> I am a madman of this happy age! The wind and the moon are my sole concern, fishing and bird hunts are my sole pleasures. Indulgence in fame and the search for wealth have never been my aim. "When served wine, one should sing": this accords with my wishes. As this fine day draws to a close, I visit my brother's elegant banquet. Here they sing, there they drink wine. In this place they have their fill of pleasure. One poet recites, another composes: the sparks of their genius mount at will to the high heavens. Chi K'ang is my friend of one thousand years. Po-lun is my drinking teacher for one night of inebriation.[17]

This does not mean, however, that Maro actually thought this way. It was probably his intention, rather, to try his hand at the role of "mad-

---

[17] [Chi K'ang (A.D. 223-62), poet, zither player, and admirer of Lao Tzu and Chuang Tzu, was one of the Seven Sages of the Bamboo Grove. Po-lun, also known as Liu Ling, was another of the Seven Sages. A poet, he displayed his love of wine in compositions like "Praise of the Virtues of Wine."—Trans.]

man," because he knew that it was common practice for Chinese intellectuals to adopt a Taoist or Buddhist posture on private occasions. This view was founded on the awareness that a Chinese poem or a Japanese uta following a precedented, special formulation—which is in fact the ideal of ga—thereby becomes a worthy composition. Although it was not necessarily regarded as a courtly pose in China, that ideal of "madness" was apparently treated as high ga in Yamato by virtue of its presence in the Chinese classics.

In fact, the concept of feng-liu (J. fūryū), a part of the Taoist view of courtliness which was associated with the world of immortals, evidently occupied a higher status in China than did the concept of madness. We might note here the Chinese characters used in the Man'yōshū to write the word "fūryū." One example is found in an exchange of poems between Lady Ishikawa and Ōtomo Tanushi:

Miyabio to	You're a man of *miyabi*,
Ware wa kikeru o	Or so I had heard—
Yado kasazu	Yet you refused to let me stay,
Ware o kaeseri	You sent me home instead,
Oso no *miyabio*.	Doltish man of *miyabi*![18]
	(*MYS*, 2:126)

Miyabio ni	Now I know I am indeed
Ware wa arikeri	A man of *miyabi*!
Yado kasazu	When I refused to let you stay
Kaeshishi ware zo	And sent you home instead,
Miyabio ni wa aru.	I was a perfect man of *miyabi*.[19]
	(*MYS*, 2:127)

Ōtomo Tanushi was evidently famous for his good looks; in an afternote to Lady Ishikawa's poem he is introduced thus:

> Ōtomo Tanushi was known by his sobriquet, Chūrō [Second Son]. He was handsome in appearance and excelled in miyabi.[20] No one who saw or heard of him could help but admire him.

The afternote continues with further information. Lady Ishikawa happened to fall in love with Tanushi. One night, she disguised herself as a

---

[18] [The first "Miyabio" is written with the characters for "man of the world" (yūshi), the second with those for "man of elegance" (fūryūshi).—Trans.]

[19] [Tanushi's use of characters for "miyabio" follows that noted for the preceding poem. —Trans.]

[20] ["Miyabi" here is written with the characters for "elegance," "fūryū."—Trans.]

poverty-stricken old woman and, carrying an iron pot with her, knocked on the door of Tanushi's house closest to his bedroom. "I am a neighbor," she croaked. "Could you let me have some coals for my fire?" Tanushi took the request at face value: he gave her the coals and sent her on her way. At dawn a deeply mortified Lady Ishikawa sent the former uta, half in jest, to Tanushi, who replied with the latter. The events recorded in this afternote appear to have been embellished in later times, in the interests of a livelier tale. The poems themselves, however, may be safely regarded as dating from the reign of Jitō (r. 687-97). The content of the story is expressed by these poems with the word "fūryū": moreover, the fact that the Chinese characters for "fūryū," together with that for "yū" (amusement, pleasure), were pronounced "miyabi" in the Japanese reading indicates that the words "fūryū" and "yū" contained a common meaning. This in turn can only be due to a contemporary association of the words with relations with a person of the opposite sex (Okazaki, 1947, 33-36).

Any consideration of the nature of fūryū must take account that a "miyabio" or "man of elegance" could be represented in characters meaning "man of the world" or "man of pleasure" (yūshi) or "man of elegance" (fūryūshi). The Japanese verb form "miyabu" literally means to behave as one would within a "miya," that is, in the royal residence or court. Its property came to consist of a refined air or appearance. A poem from Lady Ōtomo of Sakanoe to Shōmu Tennō is a self-effacing avowal that her remote village lacks miyabi:

Ashihiki no	I live in the mountains,
Yama ni shi oreba	With their sprawling foothills,
Miyabi nami	And so my ways
Waga suru waza o	Have no miyabi:
Togametamō no.	May you graciously forgive me![21]

(MYS, 4:721)

Behind the lady's modesty lies the implication that truly elegant behavior is to be found at court. Erotic love was made one of the attributes of miyabi-fūryū because highly civilized people evaluated it positively—on the condition that it represented courtly and refined behavior. But why was it evaluated positively in Yamato? Because it was in China, and the same was concluded to be true for Yamato. Why, then, did feng-liu/fūryū have a positive value in China? Because it was linked to the world of immortals.

[21] [In the Japanese, "miyabi" is written "fūryū."—Trans.]

Unahara no	Wave-tossed and dripping,
Tōki watari o	I have crossed
Miyabio no	The great expanse of sea
Miyabi o min to	To behold *men of miyabi*
Nazusai zo koshi.	At their pleasures.[22]

(*MYS*, 6:1016)

Kose Sukunamaro, the host of a private banquet, wrote this poem on white paper and affixed it, in an envelope, to the wall. It had this forenote: "The immortal ladies of P'eng-lai made this vine envelope for elegant and talented gentlemen. It is not to be opened by ordinary people!"[23] The speaker of the poem is a female immortal: "I have come," she says, "across the sea from P'eng-lai expressly to behold the miyabi of you gentlemen." It is natural to have wine and music at a banquet, but the attributes of fūryū will only be complete if beautiful women are added to the company of poets present. This banquet, however, was not open to "ordinary people," those who did not understand courtly and refined tastes. It must be composed solely of an elite belonging totally to the world of fūryū. Even Lady Ishikawa's behavior, though itself deserving of censure from the standpoint of Yamato common sense, is lent authority by a passage from the preface to the *New Songs from the Jade Terrace*:

> [Court ladies] peruse *The Book of Songs* and revere *The Book of Rites* [*Li Chi*]. They are quite unlike that lady who arranged her own marriage to her neighbor on the east. Their modesty and graceful elegance [feng-liu] do not differ in the least from the manners taught to Hsi Shih.[24]

By the measure of the elegant world, then, Lady Ishikawa's actions would have been seen in a more positive light.

A world of fūryū, in which matters uncommon to the ordinary world were evaluated positively, existed in Yamato simply because it also existed in China. Although fūryū had not existed in Yamato from ages past, it was esteemed in China, a culturally advanced country, and as such the concept definitely represented an irrefutable authority, the world of ga. Certain elements of this world may not have appealed to the sensibilities

[22] [Here "miyabio" is written "yūshi," "men of the world"; and "miyabi" is written "yū," "pleasures."—Trans.]

[23] [P'eng-lai (J. Hōrai) was one of three sacred mountains located in the sea to the east of China; immortals were said to dwell there. "Miyabi" here is written "fūryū" and translated "elegant."—Trans.]

[24] [Hsi Shih was a famous beauty (fl. late 5th cent. B.C.) from the Kingdom of Yüeh. Following the defeat of her country by the Kingdom of Wu, she served its King, Fu Cha. —Trans.]

of the Yamato people. Nevertheless, those who were highly cultured (or believed themselves to be) felt obliged to approve of a fūryū world constructed along Chinese lines. This world was, however, a conceptual one to contemporary Yamato intellectuals. Although they were aware that the most valued compositions of all, those in Chinese poetry and prose, originated within this very world, neither the Yamato composers of such pieces nor their audiences may have been capable of adequately grasping the extent of this value. They were, however, certain that eminent Chinese like the gentlemen mentioned in Yü Hsin's "K'u-shu Fu" (The Withered Tree Rhapsody) were often highly esteemed for excelling in both fengliu and proper Confucian behavior: "Yin Chung-wen was famed from sea to sea for his feng-liu and his Confucian deportment."[25] No such assurances were available, on the other hand, to aid in understanding what was considered meritorious behavior by Lao Tzu and Chuang Tzu or the Taoists. When Ochi no Hirose, vice-minister of justice and professor of the national school reminisces (*Kaifū*, 58)—

> The Classics are difficult for me,
> The *Chuang Tzu* and *Lao Tzu* are what I like.
> My life is already half over:
> Why cudgel my brains at this late date?—

one finds it very hard to believe that these are his true feelings. If he had indeed been incompetent in the "wen-tsao" (Confucius' term for "wen-hsüeh," literature), he would not have been employed as a university professor.[26] His poem was thus apparently written to conform to the Chinese conceptual pattern of venerating Lao Tzu and Chuang Tzu in one's private life. Even Ōtomo Tabito and Fujiwara Maro managed to assume a Taoist pose, or one typical of Lao Tzu and Chuang Tzu, in solely intellectual terms. On balance we may conclude that a spiritual climate conducive to the realization of Taoist thought in one's actual experience did not exist in Yamato at this time.

The world of fūryū, conceptual though it was, nevertheless possessed a system of values. The fact remains that this world did take shape in Yamato, and that certain people became aware of belonging to it and thereby creating or receiving worthy literature. The fūryū world was inhabited by talented people specially trained in literary techniques— literati, as it were. They are not necessarily to be identified with the wen-jen (literati) of later times (the Yüan and Ming Dynasties), although they

[25] *Yü Tzu-shan Chi-chu* (Ssu-pu Pei-yao ed.), vol. 1, ting 16. A photocopied edition exists (Taiwan, 1968). [Three preceding notes of the original, which amplify documentation of fine points in the text, have been omitted.—Ed.]

[26] [The "Classics" of the poem is "wen-tsao" in the original.—Trans.]

did share several characteristics. If we think of the elegant and talented intellectuals of eighth-century Yamato as literati in a broad sense of the word, then Tabito and Okura were undoubtedly the distinguished literati of their time. It must nevertheless be acknowledged that this fūryū world was still no more than an idea, and that an elegance rooted in actual experience had not yet been fully formed. Fūryū was to abandon its role as mere concept and evolve into a body of tangible literature and aesthetics with roots in experience, but only in the ensuing Middle Ages; and they will be discussed in the next volume.

At this point I wish only to note that fūryū, the governing ideal of the Early Middle Ages, was, while still in its conceptual stage, an attempt to constitute one of the spheres of expression extant in the Ancient Age. The venerable kotodama of Yamato was unavoidably obliged to retreat before the Sinified courtliness of fūryū. Unlike the feng-liu concept which, in the guise of ga, first took Yamato by storm, however, the kotodama maintained its vigor at least into the mid-ninth century. It is for this reason that we may take the Ancient Age to end there.

CHAPTER 4

The Works, Their Reception, and Their Transmission

METHODS AND AIMS OF THE WORKS

Yamato was already a literate society at the beginning of the Ancient Age. The archaic practice of composition and transmission based exclusively on oral means was gradually disappearing. Of course oral composition and transmission were not utterly done away with by the introduction of writing. For several reasons, they remained effective well into the Ancient Age. Not only was it difficult to record the Yamato language with Chinese characters, and nearly impossible to ensure its correct reproduction through these means, but instances also frequently occurred when time constraints barred a composer from writing down his work. This was particularly true for extemporaneous compositions like the following:

Hisakata no	Far-distant
Ame mo furanu ka	Rain, why not fall,
Hachisuba ni	So we might see
Tamareru mizu no	Your jewel-like waters
Tama ni nitaru min.	Gathered on these lotus leaves?

It is traditionally said of this poem:

There was once a member of the Military Guard of the Right who was a very gifted composer of waka. On one occasion, the division chief had food and drink prepared at his official residence, and gave a banquet for the officials of the Guard. The serving platters consisted of lotus leaves. Everyone became quite tipsy with sake and sang and danced, one after another. The Military Guard official was then urged to compose a poem about those lotus leaves. He immediately rose to the occasion and composed this poem (*MYS*, 16:3837).[1]

[1] [The "Military Guard of the Right" belonged to one (the hyōe) of three Guard units protecting the palace. There was the emon, which patrolled the outermost perimeter; the hyōe, which guarded the inner precincts not inhabited by the tennō; and the konoe, which protected the tennō and his surroundings. Each unit was divided into Left and Right, corresponding to sections of the palace grounds.—Trans.]

This is unmistakably an instance of an orally composed work. A further example is provided by a uta composed by Yamanoe Okura when he was lying ill:

Onoko ya mo	Is man fated
Munashikaru beki	To crumble into dust
Yorozuyo ni	Undistinguished by fine deeds
Kataritsugu beki	Like those a father tells his son
Na wa tatezu shite.	For generations everlasting?

The above poem was recited when Lord Yamanoe Okura was sick in bed. Lord Fujiwara Yatsuka sent his lordship Kawabe Azumabito to inquire after Okura's health. Okura, having given his reply, paused a moment; then, wiping tears from his eyes, he grieved and lamented, and recited this poem (*MYS*, 6:978).

It would be difficult to regard this poem as one written in advance for oral presentation. Orally composed uta were evidently not few in number, even late in the age of the *Man'yōshū*.

Nevertheless such uta do not always possess the same properties as the oral composition discussed by Parry and Lord. In oral composition, according to them, the composer relates only those contents that can be managed by means of the techniques he has on hand (Parry, 1930, 78). Compositions like those just quoted do not easily fit that conception, because they represent not a binding together of formulas but instances of the free creation of new methods of expression according to what one wishes to convey. Composition produced from the binding together of formulas has always been necessary for oral works of considerable length. It is not, however, very effective in a poetic form like the tanka, with its five lines and thirty-one syllables. Debates have also taken place over the question of whether the Parry-Lord theory can be applied to short narrative poetry like the *Romancero*.[2] It seems doubtful that this theory could have any relevance whatsoever to the tanka.

What of the chōka? Here too the Parry-Lord theory appears to have no application. We can look back to the Archaic Age for instances of formulas in chōka:

Tsuginefu ya	Where peaks abound
Yamashiro kawa o	Along the Yamashiro River,
Kawanobori	I go up the stream,

---

[2] Research by Bruce A. Beatle on the Spanish *Romancero* suggests that the Parry-Lord theory can be applied to short narrative poetry (Beatle, 1964, 92-113).

Wa ga noboreba	And as I make my way upstream
Kawa no he ni	I see growing
Oidateru	On the river's edge
Sashibu o	A sashibu, oh,
Sashibu no ki	A sashibu tree.
Shi ga shita ni	And at its foot
Oidateru	There grows
Habiro	A broad-leafed
Yutsu matsubaki	Sacred camellia.
Shi ga hana no	His countenance beams
Teri imashi	Like these bright flowers,
Shi ga ha no	He resides in a palace
Hirori imasu wa	Spacious as these spreading leaves:
Ōkimi rokamo.	Yes, my lord and sovereign.

(*KJK, Song*, 57)

The italicized lines (except for the formulaic last two) in the following *Kojiki* chōka indicate vocabulary or lines in common with the preceding song.

Yamato no	At this hilltop
Kono takechi ni	Festival in Yamato,
Kodakaru	On rising ground,
Ichi no tsukasa	On the festival hill,
Niinaeya ni	Close by the Harvest Building,
Oidateru	*Grows a*
Habiro	*Broad-leafed*
Yutsu matsubaki	*Sacred camellia.*
Shi ga ha no	*He resides in a palace spacious*
Hirori imashi	*As these spreading leaves,*
Shi no hana no	*His countenance beams*
Teri imasu	*Like these bright flowers*:
Takahikaru	Your Majesty, Child of
Hi no miko ni	The high-gleaming Sun,
Toyomiki	Please partake of
Tatematsurase	This fine sake.
(*Koto no katarigoto mo*	(*This was transmitted*
Ko o ba.)	*By word of mouth.*)[3]

(*KJK, Song*, 101)

[3] [The "Harvest Building" (niinaeya) of the fifth line was the site where the Harvest Festival (Niinaematsuri) was celebrated.—Trans.]

The following are instances of lines held in common with one or the other of these chōka:

Tsuginefu ya Yamashiro kawa	The River of Yamashiro Where mountain peaks abound
	(*KJK, Song*, 58)
Takahikaru Hi no miko	His Majesty, Child of The high-gleaming Sun
	(*KJK, Song*, 28, plus two more instances; eleven instances in *MYS*).
Toyomiki Tatematsurase	Please partake of This fine sake.
	(*KJK, Song*, 5)
(*Koto no katarigoto mo Ko o ba.*)	(*This was transmitted By word of mouth.*)
	(*KJK, Song*, 2, plus four more instances)

If such examples were to appear in great number in Yamato song, then the Parry-Lord theory would be applicable to it. The fact is, however, that there is no other instance in which this number of lines is held in common among two or more chōka. The examples given are adventitious, and we must conclude that application of the Parry-Lord theory to the chōka is unwarranted.

Yet common lines do sometimes appear in Yamato song and waka. Rather, *certain kinds* of common lines are to be found in no small number. The following chōka lines may serve as representative examples:

Yasumishishi Wa ga ōkimi Takaterasu Hi no miko. . . .	He who holds sway, Our ruler, His Majesty, Child of The high-shining Sun. . . .

These lines appear eight times.[4] The following appear six times:

Ōkimi wa Kami ni shi maseba. . . .	Because our Ruler Is indeed divine. . . .

[4] Including the following variations: waga / wago; takaterasu / takahikaru; hi no miko / waga hi no miko.

There are, moreover, several instances of related phrases; related concepts within poems are even more common.[5] Seven similar poems follow, all from the *Man'yōshū*:

Wa ga seko wa	Where might my husband's
Izuku yukuran	Journey have led him?
Okitsumo no	Is he today crossing
Nabari no yama o	The mountains of Nabari
Kyō ka koyu ran.	Far from the offing-grasses?

(1:43)

Asagiri ni	Your robe, damp
Nurenishi koromo	With morning mists,
Hosazu shite	Has yet to dry:
Hitori ya kimi ga	Are you, all alone,
Yamaji koyu ran.	Crossing on the mountain paths?

(9:1666)

Okure ite	Here I remain
Wa ga koi oreba	In longing for you:
Shirakumo no	Where the white clouds
Tanabiku yama o	Stretch in banners on the hills,
Kyō ka koyu ran.	Will you cross to come to me?

(9:1681)

Yamashina no	In Yamashina
Iwada no ono no	Near the little Iwada fields
Hahasohara	With their stands of oaks,
Mitsutsu ya kimi ga	Do you spend your time in looking
Yamaji koyu ran.	As you cross on mountain paths?

(9:1730)

Kusakage no	Do you gaze upon
Arai no saki no	The Isle of Kasa
Kasashima o	Close by Cape Arai
Mitsutsu ka kimi ga	Of shadowed grasses
Yamaji koyu ran.	As you cross on mountain paths?

(12:3192)

[5] Sasaki Nobutsuna's valuable study of repeated poems and phrases in the *Man'yōshū* (Sasaki, 1948) is the only important work on the subject. He includes poems appearing more than once as well as poems with minor variations.

Tamakatsuma	In the evening light
Shimakumayama no	On Mount Shimakuma, lovely
Yūgure ni	As a tightweave basket,
Hitori ka kimi ga	Are you, all alone,
Yamaji koyu ran.	Crossing on the mountain paths?

(12:3193)

Iki no o ni	Beloved, whose soul
Wa ga mō kimi wa	Is bound to mine,
Tori ga naku	Are you today crossing
Azuma no saka o	The hills toward the East
Kyō ka koyu ran.	Where the cocks crow?

(12:3194)

The composers of poems such as these did not make use of set conceptions only in the case of extemporaneous compositions. They might also have done so as a result of their awareness of the ga principle that beautiful expressions are those with precedents. And even in written composition, the use of preexisting phrases and conceptions as aesthetic language necessarily betokens a certain economy of thought. If, in sum, we abstract from the Parry-Lord theory the property of a regular reserve of phrases essential to extemporaneous composition, and accept the single point of economy of thought, we can appreciate that their theory is applicable, to some extent, to a genre of short works composed within an ample span of time.

I have expressly qualified the above statement with "to some extent" for a special reason. Over a lengthy period, the ancient Yamato attitude toward composition became increasingly oriented toward the refinement of expression, and this led to extremely free variations. Thus a predominance of formulas as in oral literature does not manifest itself, at least in the Man'yōshū. Take, for example, these poems by Ōtomo Yakamochi:

Two uta composed in advance, to express his feelings on meeting a nobleman or encountering a beautiful woman while visiting the capital.

Mimaku hori	Just as I was wishing,
Omoishi nae ni	Hoping for a glimpse,
Kazura kake	I have encountered
Kaguwashi kimi o	You, dear lady,
Aimitsuru kamo.	Wearing garlands in your hair.

(MYS, 18:4120)

Mairi no	It was at court
Kimi ga sugata o	That I used to see your face
Mizu hisa ni	In times long past:
Hina ni shi sumeba	Life in the countryside
Are koinikeri.	Has made me miss you so!
(*Ichi no atama ni*	(*Or, for the first two lines*)
iwaku)	
Hashiki yoshi	It was once my pleasure
Imo ga sugata o.	To glory in your charms.[6]

(*MYS*, 18:4121)

Yakamochi equipped himself with these uta so as to use them at some later date. Their expression had thus been thoroughly polished. These poems must have been written compositions, if we are to judge by the second poem, with its alternative opening lines, "It was once my pleasure / To glory in your charms," held in readiness in case he encountered a woman. Works composed in advance appear not infrequently in the *Man'yōshū*. Many of the poems composed by royal command on public occasions must have been prepared in advance. This is evident, for example, in the forenote to two poems by Ōtomo Tabito (*MYS*, 3:315-16):

> When, in late spring, His Majesty took up residence in the Yoshino Detached Palace, the Ōtomo Middle Counselor composed this chōka and its envoy at His Majesty's command. (They were never recited before the Sovereign, however.)

The forenote indicates that Tabito composed the poems in advance, expecting to present them on a future occasion. Obviously, advance compositions were generally written works.

It will be clear that the Parry-Lord concept of formulas is not applicable to conditions in ancient Yamato. At the same time it is also true that formulas exist in ancient Yamato poetry. At least the Parry-Lord definition of a formula conforms perfectly to the characteristics of the "pillow-word."[7] To give it again, Parry's definition of a formula is: "The formula in the Homeric poems may be defined as *a group of words which is regularly employed under the same metrical conditions to express a given essential idea*" (Parry, 1930, 80). As is suggested by "in the Homeric

---

[6] [Clearly the former poem could only be sent to a woman; but the second is meant for a man, unless the alternative two opening lines were substituted.—Trans., Ed.]

[7] Definition is one thing. It is yet another that one seeks far for the properties of formulas found in oral composition. Simple repetition of phrases or lines found in written composition must be considered a separate matter.

poems," Parry's definition concerns the formulas in Homer's *Iliad* and *Odyssey*, and was not intended to take into consideration such devices as the Yamato pillow-word. And yet, if we omit the qualification, "in the Homeric poems," we will see that the so-called pillow-word does not depart in the least from Parry's definition. How should this be interpreted?

According to common opinion, the bases for differentiating between the "pillow-word" on the one hand and the "preface" on the other rest chiefly on the criteria of length and the number of times they are repeated. We may acknowledge that, in principle, the pillow-word is made up of five syllables. It cannot, however, always be maintained that a preface is used only once, whereas a pillow-word is customarily repeated any number of times. Some "prefaces" are used repeatedly, like "Court officials, eighty . . ." (Mononofu no yaso) and "The warrior confronts / His target, hunting arrow / At the ready . . ." (Masurao ga / Satsuya tabasami / Tachimukau), whereas several "pillow-words" seem to have been used only once. This has led to the devising of awkward terms like the "pillow-word-like preface" (Tsuchihashi, 1960, 448). Originally, however, the pillow-word and the preface were one and the same: they served as the medium through which the kotodama was introduced into the vital words within a work or, to paraphrase Parry, introduced into a given essential word, so as to create an animated expression. It will be recalled that I have renamed these techniques "guide phrases" (dōshi). If there is a difference in meaning, the question arises *why* the guide phrase was transformed into the pillow-word in the centuries following the Ancient Age, and why the longer guide phrase (the preface) fell into decline and eventual extinction. The key to the problem will be sought elsewhere, in the development, after the Ancient Age, of formulas that differ in nature from those of the Parry-Lord theory.

The Ancient Age saw the growth of expression based on preexisting phrases and conceptions, as we have seen. This development came about from the growth in Yamato society of an awareness of ga, which had its prototype in China. Certain kinds of guide phrases were already being utilized on a repetitive basis in the Archaic Age. These differ from the ga principle of precedent by virtue of their acknowledged efficacy in invoking the kotodama. At a certain point of the Ancient Age, however, they came to be repeated out of an aesthetic awareness that expression based on preexisting diction was beautiful expression. It was for this reason that pillow-words eventually came to be used as formulas of a sort in the centuries following the Ancient Age. As guide phrases came to be used as formulas, the longer ones, which were after all difficult to memorize and had not proved efficient for repeated use, gradually disappeared. Some short, five-syllable guide phrases, moreover, had proved to be inefficiently utilized and were ill equipped to conform to formulaic conditions. They too were therefore slowly eliminated, until only a relatively small number of pillow-words remained to be transmitted to later ages. In principle, because the pillow-word is characterized by repeated use, it is differentiated from the preface which, also in principle, is used only once. To say so is to make use of conceptions reflecting the later period of decline.

This is not to say, however, that the guide phrase disappeared in the Ancient Age. The poets of the first half of the age, and Kakinomoto Hitomaro in particular, made no attempt to depart from the original qualities of the guide phrase. The number of pillow-words used by Hitomaro differs according to the method of computation, but it is thought to range from 106 examples to 122, and of these, some 64 varieties appear to have originated with him.[8] His perception that new guide phrases could be created derives from his expectation that the kotodama would function in them. If Hitomaro's age had given sole precedence to the view that an expression based on preexisting diction was a beautiful expression, he would not have made use of so many guide phrases, and he certainly would not have developed new ones. The kotodama still enlivened the guide phrase in his age.

Hitomaro's practice of creating new guide phrases ceased in the second half of the Ancient Age. Even Kasa no Kanamura, said to have been a follower of Hitomaro, uses only twenty of the conventionally styled pillow-words, and of these only two appear for the first time in Kanamura's poems. Yamabe Akahito makes use of some ten, and only one of these is new (Omodaka, 1937, 62-63). Because the number of poems composed in the later period of the Man'yōshū was far greater than that in the early period, the varieties of pillow-words employed in the later period did not decrease very much in terms of numbers. New pillow-words, on the other hand, were fewer in number than in the early age of the Man'yōshū. Ōtomo Yakamochi, for example, uses pillow-words 237 times, but only 90 varieties are employed. I have found that the frequency of pillow-words used in Hitomaro's poetry amounts to 178 times versus 106 varieties employed.[9] If these figures are compared with

[8] The number of "pillow-words" used by Hitomaro varies according to whether, or how many, poems in the *Kakinomoto Hitomaro Kashū* (a collection of poems attributed to him by the title) are accepted as genuine. The main theories propose: 140 varieties of "pillow-words" (Omodaka, 1937, 62); 118 varieties (Tsuchihashi, 1960, 417); or 106 varieties (Yamaguchi, 1964, 378-460), etc. It is not clear what criteria Omodaka uses. My view is based on Yamaguchi's work: his figures are obtained from a reexamination of works by Hitomaro and earlier poets. [The "varieties" imply reasonably distinct versions, ruling out such things as slightly different phrasing or usage.—Ed.]

[9] Using Yamaguchi, as cited in the preceding note.

those for Yakamochi's use of the pillow-word, we clearly observe the decreasing tendency of use. Even if we take into account Yakamochi's personal preferences—his inclination, for instance, to use specific pillow-words like "ashihiki no" (36 times), "amazakaru" (11 times), "utsusemi no" (10 times), and "tamahoko no" (11 times)—the fact remains that Yakamochi employs fewer varieties than does Hitomaro. Ninety poems are clearly attributed to Hitomaro versus 479 for Yakamochi.[10] In other words, along with the decreasing use of pillow-words in the later age of the *Man'yōshū* went an even greater decrease in the number of examples used.

By the later *Man'yōshū* period, then, the creation of new pillow-words had declined. This, and the fact that a few varieties came to be used so repeatedly, can only signify the evolution of the guide phrase into a pillow-word formula. Because this process occurred in the later age of the *Man'yōshū* when written composition tended to take precedence over oral, these formulas will be seen to differ in nature from those employed in epics composed orally and extemporaneously. As I have said, the pillow-word formulas were bolstered by an awareness of the ga principle, holding that expression based on precedent was beautiful expression, and these formulas undoubtedly facilitated expression in written composition as well. In this sense, the Parry-Lord theory also proves valid, "to some extent," for the sphere of written composition, an application for which the theory was not devised. Their theory does get some greater credence from the fact that even later poems in the *Man'yōshū* often relied on aural means.

METHODS AND CIRCUMSTANCES OF RECEPTION

The chief means of literary reception, even in the Ancient Age, must have been aural. This was of course true for song, but apparently waka too was uncommonly the object of visual reception. The reason is simple: paper was then a valuable commodity, and so it was difficult to produce enough manuscripts to make reading a very common alternative. There

---

[10] One theory, the reliability of which is still uncertain, identifies Hitomaro's work by distinguishing between those poems in the *Kakinomoto Hitomaro Kashū* which are set forth in Chinese characters used phonetically and those which are set forth in characters used solely as logographs (the so-called ryakutaika, short-form poems). My tentative decision is to ignore the *Kashū* and take as genuine only those poems in the *Man'yōshū* directly attributed to Hitomaro. The decision is taken faute de mieux: in fact, there is no guarantee that all those poems directly attributed to Hitomaro can be taken to be his. But too much skepticism only clogs the discussion, and I have formally recognized as Hitomaro's poems those so specifically attributed to him in the *Man'yōshū*.

was no standard method for transcribing the Japanese language, represented in this period by Chinese characters. Reading was no easy matter.
This also may serve to explain the seeming paradox that the main means
of waka reception remained aural into the second stage of the Ancient
Age, despite the marked advances made in written composition. For these
reasons, the human voice long served as the medium of poetic delivery
and reception. Although weakening with each passing year, the kotodama
managed nonetheless to survive through the Ancient Age, probably aided
by the predominant practice of aural reception.

The circumstances of waka reception may be divided into two main
categories, the formal and the informal.[11] When the tennō recited a waka
during the ceremony of beholding the country (kunimi) or at a state
banquet, or requested elegies to be recited at a funeral, the poetry recited
would have been formal. Examples of informal circumstances might be
lovers reaching a mutual understanding through an exchange of poems,
or a friend sending a poem reporting on recent happenings. Of course,
intermediate situations exist, in which neither the formal nor the informal
is exclusive, and some waka are not easily assigned to a single category.
A farewell poem addressed to someone setting off on a journey, for
instance, is an intermediate case: depending on the circumstances, it could
incline strongly toward the formal category or show signs of being informal. On formal occasions there would probably be a plural audience
for the poem, and so recitation was considered the appropriate means
of communication. The traditional favor of oral delivery obviously implied aural reception. By contrast, informal poems like those exchanged
between lovers were usually written during periods of separation.[12]

The ceremony of beholding the country consisted of surveying a certain
area from a high place and, through the utterance of auspicious language,
anticipating the advent of good fortune. It originated as a regional or
folk practice, and apparently evolved into a ceremony performed by the
head of the Yamato court (Tsuchihashi, 1965, 45-46). As Tajihi Kunihito
suggests in a few verses:

[11] I have used the terms "formal" (hyōgi) and "informal" (shigi) to distinguish stylistic
conception. Their meanings correspond to the medieval terms "hare" (official, formal) and
"ke" (unofficial, everyday). The terms "kōteki" and "shiteki" used hitherto can be misunderstood to mean "public" and "private." So I have coined terms corresponding to
"formal" and "informal" in English.

[12] [Since property was inherited matrilineally during this period, men visited women in
their own homes, and most marriages were uxorilocal. Men might reside for business in
their mother's houses or, if of wealth and place (like a sovereign), have their own establishment. It was normal to have to communicate by visit and letter between a husband and
a wife. For these and other reasons, even at this early period "love" commonly means
yearning for the person you do not presently have by you, and the verb "to meet" (au)
signifies union or reunion of lovers.—Ed.]

           Kamiyo yori   From the age of the gods
           Hito no iitsugi   It has been passed down to us:
              Kunimi suru   Mount Tsukuba,
           Tsukuba no yama wa. . . .   Where we behold the country. . . .

                                (MYS, 3:382)

The ceremony dated ("From the age of the gods") back to archaic times.
Around the sixth century, beholding the country became a ceremony
performed by the Yamato leader. The oldest example of a poem on the
subject is thought to be that by Jomei Tennō (r. 629-42; MYS, 1:2).[13]
The occasion demanded recitation, and those in attendance could therefore only have heard. It is another question, however, whether the poem
was orally composed on the spot. It seems highly likely that, aware of
the importance of the ceremony, the tennō recited a prepared text at the
scene. If we assume that various tennō may have commissioned their
poems on beholding the country from other poets, the practice might
have led to confusing the composer with the performer of the poem.

Poems somewhat like those on beholding the country were composed
by courtiers during a royal progress. On the way, the tennō would command his retinue to present poems. The request was not for lyrical,
personal poetry but rather for recitations of splendid verses in praise of
the location, uttered in the expectation that they would move the gods
and spirits to effect some auspicious action. The waka presented on such
occasions were to be carefully and prudently composed. It was forbidden
to introduce, even by chance, diction that might invite ill fortune. Thus
the safest language was that which had been frequently employed in the
past, which was acknowledged to ensure the functioning of the kotodama.
The result of this practice was the eventual resemblance of several expressions to formulas. We are not bound to the Parry-Lord theory as regards
such formulas. They need not always be connected with oral composition,
since written composition would be the most effective method of ensuring
a carefully worded poem. In fact, examples of written composition from
this period exist in some quantity.

Here is one of Okura's poems:

           Amanogawa   The Milky Way—
           Aimukitachite   All year we gaze across it;
              Wa ga koishi   But now I hear

---

[13] Although Ōjin's verses on beholding the country (KJK, Song, 40) and Nintoku's on
the same subject (KJK, Song, 53) are probably products of the Archaic Age, it is by no
means certain that they are in fact the works of Ōjin and Nintoku.

Kimi kimasu nari   My beloved is drawing nigh—
Himo tokimake na.   And I undo my skirtband![14]

(*MYS*, 8:1518)

It has the afternote, "The above was composed by royal command on the seventh of the Seventh Month, 724." Moreover, a variant line, "Kawa ni mukaite" (We face the River), appears next to the second line of the poem.[15] Since Okura would hardly have presented both options simultaneously on such an occasion, the variant was apparently conceived as an alternate possibility when the poem was composed in advance of the event, and the line chosen for entry to the text proper, "Aimukitachite," was the one recited in the royal presence.

When hearing is involved, the poet must compose in a suitable way. Even in written composition, the poet must constantly be aware of the effect written words have when presented aloud. Poets and scholars since the Meiji period have stressed their fascination with the melodic aspects of *Man'yōshū* poetry, especially that of Hitomaro. This melodiousness stems from the fact that the chief method of reception was then aural. The "Elegy for Prince Takechi" (*MYS*, 2:199), one of Hitomaro's greatest works, is at 149 lines the longest chōka in the collection.[16] Its structure is nevertheless well organized, with unequalled precision in its parallelism. If this chōka had not been composed in writing, its complexity of structure would have been out of the question. And yet the "Elegy," despite its carefully planned structure, possesses throughout a lively melodic flow that works to splendid effect. Can we not infer that this is a result of Hitomaro's concern with the aural reception of his poem? This applies not only to court elegies for state funerals but to private elegies as well. The audience for Hitomaro's "Poem Written in Deepest Mourning" (*MYS*, 2:207), composed at the death of his wife, would have been small by comparison with that in attendance at a royal funeral. Yet this chōka, like the "Elegy for Prince Takechi," was recited before a public audience and, as such, was a formal poem.

Hitomaro's "Poem to My Wife in Iwami" (*MYS*, 2:131) was written on parting from his wife when he left the province of Iwami to return

[14] [This is one of twelve poems composed by Okura for Tanabata, the festival of the seventh night of the Seventh Month, at the conjunction of two stars, Vega and Altair. They were personified respectively as the Weaver Maiden and the Herdboy, lovers who could meet but once a year, he visiting her. (See n. 12.) The speaker of the poem is of course the Weaver Maiden.—Trans., Ed.]

[15] [The River of Heaven, the Milky Way, which the Herdboy must cross.—Trans.]

[16] In this and the next paragraph the seeming titles are not from the text but are rather designations to give a sense of the poem's subject and for convenience in discussion.

to the capital.[17] Is this also a formal poem? The most appropriate method of reception for a poem of longing for one's wife, we might feel, would be to have some close friends read what one has written down. This attitude, however, emerges only with the Middle Ages, and in Hitomaro's time these poems as well were no doubt recited. The "Poem to my Wife in Iwami" is a species of farewell poem. The audience apparently consisted of Hitomaro's traveling companions, and the circumstances of recitation would have been somewhat formal. The poems were undoubtedly recited in the anticipation that the kotodama would aid the poet in controlling his emotions at parting from his wife and keep him from lapsing into irrelevant thoughts, so taking the entire group of travelers safely to the end of their journey. Such poetry differs from the lyric in the modern sense of the word. A variant version of this poem (MYS, 2:138), which differs little from the first version, may represent the text of the poem as it was composed in advance. Still another "Poem to My Wife in Iwami" (MYS, 2:135) is not to be seen as a further variant transmission but as a separate work. It was probably also recited in the course of the same journey. In any event, poems of parting occupy a middle ground between the formal and the informal, and I regard Hitomaro's "Poems to My Wife in Iwami" as an intermediate kind that tends more toward the formal category.

If we agree that poetry on beholding the country, poetry composed on royal request, and the elegy are representative of the formal category, then poetic exchanges between lovers probably offer the best examples of the informal variety. These would be quite difficult to recite before a public audience. Lady Ishikawa would certainly not have had her messenger recite this poem, addressed to Ōtomo Sukunamaro:

Furinishi	How can it be
Omina ni shite ya	That grown an aged woman,
Kaku bakari	I should act like this,
Koi ni shizuman	Sinking so deeply into love
Tawarawa no goto.	As if I were the merest girl?

(MYS, 2:129)

The written character of the poem shows us how it was transmitted.

These varying means belong to the earlier age of the Man'yōshū. In its later age, exchanges of love poems in written form grew more common,

---

[17] [For reasons given in n. 12, she would need to remain in Iwami and the couple would, in effect, be divorced. On the other hand, marriage customs in eighth-century Japan so little resemble our own that it is difficult to know what "wife" and "husband" mean in many instances, and the subject of Hitomaro's "wives" is vexed.—Ed.]

as did poetic exchanges between friends. An exchange between Ōtomo Yakamochi and Ōtomo Ikenushi exemplifies friendly exchanges, with an especially good example provided by a set of four poems (*MYS*, 18:4128-31) sent Yakamochi by Ikenushi, with a forenote dated the twelfth of the Eleventh Month, 749. Ikenushi writes, "I will now put them down in a letter and send them to you by means of the assessor." Poems sent by letter are obviously meant to be read. The poems Yakamochi wrote in reply were also sent by letter. An afternote to Ikenushi's poems records that "the poems written in reply to the above were lost and could not be recovered." Although Yakamochi had lost his drafts of the poems, and they do not survive in the *Man'yōshū* text, this incident clearly indicates the growing tendency to rely on writing and reading.

Visual reception was not limited to letters: one could also inscribe one's words on something that was bound to attract attention. A poem quoted earlier, "Wave-tossed and dripping, / I have crossed . . ." (*MYS*, 6:1016), will serve as an example. Its afternote states that "the above poem was written on white paper and affixed to a wall of the house." The use of the wall clearly implies reading. It is true that because this event occurred at a private banquet, some of the guests may have read the poem aloud. If so, however, they recited it while reading what was written, and their reception had to be primarily visual.

In China there is ample evidence of writing one's own poetry on a wall, or some other part of a house, or even on paper to attach to a tree. The evidence derives only from the T'ang period, when prefaces were supplied to poems. But the evidence is so extensive and the practice is taken as so normal that it can only be far older. Here are examples from the most famous poets.

When I went to visit Mr. Li, I wrote this poem on a wall of his house (*Ō I*, 9:1530).

Written on the wall of Mr. Tzu-yang of Sui-chou (*Rishi*, 24:1078).

Written on the wall of a building belonging to the Lung-hsing Temple of Chung-chou (*Toshi*, 14:1306).

Written on the beam of an inn, to aid my memory (*Kanshi Taikan*, 10:1707).

> At the foot of Mount Hsiang-lu
> I built a new cottage,
> Composed a poem on my surroundings
> And wrote it on a boulder.
>   (*Hakushi*, 7:1838)

There is a tree by the County Building
That flourishes in the evening and wilts in the morning.
People do not know its name;
So I wrote this poem upon it.

(Ibid., 10:1885)

Some have conjectured that the Japanese poem was an exceptional case, purposely got up to fit with its Chinese subject. We lack evidence, however, to think that true. In fact, to judge from the following example, it might be more appropriate to suppose that it was fairly common practice (*MYS*, 18:4065):

A poem written on the pillar of an inn in Imizu County.

Asabiraki	As morning breaks
Irie kogu naru	The boat is rowed from out the cove—
Kaji no oto no	The tilling oar
Tsubara tsubara ni	Sounds constant, constant
Wagie shi omōyu.	As my longing thoughts of home.

This poem was composed by one Lord Yamanoe. His given name is unknown. Some said that he was the son of Okura the governor, but it is not known if this is true.

Thinking that an inn would provide a conspicuous forum, the poet wrote his verses on a pillar. He intended to make his work public, as is indicated by the fact that he took the time to sign the poem with "Lord Yamanoe." Thanks to Yakamochi, who copied down the poem and included it in the *Man'yōshū*, the outcome for this Yamanoe's effort far exceeded its composer's expectations.

Another *Man'yōshū* passage records the writing of waka on the surface of a zither, so as to attract the attention of the musician. In another instance (*MYS*, 16:3849-50), there is a forenote: "Two poems of loathing for the mutability of this world," which have this as their afternote: "These two poems are written on the surface of a Yamato zither within the Buddha Hall of the temple of Kawaradera." Those who played this Yamato zither would encounter the two poems visually. A further example is provided by one of two poems sent Yakamochi by the maiden Awatame:

Omoiyaru	Consolation is
Sube no shiraneba	Something that I cannot find:
Katamoi no	I love without return,

| Soko ni zo ware wa | Plunged to this bowl's depths |
| Koi narinikeru. | In my longing for you.[18] |

(*MYS*, 4:707)

An afternote reads: "Written inside a ceramic bowl." The sense of "written," in this case, might be that the poem was set down and sent together with the bowl as a gift for Yakamochi. Here is an instance of a poem which is not by nature intended for wide attention, yet which presumes visual reception.

The standard means of reception in the late age of the *Man'yōshū* remained aural, although in certain circumstances visual reception made notable advances. The tendency to use writing involves circumstances more frequently requiring individual reception, an increase that occurred in addition to the presentation of compositions before public gatherings. If this process is moved one step further, we will have the situation of the poet as sole initial audience of a work. Eight "Tanabata poems" (*MYS*, 20:4306-13) written in the Seventh Month of 754, and six untitled poems (*MYS*, 20:4315-20) written that same autumn, have as their respective afternotes, "Composed while gazing alone at the Milky Way," and "A few thoughts composed while alone and lost in memories of autumn fields." The initial audience is, therefore, the creating poet, with whom no one else shares the scene. These groups of poems are undoubtedly written compositions, because they were composed in such numbers at a single time. Poetic composition in solitary circumstances stands in direct opposition to oral composition as it is found in the Parry-Lord theory. We can understand, therefore, that at the precise moment when poems came to be composed by solitary poets, waka effected its total separation from song. In song there is no such thing as a performer who, with no audience before him, takes upon himself the additional role of recipient.

FORMS OF TRANSMISSION

Transmission of Waka

Obviously a literary work is transmitted by oral or written means, but because the means of waka transmission are interconnected in several ways to the methods of composition and reception, it is in fact not always

---

[18] [There is a pun in the third line on "katamoi": a large ceramic bowl without a lid, and one-sided, unrequited love.—Trans. We omit a note in the original amplifying the evidence given earlier on publishing poems by attaching their written versions to parts of a building.—Ed.]

possible to divide waka transmission into an oral or a written category. Alternate lines of transmission and revision give rise to a wide spectrum of variance.

Examination of alternative *Man'yōshū* texts reveals two principal groups: textual variants and variants in the circumstances of composition. Textual variants generally consist of differences in a word or line, although entire variant poems are occasionally found. Larger variants appear most often in poetry from the relatively earlier part of the *Man'yōshū*, especially in the work of Hitomaro. They tend to decrease toward the later age. An examination of textual variants in 1,808 poems with known composition dates in 715 and after shows that variants are found in only forty-three.[19] By contrast, of 426 poems written in 714 and before, forty-nine have textual variants, with twenty-eight of Hitomaro's poems included in this number.[20] In proportional terms, textual variants are clearly concentrated in the earlier period. Among the various reasons given for the presence of this phenomenon, only the following are feasible:

1. A revision, made by the composer, was transmitted separately.
2. The text was altered by someone other than the poet.
3. An error in memorizing created a textual variant in the process of oral transmission.

Most of these explanations incline toward a specific reason involving the composer or the circumstances. Generally speaking, the first and third tend to be the principal causes for variants in the *Man'yōshū* and, particularly for Hitomaro, may indicate a contemporary predominance of oral over written transmissions. Writing had come into general use by the eighth century. But it would be rash to conclude therefore that written transmission was the definitive rule in Yamato. Oral transmission was hardly in decline even in the eighth century:

> An old poem (composed by Lord Ōhara Takayasu), month and year of composition unknown. It is nonetheless recorded here exactly as I heard it recited (*MYS*, 17:3952, forenote).

> This poem is recorded from a recitation made by the monk Genshō (ibid., afternote).

---

[19] One arrives at the total number of poems by excluding those without ascertainable dates from the body of poems composed between 715 and 759 (the year of the last datable poem), according to the *Man'yōshū Nempyō* (2nd ed.; Tsuchiya, 1980). [The author's specification of thirty-nine undatable poems is omitted.—Ed.]

[20] According to the *Man'yōshū Nempyō* (Tsuchiya, 1980). This excludes variant poems having their own *MYS* number (26, 89, 90, 134, 138, 139, 214, 1511, 1667, 1763) and poems representing a text identical with another (511, 1606, 1607).

When was this "recorded . . . exactly as" the editor "heard it recited"? The "month and year" of this event are also "unknown," although we may suppose that it happened later than the mid-eighth century.[21]

In Yakamochi's time, educated men were able to compose Chinese prose with considerable facility. Yet even Yakamochi on occasion required the services of Genshō, whose "transmitted recitations," or oral statements based on memory, enabled this editor of the *Man'yōshū* to procure certain poems. There is also a forenote, "Two poems composed when peace was restored after the Jinshin War," with the following afternote (*MYS*, 19:4260-61): "These two poems were heard recited on the second day of the Second Month of 752, and are recorded here forthwith."

Approximately eighty years had passed between the composition of the two poems and their being recorded in the *Man'yōshū*. If they were recited by an intellectual like Genshō, their transmission would have been reliable up to a point, although we have no way of knowing what sort of reciters came between him and the composer of the poems. Instances appear, for example, of poetic recitations performed by itinerant courtesans. Two poems (*MYS*, 19:4236-37) with the forenotes, "A poem written in sorrow at the death of his wife, accompanied by a tanka (both anonymous)," have the following afternote: "These two poems were transmitted through recitation by one Gamō, a courtesan." Several more such afternotes to poems that record the names of their reciters appear in the books of the *Man'yōshū* believed edited by Yakamochi. If it is agreed that transmission by recitation was common in the eighth century, then oral transmission could only have had precedence over written transmission in the seventh and earlier centuries.

Because oral transmission relies on memory, lapses will often bring about textual variants. This is one reason for the preponderance of variant textual transmissions in the earlier period of the *Man'yōshū*, although we should also assume that revisions could be made by the composing poet. The first kind of variant is an impromptu revision based on oral composition, while the second is a more deliberate revision. One view seeks to explain the unusually large proportion of variants in Hitomaro's poetry by assuming that both kinds of variants are represented there. But it is more natural to suppose that the popularity of his poetry led to frequent recitation, and that failures in memory in the course of recitation resulted in an increased number of variants.

Hitomaro seems to have had ample scope for oral composition. His

---

[21] Ōhara Takayasu died on 19 XII 742. Genshō's recording would have occurred at least ten years after Takayasu's death.

extant work is thought to provide several instances of poems, based on formulas [italicized in the poem that follows], which were varied slightly from one locale of recitation to another. This may have been the case for five uta recorded in Book 15 of the *Man'yōshū*, the first of which is

Tamamo karu	Passing by Otome
Otome o sugite	*Where they gather fine seagrass,*
Natsukusa no	I built a hut
Noshima ga saki ni	On the Cape of Noshima
Iori su ware wa.	*With its summer plants.*[22]

(3606)

An afternote to each poem indicates the disparities between it and a similar one by Hitomaro.[23] Oral composition gives a poet little time for reflection. Because the poet is obliged to compose almost automatically, the results may lack refined expression. The group of variant poems just described are thought to be such flawed impromptu efforts. Sometimes, however, revision seems to have produced more highly polished expression. An example is provided by the closing lines of an elegy by Hitomaro on the death of his wife. Let us compare one conclusion (*MYS*, 2:210) with a variant taken from "a certain manuscript" (*MYS*, 2:213):

Utsusemi to	For my beloved,
Omoishi imo ga	She whom I had loved
Tamakakiru	As flesh and blood,
Honoka ni dani mo	Will never be so much as glimpsed,
Mienu omoeba.	Like a shining gossamer.

(*MYS*, 2:210)

Utsusemi to	For my beloved, she whom
Omoishi imo ga	I had loved as flesh and blood,
Hai nite maseba. . . .	Has been reduced to ashes. . . .

(*MYS*, 2:213)

The variant words, "Has been reduced to ashes," directly express the powerful shock received from the insensate process of cremation. The

[22] The poem may provide supporting evidence, though of a partial nature, in favor of Bruce A. Beatle's view that the Parry-Lord theory can also be applied to short narrative poetry (see n. 2, above).

[23] [The afternote to this poem, for example, is: "Kakinomoto Hitomaro's poem has 'Passing by Minume,' and again, 'Our boat draws near to.' " The reference is to *MYS*, 3:250.—Trans.]

speaker's emotions closely dominate the diction, and seem to deny entry to all other expression. The tone of this line differs completely in nature from the rather explanatory "Will never be so much as glimpsed, / Like a shining gossamer." The new line is thought a highly deliberate revision.[24]

The transmitters of oral texts wished to memorize their subjects perfectly. They felt additional strain because the individuality of a poem demanded that the reciter maintain the accuracy of the transmission. Whenever individual expression advanced, alterations made by the transmitter would decrease. When a primitive commonality was still partially present, the functions of the composer of a poem and that of its transmitter tended to be confused. Hitomaro probably lived in an age of transition between these two stages. The *Kakinomoto Hitomaro Kashū*, or *Hitomaro Kashū* (*Collected Poems of Hitomaro*), is suspect as to authorship of individual poems, but is evidently a product of this transitional period, a time close to Hitomaro's own.

To be sure, only a few poems in the *Collected Poems of Hitomaro* exist in many versions: only 13 of a total of 332 poems have variants. We must think of the poems in the collection as having been transmitted differently from poems specifically ascribed to Hitomaro. The collection was probably compiled before the turn of the eighth century, because from the mid-eighth century people grew aware of a clear distinction between the composer and the transmitter. One may cite, as an example of this awareness, a group of poems bearing afternotes which mention a man named Wakamiya Ayumaro. The first, on the female immortal Tsuminoe (*MYS*, 3:387), has an afternote clearly stating that it "was composed by Wakamiya Ayumaro." The two travel poems that follow it (*MYS*, 3:388-89) have a differing afternote: "The above poems were recited by Wakamiya Ayumaro. The author is unknown, however." There are also instances from the mid-eighth century of complete written transmissions, that is, of the recopying of poetry previously recorded in writing. Yakamochi's afternote to eight poems by frontier guards, collected some years earlier, indicates the process whereby written poetry was reproduced and preserved: "These eight poems were composed by frontier guards some years ago. They were selected and copied by several gentlemen, including Iware Imiki of the senior seventh rank, clerk in charge of documents at the Ministry of Justice, and presented to Lord Ōtomo Yakamochi, assistant minister of war" (*MYS*, 20:4425-32, afternote).

Variants relating to the composition of a poem are more fluid than

---

[24] Poem 213 is among 427 poems dating from 714 or earlier. (See n. 19.) The reasons involve its marked signs of deliberate revision, which leads me to regard it as a work separate from 210.

textual variants. In the Archaic Age, all delivery would have been oral, and so variant attributions of authorship tended to occur. An excellent example is provided by a poem attributed both to Consort Iwanohime (*MYS*, 2:85) and to Princess Sotōri (*MYS*, 2:90), with a long discussion of the problem appearing in the afternote to the latter. These variant attributions also occurred quite frequently in the earlier period of the *Man'yōshū*. Twenty poems of the 427 composed up to the year 714 have notations indicating an alternate attribution of authorship. By contrast, variant attributions decrease sharply in the later period of the *Man'yōshū*. Only 5 poems out of the 1,808 composed in 715 and after bear notations of alternate authorship. This seems to imply a strong conviction among later *readers* that the authorship and the circumstances of composing poetry were to be clearly indicated. This emulated a recent Chinese practice, the accompaniment of a poem by a notation of the poet's name and the circumstances of composition. Underlying this was something else of importance: an awareness that waka, like Chinese poetry, was literature.

Editors of the *Man'yōshū* showed strong interest in the question of poets and composition. This is evident from matter appearing before and after poems, comments that cannot but seem somewhat excessive to us today. We respond as we do because the Chinese poetry collections contain nothing that can rival the detail with which the *Man'yōshū* records poets' names and the circumstances of composition. When the Japanese adopt a foreign practice, they tend to apply themselves more thoroughly to mastering it than ever its originators did, and by such application they amplify the distinctive features of the practice. This propensity characterized eighth-century Yamato intellectuals, as the compulsive annotation in the *Man'yōshū* shows. We see the interest in the poet and the circumstances of writing very markedly in the afternote to a poem of the later *Man'yōshū* period:

Tachibana no	Eight paths meet
Moto ni michi fumi	Beneath the orange tree,
Yachimata ni	Paths lead every way—
Mono o zo omou	As many as the ways I love you,
Hito ni shiraezu.	Though I cannot make you understand.

(*MYS*, 6:1027)

His Lordship Takahashi Yasumaro, Chief Controller of the Right, has said that this poem was copied by the late Lady Teshima. A certain manuscript, however, has it that it was composed by one Mikata, a novice monk, out of longing for his wife, Sono no Omi.

If the latter is true, then might not Lady Teshima have recited this poem when and where it was composed?

Confusion may well have arisen over the composer's name because Lady Teshima, who was present when the novice Mikata composed the poem, recited it immediately afterward. If true, this explanation implies that at a late stage in the composition of the *Man'yōshū* the writer of the afternote confused the author of a poem with its transmitter. The pains taken by the editor reveal a compulsion to establish the poet's identity.

The same zeal was evident in efforts to confirm the circumstances of a poem's composition. In Book 6 there is a forenote: "A chōka and two tanka composed by Lord Yamabe Akahito during a royal progress to the province of Kii on the fifth day of the Tenth Month, 724." One of the tanka is this outstanding example of Akahito's work:

Waka no ura ni	At the Bay of Waka,
Shio michikureba	As the tide swells on the shore,
Kata o nami	Covering the sand bars—
Ashibe o sashite	Bearing toward the stand of reeds,
Tazu nakiwataru.	The cranes cry out as they fly off.

(*MYS*, 6:919)

The afternote to this group of poems reveals a scholarly spirit: "The above poems were not dated. Mention was made, however, of 'accompanying His Majesty to Tamatsu Island.' The records of this royal progress were thus examined and, using the information provided, the date of composition was noted." The poems are described as "not dated," an indication that the editor was working with written materials. Since the only information found there, however, was that the poems were composed when Akahito accompanied the tennō to Tamatsu Island, the editor ascertained from other recorded sources that the event took place on the fifth of the Tenth Month of 724, and included this information in his forenote. The afternote emphasizes the presence of two assumptions: (1) that the date of composition should be designated as accurately as possible; and (2) that any deficiencies of transmission in the source material be supplemented. The latter point carries considerable significance. It is based on the belief that waka reception should conform to the circumstances of its composition, implicitly acknowledging that when the information has not accompanied the poem it should be supplemented by information from other sources.

Another example will provide a clearer illustration:

Onore yue	All because of you,
Noraete oreba	I have suffered strong rebuke:
Aouma no	What then does it mean
Omotakabuda ni	That you arrive triumphant,
Norite kubeshi ya.	Astride your horse of dapple gray?

(*MYS*, 12:3098)

This poem was composed in the following circumstances, according to Lord Fun'ya Masuhito, a man from Heguri: "I heard long ago that Princess Ki composed this poem after her secret love affair with Prince Takayasu had been discovered, and she had been reprimanded. Prince Takayasu, for his part, was reduced in rank to governor of Iyo Province."

Here the source material for the text differs from the source for the composition: the latter concerns Masuhito's story of what he learned "long ago," a story *heard* this time, and subsequently written down, by the author of the afternote. The process involved a linking of the heard circumstances of composition to poems delivered in writing. Insofar as stories of such circumstances were transmitted orally, the original facts easily became intermingled with extraneous elements. The next stage would involve the incorporation of fictional elements into the stories, to become that genre known as the utagatari, and this evolved before long into the utamonogatari.[25]

If the poets had known their poems would be interpreted in terms of the situation of composition, they would have set down the dates and other circumstances. But the practice of specifying dates occurs after the active period of Ōtomo Tabito and Yamanoe Okura. Okura may have pioneered the practice, since the afternote to one of his poems quoted above, "The Milky Way— / All year we gaze across it . . ." (*MYS*, 8:1518), appears to contain the first reference to a date in the *Man'yōshū*: "This poem was composed by royal command on the seventh of the Seventh Month, Yōrō 8."[26] When Tabito was posted to Tsukushi, he became a friend of Okura's and, under Okura's influence, apparently formed the habit of writing down the dates of his poems. The earliest of Tabito's

[25] [Both Japanese terms imply something like "relations of poems, and their circumstances of composition"—the utamonogatari will feature in the second volume of this *History*. —Ed.]

[26] In fact, Shōmu's accession took place in the Second Month of Yōrō 8 (724), whereupon he changed the era name to Jinki. There was therefore no Seventh Month in 724 assignable to Yōrō, and the poem had to have been composed in the Seventh Month of Jinki 1 (still 724, of course). Okura was careful to record the day—he could hardly have been without a diary or similar aid. The poem itself is discussed in the preceding part of this chapter.

poems bearing a clearly marked date specifies the year 724 (*MYS*, 3:315-16), without the day or month. In 728, perhaps three years after he had settled in Dazaifu, Tabito first appended a full date—in this case, "the twenty-third day of the Sixth Month"—to a poem (*MYS*, 5:793). Only one instance of a fully dated poem (*MYS*, 2:162) appears in the earlier period of the *Man'yōshū*, and that quite by chance: "Composed on the ninth day of the Ninth Month, eight years after His Majesty's death."[27] In addition, there are a few instances of poems bearing the month and year of composition, as in the case of formal poems composed during royal progresses. The form taken by their forenotes sometimes resembled this: "Poems composed during the progress of the former tennō and Mommu Tennō to the province of Kii in the Tenth Month, 701" (*MYS*, 9:1667-79, forenote).[28] None contains a record of the day of composition. This does not apply, of course, to poems bearing afternotes added at a later date, when the day of composition had been deduced.

Yakamochi carried on the tradition, shaped by Okura and Tabito, of recording dates. The books of the *Man'yōshū* in which Yakamochi's work is most heavily represented have, if one considers only their form, the appearance of poetic nikki. Yet these volumes cannot be called nikki, insofar as they possess no evolving narration.[29] It cannot be denied, however, that the tradition of ordering waka chronologically and appreciating them together with their circumstances of composition formed the source of works like the *Tosa Nikki (The Tosa Diary)*.

Transmission of Setsuwa

The true nature of setsuwa rests in the fact that they are orally transmitted, and even with the advent of literate times, oral transmission essentially coexisted with its written counterpart. It was standard practice for those who wrote down these prose stories still to emphasize in their records their dependence on oral transmission: "or so it was transmitted by word of mouth," "so he is reported to have said." It follows that all textual variants found in setsuwa from the Ancient Age and earlier had their origins in the process of oral transmission. We might also conclude that

---

[27] [I.e., Temmu Tennō.—Trans.]

[28] [The "former tennō" is Jitō.—Trans.]

[29] One, perhaps the last, of the editors of the collection has 204 poems in sequence in Book 4 (578-781), interpreted by some as a group serially arranged by Yakamochi to develop a love story and intended to be read as such (Itō Haku, 1975c, 448-56). It seems that there are fictional elements in the figure of the young woman who appears in the poems. That was allowed in the nikki literature of the Middle Ages. The *Tosa Nikki* is a conspicuous example of that. On the other hand, a work cannot be termed a nikki if the narrative development does not occur in the prose parts. It is for readers to decide whether to interpret the 204 poems as a narrative; the compiler seems to have encouraged such a reading by the arrangement.

revisions made by an individual composer—a process that obtains in poetry—are, in principle, nonexistent. Variant versions of circumstances of composition are similarly absent, except in the case of song.

Writing probably became widespread by the beginning of the Ancient Age. Given the ponderous writing system, however, the Yamato language could be recorded only with great difficulty. No one could possibly have expected that written setsuwa could appear in a state approximating that in which they had been narrated. Setsuwa evidently did come to be put into writing, albeit with effort, in the late fifth century.[30] The practice is not believed to have been carried out on any extensive scale, however, until the early seventh century. Several literary projects were inaugurated in the twenty-eighth year of Suiko's reign (620)—the compilation of such official histories as the *History of the Royal Family* and the *History of the State*, which were feasible, it seems, because of the availability of written materials to serve as source.[31] The difficulty of setting down in writing such materials is lamented by Ō no Yasumaro in his preface to the *Kojiki*:

> In ancient times, people both thought and expressed themselves in simple ways: it is a difficult task to put the ancient narratives into a complex prose structure and to write them out in Chinese characters. If one chooses to communicate meaning alone, the Chinese expressions one must use fail to transmit the sense of the original. And if one uses the characters for phonetic purposes alone, longer sentences are needed to express the meaning of the original (*KJK*, preface, 172).[32]

The *Fudoki (Topographies)* of the various provinces were ordered composed by Gemmei in the Fifth Month of 713.[33] These were written so as

---

[30] The *Nihon Shoki* records for the Tenth Month of the second year of Yūryaku's reign (traditionally 457), "This month the Recorder's Corporation was established" (*Yūryakuki*, 364). This corporation, the fumihitobe, was charged with recording not only the events of its time but ancient legends as well. Many of its members were probably naturalized Korean immigrants. The year of Yūryaku's death has been deduced to be 489 (Kanda, 1959, 163), so the second year of his reign would be 468.

[31] Since the works seem to have been completed in the year of their being ordered (Hayashiya, 1971, 198), they must have been based on preexisting documents.

[32] [I.e., one can use the Chinese characters for meaning, so translating into Chinese an oral narrative and losing the sounds; or use the Chinese characters phonetically, which is very cumbersome.—Trans.]

[33] "On the day of the Rat-kinoe [the second day] in the Fifth Month, an order was sent down to the Seven Districts of the central provinces and to the various regions, counties, and villages. Detailed accounts, including colors, of the following county resources were to be prepared, and their names written with Chinese characters having agreeable connotations: silver, copper, dyestuffs, plants, trees, birds, beasts, fishes, and insect life. Moreover, records were to be made and submitted concerning soil fertility; the names of mountains, rivers, and expanses, and the derivation of each name; and ancient or unusual stories related by the elderly" (*Shokuki*, 6:95).

to "communicate meaning alone," as Yasumaro puts it. That is, Chinese characters were used to express only the meaning, not the sound, of the Yamato language. For this reason, although the meaning of the legends was quite comprehensible, the kotodama—which came alive only when expressed in the Yamato language—was not adequately transmitted. Of all the *Topographies*, only that for the province of Izumo, the *Izumo Topography*, is taken to have been transcribed, albeit erratically, with the aim of preserving the Yamato language as far as possible. The following passage illustrates how the *Izumo Topography* chose to use "characters for phonetic purposes" wherever possible in its narration. In this passage, Yatsuka Mizuomitsuno, a god who is in the process of creating the Land of Izumo, ties ropes around an island, hauls it in from the sea off Shiragi (Silla), and binds it to the main island of Japan.

Takubusuma Shiragi no misaki o kuni no amari ya to mireba kuni amari ari to noritamaite *otome no muna* suki torashite *ōuo no kida* tsuki wakete *hata susuki* hōriwakete mitsu mi no tsuna uchikakete *shimotsuzura* kuru ya kuru ya ni *kawafune no* mosoro mosoro ni kuni ko kuni ko to hikikinueru kuni wa Kozu no oritae yori *yao ni* Kizuki no misaki nari.

Then he beheld a promontory jutting from Shiragi, *with shores white as mulberry cloth*, and he wondered, "Is there too much land here?" And he spoke: "There is indeed too much land here"; and he took up a spade *curved like a maiden's breast* and he thrust it hard into the land, *as if into the gills of a great fish*; and he cut away the promontory *as easily as nodding plumegrass*; and he tied it with a thrice-plied rope; and he pulled and pulled it in *like frost-withered vines*, slowly, slowly *like a river boat*; "Come, land! Come, land!" he called as he pulled it near and bound it fast; and this land now stretches from the innermost recesses of Kozu Cove to the *mounded-earth* Cape of Kizuki (*Izumo no Kuni Fudoki*, 100-102).

The frequent use of the (italicized) guide phrases served to activate the kotodama, and can only be seen as an attempt to keep the original oral tale alive in written transmission.[34] This passage and a few others, however, are exceptions rather than the rule, which tended to be represented by a writing style in conformance with the syntax of classical Chinese. The *Hitachi no Kuni Fudoki (Hitachi Topography)* is an extreme instance of the latter case: it is written in a graceful, ornate style all but ruling out the working of the kotodama.

[34] This cannot possibly hold true if one attempts to interpret the guide phrases as pillow-words, defined in the past as "conventional rhetorical phrases, each consisting of five syllables."

When Temmu Tennō commanded Hieda no Are to "recite" (shōshū) the "royal genealogy" and the "legends of antiquity," he did not mean that Are was simply to memorize some matters. She was instead to commit to memory works in the Yamato language identical to the materials handed down from the Archaic Age and to train herself to recite them accurately. "Shōshū" has been interpreted to mean either the recitation from memory of an orally transmitted text, or the performance from memory of the Japanese reading of an already extant document.[35] In either case it is important that the act was performed in the Yamato language, since the kotodama would not otherwise function. The kotodama did not lodge to an equal extent within *all* words. Because it was thought to function particularly well within certain word-sounds, such words, which required especial care in their pronunciation, were written exactly as they were to be pronounced, phonetically. Even the accentuation was indicated when necessary. "Weighty" setsuwa required a far more rigorous oral transmission than is suggested by such general pronouncements as that at the head of this discussion: "the true nature of setsuwa rests in the fact that it is orally transmitted." Unlike those kinds of "histories" that exist only to transmit facts accurately, weighty setsuwa were believed to influence the existence of the nation through the very process of oral transmission.

The transmission of weighty setsuwa was performed by the kataribe, families of reciters. As writing became fairly widespread, however, its influence spread throughout society, and even members of the kataribe, specialists in oral transmission though they were, suffered a gradual, imperceptible decline in their powers of memory.

As the results of research on oral transmission in Micronesia indicate, contact with modern civilization does not lead to the immediate weakening or extinction of oral recitation. On the other hand, oral transmission clearly cannot flourish independently within an emerging literate society, as is shown by an example drawn from an older cultural stage than that of Micronesia. The Tswana (divided into four tribes) of Bechuanaland in South Africa have transmitted many praise-poems addressed to their respective chieftains and other leaders. Those addressed to chieftains in former times, however, have far more abbreviated texts than do those of more recent times. For example, the longest text surviving from the period between the time of Masellane (r. early eighteenth century), the first chieftain of the Kgatla tribe, and that of the fifth chieftain, Pheto (r. ca. 1795-1810), consists of 21 lines, in addition to several fragmentary transmissions. With the eighth chieftain, Pilane (r. 1823-48), a praise-

---

[35] The leading theory holds that "shōshū" signifies recitation from memory of the Japanese reading of a document. This was first argued by Tsuda Saukichi; Andō Masatsugu subsequently substantiated the claim with careful factual analysis (Andō, 1939, 27-35).

poem as long as 76 lines first appears. Short texts were still plentiful at that time, and it was not until the time of the tenth chieftain, Kgamanyane (r. 1848-74), that the length was fixed at 50 or more lines, and a praise-poem consisting of 203 lines was composed. In the Kwena tribe, praise-poems varying in length from 66 to 89 lines date from the time of Sechele (r. ca. 1831-92). The longest poem prior to this consists of 25 lines. The Ngwaketsu tribe possessed praise-poems ranging from about 12 to 38 lines prior to the time of Segotshane (r. ca. 1844-46), when works between 63 and 92 lines long appear. A praise-poem 96 lines long is first found within the Ngwato tribe in the time of Kgama Sekgoma (r. 1872-1923), and by the time of Tshekedi Khama (r. 1925-59) a poem of 230 lines appears. In other words, after the mid-nineteenth century lengthier praise-poems began to appear.

This is not to say, however, that the earliest praise-poems of the Tswana tribes were short, that they grew longer after the mid-nineteenth century, and that the longest praise-poems were created in the twentieth century. Nearly all the eighteenth-century praise-poems now transmitted by the Tswana are fragments, and longer pieces are believed to have been sung at that time. Isaac Schapera points out that the Tswana praise-poems are currently in the process of being forgotten (1965, 7). One cause for this may lie in the difficulty experienced by the modern Tswana in understanding the eighteenth-century Tswana language. When Schapera asked his instructor, one of the elders, to explain a difficult point in a praise-poem, the elder replied that he could not. Despite his puzzlement at the ancient words, the elder still emphasized that they were "fine words." Thus the Tswana seem to perceive the beauty of their praise-poems as residing in a linguistic sensation rather than in rhythm or content (ibid., 22-23). Here an ancient, valued language obscure in meaning must nevertheless be employed if living expressions are to be created. This attitude was also present in ancient Yamato. The guide phrase is a case in point.[36] A given guide phrase is applied locally within a sentence, however, and is not burdened with the essential meaning to be expressed. It does not pose a very great obstacle to understanding. Ordinary vocabulary presents a different case: even the narrators will eventually be incapable of understanding expressions having no known meaning, when they are distributed throughout a setsuwa corpus. And those parts that cannot be understood will be gradually abbreviated or eliminated altogether.

A still greater influence is exerted by contact with literate societies. Caravans of Europeans arrived in the Kwena territory during Sechele's

---

[36] The guide phrase "ashihiki no," for example, seems to have lost its meaning by the time of the *Man'yōshū* (Omodaka, 1937, 65-68). In spite of that it continued to be employed, because people were aware that its use made the word "yama" (mountain or hill) into a richer expression.

rule, and the explorer David Livingstone visited there as well. Sometime around 1847, Sechele learned how to write and was converted to Christianity (Schapera, 1965, 131). It was precisely at this time that the long praise-poem came to be the fixed form. This does not mean that the praise-poem, heretofore a short or medium-length genre, had grown longer. The increased length is believed rather to have resulted from the Tswana's new ability to read and write, which facilitated the "recitation" of longer works. Because modern composers of these poems can write (although not very well), they have the advantage of being able to polish their compositions. Still, Schapera reports, they never look at written materials when they recite before an audience (ibid., 6). This attitude was shared by the poets of the *Man'yōshū*, who relied on writing while maintaining that the proper delivery of a poem could only be accomplished through vocal means. Once the Tswana became accustomed to the new transmission method, they found it difficult to remember praise-poems from their preliterate past and, moreover, lacked sufficient ability to preserve all their transmissions through writings. As a result, long poems do not survive from the past.

This modern evidence suggests that much the same things occurred with setsuwa. The praise-poem, as it is called, consists of loosely formed stanzas. Both the number of lines constituting each stanza and the number of words per line are undetermined, although the poem possesses a roughly balanced metrical form (Lestrade, 1937, 295-96). In other words, the praise-poem and setsuwa have common ground insofar as both represent an intermediate state between song and prose. They are alike in subject matter as well. Both narrate circumstances that serve to explain why an object is worthy of praise—be it a chieftain or a hero, one's own tribe or people (including women), bird or beast, plant or tree, mountain or river, an insensate thing (e.g., sacred bones) or, in modern times, a school, a railroad, or a bicycle.

It seems reasonable, therefore, to apply the situation of the Tswana praise-poem—the weakening of the transmission of its old stratum by contact with literate society—to the gradual enervation of weighty setsuwa in ancient Yamato. Temmu commanded Are to recite the royal genealogy and the legends of antiquity because by then they had reached a perilous state. Temmu's words, recorded in the preface to the *Kojiki*, probably indicate the actual conditions existing in the latter half of the seventh century: "It is our understanding that the lives of the tennō and the accounts of ancient events kept by the great families are already at variance with the truth and contain many falsehoods. If these errors are not corrected in our time, then before many years have passed the truth will have vanished altogether" (*KJK*, preface, 1:170). The kataribe's transmissions were no longer reliable.

When oral delivery was the rule, the transmitter was simultaneously the composer. According to Livingstone's records, which date from the mid-nineteenth century, the coming-of-age ceremony for children of the Kwena tribe required that each child compose and recite a praise-poem addressed to himself (Livingstone, 1857, 147). Now, however, the customs of the coming-of-age ceremony are no longer observed, and so the children are not trained in composing praise-poems. The adults occasionally compose and perform praise-poems to themselves after they have drunk beer, but they are said to use for this purpose old poems transmitted at public gatherings (Schapera, 1965, 5-6).

A period of oral transmission is characterized by the unity of three features, those of composition, performance, and transmission. By contrast, the advent of the literate period is first indicated by a debilitation of composition. The kataribe are also believed to have originally combined in their work the three features mentioned, and the inaccuracies found in the transmissions kept by the great families may well have reflected the fact that the function of composition still remained with the kataribe. Variant transmissions are not permissible for weighty setsuwa, however. Temmu's very concern that certain versions were "at variance with the truth" implies the concept of a unique or true version. The idea of a single true one may have been the result of uncertainty over the stability of written versions. For particularly esteemed setsuwa, the idea of a single true version seems to have prevented new composition and to have limited the kataribe's duties to transmission and performance.

Released from the need to compose, the kataribe were blessed with circumstances which enabled them to concentrate on performance. Although in later centuries a great art, nō, was created on the basis of just such a concept, it would be unreasonable to attribute similar aims to the seventh-century kataribe. We may readily surmise that when confronted with the power of written transmission, the kataribe lost their faith in the oral variety. In any event, writing precipitated the decline in their transmissive capacities. For what are probably similar reasons, members of the various Tswana tribes have memorized even the more lengthy of the praise-poems composed since the second half of the nineteenth century, whereas the eighteenth-century praise-poems survive only in short texts or fragments.[37] In recognizing that oral transmission was less ac-

[37] For example, a poem of praise addressed to Molefi Kgafela, the fourteenth chieftain of the Kgatla tribe, and composed by Klaas Segogwane, consisted of 120 lines. In 1931 it was presented at a tribal assembly, having been written down by the poet. Another such poem (230 lines), addressed to Tshekedi Khama and composed around 1936 by Seitshiro Mosweu, was transcribed in 1940 by Tomeletso Kgosi. In both cases, a duly memorized text was delivered orally, although the memorizing was aided by written records. This recalls the relation between a modern nō actor and his utai text. Without the assistance of writing, a modern person would be hard put to memorize such long texts.

curate than written, the Tswana may have weakened their will to memorize. We may conclude that the Tswana's situation in the last half of the nineteenth century corresponds to that of Yamato in the seventh century. As seventh-century kataribe showed a lessening ability to transmit narratives, Temmu feared for the future of the royal genealogy and the legends of antiquity. Because the kataribe were then declining in the ability to memorize, Hieda no Are's good memory stood out as something exceptional.

The kataribe had brought upon themselves the loss of two features of their office, composition and transmission. Thereafter only the performing function remained. They were evidently kept from extinction by their performances of already extant setsuwa, which they narrated in the most interesting way possible. Their studious application to this skill is believed to be the factor that extended their professional life into the Early Middle Ages. Their repertoire, however, inevitably became ever more curtailed: the "ancient passages" that were recited before a new tennō at the Ceremony of Great Thanksgiving undoubtedly offered little new either in quantity or quality. The kataribe had witnessed the advent of literate times, and accepted their fate. But unlike many veteran soldiers, they were not rejected. They continued to enjoy a certain success, at least in the seventh century, when especially appealing ways of narrating were invented for valued setsuwa. The interest we find in the written tradition that became the *Kojiki* (Figure 7), although partially due to Yasumaro's strengths as a writer, may also have owed much to the kataribe's art.

This becomes clear by a look at that portion of royal-family setsuwa that makes up Book Three of the *Kojiki*. There had been constant efforts to make the work interesting to its audience. The evidence lies in the dynamism of the narration, the use of surprises in plot, and the lengthy sustaining of suspense before resolution. These techniques, which are not present in the two preceding books of the *Kojiki*, must be the result of pains taken by the kataribe to improve the narrative. Book Three covers the period from Nintoku to Suiko. Now, if we exclude those parts which are considered to have been taken from the *Lives of the Sovereigns*, the remaining text will correspond to material from the *Honji (Accounts of Ancient Events)*.[38] It is chiefly to this latter section that the kataribe devoted their performing art. The *Lives*, being essentially a genealogical narrative, provided no opportunity to introduce elements of surprise or

[38] The *Teiki*, the royal genealogy, consisted of the following, according to the research findings of Takeda Yūkichi: (1) the tennō's relation to ancestors; (2) his or her name; (3) the location of the palace in the region and number of years of the reign; (4) consort, other wives, children, and their achievements; (5) a brief account of important royal achievements; and (6) the age at death with the day, month, and year of death, along with the location of the tumulus (Takeda, 1944, 167). Based on these criteria, sections of the *KJK* are taken to have come from the *Teiki* (ibid., 368-433).

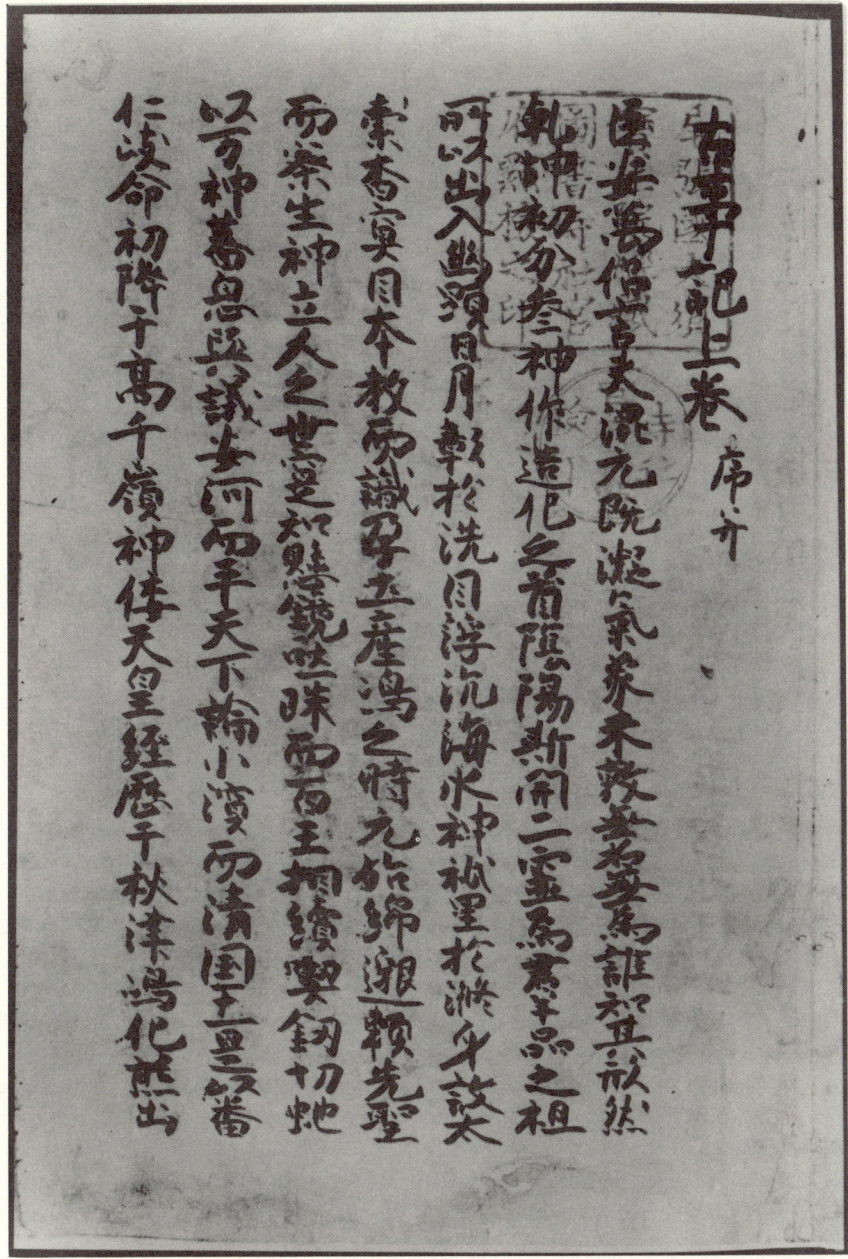

FIGURE 7. *Kojiki (Records of Ancient Matters).* The oldest manuscript (1372), at the temple Shimpukuji, Nagoya. A National Treasure.

suspense. The *Accounts*, on the other hand, consisted of setsuwa with elements far more likely to capture the interest of an audience. The *Accounts* also contained legends dealing with events in the Age of the Gods and subsequent periods. The old stratum of this material, however, would have been fixed in archaic times, so that the kataribe of the Ancient Age could not possibly have recast this section into fresher narrative. If we exclude from Book Three the portions drawn from the *Lives*, the remaining stories constitute the section based on the *Accounts*: Nintoku Tennō's exploits, the insurrection of the second prince of Suminoe, the ill-starred romance between Crown Prince Karu of Kinashi and Princess Sotōri, the revenge of Prince Mayowa, the murder of Prince Oshiwa, the flight of his two sons, and the various events connected with Yūryaku Tennō. These formed part of a body of setsuwa that drew on events from the late fourth through the early sixth centuries (Kanda, 1959, 162-63). This material was, it seems, easily embellished by the kataribe of about the seventh century.

The praise-poems of the Tswana were accompanied by "very dramatic gestures" and performed with an "elevation of the sentiment," according to a mid-nineteenth-century report (Casalis, 1859, 328-29). Since the Tswana praise-poems deal with uniform materials and have only minor differences among their texts, they were probably not very complex productions, even when dramatic gestures and displays of emotion were added. Royal-family setsuwa, by contrast, are filled with tumultuous events. If they, like the Tswana praise-poems, were performed with dramatic gestures and emotional display, their interest would certainly have been enhanced. In the *Accounts*-line setsuwa mentioned earlier (with the exception of that on Prince Mayowa) the prose is interspersed with highly technical songs, all of which are thought to have required considerable prior training.[39] The inclusion of these songs may also signify the storytellers' intent to please their audiences. When well performed, these royal-house setsuwa can only have been eagerly received. In the age of oral delivery, storytellers would have the interest of their audiences in mind, taking stock of their reactions in the course of performance and working extemporaneous improvements into the stories. The literate age was already in full flower in the seventh and eighth centuries, however, and so storytellers might have found it far more practical to plan how their expressive effects could best be heightened. This would have been done prior to a performance, by means of a thorough evaluation of the

[39] Certain terms denoting melody—"shizuuta," "shirageuta," "hinaburi," "miyahito-buri," "amadaburi," "yomiuta," and "ukiuta"—are concentrated in *KJK*, 3. Because they represent a polished repertoire of court songs, the setsuwa recited with them are also conjectured to have been performed in a technically advanced fashion. By contrast, only one kind of style, "hinaburi," is mentioned in Book 1, and that but once (*KJK*, 1:6).

plot development, the configuration of scenes, and the arrangement of songs and dramatic gestures. It is as if the process of writing made feasible the refinement of stories into texts for performance.

The story of Nintoku Tennō's courtships, for example, is composed of three sections: his courtings of Lady Kurohime, the young lady of Yata, and Princess Medori. Throughout the story, the main cause of the action is the extreme jealousy of Iwanohime, Nintoku's consort. Nintoku's courtship of the young lady of Yata results from the consort's thwarting of his affair with Lady Kurohime. Princess Medori rejects the tennō's advances because she is well aware how Iwanohime destroyed his love for the young lady of Yata. The technique of linking fairly long stories by cause and effect relationship does not appear in the old stratum of royal-family setsuwa in Book Two of the *Kojiki*. The three Nintoku sections progress from the relatively simple story of Lady Kurohime to the intricate twistings of the young lady of Yata's story to Princess Medori's tragic end, a development reminiscent of what Zeami terms the jo-ha-kyū [introduction, agitated development, rapid close]. The story of the young lady of Yata, which corresponds to the ha or development stage, is true to Zeami's theory in being more fully detailed than the other two stories.[40] One scene provides the opportunity for servants' gossip to disclose to Iwanohime the news of Nintoku's romance with the young lady of Yata. Lord Wani Kuchiko is then introduced, and this gentleman spares no effort to set matters right between the royal couple. At last the reconciliation of the royal pair takes place under the pretext of observing the metamorphosis of silkworms: such an arrangement is perfectly fitting for the ha stage. In other words, the story is unified as a whole by its developmental features.

Not only that. Further techniques incorporate surprise and suspense into the plot. Prince Oshiwa of Ichinobe is killed with an arrow shot by Prince Wakatakeru of Ō Hatsuse, who later becomes Yūryaku Tennō. Prince Oshiwa's two sons, Prince Oke and Prince Woke, flee from danger and hide themselves in the province of Harima.[41] They endure hardships on the way there—their food, for example is taken from them by an old swineherd—but the two youths, concealing their rank, eventually reach the house of a man named Shijimu, who sets them the menial task of tending the horses and cattle. In the meantime, however, Seinei, the successor to Yūryaku, dies without issue, and people search for an heir to the throne. Lord Yamabe Otate is posted to Harima and is invited to a housewarming celebration given by Shijimu. The banqueters all dance,

[40] Zeami writes, "Nō should be longest in the ha" (*Kakyō*, 91). This is a treatise on performance, but it is also applicable to the text composed.

[41] [In another context, "Prince Woke" would be normalized to "Prince Oke," but here only confusion would result.—Ed.]

whereupon two youths tending the oven fire are also made to dance. The older brother dances first; the younger brother then dances, and identifies himself in stately verse-prose.[42]

Mononofu no	Our lord,
Wa ga seko ga	A mighty warrior,
Torihakeru	Is well girded
Tachi no tagami ni	With a sword, its hilt
Ni kakitsuke	Colored red,
Sono o ni wa	And its knot
Akahata o kazari	Is hung with fine red cloth.
Akahata o tate	When he raises his red standards,
Mireba i kakuru	The enemy he sees hides afraid
Yama no mio no	Within the three-peaked mountains.
Take o kakikari	As easily as a bamboo stalk
Sue oshinabikasu nasu	Is bent for cutting at its root,
Yatsuo no koto o	As skillfully as one puts in tune
Shirabetaru goto	The eight strings of the zither—
Ame no shita osametamaishi	So our sovereign Izahowake
Izahowake no sumeramikoto no miko	Ruled the land; and his son,
Ichinobe no Oshiwa no ōkimi no	Prince Oshiwa of Ichinobe,
Yatsuko misue zo.	Has in me his son and heir.

(*Seineiki*, 280)

The astonished Otate tumbles from his seat, and drives out all the servants. He then installs the princes in a temporary palace. The younger brother, Prince Woke, is the first to ascend the throne, as Kenzō; Prince Oke, the elder brother, succeeds him as Ninken.

Kenzō searches for the burial site of his father's bones, and is shown it by Okime, an old woman who happens to know the location. Kenzō then constructs a royal tumulus and reinters the bones there. He brings Okime to live near his palace and accords her every possible kindness. He also seeks out the old swineherd who robbed the princes of their provisions during their flight, and puts him to death. Kenzō also plans

---

[42] In the *Kojiki* text this passage is written partly in Chinese used for meaning, partly in Chinese used phonetically, indicating that the compiler did not regard it as a song. Had he done so, it would have been recorded solely phonetically, one character per syllable. For a definition of verse-prose, see p. 298.

to demolish the tumulus belonging to his father's enemy, Yūryaku. The discretion of his brother Prince Oke, however, ensures that this does not come to pass.

Although this setsuwa is interspersed with other episodes relating to the same time span, it is believed to have been originally a single setsuwa plot like that just outlined. Among the characteristics of this setsuwa, there is first of all strict correspondence of events. After Prince Wakatakeru kills Prince Oshiwa, he cuts the body into pieces, puts them in a horse's feed tub, and inters the body so it is "buried level with the earth." Prince Oshiwa's grave, in other words, is flush with the ground: Prince Wakatakeru does not construct that high tumulus over the body of his victim to which a member of the royal family is entitled.

This single line of narrative leads to a later event, when Kenzō, having found his father's grave, "built a royal tumulus and interred the bones therein." It also suggests a motivation for Kenzō's desire to destroy the tumulus of Yūryaku. Kenzō may have intended to reinter Yūryaku's remains in a grave level with the earth. Moreover, Kenzō is able to affirm the identity of Prince Oshiwa's long-buried bones by certain dental idiosyncracies. Okime's speech, "He will be recognized by his teeth," indicates that the late Prince Oshiwa, true to his name, possessed crooked teeth. Only at this point does the audience realize that the prince's name will be the deciding factor in the discovery of his bones.

We observe another, similar example of how a physical peculiarity becomes the decisive factor in making a discovery. When the old swineherd takes the princes' provisions from them during their flight to safety, they respond to his action by saying, "We do not begrudge you the food, only tell us who you are." The swineherd replies, "I am a swineherd from Yamashiro." There would have been so many swineherds in Yamashiro that the right man would not be easily identified. Let us observe how the scene in which the old man appears is narrated: "Then the princes reached Karihai in Yamashiro: and while they were partaking of a meal, an old man tattooed about the eyes came and took away their provisions" (KJK, 2:249).

This careful establishment of foreshadowing and strict sequential correspondence certainly constitutes a highly evolved design. The use of surprise in plot development, moreover, is also an advanced technique for narrative of the Ancient Age. The surprise experienced by the banqueters must be extreme when a youth whom they have heretofore considered a mere drifter identifies himself with a lofty verse-prose composition totally out of keeping with his humble appearance. This display of proficiency in a literary style requiring special instruction probably astonishes the highly educated Otate most of all. That is why he topples from his seat. The other people present probably realize the gravity of the situation only by witnessing Otate's confusion.

Once the performer of the setsuwa had arrived at this part of the story, he might have interspersed his narration with dramatic gestures. Certainly he would have heightened the effect of his performance with an expressive narrative style. The audience knows from an earlier part of the story that the two youths are princes, but Otate, Shijimu, and the other characters in the story are not aware of the boys' identity. The sudden surprise is one felt by the characters alone, but if a performance is effective, the audience will have some sense of participating in the experience. Listeners will feel the characters' surprise despite their distance from that astonishment, and so be capable of enjoying the revelation. The creation of suspense is the technique through which such surprises are made effective.[43] In this case the extreme contrast between the two princes' wretched exile and the glory of the throne results in some distortion of reality, but the device works all the same.

Such ideas and techniques represent the stage eventually reached by the kataribe in the wake of their decision to attach particular attention to those improvements in performance possible only with the assistance of writing. This point is quickly understood if we compare the Oshiwa story with that of Prince Yamato Takeru's eastern expedition. Prince Yamato Takeru is a rough fellow who kills his older brother, crushing him with his bare hands. Yet when he is commanded by his father the tennō to conduct an expedition to subdue the East, he weeps and complains, "Does His Majesty think to send me to an early death?" (KJK, 2:128, 139). He is delicate enough in build to disguise himself as a girl and gain entrance to a banquet. Yet he is also daring enough to try to subdue the mountain god of Ibuki with his bare hands (ibid., 128, 142). Such nonchalant narration pays no heed to obvious inconsistencies in characterization. That, and a structural laxness in which stories follow one after another with little concern for sequential correspondence, may indicate the retention of much from the age of oral transmission.

In "The Lay of Atli" (Atlaqvitha), one of the poems from the Scandinavian collection known as the Elder Edda, King Gunnar is captured and thrown into a snake pit, where he calmly plays his harp before meeting his death. His younger brother Hogni, whose brave fighting also ends in capture, laughs as his heart is gouged from his body.[44] This lay, which is said to date from the ninth century, possesses brave figures with consistently heroic personalities. When compared with it, the legends of

---

[43] Defining suspense as expectations held by the audience of a narrative toward the unresolved events in the work, when those events concern one or more characters whom the audience is disposed to favor.

[44] [Patricia Terry, trans., Poems of the Vikings: The Elder Edda (Indianapolis and New York: Bobbs-Merril, 1969), pp. 212-14.—Trans.]

Prince Yamato Takeru are far less coherent. "The Lay of Atli," of course, cannot rival the *Kojiki* story of the two princes' wanderings for strict sequential correspondence.[45] On the other hand, "The Greenland Lay of Atli" (*Atlamál in Groenlenzco*), an early twelfth-century adaptation of the same subject matter, is more advanced in its use of climax than is the story of the princes' wanderings.[46] The *Elder Edda* apparently evolved through a complicated process involving several varieties of old and new strata. The relationship between its stage of oral composition and that of its written composition is not clearly understood. Yet the increasingly subtle structural techniques that evolved with time are the result, first, of a shift in emphasis from memorizing to performance and, second, of an abandonment of the practice of making impromptu changes before an audience in favor of revisions made through comparisons between the ancient transmitted speeches and newly devised expressions. This could not have been accomplished without the aid of writing.

Writing must have come into fairly wide use in Yamato as early as the sixth century, although this pertained to a special cultural class led by naturalized continental immigrants. The practice of the kataribe, which had originally specialized in oral transmission, could not have been infiltrated by writing until at least a century later. My earlier estimation that the terminus ad quem for the formation of royal-family setsuwa is the seventh century was founded on a consideration of these processes. Furthermore, the Hōri setsuwa, which displays a subtle structure notable even among the new stratum of deity setsuwa, may have come into existence in Yamato, in its original form, before the start of the Tumulus period. Yet its arrangement into the form in which it appears in the *Chronicles* cannot possibly be dated from the age of oral composition. It would be more appropriate to consider this setsuwa also as one that took shape in the seventh century.

[45] "The Greenland Lay of Atli" has been ascribed to the ninth-century Thorbjörn as possible author, and is said to show signs of having been a rewriting into Old Norse of an earlier Low German work (Taniguchi, 1973, *Edda*, Introduction, 298). Because written records are known to have been first kept in Iceland in the year 1117-18 (ibid., 285), this lay may be considered to date from times of oral delivery. Yet the transitions between events are smoothly handled, and there are no signs of patching variant oral traditions. On the other hand, there are also not yet any uses of foreshadowing techniques by which a listener realizes after the fact that there have been hints of an occurrence earlier in the story.

[46] "The Lay of Atli" has about 43 stanzas, compared with the 105 of "The Greenland Lay of Atli." The latter does not simply amplify the former, however. For example, the episode in which Gunnar and Hogni are captured and tortured to death is described in fifteen stanzas in "The Lay" but in only eight in "The Greenland Lay." The latter does show more skill in employing climactic techniques: various portents and warnings inform the heroes that their departure for Atli's land at his invitation will lead to their violent deaths. When they nevertheless accept Atli's invitation, the plot progresses from Gunnar's and Hogni's heroic deaths to culminate in Gudrun's unspeakably atrocious revenge.

CHAPTER 5

The Definition of Genres

As we have seen, the differentiation of lyric from narrative had already become a significant process in the Archaic Age. By the Ancient Age, the differentiation had become still more distinct, and writers grew aware of producing works in various genres. The number of genres, of course, was not large compared with those of the Middle Ages and later. Yet the people of the Ancient Age would, at the very least, have perceived the difference between song and waka. The separation of these two was completely effected when the composer of a work became also its first audience. In narrative, the clearly defined presence of prose narrative should serve to distinguish the Ancient Age from the Archaic. For the new prose narrative evolved from an intermediate stage, that of nonprose narrative expression, or narrative in verse-prose. The circumstances of these generic differentiations will be examined below.

FROM SONG TO WAKA

Court Song and Provincial Song

Some songs in the *Chronicles* have a notation in their texts signifying a musical classification: "This song is sung in the . . . Style." These are thought to have been terms used by the Bureau of Court Music in the instruction and performance of songs. The following is a list of all such terms found in the *Chronicles*:

Country Style (Hinaburi), Quiet Songs (Shizuuta), Courtier's Style (Miyabitoburi), High Ending Songs (Shirageuta), Two Levels Style (Amadaburi), Declamatory Songs (Yomiuta), Light Songs (Ukiuta).

The *Kinkafu*, which is thought to have been compiled in the ninth century, includes not only those but others as well:

High Bridge Style (Takahashiburi), Short Haniyasu Style (Miji-kahaniyasuburi), Long Haniyasu Style (Nagahaniyasuburi), Angel Style (Amehitoburi), Garden Style (Niwadachiburi), Tsugine Style (Tsugineburi), Ōshite Style (Ōshiteburi) [meaning unknown; ōshite seems to be some kind of fruit], Yamaguchi Style (Yamaguchiburi), Ayuda Style (Ayudaburi).

There also exist more specific terms for song delivery, such as "Transposed Repeats" (Utaigaeshi), "High Pitch" (Ageuta), and "Two-Pitch Melody" (Kataoroshi).[1] Song melodies and their styles of delivery probably became fairly fixed by the eighth century.

Certain songs within the *Chronicles*, however, appear in identical or similar form in the *Man'yōshū*. For example, the following two songs, taken from the *Nihon Shoki* and the *Man'yōshū* respectively, closely resemble each other.

Komoriku no	Nestled in hills,
Hatsuse no yama wa	Mount Hatsuse where streams begin
Idetachi no	Is the lovely mountain
Yoroshiki yama	I see when I leave my house,
Washiride no	Is the lovely mountain
Yoroshiki yama no	I see on running from my house.
Komoriku no	Nestled in hills,
Hatsuse no yama wa	Mount Hatsuse where streams begin
Aya ni uraguwashi	Is a splendid sight indeed,
Aya ni uraguwashi.	It is a splendid sight indeed.

(*NSK, Song,* 77)

Komoriku no	Nestled in hills,
Hatsuse no yama	Mount Hatsuse where streams begin;
Aohata no	Leafed as with green flags,
Osaka no yama wa	Mount Osaka with gentle slopes—
Hashiride no	These are the lovely peaks
Yoroshiki yama no	I see on running from my house;
Idetachi no	These the graceful peaks
Kuwashiki yama zo	I see on leaving my house:
Atarashiki yama no	Alas, that these glorious mountains
Aremaku oshi mo.	Should stand neglected!

(*MYS,* 13:3331)

There is another *Nihon Shoki* song:

Akagoma no	You, red pony,
Iyuki habakaru	Balking as you enter
Makuzuhara	A vine-choked field:
Nani no tsutekoto	Now tell me directly
Tada ni shi e ken.	What message you do bear?

(*NSK, Song,* 128)

---

[1] Additional terms include katauta, a formal distinction, in designating a part of a poem;

This appears in identical form in the *Man'yōshū* (12:3069). In neither case can a distinction be drawn between song and waka, insofar as language or text is concerned. Other examples can be added: the songs beginning "At Imaki . . . " (*NSK, Song,* 116) and "The wounded boar . . . " (*NSK, Song,* 117) exist in variant versions in *MYS,* 11:2452 and *MYS,* 16:3874, respectively. Moreover, these songs are called "uta" in their *Man'yōshū* forenotes, just as they are in the *Chronicles;* neither does the fact that the chief means of reception in the Ancient Age was aural aid us in marking a definitive point where song ends and waka begins.

This inevitably leads to the question of what waka really is, a question that will be reexamined subsequently. (See pp. 286-95.) What I would like to make clear at this point, however, is that insofar as literary works, having at least their texts in common with waka, were recited as court songs, the creation and development of waka were evidently linked to court song. "Court song" is the term used, although a considerable number of individual songs retain aspects suggestive of provincial folk song. As these songs circulated among members of the court, their melodies acquired polish and their newly composed lyrics moved toward the pure court style, losing their provincial air in the process. Is it farfetched to imagine that the literature that Ki no Tsurayuki called "Yamato uta" sprouted, grew, and bore fruit from the same soil that nourished these provincial/court songs?

The supporting evidence involves the ōuta, or great songs, of the court.[2] The three important kinds of ōuta are the kagura song, the saibara, and the fuzoku song.[3] The kagura repertoire is believed to have become fixed at some time in the early tenth century, so there is a strong likelihood that many written texts were available by the beginning of the ninth.[4] Some works, though few in number, are judged from their style possibly to date from as far back as the seventh century. The saibara are a somewhat older group, dating in general from the eighth century, and containing a considerable number of works believed to come from the seventh

---

and kamugatari, amagatariuta, Kumeuta, kunishinobiuta, and hokiuta, names referring to song content. ["Kataoroshi" indicates that a song be sung once, then repeated in a different pitch and with altered words.—Trans.]

[2] ["Ōuta," great songs, were songs preserved from archaic times and performed during the court's annual observances.—Trans.]

[3] Scholars of the Edo period normally added a fourth kind of great song, the azuma–asobiuta, to the three named to make up a canon called "Shifu," "The Four Musical Scores." Since I regard the azumaasobiuta as merely one variety of fuzoku song, I am left with three rather than four kinds of great songs.

[4] The kagura repertoire is now believed to have been fixed in the reign of Daigo, ca. 921. The earlier opinion that this had taken place in the Jōgan era (859-77) is now known to be wrong (*Kagura,* Introduction, 259-60).

century.[5] Many fuzoku songs date from the same period as the saibara. In the main, the three song groups have eighth-century origins. They are therefore considered to provide excellent data for an examination of how the *Man'yōshū* evolved from the songs of the *Chronicles*. The *Kinkafu*, cited earlier, will prove to be a still better source.

Song served various functions in archaic times: panegyrics, banquets, farewells, and dirges, in addition to lyrics recited for any appropriate circumstance. These distinctions are based on modern conceptual methods. The song designations just mentioned of course did not exist in the Archaic Age, and there were no classifications on any other basis. The songs were not then perceived as a genre. This is not to say, however, that genres did not then exist. Because they did exist, they have been given names by our contemporaries.

That termed "panegyric" includes songs in praise of places, things, and people. The first variety is best represented by songs on beholding the country [kunimi]. As I have stated earlier, the act of beholding the country was originally a regional or folk practice. And the songs recited on such occasions may have resembled an earlier form of uta like this:

Mimoro wa	People stand watch
Hito no moru yama	Over the consecrated mountain:
Motohe wa	At its foot
Ashibi hana saki	Andromeda flowers bloom;
Suehe wa	At its peak
Tsubaki hana saku	Camellias come into bloom.
Uraguwashi yama so	This is indeed a splendid mountain,
Naku ko moru yama.	A mountain watched over like a crying babe.[6]

(*MYS*, 13:3222)

Or a place-panegyric of somewhat broader scope:

Soramitsu	Is Yamato,
Yamato no kuni wa	Seen against the sky,
Kamu kara ka	A perfect place to be
Ari ga hoshiki	Because it is true to the gods' ways?
Kuni kara ka	Is it fine to dwell there
Sumi ga hoshiki	Because it is true to the land's ways?

[5] An entry in the *Sandai Jitsuroku* for 23 X 859 records that Princess Hiroi was skilled in saibara, suggesting that saibara music had come into being by the beginning of the ninth century at the latest. The verse is thought to antedate the music (*Kagura*, 268-69).

[6] [Mimoro (the consecrated mountain) is one where the gods descend to earth and where religious rites are held.—Trans.]

Ari ga hoshiki kuni wa   The land where I want to be is
   Akitsushima   The Dragonfly Islands,
   Yamato.   Yamato.

                                (*Kinka*: 12)

This song is quite conceptual. Here is a more markedly concrete place-panegyric:

   Yamato wa   Yamato
   Kuni no mahoroba   Surpasses all other lands:
     Tatanazuku   Encircled by
     Aokaki   A green hedge
   Yamagomoreru   Of mountains, range on range,
   Yamato shi uruwashi.   Yamato is lovely indeed!

                                (*KJK, Song*, 30)

The first clearly dated example of an official place-panegyric involves Jomei Tennō, who is said to have composed this song on beholding the country after climbing Kagu Hill:

   Yamato ni wa   In Yamato
   Murayama aredo   There are many hills and mountains,
     Toriyorou   But when I climb
   Ame no Kaguyama   The heavenly Kagu Hill,
     Noboritachi   Nestled by the capital,
   Kunimi o sureba   And when I behold the country,
     Kunihara wa   The mists are rising
   Keburi tachitatsu   Over the wide expanse of land,
     Unahara wa   And the gulls are flying
   Kamome tachitatsu   From the wide expanse of sea.
     Umashi kuni so   A fine land it is,
   Akitsushima   The Dragonfly Islands,
   Yamato no kuni wa.   The Land of Yamato.

                                (*MYS*, 1:2)

These uta all contain words of praise—"splendid," "a perfect place to be," "a perfect place to dwell," "lovely," "fine." The terms seem to declare to us that the songs are place-panegyrics, and yet the praise is kept in the background of the songs. Once they evolve into expressions devoted solely to descriptions of scenery, as we shall see in examples below, they become difficult to distinguish, in external appearance, from what we moderns would call scenic songs of objective portrayal.

For present purposes, however, it is more important that some place-panegyrics are considered songs while others are seen as waka, and this despite the fact that all exhibit the same essential content and external form. A fragment from the *Ise no Kuni Fudoki (Ise Topography)*, quoted earlier, contains the following:

/Masurao no	/The warrior stands before
Satsuya tabasami	His target, hunting arrow
Mukaitachi	At the ready: he lets it fly!/
Iru ya/ Matokata	Oh, Matokata,
Hama no sayakesa.	How refreshing are your shores!

(*Fudoki*, 20)

An accompanying statement reads, "His Majesty made a progress to the seashore, and he recited this song." The identity of the tennō is unknown. An uta nearly identical to that given above appears in the *Man'yōshū* (1:61). Its forenote reads, "This waka was composed by the daughter of a royal attendant who accompanied a royal progress." When a tennō journeyed to the provinces, he would call for uta to be composed on the site of his visit. These were invariably recited as invocations to the local gods and spirits, so that they might perform auspicious deeds.

It is thought that when uta were sung, lines were repeated and rhythm-marking words (hayashikotoba), like those found in the *Kinkafu*, were added to the recorded lyrics (Kume, 1979, 48-50). If we were to take our uta, "The warrior stands before . . . ," and rewrite it in the form of a song patterned on delivery methods found in the *Kinkafu*, it might look like this:

SINGER:	/Masurao no	/The warrior stands before
	Satsuya tabasami	His target, hunting arrow—
CHORUS:	Iyo	Iyo!
SINGER:	Mukai	At the ready—
CHORUS:	Iyo	Iyo!
SINGER:	Mukaitachi	At the ready: he lets it fly/
	Iru ya/ Matokata	Oh, Matokata,
	Hama no sayakesa	How refreshing are your shores,
	Hama no sayakesa.	How refreshing are your shores!

This, of course, is only an illustration, not a suggestion that songs were always sung in this format. As a matter of fact, repeated lines and rhythm-marking words differing from our hypothetical song are also to be found in the *Kinkafu*. Rather than concern ourselves with song forms, however, we should instead consider that the problem lies in the uta of the extant *Man'yōshū*: they were written down in the tanka form, but many were originally recited as songs.

The song we are concerned with uses a long guide phrase so as to emphasize the auspicious nature of the location: the burden of the uta, apart from this emphasis, is: "Matokata, how refreshing are your shores!" Once the long guide phrase had introduced vitality into the shores of Matokata, its landscape would have become tinged with spiritual qualities. People of the time would have regarded the shores of Matokata, where auspicious events were bound to occur, as unsurpassingly, vivaciously "refreshing." Modern Japanese cannot possibly perceive what was actually signified by the word "sayakesa" (refreshing), because they have grown estranged from the kotodama. And not only we modern Japanese: did not the people of the Ancient Age too gradually lose their ability to perceive its significance? In other words, those capable of vividly perceiving the auspicious character of a location solely by means of that guide phrase, a "meaningless preface" if you will, lived at a time when a primitive mentality still flourished.[7] As the kotodama lost vitality, people grew unable to grasp the auspicious quality of a location unless it was described.

Let us consider this kagura song:

Motoe	*Opening*
Yūshide no	Blessed by the gods, this fertile paddy,
Kami no sakita ni	Hung with sacred mulberry strips,
Ina no ho no	Yields ears of rice;

Sue	*Close*
Ina no ho no	May the ears of rice
Moroho ni shide yo	Be many, and heavy-bent with fruit,
Kore chiho mo nashi.	And may there be no stunted ears.

(*Kagura*, 36)

---

[7] With that variety of guide phrase hitherto known as the preface there is identified a subcategory, the "meaningful preface" (ushin no jo), which logically joins the scene depicted by the poet in the preface to what follows in the poem. There is no name for a preface that does not do so; to give it a name for discussion I offer "meaningless preface" (mushin no jo), inadequate as these terms are.

The song appears in a closely similar version in the *Kinkafu*, under the heading of "Two-Pitch Melody." Here is its singing version:

Yūshide no	The gods' promontory,
Kami ga saki naru	Hung with sacred mulberry strips,
Ina no ho	Yields ears of rice—
Aya	*Aya*!
Ina no ho no	May the ears of rice
Moroho ni shide yo	Be many, and heavy-bent with fruit,
Kore chifu mo nashi.	And may there be no stunted ears.

(*Kinka*, 3)

A folk song may have been incorporated into the group of kagura songs, or again, this kagura song may have been arranged into a kinka, a song performed to zither accompaniment. It simply is unclear what became what. In either case, these songs undoubtedly were recited in the expectation that vocalizing the auspicious nature of the rice paddy would give rise to occult forces that would in turn improve the rice harvest. In other words, this is an example of a panegyric addressed to a thing. But unlike the uta cited earlier, "The warrior stands before . . . ," which used a guide phrase unconnected with nature, this song gives a very concrete description of a paddy prior to a rich harvest.

This little detail deserves notice. When such concrete specification is taken one step further, it evolves into what we might call a descriptive mode, as is displayed by the following song:

Motoe	*Opening*
Naniwagata	High tide comes to
Shio michikureba	The sand bars of Naniwa:
Amagoromo	Fishermen's rain capes—
Sue	*Close*
Amagoromo	Fishermen's rain capes—
Tamino no shima ni	The cranes veer off in flight
Tazu tachiwataru.	To the Isle of Tamino.

(*Kagura*, 37)

This too can only be a kotoage, uttered in the expectation that a desirable phenomenon will be effected here through praise of the auspicious qualities of the location.

Yet uta like the two that follow, the one by Takechi Kurohito and the next by Yamabe Akahito, are interpreted as simple nature poems by many modern Japanese readers, who tend to be impressed by the brilliant objective portrayal of a scene:

> Sakurada e
> Tazu nakiwataru
> Ayuchigata
> Shio hinikerashi
> Tazu nakiwataru.

> Cranes fly crying
> Toward the Sakura paddies:
> It must be ebb tide
> At the inlet of Ayuchi,
> And the cranes fly crying.

> (*MYS*, 3:271)

> Waka no ura ni
> Shio michikureba
> Kata o nami
> Ashihe o sashite
> Tazu nakiwataru.

> At the Bay of Waka,
> As the tide swells on the shore,
> Covering the sand bars—
> Bearing toward the stand of reeds,
> The cranes cry out as they fly off.

> (*MYS*, 6:919)

The common notion that this is objective description involves modern Japanese readers led astray by the objective-description theories of Saitō Mokichi and Shimagi Akahiko. The fact is that objective portrayal could not have existed in Yamato at that time. It is unlikely that Kurohito and Akahito composed their poems without a prior knowledge of the place-panegyric to the Naniwa region given above, a song selected as a kagura song. Nor is it easily imagined that the poets were unaware of the expectations of, and wishes for, good fortune—effected by the action of the kotodama—which were implicit in the Naniwa song. Yet the last half of the Ancient Age saw the weakening of poetic reliance on the kotodama, and a gradually developing experience of pleasure in the beauty of nature for its own sake. With this in mind we can probably say that the nature uta of the Ancient Age developed from place-panegyrics.

Poems of praise for individuals include personalized deities and tennō [commonly more a distinction than a difference]. I would like to call this group of poems the personal panegyric. Scenery is frequently used in this kind, which differs little in that respect from the place-panegyric, as the example of a song shows.

> Tsuginefu ya
> Yamashiro kawa o
> Kawanobori
> Wa ga noboreba
> Kawa no he ni
> Oidateru

> Where peaks abound
> Along the Yamashiro River,
> I go up the stream,
> And as I make my way upstream
> I see growing
> On the river's edge

Sashibu o	A sashibu, oh,
Sashibu no ki	A sashibu tree.
Shi ga shita ni	And at its foot
Oidateru	There grows
Habiro	A broad-leafed
Yutsu matsubaki	Sacred camellia.
Shi ga hana no	His countenance beams
Teri imashi	Like these bright flowers,
Shi ga ha no	He resides in a palace
Hirori imasu wa	Spacious as these spreading leaves:
Ōkimi rokamo.	Yes, my lord and sovereign.

(*KJK, Song,* 57)

This song implies an expectation, a desire that, through an arrangement of auspicious language, the honored person will receive the voice of the singer into his body and experience good fortune. In fact it is said to have been presented to Nintoku Tennō by his consort, Iwanohime (*Nintokuki,* 206). But it was very likely composed by a skilled poet. The Tswana tribes provide instances of chieftains who compose their own praise-poems. Normally, however, the poems are composed for the chieftain by trained tribesmen who are then rewarded with oxen (Schapera, 1965, 5-6).

It is not known whether rewards were given for songs in archaic Yamato. We may nevertheless conclude that skilled composers were always present to receive the royal command. Such court positions would also have existed in the Ancient Age, and might have been occupied by poets like Kakinomoto Hitomaro. The panegyrics composed by him and his fellow poets followed a tradition established in the Archaic Age. Instead of singing about brilliant accomplishments to extol the person praised, they sought to activate the kotodama. Their works may thus be fittingly called panegyrics to good fortune. The following personal panegyric was presented to Prince Naga (d. 715) by Hitomaro:

Yasumishishi	Our Prince, Child
Wa ga ōkimi	Of the high-gleaming Sun,
Takahikaru	Scion of our lord
Wa ga hi no miko no	Who rules the land in peace—
Uma namete	When His Highness,
Mikari tataseru	Leading horsemen, rides to hunt
Wakakomo o	Into the fields
Kariji no ono ni	Where young reeds are gathered,
Shishi koso ba	The wild beasts

Ihaiorogame	Crawl along in adoration;
Uzura koso	Even the quails
Ihaimotōre	Creep around and around.
Shishi ji mono	Like the wild beasts,
Ihaiorogami	We too crawl in adoration;
Uzura nasu	We are as quails,
Ihaimotōri	Creeping around and around:
Kashikomi to	With reverence
Tsukaematsurite	We dedicate our services;
Hisakata no	And we look on his face,
Ame miru gotoku	Like the sight of a pure landscape—
Masokagami	As if we beheld
Aogite miredo	The far distant heavens;
Harukusa no	But he is more splendid still—
Iya mezurashiki	A plant grown finer with each spring:
Waga ōkimi kamo.	And we know this is our lord!

(*MYS*, 3:239)

If we compare this with the *Kojiki* song that begins, "Where peaks abound / Along the Yamashiro River," we see that Hitomaro's poem differs appreciably in the ingenuity of its repetitions, parallelism, and freshness of imagery: "wild beasts," "quails," "A plant grown finer with each spring." It is, however, identical to the earlier song in its implicit evocation of the kotodama to bring about agreeable events.

"Banquet poems" is the term I have given to songs recited at formal collations. They were of course intended as entertainment for the banqueters, although this was not the sole aim of such songs. They, too, originated from the desire that the kotodama, borne by the singing voice or voices, might bring good fortune to everyone present. To assume otherwise is to conclude that the compilers of the *Chronicles* did not recognize the value of what they so painstakingly recorded. One variety of banquet uta is the farewell poem: it was intended to be recited in sending off a traveler. Since, however, farewell songs celebrated in advance the good fortune to be encountered on a journey, their composers avoided, with a caution bordering on the neurotic, any vocabulary that might invite unpleasant circumstances. This was due to the nature of the kotodama, which could bring about not only good but evil results as well. Such concerns also survive to a certain extent in modern Japanese society, although, as we know from the tenth-century *Tosa Diary*, they were far more rigorously observed in the Middle Ages. Like the panegyric songs (panegyrics to places, things, and people), both banquet poems and farewell songs share recognizable features with the songs of the

Chronicles and the waka composed in the first half of the Ancient Age. We may thus conclude that waka dating from the first half of the Ancient Age represent a direct extension of the songs of the *Chronicles*.

Dirges differ somewhat in tenor from the varieties of song hitherto discussed. In archaic times, dirges were sung during the period of mogari (written with characters signifying "suspension of mourning" in the *Wei Chih*, "Account of the People of Wa"), that is, during the ceremony of laying out the deceased (in a temporary mausoleum prior to the permanent entombment) and of gathering surviving relatives at this mausoleum. The singing of dirges in these circumstances is considered to be an incontrovertible fact, borne out by the *Kojiki* description of Ame no Wakahiko's funeral. Of course, we do not know the nature of third-century dirges, although the four songs associated with the death of Prince Yamato Takeru are said to have been recited at the funerals of tennō in succeeding generations. We can accept the *Kojiki* statement that they were recited even in its day, because if this were not fact, it would have been subjected to harsh criticism by the people of the time.[8] Yet the texts of these four songs differ strikingly in their form of expression from the public and private elegies composed in the first half of the Ancient Age. That is, we cannot say that the dirges developed directly from the songs of the *Chronicles*. This may be because they were fixed into specific texts such as those transmitted by the *Kojiki*, and no new ones were composed.

With the commencement of the age of the *Man'yōshū*, elegies came to be frequently presented on occasions other than that of the mogari.[9] Instead of remaining a text with the occult powers to call back the souls of the dead, the elegy moved closer to the lament, in which the poet mourns his eternal separation from one near to him. Other features were added to the expression of grief: for example, the deeds and benefactions performed by the deceased were here extolled. Elements of the panegyric remain in the formal elegy—as is shown by Hitomaro's "Elegy for Prince Takechi" (*MYS*, 2:199)—and occult characteristics still survive. But the elegy was moving chiefly in the direction of lyric poetry.

The highly emotional nature of Yamato poetry is emphasized by the way in which the dirges came to be supplanted by lyric elegies. Moreover, nearly all ancient waka developed on lyric lines, a fact manifest in subsequent developments for waka. The old songs appear to have taken on the expressive characteristics of waka when the songs were polished for

---

[8] "These four songs were all sung at his funeral. Up to the present day, therefore, these songs have been sung at royal funerals" (*KJK*, 2:143-44). "Up to the present day" refers to the time when the Yamato Takeru setsuwa became fixed, not to the eighth century, when it was recorded in the *Kojiki*.

[9] A few elegies were used at the mogari ceremonies (see Chapters 3, 7, 9), e.g., *MYS*, 2:151, 167, 196, 199.

court performance. Part of the royal-family setsuwa in the *Kojiki* describes how Crown Prince Karu of Kinashi becomes the lover of his full sister, the elder princess of Karu. This leads to public commotion and culminates in the capture and banishment of the crown prince and the lovers' subsequent deaths. The narrative of this story, which one is tempted to call a Yamato *Aïda*, is interspersed with thirteen songs (*KJK*, 2:238-41). Among them is this [short guide phrases italicized, long set off by slashes]:

/Ashihiki no	/To make paddies in the mountains,
Yamada o tsukuri	*With their sprawling foothills,*
Yamadakami	We need water, yet the hills are high;
Shitabi o washise/	Thus conduits run in the earth concealed/
Shitadoi ni	Concealed was my visit,
Wa ga tou imo o	The visit paid my beloved;
Shitanaki ni	Concealed were her tears of joy,
Wa ga naku tsuma o	The tears shed by my wife;
Kozo koso wa	But tonight, free from fear,
Yasuku hada fure.	We'll hold each other, skin on skin.

(*KJK, Song*, 78)

This uta is represented as recited by the crown prince at the beginning of his affair with the elder princess. Yet the *Kojiki* significantly notes that "This is a High Ending Song" (shirageuta). The song is also found, with slight variations, in the *Kinkafu* and, again, it has the heading, "High Ending Song." This kind of song was apparently named for the higher pitch in which the concluding lines were sung. The problem, however, rests not so much in the meaning of "shirage" as in the fact that the term designated music transmitted and taught as court song. The appearance of this uta in the *Kinkafu* indicates that it actually was sung as a court song.

It is also noteworthy, however, that each of the thirteen songs mentioned above is labeled in the *Kojiki* with a term like "High Pitch, Country Style," "Courtier's Style," "Two Levels Style," "Two-Pitch Melody, Country Style," or "Declamatory Song." Of these, the terms "Two-Pitch Melody" and "Declamatory Song" also appear in the *Kinkafu*. All thirteen songs pertaining to the ill-starred love of Crown Prince Karu of Kinashi were probably learned and performed at court. One song is recited in the *Kojiki* by the elder princess of Karu when, out of longing for her brother, she sets off for his place of exile in Iyo. It appears in identical form in the *Man'yōshū* (2:90):

Kimi ga yuki	The journey of my lord
Ke nagaku narinu	Has lasted many days:
Yamatazu no	As elderberry leaf meets leaf
Mukae o yukan	I shall go out to meet him.
Matsu ni wa mataji.	I cannot wait, I'll wait no more!

(KJK, Song, 88)

The song appears again in the *Man'yōshū* (2:85), with some variations, as the composition of Iwanohime, consort of Nintoku.

There is another example from this cycle of story and song. Later Prince Karu is joined in Iyo by the princess, and he sings of his longing for home, prior to their joint suicide:

/Komoriku no	Nestled in hills
Hatsuse no kawa no	Is Hatsuse where streams begin
Kamitsuse ni	Upstream
Ikui o uchi	I raised a sacred post,
Shimotsuse ni	Downstream
Makui o uchi	I raised a fine post.
Ikui ni wa	On the sacred post
Kagami o kake	I hung a mirror;
Makui ni wa	On the fine post
Matama o kake/	I hung fine jewels./
Matama nasu	Like fine jewels
Aga mō imo	Is my darling, whom I cherish;
Kagami nasu	Like a mirror
Aga mō tsuma	Is my wife, whom I cherish—
Ari to iwaba koso yo	If you were in the city,
Ie ni mo yukame	I would go to your house,
Kuni o mo shinowame.	I would yearn for home.

(KJK, Song, 90)

This song also appears in the *Man'yōshū* (13:3263), with some insignificant differences. We may deduce from these examples that many other uta now found only in the *Man'yōshū* once existed as songs that were taught and performed at court.

We may term song-setsuwa (utasetsuwa) those setsuwa narratives interconnected with a number of songs. No small number of such story and song cycles can be found in the *Chronicles* along with that on Prince and Princess Karu. Other important examples of song-setsuwa include that of Nintoku Tennō, who, as we recall, is subjected to Iwanohime's unusually violent jealousy (*Nintokuki*, 201-17), and those portions of the Yūryaku Tennō setsuwa that concern the steadfast Akaiko (*Yūryakuki*, 267-68) and the protagonists of the palace banquet episode, the court lady from Mie and Princess Odo of Kasuga (*Yūryakuki*, 270-72). Once again we discover that songs contained in the narratives are designated with terms like "Quiet Song with Transposed Repeats," "Song of the Amagatari" (Amagatariuta), "Quiet Song," and "Light Song." Of these, Akaiko's song, "Lovely fence, built round / The gods' preserve . . ." (*KJK, Song*, 94), also appears in the *Kinkafu* as a Quiet Song (*Kinka*, 1), signifying that the corpus was sung at court.

Yet such songs, which were eventually taught and performed at court, are believed to have been transmitted at some earlier time by the kataribe. The three songs that pertain to the story of the court lady from Mie (*KJK, Songs*, 100-102) are labeled "Songs of the Amagatari," evidently songs transmitted by a kataribe which, because it had originated from the Fishermen's Corporation (Amabe) of Ise, took the name Amagataribe, "The Fishermen's kataribe" (*KJK, Song*, 102, supplementary note). In the period prior to their emergence as court performances, the songs, and the related setsuwa, were undoubtedly transmitted by the Amagataribe of Ise. The fact that the protagonist is a court lady from Mie (i.e., Ise) reflects the local origin of this setsuwa. In other words, songs and setsuwa that had originally been transmitted by provincial kataribe were brought to court and, in the process of repeated performances there, must have undergone a gradual refinement of expression.[10]

All three songs concerning the court lady from Mie have as their concluding lines, "*This was transmitted / By word of mouth*," a formula they share with three songs pertaining to the God of Eight Thousand Halberds (*KJK, Songs*, 2-4). The first song of this latter group contains the lines, "By the court servant Ama / Whose fishing forebears plumbed the depths," clearly indicating that it was originally transmitted by the Fishermen's Corporation ("Ama" meaning "fisherman.") Let us review this song.

Yachihoko no	The divine Lord
Kami no mikoto wa	Of Eight Thousand Halberds
Yashima kuni	Cannot find a fitting bride
Tsuma makikanete	In all the Isles of Yamato.

[10] In addition, fuzoku songs are essentially provincial songs, and several saibara use the words of provincial songs.

Tōdōshi	Then, hearing that
Koshi no kuni ni	In the distant
Sakashi me o	Land of Koshi
Ari to kikashite	A clever maiden dwells,
Kuwashi me o	Then, hearing that
Ari to kikoshite	There a lovely maiden dwells,
Sayobai ni	He sets off
Aritatashi	To pay her court,
Yobai ni	He comes calling
Arikayowase	To court her.
Tachi ga o mo	He does not pause
Imada tokazute	To loosen his sword knots,
Osui o mo	He does not pause
Imada tokaneba	To loosen his cloak.
Otome no	Does the maiden sleep
Nasu ya itato o	Behind that wooden door?—
Oshisoburai	As I stand
Wa ga tatasereba	And as I push against it,
Hikikozurai	And as I stand and
Wa ga tatasereba	As I pull upon it,
Aoyama ni	A tiger thrush calls
Nue wa nakinu	From verdant hills;
Sanotsutori	Bird of the fields,
Kigishi wa toyomu	A pheasant cries out;
Niwatsutori	Bird of the garden,
Kake wa naku	A rooster crows.
Uretaku mo	How vexing is
Naku naru tori ka	The racket of these birds!
Kono tori mo	If only I could
Uchiyamekosene.	Make them stop!
Ishitau ya	*By the court servant Ama,*
Ama hase tsukai	*Whose fishing forebears plumbed the depths,*
Koto no katarigoto mo	*This was transmitted*
Ko o ba.	*By word of mouth.*

(*KJK, Song*, 2)

The orderly parallelism of this song indicates that it, together with three others concerning the God of Eight Thousand Halberds (*KJK, Songs*, 3-5), must be regarded as belonging to the more ancient part of the new stratum.

Let us consider with it a *Man'yōshū* uta based on similar concepts:

Komoriku no	Nestled in hills
Hatsuse no kuni ni	Is Hatsuse where streams begin,
Sayobai ni	And having come
Waga kitareba	To court you, I find
Tanagumori	Clouds cover the sky
Yuki wa furiku	And the snow falls down;
Sagumori	Clouds lift a bit
Ame wa furiku	And the rain falls down.
Notsutori	Bird of the fields,
Kigishi wa toyomu	A pheasant cries out;
Ietsutori	Bird of the house,
Kake mo naku	A rooster crows.
Sayo wa ake	The day dawns,
Kono yo wa akenu	This day has now begun.
Irite katsu nen	Quick, let me into your bed,
Kono to hirakase.	Open your door to me—oh, do!

Envoy

Komoriku no	Nestled in hills
Hatsuse oguni ni	Is Hatsuse where streams begin,
Tsuma shi areba	Where I have a wife:
Ishi wa fumedomo	And though the road was rocky,
Nao shi kinikeri.	I have come to be with her.

(*MYS*, 13:3310-11)

The two uta following these are replies from the woman (3312-13). They correspond to Princess Nunakawa's answering uta in the *Kojiki* (*KJK, Song*, 3). This correspondence is made more evident by part of poem 3312 in the *Man'yōshū*, in which the speaker addresses her lover as "Yobai sesu / Aga sumeroki yo" ("My sovereign / You who seek my hand"): here it is a tennō who has come to see the woman. This creation of a character who possesses equal status with the God of Eight Thousand Halberds is also a sign of correspondence between *Man'yōshū* poems and *Kojiki* songs 2 and 3. The *Man'yōshū* uta 3310-13 are all anonymous, although the presence of envoys indicates a composition date later than the mid-seventh century, as does the fact that the envoys were clearly composed on the waka model.

One might conclude that these *Man'yōshū* uta represent a reworking into waka form of the songs concerning the God of Eight Thousand Halberds. But in refinement of language the *Kojiki* group is appreciably superior. So clumsy is the style of the *Man'yōshū* uta group that the reader might suppose they are late fifth-century compositions. The author of the *Man'yōshū* group may not have known the *Kojiki* songs relating to the God of Eight Thousand Halberds at the time of composing these uta. Nevertheless, the considerable resemblance between the two groups is possible only by the presence of a common ancestor, a song group the form of which served as the source of both the God of Eight Thousand Halberds songs and the *Man'yōshū* uta. During the process of court instruction and recitation, the songs of the God of Eight Thousand Halberds became more refined in their expression. But the composer of the *Man'yōshū* uta, deprived of a similar environment, could apparently produce only lyric expression so inept as to create the illusion of old-stratum language.

Differences in refinement of expression are not always as striking as this, but there are instances of provincial songs that serve as the common ancestor for court songs on the one hand and *Man'yōshū* uta on the other. A song has been recorded from a now lost passage of the *Hizen no Kuni Fudoki (Hizen Topography)*. It was performed, with a dance, by the village young people, in the course of a banquet they gave every spring and autumn on Mount Kishima. [Guide phrases will be italicized until further notice.]

Arare furu	*Where hail falls*
Kishima ga take o	At the peak of Kishima
Sagashimi to	It is so very steep to climb:
Kusa torikanete	I cannot cling to its grasses,
Imo ga te o toru.	So I'll take my sweet girl's hand instead.

(*Fudoki*, 19)

The speaker attempts to climb the peak by clutching the grasses that grow on its slopes. He loses his grip (or pretends to) and instead grasps the girl's hand. Such is the sum of the song. It is understandable in this case, since the sweetheart of the song is a sturdy country lass. If she were a capital-bred girl, however, the song would not succeed. When Nintoku Tennō falls in love with his half-sister Princess Medori and wishes to make her his wife, he asks his half-brother Prince Hayabusawake to serve as his intermediary. But Princess Medori, well aware of the violently jealous nature of Iwanohime, the tennō's consort, rejects his offer and marries Prince Hayabusawake instead. When Prince Hayabusawake fails to report back to Nintoku, the tennō goes directly to Princess Medori; he finds her at her weaving, and asks her in a song, "For whom are you weaving that cloth?" The princess replies with a song to the effect that the cloth will make a garment for Hayabusawake, and Nintoku, now aware of the situation, returns to his palace. Princess Medori later recites a song to Hayabusawake suggesting that he attack Nintoku. On getting wind of this, Nintoku sends a punitive force against the couple. In their flight from the royal army, they climb Mount Kurahashi, and Hayabusawake sings:

> *Hashitate no*   *Like an upright ladder,*
> Kurahashiyama o   Mount Kurahashi
>   Sagashimi to   Is so steep to climb:
> Iwa kakikanete   You cannot cling to its rocks;
> Waga te torasu mo.   Please grasp my hand instead.
>
> (*KJK, Song,* 69)

But in the end they cannot elude Nintoku's forces. Both are eventually killed in Uda. In Hayabusawake's song it is the woman, Princess Medori, who grasps her companion's hand. A modern Japanese would respond believingly to the woman's gesture. A very similar uta is attributed to the female immortal Tsuminoe:

> *Arare furi*   *Where hail falls*
> Kishimi ga take o   At the peak of Kishimi,
>   Sagashimi to   It is so very steep to climb:
> Kusa torikanawa   I cannot cling to its grasses,
> Imo ga te o toru.   So I'll take my lady's hand instead.
>
> (*MYS,* 3:385)

Since the last line sounds odd coming from a female immortal, the afternote contains an alternate attribution which states that the uta was given to Tsuminoe by a man named Umashine. In any case, we have established the existence of a process whereby an antecedent provincial song form evolves at court into refined expression and, furthermore, whereby uta are created which are later selected for inclusion in the *Man'yōshū* as waka.

Such evidence reveals two important phenomena. The first is that the song-setsuwa genre, in which an emotional climax is celebrated in lyrical recitation by one or more characters, flourished chiefly in the sixth century, although epic, with its recitation of an entire setsuwa corpus in verse-prose, did not come into being.[11] The several song-setsuwa narratives cited above do not have events from the "Heroic Age" for subject

---

[11] "Epic" is often used synonymously with "heroic poetry." I have followed E.M.W. Tillyard in defining epic as "verse narrative of deeds," and heroic poetry as a subgenre within the epic and a kind having as subject events from the heroic age as well as a "heroic impression" (Tillyard, 1954, 10-11).

matter, and so they could not have become heroic poetry in the Homeric style. These narratives might nevertheless have evolved into an epic centering on the royal succession. Despite the presence, in sixth-century Yamato, of subject matter ideally suited to the creation of such a genre, an epic corresponding to the *Edda* did not in fact emerge. The reasons for this have been discussed above, but the preferences of the Yamato people are strongly reflected in this phenomenon. Blessed with excellent subject matter, the Yamato people chose not to develop it as epic, but rather to turn it into the lyric poetry of the *Man'yōshū*.

The second phenomenon is the rise in the level of waka expression which accompanied the textual refinement of courtly song libretti in the course of instruction and performance. Book 13 of the *Man'yōshū* contains several waka with extremely ancient forms of expression. Here is one:

Tsuginefu	*Where peaks abound,*
Yamashiroji o	On the road to Yamashiro
Hitozuma no	Other women's husbands
Uma yori yuku ni	Travel on horseback;
Onozuma shi	Only my husband
Kachi yori yukeba	Travels on foot.
Miru goto ni	When I see him walking,
Ne nomi shi nakayu	All I can do is cry;
Soko omou ni	The very thought of it
Kokoro shi itashi	Grieves me no end.
Tarachine no	Here, husband, take
Haha ga katami to	This clear-reflecting mirror,
Waga moteru	A cherished keepsake of my mother,
Masomi kagami ni	*She with withered breasts*;
Akizuhire	Add to it my shawl,
Oinamemochite	Delicate as dragonfly wings,
Uma kae wa ga se.	And buy a horse, my love!

Envoy

Izumikawa	The ford was deep
Watarize fukami	At the Izumi River,
Waga seko ga	And so my husband's
Tabiyukigoromo	Clothes taken for his travel
Nurehitan kamo.	Were soaked from top to bottom!

(*MYS*, 13:3314-15)

Uta like these impress the reader as being ancient, simple songs, but this does not always mean that they are the products of an ancient time.

Rather, old forms were probably preserved among provincial composers who rarely came into contact with courtly expression. By contrast, poets like Hitomaro must have learned how song libretti were refined at court, and so courtly refined styles would be reflected in their waka.[12] It is a marvel that Hitomaro could express the kotodama of the Archaic Age by the new courtly techniques; that could have come about only under the circumstances of his familiarity with the court—although we are still left with the question of what process made possible the birth of waka as an individual entity out of folk expression.

Recognition of Poetic Qualities in Waka

I have been proposing that sophisticated waka expression was brought into being through the agency of polished court song libretti. Inasmuch as my view contradicts the commonly held distinction between an aurally received song and a visually received waka, I must address myself to the question of how song and waka are to be differentiated. Songs in the *Chronicles* are designated in narrative passages by words like these: "The uta . . . ," "The uta was . . . ," ". . . composed an uta," ". . . said in an uta," or ". . . replied with an uta." The prefaces to the *Man'yōshū* poems designate their works in similar fashion: "The uta . . . ," ". . . composed an uta," ". . . presented an uta," ". . . an uta in reply to the presented uta." Thus song cannot be distinguished from waka in this respect. Certain statements in the *Chronicles*, such as "Then he sang, saying . . . " (Sunawachi kuchitsuuta shite iwaku), provide clear indications that works were sung (e.g., *NSK, Song,* 123).[13] But similar expressions are also found in the *Man'yōshū* (e.g., *MYS,* 18:4044). Even the term "kuchitsuuta" (signifying an uta without musical accompaniment) does not clarify whether its content is a song or a waka. Moreover, as we have just been seeing, certain songs in the *Chronicles* also appear in identical or very similar form in the *Man'yōshū*, so it is also difficult to discover anything conclusive in regard to content and form that will differentiate song from waka. Where, then, might we hope to find such distinctive factors?

According to one view, we can differentiate song and waka in this fashion: whereas in the Archaic Age the word "uta" signified a regularly rhythmic song possessing melody, the same word in the *Man'yōshū* signifies a recitation with fluctuating rhythm, frequently indicated by terms

[12] We can easily believe that provincial songs were familiar to court literati around the time of Hitomaro from the fact that Temmu ordered, in 625, the various provinces to send to the capital a hundred men and women talented in song (*Temmuki,* 336).

[13] There is also Chinese evidence: "Recitation shown to P'ei Ti" (*Ō I,* 13:1559); "Recited on leaving the Tzü-ch'en Palace" (*Toshi,* 6:1157); "Recited and presented to Scholar Hung, who was summoned to the court" (*Rishi,* 8:922). According to these and other prefaces, poetry in the T'ang period seems to have been recited orally on occasion, being memorized for later transcription. The same probably applies to examples in the *Man'yōshū*.

like "gin," "shō," and "shōei." If these criteria were applicable, the matter would be settled most lucidly. Unfortunately, there is strong evidence to the contrary. As we have seen, musical scores in the *Kinkafu* reveal that from the Archaic to the Ancient Age, song was recited to fluctuating rhythms. The single exception is the saibara, a type of song derived from subjecting the Yamato-style fuzoku song to a musical arrangement in conformance with T'ang melodies and rhythms. This being the case, how can we differentiate between song and waka? I shall subsequently attempt to present criteria that make this differentiation possible, although they will represent, in essence, no more than a definition, which is to say an understanding, of waka and what it signifies. We do not even know how strictly the *Man'yōshū* poets themselves discriminated, as individuals, between song and waka. As a result, we cannot hope for greater validity than that contained in a definition.

Ki no Tsurayuki and his circle conceived of the waka as the "Yamato uta," in the sense, that is, of poetry from the Land of Wa. This, however, does not mean that the concept existed throughout the age of the *Man'yōshū*, a time when "waka" signified a sung response to someone's uta. From Okura's time onward, people had gradually grown conscious of the "poetry from the Land of Wa." But for them to call it "waka" indicated that this poetry must have been seen as "worthy expression" like Chinese poetry and, moreover, as equal in worth to Chinese poetry. In other words, this variety of uta, which was later termed the "Yamato uta," was thought to have certain features.

1. Realization of individuality
   a. The composer as subject (identification or nonidentification of the composer)
   b. The specificity of the work (a specific scene, date, and/or circumstance of composition)
2. Communal awareness
   a. Expression based on precedent (similar uta, similar diction)
   b. A commonly held code of reception (agreement based on feelings of solidarity)
3. The union of visual reception and written composition
   a. The tendency to rely on the expressive properties of Chinese characters (the "shih form" and rebus script)[14]
   b. The reception of grouped uta (uta in collections and standing alone)

[14] [The "shih form" (shitai) was one of several ways of writing Japanese poetry with Chinese characters. In this form, the Japanese poem was "translated" solely into Chinese rather than written phonetically with Chinese characters. The poem therefore resembled a shih, or Chinese poem. Nonetheless, it was read and recited in Japanese. See also n. 18 below.—Trans.]

I should like to take up each point in turn.

Chinese poetry became fixed in its identity as "worthy expression" with the evolution of a tradition requiring the clear identification of the composer of each poem. If the Yamato people were to produce "worthy expression" on an equal level, they too would be obliged to identify the composer of a given work. This did not mean that people found it preferable to know the name of the author of a work, but rather that the act of identification was a formal necessity. It was generally proper form to have the name of the composer precede an uta, as in these cases: "An uta by Princess Nukada," or "Three uta by Lord Kakinomoto Hitomaro." When a more ceremonious tone was called for, the composer's official title would be given too, as in this case: "Two uta by the royal attendant Lord Ishikawa Hironari." The composer's name might also appear in an afternote. In poetry collections, the poet's name often appeared in this fashion: "The above two uta are by Lord Abe no Mushimaro," or "The above two uta are by a lady from Tsushima whose name is Tamaki." Instances also appear of the poet (as compiler) recording his own name, as in "This was composed by the Assistant Minister of War, Lord Ōtomo Yakamochi."

In some special cases the composer's name is either unknown or not given because of his lowly status, as in "Two uta by an instructor of Go," "An uta by a fisherman from Buzen Province," or "An uta recited by a beggar." Behind such notations was an awareness that, properly speaking, the composer's name should have been given.[15] Other notations—"An anonymous uta," or "The name of the composer of the above nine uta is unknown"—are based on a similar awareness. This signified a recognition that the Yamato uta was a sufficiently "worthy expression" to disclose both its composer's responsibility and the honor due the poet by the act of indicating the name. This can only be one manifestation of the fact that the "Yamato uta"—regardless of what it was then called—was perceived, at least in essence, as that contrasting with Chinese poetry.

In many instances, however, the name of the composer is duly revealed by an accompanying description of the situation when the uta was composed. The scene, date, and circumstances of composition often appear in forenotes and afternotes. For example:

Crown Prince Shōtoku, on his way to visit the well of Takahara, saw a dead man on Mount Tatsuta. Deeply grieved, he composed this uta (*MYS*, 3:415).

[15] "The composer of the above poem is not named here because of his lowly status" (*MYS*, 8:1428, afternote). Such statements reveal the awareness that the poet's name should be given with the poem, and that a reason was required for an exception. [In fact, elsewhere in the *MYS* lowly people—even animals—are identified as poets.—Ed.]

An uta composed by Prince Shiki on the occasion of his visit to the Naniwa Palace in [704] (*MYS*, 1:64).

On the fifth day of the Fifth Month [749], a banquet was held for the monk Hyōei and others who were messengers sent from the temple of Tōdaiji to take possession of some reclaimed rice fields. Lord Ōtomo Yakamochi, who was at that time governor of the province, offered sake to the monks and recited this uta (*MYS*, 18:4085).

Each was composed in a specific time, place, or circumstance peculiar to itself: that is, the prose remarks indicate that each uta came into being under conditions that occurred only once. In its turn, the audience of each uta was expected to honor the given conditions.

The prose accounts are not to be confused with setsuwa narratives relating how long, long ago, in a certain place, a certain person did a certain thing. Instead the accounts of poems emphasized that the work was composed by an actual, specific individual in a specific situation. In cases where not all these conditions were known, the forenote would give what information was available, and the afternote would contain whatever caveats were deemed necessary. For example, the forenote to one of Akahito's waka reads, "One uta on the warbler by Lord Yamabe Akahito," while the afternote observes, "The date and place of composition of the above waka have not yet been ascertained. It is recorded here, however, exactly as it was heard recited" (*MYS*, 17:3915). Again, such notations reveal an awareness that, properly speaking, the date and place of composition should have been given [and that waka were typically transmitted vocally].

This awareness—that the name of a specific poet and the time, place, and circumstances of composition must be disclosed with a poem—was also linked to a desire to discriminate among uta styles. A group of *Man'yōshū* poems bearing the forenote "Three uta—one lengthy, two short—in longing for a boy named Furuhi" have the following afternote referring to the last of the three: "Given that the fashioning of the poem resembles Yamanoe's, it is placed here after the two others" (*MYS*, 5:904-906).[16] The emergence of the question of "fashioning," that is of style, can only reflect the contemporary perception that an uta was the work of a specific individual. Furthermore, as people became more strongly conscious of the specificity of poetry, another attitude emerged which held that, properly speaking, textual departures should not be tolerated. It has already been pointed out that notations of variant textual trans-

---

[16] [The reference is of course to Yamanoe Okura, several of whose poems immediately precede these.—Trans.]

missions abound in the *Man'yōshū*. Their presence, however, did not in the least mean that variants were welcome; they must have owed their place in the *Man'yōshū* to the concept of the literary work as the product of a unique process.

These assumptions of individuality and specificity did not signify a prevailing assumption that each poet worked independently of others. Cooperation and solidarity was a concurrent aim. As we have seen, similar poems and poetic diction are frequently found at the time of the *Man'yōshū*. The Japanese situation involves features unlike those assumed by the Parry-Lord theory, in that Japanese poems tend in many ways to be based on an awareness of ga, that principle holding that beautiful expression must have a precedent. For example, this waka:

Momoshiki no	I have forgot the year when
Ōmiyahito no	Gentlefolk from the Palace
Nikitatsu ni	*Built with stone and wood aplenty*
Funanorishiken	Boarded, long ago, their ship
Toshi no shiranaku.	In Nikitatsu harbor.

(*MYS*, 3:323)

It is clearly based upon an earlier uta, said to be the work of Princess Nukada:

Nikitatsu ni	We've waited for the moonrise
Funanorisen to	Before boarding ship
Tsuki mateba	In Nikitatsu harbor;
Shio mo kanainu	Now the tide is full—
Ima wa kogiide na.	Let us row out to sea!

(*MYS*, 1:8)

It was expected that the audience of "I have forgot" would consist of people possessing a prior knowledge of Nukada's uta. The composer of "I have forgot" is not attempting, however, to skimp by reliance on formulas. Instead, the end is to overlap the new uta with the scene evoked by Princess Nukada's, bringing out a new motif, one absent in hers.

The use of this technique creates effective expression in direct proportion to the degree of excellence possessed by the diction borrowed from the antecedent uta. Whether the ancient technique of producing an individual freshness based paradoxically on obviously antecedent diction was employed with the same awareness as was the technique of honkadori, or allusive variation, in the Middle Ages, is something that cannot be ascertained. We have no way of conversing with inhabitants of either period. It probably cannot be denied, however, that reception in the Ancient Age, as in later times, was consciously effected through contact among people possessing a common knowledge of antecedent poetic diction. Without this assumption, we would be quite unable to comprehend the abundance of similar concepts and diction in the *Man'yōshū*.

The turn to preexisting diction may have been in search of an "understanding" effecting mutual comprehension among the members of the audience, the poet included. If the question had been one of simply interpreting an old poem, the poet could probably have managed on his own. But without means shared with a contemporary audience, there was no way for a poet to judge the effectiveness of a given use of prior diction.

The guide phrase provides an excellent example. At one time, everyone knew that the kotodama would be introduced into the word "yama" (mountain, hill) through the use of the guide phrase "ashihiki no" (with its sprawling foothills), and the result would be lively expression. An "understanding," which effected a mutual comprehension of the word "ashihiki," did exist, although it may never have been clearly articulated. In later ages, as the working of the kotodama lost in strength, it seems to have been operated with some force by exertion of mental effort. Having heard the phrase "ashihiki no" pronounced, an audience realized that the word "mountain" was expected somehow to acquire vitality.[17] This realization was probably sustained less by individual efforts than by feelings of communal solidarity: each member of an audience assumed that individual and group response were one. This sense of solidarity brought into being the concept of sama, elegant style, stressed later by Ki no Tsurayuki. In this were the origins of literary promise for all waka.

Although modern readers probably find it easiest to conceive of the distinction between song and waka as that between aural and visual reception, the distinction would have confused people of the Ancient Age. As we have seen, up to the second half of the Ancient Age waka was orally presented and heard. Although reading increased with the passage of time, it never managed to reverse the ascendancy of oral delivery and aural reception. To the proposition that "song is the form which is aurally received," people from the Ancient Age would protest that waka was usually like that, too. Like Chinese poetry, waka was undeniably written down and often taken in visually. The question is not whether little or much visual reception took place. Waka and Chinese

---

[17] The guide phrase, "ashihiki no," appears thirty-six times in Yakamochi's poems, so that he must have had a definite belief in its efficacy. The original meaning of "ashihiki no" had probably been lost even by Hitomaro's time (Omodaka, 1937, 65-68), but a new or misunderstood meaning was justifiable as long as the conviction remained that the guide phrase would bring the kotodama to function.

poetry differ from song in that they are set down in writing, so requiring visual reception. Some earlier songs had been recorded in writing, but they were still delivered orally. Yet the fact of the songs having been preserved in writing inexorably relates them to written poetry. Their being transmitted by writing, even if for oral delivery, necessarily bound them to the Chinese characters then used for transcription. The "shih form" of transcription provides a particularly good example of oral songs preserved in writing.[18]

Until they later invented their own writing system, kana, the Yamato people had only Chinese characters with which to write their language. It will be obvious that this made it extremely difficult to produce a faithful recording of song and waka texts. It is also well known that, as a result, various methods were devised to record the Japanese language with Chinese characters. The categories used are as follows:

1. The use of Chinese characters solely as graphs to communicate meaning (as in *MYS*, 11:2499).
2. The use of Chinese characters both as graphs for meaning and as phonetic symbols (as in *MYS*, 2:90).
3. The use of Chinese characters solely as phonetic symbols (as in *MYS*, 20:4296).

The shih form of transcription belongs to the first category, although we have no clear evidence whether this provided a convenient means of jotting down the important words of a poem as an aide-mémoire, while omitting the rest, or whether it followed a system like that used for the Chinese shih, with inflected word endings and grammatical particles supplied by the reader. Yet that first "shih form" may be correctly interpreted as a text which requires or anticipates that it be read by means of a system similar to that used in reading the Chinese shih. The syllabic system of the third category was the most accurate and the simplest means of transcription, and also remained faithful to the spoken sounds of the words. For this reason the songs of the *Chronicles* were transcribed according to the third form. Despite the accuracy of transcription achieved by the syllabic system, the large number of homonyms in the Japanese language led to lexical confusion. The second form was created as a result: here the number of Chinese characters deemed necessary to communicate meaning appeared together with the syllabic means of transcribing inflections [and particles]. The people of the Ancient Age seem

---

[18] "Shih form" (shitai) is usually referred to in scholarly circles as "abbreviated form" (ryakutai). This term suggests, however, the existence of an original form prior to an abbreviation, which is not the case. I have therefore followed Itō Haku in reviving Kamo no Mabuchi's term for this form. It corresponds to method (1) in the next paragraph. [See n. 14, above.—Ed.]

to have considered this method of transcription the easiest to comprehend. As is indicated by Kamo no Mabuchi's name for this method, "the
standard form" (jōtai), this second form enjoyed great popularity
throughout the time of the *Man'yōshū*, the result perhaps of the facility
it provided its audience.

By contrast, the first form is not readily understood. The practice of
providing only the most important words, while leaving the inflective
word endings and grammatical particles to be supplemented by the reader,
resembled in essence another Japanese reading system which would come
into use from the ninth century. In this, Japanese readers of Chinese
classics supplemented a Chinese text with inflective word endings and
grammatical particles provided by kana or the guide marks called kunten.
The earlier, first category demanded more flexible readings, and for the
following reason. The kunten system, which was devised as a means of
transcribing supplementary inflective word endings and grammatical particles, resulted in a fixed method of reading a given sentence. Prior to the
invention of that system, however, inflective word endings and grammatical particles were products of each reader's thought. Fixed readings
were infeasible.

To employ an analogy, these two methods of reading can be likened
to two kinds of chess games: not even a beginner has trouble lining up
men on the chessboard and playing a game, but only an experienced
player is capable of carrying on a game in the mind, unaided by board
or chess pieces. The composer of a work written in the first form required
or anticipated that readers would have an interpretive ability on a par
with that of the chess player who uses neither board nor men in the
game. It was clearly more difficult than the second and third forms. The
first is thought to have been the method of transcription used for audiences which the composer assumed were accustomed to reading Chinese
shih transcribed solely in Chinese characters. As such it is a good example
of what I have called "written composition that anticipates visual reception."

This property of written composition anticipating visual reception is
still more clearly perceived within certain transcription methods that
utilize Chinese characters as indicators of meaning. For example, the
Yamato word for mist is "kiri," but the two Chinese characters sometimes
used to express this word were read in Chinese as "pai-ch'i," signifying
"white vapor." If this text was read, the reader would realize that the
pronunciation of these two characters differed from that for the Yamato
word they symbolized, and observe that the word in question corresponded in meaning to "white vapor." Taking all this into consideration,
the reader would understand that the Yamato word "kiri" was expressed
here by the two Chinese characters.

To give another example, the Yamato word for hail, "arare," was sometimes expressed with two characters read "wan-hsieh" in Chinese, and signifying "round snow." Reflecting on what "round snow" might be, the reader would understand that "hail" was intended. In another instance, the word for beast is expressed through the use of two characters read "shih-liu" in Chinese, which signify "sixteen." The Yamato word for beast is "shishi"; and since "shi" signifies "four" in the Yamato language, "shishi" (four fours) would equal "sixteen." Thus the reader would understand that the character compound for "sixteen" signified "beast." This system—which has the intellectual appeal of wordplay and rebus puzzles—is certainly an example of written composition anticipating or requiring visual reception.

Uta possessing a literary quality commensurate with Chinese poetry were not meant to be appreciated only as individual works. It was also considered proper that they be collected and appreciated as groups. The presence of poetry collections in China may well be deemed the rational prerequisite for the evolution of the idea, in Yamato, that uta collections were indispensable. Yet the choice of a form like the uta collection can only indicate an assumption that the work would be visually received, read. It is most unlikely that all 234 poems included in Books 1 and 2 of the extant *Man'yōshū* were ever recited and aurally received as a single corpus. This would apply to later books as well. Moreover, the nonextant poetry collections dating from this time—the *Collected Poems of Kakinomoto Hitomaro, The Grove of Poetry, Arranged by Topic (Ruiju Karin), The Anthology of Ancient Uta (Kokashū), The Anthology of Kasa no Kanamura, The Anthology of Takahashi Mushimaro, The Anthology of Tanabe Sakimaro*—could only have been appreciated in their entirety by reading, at least if we assume that they contained a considerable number of uta.

In other words, uta possessing literary worth comparable to that of Chinese poetry were presented in groups so that they could be visually received as a corpus. Despite the fact that the predominant reception was aural, poetic awareness at the time somehow linked the concept of the uta as a worthy expression to the act of visual reception. Many uta collections, moreover, were arranged by categories according to a certain plan. The group of uta making up Books 1 and 2 of the *Man'yōshū*, for instance, is divided into miscellaneous poems, love poems, and elegies, and follows a chronological order within each category.[19] Oral delivery

---

[19] One view has it that within Book 2 certain poems are organized in groups and were intended to be so read, with the group connected with Prince Ōtsu given as an example (Itō Haku, 1975c, 438-48). This theory holds that six poems (2:105-10) were ordered into a monogatari-like sequence. The editor of this section may have had simple chronology in mind but may also have anticipated the pleasure that readers would have in following the

would have been wholly inappropriate for anyone conscious of such a structure. In short, elements of visual reception had to be added to the text so that the Yamato uta might be appreciated in a manner commensurate with "worthy expression."

If we agree that those Yamato uta which were the literary equivalents of Chinese poetry, namely waka, possess the characteristics just described above, then the next question is, when did such waka come into being? This ultimately becomes a question of Yamato uta as a conceptual object, and ignores such factual questions as whether the waka was recited to listeners.

VERSE-PROSE AND PROSE IN NARRATIVE MODE

As this question shows, lyrics involved two separate forms, song and waka. With the narrative genre, by contrast, the eventual differentiation was between verse-prose and prose. The former seems to have evolved from some kind of "recited text," the contents of which were neither song nor setsuwa. Its course of development differed from that followed by the latter form, prose.

The progress of verse-prose can be deduced from an extremely useful source: the text of the congratulatory speech (murohoki) offered by Prince Woke—who will subsequently use this opportunity to reveal his true identity—on the occasion of his master Shijimu's housewarming.[20] Earlier in the narrative, it will be remembered, the prince wanders with his elder brother Prince Oke to the province of Harima, where they are reduced to serving as stableboys for Shijimu's cattle and horses. Prince Oke dances at the housewarming; then Prince Woke "straightened his robe and sash and pronounced a murohoki." His recitation (*NSK*, 1:402-403) follows. [Here nonmetrical lines are italicized—although some hypometric lines may have been thought regular—and in the rest of this chapter any guide phrases will not be so designated.][21]

Tsukitatsuru	This new house is built
Wakamuro kazune	With beam vines
Tsukitatsuru	And built
Hashira wa	*With pillars that*
Kono iegimi no	*Bespeak the steady nature of*

---

unfolding of a story. This interpretation covers all of Book 2. If true, we must allow yet greater importance to visual, reading reception of poetry in this period.

[20] A summary of this story has been given toward the end of Chapter 4. This murohoki appears in the *Nihon Shoki*; it was clearly not regarded as a song, because the syllabic method of representation was not used to record it.

[21] [The "metric lines" of the transliteration are put in roman and "prose lines" in italics, both here and in the next example.—Ed.]

Mikokoro no shizumari nari	The master of this house.
Toriaguru	The roof beams,
Muneutsuwari wa	Rising high,
Kono iegimi no	*Bespeak the generous nature of*
Mikokoro no hayashi nari	The master of this house.
Toriokeru	*The rafters*
Haeki wa	Aligned in rows
Kono iegimi no	*Bespeak the orderly nature of*
Mikokoro no totonōri nari	The master of this house.
Toriokeru	*The under-thatch*
Etsuri wa	Covering the rafters
Kono iegimi no	*Bespeaks the tranquil nature of*
Mikokoro no tairagi nari	The master of this house.
Toriyueru	*The stout vine ropes*
Tsunakazura wa	Binding the roof joints
Kono iegimi no	*Strengthen the life of*
Miinochi no kataki nari	The master of this house.
Torifukeru	Thick-bunched grasses
Kaya wa	*For the roof thatch*
Kono iegimi no	*Bespeak the ample fortune of*
Mitomi no amari nari	The master of this house.
Izumo wa	*Izumo, famed for*
Niibari	*Reclaimed fields—*
Niibari no	Newly reclaimed fields produce
Totsukashine no ho o	*A plentiful rice harvest,*
Asarake ni	Rice placed in a shallow vat
Kameru ōmiki	And brewed to make fine sake.
Umara ni o	What a joy it is,
Yarafuru ka wa	My lads,
Aga kodomo	*To drink it down!*
Ashihiki no	And when I dance,
Kono katayama no	My mask adorned with
Saoshika no	*The antlers of a stag*
Tsuno sasagete	From this secluded mountain
Aga maisureba	With its sprawling foothills,
Umasake	*Then you who drink here sake*
Eka no ichi ni	*Finer by far than what they sell*
Atai mochite kawanu	*In the Eka markets,*
Tanasoko mo yarara ni	*You must clap your hands*

| *Uchiagetamawane* | Merrily in time, |
| *Aga tokoyotachi.* | My long-lived gentlemen![22] |

Since the text is not set down according to the syllabic system, we cannot be sure that it was recited exactly as it appears in this romanizing. But the original would not have differed greatly. As is no doubt apparent, the text is a mélange of five- and seven-syllable lines on the one hand and, on the other, lines with syllable counts other than five and seven. Now, if we agree to call the former group "metric lines" and the latter "prose lines," we find that the ratio of metric lines to prose lines in the text of this murohoki is roughly 6:5.

Having finished his murohoki, Prince Woke finally reveals his true identity, again in verse-prose. Here the ratio of metric lines to prose lines is roughly 5:7, and the announcement reads like this:

Isonokami	Sacred cryptomeria of Furu
Furu no kamisugi	In Isonokami:
Moto kiri	*Their trunks were cut down,*
Sue oshiharai	Their limbs sawed off,
Ichinobe no miya ni	*To build the Ichinobe Palace*
Ame no shita shirashishi	*Whence all the world was governed—*
Ame yorozu	Throughout the heavens,
Kuni yorozu	Throughout the earth—
Oshiwa no mikoto no	*By the royal Oshiwa.*
Mianasue	His son and heir
Yatsukorama kore nari.	*Stands before you: it is I![23]*

(NSK, 1:403-404)

A longer declaration (given above) by the prince appears in the *Kojiki*, and its ratio of metric lines to prose lines is about 5:4. The ratios calculated above are, in effect, only tentative calculations, since the readings of the lines themselves are not definite. Nevertheless, the standard ratio is seen to be about 5:5, with higher or lower values indicating some degree of oscillation. I would like to assign the term "verse-prose" to texts like these in which metric lines, in an amount sufficient to be deemed a prominent characteristic, constitute an essential structural element.

The verse-prose we have just examined, however, displays another characteristic in addition to that of metric lines: frequent use of repetition.

[22] Tsuchihashi Yutaka considers "umasake" (sixth line from the end) to be a pillow-word (*NSK, Song*, 180, headnote), but it is better viewed as a substantive. [The "beam vines" (second line) were vines used to lash house beams in the Archaic Age.—Trans.]

[23] ["Royal Oshiwa": he is not recorded as a tennō and must have been a local king.—Trans.]

In the first example, the most frequently repeated line, "Kono iegimi no" (The master of this house), occurs six times, and "Tsukitatsuru" (Built) twice. The line "Mikokoro . . . nari" (Bespeaks the . . . nature of) may also be counted as a repetition, because it contains only one place where a word is substituted into a pattern: "shizumari" (steady), or "hayashi" (generous), for example. If we add to this the lines "Miinochi no kataki nari" (Strengthen the life of) and "Mitomi no amari nari" (Bespeak the ample fortune of), which correspond to repetitions, the repeated line occurs a total of six times. If we admit as well the form "Tori- . . . -ru," there are another five occurrences. One such semirepetition involves the words "Moto kiri" (Their trunks were cut down) and "Sue oshiharai" (Their limbs sawed off). But these lines smack more of parallelism in that they differ within common syntax and sense. The disparity, however, is so small that examination of primitive song would reveal parallelism of equivalent simplicity.[24] The subsequent lines "Ame yorozu" (Throughout the heavens) and "Kuni yorozu" (Throughout the earth) should, on the other hand, be called a semiparallel repetition. The verse-prose with which the prince, in the *Kojiki* version of the narrative, reveals his identity, has indeed been regarded as tending toward parallelism, although its style is not sufficiently evolved to possess orderly parallel antithesis.

We may conclude that, in essence, the two chief characteristics of verse-prose are a mixture of metric and prose lines, and the use of repetition or of a parallelism that verges on repetition. The appearance of the guide phrases "Ashihiki no" and "Isonokami" also attract our notice. The guide phrases cannot be claimed as a characteristic peculiar to verse-prose, however, since they also occur frequently within prose of the Ancient Age.

Verse-prose is, therefore, of an entirely different character from prose narrative (setsuwa). If we take narrative to be the temporal relation of phenomena and events, or their successive states, we shall discover no

---

[24] For example, the lines below occur in a song recited by an Andaman Islands aborigine who went on a pig hunt and caught no game (Kurtz, 1922, 100-102). Italics indicate choral repetition.

> Lelmo beetles my-much-rough,
> Cicadas my-much-rough-O,
> My-much-rough-O, buzzing-O.
> *My-much-rough-O, buzzing-O.*

The first and second lines exhibit small disparities but not sufficient ones to be termed parallel. "Lelmo beetles" and "cicadas" are approximate translations for "lelmo-le" and "jiramāū-le": their precise meanings are unknown. "My-much-rough" is a literal translation making no sense. Kurtz states that it means "My ears are rasped." He explains that the man had let the pig escape because he was distracted by noises which made him unable to follow his quarry's movements.

such narrative in the verse-prose works just considered. The elimination of five- and seven-syllable metric lines, of repetition, or of parallelism from verse-prose would therefore not yield prose narrative. Verse-prose belongs to the declarative mode, in which circumstances or thoughts are directly expressed without regard for chronological order. This mode probably followed a different formative process from that of narrative. From their very origins, then, verse-prose and prose were functionally dissimilar. Verse-prose is used when the speaker needs to express an unusual or special attitude. For example, when God creates a woman out of the rib taken from Adam's side, and brings her to Adam, the man cries,

> Now this, at last—
> bone from my bones,
> flesh from my flesh!—
> this shall be called Woman,
> for from man was this taken.
> (Genesis 2:23; New English Bible)

Or again, when King Croesus asks the oracle of Delphi how long his reign will last, the priestess gives Apollo's answer (*Historia* 1:55):

> When comes the day that a mule shall sit on the Median throne,
> Then, tender-footed Lydian, by pebbly Hermus
> Run and abide not, nor think it shame to be a coward.[25]

In other words, verse-prose is a formal style. A given work might be generally informal, but only when formal expression is required within some part of it will verse-prose be utilized. The *Historia* of Herodotus contains a large number of divinely inspired dream oracles expressed in verse-prose, together with oracles and prophecies given by priestesses and soothsayers. Inscriptions on Greek temple offerings—tripods, paintings, chariots—and tombs were also written in verse-prose, usually in hexameter but occasionally in trimeter. Verse-prose was used in Yamato under similar circumstances. The difference between Greek and Yamato verse-prose lay, first, in the rather strict observance of the foot in the Grecian variety, in contrast to Yamato verse-prose, which contains a considerable proportion of prose lines; and second, in the fact that the Greek variety has fewer repeated lines and less parallelism than does that of Yamato.

The use of a special style for circumstances perceived as sacred is a

---

[25] [Aubrey de Selincourt, trans., *Herodotus: The Histories* (Penguin, 1954; rpt. 1955), p. 33.—Trans.]

practice found among many peoples. Ancient Egypt apparently distinguished between the sacred and the profane to the point of having separate writing systems for each (Matsudaira, 1967, 2-36). Similarly, the Yamato people used special forms of speech in sacred circumstances, though the question of special forms of writing does not apply. The special style of speech did not become a fixed, chiefly metric form in the Archaic Age but probably in the early Ancient Age. It has been noted above that nonmetric lines appear in such archaic works as the verse dialogue of the gods Izanagi and Izanami:

IZANAMI:	Ana niyashi	My, oh lovely,
	E otoko o	What a fine man!
IZANAGI:	Ana niyashi	My, oh lovely,
	E otome o.	What a fair maid!
		(*JDK*, 178)

When a yet more formal statement was necessary, song was generally employed. The *Harima no Kuni Fudoki* (*Harima Topography*) also transmits the story of Prince Oke's and Prince Woke's wanderings, although Prince Woke's declaration of his true rank takes this form (*Harima no Kuni Fudoki*, 351):

Ōmi wa	Ōmi is
Mizu tamaru kuni	A land rich in waters;
Yamato wa	Yamato is
Aogaki	Green-hedged,
Aogaki no	Green-hedged with
Yamato ni mashishi	Mountains, Yamato where dwelt
Ichinobe no	Our sovereign Ichinobe,
sumeramikoto ga	
Mianasue	Whose son and heir
Yatsuko rama.	I am!

This work is simpler than the *Nihon Shoki* version. Yet the language of the first half might well make a fitting song, and we probably have here the most ancient form of Prince Woke's declaration.[26] The expression of the *Kojiki* version is of far later date. Because provincial transmissions are more likely to retain old forms than are those from culturally central

---

[26] That is to say that the characteristics are reminiscent of the old stratum. I do not suggest a time of composition. The *Harima no Kuni Fudoki* was compiled about 713 and so is a year or so later than the *Kojiki*, compiled in 712. The *Kojiki* version of the princes' wanderings is better ordered, however, and so more characteristic of the new stratum.

areas, we may conclude that the version in the *Harima Topography* displays the earliest form.

Now, Kenzō Tennō, the subject of this setsuwa, is believed to have acceded to the throne in the early sixth century, or about fifteen years later than the year of accession mentioned in the *Nihon Shoki*. This suggests that the *Harima* revision must have evolved at some time after the mid-sixth century. If we tentatively take the late sixth century as the formative period for this text, then the verse-prose-like declaration of the prince in the *Kojiki*, which exhibits a later style, cannot easily be dated earlier than the seventh century. In other words, although a definite conclusion is beyond our reach, we can estimate that the formation of verse-prose may have occurred at some point in the early seventh century. The text of the murohoki does contain rather polished expression for verse-prose. Notwithstanding our estimate of date for Prince Woke's declaration of identity—which exhibits a somewhat older style in the *Nihon Shoki* than in the *Kojiki*—the murohoki, and it alone, is probably a product of a slightly later stage, the terminus a quo of which is perhaps the mid-seventh century.

Our inquiry has shown that verse-prose was undoubtedly used in formal situations, and especially in those perceived as sacred. Norito, a conspicuous form of verse-prose, also developed under such circumstances. The great majority of norito appears in the *Engi Shiki*, although several, including the norito "Toshigoi no Matsuri" (Celebration of Prayers for the Coming Year), "Ōharae" (The Great Purification), and "Ōtonohokai" (Celebration for the Palace) have been called works of the late seventh century.[27] Norito expression can be divided, for purposes of consideration, into a prologue, which states the object of the prayer, and the main text, consisting of a statement to the divinity. When a norito is so divided, the incidence of metric lines is found to be higher in the main text. The main text of "Celebration for the Palace," for example, is as follows:

Kore no shikimasu	*The great palace*
Ōmiyadokoro no	That stands here
Sokotsuiwane no	*Has foundation cables*
kiwami	
Shimotsutsuna ne	*Plunging down to bedrock:*

[27] Takeda Yūkichi has deduced, from examining inception years for Yamato place names, that the norito "Toshigoi no Matsuri" dates from between 672 and 710. He also states that the norito "Ōharae" and "Ōtonohokai" are "regarded as possibly ancient" (*Norito*, "Kaisetsu," 373-74). It is not clear what period is meant by "ancient"; if "regarded as" refers to Shiraishi Mitsukuni's theory (Shiraishi, 1941, 432-34), then "Ōharae" is taken to antedate 701, and "Ōtonohokai" to be a work of "an extremely ancient period."

Hau mushi no wazawai naku	May they suffer no harm from creeping serpents;
Takama no hara wa	May the abundant sky
Aokumo no	That reaches into
Tanabiku kiwami	The clouds and blue
Ame no chidari	Of the Plain of Heaven
Tobu tori no wazawai naku	Suffer no harm from flying birds;
Horikatametaru	May the placement of the firmly fixed
Hashira keta utsubari to mado no kikai	Pillars, girders, beams, doors, and windows
Ugokinaru koto naku Hikiyueru	Suffer no shifting or rattling; May the knots of
Tsuname no yurubi Torifukeru	The thatch ropes not slacken, And the roof thatch
Kaya no sosoki naku	Suffer no loss of grasses;
Miyukatsuhi no sayaki	May there be no clamor of floor-ghosts,
Yome no isusuki	And may we suffer no fright
Itsuzushiki koto naku Tairakeku Yasurakeku	From the errant Evil Eye; Keep us in peace And in tranquillity,
Mamorimatsuru kami no na wa	O guardian divinities
Yafune Kukuchi no mikoto	Whose names we invoke:
Yafune Toyouke hime no mikoto to	The male Housetimber,
Mina o ba tataematsurite	The female Housethatch.
Sumemima no mikoto no miyo o Kakiwa ni Tokiwa ni	May the reigns of our Sovereigns, the Scions of Heaven, Be always secure, A solid rock,
Mamorimatsuri	An everlasting rock;
Ikashi miyo no	Through our prayers for good fortune—
Tarashi miyo ni	That they be glorious reigns
Tanaga no miyo to	And satisfactory reigns,
Sakiwaematsuru ni yorite	Reigns that endure forever—
Imitama tsukurira ga	The fashioners of sacred jewels
Mochiyumawari	Perform fasts and
Mochikiyomawari	Purify themselves
Tsukuritsukaematsureru	So that they may create

Mizu no yasakani no	A necklace eight feet long, with five
mifuku no	hundred jewels of blown glass,
ihotsumisumaru	filled with life,
no tama ni	
Akaru nigite	Hung with lustrous cloth
Teru nigite o tsukete	And with glossy cloth.
Imibe no Sukune	Lord [name insertable] of the Imibe
nanigashi ga	
Yowakata ni	Takes up and places
Futodasuki	The great sash
Torikakete	Over his feeble shoulders and
Kotohoki	Speaks the words to activate its
shizumematsuru	spiritual power;
koto no	
Moreochimu koto o ba	But if they fall short,
Kamunaobi no mikoto	I pray to the god Kamunaobi
Ōnaobi no mikoto	And to the god Ōnaobi
Kikinaoshi	To hear my words and correct them,
Minaoshite	To see my actions and correct them,
Tairakeku	And to govern our world
Yasurakeku	So as to bring it peace
Shiroshimese.	And tranquillity.[28]

(*Norito*, 419)

If we exclude lines with proper nouns or nouns treated as such, the ratio of metric lines, five or seven syllables long, to prose lines is roughly 10:14. Metric lines appear at a lower rate of incidence than in Prince Woke's murohoki. Within the norito itself, however, metric lines appear at a higher rate of incidence in the main text than in the prologue. We can interpret this as the result of extant norito having frequently been performed in situations where their presence required one or another explanation: the prologues, with their high incidence of prose lines, were developed so as to explain the main text. The main text, on the other hand, served to activate the kotodama, and so had to maintain a high incidence of metric lines. The main text of "Celebration for the Palace" nevertheless contains a lower incidence of metric lines than does Prince Woke's murohoki, a fact which indicates that even the "Celebration," which is held to belong to an "extremely ancient period" within the norito corpus, can hardly predate the mid-seventh century.

A further criterion for measuring the properties of verse-prose, in ad-

---

[28] [Once again, in the transliteration italics represent "prose lines" and roman "metric lines."—Ed.]

dition to the incidence of metric lines, is the incidence of repeated lines and parallelism in a work. In this respect too, norito can be said to represent expression on a rather advanced level; parallelism predominates over repetition in the norito. Moreover, norito parallelism consists not only of likeness verging on repetition, as in the couplets "Tairakeku / Yasurakeku" or "Kakiwa ni / Tokiwa ni," but also in the more complex constructions:

(1) Ōmiyadokoro no	(1) Takama no hara wa
(2) Sokotsuiwane no kiwami	(2) Aokumo no tanabiku kiwami
(3) Shimotsutsuna ne	(3) Ame no chidari
(4) Hau mushi no	(4) Tobu tori no
(Wazawai naku)	(Wazawai naku)

These instances of antithetical parallelism, although differing considerably in meaning, share a great many characteristics. Antithetical parallelism has, as its two poles, direct opposition—in which words display a clear contrast, such as "heaven" and "earth" or "eastern fields" and "western gardens"—and significant opposition, in which the significance expressed by each word provides a contrast: "refreshing breeze" and "year's end," for example, or "flying birds" and "falling blossoms."[29] In our example, the only direct opposition is provided by "Hau mushi no" and "Tobu tori no" (From creeping insects, From flying birds); all the other couplets represent significant opposition. Because significant opposition is a more advanced technique than direct opposition, its appearance in norito demands notice.

Yet an even more noteworthy characteristic of norito is alternating parallelism (kakku tsui).[30] The numbers that precede the lines in the example just given indicate corresponding lines: thus line 1 in the left column does not correspond to the line which immediately follows it (line 2 in the left column), but rather to line 1 in the right column. This is alternating parallelism, although the example given does not necessarily provide a typical instance. We can observe, as a more representative example of alternating parallelism, a passage from another norito held to be ancient, "Celebration of Prayers for the Coming Year":

Kushi Iwamato no mikoto	When we invoke the august names of
Toyo Iwamato no mikoto to	*The god Kushi Iwamato and*

[29] According to the *Wen-pi Shih*, written in the early T'ang Dynasty (Konishi, 1953, 91, 102).
[30] This term is also found in the *Wen-pi Shih* (ibid., 93). The technique of alternating parallelism was widely known in medieval Japan, however, and is discussed in several works on poetics.

Mina wa mōshite	*The god Toyo Iwamato, and*
Kotooematsuraba	When we worship them,
Yomo no mikado ni	They block the way,
Yutsu iwamura no gotoku	*Like groups of sacred boulders,*
Sayarimashite	*To every palace gate.*
Ashita ni wa mikado o kikimatsuri	They open the gates in the morning,
Yūbe ni wa mikado o tatematsurite	They close the gates in the evening;
Utoburu mono no	And if loathsome demons
Shimo yori yukaba	Try to slip beneath the gates,
Shimo o mamori	*Our gods will guard below the gate;*
Ue yori yukaba	If demons try to mount the gate,
Ue o mamori	*Our gods will guard above the gate.*
Yo no mamori	They protect us by night,
Hi no mamori ni	*They protect us by day:*
Mamorimatsuru ga yue ni	*Because they guard so constantly,*
Sumemima no mikoto no	*The Sovereign, Scion of Heaven,*
Uzu no mitegura o	*Praises them, presenting*
Tataegoto oematsuraku.	*Wondrous offerings.*[31]

(*Norito*, 389)

If a portion of this, from "Ashita ni wa" through "Mamorimatsuru ga yue ni," is arranged so that its parallel configuration can be easily perceived, it will look like this (italicized lines represent the alternating parallelism):

Ashita ni wa mikado o kikimatsuri ⎫
Yūbe ni wa mikado o tatematsuri   ⎬ -te / Utoburu mono o

(1) *Shimo yori yukaba* / (2) *Shimo o mamori* ⎫ Yo no mamori ⎫ ni / Mamorimatsuru
(1) *Ue yori yukaba* /   (2) *Ue o mamori*   ⎬ Hi no mamori ⎬ ga yue ni

China developed parallelism early in its literary history. It was already being used in various works of the Chou period (Liu, 1936, 11-24). Alternating parallelism is first found, however, in the "Tzu-hsü Fu" of Ssu-ma Hsiang-ju and the "Tung-hsi Fu" of Wang Pao (died after 59 B.C.). These instances occur in poetic works, however. It was not until the Chin Dynasty and the compositions of Yang Hu (A.D. 220-78) and Lu Chi (261-303) that alternating parallelism first appeared in prose

---

[31] [The two gods invoked at the opening of the poem are guardian deities of the gates of the royal palace.—Trans.]

(Suzuki, 1936, 81 and 102). Alternating parallelism is found in Yamato song as far back as the Archaic Age. But the appearance of alternating couplets in norito, with their rather high incidence of prose lines, can hardly be said to have developed independently in so short a period of time. Especially when we consider how long it took for even the Chinese—a people seemingly endowed with an instinctive love of parallelism—to evolve the use of alternating parallelism in prose. Norito were evidently influenced by Chinese styles of composition. The Imbe and Nakatomi clans were the chief administrators of norito, although the Kuni no Miyatsuko, in their function as provincial officials, also seem to have participated. The Imbe and Nakatomi clansmen and the Kuni no Miyatsuko were all members of the contemporary intelligentsia who served as quasi-priests. Therefore it would not be unusual for such men to be proficient in Chinese composition. The quality of norito parallelism, as demonstrated by the manifestation of rather advanced instances of significant opposition, suggests that those who made or refashioned them were also masters of Chinese composition.

It would be no easy matter, however, to attain skill in foreign classics sufficient to incorporate their expressive techniques into one's own language and style. For this reason the late seventh century seems the most natural point at which Yamato intellectuals would have become capable of achieving wide-scale proficiency. The results of our inquiry into Prince Woke's murohoki and the several versions of his declaration of identity are also in general conformance with this conclusion. Takeda Yūkichi has deduced, from research into the years of inception of Yamato place names, that the norito "Celebration of Prayers for the Coming Year" evolved during the period when the capital was located at either Asuka or Fujiwara (672-710) (*Norito*, "Kaisetsu," 373), an estimation also in accord with my conclusion. Our recognition that the new strata of deity and royal-family folklore, as well as verse-prose and norito, share a common characteristic in their aim for more refined structural and expressive techniques will yield us further crucial information about the Ancient Age.

PART THREE

The Ancient Age: The First Stage

CHAPTER 6

The Study and Composition of Chinese

COMPOSITION ON THE CHINESE MODEL

The spread of Chinese, and especially Confucian, culture in Yamato society was probably the greatest factor in bringing about the enervation of an indigenous Yamato expression relying on the working of the kotodama. Confucianism is an intellectual and rational form of humanism. It places great importance on "li" (J. ri), "reason," "fundamental principles." Indeed, so closely are Confucian principles connected to a perception of reality that they transformed even the practice of augury, originally no more than a means of fortunetelling, into a systematic method and principle. The gradual infiltration of Confucianism into Yamato could only signal the unavoidable enervation of the kotodama, a rich repository of primitive elements. Although kotodama slowly began to yield its preeminent position to the new ga literature, the infiltration of Chinese culture was not an abrupt process.

The first official negotiations between Yamato and China occurred, according to Chinese records, in A.D. 57, at the time of the Later Han Dynasty (*Gokanjo Waden*, 84-85). A period of roughly four hundred and twenty years elapsed from the time of "Queen Himiko's" embassy to China until the normalization of diplomatic relations by the "Five Kings of Wa." Since the two countries would have entered into diplomatic correspondence during this period, the assistants of the Yamato rulers undoubtedly possessed a considerable knowledge of the Chinese language and its writing system. The *Sung Shu* records a memorial sent to the ruler of the Liu Sung Dynasty in 478 by "King Wu of Wa," Yūryaku Tennō (*Sōjo Wakokuden*, 86-87). The style gives the impression of being still too plain to qualify as proper p'ien-wen [parallel prose of the Six Dynasties], but the official Chinese in which the document is written employs correct diction and so is quite intelligible.[1] Fifth-century Yamato natives could hardly have been capable of writing Chinese on this level. The memorial was probably composed for Yūryaku by a Korean immigrant.

---

[1] [The parallel prose style, an ornate and highly formal Chinese variety, was popular during the Six Dynasties Period (ca. 222-589) in China and subsequently in Korea and Japan.—Trans.]

The Recorders' Corporation (fuhitobe) was established by Yūryaku in the second year of his reign (legendary 468); he apparently singled out two of its members, Suguri Ao of Musa and Tamitsukasa Hakatoko of Hinokuma, for special favor (*Yūryakuki*, 364). The names of these Recorders clearly suggest that they were immigrants from Korea.[2] The presence of such clerks must explain how the Yamato people were able to draft official documents addressed to the Sung court (Hayashiya, 1971, 196). Native Yamato citizens would have found the mastery of Chinese composition onerous, surely requiring another century or two before it was possible to absorb Chinese culture through the medium of Chinese letters.

Korea, by contrast, adopted Chinese culture much earlier than did Yamato. A national school was established in the second year of the reign of King Sosurim of Koguryŏ (372), and aristocratic youths were taught the Chinese classics there (Kim Sa-yŏp, 1973, 89). By the fifth century, therefore, the Koreans had become skilled in expressing themselves in Chinese. The Monument to King Hot'ae (Kwanggaet'o), erected in 414, bears an inscription with a total of 1,779 characters: 207 of these are damaged and thus illegible, but the surviving text, like King Wu's memorial, can be termed a correct and intelligible composition.[3] We cannot possibly evaluate the respective expertise demonstrated by Koguryŏ and Wa in Chinese composition by comparing the 1,779-character inscription to King Hot'ae with the 267-character text of King Wu of Wa's memorial. Very generally speaking, however, the Korean intellectuals who entered Yamato toward the end of the fifth century must have been capable of writing Chinese prose on a level little different from that found in Koguryŏ cities in the early fifth century. Yet this statement must apply to Korean immigrants alone: by no stretch of the imagination could any member of the Yamato nation have written Chinese with similar success.

By the sixth century, however, the Yamato people seem to have made relatively rapid progress in the art of Chinese literary expression. This belief is founded on the appearance, in 604, of Crown Prince Shōtoku's *Jūshichijō Kempō* (*Constitution in Seventeen Articles*), which is written in correct Chinese prose. Shōtoku cites the important Chinese classics, *The Book of Songs*, *The Book of Rites*, the *Tso Chuan* (*The Tso Commentary*), the *Hsiao Ching* (*The Classic of Filial Piety*), the *Lun Yü* (*The Analects*), *Records of the Historian*, and *Selections of Refined Literature*, as literary authorities (Okada, 1929a-b, 23). These references clearly indicate an awareness that beautiful expression consists of writing based on preexisting diction.

---

[2] See Okada, 1929a, 15-20.
[3] According to Mizutani Teijirō's interpretation (Mizutani, 1977, appendix).

Apart from the excerpts in the *Nihon Shoki*, no version of the *Constitution in Seventeen Articles* survives. This fact, together with the presence in the text of the *Constitution* of references to events that are believed to have occurred after Crown Prince Shōtoku's death, have long led to suspicions that the *Constitution* is not the work of Shōtoku or, if one assumes it is, that the text selected for inclusion in the *Nihon Shoki* was revised by a later hand.[4] The *Nihon Shoki* nevertheless clearly states that "the Crown Prince himself composed, for the first time, a *Constitution in Seventeen Articles*" (*Suikoki*, 142). We might do better, then, to conclude that this statement cannot be refuted by extant data. The *Constitution* may well be Shōtoku's work, but Korean immigrant intellectuals in his entourage must also have made major contributions. I would like to think that the solicitation of cooperation from these intellectuals and the consolidation of a composition of such speculative force could only have been effected if Prince Shōtoku himself was the author of the work. This is not to say that the extant text does not contain revisions by a later hand (e.g., an editor of the *Nihon Shoki*). But we may conclude that the extant *Constitution* remains essentially a work of Suiko Tennō's time.

Prince Shōtoku was undoubtedly proficient in Chinese literary expression, a fact borne out by his compilation of the *Hokke Gisho* (Figure 8), a commentary on the *Lotus Sūtra* (J. *Hokkekyō*). This has also been seen as the work of another writer (Tsuda, 1930, 129-38) for the following reason: "When we consider that such a work unexpectedly manifested itself very early in the history of Japanese Buddhism, and that works of a similar nature disappeared entirely after a period of some years, the reasons for the events must be fully explained" (ibid., 137). This, however, may be too negative a statement to serve as the basis for refuting authorship.[5] The main text of the *Hokke Gisho* (called pen-

---

[4] Kariya Mochiyuki (*Bunkyo Onko Hikō*, 124) was the first to question Prince Shōtoku's authorship; his theory was further developed by Sakakibara Yoshino in *Bungei Ruisan* (vol. 4, *Kokambun*, fol. 4r-v). A lucid refutation of Prince Shōtoku's authorship, based on principles of textual criticism, has been given by Tsuda Saukichi (1930, 1933). Kakimura Shigematsu wrote criticism of a similar nature prior to 1930, but his work was not published until sixteen years after his death (Kakimura, 1947).

[5] The external evidence in favor of Shōtoku's authorship includes the following: (1) he is said to have "lectured on the *Lotus Sūtra* at Okamoto Palace" (*Suikoki*, 148) in 606; (2) the *Hōryūji Engi Shizaichō*, compiled in 747, notes that three commentaries, including that on the *Lotus Sūtra*, "are the work of the Cloistered Prince Shōtoku" (*Dai Nihon Komonjo*, 4:511); and (3) the *Jōgū Shōtoku Hōō Teisetsu* records that the prince "composed a seven-volume commentary on the *Lotus Sūtra* and other subjects, known as the 'Commentary Written by the Crown Prince'" (*Hōō Teisetsu*, 44). There is internal evidence, moreover: (1) the style of writing and the paper used for the manuscript in the possession of the royal household seem to date from the seventh century; and (2) corrections and revisions are acknowledged to have been made by the prince. In the face of this evidence, Tsuda's theory is hardly persuasive.

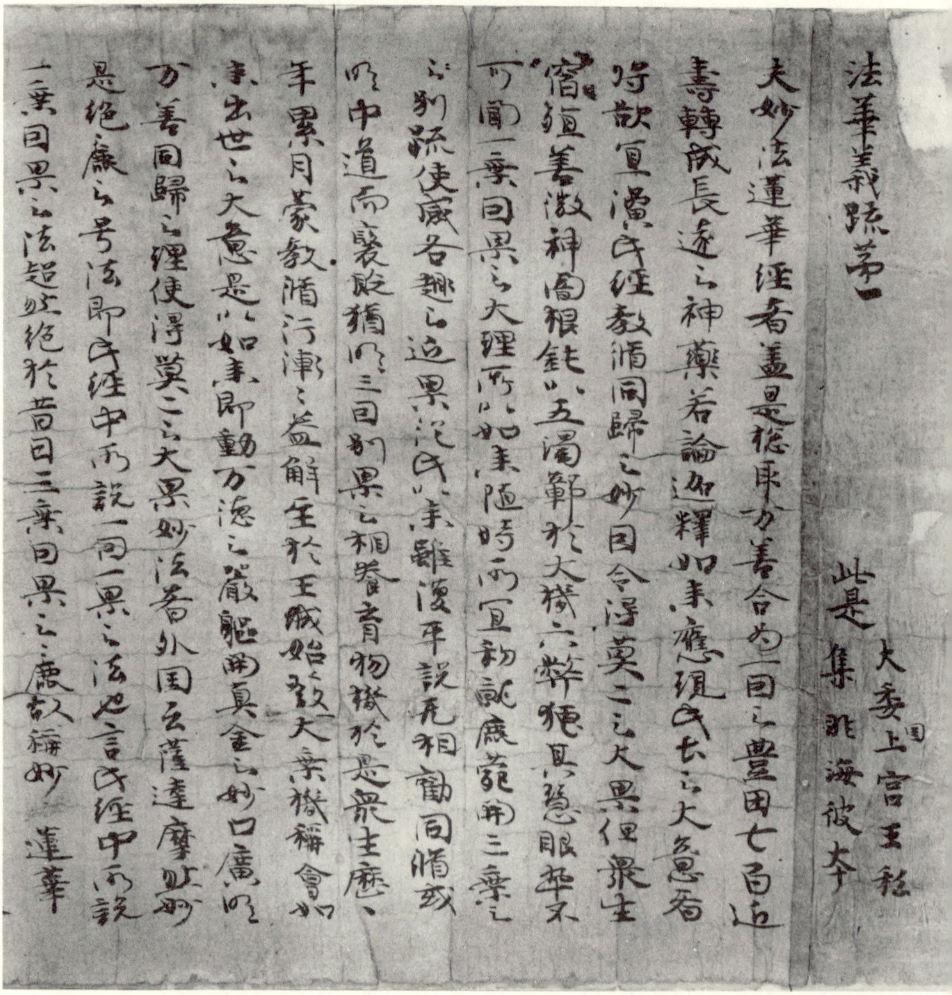

FIGURE 8. *Hokke Gisho* (*Commentary on the Lotus Sūtra*, 7th century). Autograph by Prince Shōtoku. Property of the Royal Household.

su, pen-i, etc.) is made up of Chinese commentaries on the *Lotus Sūtra*, among which the *Fa-hua I-chi*, written in the Liang Dynasty by Fa-yün (abbot of the Kuang-chai temple), figures largest.[6] Shōtoku's own presentation appears as an appendix that is shorter than the main text.[7] He

[6] [The Liang, 502-57, is one of the Six Dynasties.—Trans.]

[7] In the Hanayama Shinshō edition of the *Hokke Gisho*, the section that contains the prince's own thesis is clearly distinguished from the pen-su and pen-i of Fa-yün and his circle and is therefore convenient to use.

writes at some length, however, when he casts doubts on Fa-yün's theories with comments like, "But I do not understand this," or "I cannot assent to this, however," or when he states, "I do not agree, however," preparatory to advancing his own ideas. Here Shōtoku was required to draw on his own powers of composition so as to manage the relatively complex speculative argument. The target of his dispute was an advanced form of religious speculation based on the sutras; the fact that his rebuttal was written in Chinese can only be attributed to Shōtoku's high level of competence in Chinese composition.

Tsuda doubts that Shōtoku was the author of the *Hokke Gisho*: he suggests that the prince was assisted in his work by a Buddhist priest named Hyeja, an immigrant from Koguryŏ, and asks why the *Constitution* should then be regarded as the work of Shōtoku (ibid.). The *Constitution*, however, may be acknowledged as Shōtoku's own work, at least in its composition. Japanized syntax is frequently found in those sections where the prince states his own views, and such prose would not have been written by a learned priest like Hyeja.[8]

Prince Shōtoku's demonstrated ability in Chinese composition serves to indicate the considerable degree of skill with which Yamato intellectuals had come to express themselves in Chinese prose. Without such advances within his society, Shōtoku would not have been capable of discoursing upon ethics in Chinese, no matter how outstanding his individual talents might have been. A man may possess rare genius, but if he is born into a backward age, his achievements are not likely to soar far beyond the general level of culture. The *Hokke Gisho* certainly contains Japanese stylistic idiosyncrasies, yet these are not so pronounced that Shōtoku's exposition could not be understood in Korea and China. This is supported by evidence that, on returning to Koguryŏ in the Eleventh Month of 615, Hyeja took along the *Hokke Gisho* and circulated it in his native land.[9]

Of course, when one compares the somewhat Japanized Chinese of the *Hokke Gisho* with the correct prose style of the *Constitution in Seventeen Articles*, doubts about the authorship of the *Constitution* are inevitable. Apparently several Korean intellectuals residing in Yamato—men like Hyeja, Kakka, Hyech'ong, Kwallŭk, Sŭngyung, and Unch'ong—participated in revising the *Constitution*.[10] Without the linguistic powers

---

[8] Analysis of several passages has shown that word order does not always conform with Chinese grammar, and that auxiliary verbs and conjunctions are frequently used in nonstandard ways (Hanayama, 1933, 5, 46-47).

[9] "When the priest Hyeja returned to his native land, he took with him the prince's *Commentary* and circulated it there" (*Hōō Teisetsu*, 44).

[10] All are mentioned between 592 and 603 (the first twelve years of Suiko's reign: *Suikoki*, 136-42). Hyeja served as the prince's instructor in Buddhism, and Kakka filled a similar post in Confucianism. The others were emigrant Buddhist priests from Koguryŏ and Paekche;

commanded by the Korean intellectuals, Prince Shōtoku would have been utterly incapable of writing a work like the *Constitution*. His advisers must have found it necessary to correct, time and again, Shōtoku's Chinese expression, to the extent of choosing language in conformance with what he wished to say.

Shōtoku's writing may have begun with the composition of a rough draft, this being subsequently revised by the immigrant scholars and then subjected to further revision under Shōtoku's direction. Such a process could have been reasonably described as "The Crown Prince himself composed, for the first time, a *Constitution in Seventeen Articles*." The cultural level so attained by the people of Yamato enabled them to express themselves in a writing system—literary Chinese—shared by the Chinese and Koreans: this is the reason why I have chosen the twelfth year of Suiko's reign (604), the year the *Constitution in Seventeen Articles* was written, as the symbolic point of division between the Archaic and the Ancient Ages. (See Chronological Table at the end of this volume.)

Other extant compositions date from Suiko's reign. One of these is known as the Dōgo Hot Springs Monument inscription of Iyo province. An inscribed stone monument was erected in the fourth year of Suiko's reign (590) in commemoration of a visit made by Prince Shōtoku, the priest Hyeja, and one Lord Kazuraki to a palace located near the Dōgo hot springs in Iyo. The monument itself no longer exists, but the inscription is quoted in a fragment from the *Iyo no Kuni Fudoki* (*Iyo Topography*, 493-96). It begins with this passage: "Our Cloistered Prince visited Iyo with the priest Hyeja and Lord Kazuraki. . . ." The third-person usage suggests that the author of the inscription is someone other than the two people mentioned along with the prince on his progress to Iyo. The extant version contains numerous miscopyings and is not always easily interpreted. Nonetheless it is written in parallel prose, and the style, with its frequent allusions to historical precedent, may be regarded as deriving from works of the Ch'i and Liang Dynasties (Okada, 1929a, 31-32). This inscription indicates that an awareness present in late Six Dynasties China, that beautiful expression possessed a definite form and used diction with literary precedents, had also sprung forth in the writings of Prince Shōtoku and his circle of Yamato intellectuals. Despite the small number of works, and despite their not having been written in the Yamato language, their presence announced the birth of ga writing in Yamato.

This period may be taken, then, as the symbolic beginning of the Ancient Age in Japanese literary history. Still another inscription, the *Tenjukoku Mandara Shūchōmei*, records the provenance of an embroi-

---

one of these, Kwallŭk, was also a teacher of calendrical principles, astronomy, geography, and magic.

dered mandala depicting the Buddhist Paradise.[11] It was commissioned by Prince Shōtoku's consort, Princess Tachibana, after the death of her husband, as a representation of his rebirth in paradise. The inscription consists of approximately four hundred characters. Had it been taken to China, its lack of conformance to the parallel prose standard and its phonetic transcription of Yamato proper nouns might have rendered it unintelligible. The author of the inscription nevertheless clearly attempted to use established diction in the composition.

AN APPROXIMATION OF A POETIC CIRCLE

During Suiko's reign, Chinese prose was composed in the fashion described. From that we might presume that considerable advances were also made in the composition of Chinese poetry (shih) in the early seventh century. The earliest extant shih composed by Japanese, however, date from the reign of Tenji (668-671). The preface to the *Kaifūsō* contains the following passage dealing with Tenji's efforts.

> The peerage was established and official ranks were set up in Crown Prince Shōtoku's time; it was then that court etiquette was first instituted. People devoted themselves solely to Buddhism, however. They had not time as yet for the composition of literature. When the Ōmi Sovereign [Tenji] ascended the throne, he broadened the scope of the royal functions and laid far-reaching plans. His ideals of government embraced both heaven and earth, and his results shone throughout the universe. Some time thereafter, he concluded that nothing surpassed literature in giving order to the behavior of the people and improving its ways, and that scholarship was preeminent in terms of moral enrichment and personal enlightenment. Then he established a court school [daigaku] and summoned the best young men to study there (*Kaifū*, 59-60).

This may well be an accurate report. In Prince Shōtoku's day—that is, in the early seventh century—intellectual interest was still focused on writing devoted to practical learning. Attention had not yet turned to the composition of belletristic p'ien-chang (literary works). If, however, Tenji did indeed establish a school for talented youths so as to further the literary arts, then the art of shih composition was given an opportunity to flourish in Yamato after the mid-seventh century.[12]

The *Kaifūsō* passage continues describing Tenji's actions:

---

[11] The embroidery survives only in fragments, but the inscription is quoted in *Jōgū Shōtoku Hōō Teisetsu*.

[12] No pertinent entry appears in the *Nihon Shoki*. Perhaps Tenji established a court school on an experimental basis, without systematizing it.

He often invited men of letters to attend his frequent formal gatherings. On such occasions he personally wrote down his compositions, and his wise nobles presented panegyrics. More than one hundred works of fine craftsmanship and splendid writing were composed, but all were reduced to ashes at the time of the Civil War (*Kaifū*, 60).

Three important points are made here. The first is the acknowledgment by aristocratic society that the presentation of shih at a "formal gathering"—an official banquet—was a worthy act. This was apparently no more than an imitation by the Yamato court of a long-established Chinese tradition. Momentous changes in Yamato writing circles were nonetheless engendered by a fundamental, growing consciousness that the shih represented worthy linguistic expression. It was common practice in Yamato from the Archaic Age to present uta on public occasions, but the contents of such uta were not perceived as having an intrinsic worth. Rather, they played a partial role, in making a banquet interesting. What was perceived as worthy was the anticipation of an auspicious effect from the kotodama lodging within an uta recited to express an intention or desire. In such cases, worth *was* attached to the actions of the kotodama, whereas the language of the uta was probably not perceived to possess a worthy existence of its own. The formation of a new awareness, that poems were to be presented before the tennō because they represented worthy language, may be seen as the first step toward a literature different from that found earlier in Yamato.

The second point is that cognizance was taken of expressive techniques. Literary language was intrinsically worthy because it possessed refined techniques, and because people were moved by the beauty of its expression. Such language created "works of fine craftsmanship and splendid writing," and was therefore the object of appreciation at official banquets, whereas careless or crude compositions were ignored. Incidentally, the very fact that a composition was regarded as finely crafted and splendid, or careless and crude, indicates the emergence of a critical consciousness. For the first time, excellent or poor compositions were distinguished by judgments based on some criteria. The criteria did not preexist in Yamato and could only be adduced from study of Chinese criticism.

In other words, the consciousness of belles-lettres was imported from China. And let me make clear that by "China" I particularly mean the expressive ideals of the literature of the Six Dynasties period. If the concept of "beautiful expression" dominates the whole of Chinese literature, it is particularly marked in the Six Dynasties. Literary trends during that period are represented by the contributions of two men, Hsiao T'ung (501-31), an editor of the *Selections of Refined Literature*, and his younger brother Hsiao Kang (503-51), an important contributor to another collection, *New Songs from the Jade Terrace*. The former man held that the best works combine ornate beauty, ch'i-li (J. kirei) with substance, chih-shih (J. shitsujitsu), whereas the latter contended that a work need only have beauty to be superlative literature (Suzuki, 1927, 76-77). In either case ornate beauty was taken as a positive criterion, because of the central position occupied by the concept of "beautiful expression" in Six Dynasties literature. Yamato intellectuals, of course, would have absorbed such critical attitudes directly from works like the *Selections*, but we cannot overlook a further factor, the active role played by Korean newcomers as influential consultants in literary matters.

The third point is that literary works were written down. We do not know the actual number of compositions indicated by the words "more than one hundred works." It is nonetheless worth noting that they were written down. The "Civil War" referred to in the *Kaifūsō* passage is the Jinshin War (672), during which the seat of the court at Ōmi was razed by dynastic rivals. Because these compositions were destroyed by fire, they were obviously written works. Paper was already in use at that time, although it remained an extremely precious commodity, reserved for the reproduction of such vital works as important national documents or Confucian and Buddhist scriptures. It is an indication of the high value accorded to Chinese poetry and prose that they too were written down. To put it another way, a work came to be acknowledged before the world as worthy expression by one important method: the act of recording it in writing.

Whether such a work was visually received or not is another question. The method of reception for compositions in Chinese was probably aural at this time. But with the inception of writing as a means of transmission, at least in the case of the most highly valued works, the Yamato people undoubtedly altered somewhat their awareness of literature. What is more, oral composition in Chinese was clearly far more difficult for a Yamato nobleman than the recitation of an uta in his own tongue, because then he composed in a foreign language requiring a complex writing system. It is not known what materials were used to record the works, but we may infer that written composition was the rule. This must have exerted a great, albeit indirect, influence on the writing and reading of waka in later centuries.

The extant preface to the *Kaifūsō* was written in 751, so its reliability as a transmission of mid-seventh century events cannot be guaranteed. On the other hand, it is no easy matter to fabricate such items as its description of the Ōmi court's admiration for shih. Ki no Tsurayuki and his associates later wrote of waka composition in the preface to the *Kokinshū*: "Some poets set off for lonely spots to compose waka on the blossoms there, and others wandered alone in the dark of night, seeking to improve on their poems about the moon. Our sovereigns observed the various aims of the waka produced, and they passed judgment on their superior or inferior quality." If shih in the reign of Tenji were appreciated in a fashion similar to that described by Tsurayuki for waka, this would mean that reception was accompanied by criticism in the mid-seventh century, and that something like a poetic circle had been formed.[13] This was only an approximation of a poetic circle, however. Although we do not know whether it performed all the functions of that kind of group proper, surely its members would have been aware of the difference between a good work and a poor one. When a poet presented a composition to this circle, he probably anticipated, inwardly at least, that his work would be praised as fine composition.

Let us examine, for example, a shih entitled "Quatrain in Five-Character Lines, Composed on Attending a Royal Banquet," by Crown Prince Ōtomo (648-72), who later reigned as Kōbun (*Kaifū*, 1):

> The Sovereign's wisdom shines bright as the sun and moon;
> The royal virtues spread far as heaven and earth.
> All Three Sources are at peace;
> Ten thousand lands express their fealty.[14]

Okada Masayuki's glowing appraisal of this poem has given it a seemingly unshakable standing as a masterpiece.[15] Yet no one has indicated what critical standards have enabled these scholars to acknowledge Prince Ōtomo's poem to be so superlative.

Okada has asserted that it surpasses the work of Sui and T'ang poets. If so we can compare the poem with similar compositions of the Sui and T'ang periods to show how and where it excels. The following shih will serve as an object of comparison (*Shōseki*, 385):

> The sun and moon shine bright as the imperial virtues;
> Mountains and rivers are rivaled in splendor by the Emperor's palace.
> Peace reigns, no business comes before the Throne:
> We offer instead books that teach eternal life.

---

[13] "Poetic circle" is taken to mean a social situation in which poems are composed and presented to people who criticize as well as hear or read them.

[14] [The "Three Sources" are heaven, earth, and the human race.—Trans.]

[15] "The diction is graceful, the concept grand; the poem seems to absorb the world and encompass the globe. No manner of expression but this would have sufficed to praise the renowned virtues and high deeds of Tenji Tennō" (Okada, 1929a, 181; see also Sugimoto, 1943, 8-9, and Hayashi, 1944, 23, among others).

I would like to pass over, for the moment, the question of the poet's identity and the circumstances under which this poem was composed, and begin solely with an examination of the writing.

The first two lines are very clear indeed; they are cited in the *Shih I* of Chiao-jan (Konishi, 1953e, 92). Although the imagery resembles that in Prince Ōtomo's poem, the technique of antithesis is employed so systematically in these two lines that they become a model of direct opposition; this harmonizes well with the tone of a stately paean to the royal virtues, and is irreproachable.

In Prince Ōtomo's poem, by contrast, the character for "bright" (ming) in "The Sovereign's wisdom . . . bright" is placed too close to "sun and moon" (jih yüeh) [which together constitute "ming"]. Furthermore, Prince Ōtomo establishes a connection between "royal virtues" and "heaven and earth" by regarding both as the foundation of all existence, but the characteristics held in common by these two word-groups cannot be grasped unless one takes the time to compare them in one's head. The image of the "sun and moon" in the second poem serves as a metaphor for the abstract concept of "imperial virtues" while still maintaining a proper distance. An easy correspondence is also formed there between earthly phenomena—"mountains and rivers"—and a dwelling place—"the Emperor's palace"—while their common characteristic, "splendor," is immediately apparent. When Prince Ōtomo's composition is considered in connection with such finely wrought work, it obviously lacks polish in important respects.

The meaning of the third and fourth lines of the Chinese poem is truly witty, displaying the kind of originality only this composer can command: it is so peaceful these days, writes the poet, that we have no business to present to Your Majesty, so we shall report instead of books, which, we hope, will enable you to sustain this country forever. The third and fourth lines of Prince Ōtomo's poem, by contrast, are nothing more than a statement of peace on earth. There is a felt difference of intensity between the two sets of lines. Now, the second poem quoted is the work of the deposed Emperor of the Ch'en Dynasty and is entitled, "A Poem Composed at His Majesty's Request While Attending a Sui Banquet." Scholars have tended to treat this poem negatively because of the obsequious attitude taken by its composer toward the conquering dynasty.[16] If the work is separated from these circumstances, however, and considered solely on the grounds of critical reading, it is difficult to conclude that

---

[16] The former Emperor of the Ch'en Dynasty, whose throne had been usurped by Wen Ti (the "Cultured Emperor") of the Sui, attended an official Sui banquet and offered this panegyric to the new dynasty. His lack of self-respect in doing so has brought criticism on his poem as well: "It somehow withers in comparison with Prince Ōtomo's magnificent work" (Hayashi, 1944, 23).

Prince Ōtomo's composition occupies an equal status with the best poetry of China.

I did not give a very high evaluation to Prince Ōtomo's composition because I have sought to temper the excessive, overstated praise heretofore awarded this poem. Yet if we consider that it appeared some ten years after shih composition was inaugurated in Yamato, we can only be astonished at the progress made in this short time. In any event, Prince Ōtomo assimilated the forms of expression characteristic of the Six Dynasties period, a point that has also been acknowledged by Chinese scholars (Wu, 1955, 3). A great deal of training is required to master forms of expression in a foreign poetic medium. The following poem, "The Oriole's Song," is the oldest extant shih composed by a Korean:

> The wings of orioles flutter
> As they nestle near their mates.
> I ponder my loneliness:
> Will she not return with me?[17]

This poem has clearly adopted and mastered forms of expression found in *The Book of Songs*. Its maturity of expression renders it difficult to believe the traditional attribution of the poem to King Yuri, who composed it in the third year of his reign (17 B.C.). On the other hand, we must conclude that the work predates the period when Korean culture became significantly influenced by the Six Dynasties style, and that even more advanced composition must have developed once this style became familiar in Korea.

The second-oldest Korean shih extant is the "Poem Sent to Yü Chung-wen"; it is written in five-character lines and is attributed to a Koguryŏ general, Ŭlchi Mundŏk, who is said to have composed it in the twenty-third year of King Yangyang's reign (612). The poem:

> For godlike plans you study the heavens;
> For marvelous stratagems you scrutinize the earth.
> You triumph in battle, your fame already great;
> Be satisfied with this, I pray: withdraw your troops from here.[18]

[17] It appears in the section on King Yuri in Book 13, "Biographies of the Royal Family of Koguryŏ," in the *Samguk Sagi* (*Sangoku Shiki*, 148). The circumstances of composition are said to be: while King Yuri was absent on a hunting excursion, his favorite consorts, Lady Rice and Lady Pheasant, quarreled out of jealousy, and being vilified by Lady Rice, Lady Pheasant fled the palace. When the King returned and learned of the incident, he spurred his horse and galloped after her but was unable to bring her back. As he rested under a tree, he saw orioles flying in its branches and composed the poem.

[18] It appears in Biography 25 (Yü Chung-wen) of the *Sui Shu*, Book 60 (*Sui Shu*, 1455).

Some have doubted that a warrior could produce a poem of this caliber, and there has been speculation that the poem was composed by another person on the general's behalf. This shih has nevertheless always been regarded as a masterpiece (Yi Ka-wŏn, 1961, 22-23). Whatever its authorship, the shih can clearly be dated as a work of the early seventh century because it is cited in one of the Chinese histories, the *Sui Shu* (compiled in 636).

Yet I cannot conclude that it merits an evaluation like "The concepts in this poem are sublime" (Kim Sa-yŏp, 1973, 35). Its intent is indeed ingenious: the poet urges an honorable end to the fighting by praising the enemy general and by reasoning that he would do well to withdraw victoriously. Surely the poem is lucid, but it lacks beauty as poetry. The first and second lines obey all too faithfully the rule of direct antithesis: no interest is generated by some "distancing." The third and fourth lines are directly declarative, and no intricate turns of phrase are to be found. This poem differs so greatly in subject matter from that of Prince Ōtomo that it would be difficult to compare them in terms of skill. It is at least apparent, however, that Ŭlchi Mundŏk's poem is deficient in the most representative characteristic of the Six Dynasties style, the expression of ornate beauty.

Not long after the time of Prince Ōtomo, however, the poetry of Prince Ōtsu (663-86) demonstrated that beautiful expression in the style of the Six Dynasties had already become established. His "Poem in Five-Character Lines, Recited at a Banquet in a Spring Garden" (*Kaifū*, 4) no doubt postdates Prince Ōtomo's "Quatrain in Five-Character Lines, Composed on Attending a Royal Banquet" by some ten or fifteen years, yet the newer poem brilliantly reflects the poetic style of the Ch'i and Liang Dynasties, which is to say, the later Six Dynasties style:

> Opening my collar, I pause at the royal lake;
> Feasting my eyes, I stroll through golden gardens.
> Moss lies deep beneath the limpid waters;
> Distant peaks rise dimly through the mist.
> The lapping of waves blends with the sound of the zither;

The Sui general Yü Chung-wen used ingenious stratagems to defeat Koguryŏ forces; Ŭlchi Mundŏk thus feigned surrender and proceeded to the headquarters of the Sui army. Yü Chung-wen was under orders to capture Ŭlchi on sight, and tried to do so. But the civil administrator for the territory, Liu Shih-lung, forbade Ŭlchi's capture, permitting him to go free. On realizing his error, Liu sent a messenger to invite Ŭlchi to return, but instead he set fire to his camp and fled. The poem quoted here was presented by Ŭlchi to Yü Chung-wen outside the Sui camp. The incident is also described in Book 20, "Biographies of the Royal Family of Koguryŏ," 8 (*Sangoku Shiki*, 205-6). But this is actually no more than an embellishment of the *Sui Shu* account and fails to include the poem.

The singing of birds is borne on the breeze.
Assembled lords, prostrate with drink, are brought home in
    carriages:
Who now will bother to speak of the P'eng-tse banquet?[19]

Like Prince Ōtomo's composition, this is a banquet poem, but Prince
Ōtsu's work clearly differs in one respect: it is essentially descriptive. The
style is also different from that of "The Oriole's Song" and the "Poem
Sent to Yü Chung-wen." Moreover, the inlay of language brimming with
visual beauty—"golden gardens," "moss . . . beneath the . . . waters,"
"peaks . . . through the mist"—makes full use of the late Six Dynasties
poetic style. Lines five and six, which represent a transition to auditory
imagery, exhibit a subtle intellectual refraction that is still more reminiscent of expressive techniques found in the late Six Dynasties. The
conception of these lines—that the melody of the zither is enhanced by
the lapping of waves, and the voice of the wafting breeze is made pleasant
to the ear by the singing of birds—is achieved through opposing the
sounds of nature in a garden to the sounds of courtiers' music in a subtle
cause-and-effect relationship, rather than through stating directly how
splendid the poet finds the musical performance. Prince Ōtsu's attempt
to give form to auditory beauty is an expressive technique developed in
the late Six Dynasties period.

A Chinese scholar declares these lines to be "on a level with the best
poetic works of the Liang and Ch'en Dynasties" (Wu, 1955, 4). Even
lines seven and eight, which are not descriptive, avoid making a direct
statement of their import, namely that no scene can match that of a
successful gathering with its pleasantly tipsy participants. Precedents are
invoked instead, of Shan Chien who, when thoroughly drunk, was always
loaded feet first into his carriage and driven home, and of T'ao Ch'ien
(Yüan-ming), the extraordinary poet and fabled drinker. When the indirect expression in these lines is compared with lines three and four of
Ŭlchi Mundŏk's poem, the Japanese appears far more characteristic of
the Six Dynasties style. Several instances of late Six Dynasties poetic
vocabulary also appear in the Japanese poem.[20] "Poetic expression based
on literary precedent is beautiful expression": by Prince Ōtsu's time this
traditional Chinese dictum had tentatively rooted itself within the Yamato
shih, and represented nothing less than the birth of ga in Yamato.

This is not to say that shih composed in Yamato ranked with the best
Chinese compositions, a point that was made in discussing Prince Ōtomo's poem. This should be kept clearly in mind in considering the his-

[19] [P'eng-tse is a district of Kiangsi Province where the poet T'ao Ch'ien, 372?-427),
serving as magistrate, gave one or more famous banquets.—Trans.]
[20] Much of the diction of the poem had also appeared in the Wen Hsüan.

torical significance of the birth of ga. I have drawn attention to what can only be the superior adaptive capacity of the Yamato shih, a literary form that assimilated the expressive forms typical of the Six Dynasties in a relatively short period. The faults inherent in the poetry itself completely disqualify it as literature of the first rank. One particularly conspicuous fault is metric irregularity. In the T'ang period, Chinese poetry perfected a form, regulated verse (lü-shih), that was capable of displaying the utmost euphonic beauty. Prince Ōtsu's poem cannot of course be discussed in terms of the codes of regulated verse: this seventh-century prince would quite naturally not have been aware of the rules of regulated-verse composition. The Yung-ming style of poetry, led by the theoretician Shen Yüeh, nevertheless flourished during the Ch'en and Liang Dynasties (Kuo, 1970, 69-83), and euphonic beauty, though differing in tenor from that found in regulated verse, was a special characteristic of late Six Dynasties poetry. When Prince Ōtsu's banquet-poem is considered in terms of late Six Dynasties metric standards, it cannot after all be pronounced fully beautiful. These are the limits of poetry composition in a foreign language. Prince Ōtsu adopted the *late* Six Dynasties poetic style rather than the style of the early Six Dynasties seen in Ŭlchi Mundŏk's composition of shih, a point we ought not forget. On the other hand, of course, we must also consider the great amount of assistance provided to this end by Sat'aek Chomyŏng (a cultural assistant of Prince Ōtomo) and his fellow Korean immigrant intellectuals during and after this period.[21]

[21] "Sat'aek Chomyŏng, T'appon Ch'unch'o, Kil T'aesong, Ho Solmo, and Mokso Kwija were chosen from among many to serve as consultants" (*Kaifū*, 70).

CHAPTER 7

Waka Expression

The Rise of Ga and the Fall of Kotodama

It is believed that Japanese groups approximating poetic circles and formed to compose shih exerted an influence on waka, although it is not clear when or through what processes this influence took place. There is an uta beginning, "Fuyugomori/Haru sarikureba" (With the coming of spring/ After winter's confinement; MYS, 1:16). It was composed during the reign of Tenji and has the following forenote:

> His Majesty commanded the First Minister, Lord Fujiwara, to compare spring with autumn and determine which was the more lovely, the sight of a myriad blossoms in the spring mountains, or a scene of colored leaves by the thousands in the autumn mountains. Princess Nukada stated her verdict on this occasion with the following uta.[1]

The author of the forenote has taken care to record that the princess "stated her verdict . . . with the following uta," perhaps because the other participants presented shih instead. The practice of presenting shih at official banquets probably began during Tenji's reign, as has been discussed. But the fact that a waka appeared together with shih on such an occasion can only indicate that waka was also acknowledged as worthy composition. In other words, the worthiness of waka resided in its very expression. No consideration was given to other areas of possible worth, such as the bringing about of some kind of auspicious event through magic properties contained in the words of a waka. In short, the writing of waka now required beauty above all. [Unless for special purposes, guide phrases are not italicized in this chapter.]

Fuyugomori	With the coming of spring
Haru sarikureba	After winter's confinement,
Nakazarishi	Birds that did not sing
Tori mo kinakinu	Now come and sing;

[1] The First Minister, Fujiwara Kamatari, lived 614-69, dying in the eighth year of Tenji's reign; the episode therefore occurred between 662 and 669. [Kamatari, who owed his rise to the tumultuous events surrounding the Taika Reform of 645 (see n. 4, below), was the maker of the fortunes of the Fujiwara house. Trans., Ed.]

Sakazarishi	Flowers that did not bloom
Hana mo sakeredo	Now burst into bloom.
Yama o shigemi	But the mountain undergrowth is dense:
Irite mo torazu	I cannot enter and gather the blossoms;
Kusa fukami	The grasses grow tall:
Torite mo mizu	I cannot pick and admire the blossoms.
Akiyama no	When I behold the foliage
Ko no ha o mite wa	On autumn mountains,
Momichi oba	The yellow leaves
Torite so shinobu	I gather and admire;
Aoki o ba	Those leaves still green
Okite so nageku	I pass by with a sigh
Soko shi urameshi	(That alone is hateful):
Akiyama so are wa.	I find for the autumn mountains!

(*MYS*, 1:16)

It will be immediately observed that twelve of the eighteen lines are involved in parallelism and, moreover, that all instances constitute parallelism in alternation of lines. Alternating parallelism also appears in the new stratum of archaic song, but lyric poetry that is principally made up of alternating parallelism, and very skillful parallelism at that, probably postdates the composition of shih in Yamato. To illustrate:

Nakazarishi	A	Birds that did not sing
Tori mo kinakinu	B	Now come and sing;
Sakazarishi	A	Flowers that did not bloom
Hana mo sakeredo	B	Now burst into bloom.

The ABAB pattern in the four lines provides an alternation of parallelism that constitutes a unit of four lines. That is not all. The alternating parallelism is redoubled by the replay, within juxtaposed rather than alternating lines, of forms of the verbs "naku" (sing) and "saku" (bloom). If we number the lines by their use of the repeated verbs, retaining the AB pattern, the result is A1 B1 A2 B2. This technique is termed "shuang-ni tui" in the early T'ang treatises *Wen-pi Shih* and *Pi-cha Hua-liang* (Konishi, 1953e, 94-95). Instances of its use appear already in Six Dynasties poetry, and it was evidently much used by Yamato court poets.

The first extant instance in Yamato of this technique appears in a shih by Prince Kadono (661-705) bearing the title, "A Poem in Five-Character Lines, in Celebration of Warblers and Plum Blossoms on a Spring Day" (*Kaifū*, 10):

White plum blossoms open—*white* dimples;
Lovely warblers sing—*lovely* voices.

Four more examples of shuang-ni tui are to be found in the *Kaifūsō* (27, 30, 32, 59). By utilizing this technique in her waka, Princess Nukada may have sought to create a stir among the men present, who were no doubt confident of their standing as shih poets. Yet in her lines on autumn, which she maintains is superior to spring, the princess establishes her focus through the use of a model form of direct parallelism.

(A1) Momichi o ba/(B1) Torite so shinobu
(A2) Aoki o ba/(B2) Okite so nageku

(A1) The yellow leaves/(B1)I gather and admire;
(A2) Those leaves still green/(B2) I pass by with a sigh

The technique of contrasting the colors "yellow" and "green" in the lines marked A and the actions "gather" and "pass by" together with the emotional displays "admire" and "sigh" in the lines marked B is also highly characteristic of direct parallelism according to Chinese poetic criteria.

Such instances suggest most persuasively that expressive techniques, corresponding in substance to those used in writing shih, were employed in waka composition in the course of official banquets and other formal occasions, and that in this way the Ōmi court became aware that waka as well as shih was capable of being "worthy expression." As we have seen, the shih of the Ōmi court were modeled chiefly on the poetic style of the late Six Dynasties, and tended to be objects of beautiful verbal technology. The following lines appear in a shih by the priest Chizō, "A Poem in Five-Character Lines, Celebrating the Blossoms and Warblers" (*Kaifū*, 8):

And though I revel in this amusement,
Lack of artifice is cause for shame.

The poet's feeling of shame for not having enough "artifice" (tiao-ch'ung), which is to say polished expressive techniques, is indicative of the contemporary desirability of these techniques.[2] The expectation that, by

---

[2] A refined literary style was traditionally regarded with suspicion: in the "Wu Tzu" chapter of Yang Hsiung's *Fa Yen*, the master is asked, "Have you loved rhapsodies [fu] from your youth?" He replies, "Yes, as a child I loved artifice and elaboration," quickly adding, "When I grew up I no longer practiced them." By the late Six Dynasties, an elaborate, refined art was looked on favorably. Chizō is an exponent of this new literary awareness.

composition for official banquets and like occasions, waka should also possess refined expression, was a natural consequence of this aesthetic aim. Kakinomoto Hitomaro inherited this awareness of expressive techniques, and he crystallized it in the famous uta that mark the apex of the period of the *Man'yōshū*.

All the same, it is difficult to imagine that waka offered no resistance whatsoever to being infused with the new Yamato awareness of shih expression. An awareness of Six Dynasties expression was linked to the waka only under extremely limited circumstances or in extraordinary situations, as, for example, when a tennō invited shih poets and waka poets to the same gathering and commanded each to display specialized gifts. In principle, waka and shih seem to have had separate functions. Alternatively, the Six Dynasties' criterion—that a work was evaluated either positively or negatively depending on whether its expression was polished—was not the only force in waka: the Ōmi court continued to maintain a belief in the kotodama, through which auspicious or inauspicious events occurred as a result of certain turns of phrase.

Ama no hara	As I cast my gaze
Furisakemireba	Across the Plain of Heaven,
Ōkimi no	I see that our Lord
Miinochi wa nagaku	Will be provided with long life
Ama tarashitari.	By the favor of the skies.

(*MYS*, 2:147)

To judge solely from its text, this might appear to be an auspicious congratulatory poem. The uta is, however, included in a section of the *Man'yōshū* devoted to elegies; its forenote reads, "An uta offered by the consort at the time of the Sovereign's illness." This uta was presented by Yamatohime, the consort of Tenji, when he was bedridden. So, if this uta was recited near the sickbed of the tennō, the breath of the reciter was expected to reach the sick man and, through the action of the kotodama, effect a recovery (Itō Haku, 1975c, 274).

We may conclude from its similarities that another poem is also a kotodama uta, one composed in this instance by Princess Nukada on behalf of Saimei Tennō in anticipation of her having a calm sea voyage (Itō Haku, 1975a, 188-90):

Watatsumi no	The setting sun is bright
Toyohatakumo ni	Against the Sea God's
Irihi sashi	Flowing banks of clouds:

Koyoi no tsukuyo   May the moon tonight
Sayakeku ari koso.   Shine pure and clear.

(*MYS*, 1:15)

Another uta, also thought to have been composed by Princess Nukada
on behalf of Saimei (ibid., 152-56), was probably recited under the same
circumstances as the preceding poem, and again anticipated the action
of the kotodama:

Nikitatsu ni   We've waited for the moonrise
Funa norisen to   Before boarding ship
Tsuki mateba   In Nikitatsu harbor;
Shio mo kanainu   Now the tide is full—
Ima wa kogiide na.   Let us row out to sea!

(*MYS*, 1:8)

We may consider one more poem attributed to Princess Nukada, who is
thought to have composed it in longing for Tenji:

Kimi matsu to   I wait for you,
Aga koioreba   And as I fill with yearning,
Waga yado no   Along my house
Sudare ugokashi   The blinds begin to move at last—
Aki no kaze fuku.   As the wind of autumn blows.

(*MYS*, 4:488)

This is not simply a lyric poem. The movement of the blinds is a sign
that the awaited lover has arrived. The uta can only reflect the expectation
that, with recitation, the kotodama within the reciter's breath will mag-
ically transform her dwelling into a place her lover will visit.[3]

If we assume that the kotodama was still active in the early period
represented by the *Man'yōshū*, then the following two uta should probably also be read in the same terms. Their composer, Prince Arima (640-
58), was enticed into committing treason, perhaps in connection with
Fujiwara Kamatari's plot.[4] He was arrested and taken to Yunosaki in

---

[3] One view has it that this uta, "Kimi matsu to," is written in a style too sophisticated
for a seventh-century poet like Princess Nukada. If so, the poem may be a work of the
eighth century or later that was composed under Princess Nukada's name (Itō Haku, 1975a,
191). If, however, we follow my interpretation and read this uta as a possessor of magic
properties, there is no need to strain in the effort to reject it as a work of the earlier
Man'yōshū period.

[4] [In 644 Nakatomi Kamako (who later took the name Fujiwara Kamatari) plotted with

Kii Province, where Saimei Tennō was in temporary residence. After his case had been heard, the prince was brought back to the hill of Fujishiro and strangled to death (*Saimeiki*, 267-68). His uta were probably composed at the time he was taken to Yunosaki:

Iwashiro no	Today I bind together
Hamamatsu ga e o	The branches of an
Hikimusubi	Iwashiro beach pine:
Masakiku araba	If fortune favors me,
Mata kaerimin.	I shall return to see them once again.

(*MYS*, 2:141)

Ie ni areba	Rice that, were I home,
Ke ni moru ii o	Would fill a dish
Kusamakura	Is in travel—
Tabi ni shi areba	Grasses for my pillow—
Shii no ha ni moru.	Served upon oak leaves.

(*MYS*, 2:142)

The forenote to these poems (which appear in a section of elegies) states that they are "two uta recited by Prince Arima when, feeling troubled at heart, he bound together two pine branches." These are not simply uta recited by the prince in his misery. The former was composed in accordance with a belief that an auspicious event would result from the binding together of pine branches. In it, the prince tells the pine tree that his act will ensure a safe return, and if fortune protects him, he will revisit the tree to see its bound branches. The poet anticipates that the kotodama within his poem will manifest magic powers through the pine tree and rescue him from danger. Similarly, the significance of the latter uta is not that rice served in dishes at the prince's house is eaten on oak leaves now that he has been obliged to make this journey. Instead, the uta was probably recited as an invocation to the spirit of the pine tree, and was accompanied by an offering of rice.

Prince Nakanoōe to overthrow Soga no Emishi and Soga no Iruka, powerful men who were apparently intent on destroying the reigning dynasty. Iruka was assassinated, and Emishi and his party either fled or were put to death. Kōgyoku Tennō, who had had the Sogas' backing, abdicated in favor of Kōtoku, Prince Arima's father. Kōtoku's enthronement in 645 marked the beginning of the Taika Reform that strengthened the centralized powers of the state.

Prince Nakanoōe was named crown prince; following Kōtoku's death in 654, Nakanoōe's mother (the former sovereign Kōgyoku) ascended the throne for a second time as Saimei. Her son Nakanoōe was de facto ruler, however, and succeeded her as Tenji Tennō. The nature of Prince Arima's treason is unknown. He was probably caught on the opposing side in these events, and may have conspired to overthrow Saimei.—Trans.]

I wish to interpret the poems as addresses to the pine tree. The prince admits to the tree that a proper rice offering should be placed on a dish, and excuses his use of oak leaves by referring to his transient situation: oak leaves would have been much too small to serve as a rice vessel for the poet himself. It might seem strange that two poetic supplications for good fortune are included in an elegy section of the *Man'yōshū*. To its editors, however, they corresponded to lament and were treated as elegies because the circumstances ended in the poet's death. An uta cited earlier, "As I cast my gaze/Across the Plain of Heaven" (*MYS*, 2:147), must have been similarly treated. Although it invoked the longevity of the tennō, his death ensued, and it too was entered in the elegies section.

This evidence suggests that it was common practice at the Ōmi court to anticipate the action of the kotodama in uta. The attitude coexisted, however, with another which we have already seen reflected in Princess Nukada's "Uta on the Relative Merits of Spring and Autumn" (*MYS*, 1:16): that the uta had its raison d'être in its acknowledged worth as poetic expression and the emotion evoked in response to that expression. When Princess Nukada's uta rely on the kotodama, they also display a respect for expression, a fact that might lead one to conclude that their composition took place in a period of transition between (as it were) periods of kotodama and fūryū.

Numerically speaking, however, few uta of this time demonstrate a high regard for expression, and we must conclude after all that the period is in general that of kotodama. Within the realm of shih composition, expression was recognized to have an intrinsic worth. In the case of waka, this attitude was limited either to special occasions or specific poets. "Specific poets" means Korean immigrant poets and those directly influenced by them. For example, Crown Prince Nakanoōe heard a false report made against the Minister of the Right, Yamada Maro of the Soga clan. The prince believed the slander and attacked the minister, who thereupon committed suicide with eight members of his family. One of Maro's daughters, Lady Miyatsuko, was the prince's consort, and she died of grief after this incident. By this time the prince was aware of Maro's innocence. When he was further confronted with the death of his beloved consort, he experienced the deepest regret and sorrow.

Kawara Maro of Nonaka, a member of the Recorders, then presented the prince with the following two uta (*Kōtokuki*, 244-47):

Yamagawa ni	In a mountain stream
Oshi futatsu ite	A pair of mandarin ducks
Tagui yoku	Keeps devoted company;
Tagueru imo o	Beloved, once by my side,
Tare ka iniken.	Who has taken you away?

Motogoto ni	Blossoms are opening
Hana wa sakedomo	On every tree:
Nani to ka mo	Why then, oh why,
Utsukushi imo ga	Will that dear and lovely one
Mata sakidekonu.	Never blossom forth again?

(*NSK, Song*, 113-14)

As the commentators indicate, the former uta is clearly based on the first poem in *The Book of Songs*, "Kuan-chü" (The Ospreys Cry):

> Kuan-kuan, softly cry the ospreys
> Resting on a sandbar in the river.
> Serene and fair is the maiden,
> A fine wife for the gentleman.

The uta undoubtedly employed such expression on the assumption that the recipient, the prince, would recognize the allusion to *The Book of Songs*. The presence within waka of language based on Chinese poetic diction aided in fostering the perception that waka and shih were qualitatively similar. Waka itself was eventually transformed by this, changing from messenger and conveyor of the kotodama to works of worthy expression.

Kawara Maro's second uta is not a direct statement of sorrow for the beautiful consort.[5] Instead, it is presented indirectly: every year the blossoms open, but my consort, who was as beautiful as any blossom, will never return—why must that be? The intent of the poem, to contrast the repetitive characteristic of one possessor of beauty with the single appearance of another, makes it possible to incorporate into this waka that rationalism or reasoning (li) so conspicuously present in late Six Dynasties poetry. This characteristic does not appear as distinctly as in poetry from the period of the *Kokinshū*, but it may be regarded as constituting a distant source for expression typical of the *Kokinshū*. Now, Kawara Maro, the composer of these poems, was a member of the Recorders, which was formed from continental immigrants. He would have been proficient in Chinese poetry and prose.[6] The first compositions containing

---

[5] One theory has it that the story of Lady Miyatsuko is a fabrication based on the Han Dynasty Lady Li (d. 120 B.C.), whose story Kawara Maro found in the *Sou-shen Chi* (Tsuchihashi, 1976, 451, 362-63). The Chinese story was very likely used to embellish sections of the *Chronicles* during the process of compilation, but there are no grounds to hold Lady Miyatsuko's story an outright fabrication.

[6] [Recorders: "fubito" is the usual modern designation, "fumfito" the Old Japanese. In any event,] many of them were immigrants who could write Chinese. Kawara may be associated with the shoban (immigrant family) names of Kawachi Province (*Shinsen Shō-jiroku*). Nonaka was also in Kawachi and was similarly associated with immigrants and

expression that was perceived as intrinsically worthy were produced by intellectuals of immigrant descent in the genre of Chinese writing, and this process apparently came to include waka expression as well as shih.

The process just described is concerned with the infiltration of what one might call the inner character of Japanese literary expression by Chinese or Sinified perceptions. The external character was similarly affected. It seems to have been assumed that in its standard form the chōka, or long uta, should possess one or more envoys (hanka). Of the eighteen chōka (including variants) taken to be by Hitomaro, all have envoys, whereas of the fourteen chōka of what might be termed the pre-Hitomaro period of the Man'yōshū, none has an envoy. In other words, the later the chōka, the more fixed was the practice of appending an envoy. This seems to prove that there was a growing awareness that a proper chōka was to be accompanied by one or more envoys. Now, the envoy is similar in its properties to the luan of the Chinese rhapsody (fu), as Edo scholars indicated. A luan is a short text that follows the rhapsody and sums up the meaning of the entire poem. It is functionally similar, therefore, to the envoy. Eight rhapsodies with luan are included in the Selections of Refined Literature, the likeliest source for Yamato gentlemen of the Ancient Age.[7] Yet the chōka was not recognized as the Yamato equivalent of the rhapsody until the time of Ōtomo Yakamochi, in the second half of the Ancient Age.[8] No such awareness is to be found in the first half. The chōka of the early period of the Man'yōshū, moreover, were in fact not much longer than tanka, and as such did not bear comparison with the monumental rhapsody. It is therefore difficult to imagine that the envoy was originally devised in imitation of the rhapsodic luan, and another source must be sought.

The Korean hugu (concluding lines), verses appended to the hyangga, deserves consideration as a source. Many hyangga are accompanied by a hugu, which repeats or emphasizes the import of the poem—as with chōka and hanka. An example of a hyangga with hugu is furnished by "Hyesŏng Ka" (Song of a Comet), a work thought to date from the late sixth or early seventh century. Because there is no certainty as to how Old Korean was pronounced, it is only possible to present the poem with

their names (Wamyō Reijūshō). [The Recorders were one of a number of court officers inclusively termed "kabane." As time went on, some titles dropped from use and others (e.g., "ason" from "asomi") acquired a different meaning. To this point—with the author's agreement—all such court office ranks have been translated simply "Lord" or "Lady." The titles involved were, at that time, part office titles and part names.—Ed.]

[7] The ch'ung, ch'ang, hsi, and sui are similar in function to the luan. The fan-tz'u found in the Hsün Tzu differs in nature from the hanka (Nakanishi, 1963, 598-602).

[8] Yakamochi presented "In place of a luan," a regulated-verse poem in seven-character lines (Book 18); and he refers to hanka [envoys] as tanka in "A Fu on Mount Tachi, Together with Two Tanka" (MYS, 17:4,000), not calling them luan.

a translation and with a transcription in the Korean prototype of man'yōgana. From the latter, the reader will gain some sense of the intellectual achievement of the Koreans in adapting a noninflected to an inflected language—and some sense also of the difficulties of the system for Japanese and Koreans alike. In the poem the comet is a metaphor for the Japanese invaders, and the governing moon for Korean might.[9]

SONG OF THE COMET

There is a *castle* by the *Eastern Sea*
Where Gandharva used to *play*.
Japanese soldiers came there;
Torches were burnt, and *rockets* were fired.

As the *moon* heard that *three knights* visited this *mountain*,
She *zealously* lit her lamp
And *someone*, looking at a *star* that *swept* a *path*,
Said, "Behold, a *comet!*"

Hugu

The moon has already *gone down*:
Where *is* that *comet* now?

旧理東尸汀叱
乾達婆矣遊烏隠城叱肹良望良古
倭理叱軍置来叱多
烽燒邪隠辺也藪耶
三花矣岳音見賜烏尸聞古
月置八切爾数於将来尸波衣
道尸掃尸星利望良古
彗星也白反也人是有叱多
　　　後　句
達阿羅浮去伊叱等邪
此也友物比所音叱彗叱只有叱故

⁹ *Iji*, 5: "Divine Response," 7. [Note curtailed. Translation adapted from that by Peter H. Lee, *Anthology of Korean Poetry* (New York: John Day, 1964), p. 34.—Ed.]

In the text reproduced here, the underlined Chinese characters (corresponding to the italics of the translation) are used for their *meaning*, and those not underlined are used for their *sounds*. The functional resemblance between this hugu and the Yamato envoy was pointed out long ago by Ogura Shimpei in the early years of hyangga research (Ogura, 1929, 52). I would prefer, however, to consider this on a level other than that of resemblances, and as a conscious imitation.

In place of the indicator hugu, an interjection, "aya" or "ayaya," is sometimes employed; the hugu is also known by the explanatory term "t'an wal." These terms signify that the hugu condenses the general meaning of the main body of the poem and expresses this meaning emotionally: thus its function is equivalent to that performed by the Yamato hanka (envoy) to chōka. The main body of the hyangga, moreover, is shorter than the Chinese fu, or rhapsody; it is not much different in length from chōka of the early period of the *Man'yōshū*, a further indication of the close relationship between the hugu and the envoy. There is no way to determine whether the hugu derives from the luan of the Chinese fu, given the present circumstances of the hyangga. Only twenty-five hyangga survive from the entire corpus, and the course of development of this genre is unknown. On the other hand, the likelihood that the Yamato envoy is linked to the hugu rather than the luan is virtually certain.

One can hardly conclude that the envoy is modeled on the hugu simply on the basis of their functional similarities. This assumption can be supported, however, by citing the common features found in the principal method of transcription used in the age of the *Man'yōshū* and that used in the transcription of hyangga.[10] In the Korean "Song of a Comet" just given, the underlined parts of the text represent areas where Chinese characters are used in accordance with their meaning in the Chinese language; these characters are, in other words, used as semantographs. The characters not underlined represent that part of the text which expresses the Korean language with Chinese characters having sounds that approximate Korean pronunciation—a phonetic use of Chinese characters. This method of mixed transcription, using Chinese characters as

[10] Ōno Susumu seems to have been the first to pronounce his views on this matter. In a symposium on "The Language and Writing System of Ancient Japanese," *Gengo Seikatsu* (Chikuma Shobō, no. 292, January 1976), he proposed in essence that Koreans employed a method of transcription using Chinese characters for both semantic and phonetic functions in setting down hyangga, that this method dates from the Koguryŏ period, and that it was imported into Yamato. That is, that the Japanese received information on the pronunciation of characters directly from China, whereas the practice of using characters both semantically and phonetically came from Korea (p. 15). Because these statements were made in a symposium, no evidence was presented. A rebuttal of Ōno's theory holds him mistaken in concluding that the pronunciation of Chinese characters was taken solely from China, because a large number of Sino-Korean pronunciations have also been taken into Japanese (Fujii Shigetoshi, 1976b, 99).

both semantographs and phonetic units, was also the most widely accepted practice during the age of the *Man'yōshū*. I will give as one example the following poem. As in the case of the hyangga given above, italicized areas in the Japanese text indicate the use of Chinese characters as semantographs.

Kimi ga *yuki*	The journey of my lord
Ke *nagaku nari*nu	Has lasted many days:
Yama tazune	Shall I go
*Muka*e ka *yuk*an	To meet him in the mountains,
Machi ni ka *mata*n.	Or shall I wait, wait here for him?

(*MYS*, 2:85)

Most scholars are in agreement with Kamo no Mabuchi—who termed this method of transcription the "standard form"—when they acknowledge that it was the most widely accepted such method of its time.

It has been suggested that the same transcriptive device developed independently in Silla and Yamato. According to this argument, the Japanese and Korean languages, which have similar grammatical structures, could reasonably be expected to use Chinese characters both as semantographs and as phonetic units when transcription is effected through the Chinese writing system, because the Chinese language for which this system was developed is totally unrelated to either Japanese or Korean. This line of thought is not implausible. On the other hand, Korean immigrants indisputably played a leading role in demonstrating to the Yamato people the practical use of documents and books written in Chinese with Chinese characters. And because the semantographic-phonetic method of transcription was used in Korea, it is not easily explained how the same system would have originated among Yamato intellectuals, unless we presume the simplest explanation of Korean influence.

This explanation is further supported by the fact that a great many of the Chinese characters used phonetically and employed as man'yōgana are pronounced in the Korean manner, not the Chinese. Research on this subject has been advanced by Fujii Shigetoshi, Pak Pyŏng-ch'ae, and Yi Sung-nyŏng, among others, and even richer results are anticipated in the near future. According to an excellent recent study, that conducted by Yi (Yi Sung-nyŏng, 1955, 62-166), Korean pronunciation of Chinese characters has changed considerably since the early Yi Dynasty (late fourteenth century). Although at the present stage of research it is difficult to reconstruct the pronunciation system during the Silla period, Yi classifies the Korean methods of transcription in this manner:

$\left\{\begin{array}{l}\text{Transcriptions of proper nouns} \\ \quad \text{(place names, official titles, names of people)} \\ \text{Transcriptions of texts} \left\{\begin{array}{l}\text{Songs (hyangga)} \\ \text{Writing in general (later source materials)}\end{array}\right.\end{array}\right.$

When the results of Yi's inquiry into Korean transcription methods are collated with studies conducted by Japanese on the *Chronicles*, the *Man'yōshū*, and the *Topographies* among other works, the probable conclusion is that Chinese characters used phonetically by Yamato intellectuals in the Ancient Age were pronounced, in many cases, according to the Korean fashion.[11] Korean influence is also apparent in Japanese vocabulary: the appearance of words of Korean extraction—such as "marihishi" (south), "kasasagi" (magpie), "kuchi" (hawk), "kokishi" (king), "seshimu" (prince), "sashi" (fortress), "nare" (river), "bure" (village), and "mure" (mountain)—in documents of the Ancient Age seems to imply the participation of large numbers of Korean immigrants in the management of Yamato writings.[12] It seems fairly certain, then, that the transcription method used in hyangga was brought into Yamato by these same Korean intellectuals.

When the hyangga transcription method was brought into ancient Yamato, information would also have been transmitted about its expressive form. If we connect this fact to the other, that the hugu with the hyangga and the envoy with chōka closely resemble each other in form and function, we can safely assume that the hugu served as model as the envoy evolved. This view is also reasonable in chronological terms. The number of envoys gradually increased during the reign of the Ōmi court in the mid-seventh century. Moreover, the "Song of a Comet," the oldest extant documented hyangga, is considered to date from the late sixth or early seventh century. If any questions remain, they concern the reliability of the primary hyangga sources as faithful recorders of seventh-century song: the *Kyunyŏ Chŏn*, which records eleven hyangga, dates from the year 1075, and the *Samguk Yusa*, containing fourteen hyangga, dates from the first half of the reign of King Ch'ungnyŏl of the Koryŏ Dynasty (ca. 1275-81). These sources appear more reliable, moreover, by our knowledge that a collection of hyangga, the *Samdaemok*, was compiled in the second year of the reign of King Chinsŏng (888) of the Silla Dynasty (Kim Sa-yŏp, 1973, 113). Although it is no longer extant, people of the Koryŏ Dynasty are believed to have quoted from it; so the extant texts are less dubious than they seem at first glance.

Thus we see that, in the late seventeenth century, Chinese literature—reaching Yamato directly from the continent or through Korea—came

---

[11] The statement is based on work by Hashimoto Shinkichi, Arisaka Hideyo, Takagi Ichinosuke, and others. [See also n. 10—Ed.]

[12] See *Jidaibetsu Kokugo Daijiten*, "Jōdai Hen," p. 49. [And n. 10.—Ed.]

to pervade waka expression in both form and substance, and that the characteristic Yamato kotodama seems to have retreated from the poetic arena. On the whole, however, the kotodama continued to flourish in the sphere of waka. The imported concept of ga had not yet become the dominant ideal. This period corresponds roughly to Kakinomoto Hitomaro's most active years.

THE WORLD OF HITOMARO

There are two extreme positions taken by critics of Hitomaro. One reveres him as a sage of poetry, and considers him not only the supreme composer of uta in the period of the *Man'yōshū* but also the supreme poet in the entire history of waka. This view has been held by Saitō Mokichi, Shimagi Akahiko, Tsuchiya Bummei, and other writers associated with the tanka journal *Araragi*. Omodaka Hisataka, who made highly significant contributions to the study of the *Man'yōshū*, also sided with this view. The opposite extreme maintains that Hitomaro was no more than a poet in the employ of the court, and that his work is devoid of content and bedecked with pompous rhetorical flourishes; its principal proponent has been Hasegawa Nyozekan. Apparently his stance has not received unequivocal approval from any scholar, but quite a few specialists with certain ideological beliefs have approached it with some sympathy.

These two extreme positions share a common attitude, however. Both attempt to criticize Hitomaro by applying nineteenth-century values to his work, and both insist, moreover, on the absoluteness of their criteria. Attitudes like these are unlikely to be thought legitimate in the twenty-first century. We moderns rightly criticize the classics in terms of our modern conceptions. Yet minute by minute our present age moves into the past, and the year 1983, for example, cannot be the one and only present. In the year 2001 a present age will exist that is different from the present of 1901. In 2001, however, scholars will doubtless be right in seeking to grasp, as best they can, conditions that will inform them of the nature of the expressive awareness under which eighth-century waka poets wrote, and the manner in which these poems were received by their contemporaries, as also to search for intellectual coordinates of those ancient conditions and the concerns of a new present time. The condition for Hitomaro, in *his* time, was apparently the coexistence of kotodama and ga, just discussed.

The Exaltation of Kotodama

Hitomaro's most active period differed little from that of the Ōmi court period, in that for both the kotodama performed a vital function. During

Suiko's reign, Buddhism enjoyed only superficial success. But its gradual diffusion throughout Yamato daily life could not but alter to some degree the characteristic kotodama of Yamato. When Tenji Tennō was on the verge of death, his consort offered an uta that prayed for his resuscitation, as we have seen. Yet when Temmu Tennō became gravely ill, he ordered that sermons be preached on the *Medicine King Sūtra* at the temple of Kawaradera, and Buddhist priests were installed in the palace. In addition, Temmu sent a messenger to the temple of Asukadera with this announcement: "My health has worsened of late. I hope that, through the power of the Three Treasures, my health will be restored." He also had lamplight masses performed at Kawaradera (*Temmuki*, 383-84).[13] It is not known whether uta were presented on the occasion of Temmu's illness. But a practice of such antiquity was not likely to disappear quickly. As Buddhist prayers gained ever wider credence among the Yamato people, the kotodama was made to recede from the area of prayer for recovery from illness, not to mention from the panegyric and the elegy. This retreat did not occur until the end of Genshō Tennō's reign, however, and in Hitomaro's time the kotodama evidently still possessed active properties.

Hitomaro's poetry relied thoroughly on the kotodama. Unless this facet of his work is acknowledged, many of his uta cannot be properly interpreted. Let us first consider one of his panegyrics, recited when the poet was in attendance on Jitō Tennō:

Yasumishishi	She who holds sway,
Waga ōkimi no	Our Sovereign Lady,
Kikoshiosu	Is pleased to rule
Ame no shita ni	The many provinces
Kuni wa shi mo	That make up the land
Sawa ni aredomo	Lying beneath the heavens;
Yamakawa no	Yet her heart is drawn
Kiyoki kafuchi to	To the mountains and the streams
Mikokoro o	That make the pure landscape
Yoshino no kuni no	Of the province of Yoshino:
Hanajirau	There, upon the fields of Akizu,
Akizu no nobe ni	Where cherry blossoms fall,
Miyahashira	She causes the great pillars of
Futoshikimaseba	Her dwelling to be firmly placed.
Momoshiki no	Courtiers from the palace,
Ōmiyahito wa	Built with stone and wood aplenty,

---

[13] [The Three Jewels (or treasures) are the Buddha, the sutras, and the priesthood.— Trans.] An attempt was made to use Buddhist prayers for the recovery of Yōmei Tennō (r. 585-87) from an illness.

Fune namete	Cross the morning river
Asakawa watari	In boat after boat;
Funagioi	Cross the evening river,
Yūkawa wataru	Boat racing against boat.
Kono kawa no	May her reign be everlasting
Tayuru koto naku	As the flow of this river;
Kono yama no	May her power be more exalted
Iya takashirasu	Than the heights of this mountain.
Mina sosoku	Detached Palace of the Torrent,
Taki no miyako wa	Where waters plummet,
Miredo akanu kamo.	I never tire of beholding you!

Envoy

Miredo akanu	I never tire of beholding
Yoshino no kawa no	The river Yoshino where
Tokoname no	Evergreen mosses grow,
Tayuru koto naku	Perpetual as our lady's reign:
Mata kaerimin.	May she return to view it countless times.

(*MYS*, 1:36-37)

The purpose these poems served was not simply to praise the fine scenery. The most convincing explanation for Jitō's repeated excursions to Yoshino may be that they were carried out to bring her into contact with the wealth of supernatural forces within the Yoshino landscape, so that she might experience ochikaeri, rejuvenation (Yamamoto, 1962, 106-7). Temmu journeyed to Yoshino twice, Mommu twice, Genshō once, and Shōmu three times. By contrast, Jitō went to Yoshino thirty-one times (in addition to two earlier visits there as Temmu's consort). Her unusually frequent progresses to Yoshino are well explained by Yamamoto Kenkichi: his theory is that Jitō, who loved everything that was colorful and grand, harbored a wish "To be perpetually/An immortal maiden" (Tsune ni mo gamo na/Toko otome nite"; *MYS*, 1:22). By verbalizing each aspect of the Yoshino landscape and reciting these words as poetry, Hitomaro established, through the medium of his breath, a contact between the local supernatural powers and the person of the sovereign. The words used in this process were carefully chosen to include only those with auspicious meaning.

If this poem is interpreted according to modern sensibilities, Hasegawa Nyozekan might well be right to criticize its content as a mere assemblage of hollow encomiums. Such perceptions, however, are those of modern people, people who have isolated themselves from the spiritual aspects of mountains and streams. Hitomaro's contemporaries saw each word of his poem as a separate living entity. When he sings of "the mountains and the streams/That make the pure landscape," he does not use the word "pure" as a concept. Instead, the fresh purity of the mountains and streams is to enter Jitō as a vital force. Again, the line, "Where cherry blossoms fall," is quite unconnected to that medieval Japanese symbol of evanescence, the melancholy falling of blossoms. To the contrary, the splendid sight of scattering cherry blossoms was perceived as a dynamic force, an event filled with vitality, and was evoked in the anticipation that the healthy beauty of Jitō would be further enhanced.[14] The *Araragi* group's interpretation of this uta as "concrete and objective" and therefore excellent is accordingly misplaced.[15] Such critical conceptions did not exist in Hitomaro's time.

These kotodama-centered uta were heirs to an archaic legacy, the uta on beholding the country, a point which has been made by several scholars. Hitomaro's conclusion of his chōka with the line, "I never tire of beholding you!" (Miredo akanu kamo), which is repeated in the first line of the envoy, "I never tire of beholding" (Miredo akanu), is particularly indicative of the vitality within these uta of the word "mi" (behold); this word also appears in the term "kuni*mi* uta," uta on *beholding* the country. The tradition of beholding the country is thought to have been unique to Yamato and devoid of foreign elements.

A comparison of Hitomaro's uta with a shih recited, again, at Yoshino, but this time by Fujiwara Fubito (659-720), may serve to illustrate this fact:

> I compose my poems in a realm of peaks and waters,
> And I order banquets set within my ivy walls.
> Here the Dame of Nuribe flew skyward with a crane:
> Trapped in a weir, Tsuminoe married a mortal man.
> Haze on the mountain crags is emerald in the light;
> Sunlight gleams scarlet by the banks of the river.
> The abode of the immortals is less distant than I thought:
> We join in celebration of the wind in the pines.
>
> (*Kaifū*, 31)

The auspicious nature of the locale is expressed here as the realm of the immortals. The Dame of Nuribe tasted the herbs of the immortals and

---

[14] Ide Itaru has observed that flowers appear in uta from the Archaic Age forward as fetishes bearing vital force (Ide, 1973, 13-16).

[15] This characterizes the usual stance of the *Araragi* group rather than any particular member's expressed view, although Tsuchiya Bummei has referred to the "concrete and objective" qualities of this work in his criticism (Tsuchiya, 1951, 176-77).

flew into the heavens.[16] Tsuminoe was an immortal who descended to the world of men.[17] These legends were always cited in shih about Yoshino. Even when they were not the objects of direct reference, it seems to have been common practice to celebrate Yoshino as the realm of the immortals:

> Desirous of visiting the immortals' haunts,
> The royal party came to the banks of the Yoshino. . . .
>
> *(Kaifū, 48)*

> This is land inhabited by immortals:
> What need have we of those in Hakoya?
>
> *(Kaifū, 73)*

It is not known when Taoist thought was imported into Yamato, although Kwallŭk, a Paekche native serving at the court of Suiko, is recorded to have been a teacher of magic, which is to say that he taught the art of becoming an immortal.[18] Stories about immortals may thus have been brought into Yamato by Korean and Chinese immigrants and by Yamato youths returning from study on the continent. Such stories seem to have been combined with ancient legends about the Yoshino area, and, perhaps in the seventh century, a story evolved that conceived of this region as the realm of the immortals. Needless to say, eternal youth and immortality are the most important ideals of Taoism. Once the presence of female immortals in Yoshino was ascertained, then, it would have been a natural consequence for a female tennō desirous of eternal youth to make frequent progresses to that area. Yet Hitomaro, who accompanied her on these progresses, did not choose in composing his poem to mention the Dame of Nuribe or Tsuminoe, both affiliated with foreign concepts of immortals. I surmise that Hitomaro believed instead that his duty was to create expression that relied on the kotodama

[16] This seems to be founded on similar stories: cf. *Ryōiki*, 104-7, telling of a woman from the village of Nuribe in Uda, Yamato Province, who ate the herbs of the immortals and flew into the sky.

[17] This tale seems to tell of a friendship between Imashine, a man living near the Yoshino River, and a female immortal who temporarily changes herself into a wild mulberry branch (tsumi no e). The details of the story can only be inferred from ancient poetic references— that is, poems in the *Kaifūsō* (numbers 45, 72, 98-100, 102, in addition to that given here)—and three poems in the *Man'yōshū*, 3:385-87 (Takeda, 1927; Kojima, 1954).

[18] "Then Kwallŭk, a Buddhist priest from Paekche, arrived in Yamato. He presented books on the calendar with others on astrology and geography; he also presented books on the arts of invisibility and magic. At this time three or four were chosen to study these arts with Kwallŭk. Lord Tamafuru, founder of the Yako family of Recorders, studied calendrical art. Ōtomo Kōsō, village headman, studied astrology and the art of invisibility. Lord Yamashiro Hinitate studied the art of magic. All attained proficiency" (*Suikoki*, 140).

unique to Yamato, an expression putting into kotoba or language the spiritual aspects of the region, and to recite those kotoba.

Waka poets of a slightly later time than Hitomaro's were, by contrast, quite eager to use Taoist-style female immortals as poetic subjects. Three uta based on the Tsuminoe story appear in the *Man'yōshū*, and one of these (*MYS*, 3:387), composed by Wakamiya Ayumaro, is thought to date from about 738 (Tsuchiya, 1932, 270). Regardless of the validity of the particular dating, the concept of the immortals had clearly made its way into waka by the mid-eighth century. Hitomaro nonetheless kept to the ancient ways, perhaps because the celebration of foreign things was not only devoid of spiritual properties but would also weaken the activity of the Yamato kotodama by intermixing foreign words and concepts with the Yamato.

Hitomaro's elegies are another instance of his manifold reliance on the kotodama in his poetry. The various kinds of laments known as elegies (banka) in the *Man'yōshū* include poems presented at funerals, and they imply a wish that the deceased will return to life. The world of the dead in archaic Yamato had always been contiguous to the world of men, a fact reflected in the folklore of the gods Izanagi and Izanami at the Hill of Hira in the Land of the Dead (*JDK*, 194-95). People believed that even souls departed from their bodies could somehow be brought back. This was why the mogari ceremonies were instituted. From the late seventh century on, however, these ceremonies showed signs of becoming increasingly routine, perhaps because of a Buddhist influence that fostered a strong awareness of the reality of death. The first funeral of a tennō to include Buddhist rites was that of Temmu. By Jitō's time, Buddhist rites made up the majority of the funeral ceremonies, and with Genshō's funeral nearly all the rites were Buddhist (Itō Haku, 1975, 256-62). This tendency was accompanied by the adoption of cremation over burial: cremation was first performed at a royal funeral with that of Jitō. Mommu, Gemmei, and Genshō were also cremated. This must relate to the fact that no mogari elegies were composed after the time of Jitō (Kanda, 1972, 39-44). This in turn may aid us in understanding why Hitomaro did not present mogari elegies for either Jitō or Mommu, and why the elegy gradually underwent a transformation into the lament. The kotodama nevertheless maintained its vitality in the elegies of Hitomaro.

In Hitomaro's "Elegy for Crown Prince Kusakabe" (*MYS*, 2:167), the poet anticipates the beneficial action of the kotodama in his evocation of the line from remote antiquity, when heaven and earth were created, down to Prince Kusakabe's time. Genealogical narrative is one of the literary genres found among nomadic tribes, such as those of ancient Israel (Sekine, 1978, 141-42). Similar circumstances obtained in archaic

Yamato: when the royal genealogy was recited, its recipients definitely did not perceive it as a dry and meaningless array of proper nouns. An uta, however, cannot be formed solely from the enumeration of proper nouns; and, in its stead, the celebration of past royal deeds may have originated with Hitomaro. The words describing the illustrious royal line were inhabited by the kotodama, which was hoped to reach Crown Prince Kusakabe and effect his soul's return to life. If the prince would consent to return to life and, in time, to become tennō, then his rule would flourish like the "flowers in spring" (haru no hana) and the "full moon" (mochi-tsuki); the poet eagerly awaited, as for "rain from heaven" (amatsumizu), the prince's return, for then the people might trust in him, as in a "mighty ship" (ōfune). Hitomaro shows his disposition toward expression that relies on the kotodama in his array of highly auspicious guide phrases as well as in his plea for the return of the prince's soul: the poet laments the confusion among the prince's attendants in the now masterless palace.[19] This is most definitely not a lyric poem expressing simple grief.

All the uta mentioned above are formal and, as will be discussed subsequently, are considerably infused with Sinified expressive techniques. Yet the poet shows his reliance on the kotodama, a tendency still more pronounced in the informal uta. It is particularly conspicuous in those uta in which guide phrases play a major role. [They are, therefore, designated again by slant lines and italics.]

/Iwami no umi	/The Bay of Tsuno curves
Tsuno no urami o	In the Iwami Sea:
Uranashi to	People may well think
Hito koso mirame	That bay a poor one;
Kata nashi to	People may well think
Hito koso mirame	That beach a poor one.
Yoshie yashi	Well then, never mind!
Ura wa naku to mo	That bay may be poor indeed—
Yoshie yashi	Well then, never mind!
Kata wa naku to mo	That beach may be poor indeed,
Isana tori	But when the seagrass nears
Umihe o sashite	The shoals of Nikitazu,
Nikitazu no	By the stretch of sea
Ariso no ue ni	*Where whales are caught*;
Ka ao ouru	Grown a vibrant green,
Tamamo okitsumo	The jewel-like offing seagrass
Asa ha furu	Like morning wings

[19] "Harukusa no" (Spring plants)—a guide phrase similar to "Haru no hana" (Spring flowers)—was also used to evoke an auspicious event by kotodama.

Kaze koso yoseme	Is brought landward by the wind,
Yū ha furu	Like evening wings
Nami koso kiyore	Is brought landward by the waves;
Nami no muta	As, together with the waves,
Ka yori kaku yoru/	It is drawn first here, then there,/
Tamamo nasu	*As if jewel-like seagrass*
Yorineshi imo o	You drew near to me to sleep,
Tsuyu shimo no	You whom I have left behind
Okite shi kureba	*Like dew and frost on grass.*
Kono michi no	Ten thousand times I turn,
Yaso kumagoto ni	Pausing at each bend
Yorozu tabi	Of this myriad-twisting road
Kaerimisuredo	To catch a glimpse of you,
Iya tō ni	But the distant village
Sato wa sakarinu	Grows ever farther from me,
Iya taka ni	And the mountain path I tread
Yama mo koekinu	Climbs to ever greater heights—
Natsukusa no	Does my beloved,
Omoishinaete	Longing for me, hang her head,
Shinoburan	*A drooping summer plant?*
Imo ga kado min	That I may behold her gate,
Nabike kono yama.	Bend down, o you mountains!

(*MYS*, 2:131)

This is one of Hitomaro's finest works, the first of his "Poems of Longing for My Wife in Iwami." The first half of the uta, that is, the first twenty-two lines from "Iwami no umi" through "Ka yori kaku yoru," serves as one great guide phrase to evoke the line "Tamamo nasu" (As if jewel-like seagrass). Such sections have heretofore been called jo-kotoba, "prefaces," and uta having them were called "joka."

These so-called joka are to be found as early as the songs of the *Chronicles*: a good example is this one song sent by Nintoku to his consort, Iwanohime:

/Mimoro no	/In Ōiko Field,
Sono takaki naru	That sacred ground
Ōiko ga hara	Set high upon the butte,
Ōiko ga	There stands a mighty boar,
Hara ni aru	And in his belly side by side
Kimo mukau/	The two lobes of his liver lie:/

Kokoro o dani ka   In heart if not in body,
Aimowazu aran.   You surely wish to be with me?[20]

(KJK, Song, 60)

In the *Kojiki* episode that precedes this song, Iwanohime learns of Nin-toku's secret involvement with the young lady of Yata. Enraged, she goes to stay in the house of a Han Korean, Nurinomi, in the village of Tsutsuki, and refuses to return to the palace. The "preface" makes up the first six lines of the uta, but the import of the song rests only in the last two lines, "Kokoro o dani ka / Aiomowazu aran" (In heart if not in body, / You surely wish to be with me?). The guide phrase for "kokoro" is "kimo mukau"; and the guide phrase for the last two lines consists of the previous six. Added to this complexity, there is a further play in "Ōiko ga hara," which represents both the place name, Ōiko Field, and, by homonym, a mighty boar's belly. This image is, in its turn, enhanced by "That sacred ground / Set high upon the butte" [representing the first two lines of the original]. The result is a structure made up of a single-complex guide phrase.

A similar structure is to be found in "A Poem of Longing for My Wife in Iwami," although there it is expanded into a thirty-nine-line passage. The addition of a lengthy guide phrase, "Iwami no umi / . . . / Ka yori kaku yoru," to a short guide phrase, "Tamamo nasu," infuses the short one with vitality. The short guide phrases, "Kimo mukau" and "Tamamo nasu," are points of contact linking their respective long guide phrases to the import of the uta. Thus the "preface" appears to have been an archaic device that was expanded by the *Man'yōshū* poets.

This is further corroborated by the inclusion of uta with long guide phrases (fourteen chōka and four tanka) in Book 13 of the *Man'yōshū*, a book that resembles a collection of sixth- and seventh-century provincial songs. The *Collected Poems of Hitomaro* include seventy-one tanka and one sedōka (all of dubious authorship). There are also nine chōka and six tanka clearly marked as the work of Hitomaro, and these belong to the "joka" category.[21] And in tanka, a long guide phrase may perform the same function as it would in a chōka, as these examples from the *Collected Poems of Hitomaro* illustrate:

[20] ["Ōiko no" is a homonym for the word meaning "mighty boar" (ll. 3 and 4). "Kimo mukau" (The two lobes of his liver lie) is a guide phrase for "kokoro" (heart)—as in many cultures, the liver was thought the location of the emotions. Besides the one-line guide phrases of the first six lines, their entirety functions as a lengthy guide phrase for the last two.—Trans., Ed.]

[21] The numbers calculated are taken from *Man'yō Jokahyō* (Itō Haku, 1976, 282-300).

/Idete miru	/I go out and behold
Mukai no oka ni	The hills before me all abloom
Moto shigeku	With trees of every kind:
Sakitaru hana no	As they bear fruit,/ how can I not
Nara/zu wa yamaji.	Bring to fruition my great love?

(*MYS*, 10:1893)

/*Nubatama no*	/*Black as lily seeds,*
Kurokamiyama no	The Blackhair Mountains
Yamasuge ni	Where the mountain sedge
Kosame furishiki/	Is rained upon continuously/
Shikushiku omohoyu.	Continuous as my thoughts of you.

(*MYS*, 11:2456)

The import of both uta is contained in their final lines. But the addition of their four-line guide phrases infuses these conceptual statements with individualized vitality. These uta imply an anticipation that their kotodama will reach the person addressed in each poem, and so make the speaker's aspirations a reality.

The actual state of things was probably somewhat different. If the poet had previously been affected by Sinified ideas, he would have had little confidence in the capacity of an uta to remove the many obstacles from his path of love. But might it not have been the most moving of all experiences, even for those *Man'yōshū* poets given to new and foreign ways of reasoning, to bring their deepest selves into contact with the vital forces bestowed by the kotodama? If one says, "As I leave my house, I see that a great many trees are growing on the hills in front of me, and that those trees are in bloom," one has done no more than make an extremely ordinary statement: nothing in it would seem to evoke emotion. If, on the other hand, we read the poem as an association of ideas—flowers are followed by fruit, and love, like fruit, will grow—that concludes with ". . . how can I not / Bring to fruition my great love?" then the poem risks being denounced as mere word play.

Surely a modern Japanese need not be Hasegawa Nyozekan to feel like criticizing this poem as a piece of triviality. This, however, would be true only for the inhabitants of modern Japan, where the kotodama has reached its nadir. These two tanka may well have been profoundly moving to the people of Yamato in the Ancient Age. The trees mentioned in the first poem are not just any trees, but the trees that watch over the speaker's house. Because he has made the blossoms on those trees into words, the vitality produced by the blossoms as they, in due course, form fruit is certain to transfer itself to the object of the speaker's love, and to bring it to fulfillment. This assertion evidently moved not only the composer but his Yamato audience as well. Flowers brimmed with vitality and harbored spiritual forces capable of bringing good fortune.

A similar use of long guide phrases appears in tanka held to be the work of Hitomaro. The long guide phrase in his "Poem of Longing for My Wife in Iwami" undoubtedly relies on the kotodama, as it does also in this tanka by Hitomaro:

/Natsuno yuku	/The antlers of young deer
Oshika no tsuno no	Roaming the summer fields
Tsuka/ no ma mo	Are short / yet even for the
Imo ga kokoro o	Shortest time, would I forget
Wasurete omoe ya.	The memory of my love?

(*MYS*, 4:502)

If we examine the explicit statement "Tsuka no ma mo / Imo ga kokoro o / Wasurete omoe ya" (yet even for the / Shortest time, would I forget / The memory of my love?), we can only evaluate the expression as childish in the extreme. Yet with the addition of the guide phrase, "Natsuno yuku / Oshika no tsuno no," to these lines, the people of ancient Yamato would have been deeply moved. Newly emerging antlers are short and stubby, but because they soon develop into splendid structures, their early shortness is filled with the life force. The summer fields that form the background for this scene are likewise filled with the vitality of plants at their most vigorous stage of growth.

So it is that the simple declaration which forms the import of the uta is transformed into a moving expression. This process is not to be interpreted rhetorically: the guide-phrase section of an uta, for example, does not serve as a symbol of the import. The guide phrase "The antlers of young deer / Roaming the summer fields / Are short" is not a symbolic vehicle, not a mere semiotic signifier, but a lodging-place for entelechy. If spiritual qualities that cannot be captured by conscious language are considered "divine," then the guide phrase, which expresses the divine in a way incapable of reduction by deliberate rationality, becomes a condensation of myth.[22] The guide phrase may be thought to resemble proper nouns like "Omodaru" or "Ayakashikone," which comprise within themselves, in their identities as instantaneous deities, an "untold setsuwa."

Hitomaro's guide phrases are from a mythic language: the Archaic

[22] My conception of myth relies on Wellek and Warren's, but I have altered their definition to include narratives not necessarily concerned with the factual. My "myth" therefore involves accounts that express, from a suprarational standpoint, profound knowledge, and explanations, of natural and human phenomena.

Age bequeathed them a wealth of mythic qualities, and these guide phrases therefore possess properties different from those of the medieval preface and pillow-word. In this sense, the "Poem of Longing for My Wife in Iwami" is filled with mythic language. Up to now the section from "Iwami no umi" through "Ka yori kaku yoru" has been interpreted simply as a preface to "Tamamo nasu." This interpretation, however, cannot possibly explain why twenty-two of a total of thirty-nine lines are allotted to the "preface," and why three of the remaining seventeen lines are taken up by "pillow-words." Yamamoto Kenkichi made a crucial suggestion when he noted that, in uta with guide phrases and other matter so allotted, the section conveying the import possesses only a contextual subject: the true poetic subject rests within the allegedly subordinate section, and most especially within the pillow-words of this section (Yamamoto, 1962, 69-71). The most open expression Hitomaro can make of his poignant feelings for the wife who cannot accompany him is to describe her as "Yorineshi imo" (You [who] drew near me to sleep). He expresses his wife's gently reclining form with the image of "tamamo," jewel-like seagrass; and, so as to transfer vitality into that jewel-like seagrass, the poet begins with successive features of the Iwami coast, where he lived briefly with her. The resulting long guide phrase is certainly not a subordinate embellishment.

It is a matter of common knowledge that Hitomaro created many of the guide phrases he used, and this can only reflect the importance he attached to poetic expression based on the guide phrase, as it is surely indicative of a healthy and vigorous kotodama. After the end of the Ancient Age, newly composed guide phrases declined in number, as did the use of guide phrases in general. This, together with the increasing formality of the guide phrase, paralleled the gradual enervation of the kotodama.

Contact with Ga

Buddhism was not the only ideology to affect the ancient kotodama of Yamato. Confucianism and Taoist thought, those products of Chinese culture typical of the Han people, also had their effect.[23] This influence might best be represented in Hitomaro's time by the lines "Ōkimi wa / Kami ni shi maseba . . . " (Because our Ruler / Is indeed divine). Six examples, including variant transmissions, of this diction are found in uta, and all date from the reigns of Temmu and Jitō.

[23] This does not imply full Taoist scope. Taoism can exist only with the combined presence of the adepts, tao-shih, who specialize in ceremonies and austerities, along with tao-kuan, who assist in their operation. Neither kind of adept was present in Japan (Shimode, 1975, 176).

Ōkimi wa	Because our Ruler
Kami ni shi maseba	Is indeed divine,
Amakumo no	She makes her dwelling
Ikazuchi no ue ni	Far above the Thunder,
Iori seru kamo.	Among the heavenly clouds.

(*MYS*, 3:235)

This uta is thought to have been presented to Jitō by Hitomaro on the occasion of her progress to Thunder Hill (Ikazuchi no Oka). The uta is based on the poet's faith in the kotodama: his declaring that the tennō is superior to the Thunder God was expected to come true for her. Yet the emphasis placed on such content in this period requires us to consider a factor other than ancient Yamato tradition: the impact of Chinese civilization.

The ruler of Yamato was known as ōkimi up to the sixth century; this title was written with the characters for great ruler, ta-wang, in Chinese. The change from ōkimi/ta-wang to t'ien-huang (J. tennō, Heavenly Sovereign) apparently took place around the seventh century.[24] The statue of the Medicine King enshrined in the Kondō of Hōryūji has a halo bearing an inscription dated 607, in the reign of Suiko. The inscription contains the expressions "Heavenly Sovereign who rules the land" and "Great Ruler, Heavenly Sovereign."[25] Yet the Chinese rarely used the term "t'ien-huang" (tennō) for their rulers, nor are there any instances of its use in Korea.[26] Tsuda Saukichi has noted, however, that the supreme deity in the Taoist heaven is called t'ien-huang ta-ti, "Heavenly Sovereign, Great God," a term with religious connotations, and that this deity was also compared at times to earthly rulers (Tsuda, 1920, 474-91).[27] Because

[24] [Ever since this early designation, Japanese sovereigns have been known as "tennō." Since the term has nothing to do with empire—a nonclassical, and indeed a brief modern notion—"emperor," "empress," "imperial," and related terms are excluded from use in this *History*. "Tennō" or "sovereign," "consort," "royal," etc. are used when some designation must be given. "Emperor" will of course be appropriate in Vol. 5—Ed.]

[25] In recent decades a debate has continued over the authenticity of the Medicine King (Yakushi) statue as a work from Suiko's reign. Perhaps the most convincing explanation is one holding that the statue was purposely made in an antique style when Hōryūji was rebuilt (Machida, 1977, 268-80). Another explanation admits that the statue may be a later work but holds that the inscription dates from Suiko's reign (Takeuchi, 1952, 32-33). Whichever the case, the present concern turns on Hitomaro's celebration of the ōkimi and so is immune from major difficulties posed by this debate. A photograph of the inscription appears in *Hōryūji Meimon Shūsei* (Machida, p. 11).

[26] A single exception appears in 674 for the reign of Kao-tsung of the T'ang Dynasty. He is referred to as "t'ien-huang" (tennō) and his consort as "t'ien-hou" (heavenly consort).

[27] The passage is found in the "Ho-ch'eng T'u" of the Book of Prophecy attached to the *Ch'un Ch'iu (Spring and Autumn Annals)*: "The Heavenly Sovereign and Great God (t'ien-huang ta-ti) is the Pole Star." In other words, the t'ien-huang (tennō) was the Pole Star god who ruled over the Five Kings of Heaven. This god was identified with Fu-sang Ta-ti Tung-wang Kung, the supreme being (essentially an immortal) of Taoism.

the T'ang court had a high regard for Taoism, these concepts were also transmitted to Yamato, but probably not before they had become somewhat conflated with the Confucian precept that the Emperor (huang-ti) or Son of Heaven (t'ien-tzu) ruled by virtue of his having received the mandate of heaven. Yet the Chinese huang-ti (t'ien-tzu) was in all circumstances a real person executing the mandate of heaven in a real society: he was not a god. By contrast, when Hitomaro and his fellow poets recited, "Because our Ruler / Is indeed divine," they indicated that their "Ruler," unlike the Chinese huang-ti, was a divinity. In China the term "Heavenly Sovereign" did not signify the ruler of a nation; its use in Yamato to signify a ruler descended from the gods must be seen as having a Taoist basis.

For nearly two thousand years, Japan has eagerly adopted Chinese culture. Yet that continental culture has also contained certain elements that the Japanese have unconditionally rejected. Surely one such element was the concept that the mandate of heaven would be transferred to the most worthy leader, regardless of family connections to the previous sovereign. The Chinese huang-ti received the mandate of heaven and was able to maintain his dynasty as long as the mandate was faithfully executed. If his behavior ran contrary to the mandate of heaven, he would be immediately overthrown, and someone from another family would establish a new dynasty. The social origins of the new huang-ti were of no concern, if only he possessed both the sincere desire to obey the mandate of heaven and the power to carry it out in his government. The founders of the Chinese dynasties often came from the lowest classes of society; T'ai-tsu (the Grand Progenitor, i.e., Chao K'uang-yin) of the Sung Dynasty may serve as a representative example. Such things would not do, however, for the ōkimi of Yamato. It was absolutely necessary that the sovereign be a descendant of the gods. Therefore it was also necessary that he, or she, unlike the Chinese ruler, bear the title of a god, tennō (t'ien-huang.)

This belief did not originate in Hitomaro's time but evidently dated far back into the Archaic Age. Yamato contact with Chinese culture may, however, have given it added significance. In the third century, Yamato was in a state of enormous upheaval, which was remedied by the accession of "Queen" Himiko to a sovereign-like position. Her ability to quell the rebellion was not due to expertise in military tactics and strategy, nor to talent in planning and administration, but was solely a result of her extraordinary command of kuei-tao, shamanism.[28] This is at the very heart of the Yamato ōkimi's persona, and forms the source from which

[28] "They chose a woman named Himiko for their queen. She was skilled in shamanism and bewitched her people" (*Gishi Wajinden*, 81).

the deity setsuwa of the Plain of Heaven was narrated. At all costs, the Yamato ōkimi was to be linked by blood to the ancestral divinities in heaven, and absolutely no one outside the royal family was permitted to ascend the throne. This belief, which stood in direct opposition to the Chinese principle of a justified change of dynasties, became more clearly perceived through the Taoist concept of a heavenly sovereign. The result appears in the poetry of Hitomaro and his colleagues: "Because our Ruler / Is indeed divine. . . ." One might say, then, that Yamato confirmed itself as Yamato by contact with Chinese culture.

In Hitomaro's poetry we recognize a new awareness of Yamato ways brought about by contact with Chinese culture, with a resulting formation of a new Yamato literature. This can be seen, first of all, in his extended chōka structure and refined use of parallelism. In the early period of the *Man'yōshū*, chōka were ten or so lines long at most; these may be called small-scale chōka.[29] Hitomaro's average chōka was some tens of lines long, not to mention his longest work, the "Elegy for Prince Takechi" (*MYS*, 2:199), which runs to 149 lines. Since such large-scale chōka appeared quite unexpectedly, their presence may have been due to some special factor. This factor, I believe, was the influence of Chinese civilization, and that of the fu (rhapsody) in particular. We do not know which Chinese shih collections were available to Hitomaro, but if we recall that the shih and Chinese prose written at the Ōmi court were modeled on Six Dynasties literature, then very likely Hitomaro was aware not only of shih but of fu as well. Chinese shih are not considered long works, but this is true only in comparison with the fu. A shih is of course written in Chinese, an uninflected language made up of monosyllabic words; and even a rather short shih, if rewritten in the Yamato language, attains an impressive length. It is not inconceivable, therefore, that large-scale chōka were without parallel in Yamato poetry, and their sudden appearance leads one to presume that behind it lay a strong stimulus. It would be far more reasonable to conclude that this stimulus was provided by the fu, a literary form that must have seemed extraordinarily long to the people of Yamato.

If the chōka had undergone a *gradual* process of expansion, it would not be necessary to postulate the probable influence of the fu. But the expansion of the chōka occurred suddenly, and the composition of lengthy ones rapidly declined after Hitomaro's time. Yakamochi composed large-scale chōka in conscious imitation of Hitomaro, but these must be considered exceptions. Otherwise, in the last half of the Ancient Age the

---

[29] The only exception is "An Uta by Ikusa Ōkimi on Beholding a Mountain" (*MYS*, 1:5), which is twenty-nine lines long. Ōkimi appears to have been an immigrant (Itō Haku, 1975a, 25-26), sufficient reason for the exceptional length. The rest are from eleven to eighteen lines long.

chōka, whether the large-scale or the small-scale variety, fell into a decline. As we have been seeing, one of the chief characteristics of Japanese literature is brevity. From this perspective, the decline of the chōka was evidently a natural process. The composition of large-scale chōka, a practice that ran counter to this natural process and lasted less than twenty years, can be explained only if we consider it as having resulted from the strong impetus provided Hitomaro by the vast scope and overflowing welter of fu expression. This point is further strengthened by Hitomaro's apparent habit of drawing on fu techniques in forming antithetical parallelism for large-scale chōka.

Hitomaro's free use of these techniques in his chōka has been well known to scholars since the Edo period—so well known, indeed, that further elucidation seems strange. To think so, however, is to think of our present superfluity of studies of the Japanese classics. If we were to push back our awareness to a time between the late seventh and early eighth centuries, we might realize that Hitomaro's techniques are so innovative that they can only be termed extraordinary. To begin, Hitomaro's parallelism often results in antithetical parallelism in the strict sense of the term. Up to now in this discussion, the word "parallelism" (taiku) has been used in a rather broad sense.[30] I have taken parallelism to mean any two consecutive lines that correspond syntactically and semantically while differing in some way, large or small—since without difference they would be identical and constitute repetition. So that we may more closely observe parallel usage, however, it will be beneficial to narrow the boundaries of the definition and limit "couplet parallelism" only to corresponding consecutive lines that do not depict simultaneously existing things.

Let us consider, for example, these lines from the "Elegy for Prince Takechi":

> Ōmimi ni / Tachi torihakashi
> Ōmite ni / Yumi torimotashi
>
> You wear a sword / Clasped to your mighty person,
> You hold a bow / Clenched in your mighty hand.

---

[30] [Parallel constructions are a conspicuous feature of Chinese poetry. The author's argument now again turns on close distinctions. Following James J.-Y. Liu's discussion of parallelism in Chinese poetry, he uses "taiku" or "tsuiku" for Liu's "antithetical couplets." To this point in the translation, "parallelism" has been used to translate "taiku" and that will continue to be the case when the general phenomenon is meant. For the strictest kind of parallelism, "couplet parallelism" will be the term; for the less strict, "layered parallelism" (jōku) and "alternating parallelism" will continue to be the term for the ABAB form discussed earlier.—Ed.]

In this case the "hand" of the second line exists as part of the "person" of the first line; again, "sword" and "bow" are weapons belonging to the same man. Therefore this cannot be deemed strict couplet parallelism. Oppositions of this sort have been termed "layered parallelism" to distinguish them from couplet parallelism (Shirakawa, 1979, 158-59). Layered parallelism may be seen as occupying an intermediate position between repetition and strict couplet parallelism. With matters thus defined, we see that the parallelism found in the songs of the *Chronicles* and in norito is actually layered parallelism, and that couplet parallelism first appeared in the early age of the *Man'yōshū*.[31]

An early example appears in a passage of Princess Nukada's "Uta on the Relative Merits of Spring and Autumn":

> Nakazarishi / Tori mo kinakinu
> Sakazarishi / Hana mo sakedomo
>
> Birds that did not sing / Now come and sing;
> Flowers that did not bloom / Now burst into bloom.

This is an exception, however, and the frequent use of strict couplet parallelism began with Hitomaro. Even in his usage, couplet parallelism appears only in uta that have a ceremonial tone. By contrast, layered parallelism predominates in uta that express the poet's personal feelings (Shirakawa, 1979, 158-59). Hitomaro's "Uta in Praise of Yoshino," for example, has

> Fune namete / Asakawa watari
> Funagioi / Yūkawa wataru
>
> Cross the morning river / In boat after boat;
> Cross the evening river / Boat racing against boat.

The contraposition of "morning river" and "evening river" qualifies this as strict couplet parallelism, since a morning event cannot occur simultaneously with an evening event.

We should not fail to observe the ceremonial tone: this is a magic uta presented to Jitō by Hitomaro in the course of a progress to Yoshino, a journey she made to pray for eternal youth and longevity. Hitomaro, who attempts in this uta to move the local gods by the power of the kotodama, held that special Yamato faith. Yet in adopting a ceremonial and formal tone with which to invoke the local deities, he demonstrates an awareness that the appropriate technique under these circumstances

---

[31] Kakimura Shigematsu noted (1947, 252-57) that the songs in the *Chronicles* employ layered parallelism and that couplet parallelism appears only in the period of the *Man'yōshū*.

is that of Sinified strict couplet parallelism, and this awareness identifies him without doubt as a poet of the Ancient Age rather than of the Archaic Age. Moreover, Nukada's "Uta on the Relative Merits of Spring and Autumn" was presented at an elegant banquet before an audience highly sensitive to Chinese culture. If these two points are considered together, we ought to conclude that, as early as the time of the Ōmi court, experience counseled poets who required a ceremonial tone to employ as efficacious devices those techniques of couplet parallelism that were fixed in Chinese literature. Hitomaro undoubtedly placed an even more definite emphasis on this precept.

Chinese literature apparently had an impact on Hitomaro's work in another respect, the use of alternating parallelism. As we have seen, alternating parallelism is a technique in which the first and third lines make one contraposition and the second and fourth lines make another. The examples cited above, the "Uta on the Relative Merits of Spring and Autumn" and the "Uta in Praise of Yoshino," both employ strict couplet parallelism so far as meaning is concerned. At the same time, both use the technique of alternating parallelism in their form. This would apply, however, only to waka, which have as their units lines of five and seven syllables. If those examples were translated into Chinese, the sum of five and seven syllables, that is twelve syllables, would be roughly equivalent, in the amount of meaning conveyed, to a single five-character line of a shih.

If, then, we consider the shih as our standard, the instances cited above would each correspond to a single parallelism, and alternating parallelism in the waka could not easily correspond to alternating opposition in the shih unless the relevant waka lines were at least as many as the following, which are taken from the "Elegy for a Court Lady from Kibitsu" (*MYS*, 2:217):

1

Tsuyu koso ba / Ashita ni okite / Yūbe ni wa / Kiyu to ie
Kiri koso ba / Yūbe ni tachite / Ashita ni wa / Usu to ie

Though dew / Forms in the morning / And fades / In the evening;
Though mist / Rises in the evening / And vanishes / In the morning. . . .

The "Elegy for Princess Asuka" (*MYS*, 2:196) also contains alternating parallelism that extends over several lines:

2

Iwahashi ni / Oinabikeru / Tamamo mo zo / Tayureba ōru
Uchihashi ni / Oiōreru / Kawamo mo zo / Karureba hayuru

By the stone bridge / Lovely waterplants / Bend and grow: /
   Though cut, they grow anew;
By the plank bridge / River plants / Grow thick: / Though
   withered, they sprout anew. . . .

Alternating parallelism appears as well in the "Elegy for Prince Takechi":

3

Totonouru / Tsuzumi no oto wa / Ikazuchi no / Koe to kiku made
Fukinaseru / Kuda no oto mo / Ata mitaru / Tora ka hoyuru to

Your troops form ranks / To the sound of drums, / So loud we
   mistake it / For the voice of the thunder;
Shrill and sharp / Is the sound of fifes: / Could it be a tiger /
   Howling as he sees his foe?

4

Sasagetaru / Hata no nabiki wa / Fuyugomori / Haru sarikureba /
   No goto ni / Tsukite aru hi no / Kaze no muta / Nabikau
   gotoku
Torimoteru / Yuhazu no sawaki / Miyuki furu / Fuyu no hayashi ni /
   Tsumiji kamo / Imakiwataru to / Omou made / Kiki no
   kashikoku

The fluttering / Of banners raised aloft / Is like the flicker / Of
   windblown flames / Set by farmers / In every field / When spring
   has come / After winter's confinement;
The resonant sound of / Firm-held bows in use / Is fearsome to the
   ear: / We mistake it for / A whirlwind / That sweeps into / A
   wintry forest, / Scattering the falling snow.

The second example is a joka (preface poem) with respect to its meaning, but its form is that of alternating parallelism. The fourth example is made up of so many lines containing components so distant from their corresponding elements that, in terms of meaning, a syntactic reprise is not easily recognized. [Our translation does not reproduce the extraordinary ABAB adjustment of four sets of four lines.] The poet's formal aim was clearly to construct a large-scale alternating parallelism.

Despite the Han Chinese fondness for parallelism, which verges on the automatic, alternating parallelism did not appear in China until several centuries after the age of single opposition, a point I have mentioned before. Its sudden manifestation in Hitomaro's day can only be understood as the result of his having received some special stimulus. This stimulus, like that which motivated Hitomaro toward longer works, was

provided by the fu. This can be said because one of the chief characteristics
of Six Dynasties fu, known as p'ien-fu (couplet rhapsodies), is the heavy
use of couplet parallelism (Suzuki, 1936, 99-100). Whether this device
was Hitomaro's alone is still a matter of some question: the text of the
norito "Celebration of Prayers for the Coming Year," a composition
believed to date from the same period (that is, from the late seventh or
the early eighth century), is also interspersed with alternating parallelism.
Intellectuals connected with the Yamato court might somehow have developed a sudden interest in fu, although this is difficult to substantiate.
We should therefore take note of this fact alone, that during Hitomaro's
active period both the aim to create large-scale chōka and the use of
parallelism suddenly increased, only to decline in the age that followed.
My earlier description of Hitomaro's parallel techniques as "extraordinary" was meant to emphasize this fact.

Contact with Chinese culture acted in a second way to form a new
Yamato literature in the formalizing of realism and fictitiousness in Hitomaro's poetic expression. In archaic song, as in waka composed before
Hitomaro's time, the subject of the work was seen as a real person or
thing. When the God of Eight Thousand Halberds gets in a tangle over
his love affairs and is roundly scolded by his consort Suseribime, or when
Kenzō Tennō rewards Okime, the old woman who shows him the burial
site of his father's bones, with exceptionally kind treatment, the people
of the Archaic and Ancient Ages would have taken these as actual events.
Thus the uta in these stories were also thought to be based on real events.
This was true for Hitomaro as well: his exposition of the royal line in
the "Elegy for Prince Kusakabe" (MYS, 2:167), from the far-distant
creation of heaven and earth and the descent of the Heavenly Grandchild
down to the reign of Temmu, was undoubtedly presented as reality. Yet
this "reality" of the royal line was real to the poet because the Yamato
people firmly believed it to be a faithful representation from remote times
and therefore true beyond doubt. It was not a reality experienced by
Hitomaro himself. Literary works in this period that concern a reality
experienced by the composer himself, as well as by many in his audience,
correspond to kabuki plays on contemporary subjects (sewamono), whereas
the past reality that formed the subject matter for archaic and ancient
works may be attributed the reality of a historical kabuki (jidaimono).
Hitomaro seems to have been the first to create poems that concerned
experiences shared by his contemporaries.

The poetic recitation of past events took the place of genealogical
narrative as a result of an expressive awareness dating from remote times
and an anticipation of the action of the kotodama. The use of experienced
reality as subject matter, however, has a different significance. In the

"Elegy for Prince Takechi" (*MYS*, 2:199), Hitomaro relates, in a descriptive-narrative mode not seen elsewhere in chōka, the extent of the prince's heroism during the Jinshin War. A lengthy passage follows [guide phrases again marked]:

Ōmimi ni	You wear a sword
Tachi torihakashi	Clasped to your mighty person,
Ōmite ni	You hold a bow
Yumi torimotashi	Clenched in your mighty hand,
Miikusa o	As you issue commands
Adomoitamai	To the royal forces:
Totonouru	Your troops form ranks
Tsuzumi no oto wa	To the sound of drums,
Ikazuchi no	So loud we mistake it
Koe to kiku made	For the voice of the thunder;
Fukinaseru	Shrill and sharp
Kuda no oto mo	Is the sound of fifes:
Ata mitaru	Could it be a tiger
Tora ka hoyuru to	Howling as he sees his foe?
Morohito no	The sound strikes terror
Obiyuru made ni	Into every soul.
Sasagetaru	The fluttering
Hata no nabiki wa	Of banners raised aloft
Fuyugomori	Is like the flicker
Haru sarikureba	Of windblown flames
No goto ni	Set by farmers
Tsukite aru hi no	In every field
Kaze no muta	When spring has come
Nabikau gotoku	*After winter's confinement*;
Torimoteru	The resonant sound
Yuhazu no sawaki	Of firm-held bows in use
Miyuki furu	Is fearsome to the ear:
Fuyu no hayashi ni	We mistake it
Tsumuji kamo	For a whirlwind
Imakiwataru to	That sweeps into
Omou made	A wintry forest,
Kiki mo kashikoku	Scattering the falling snow.
Hikihanatsu	Your forces shoot
Ya no shigekeku	Volleys of arrows
Ōyuki no	That fall on the enemy,
Midarete kitare	A great snowstorm;
Matsurowazu	And when the rebels
Tachimukai shi mo	Confront you, bound to die—

Tsuyu shimo no	As fade the dew and frost—
Kenaba kenu beku	If die they must,
Yuku tori no	And armies vie against each other
Arasou hashi ni	*As do birds in flight*,
Watarai no	Divine winds blow
Itsuki no miya yu	From the Great Shrine
Kamukaze ni	Of Watarai,
Ifuki matowashi	Sowing confusion
Amakumo o	Among the enemy,
Hi no me mo misezu	Covering the sun's eyes
Tokoyami ni	With heavenly clouds,
Ōitamaite	And bring darkness to the earth:
Sadamete shi	Subduer of the enemy,
Mizuho no kuni o. . . .	Our land, with its nodding ears of rice. . . .

Because a battle scene is depicted here, several writers have linked this mode to expression in heroic poetry. But heroic poetry is, so to speak, historical drama, and clearly differs from expression such as is found in this poem. This poem has its essence in the emotional evocation of a reality that is known to Hitomaro's audience through contemporaneous experience. Each phrase and line was thus newly created so as to make the audience feel it had actually experienced the scene. The poem bears no resemblance whatsoever to heroic poetry or to any other orally composed works that rely on formulas.

The "Elegy for Prince Takechi" contains examples of alternating parallelism on a large scale, as we have seen. In this there lies a meticulous design. In formal terms these examples of alternating parallelism form antitheses, but when meaning is considered, the elegy is discovered not to contain any real couplets (what was termed strict couplet parallelism). Five years before he composed this elegy, Hitomaro employed strict couplet parallelism in his "Uta in Praise of Yoshino" (*MYS*, 1:36). Obviously he could not have been ignorant of parallelism formed from the opposition of such nonsynchronous phenomena as "morning" and "evening," "spring" and "autumn." The 149-line "Elegy for Prince Takechi" utilizes the complex alternating parallelism form, and yet strictly defined parallelism in adjacent lines is completely absent. This can only mean that Hitomaro deliberately avoided its use.

His reason may have been that strict couplet parallelism was not appropriate for expressing actual sensations (Shirakawa, 1979, 159). For example, a line of an uta describes a morning scene: if a line describing evening is then placed in opposition to the line concerned with morning, this description of evening would be a conceptual matter, and so dilute the actual sensation of "morning" to which it was counterposed. Again, if two lines opposing spring and autumn are used in connection with action in a summer scene, the conceptual nature of this parallelism would greatly weaken the audience's sense of being present at the scene evoked in the work. In certain kinds of literary expression, the emotions evoked by the work have their roots in experiences common to both the composer and his audience. These works do well to avoid an overconceptualizing that would attenuate the audience's sense of immediacy. Hitomaro evidently felt this.

This manner of presentation makes Hitomaro seem as though he might have made use of that literary expression which the *Araragi* group called "objective portrayal." This group labored under a delusion, however, when they assumed that objective portrayal existed in Hitomaro's time. For this reason, I have spoken of kabuki on contemporary subjects expressly so as to avoid similar misconceptions. The scenes performed in kabuki on contemporary subjects belong to the same period as that of the audience, and the emotions evoked by these scenes are rooted solely in realities shared by the members of the audience in their daily experiences. In other words, actual events do not always form the subject of a performance. On the contrary, fictional events are the norm. Through Hitomaro's poems, the members of his audience sought a source of emotion in the depicted phenomena that would enable them to regain their own experience. Yet the very phenomena Hitomaro describes, and the manner used to describe them, are not without their fictitious elements.

Some of the important works within Hitomaro's canon of informal poems include the group known as the "Poems of Longing for My Wife in Iwami" (*MYS*, 2:131-39). The first chōka of this group has been given, and one of its envoys is especially renowned:

Sasa no ha wa	Rampant on the mountain,
Miyama mo saya ni	Bamboo leaves rustle
Sayagedomo	Restless in the wind—
Ware wa imo omou	Yet steadily do I long for her,
Wakarekonureba.	For we have just parted.

(*MYS*, 2:133)

This entire subgroup of one chōka and three envoys (131-34) has been thought to brim with the poet's true emotions. One interpretation, however, contends that a consideration of this subgroup in relation to variant transmissions and in correspondence with the second subgroup of the series (135-39) reveals that its audience consisted of palace ladies, and that the subgroup itself was presented before this audience a second time in a revised version. According to this reading, then, Hitomaro was not necessarily describing an actual event. He probably was actually posted to Iwami and actually did form an attachment there to a certain woman. But this is not to presume a fact for every detail of the poems.

Moreover, the traditional idea that the woman of Yosami, whose envoy (MYS, 2:140) follows this group, is Hitomaro's Iwami wife, is labeled pure fiction (Itō Haku, 1975a, 279-303). Another group, the "Poems Written in Deepest Mourning" (MYS, 2:207-16), has been interpreted as an expression of Hitomaro's true feelings, an overflowing of boundless grief over the death of his wife. The unified structure of the whole, however—despite a perceptible time difference between the first and second set of chōka and envoys—is attributable to the poet's awareness of onlookers besides himself. This seems to have resulted from Hitomaro's undeliberate projecting into his work techniques that were employed in the composition of uta to be presented at court salons. This poetic group, then, should probably be regarded as possessing some fictional content (Itō Haku, 304-26). Again, the "Deathbed Uta of Hitomaro" (MYS, 2:223) and the two uta recited at that time by his wife, the woman of Yosami (MYS, 2:224-25) inform us that Hitomaro met his death on the road, with a rock for his pillow, at a place called Kamo Mountain in Iwami Province. Here is his presumed deathbed poem:

Kamoyama no	Here I lie, alas!
Iwane shi makeru	With my head laid for its pillow
Ware o kamo	On Mount Kamo's crags,
Shirani to imo ga	While my beloved, unaware,
Machitsutsu aruran.	Must anxiously await me.
	(MYS, 2:223)

And here are the woman of Yosami's two poems on Hitomaro:

Kyō kyō to	Today he'll come, today:
Aga matsu kimi wa	Thus have I awaited him.
Ishikawa no	Tell me, are his ashes not
Kai ni majirite	Mingled with the shells
Ari to iwazu ya mo.	Of the Ishikawa River?[32]
Tada ni awaba	I would meet him face to face,
Aikatsumashiji	But such a meeting cannot be:
Ishikawa ni	Ishikawa River clouds,
Kumo tachiwatare	Rise and show yourselves, so that
Mitsutsu shinowan.	By seeing you, I might think of him.
	(MYS, 2:224-25)

[32] [Following cremation, the ashes were apparently scattered upon a river.—Trans.]

The tradition of meeting an untimely death on the road and leaving behind an uta bemoaning one's fate had been in existence since archaic times. Prince Yamato Takeru stands out as the first poet to compose in this vein. Crown Prince Karu and Prince Arima might also be mentioned. Hitomaro may have seen himself as another member of this tradition. Imagining himself to be a character within a play who, on the verge of death, recites a lament, Hitomaro would have presented his uta to the court salon. This would mean that the woman of Yosami, Hitomaro's Iwami wife, did not exist except, perhaps, as a part to be played by one of the court ladies (Itō Haku, 327-47).

Itō bases his theory on the view that Hitomaro received court favor for his recitations of new poems and that he was, so to speak, a leading performer of uta. If the scene of his presentation was a royal progress or a state funeral, Hitomaro might have created a panegyric or a formal elegy. If a court salon gave an elegant banquet, he might have composed informal elegies or love poems, literary forms that allowed fictitious elements. Whether the occasion was formal or informal, he would have given a poetic "star performance." This method of interpretation will probably never meet with the concurrence of those scholars of Japanese literature imbued with the *Araragi* group's objective-portrayal theory. Yet this view, that Hitomaro drew his poetic subjects directly from his own experience, resembles the late nineteenth- and early twentieth-century "I-novel" (shishōsetsu) and *Araragi*-group tanka—neither of which could distinguish between author and speaker—in its adoption of a partly erroneous version of nineteenth-century Western realism.

In both the Archaic and the Ancient Ages, the norm was instead to create in one's composition a speaker separate from the composer. The God of Eight Thousand Halberds adopts an aggressive stance and tells Suseribime, "If I were drawn away from here, / Then you might say, / 'I'll never cry,' " but the truth is that she would surely burst into tears. His consort replies, "I am, alas, / Only a woman, / And but for you, / I have no husband," and begs him to stay with her that night. To judge solely from the narrative context and the verse in which these songs form a first-person dialogue, one might conclude that the God of Eight Thousand Halberds and Suseribime composed and recited their own work. This is obviously wrong, however: both the god and Suseribime are no more than the speakers of the work, and are certainly not its authors.

The separation of author from speaker exists throughout the songs of the *Chronicles* and was inherited by Hitomaro. Kanda Hideo detects such a separation in the uta Hitomaro dedicated to royal patrons. One such group, which bears the forenote "Two uta dedicated to Princess Hatsusebe and Prince Osakabe by Kakinomoto Hitomaro" (*MYS*, 2:194-95), contains the following passage [with guide phrases indicated]:

Tamamo nasu	The prince my husband,
Ka yori kaku yori	Whose body bent to mine,
Nabikaishi	Moving first here, then there
Tsuma no mikoto no	*Like jeweled water grasses,*
Tatanazuku	Whose skin was soft to touch
Nikihada sura o	*As folded silk,*
Tsurugitachi	No longer does he lie near me
Mi ni soeneneba	*Close as a sharp-edged sword,*
Nubatama no	And so our bed is lonely in
Yotoko mo aruran	The night—*black as lily seeds.*
Soko yue ni	These are the reasons why
Nagusamekanete. . . .	I cannot be consoled. . . .

(*MYS*, 2:194)

This love scene might appear unduly prying and insulting to the princess. But Kanda argues that this passage is not at all unnatural if it is read as a poetic expression of Princess Hatsusebe's own feelings for her deceased husband, Prince Kawashima (Kanda, 1972, 233).[33] In analytical terms, this "poetic expression of the princess' feelings" is the creation within a work of a speaker separate from the author. On the other hand, Hitomaro's appearance as the speaker within one of his own compositions, where he dies on Kamo Mountain with a rock for his pillow, suggests that there is no separation between composer and speaker when both have the same identity. The Hitomaro within the work, however, is a fictional character modeled on Hitomaro the poet, just as the kabuki playwright Namiki Shōzō, a character in the kabuki play *Yadonashi Danshichi Shigure no Karakasa*, is modeled on the author of the play, Namiki Shōzō (1730-73).[34] In both cases the author and the speaker must be taken to possess separate individualities.

Despite the archaic heritage, this technique of radical separation probably encountered considerable opposition from Hitomaro's audiences. He employed it nonetheless, perhaps because the presence of certain conditions ensured a receptive audience. These conditions were probably created by the diffusion of Chinese shih and fu into Japan. Let us begin by considering poetry in which the speaker of a work has an identity separate from the composer. Shih Ch'ung (249-300) composed a yüeh-

---

[33] Further examples exist of a speaker who is not the composer: *MYS*, 9:1683-84 and 1701-3.

[34] The kabuki playwright who appears in the play was named Heiuemon when it was performed in the intercalary Ninth Month of 1767. This character was evidently renamed Shōzō, like the dramatist, in 1790, and the latter name has been used ever since in performance, including the most recent staging in August 1980 at the National Theatre in Tokyo.

fu (ballad) entitled *Wang Ming-chün Tz'u (Wen Hsüan*, 27). This tells the story of Wang Chao-chün, who was married, out of Han policy considerations, to Ch'an-yü, the King of Hsiung-nu. The poem is expressed in the first person, and the speaker is Wang Chao-chün: "Though born into a Han family, / I now depart for Ch'an-yü's house."

Several instances of speakers who are not the composers also appear in Six Dynasties poetry. Lu Yün (262-303), in his "Poem Sent by Ku Yen-hsien to His Wife" (*Wen Hsüan*, 24) establishes a speaker (Ku Yen-hsien's wife) whose husband has left her behind in Wu to enter government service in Loyang. She speaks with some bitterness of her conviction that her husband is enjoying himself in a capital teeming with beauties.[35] The motif of a wife expressing bitterness at being separated from her husband is found frequently in Six Dynasties poetry by men, and if we assume that this separation might have resulted from the husband's death, we have before us Princess Hatsusebe's situation. If Yamato audiences were aware that Chinese poets often employed a technique creating a female speaker pining for her lover and used a female speaker in their poetic presentations, then Hitomaro and his fellow poets may not have had to fear complaints about excessive prying or lese majesty—even if the poetic subject was the conjugal emotions of a princess.

Was it really possible at this time for a poet like Hitomaro to fictionalize himself as a character in one of his poems? This question can only be addressed by citing examples of fu in which speakers far more fictitious than the dying Hitomaro appear. In "The Rhapsody of Master Imaginary" (Tzu-hsü Fu) and "The Rhapsody on the Imperial Park" (Shang-lin Fu; *Wen Hsüan*, 7-8) of Ssu-ma Hsiang-ju, there are three speakers, Master Imaginary (Tzu-hsü), Master Nonexistence (Wu-yu Hsien-sheng), and the Duke of Nothingness (Wu-shih Kung): the very names bespeak the fictitiousness of the characters. Again, Yang Hsiung (53-18 B.C.) creates two speakers named the Master of Writingbrush Grove (Han-lin Chu-jen) and Master Ink Visitor (Mo Ko-ch'ing) in his Chang-yang Fu (*Wen Hsüan*, 9). Okura may have borrowed this technique in creating the Poor Man and the Destitute Man for his poem "A Dialogue on Poverty" (*MYS*, 5:892). We may best conclude, then, that by Hitomaro's day poets were familiar with fu that possessed fictitious speakers. Very well, the poets certainly created obviously fictitious speakers. But could a poet also appear in his own work as a fictitious speaker? Ts'ao Chih (A.D. 192-232) writes in his preface to "Rhapsody on the Goddess of the Lo" (Lo-shen Fu; *Wen Hsüan*, 19:402):

---

[35] The title in the *Wen Hsüan* is wrong. Two titles actually exist in the *Anthology of Lu Shih-lung*: "A Poem Sent by Ku Yen-hsien to His Wife" and "The Wife's Reply." The title of the former was apparently attached to the latter.

In the third year of Huang-ch'u (222) I traveled to the capital to attend court, and on the way back I crossed the Lo River. The ancients have said that the goddess of this river is named Princess Fu. Inspired by Sung Yü's reply to the King of Ch'u, in which he told the story of this goddess, I have composed this fu.

The fu itself also commences in the first person: "As I was coming from the capital, / Returning to the Eastern Provinces. . . ." The speaker is the poet, but his affair with the goddess, who appears later in the fu, is no ordinary experience. When the events within a work are unmistakable fabrications, one must obviously interpret the "I" whose actions are described in the work not as identical to the poet but rather as a fictitious speaker who reflects the composer's identity.

If, then, Hitomaro's audience was well aware (and Hitomaro knew they were) that the technique of creating fictitious speakers appeared in fu, the poet could have safely fashioned himself into the speaker of one of his own compositions. I do not mean to argue that he adopted the technique of a fictitious speaker from Ts'ao Chih's fu. This technique is found in songs predating the Ancient Age, as we have seen. We may safely say that Hitomaro continued that native tradition in his waka. The problem lies, rather, on the side of the audience. If Hitomaro had not composed for people with a wide knowledge of Chinese shih and fu, he might not have been able to experiment on quite such a radical scale. The same can be said for his use of guide phrases, his experiments with narratives that resemble drama on contemporary subjects, his development of large-scale parallelisms and strict couplet parallelism—and, moreover, his praise of the ōkimi as tennō (t'ien-huang), the Heavenly Sovereign. In all these respects, his poetry was based on traditions handed down from archaic times. On the other hand, his audience had a considerable understanding of Chinese civilization and strove to bring Yamato closer to it. It was from the combination of these two forces that Hitomaro's poetry came into being.

CHAPTER 8

Setsuwa Expression

FROM ORAL TO WRITTEN NARRATIVE

Works like the *Kojiki* have provided us with the main materials for studying stories of the gods and of the royal house, and the setsuwa hitherto discussed are presumed to have been handed down as oral tales from the Archaic Age. We presume oral transmission, because even if we grant the existence of literacy, stories to which special value or authority was attached were, in general, made known orally. On the other hand, it is a fact that written texts of setsuwa predated the compilation of the *Kojiki*. The people who possessed and read them must have constituted an extremely small number of persons of position, but it cannot be denied that the works were read. Yet it was the original nature of setsuwa to be orally delivered and aurally received. The written and visually received versions were as shadows compared with the original brightness of orally delivered and aurally received setsuwa.

Oral relation may decline, and when it is no longer possible to recover the so-to-speak music of works experienced in oral delivery, the result is a body of setsuwa transcribed in texts that amount to no more than information written down and restricted in value to supplementary material for historical and folkloristic study. If, however, in writing down the story, the writer commands language suitable for written literature and if the writer works with a lively image of oral literature, then the result, even when the original version has been lost, will retain its vitality as interesting narrative handed down in writing. Setsuwa collections like the medieval *Uji Shūi (A Collection of Tales from Uji)* are good examples of this.

The line of setsuwa delivered in writing probably originated from what remains in the *Hitachi Topography* (pp. 72-74). There is a story that to the south of the village of Karuno in the district of Kashima there once was a place called the pine grove of Unai. Once long ago, a lad named Iratsuko of Sanuta in Naka loved a lass named Iratsume of Aze in Unakami. Meeting her unexpectedly at a betrothal or mating gathering, he addressed a poem to her.

Iyazeru no	Excuse me, please—
Aze no komatsu ni	On the small pines of Aze
Yūshidete	Tree offerings hang down,

Wa o furimiyu mo	Looking as though they wave to me—
Aze to koshima wa mo.	Oh, lovely small isle of Aze!

To which she replied:

Ushio ni wa	"When the tide is full,"
Tatan to iedo	I said, "I will stand up for you."
Nase no ko ga	O you boy of Nase—
Yasoshima kakuri	While I was hidden among eighty isles,
Wa o miseba shirishi.	You sought me out and showed you care.

(*Fudoki*, 7, 8)

Thereafter the pair left the site of the party and, in order to avoid being seen by others, entered the pine grove, free from observation, pledging each other their love, and, as the story runs:

Hands held in hands, knees joined with knees, they gave full vent to their yearnings and whispered their anxieties. The yearnings they had felt for so long now had relief, and they laughed again and again with their new-found joy. It was just the hour that the dew begems the tree fronds, just the season of the golden autumn breeze. Where the moontree shone in its full brilliance off at the western shores the cranes were crying out in flight, the voice of the wind in the pines hummed and hummed its song as migrant geese bore off on their northern flight. By the deserted and silent peak an old spring trickled from the rockface, and in the deserted night the newly accumulated frost could be seen even through the foggy air. On the nearby hills, the leaves of the woods shone full with a color that gazed on itself, while at the sea beyond there was no sound save the voice of the surf on the rocky shoreline. To be there this evening was a joy beyond which there is no other, and the pair savored to the full the sweet joys of mutually opening their hearts, forgetting in their devotion that dawn would soon break. Suddenly the cocks were crowing, and dogs barked as the sky began to glow, and it was day. At this the young pair felt helpless, and feeling deep shame at being seen, they were transformed into a pair of true pines.

There is much in this that shows a Japanese hand.[1] But the main style involves just that level of mastery of ornate Chinese prose then typical. It has been speculated that the author may have been Fujiwara Umakai,

---

[1] Some phrases are not genuinely parallel and others are unprecedented in their grammar. The idea of the sweetness of talk is distinctly Japanese. And some combinations of Chinese characters are simply mistaken.

the governor of Hitachi.[2] The evidence of authorship is not conclusive, but the writer had certainly received standard training in Chinese verse and prose. Here is a style that, far from preserving in folk tales the smell of the earth, has so embellished matters with the rhetoric of Chinese prose that the rich beauty of the telling in the folk original has been gravely marred. Such at least was the heated judgment of Motoori Norinaga and others.

The work is certainly open to such criticism. But we must think of the age. People had not yet developed feasible methods for writing prose in natural Japanese. Writing Chinese prose was the one method showing promise, and the only model available to the age was the ornate style of the Six Dynasties. It should be thought an entirely natural development that this kind of prose should have come into being. Rather than criticize the overblown language, I should think it better to observe the birth of an awareness that there was a value in writing down even provincial folk tales as something amounting to genuine literature. It was because this attitude existed that Yamanoe Okura could base a chōka and hanka on the legend of the magical stones of Jingū (consort of Chūai Tennō and regent) as she was setting off to invade Korea (*MYS*, 5:813-15), prefacing his chōka with Chinese prose. It was not just Okura. Many other writers of the time took delight in drawing on popular stories for their poems. A reflection of their pleasure can be found in the run of legendary poems ("Yoshi aru uta") in Book 16 of the *Man'yōshū*. There is also the story of Urashima (*MYS*, 9:1740-41), which is based on a story found in the *Tango no Kuni Fudoki* (pp. 70-77; *Tango Topography*).[3] This is just one of the many examples of provincial setsuwa of the common people being taken over by waka, and it should also be observed what an elaborate style is used for it.

The compilers of the *Topographies* did not try to drape everything with Chinese-style brocades. There were occasions when the dominantly ornate style of the *Izumo Topography* required intermission in favor of native Japanese, and then there was no need to stick at all costs to the proprieties of Chinese prose. We have already noted the story of how the god Yatsuka Mizuomitsuno could rope an island, pull it to the mainland, and create the province of Izumo. In this story the Yamato language is set down phonetically to the extent feasible, and guide phrases are used to activate the kotodama. For its musical key, the *Izumo To-*

---

[2] The first to suggest that the author might be Umakai was Suga Masatomo (1824-97); see *Suga Zenshū*, p. 631. There is also a theory that the story was composed by the poet Takahashi Mushimaro (Kawara-Kojima, 1937), 56-57), but this has not won acceptance.

[3] [This story of Urashima's luxurious stay with the Sea God's daughter is resembled in outcome by the story of Rip Van Winkle and is popularly known in Japan today as "Urashima Tarō"; the poem is far more caustic (than modern revisions) about Urashima's giving up his fine life in an immortal world.—Ed.]

pography does tune to the proper pitch of Chinese prose, and the elaborated style incorporates not a few Chinese quotations (Kojima, 1962, 638-50). Yet here and there appear sections in which the pulse of Japanese prose is also felt.[4] The fact probably testifies to the need for Japanese to be used in weighty setsuwa if the kotodama were to work. In the part on pulling the island to form the province, certain phrases such as "Come, land! Come, land!" are repeated in four instances, as the following excerpt shows by example:

> ... and he wondered, "Is there too much land here?" And he spoke: "There is indeed too much land here"; and he took up a spade curved like a maiden's breast and he thrust it hard into the land, as if into the gills of a great fish; and he cut away the promontory as easily as nodding plumegrass; ... and he pulled and pulled it in like frost-withered vines, slowly, slowly like a river boat; "Come, land! Come, land!" he called ... " (*Izumo no Kuni Fudoki*: 100-102).

Obviously the repeated phrases are expressions possessing kotodama. Had this been thought a trivial story, there would have been no need of the Yamato way of narrating.

Another story will illustrate the decorum involved. There was in Yasuki a storyteller named Imaro. When the daughter who was his heart's delight was swimming in free pleasure along the seashore, she was attacked by a wanizame [a shark or sea lawyer say the Japanese-English dictionaries], which bit off her legs, killing her. The father stood by her corpse [at the mogari] in great agitation, at last addressing himself to the gods. Here is the account:

> At Himesaki, where the remains of his assaulted daughter had been placed, the father was seized by a grievous anger, shouting to the heavens, stamping the earth; when he walked he groaned, and when he sat he wept. In daytime and in nighttime he agonized, unable to leave the place of her temporary enshrinement [i.e., mogariya]. Some days passed in this fashion. Now, as he filled with resentment, he sharpened his arrows and honed his halberd; and he chose a suitable place, one where he could raise up his invocation: "You fifteen million deities of the sky, you fifteen million deities of the earth, venerated throughout this land in the holy quiet of three hundred

---

[4] Whenever divinities are expected to appear, the style used is always basically Japanese. This can be seen throughout the place-name setsuwa: Sada no Ōkami (p. 184), Tagitsuhiko no Kami (p. 172), Ajisukitakahiko no Kami (p. 225), etc. There are two exceptions—that of Sayū (p. 204) and Ayo (pp. 236-38)—but in the former human characters appear along with the goddess Izanami, and in the latter the concern with spirits leads to a style like that used to describe the appearance of divinities.

and ninety-nine shrines, and with them, you others of the ocean depths, may the gentle sides of all you gods remain in peace, may the active sides of all young gods attend to what Imaro beseeches in this place. If there truly be a divine spirit, take pity on my sore heart that I may know that the divine spirit is a god indeed" (*Izumo no Kuni Fudoki*, 104).

Up to the point where Imaro speaks, the style follows the requirements of Chinese prose—to be sure not in a manner matching that of the *Hitachi Topography*, but at least more or less proper as Chinese. What ensues is nothing other than Yamato words recorded in Chinese: in fact, as Chinese it is nearly devoid of meaning. This may have something to do with the speaker's being a storyteller, but essentially it is because prayers to the gods (here in both their nikimitama, or gentle, and aramitama, or active, roles) are of such gravity that for the kotodama to work, the Yamato language must be employed. The shift in style is founded on this assumption, which is reflected in the styles of the *Kojiki* as well. This evidence tells us that the first stage of the Ancient Age was a period of transition from the indigenous Yamato culture to that of a foreign civilization.

The World of Yasumaro

When Ō no Yasumaro compiled the *Kojiki*, his sources were the *Royal Genealogy* and the *Legends of Antiquity* that Hieda no Are had committed to memory. Regardless of whether or not parts of what Are had "committed to memory" had a basis in written records, there is no doubt that Yasumaro shouldered the responsibility of turning what she told him into written literature. In his work, Yasumaro showed a basic attitude toward shaping his material that differed from that in the account of the lovers' idyll in the *Hitachi Topography*. His method was one shared by the *Izumo Topography* in those sections of setsuwa dealing with the deities of heaven and earth. In other words, Yasumaro's basic attitude was that he should arrange his narrative so that the functioning of the kotodama could be maintained. For this there was story matter, inherited from a distant past, in which it was believed the kotodama worked to extraordinary effect. The safest measure was, therefore, to give his material literary shape in just the form in which he had inherited it, the fear being that to alter things to suit the new tastes of the age would weaken the kotodama.

The text of the *Kojiki* as we have it is not an amalgam of the *Royal Genealogy* and the *Legends of Antiquity* memorized by Are. Integral transmission of them was not required. It seems to have been thought enough to make a whole, as it were, by scissors and paste. In the process, according to Takeda Yūkichi and others, a distinction was made between the *Genealogy* sections and the *Legends* sections—the study of which has led to modern scholarly benefits (Takeda, 1944). From another standpoint, the failure to amalgamate probably derived from Yasumaro's lack of freedom to mingle the two sections.

In the West, stories mingling genealogy and narrative have existed from ancient times. In his *Theogony*, Hesiod—who lived thirteen or fourteen centuries before Yasumaro—brought off a striking integration of elements similar to those in the *Royal Genealogy* and the *Legends of Antiquity*. This 1,022-line narrative poem depicts the actions of the gods in a unified cosmos. The means of tying it all together are the births and genealogies of the gods. The telling does not proceed in natural chronology from the oldest to the latest time, but starts instead from a point somewhat beyond the creation of the cosmos (recounted in ll. 116-36). Hesiod's status in the course of telling the story is that of listener to stories of the gods told him by the Muses of Olympus. And the earliest stage of the narrative as related by the Muses (ll. 36-115) tells of the father of the gods, Zeus, which logically or chronologically follows the creation of the cosmos that ensues in the story. From the revision of natural chronology to another, narrative order it is evident that Hesiod artfully designed a narrative structure and that he was far more skilled than Yasumaro. Since his poem orders the world of the gods genealogically, in whatever he touches on, lineage is related. As genealogies, Hesiod's do not differ fundamentally from the *Royal Genealogy*. At the same time, there is this great difference: in Hesiod's telling, the actions of the gods are related *with* the lineages, as if he were amalgamating genealogical and legendary matters. We can only judge the *Theogony* to be the more impressive. Moreover, its narrative technique works marvels of tone as bit by bit a tense passage is heightened.[5] For example, there is that scene of battle between the Titans and the sons of Chronos (ll. 674-712), with depictions such as these:

> On the other side the Titans prudently strengthened their ranks. Both sides employed all the strength in their hands. The limitless expanse of the sea echoed terribly; the earth rumbled loudly, and the broad area of the sky shook and groaned. Mount Olympus trembled from base to summit as the immortal beings clashed, and a heavy quaking penetrated to the gloomy depths of Tartarus—the

[5] It is not being argued that Hesiod's language is wholly his own. Excluding personal nouns, about 83% of his vocabulary is borrowed from the Homeric epics. This was discussed by Murakawa Kentarō at the 1952 meeting of the Society for Historical Research (Rekishigaku Kenkyūkai, Report 18).

sharp vibration of innumerable feet running and missiles thrown. While the weapons discharged at each other whistled through the air, both sides shouted loud battle cries as they came together, till the noise reached the starry sky.

Then Zeus decided to restrain his own power no longer . . . (ll. 674-87; trans. Norman O. Brown).

Writing like this would be better compared with Hitomaro's "Elegy for Prince Takechi," and it is not really appropriate for comparison with the prosaic *Kojiki*. The point I am trying to make, however, does not concern the level of tension or sublimity, but rather that Hesiod's relation of genealogy and the accounts of actions are so skillfully *joined* as a totality that the design gives great pleasure to the reader.

Hesiod is said to have been a farmer whose means extended to no more than a few slaves and some part-time help.[6] Why was Yasumaro— by contrast an important Yamato writer with the backing of the court— unable to do more than assemble a clumsy pastiche of sections from the *Royal Genealogy* and the *Legends of Antiquity*? In my opinion, he wrote as he did not because he could not have done otherwise but deliberately. The dedication he wrote in presenting the *Kojiki* to Gemmei is in a consistently ornate style. If he had wished, he could have written the *Kojiki* with the elaboration of the *Hitachi Topography*. In fact of practice, the work is set forth in a style shared with those portions of the *Izumo Topography* which present stories of the gods. And his reason for doing so was that in setting forth weighty Yamato setsuwa he thought himself forbidden to use language in which the kotodama would not work. In order to make it work, it was important that the narration not lose the atmosphere pervasive and appropriate to each part. In order that the differing qualities of the genealogical and legendary passages be understood, he had to keep the elements separate on his plane of narration. It follows that it was necessary to distinguish the two narrative lines on the basis of external qualities and not to mix the relatively free style of the *Legends of Antiquity* with the set style of the *Royal Genealogy*.[7] Since neither of them was in the really ornate style, they formed the basis, in combination, of a characteristic style of Japanese composition.

It could hardly have been easy to convert this vein of Japanese narrative to writing using Chinese characters. The discovery of the means to do it was not Yasumaro's alone but rather required the efforts of many Yamato writers. As I have said earlier, I believe that the conception of using Chinese characters to some extent for their meaning, and yet also when necessary for phonetic conveyance of the inherent language of Yamato,

---

[6] See the paper by Ōta Shigemichi (ibid., Report 2).
[7] Referring to the theory of Takeda Yūkichi; see Chapter 4, n. 38.

was something learned from Korean immigrants. As the method was extended from words to phrases and to whole sentences, the full discovery became possible: a new style of Chinese prose based on inherent Japanese principles of composition. To make that possiblity a reality, it was necessary to overcome many uncommon obstacles, and surely the achievement required the assistance of immigrants. In practice, this must have involved Japanese learning gained in the study of Buddhist sūtras.

It was made evident long ago by Kanda Hideo and Kojima Noriyuki that, considered as Chinese prose, the style of the *Kojiki* abounds in grammatical features not indigenously Chinese but derived in all likelihood from the style the Chinese used in translating sūtras.[8] Because Chinese intellectuals felt that fictional stories held little value, Japanese writers of divine or royal setsuwa seeking an appropriate style in Chinese prose would have found it very difficult to discover anything suitable in what were thought the Chinese classics. Yet there were sūtras well known in seventh-century Yamato, and in both the *Lotus Sūtra* and the *Vimalakīrti Sūtra* (J. *Yuimagyō*) many fictional stories are skillfully told.[9] In these Buddhist scriptures, then, there were various methods of expression useful as guides for converting Yamato setsuwa into Chinese prose. Moreover, since there are numerous examples in the Chinese versions of the sutras of written characters used phonetically to represent Indian words, the possibility is truly great that those scriptures were Yasumaro's source for the use of Chinese characters and phrasing. More than that, there are grounds for at least suspecting that the very ways of mingling song and prose in the *Kojiki* emulated sutras (Kanda, 1959, 106-9). A mingling similar to that which occurred in Yamato from the Archaic Age—or primitive times—will be found in the writing of primitive people today and can be taken analogically as confirmation.[10] In any event, there is no denying the influence of Buddhism in stylistic matters.

It was not just Yasumaro who was sufficiently proficient in analyzing sutras to use their linguistic methods to write works like the *Kojiki*. A considerable number of other Yamato writers must have acquired the ability by virtue of the same assistance of immigrants. But it is not enough to say "immigrants." As we can infer from the standard adaptation of Chinese characters that waka shares with Korean poetry, the majority of those immigrants must have been Korean intellectuals. Silla, the tardiest of the Korean kingdoms to accept Buddhism, had embraced it by

[8] See Kanda, 1950; Kojima, 1951; Kanda, 1951; Kanda, 1959, 104-20; Kojima, 1962, 227-53.

[9] [The "fictional stories" are commonly extended parables or exempla such as teachers use in many religions. And just as the exempla of medieval Europe gave impetus to vernacular narrative, so did the Buddhist stories exercise immense influence on Asian literatures.—Ed.]

[10] For example: Bleek-Lloyd, 1911; Bleek, 1928; Berndt, 1963; Guisinde, 1975 and 1977.

528, and thereafter any influence Korea exerted on Japan would involve Buddhist teachings. We should not suppose, however, that a Yasumaro's use of the civilization of the Korean peninsula or of the larger continent betokens merely an enthusiasm for an imported culture. To the contrary, foreign writing was drawn on and adapted in order to invigorate the kotodama, which had existed in Yamato from its distant past. In that respect Hitomaro, who also borrowed various foreign kinds of expression to make the kotodama work, can be said to stand on the same footing as Yasumaro.

PART FOUR

The Ancient Age: The Second Stage

CHAPTER 9

The Composition of Poetry and Prose in Chinese

THE FORMATION OF A POETIC CIRCLE

We can distinguish the second from the first stage of the Ancient Age by the role accorded to kotodama. Whereas in the first the kotodama had held a preeminent position, in the second it quickly attenuated and was replaced by a strong awareness of "literature as literature" for an audience that took writing itself as its object. The reason for this change can only be the concept of ga, which, in the second stage, became a Yamato standard. The rapidity of the advance of Chinese literature probably derived from the prosperity of the poetic circle centered on Prince Nagaya (684-729).

In the *Kaifūsō* there appear a number of poems written at royal request for celebrating banquets and excursions, poems dating from the late years of the seventh century and the early years of the eighth. But both in quantity and in quality these are far exceeded by works composed in gatherings at the prince's residence. The time we are seeking to recapture—no doubt involving poetic gatherings, when the flowers of the prince's gardens were at their height, to entertain honored and learned guests from Silla—did not last more than the ten years between 721, when the prince became the Minister of the Right, to his untimely death in 729, when he committed suicide because of involvement in a rebellion.

In the poetic garden of this decade a new style of literature was developed. It resembles the group of so-called eight friends of Ching-ling, which gathered at the western residence of Hsiao Tsu-liang (460-94), King of Ching-ling at the time of the Southern Chi Dynasty. The group produced a new kind of poetry named the Yüng-ming style. Its name (which suggests enduring brightness) was derived from the dates when literature prospered in Hsiao's western residence between the fifth and tenth years of the Yüng-ming era (487-92; Suzuki, 1928, 20-52). It may be that Prince Nagaya knew about Hsiao Tsu-liang and deliberately emulated him. If so, he could not have foreseen that his own splendid enterprise would end in under ten years, as had his predecessor's.

An international coloring is one of the most distinctive features of Prince Nagaya's poetic garden. Among the works composed there are nineteen extant by the prince himself—ten of which were written in the presence of guests from Silla. In the acquisition of Chinese culture, Silla was much in advance of Japan. Yet Japanese could now exchange poems with Korean intellectuals, testifying unmistakably to the newly found true ability and self-confidence of Japanese courtiers. These poems were *not* written ahead of time for presentation on a certain day; they were composed on the spot. The impromptu nature of composition is clear from the fact that of those poems by the prince, ten are so-called fu-yung (J. fuei). That is, they bear headnotes indicating the receipt of topics: "A Fu Written on Receiving the Topic *Wind*," "A Fu Written on Receiving the Topic *Rare*" (*Kaifū*, 60, 63), etc.[1] Moreover, for the host and guests to be compatible in their exchanges of poems, both sides had to possess common knowledge and techniques. If the Yamato side employed allusions not understandable to the Silla side, or if the Silla side took deliberate pains on imagery the Yamato side did not understand, their joint efforts would not have prospered. It follows that common purposes and shared poetic techniques were essential. These could only be found in Chinese literature. In it were the standards for judging whether something was proper or wrong, skillful or clumsy. On both sides, individuals had to suspend awareness of themselves as people of Yamato or Silla and conceive of themselves as Chinese poets. This must have been an enormous stimulus to a conception of writing for the Yamato participants, explaining how it was that the Chinese conception of ga made such rapid progress in Japanese culture at that time.

There was another highly significant factor at work on the conceptions of writing held by the Yamato poets composing in Chinese at those international parties. The question was not so much "What shall I say?" as "How shall I say it?" For the poems composed at the parties, the conditions for a given occasion were determined from the outset, and the supporting structure—the "What shall I say?"—was already in place. Within such architecture, the only way possible to write poems that one's companions would find interesting or impressive was to strain for a finished design in minute decorations of language.

The Chinese poetry making up the textbook was the Six Dynasties poetry available at the time. The textbook poems were themselves products of a linguistic technology that had reached an advanced state of art in making minute "How shall I say it?" calculations. Small wonder, then, that Yamato poets should raise the same question. Those concerns seem

---

[1] Fuei involve selecting a line from a famous poem and dividing up its character-words among those participating at the banquet, each of whom was to compose an impromptu verse in Chinese rhyming correctly with the word received. In the supervision there was also great responsibility for later adjustment or correction by the person handing out the words.

unlikely to have been restricted to occasions when foreign guests were one's companions, but to have extended to court banquets and excursions as well. In the *Kaifūsō* there are twenty-two poems composed at royal request. All treat the same subjects: the peace of the land and the great virtues of the tennō. Obviously the concern of the poets was "How?" And the poets addressing themselves to royal merits would be the more sensitized to the problem of "how" after their experience of exchanging poems with foreign-born residents.

In composing their poems in a foreign language, poets must have found it most troublesome to establish models for proper phrasing. It was natural that they should turn for their models to poems esteemed in the country of origin. Since, for late seventh- and early eighth-century Yamato, late Six Dynasties poetry set the pattern, most of the diction appears in *Selections of Refined Literature* and *New Songs from the Jade Terrace*. There are also instances of phrasing taken from early T'ang poets. It is clear from headnotes to poems that the two T'ang poets chiefly drawn on were Wang Po (650-76) and Lo Pin-wang (d. 684).[2] At the Shōsōin there is an incomplete copy of the *Wang Po Collection* inscribed with the date 704, just thirty-one years after the death of the poet. In all likelihood, the head of the seventh embassy to T'ang China, Awada Mahito, was the one who got it to Japan.[3] This embassy left in 702 and returned, probably, in 704. On that trip were also Priest Benshō and Yamanoe Okura. It should not be thought that, in drawing on the authority of early T'ang poets, Japanese poets departed from the poetic model of the Six Dynasties. The early T'ang poet Ch'en Tzu-ang (661-702) was exceptional in aiming at the simpler styles of the Han and Wei Dynasties rather than the magnificence that so appealed to Six Dynasties taste (Aoki, 1935b, 56-57). Although his advocacy of a new style has consequence to a historical perspective, at the time it would have seemed no more than a local occurrence. We cannot possibly imagine that on their infrequent visits to China the people of Yamato were situated to understand the values and assumptions of a new style. The poets whose collections the seventh T'ang embassy concentrated on for purchase and return were no doubt those who were then of repute in Ch'ang-an: Wang Po, Lo Pin-wang, and Yü Hsin (513-81) of the Northern Chou.[4] The

---

[2] The use of the *Wang Po Collection* has been demonstrated by Okada Masayuki (1929a, 228-29) and has been the subject of a deep and thorough study by Kojima Noriyuki (1965, 1286-1307).

[3] The sixth T'ang embassy went in 669. Wang Po was then but twenty and his works were hardly likely to have been collected by then.

[4] The *Shashō Sōmokuroku* of the Shōsōin [the royal museum and library in Nara] gives, under the year 748, the titles: *The Collected Works of Hsü Ching-tsung* (10 parts) and *The Collected Works of Yü Hsin* (20 parts, according to the *Dai Nihon Komonjo*, 4889).

result was that, until about the ninth century, the styles of Chinese poetry in Yamato were modeled on those of the Six Dynasties.

A number of important consequences flowed from the events just described. One was the rage for a kind of nature poetry. The traditional character of Chinese poetry had derived from the injunction to state one's intention, and as a result nature was almost wholly ignored until the Han and the Wei Dynasties. In the Chin and the Liu Sung Dynasties—about the fourth and fifth centuries—nature poetry began to appear almost accidentally and in no sense as a major movement in taste. With the Southern Ch'i, however, poetry on nature did become popular. Among the poets who frequently composed in the new way were Hsieh T'iao (464-99) and Wang Jung (467-93), and in the Liang Dynasty there were Shen Yüeh (441-513) and Ho Hsün (d. 518). The apex of this kind came in early T'ang poetry, as is shown conspicuously in the one hundred and twenty poems "On Miscellaneous Subjects" by Li Ch'iao (645-714).[5]

Although this Chinese poetry is termed nature poetry, much of it offers only objective description of individual things—from celestial phenomena such as the moon, clouds, rain, and snow to flora and fauna such as pear blossoms, falling plum blossoms, the wu-t'ung tree, roses, cicadas, wild geese, monkeys, and cranes; and also objects of human craft such as zithers, mirror stands, candles, or fans. Other poems are marked by inclusion of the poet's feelings with the description. Both the simply descriptive and the descriptive lyricized by personal response are Six Dynasties styles, with the simply descriptive emerging first (Ami, 1960, 234-46). Both kinds appear in Japan as well. Against Nakatomi Ōshima's "On a Lone Pine" in the descriptive-lyric mode (*Kaifū*, 12) we may set the following, Mommu Tennō's "Composed on Snow," in the simply descriptive style.

> The silk gauze of clouds enwraps jewels as it rises;
> The petals of snow take on color and freshness.
> In the grove it makes willows fluff like cotton;
> On the ridge beam it resembles the dust of songs.
> It replaces a lamp to illuminate the evening's writing;
> It drives off the wind as it circles the banks of the Lo-shui.
> At the back of the garden the apricot has flowered;
> On winter branches is tied the sash of spring.
>
> (*Kaifū*, 17)

It is also possible that they were brought back by the eighth embassy (left in 717) or the ninth (left in 733).

[5] This collection of Li Chiao's poems was lost in China, but the first few pages of a ninth-century copy of the text survive in Japan.

The clear aim is to present various ways snow may be conceived. In this description, the minute examination of the conditions of the object requires continuous development of descriptive fineness. Along with those features, we must observe the implicit awareness of a separation between nature and the poet. In archaic Yamato, the deliberate ideal was to speak well and exhaustively of plants and trees. Because there was no separation between the human and the natural, there could be no conception that nature existed as something viewed objectively outside the poet. It appears that with the new nature poetry there arose a conception of a nature to which the poet's and reader's selves were not bound. It is not clear whether the separation was fully conceived by Mommu's age, but at the very least a beginning had been made.

It must also be remarked that the simple description we find in Mommu's poem should not be confused with so-called objective description. We should not think that the description is of some reality that the poet has personally experienced—if for no other reason because the poem includes some impossibilities. For instance, Mommu speaks of the snow piling on the ridge beam (probably he has in mind powdery snow filtering through a hole in the roof) as something resembling "the dust of songs." It is impossible to believe that Mommu himself ever beheld conditions, as the old phrase put it, when a troubled minister sang and the dust danced on roofbeams.

The advent of this kind of nature poetry to Yamato poetic circles had its influence on waka as well. In a number of poems from the *Collected Poems of Hitomaro* there are title-like topic notes such as "Composed on the Sky," "Composed on the Mountains," or "Composed on Flowers." It is quite clear that these designations imitate those used for Chinese compositions. It cannot be known, however, whether all waka so labeled were composed on the topic specified or whether the designations were added subsequently. With the *Collected Poems of Hitomaro* at least, we can probably conclude that the forenotes were there from the beginning, because there are in the collection other nature poems of essentially the same kind that are categorized as miscellaneous and are untitled (10:1812-18, 2313-15, etc.). If the editor of Book 10 is thought responsible for the existence or nonexistence of the designations, we would expect consistency one way or the other. There is no proof that Hitomaro compiled the collection to which his name is attached, but it is the product of his age or of one close to it. Which is to say that about the same time that Mommu was writing "Composed on Snow," a conception of nature poetry emerged for waka as well. We find, as in Chinese composition, both poems of simple description and others in which infusion of the poet's feelings adds lyricism to description. Here are examples of plain description [guide phrases not italicized]:

COMPOSED ON FLOWERS

Yū sareba	As evening falls,
Nohe no akihagi	Along the fields the soft underleaves
Urewakami	Of autumn bushclover
Tsuyu ni karekeri	Have been withered by the dew.
Aki machigate ni.	Autumn being too long to wait.

(*MYS*, 10:2095)

COMPOSED ON SNOW

Ashihiki no	Where foothills sprawl
Yamagawa no se no	The mountain stream falls in rapids,
Naru nae ni	And with the water's sound,
Yutsuki ga take ni	Upon the peak of Yutsuki
Kumo tachiwataru.	The clouds hang in full layer.

(*MYS*, 7:1088)

Readers may find it difficult to understand why the Japanese have not recognized the very similar features that appear suddenly in the descriptive poems of the *Collected Poems of Hitomaro* and that mark the descriptive style of Mommu's "Composed on Snow." The explanation lies in the assertion, made by modern tanka poets of the *Araragi* school, that "objective depiction" is the distinguishing feature of descriptive waka. That is a misconception. Nature poetry is simply that using natural phenomena for materials; it is not necessary that the poet always be concerned with actual space and actual living things. Not long after poets were writing "Composed on Flowers" and "Composed on Snow," the form of such forenotes or titles shifted to "A Poem Written on a Warbler in Spring" or "Written on the Hototogisu," and from those forms to "A Poem on Plum Blossoms" or "A Poem on the Crescent Moon." Whatever the phrasing of these designations, their characteristics as nature poems remain the same.

Nature poetry in Chinese need not always be concerned with real things and real space or be composed at the site described. When in the course of describing the appearance of things the poet turns also to include related objects, it is easy to think that what is described was actually present and visible. That is an illusion, because as we have seen with Mommu's poem, no real scenery is described. So much is clear, line by line, from the presence of things that cannot coexist temporally or spatially. Of course natural objects and scenes might be introduced to a degree into Chinese poems of lyric feeling. To the extent that details of that kind increase and pure description emerges in nature poetry, the proportion of human feeling decreases, and in extreme instances an entire work may be concerned with natural objects and scenery. Prince Nagaya's "Early Spring Banquet at Sa-ho's Jeweled Tower" (*Kaifū*, 69) is a banquet poem properly speaking, not a poem of natural description. But a close look shows that to some extent actual features of the location have become the subject matter.

The scene is lovely, in Gold Valley the room
Where the year opens Piled Grass Pond to spring;
The pines and the haze together breathe greenness,
The cherry and willow separately display youth.
The peaks are lofty, and it grows dark on the cloud path:
Fish are startled, raising havoc with the duckweed by the banks.
In the gushing spring move the sleeves of the dance,
And the sound of the stream fills the pines and bamboos.

The lines contain a number of allusions. "Piled Grass," for example, does not refer to plants in the prince's garden overlying each other in their luxuriant growth but to the appearance imagined to exist at Piled Grass Pond at Sa-ho, which, from the Han period on, was the prince's residence at the detached palace at Ch'ang-an (Kojima, 1965, 1282-83). Many other recognizable expressions are interwoven into the description of the scene, making it difficult to guarantee that the garden was as the lines describe it. It should be noticed perhaps that the aims shown here are related to what was being practiced in waka.

In truth, this is the single poem in the *Kaifūsō* with so marked a degree of natural description. Natural description appears in Six Dynasties poems, but, as is well known, every period of Chinese poetry has "Express your intention" as its motto. It was suggested earlier that the advance guard of late Six Dynasties nature poetry was led by T'ao Ch'ien and Hsieh Ling-yün (385-433; Aoki, 1935a, 578-79). Yet in the work of both poets personal, emotionally expressed lyricism remains an important component, and poems consisting almost entirely of natural description appear only with the Liang period—Hsiao Kang (503-51) being a conspicuous example (Ami, 1960, 343-46). Since many poems with strong elements of natural description were written in China, they must have been familiar to Yamato intellectuals. How, then, are we to take the fact that there is only one Chinese poem of that kind in the *Kaifūsō*?

The answer may involve the Korean teachers, but since only some half-dozen poems in Chinese are extant from pre-eighth-century Korea, decisive examination is impossible.[6] We can imagine that those people of

---

[6] "Ku Sok," a work said to be by the Koguryŏ priest Chong (late sixth century), is a

Yamato, whose experience of writing poems in Chinese was at most of a hundred years' standing, would have found it difficult to respond warmly to poems whose conception was limited to natural description without an expression of personal feeling. The one person who could make the change was none other than the chief organizer of Yamato poetry circles, Prince Nagaya.

We should observe one last feature of poetry in the brief heyday of Nagaya's salon. It was there, for the first time, that prefaces in ornate parallel prose were added to poems and that methods were devised for understanding the practical connections establishable between a preface and a poem. [These prefaces in ornate Chinese should not be confused with introductory guide phrases in Japanese.] It will be more convenient, however, to treat this matter in discussing Okura, Tabito, and Yaka-mochi.

INDIVIDUAL EXPRESSION

In 704, or possibly 707, Okura returned to Japan with the seventh T'ang embassy. As an intellectual who had had contact with Chinese literary circles, he appears to have gained admission to Prince Nagaya's salon. None of his poems appears in the *Kaifūsō*. There is a note to a poem by him in the *Man'yōshū* (8:1519): "This poem was written on the evening of the Seventh Night festival at the residence of the Minister of the Left [Prince Nagaya]." Evidence shows he appeared at Prince Nagaya's salon (in 724) when the poetry garden was at its full bloom. We may surmise that the regular members of the prince's group were not a little affected by the *Wang Po Collection* and "The Visit to the Immortals' Dwelling."[7]

In their styles, the poetry of the late Six Dynasties and the early T'ang are so much alike that for most purposes "Six Dynasties style" is an adequate description. Early T'ang poetry does have, however, some noteworthy features of external form. One is just that preface-writing referred to. As opposed to titles or to headnotes designating topics, the preface is sufficiently independent to be appreciated for itself, and yet it can also be enjoyed along with its ensuing poem. Prefaces had begun to appear

---

simply descriptive lyric. But it is mentioned in the *Haedong Yŏksa* (late eighteenth century) as deriving from the *Koshiki* (a lost work), and its date and authorship are questionable.

[7] "The Visit to the Immortals' Dwelling" "Yu Hsien-k'u"; J. "Yūsenkutsu") is said to have been written by Chang Wen-ch'eng (660?-740) when he was twenty. At the time of the sixth T'ang embassy he was only about ten, so the work must have been brought back by the seventh, which went to China in 702. In China the work was looked down upon as a piece of trivial writing. It was quickly lost, remaining extant only in Japan. Concerning Wang Po, see n. 2. [The work is conspicuous as one of the most popular Taoist works in early Japan.—Ed.]

from about the time of Wang Hsi-chih (307?-63?), but it was not till the early T'ang that their practice flourished. The preface to Yamada Mikata's "At a Banquet at Prince Nagaya's Residence with Guests from Silla on an Autumn Day" (*Kaifū*, 65) has so many points in common with prefaces to poems in the *Wang Po Collection* and with prefaces by Lo Pin-wang (Kojima, 1965, 1286-90). Shimotsuke Mushimaro's preface (*Kaifū*, 65) is in much the same vein. The presence of these particular prefaces may be owed to the fact that Mikata was head of, and Mushimaro a teacher at, the national school. They use many allusions and conform to the rules for the ornate style. Yet what they mean to say they say directly, and their work is more appealing than Yasumaro's prose dedication of the *Kojiki* some fourteen years earlier. There are prefaces to other poems: to Fujiwara Umakai's "A Little Banquet by the Southern Pond in Late Spring" (*Kaifū*, 88) and "Sent, while in Hitachi, to Lord Yamamoto in the Capital" (89); as also to Fujiwara Maro's "Late Spring at a Drinking Party at the Garden Pond of My Younger Brother" (94). As with the prefaces by Mikata and Mushimaro, these depend on the phrasing of early T'ang prefatory prose. The practice in poetic circles after Prince Nagaya is very similar (Kojima, 1965, 1314-20).

One whose tastes had been refined by the prefaces to poems in the *Kaifūsō* would discover something obviously different in Okura's preface to his "Japanese Lament" (*MYS*, 5:794). In a word, it is not beautiful. The prose prefaces we were considering earlier were all written in poetic diction. These are the terms, for example, in which Umakai describes the circumstances of the banquet:

> This is the day: people assemble on a fragrant night, and the season has reached late spring. Reflected on the waters are red peach flowers, and halfway droop gauze flags which, low by the bank green willows begin to sweep with their long threads. And here: at the grove, pavilion guests inquire after me, coming and going by the flowers' edge and on a poolside platform my entertainment is fostered— whether left or right are zithers and winecasks. Beneath the moon perfumes give fragrance, as we pass time with poetry and gesture to friends with fans; before the breeze my spirit stirs, and I walk to the dancing area loosening my collar.

The diction of the preface derives without exception from the word-hoard of Six Dynasties poetry. To the extent that we accept the critical principle that precedented expressions are the beautiful ones, we must say Umakai's are certainly lovely. Then there is the ordering: the four-character and six-character phrasing that is the basis of the ornate style has been skillfully arranged. Using the four-character lines, he can employ simple parallelism: "people assemble on a fragrant night,/and the season has reached late spring." Alternating parallelism follows.[8]

A   Reflected on the waters are red peach flowers (4)
B   And halfway droop gauze flags (4)
A   Which, low by the bank green willows (4)
B   Begin to sweep with their long threads. (4)

Next we discover yet heavier parallelism:
A   At the grove pavilion guests inquire after me (6)
B   Coming and going by the flowers' edge (4)
A   And on a poolside platform my entertainment is fostered (6)
B   Whether left or right are zithers and winecasks (4)

Thereafter the alternating parallelism is again lighter:

A   Beneath the moon perfumes give fragrance (4)
B   As we pass time with poetry and gesture to friends with fans (6)
A   Before the breeze my spirit stirs (4)
B   And I walk to the dancing area loosening my collar (6)

With these rhythmical clauses are auxiliary phrases: "This is the day," "And here," to relieve the monotony of the carefully modulated phrases. It is a wonderful rhythm.

Compared with such a style, Okura's is utterly lacking in beauty. Let us consider its first half.

They say: the four vitalities rise and die, resembling dreams entirely empty: the three existences whirl in a flow, just like a cycle never ending. Moreover, Vimalakīrti the great master, staying or going from his sacred quarters, was caught by an outbreak of plague and its afflictions; Śākyamūni, accomplished in benevolence, agonized over extinction among the sal trees, and could not escape the suffering of this murky swampworld. Moreover, the two saints, at virtue's limits, lacked strength to sweep away strong death which comes in the end; in three thousand world spans, who could escape black grief when it come searching? Two rats vie in running, moreover, before our eyes cross birds that will fly tomorrow, and four snakes struggle crawling in, moreover, its brevity resembles a speeding night-horse seen through a wall-chink.

[8] [In what follows, the simple quotation by the author has been diagrammed to show alternating parallelism (ABAB) and the number of characters in the Chinese phrase (four or six). The punctuation in our translations from Chinese is meant to emphasize the clauses of the original more than English syntactic units.—Ed.]

It is not that these sentences lack poetic allusions, but that their sources are all in sutras. It follows that Okura uses no *poetic* language. And to the extent that we postulate as the canon of beauty the language appearing in *Selections of Refined Literature* and *New Songs from the Jade Terrace*, Okura's poetry is destitute of appeal. If we account Umakai's phrases to be richly colored, the words of Okura are ashen. Most of his clauses are didactic, and images with vitality are so scarce that one is hard pressed to give the composition a high grade. We must take, to some extent, as dynamic images "before our eyes cross birds that will fly tomorrow" and "a speeding night-horse seen through a wall-chink." But these are also from sutras and so familiar as to have grown proverbial. Feeble imagery, really. Although the phrases are consistently of four and six characters, they lack the trim poise of Umakai's. The insistent, heavy "moreovers" that follow also testify to a style no one would confuse with the ornate: "Two rats vie in running, / *moreover*, before our eyes cross birds that will fly tomorrow, / and four snakes struggle crawling in, / *moreover*, its brevity resembles a speeding night-horse seen through a wall-chink." This transitional expression is altogether ordinary in sutras. A few of the abundant examples may be offered from the *Lotus Sūtra* (*Hokkekyō*, 1962-67).

Now the World-honored one shows an extraordinary appearance. What can be the cause or reason, *moreover*, that there are portents? (Introduction)

These future Buddhas shall enter the world with infinite and un-countable devices, using variety on variety of reasonings, offering many parables, *moreover*, for all living things expounding the dharma (Chapter 2).

> Medicine King, I now make known to you
> The various scriptures I have taught;
> *Moreover*, among these writings
> The lotus dharma is of very first import.

(Chapter 10)

The poison has penetrated so deeply that they have lost their proper minds, and even of this my fine-colored fragrant medicine, *moreover*, they say it has no appeal (Chapter 16).

We must acknowledge that Okura's language has precedent. But the precedents are alien to the ga standard refined by Chinese poets and composers of fu. Since the Chinese translations of the sutras also use colloquialism from time to time, we might even say they present a zoku precedent. To the extent that we rely on the standards of Chinese poetry and fu, Okura's preface has nothing beautiful about it.

That judgment holds not simply for Okura's preface but also for his four Chinese verses between the preface and the chōka.

> On love's river the broken waves have already gone to collapse;
> On pain's sea evil passage will never again entangle me.
> From long ago this soiled world has been hateful, repellent;
> By the Original Vow my rebirth will be in the Pure Land.

Too doctrinaire, too given to stringing along allusions lacking in beauty, this kind of thing hardly arouses or stirs a reader. The images are few, and those in conventional phrases—"love's river" and "pain's sea"—are dead metaphors both. And as for that "broken waves," we must pronounce it at least half dead, so far has it lost most of the vitality it once had.

Yet we must also realize that this is the first poem in Yamato made of the stuff of philosophical thought. The doctrines of Buddhism were known in Yamato from the sixth century, but this is the first poem to deal with them in terms of the poet's own experience. By contemporary Japanese standards of Chinese verse, it is decidedly deficient.[9] But something else was to be expected from Okura, who had gone to China in 702. The current style of regulated verse was then established by Shen Chüan-ch'i (650-713?) and Sung Chih-men (d. 712), who were flourishing while Okura was in China. But as I have observed before, when a new style is propagated in a culturally advanced area, it is not likely that a person from a culturally laggard area will possess the awareness and values to make appreciation possible. Even so, Okura expressed himself with some adequacy in the seven-character quatrain, and he deserves credit for his ability to use the new medium intelligibly.

This feature—not beauty but intelligibility—is yet clearer in "Composed While Sunk in Illness and Lamenting My Lot."[10] The composition is studded with allusions sufficiently difficult for Okura to have added a

---

[9] The complex prosodic rules are not always followed. Chinese regulated verse, lü-shih, consists of eight lines of five or seven syllables (and usually words) each. The prosodic rules involve two levels of tones (plain and accented), and there are four rules governing their usage. One rule holds that the second and fourth syllables must not have the same accent; a second that the second and sixth should be the same; a third that the same tone should not be used for the third and fifth syllables; and a final one that the accents in the second and fourth syllables in even numbered lines should be matched in those syllables in the line following. Each of these rules has its Chinese name, and the third was the only one for which violation was thought merely venial. [This note is a composite of the author's original note and information sent separately.—Ed.]

[10] [Under this title there are a lengthy prose preface in Chinese, a regulated-verse quatrain in Chinese, a chōka, and six hanka. The author refers to the preface alone here.—Ed.]

large number of notes in a manner foretelling T. S. Eliot's practice with *The Waste Land*. There is not much beauty in the precedented phrases piled up by Okura. They were not taken by him, as one might say, from the first-class flower gardens of Chinese classics but from some weedy plot, certainly nothing to which one could attribute the refinement of ga. In spite of this, Okura does express himself clearly. No little training is required to do so in a foreign language, to which the safest approach is to lift lines and phrases from writing in the other country, patching them together more or less appropriately. Others at the time, if not Okura, followed that safe path, so discovering what was, to some extent, the beautiful.

There are times, however, when Chinese sources lacked phrases to enable one to say something urgent. It then became necessary either to sacrifice what one wished to say in favor of a set expression or to say what was deeply felt at the hazard of being thought strange by people born in the other culture. Okura made the latter choice, and if Chinese would have furrowed their brows over his style, it was cause for no great concern. His ability to carry on forcefully shows, in the form assumed in his writing, his experience of Chinese conversation on its home ground, something more commanding than composition based solely on written evidence. Okura's Chinese composition—at least in "Sunk in Illness"— is that of a person who speaks Chinese. We may doubt the quality of his Chinese. We may think him often awkward in its use. That is, he often uses strange phrases and yet—even in a somewhat huddled-up manner—he gets out what he wishes to say.

Okura was allowed into Prince Nagaya's salon because his feet had actually trod Chinese ground. But any poems he wrote at the salon do not appear in the *Kaifūsō*. This is only to be expected, since to those who conceived of meritorious writing in terms of the ga standard determined by Six Dynasties poetry, Okura's writing was just too odd. Regarded from another view, however, individual expression in Chinese verse begins with him. In waka there had been those before him who had given expression to their personal feelings, but by conveying the implication that in such-and-such a situation anyone would feel that way. Assuming that what they felt was felt by all, those poets gave in fact little attention to others. Coming right out with what one thinks may look rather feeble next to the individual expressiveness of Western Romanticism centuries later. But that way is a feature of his Chinese composition, and the same quality makes his waka very Okura-like. The second envoy to Okura's lament over the death of his son Furuhi (*MYS*, 5:906) is of uncertain authorship. As an afternote puts it, "Given that the fashioning of the poem resembles Yamanoe's, it is placed here after the two others."

When Book 5 of the *Man'yōshū* was being edited, Okura's individualistic style was assumed in poetic circles.

By comparison with Okura's, the Chinese compositions of Ōtomo Tabito are distinctly beautiful. His "In Attendance at the First Banquet of Spring" has already been mentioned. Because it was composed at a court feast, it is to be expected that Tabito would have culled beautiful words and ornate phrases. Yet even in so personal a work as the "Preface to an Excursion to the Matsura River" (prefixed to *MYS*, 5:853), he uses the beautiful syle of the Six Dynasties.[11] Here is the first half:

I went for a brief stroll to the region of Matsura, and by the pools of Tamashima where I was feasting my eyes, there on a sudden I met a bevy of young women angling. The bloom of their faces was beyond compare; their radiant forms had no rival. Unfolding willow leaves seemed to be their brows, and blossoming peach flowers were on their cheeks. Their demeanor was more stately than clouds, and their elegance would exhaust words. I spoke to them asking, "Of what village, of what house are you the delights? Perhaps you are young goddesses, or immortals?" The young women all joined in laughing at me, saying, "We are countrified offspring of fishers, people who live in a grass-thatched hut. Village we have none and house we have none, nothing at least worthy those names."

Journeying to an unknown place, meeting there beauties who are im-mortals (whether openly or in disguise), entering into love with vows that will not be kept—these motifs had already appeared in the "Fu on the Kao-t'ang Viewing Tower" (Kao-t'ang Fu), "The Fu on a Goddess" (Shen-nü Fu), and the "Fu on the Goddess of the Lo" (Lo-shen Fu) in *Selections of Refined Literature* (*Wen Hsüan*, 19). There were also various prose works composed along these lines, of which the most important for Japan is "The Visit to the Immortals' Dwelling." This work had been brought back, some twenty-three to twenty-six years before Tabito wrote, by Okura and others, and from about 730 it circulated widely among Yamato intellectuals. Allusions to it were unlikely to go unrecognized. In fact it provides the chief basis for Tabito's preface, and it has been shown that he uses phrases recalling the Chinese story (Kondō, 1936). He also draws on poems in the *Selections*. All this shows that Tabito's style is typical of its age, and that by its standard Okura's is distinctly odd.

Ōtomo Yakamochi's composition in Chinese utilizes most of the ele-

---

[11] Tsuchiya Bummei had a theory that this preface was by Okura, but it differs markedly from Okura's distinctive style. I follow the interpretation of Doi Kōchi, who held that Okura, who had never been to Matsura, would not have said what is said in the opening clause (Doi, 1960, 176-77).

ments we have seen in the writings of his father. Yet there are also some noteworthy expressions of individualism that will not be found in Tabito's writing. Among the poems in Chinese and Japanese that Yakamochi exchanged with Ōtomo Ikenushi, there is this one in Chinese (*MYS*, 17: prefixed to 3976).

> Treetops in spring intercalary days make an enticing
>   landscape of great beauty;
> The first third of the month the mild breeze brushes,
>   gently of itself.
> Swallows arrive at their mud nests at the eaves
>   in auspicious entrance;
> Great geese return, picking reeds to bear far out
>   on the offing.
> I would listen, Sir, as you whistle that new and fashionable
>   song at my side;
> And to cleanse the wine cup, lend it
>   to the pure flowing stream.
> Let me say how I wish to attend your wonderful banquet;
> But I do not know how to go, stained with sickness,
>   with uncertain legs.

If we compare this with Okura's Chinese poetry, this seems like the real thing. Even the prosody seems better attended to.[12] The phrasing is, by and large, what we would expect for this occasion. It all seems quite reasonable—except for the problem of the last two lines. Of course, the preceding six are made of elements that matter little to the speaker of the poem, so that there is inevitably little force in those fine precedented phrases. The last two lines, however, touch on the fact that Yakamochi had been sick to his stomach since the twentieth of the previous month, and the prospect of going to the musical banquet on the third of the Third Month, with such weakened legs—well, it's impossible. The individualistic feeling these two lines convey represents a kind of poetic subject for which appropriate phrases are not to be found in the *Selections*, or the *Jade Terrace*. There was nothing he could do but use his own phrasing, with the result that the last two lines do show a lack of craftsmanship. With whatever strain, he has joined Okura to some extent in attempting to adapt actual feeling in individual daily life to poetry.

Yakamochi's Chinese poetry has nothing outstanding about it. To appreciate the lowness of its level, we may compare with his poem another

[12] Yakamochi fairly well observes the rules for the New-Style Poetry (hsin-t'i shih), for example that the second and fourth possible rhyme words should not rhyme on level tones, but that the second and sixth should. See n. 9. [Note abbreviated.—Ed.]

in Chinese by a Korean writing at about this time. The poem is by the
Silla poet Kim Chi-jang writing in T'ang China about 756.[13]

Seeing a Boy off from the Mountain

At the empty gate you yearn, lonely, quietly for your home;
With polite parting at the room in the clouds, you descend Mount
    Kukwa.
How dear is the bamboo railing you turn to, the bamboo horse you
    ride,
Tired of the golden earth and of scooping golden sands.
Taking the bottle to the house by the valley stream, ceasing to invite
    the moon;
Boiling tea is left in the pot, and you cease to be invited with
    flowers.
As you depart happily, there is no point to tears constantly falling,
The old priest claiming as companion only smoky haze.

It may be unjust to compare the Chinese verse of Yakamochi with the
composition of someone with experience of China. But even if granted
a considerable handicap, Yakamochi cannot be said to equal that lonely
Korean poet.

[13] Kim Chi-jang was a Silla prince. At the time of Hsiao Tsung he went to China and
lived at Chiu Hua Mountain. The poem has the distinction of being included in *The
Complete T'ang Poems (Ch'üan T'ang Shih).*

CHAPTER 10

Waka Composition

FROM KOTODAMA TO GA

Hitomaro's chief intent was to use contact with the advances of Chinese civilization to give him personal insight into the indigenous Yamato culture. And when he turned to express himself in poetry, his guide phrases, which maintained kotodama, played a crucial role. During the second stage of the Ancient Age, waka poets held to the same way of thought, although there are not a few differences in the poetic styles of the two stages. During the second, poets believed they could use Chinese writings, to some degree, to act as agents of Yamato expression. In putting that aim into practice they conclusively weakened kotodama.

The poets did not lose faith in kotodama. We recall that it was Okura who called Yamato "A land where the kotodama / Brings us good fortune." He was not alone in thinking so. In the seventh intercalary month of 746, as Ōtomo Yakamochi was on his way to the governorship of Etchū, he received a poem from his aunt, Lady Ōtomo of Sakanoe [in this chapter, guide phrases are italicized]:

Kusamakura	*Grass for your pillow,*
Tabi yuku kimi o	Your journey takes you afar.
Sakiku aredo	I pray you prosper
Iwaie suetsu	To the length of sacred cords
Aga toko no he ni.	That adorn my bedside.

(*MYS*, 17:3927).

Although there is some doubt that things were to go as well as she hoped, the poem itself is definitely affirmative. If a messenger recited the poem in Yakamochi's presence, the orally delivered kotodama would reach him, amplifying his prospective good fortune. On New Year's Day 759, as he was ending his service as governor of Inaba, Yakamochi composed a poem at the banquet to which his staff treated him.

Atarashiki	Once more it is new,
Toshi no hajime no	The year that begins today
Hatsu haru no	With the start of spring,

Kyō furu yuki no	And may the snow that falls this day
Iyashiku yogoto.	Be good auspice to the land.

(*MYS*, 20:4516)

Here is the last datable poem in the collection, and presumably there-fore Yakamochi's latest one included in it. Because it considers the snow a good omen, that falling on New Year's Day is invoked to increase the blessings on Yamato, an invocation of the kotodama by whose working this year, too, will be accompanied by good fortune. There is no question but that this is a pretty feeble poem by modern critical standards. But to Japanese, including myself, who possess traditional feelings, the aus-picious life that is assumed will run throughout the new year causes profound sensations. That the same Yakamochi who could write other poems judged outstanding by modern standards should also have written this shows that the *second* stage of the Ancient Age was after all part of that Ancient Age—a time when the kotodama did retain validity. None-theless the difference between the two stages is that the kotodama which had flourished so in waka for the world inhabited by Hitomaro would shortly be gone. Why?

When Okura wrote of "A land where the kotodama / Brings us good fortune," it was at the time the ninth T'ang embassy was embarking. In order that the kotodama invoked might promote the peace and prosperity hoped for, he also wrote of it as "From the Age of the Gods." This stress shows the emphasis upon the Yamato character deliberately invoked for the kotodama. Similarly, the words of invocation had to be Yamato-kotoba, Yamato words, because the kotodama would not function in a foreign language. There is something of a problem with the words Okura prefixed to his poem, "A Poem of 'Good Departure, Good Return.' " In the Archaic Age and the earlier stage of the Ancient Age, poems had no topical title at all. Okura's should be contrasted with the forenote to the second poem in the *Man'yōshū*: "A Poem, composed when the Tennō ascended Kagu Hill to behold the country." There are many poems with "titles" like this, "titles" supplied by a compiler to explain the circum-stances of *another* person's composing a poem. This is not at all the same kind of "title" in which an individual author supplies information about the subject or character of the work. For example: "Prostrate with Grief before the Education Ministry" (*Wen Hsüan*, 30:674) or "There is Grief in a Spring Bedroom" (*Gyokudai*, 6:540). Of this variety of headnote the first seen in Japan is Okura's "Japanese Lament" (*MYS*, 5:794), no doubt reflecting Chinese usage. This returns us to the difficulty with headnotes that state a theme in the manner of Okura's "Poem of 'Good

Departure, Good Return.' "[1] For kotodama, Yamato words must be used. Of course Okura's *poem* is written in Yamato words. When he stated his topic in a *Chinese* headnote, Okura may well have been unaware of doing anything special, but the thought must have been hidden somewhere that it might be possible to work the Yamato kotodama in Chinese. In the T'ang Dynasty, "good departure" had something of the feeling of "goodbye," a rather colloquial flavor, and even a nearly one-to-one equivalence with the Yamato "Fare well ahead / And come back soon" (*MYS*, 5:894).[2] Perhaps the kotodama would not fail even in the Chinese of "Good Departure, Good Return." So much seems implied by Okura's later Chinese composition, "Sunk in Illness and Lamenting My Lot."

> "What people desire, Heaven bestows." If there be truth in that saying, what I beg and entreat is quickly to be free from this illness, and I pray to be normal again.[3]

This Chinese prose does not simply set forth the state of the illness. Depending on the eloquence used in these words, Okura could hope to be relieved in his suffering. Because he was also a Buddhist he may also have held in the back of his mind the idea that reading sūtras would assist his recovery.[4] We may also wonder if he, who could write about the kotodama in his poetry, did not think in more general terms that incantations delivered in spoken words would have results commensurate with the words, and if so, would that not be true in lands other than Yamato?

That would be to look at Yamato from the perspective of the world. Of course to the country at that early time the rest of "the world" constituted China, Korea, and India. The placing of Yamato in that larger "world" must have betokened a considerable alteration in the way the Yamato people regarded themselves. One of the signs is that Yamato was now internationally recognized as a state. This self-awareness of living at the eastern verge of the "world," as if at the origin of life, led to a desire to change the name by which China and Korea had called

---

[1] [The author's argument, which had turned on who wrote the headnote, now turns on the language in which it is written: Okura uses Chinese. Neither a third-party editor nor Chinese had traditional connection with the working of the kotodama.—Ed.]

[2] This colloquial element was pointed out by Kojima Noriyuki (1952, 82-83). Since we observe the same colloquial "hao-ch'ü" in "Seeing a Boy off from the Mountain" [at the end of Chapter 9], it is impossible to exclude the expression altogether from poetic diction. But since that poem is by a Silla priest, we also cannot say the expression is poetic and leave it at that.

[3] [This prose piece follows *MYS*, 5:894, just discussed.—Ed.]

[4] An early example is that of services for the cure of Temmu Tennō from a serious illness. According to the *Temmuki* (dating the event at 686; p. 385), there was a general court recitation of the *Konkōmyōkyō* (*Suvarnaprabhāsottma Sūtra*). It was believed that the strength of the rite lay in *vocal* recitation.

the country, from the "Wa" [Ch. Wo] used earlier to a word connoting the land where the sun originates: Nihon.[5] At the time of one of the T'ang embassies, the Chinese thought very arrogant the desire of representatives of Wa or Yamato to be referred to as people of Nihon. Many records from that time remark on the stated desire with irritation.[6] If in the Chinese view the Japanese preference was arrogant, to those of Yamato it was in the nature of an announcement of arrival on the international stage.

This current had already begun to run in the seventh century, and by the beginning of the next its flow was visible in literature as well. There is an example in a poem by Priest Benshō, "In the T'ang, Longing for My Proper Home." He had gone with the seventh embassy to study, and wrote:

> In the region of the sun I look for Nihon;
> At the bank of clouds I hope for a cloudbreak.
>
> (*Kaifū*, 27)

This was probably the first literary usage of "Nihon" in history. Not long after this poem was written, Okura, who was on the same embassy, wrote a poem in Japanese for Tabito with the title, "Nihon (no) Banka" (A Japanese Lament). A "banka" was taken to be a poem written for a funeral, and there are examples of such usage in *Selections of Refined Literature*. Okura's use is not that of the Chinese, who recited the verses

[5] [The two characters for "Nihon" mean "sun's origin." In modern times they have been pronounced "Nihon" or "Nippon." At the time of the Taika Reform in 645, those characters were used but read "Yamato," and in some poetic usages, as in renga, are pronounced "Hi no moto," which is a non-Sinified reading. The author uses only the characters, without indication as to their pronunciation, and therefore "Japan" will be the translation hereafter. The presumption that he means "Nihon" derives from the fact that modern Japanese dictionaries use that pronunciation for their main entry—"Nippon" having somewhat nationalistic overtones. There are numerous other words used poetically or periphrastically for Japan: "Akitsushima," "Shikishima," and, indeed, "Yamato." For "Yamato" the author uses katakana throughout rather than the usual two Chinese characters, the second of which is often read "wa" and used to designate "Japan" in character compounds. That "wa" is not to be confused with the other "wa" which is the Japanese pronunciation of the Chinese "Wo" used to designate Japan by the Chinese and Koreans: see the next note.—Ed.]

[6] For example, in a kind of account or preface to the papers presented by the seventh T'ang embassy, a Chinese recorded in 703: "The country of Jih-pen [characters for 'Nihon'] is another name for 'The country of Wo' [J. Wa]. Because that country is near where the sun rises, they give it the name of Jih-pen ['country where the sun originates']. Others say that those people do not like the name of 'Wo' [which literally means 'dwarf'] and so changed to the new name. Others say that Jih-pen was originally a small country but that it has now swallowed up Wo. We do find that when they come on embassy, they are excessive in their talk about their country, which is why we Chinese cannot trust them" (*Kyū Tōjo*, 93). Actually it was the sixth rather than seventh embassy that had seemed conceited to the Chinese.

as the remains of the deceased were being taken to burial. Instead he laments an absent dead person. Perhaps he was aware of his departure from Chinese usage and that is why he insists on a *Japanese* lament. Recognizing the difference, he offered the novel "Nihon no Banka" to clarify the differences. To make possible this usage, this sense of national comparability, he must have held a prior premise, "Chinese shih and our waka are the same in being poetry." Waka was not simply Yamato uta but in fact had ceased to be something essentially different from Chinese poetry.

Until this point in my *History* I have been using "Yamato" to designate Japan. This decision was reached after lengthy consideration of the nature of both the Archaic Age and the Ancient Age in its first stage. Henceforth the term to be used in the discussion reflects the change in attitude just described: the country is now to be considered Nihon.[7]

The boat of the seventh T'ang embassy carrying back Okura and the priest Benshō also bore the *Wang Po Collection* and "The Visit to the Immortals' Dwelling." This embassy had great influence on the second stage of the Ancient Age, as is shown by that rising awareness at the time of an internationally conceived "Nihon," Japan. The question this raises for waka is: what in fact were the changes, in practical terms? In what follows I wish to distinguish four.

One external innovation is the composing of waka with an accompanying preface in Chinese prose. It has been observed how the Japanese wrote Chinese prose prefaces for their Chinese poems, after the manner of early T'ang practice. Tabito and Okura's group were now going so far as to write Chinese prefaces for Japanese poems. The best example is no doubt one we have considered, Tabito's "Preface to an Excursion to the Matsura River." There is no question but that the preface itself had to be sufficiently independent to be appreciated for its fine prose. But it also had to participate in a structural plan that would render integral, as one expressive world, the preface-and-poem. It is one thing to write a preface for a Japanese poem in the presumption that a single expressive integer will result. Without the assumption mentioned earlier—that the Chinese shih and Japanese waka are the same in essence—as an explicit basis for the practice, the integration would not be feasible, either for the literary expression or for its readers. In the plum-blossom viewing banquet held by Tabito at his private residence on the thirteenth of the First Month in 730, thirty-two poems were composed. It was an epoch-making event to join to them a preface in Chinese. Edo-period commentators on the *Man'yōshū* made the connection between that pref-

---

[7] [The nearest we can approximate the shift is to change from "Yamato" (except when the author uses the term to designate the earlier state) to "Japan."—Ed.]

ace and Wang Hsi-chih's own to his "Record of the Orchid Pavilion Gathering" (Lan-t'ing Chi). We must go further: not simply the prose preface, but the plum-blossom viewing banquet itself was modeled on the assembly of poets at the Orchid Pavilion.[8] Tabito's banquet seems to have excited contemporary fame in the capital, and there have come down to us the poems written as later response by Yoshida Yoroshi and Ōtomo Fumimochi (MYS, 5:864; 17:901-6). These are the reasons why this banquet of Tabito's was chosen as the symbolic dividing-point between the two stages of the Ancient Age.

A second change for waka involves the individualism that entered into poetry. The adding of a preface in Chinese was, for Yakamochi, a way of substituting a bit of correspondence for a proper preface. The sedōka he composed with Ikenushi (MYS, 17:3965) has that air. The contents of the correspondence run much like, "Because of illness, I have not been able to attend to my affairs," or "Let me acknowledge receipt of your excellent poem." That being the way of letters, Yakamochi may have thought waka should resemble them in tone. In the earlier stage of the Ancient Age poems had such personal elements, but the feeling that informed the poetry was that which anyone might have had in such a situation, and the poet acted as a representative for all. But to Yakamochi and other later ancient poets, the feeling expressed is commonly that of the response or circumstances personal to the writer at that time. The poems by Hitomaro offer us little insight into his biography, and it is seldom clear as to the circumstances in which he wrote, although modern Japanese find them impressive. Few modern readers find Yakamochi's poems consistently impressive in themselves. To appreciate them, it is necessary to savor them in the discoverable context of his life and the immediate background. Since in fact we can know so relatively little about the circumstances when he composed, it is easy to undervalue them.

Yakamochi was not the first to feature individual feeling. Tabito and Okura had their tries before him. But those poems usually express shared thoughts and feelings in a private situation. For example, there are Tabito's thirteen "Poems in Praise of Wine" (MYS, 3:338-50). These express ideals of reclusion that derive from Taoist thought, and it is Tabito whom we must credit for first using established Chinese thought as material for waka. In his "Poem to Set a Confused Heart Straight," Okura draws freshly on Confucian logic and realism, even if nothing strikes the eye as philosophically new. It is difficult to know how seriously to take the

---

[8] On the third of the Third Month 353, Wang Hsi-chih held, along with purification rites, a garden party for composing poems, with forty-one famous guests in attendance (Shih-wen Lei-chü, pt. 1, vol. 87). There are also some prefaces for poems celebrating similar parties held by Yen Yen-chih and Wang Jung in the Wen Hsüan (46:1008-19).

more or less Taoist outlook of elite profession that Tabito flaunts, but Okura sets forth in his poem a fictional, Tabito-style Professor Disdain, adopting a position that seems to mount indirect opposition to Tabito's "Elite Profession" in his "Poems in Praise of Wine" (Takagi Ichinosuke, 1941, 414-16).[9] This resistance derives from the distance in individual outlook between Tabito and Okura. That is not to say that either of them falsified their personal views. Take this poem by Tabito:

Yo no naka wa	Each time that I realize
Munashiki mono to	The transience of
Shiru toki shi	This world,
Iyoyo masumasu	The more, the harder
Kanashikarikeri.	I am struck with sadness.

(MYS, 5:793)

This of course proclaims the familiar moral that the world is a vain and insubstantial thing.[10] And although expressed in religious terms—which should have alleviated his sense of bereavement—we find "The more, the harder / I am struck with sadness." This is Tabito's special, private outlook.

There is also Okura's "Poem on Thinking of His Children" with its preface.

Śākyamūni expounds truthfully from his golden mouth, "I love all things equally, the way I love my child, Rāhula." He also teaches us, "No love is greater than the love for one's child." Even the greatest of saints cherishes his child. Who, then, among the living creatures of this world could fail to love children claimed as one's own?

Uri hameba	When I eat melon,
Kodomo omōyu	I long for my children;
Kuri hameba	When I eat chestnuts,
Mashite shinowayu	I yearn all the more.

[9] The "Tzu-hsü Fu" and the "Shang-lin Fu" introduced fictional speakers and a dramatic mode into Chinese writing. [We have taken the translation of the title of Okura's work from Levy. The author in his Japanese plays off Okura's "Baizoku Sensei" (we take Levy's "Professor Disdain" as the translation) with his own Taoist-like coinage, "hanzoku." So in the spirit of the author's wordplay, we contrast to Okura's "Professor Disdain" (Baizoku Sensei) Tabito's outlook of "Elite Profession" (Hanzoku).—Ed.]

[10] One may recall: "Although when I was young I thought this world beautiful, the world is really false, errant, and an illusion," Ch'ih-shih Ching, pt. 2; or, from the T'ien-shou-kuo Hsiu-chang Ming, there is also "The world is false and transient; the Buddha's retort is the truth." But Okura's is so pervasive a Buddhist assumption that it seems unlikely to derive from any particular scriptural passage.

Izuko yori	Where could it be
Kitarishi mono so	That they come from to me?
Manakai ni	They and their doings
Motona kakarite	Are visions before me,
Yasui shi nasanu.	And I cannot sleep at ease.

Envoy

Shirokane mo	What could I do
Kogane mo tama mo	With either a heap of silver
Nani sen ni	Or with gold and pearls?
Masareru takara	The greatest treasure world of all
Ko ni ikame yamo.	Would not equal a child of mine.[11]

Okura expresses orthodox morality in his preface and a personal feeling all his own in phrases of his envoy—"When I eat melon" and "When I eat chestnuts." Okura's poems include some with headnotes like "A Poem Boldly Expressing My Own Feelings," well revealing the individualism that had grown so much by this time.

The third innovation is the development of fictionality. The technique of using a fictional speaker had already been used by the time of Hitomaro. But, as in the Archaic Age, it was still often unclear whether the speaker was fictional or represented the author. In contrast, during the latter stage of the Ancient Age, an unquestionably fictional character may appear before us, much like a member in a theatrical cast, as a distinct person. As evidence we can take the poems written on the twenty-eighth of the Third Month of 739. The occasion was Isonokami Otomaro's arrest and banishment to Tosa for getting into trouble with a woman.[12]

Isonokami	*Isonokami,*
Furu no mikoto wa	You great man from Furu,
Tawayame no	Because of your mistake,
Matoi ni yorite	Getting that woman in trouble,
Umajimono	You are like a horse
Nawa toritsuke	Drawn along by a rope,
Shishijimono	You are like a boar,
Yumiya kakumite	Hemmed in by bows and arrows.
Ōkimi no	By the command
Mikoto kashikomi	Of our dread Sovereign,

[11] *MYS*, 5:802-3. [The translation of the preface is by Levy.—Ed.]
[12] Ibid., 6:1019-22. The cause of Otomaro's exile was adultery with the [a?] wife of Fujiwara Umakai (*Shokuki*, vol. 13). While in Tosa, Otomaro composed four poems in Chinese that were selected for the *Kaifūsō*.

Amazakaru	You must depart for a province
Hinae ni makaru	*Distant as the heavens*
Furukoromo	Off there on the tatters
Matsuchiyama yori	Of Matsuchi Mountain—
Kaerikonu kamo.	Will you come back from there?

*   *   *   *   *

Ōkimi no	By the command
Mikoto kashikomi	Of our dread Sovereign
Sashinarabu	You are taken off,
Kuni ni idemasu	Going away to some province.
Hashikiyashi	Dear and beloved,
Waga se no kimi o	My lord husband,
Kakemaku mo	May the fearsome gods
Yuyushi kashikoshi	Dwelling at Suminoe
Suminoe no	Take on human shape
Araitokami	And condescend to guard
Funa no e ni	At the prow of your boat,
Ushihakitamai	Staying close beside you
Tsukitamawan	Delivering you safe
Shima no sakizaki	From the juts and points of isles,
Yoritamawan	Preserving you safe.
Iso no sakizaki	From the juts and points of shores,
Araki nami	Keeping your boat free
Kaze ni awasezu	From the rough waves and the winds,
Tsutsumi naku	Kept in good health
Yamai arasezu	And protected against disease,
Sumuyakeku	And with no delay
Kaeritamawane	Bring you back home again
Moto no kunihe ni.	To your native land.

*   *   *   *   *

Chichigimi ni	My lord and father
Ware wa manago zo	Held me his beloved son,
Hahatoji ni	My lady mother
Ware wa manago zo	Held me her beloved son.
Mainoboru	Travelers from the eighty clans
Yasoujihito no	Come back to the capital
Tamuke suru	Up the awesome Kashiko Slope,
Kashiko no saka ni	Making offerings at the shrines
Nusa matsuri	Tugging at the sacred rope,
Ware wa zo oieru	While I press on and on
Tōki Tosaji o.	Over the road to distant Tosa.

Envoy

Ōsaki no	The Ōsaki strand
Kami no obama ni	Where the god rules the shore
Sebakedo mo	Is a constricted place—
Momofunabito mo	Unlike the many boatmen going forth,
Sugu to iwanaku ni.	I must remain in exile here.

The first poem is related from the external viewpoint of a narrator, the second from the point of view of Otomaro's wife, and the third that of their child.[13] The envoy is presented as if Otomaro himself is speaker. This dramatic mode had been experimented with about seven years earlier by Okura in his "A Dialogue on Poverty" (*MYS*, 5:892-93). The development of the technique of distinct fictional speakers had as one of its causes the emergence in China of fu that introduced fictional speakers. There are, for example, the "The Rhapsody of Master Imaginary" and "The Rhapsody on the Imperial Park," by Ssu-ma Hsiang-ju. In 728 the court school introduced a new literary curriculum with *Selections of Refined Literature* as principal textbook. With such a resource, nearly every Chinese technique could become known quickly.

If Hitomaro's use of fictional speakers constituted a development of elements from songs of the Archaic Age, during the period of Tempyō culture the models for fictional speakers were found in Chinese literature.[14] If there was a problem in this, it was not the civilized attainments of individual poets but the general level of the literary audience. Tabito's "Poem on a Japanese Paulownia Zither" (*MYS*, 5:810-11) involves a dialogue, in a dream, between the spirit of the zither and the poet, so that in this instance it is not simply the speaker who is fictional. The poem was composed for presentation to Fujiwara Fusasaki, a person of such learning that it was unnecessary for him to attend the national school, and of sufficient talent for three of his Chinese poems to survive in the *Kaifūsō* (85-87). Tabito also makes use of a fictional speaker in his "Preface to an Excursion to the Matsura River" (*MYS*, 5:853-63). This was presented to Yoshida Yoroshi, again a person whose sophistication is not in question, since he also has poems in the *Kaifūsō* (79-80). The Otomaro poems differ in seeming to be intended for a readership possessing no special acquaintance with Chinese poetry. To the extent that the Otomaro poems caused no contemporary perplexity, we can see

[13] There is a possible problem with the text of the tenth line of the third poem. Kamo no Mabuchi glossed the line in a way making Otomaro speaker. The age requisite for adultery and other considerations makes that interpretation odd.

[14] ["Tempyō Culture" is a phrase often used for the flowering of court culture from ca. 729-757, when the era names for part of Shōmu's reign and all of Kōken's had "Tempyō" designations: "Tempyō-Kampō," etc.—Ed.]

that people brought up on the new learning in such books as the *Selections* had grown in number, producing many more sophisticated readers of Japanese poetry.

The fourth change involves the alteration in guide phrases. The expressive aim of late Six Dynasties poetry centered on how beautifully something might be said, and that "how" was dependent on the originality and freshness of the individual author. When that expressive aim became widespread in Japan, authors chose to rely less on the kotodama, which epitomized the ancient linguistic usage of Yamato, and to turn instead to a subjectivity by which the author as an individual wrote with that individual's own words. The result was the deterioration in guide phrases. For those consisting of a five-syllable line, there was a weakening of the kotodama—although of course they gave ornamental emphasis to the words that followed. They became the so-called pillow-words (makurakotoba). For those guide phrases consisting of a number of lines—now the so-called prefaces (joshi)—the function changed from the older one of leading into the lines expressing the main predication. They became instead meaningful prefaces (ushin joshi, ushin no jo). For both, the decrease was in quantity as well as quality. The conclusion of this trend occurs only in the Middle Ages, but as early as this later stage of the Ancient Age, the direction of change is clear. To distinguish the expressions in which the working of kotodama has weakened from its strength in those guide words and phrases of earlier times, I should like to identify the new usage of guide words and phrases by their familiar terms: pillowwords and prefatory words (jokotoba). A variety of confusions has arisen from conceptual imprecision in distinguishing between usage in medieval waka as opposed to that in the earlier Ancient Age and before.

In many respects it is easy to apprehend the damages implied by the shift to makurakotoba. The poems chosen to symbolize the dividing line between the former and latter stages of the Ancient Age, the "Poems from the Plum Blossom Banquet" by Tabito and others, include some forty-five—of which only one uses a pillow-word. That poem is by Tabito (*MYS*, 5:822):

Waga sono ni	In my garden
Ume no hana chiru	Fall the blossoms of the plum;
Hisakata no	*From distant reaches,*
Ame yori yuki no	From the heavens the snow
Nagarekuru kamo.	Seems to come in a stream.

"Hisakata no" is a very old, now conventionalized expression prefixed to celestial phenomena. It could be omitted from the poem with no alteration in meaning. Because omitting the guide phrase "Tamamo karu"

(Where they gather fine seagrass) from Hitomaro's poem (*MYS*, 3:250) would alter the meaning of the poem, its function is altogether different.

Or again, in the eighty-two lines making up Okura's chōka and hanka in "A Dialogue on Poverty" (*MYS*, 5:892-93), there is but one pillow-word-like expression, "Nuedori no" (The tiger thrush)—and if we follow Takagi's analysis, even that is not a pillow-word (Takagi Ichinosuke, 1941:104-5). This evidence suggests that in a situation dominated by Sinified expressive aims it became difficult to use pillow-words. The decrease in the frequency of use of pillow-words is an unmistakable feature of the second stage of the Ancient Age. Moreover, at this time, when surviving poems are relatively numerous, there is also a decline for the first time in the number of individual pillow-words used. Whereas Hitomaro used 106 individual "pillow-words" a total of 178 times, Yakamochi uses but 90 individual pillow-words a total of 237 times.[15] This must surely be taken as a development characteristic of literature at the time. As part of that development, pillow-words are becoming decorative language.

With prefatory words and phrases, the development was toward the so-called meaningful prefaces. With the weakening of that imparted vitality which had been the original purpose of these phrases, it became uneconomical to waste several lines on that which now seemed unrelated to the main body of the poem. This practicality became the main concern, so that along with the extinction of Hitomaro-style lengthy guide phrases, there is in tanka only the meaningful preface, whose scene and situation are described in ways painstakingly related to what follows. The practical spirit first appears in circumstances involving Sinified expressive aims. As we have seen, there is the atmosphere of hovering over the poems related to Tabito's "Preface to an Excursion to the Matsura River." In the eleven poems of this group, there is not one use of a pillow-word. The sole use of a preface follows.

/Wakayu tsuru	/Like the Matsura
Matsura no kawa no	Where we angle fish
Kawanami no/	In the river waves/
Nami ni shi mowaba	If I loved you as is usual,
Ware koime yamo.	Would I yearn for you like this!

(*MYS*, 5:858)

The preface in the first three lines has as its juncture with the last two a play on "kawa*nami*" and "*nami* ni" [in the translation "river waves,"

---

[15] [The author's contrast can be fully appreciated only by virtue of its involving by nineteen chōka by Hitomaro vs. forty-six by Yakamochi.—Ed.]

"as is usual"]. But along with this traditional device we have verisimilar description of activities at a riverside.

When juncture is effected by homophony, something of the old-style usage remains. We find completed specimens of the meaningful preface when the connection is effected metaphorically. A poem by Yakamochi (*MYS*, 4:785) will serve as example:

/Waga yado no	/The dew settles
Kusa no ue shiroku	White upon the plants
Oku tsuyu no/	About my house/
Inochi mo oshikarazu	Insubstantial life means nothing
Imo ni awazareba.	When I cannot have her I love.

This use of the familiar emblem of dew for life's evanescence lacks that infusion of vitality which is the essence of how the kotodama works.

Of course none of this implies that poets had grown wholly dissatisfied with old styles of thought or with their expression in verse. Here is a poem by Fujiwara Kusumaro in reply to poems sent him by Yakamochi (*MYS*, 4:791).

/Okuyama no	/In distant mountains
Iwakage ni ouru	Under shade of boulders grows
Suga no ne ni/	The fine-rooted sedge/
Nemokoro ware mo	With what great depths do I
Ai omowazare ya.	Not also yearn to be with you.

But the poetic trend was in general toward the meaningful preface. That trend would be a legacy to the *Kokinshū*. And the poets who gave the trend its force—Okura, Tabito, Yakamochi, among others—had been imbued with the Sinified aim of individualistic expression.

POETRY OF THOSE AT THE CAPITAL

More poems in the *Man'yōshū* come from the period of Yakamochi than from any other. The style of this large body of poems does not differ much from the style of poetry at the time of Tabito and Okura, so that if a distinction is to be made, this corpus of poems has an air of refinement and may be called "poetry of those at the capital."

In the poems by Yakamochi and other later writers, we often find contrasts between the capital and rusticity, or expressions of longing for the capital at Nara from courtiers posted to the provinces. Both Tabito and Okura have a poem of such a general kind (3:331; 5:880). But their numbers are so small that generalization is not feasible. There is also the expression "the countryside, *distant as the sky*" (*amazakaru* hina), which appears twenty-three times in the *Man'yōshū*, with eighteen from poems in Yakamochi's time. The capital was much preferred.

Aoniyoshi	*Lovely in colored earth*
Nara no miyako wa	Nara the royal capital
Saku hana no	Abloom with flowers—
Niou ga gotoku	As if they set it all aglow—
Ima sakari nari.	Now at their height of bloom.

(*MYS*, 3:328)

The Nara of the time referred to by this poem was a city modeled, in its checkerboard of streets, on Ch'ang-an, and along those regularly crossing streets were planted willows (*MYS*, 19:4142). To the east and to the west were markets, and people of the time felt an urban bustle (*MYS*, 3:310; 7:1264). The nobility went to and fro on proud horses. When they described those scenes, the Japanese had in mind poetic descriptions of the prosperity of Ch'ang-an. Here is some Chinese nostalgia, "On the Ch'ang-an of Old," by Lu Chao-lin (635-84).

The southern streets and northern palaces join in the northern
   quarter,
The five-branched roads and the three avenues set bounds to the
   three markets.
Tender willows and green pagoda trees sweep the ground where
   they droop.
Fresh breezes raise red dust, darkening the expanse of sky.
                              (*Ch'üan T'ang Shih*, 41:5-9)

After they had become accustomed to broad avenues like those of the capital, the difficulty of walking in the country must have come as a shock.

Aoniyoshi	*Lovely in colored earth*
Nara no ōchi wa	Nara has wide avenues
Yuki yokedo	Where it is good to go,
Kono yamamichi wa	But this mountain path out here
Yuki ashikarikeri.	Makes the going very bad.

MYS, 15:3728)

After living for a time in the country, one's spirits flag.

Shiratama no	*As dear as pearls,*
Migahoshi kimi o	You whom I wish to see and yet
Mizu hisa ni	Do not this long while—
Hina ni shi oreba	Oh, this being in the country,
Ikeru to mo nashi.	You cannot call it life at all.

(*MYS*, 19:4170)

For these poets, real life existed only in the capital. From this attitude, as a remote source, was born the conception of "travel" (tabi) codified in the renga of the High Middle Ages—a travel stanza was one dealing with passage from the capital to the country or from province to province: to go from the country to the capital was to return, not to travel at all. In the earlier stage of the Ancient Age there was no such literary awareness of life in the capital. The concept of "poetry of those at the capital" is one that first appears during Yakamochi's time. And what were the special characteristics of those at the capital? What implications did the capital have for their writing?

Among the special characteristics of those people at that time, the very first requiring mention is that they were educated in the culture of a foreign country. It was essential that they have the most up-to-date information about T'ang China. They made some misjudgments, as in bringing home from China "The Visit to the Immortals' Dwelling" as a presumed classic, whereas to the Chinese it was a trivial bit of zoku writing; or in taking as their poetic model the declining phase of Six Dynasties poetry. Such distortions were inevitable, however, and their awareness certainly led them to aim at what was newest in the culture of the T'ang Dynasty. Yakamochi and perhaps others were brought up in Tabito's residence, living with a nun from Silla (*MYS*, 3:460-61). He could only have had the warmest affection for that foreign culture from his childhood.

These people of the capital, with their information about the continent, assumed they had a mutual possession. The premise for poetic composition in Yakamochi's time was that "the people I know possess the same knowledge I have of Chinese literature." Perhaps before he turned twenty, Yakamochi sent a number of love poems (sōmonka) to the girl later his wife, Ōiratsume (the Eldest Daughter) of the Sakanoe house. Here are the first two of one run of fifteen (*MYS*, 4:471-472).

Ime no ai wa	Loving in a dream,
Kurushikarikeri	What suffering has it brought—

Odorokite	For I awake,
Kakisaguredo mo	And though I reach about for you,
Te ni mo oreneba.	I cannot feel you with my hands.

Hitoe nomi	The sash, remember it?
Imo ga musaban	The one, my dear, that you tied
Obi o sura	Just once about me—
Mie musabu beku	So much my yearning wastes me
Waga mi ga narinu.	It goes around me three times now.

These are poems in the wake of works like "The Visit to the Immortals' Dwelling," writings redolent of predecessors.[16]

As Yakamochi wrote, Ōiratsume was ten years old, obviously with no conception of Chinese literature. On the other hand, her mother—Lady Ōtomo of Sakanoe—welcomed with enthusiasm the prospect of her daughter's becoming Yakamochi's wife, and it appears that she stood in for her daughter, responding poetically to Yakamochi (Yamamoto, 1971, 152). Yakamochi no doubt also believed that the mother would acquaint her daughter with "The Visit to the Immortals' Dwelling." Mother and suitor composed poems on the same topic, "The Crescent Moon." His precedes hers (MYS, 6:993, 994).

Tsuki tachite	The moon comes up,
Tada mikazuki no	And just like the crescent moon,
Mayone kaki	My eyebrows as they itch—
Ke nagaku koishi	And having yearned for you so long
Kimi ni aeru kamo.	I find that at last I have you.

Furisakete	Casting my gaze about
Mikazuki mireba	I see the crescent moon,
Hitome mishi	And just one look
Hito no mayobiki	Upon those blackened eyebrows
Omowayuru kamo.	Is enough to make me yearn.

The reference to blackened eyebrows derives from knowledge about Chinese cosmetics, about customs that probably originated in Iran or India. Sim-

---

[16] MYS, 4:741-42. With 741, cf. "For a moment I slept as I sat, then I had a dream of the Ten Beauties and the surprise awoke me in distraction, suddenly empty-handed. My heart was filled with a wan pleasure. I returned—what could I say?" ("Yūsenkutsu," p. 119). And with 742, cf. "These eyes were wholly certain, both wild ducks were lost together. Day after day my robes seemed larger, morning after morning my sash loosened" (ibid., p. 188). These passages have been mentioned as sources since Keichū [d. 1701, one of the great Japanese scholars]. But the conception of the latter can be found in several poems, in both the Wen Hsüan and the Yü-t'ai Hsin-yung, so the connection cannot be called certain (Kojima, 1974, 1021).

ilar kinds of exotic depiction can be found in holdings in the Shōsōin—a picture of a beautiful woman standing beneath a tree, or a folding screen depicting a woman whose head is decorated with feathers.[17] Chinese poets refer solely to women's eyebrows as moths' eyebrows—that is, broadly painted ones—and sometimes the moon is compared to them, as in a couplet from Ho Tzu-lang's "In Reply to Mr. Miao's Poem, 'On the Moon' ":

> Brilliant and lucid sparkle the pool's waters,
> The reflection seen is the moth-browed moon.
>
> (*Gyokudai*, 5:529)

There are no examples of moons compared to thinly drawn eyebrows. And if Lady Ōtomo and Yakamochi wrote from shared knowledge, that does not mean they were simply drawing on the exotic appeals of another country, but that their writing had the specific aim of giving expression to "the new" (atarashimi).

Seventeen years later, Yakamochi wrote two poems under the heading "Gazing Intently at the Peaches and Plums in My Spring Garden" (*MYS*, 19:4139, 4140).

Haru no sono	The garden in spring
Kurenai niou	Glows with the crimson
Momo no hana	Of the peach flowers,
Shitaderu michi ni	And on the brightened path beneath
Idetatsu otome.	A young woman stops to gaze.
Waga sono no	In my garden
Sumomo no hana ka	They are plum flowers, are they?
Niwa ni chiru	There they fall,
Hadare no imada	Or is it a patch of snowflakes
Nokoritaru kamo.	That somehow still remains?

It is well known that the former poem uses the same motif as the picture in the Shōsōin, a beautiful woman standing beneath a tree.[18]

---

[17] In early [eighth-century] T'ang China, there were more than ten styles of makeup for women's eyebrows. But in general they can be distinguished as either thick and dark or fine and light. The style for the painting of the beautiful women under a tree and the woman on the screen is the thick and dark ("moth eyebrows"); Fujii Kiyoshi, 1966, 146-48. However, in the painting of the beautiful woman in foreign dress from Turfan [northern Sinkiang province in China] and the women pictured on the walls of the Takamatsuzuka tumulus [the Nara-Asuka area] the painted eyebrows are of the fine and light kind.

[18] [See the frontispiece to this volume.] The Shōsōin picture referred to is believed to date from 752, and Yakamochi's poem from two years before that. Pictures of beautiful women under trees have been discovered in Astana in central Asia and in eastern Turkestan,

Taken together the two poems function like parallel lines in Chinese verse, although no doubt their chief aim is to appreciate the rich coloring projected. A poem by Hsiao Kang, "In Reply to the Prince of Hsiang-tung's Poem, 'A Famous Scholar Likes Beauties,' " contains these lines:

> The window where she makes up is screened by the willow's color,
> On the well water shines the peach blossom's crimson.
>
> (*Gyokudai*, 7:559).

Yakamochi's poems seem to make use of these lines. Yet it must be said that in late Six Dynasties or early T'ang poetry, when the subject is a beautiful woman in a lovely scene, she is shown applying makeup, walking, dancing, or somehow moving, whereas Yakamochi's pictorialism records a woman in an arrested pose. It may well be that, to a readership well versed in Chinese poetry, that halted pose held appeal for its novelty (atarashimi).

The expressive attitude, the implicit tone of the poetry of Tempyō era culture, is a second important characteristic. From the beginning of this *History*, implicitness has been postulated as one of the characteristics of all Japanese literature. It is a quality that becomes fully marked with the poets of the capital. We can begin with the admission of conceptual similarities as a first manifestation of that implicitness. Here is a poem from Yakamochi's earliest period, when he was perhaps twelve (*MYS*, 8:1441).

Uchikirashi	White haze comes to the sky
Yuki wa furitsutsu	And the snow falls on and on—
Shikasuga ni	Be that as it may,
Wagie no sono ni	In the garden of my house
Uguisu naku mo.	The warbler already sings.

In a poem written some two years before and included among the "Poems of the Plum Blossom Banquet" arranged by Tabito, Ōtomo Momoyo had written similarly (*MYS*, 5:823):

Ume no hana	Blossoms of the plum,
Chiraku wa izuku	Where is it that they fall?
Shikasuga ni	Be that as it may,
Kono Ki no yama ni	Here at Ki among the hills
Yuki wa furitsutsu.	The snow falls on and on.

and there must have been numerous T'ang examples (Fujii Kiyoshi, 1966, 136-38). It seems very possible that Yakamochi had seen the motif in materials imported from China.

Of course Yakamochi must have known Momoyo's poem, and one can easily multiply examples of this kind.[19]

Uchinabiku	At last signs beckon:
Haru sarikureba	Spring has definitely come;
Shikasuga ni	Be that as it may,
Ama kumo kirai	From the clouds that mist the sky
Yuki wa furitsutsu.	The snow falls on and on.
Ume no hana	Blossoms of the plum
Sakichirisuginu	Have opened and already fallen;
Shikasuga ni	Be that as it may,
Shirayuki niwa ni	The white snow in my garden
Furishikiritsutsu.	Falls on and on and on.
Yama no ki ni	At the mountain's edge,
Yuki wa furitsutsu	The snow falls on and on;
Shikasuga ni	Be that as it may,
Kono kawayagi wa	The willows by this riverbank
Moetekeru kamo.	Have begun to shine with green.

(*MYS*, 10:1832, 1834, 1848)

A variety of criticism of such practice has been entered by practitioners of modern tanka. But if we treat the poems as examples of literary practice in this later stage of the Ancient Age, what we see is no less than the emergence of the poetry of those at the capital. We see poets whose thoughts and feelings have been refined by contact with an advanced culture. Their temper reflected some desire to escape from the increasing complexity of the social environment of the capital, and probably they became increasingly sensitive as well. So sensitive a temper recoils in particular from the stimulus of the excessive.

It was not like these people of the capital to hold that intense speaking was requisite to move the feelings. On the contrary, to a ripe sensibility the smallest stimulus could provide one with a suitable degree of agitation. There was, as a consequence, no need to search for novelties of material or design. Poets sanctioned the joining of largely similar phrases. With the large-scale, sophisticated entropy of the time, the people of the

[19] See Yamamoto, 1971, 34-36. [The "kind" of motif referred to is one not simply involving shared diction and imagistic features of these two and the next three poems, but an implicit resemblance, as when—with elegant confusion—plum blossoms and snow petals are taken for each other. It will be clear that the poem by Yakamochi takes its second and third lines from Momoyo's fifth and third, sharing a common language but not making an allusion.—Ed.].

capital must have taken pride in the minute differences they so efficiently perceived and communicated. That is why poets relied on a readership likewise sensitive and able to pursue minute variations among a number of models.[20] This is at one with the expressive awareness found in the *Kokinshū*: the later stage of the Ancient Age includes the vanguard of the Middle Ages.

The implications typical of those at the capital often found expression in sadness (shūshi). From the observation that human existence could not escape eventual extinction in the infinite flow of time and the vast reaches of the cosmos, there was born a sense of transience (hakanasa). With that came a change in the workings of contemplative reasoning. As early as the Archaic Age, there had been poems speaking of the sorrow (kanashimi) leading to shedding tears of blood over the death of one's spouse. In the new age, however, despair or bereavement directly conveyed were not the affective materials of poetry. Rather, in both rational and emotional response to the quality of human life in its entirety, the implicit sense of transience led to expressions of sadness.

Here are three poems by Yakamochi on the twenty-third and twenty-fifth of the Second Month of 753 (*MYS*, 19:4290-92).

Haru no no ni	Over the spring fields
Kasumi tanabiki	The haze trails in banners,
Urakanashi	And it is all so sad,
Kono yūkage ni	While from this evening's shadows
Uguisu naku mo.	The warbler also sings its song.
Waga yado no	Here at my house
Isasa muratake	Stands a meager bamboo grove;
Fuku kaze ni	In the wind that blows
Oto no kasokeki	The sound itself turns dark
Kono yūbe kamo.	As this evening falls.
Uraura ni	Softly, softly,
Tereru haruhi ni	The spring sunlight shines,
Hibari agari	A lark rising in it;
Kokoro kanashi mo	And there is sadness in my heart
Hitori shi omoeba.	That I should feel these things alone.

[20] There was deliberate pursuit of associated images [such as the warbler and snow in Yakamochi's poem—Ed.]. For instance, the associated imagery for the hototogisu (a "summer" bird) includes: the mandarin orange (tachibana), appearing most often (sixteen times); thereafter deutzia (unohana, nine times), iris (ayame, eight times), and wisteria (fuji, six times). Infrequent associations are with the Japanese bead tree (ōchi, twice) and bush clover (hagi, once).

These three are among Yakamochi's very finest poems. The sensitive description offers a feeling of deep loneliness aroused by faint sounds greeting the ear. That feeling is heightened the more for being aroused amid the overflowing brightness of spring. Many critics have pointed out acute sensations of a modern kind in these poems and have so praised them. Certainly it is possible to appreciate these poems on the basis of their having a modern sense of isolation: undeniably that is one way of access to them. On the other hand, it is obvious that Yakamochi is not a modern poet, and if we account for the *ancient* character of the isolation expressed in the three poems, we shall get closer to their original conception.

About the middle of the Six Dynasties in China there emerged an aesthetic understanding that human life takes place within a vast natural scene. One feature of this was the view of human life as something floating on an eternal temporal stream. Perhaps the first poem of this kind was the "Fu Lamenting Time's Passage" by Lu Chi (261-303). Another feature was the transience of life derived from consideration of human drifting through the boundless reaches of the cosmos. This was first observed in "A Preface to the Orchid Pavilion Gathering" by Wang Hsi-chih (Shiba, 1958, 114). However, this kind of thought was presented as explicit thought, and writing that depicts human transience melting away in natural description was not seen until later, in T'ao Ch'ien. The poem he wrote—"A Poem Given to My Cousin, Ching-yüan, Composed in the Twelfth Month [of 403]" (*Tōshi*, 3:423-24)—consists of twenty lines, of which the fifth through eighth are:

> Frigid, frigid, the year ends in wind;
> Dark, dark, the whole day wears out in snow.
> Though I incline my ear, there is not even a faint voice:
> What reaches my eye is stark white and certainly pure.

This is not vernal sadness but wintry severity.

If this writing about the silent, endless fall of snow that heightens human isolation is transposed to the scenery of spring, it would be at one with Yakamochi's "That I should feel these things alone." It is not that Yakamochi was using this poem by T'ao Ch'ien. Because there is no lack of other Chinese poems on the subject, it is meaningless to point to a given poem as source. But if Yakamochi knew of the poetic motif of sadness treating the isolation and desolation which Chinese discovered in the human position between heaven and earth, then his molding his own impressions into the motif must show how aware he was that he was writing the poetry of the people at the capital. Surely his three poems show that just as in another poem he could exchange, for his own wife's stepping into their garden, the view of a Chinese woman amid the splendor of peach blossoms, so also he could write about his sensations of a spring day as if he had become a Chinese poet possessed by sadness. It is much too modern a notion that all he wrote about was his own immediate feelings. We shall not find poems like these three in the rest of Yakamochi's oeuvre, nor in writing after him. Their achievement occurred incidentally, touched off by Chinese poems of sadness. It does seem better to interpret them so rather than believe that Yakamochi had labored and labored, at last managing to drag his feet across some final poetic boundary.

There was a third feature. In addition to being, at any cost, people of the capital, these poets were never to forget an attitude of "play" (asobi) in every last aspect of their life, including poetry. There was in this an inclination to scorn as rustic those who knew no better than to be dead serious, taking everything with an open mouth. This was not to reject earnestness itself, however. One would wear a sober face when earnestness was required, just as one knew the right occasion to depart from the serious by exercising "latitude" (yutori): knowledge of decorum was essential to people of the capital. In matters literary, this meant protecting ga to the end in formal situations, although it could also be desirable, according to circumstances, to infuse zoku into informal situations. Obviously, that zoku was never to overwhelm the standard ga, and it was always from an awareness of ga that one judged the occasion, the degree, and the quality of zoku that might be hazarded. The fact that the zoku was always considered in terms of its dominance by ga relates to the "ga-zoku" defined in the General Introduction to this *History*.

This realm of ga-zoku first appears in the use of Sinified diction in waka. In theory, waka was to be composed solely in Yamato words, with no intermingling of foreign diction. We can find, however, examples of waka using Indic words translated into Chinese and taken by Japanese as Sinified loanwords [which are italicized but are not guide phrases].

Baramani no	It is *sacerdotal*,
Tsukureru oda o	Yet the well-worked field
Hamu karasu	Is raided by the crow
Manabuta harete	Perched with swollen eyelids
Hatahoko ni ori.	On the sacred banner box.

(*MYS*, 16:3856)

Kono koro no	If these were times
Aga koi chikara	When what I exert for love
Shirushiatsume	Were totaled and recorded,

Kū ni mōsaba   And I could tell of my whole *anguish*,
Goi no kagafuri.   I would be promoted to *fifth rank*.

(*MYS*, 16:3858)[21]

It is not certain when these poems were written, but they seem to be products of the later stage of this period.

Ga-zoku did not depend solely on the use of outlandish diction, since that which was productive of comic effect would also serve.

Teradera no   Passing many temples,
Megaki mōsaku   The famished she-demon said,
Ōmiwa no   "Find me Ōmiwa,
Ogaki tabarite   A famished he-demon like myself,
Sono ko umawan.   And I'll bear him one like us."

(*MYS*, 16:3840)

Now, these verses were addressed by Lord Ikeda to his butt, Lord Ōmiwa Okimori, who was not to be denied his turn.

Hotoke tsukuru   For the Buddha statue,
Masoho tarazu wa   You lack enough vermilion—
Mizu tamaru   So there is the puddle
Ikeda no Aso ga   Of Lord "Pond Field" Ikeda,
Hana no ue o hore.   Dig in that big red nose.

(*MYS*, 16:3841)[22]

Countering the charge of being a hellish demon, Okimori declares Ikeda (Pond Field) to have a red nose—like many a pictured demon in Japan. Neither allegation involves the use of loanwords from other tongues but rather uses highly colloquial language like "Dig in that big red nose" (Hana no ue o hore) that is not at all appropriate to waka. All in all, we discover three kinds of "okashimi" (oddness, the diverting) that would define haikai in a later age: the use of Sinified words; the use of common, low language; and humorous content. By such criteria, we can say that haikai originates in the later stage of this age.

[21] The italicized words are borrowed, with "Baramani" being ultimately Indic (via China) and the others Sinified. [The fifth rank was crucial in being the first of the upper nobility, at a wide gap above ranks below.—Ed.]

[22] Poem 3841 may have been written about 752. If so, that would more or less fix the date of the poem to which it replies. ["Gaki" (male or female) are properly souls from the Buddhist hell, where they are so famished and endure such pain that they would like to get back to the human world. But the demonic and evil are what is more generally implied by the poem.—Ed.]

Although these examples clearly have elements in common with haikai, it was not necessary to go to such extremes to produce haikai-like exchanges among close friends. For example, Yakamochi sent the following to a young woman:

Hanekazura	The maiden who put on
Ima suru imo o	The garland of her debut
Ime ni mite	In my dream comes now to view,
Kokoro no uchi ni	And here within my yearning heart
Koi wataru kamo.	Longings tear me all apart.

(MYS, 4:705)[23]

Nobody knows what a "hanekazura" is, but it must have been some kind of head ornament used for a young woman's coming-of-age ceremony. So Yakamochi is saying: in spite of your having done with coming-of-age, you insist on wearing that garland in my dreams, so casting me into the most agitated yearning for you. For her part, the young woman replies:

Hanekazura	A maiden who now wears
Ima suru imo wa	The garland of her debut
Nakarishi o	Never will come to view,
Izure no imo so	But how many merry maidens
Sokoba koitaru.	Do you take to stir that heart?

(MYS, 4:706)

She replies: "That 'you' you spoke of as wearing the garland is not to be found here and where, then be that 'you' whom you go on so about? Lord Yakamochi, I am one thing, but you seem to take other young ladies as your lovers, and really such inconstancy. . . ." So the teasing goes. It seems likely that the young woman addressed did not write the reply, but rather her mother or an elder sister on her behalf. Both sides realize that the business is made up. This technique of speaking of the fictional as real will be one that flourishes in the Early Middle Ages, taking its origin here in the late stage of the Ancient Age.

This world of humor and play, with its objective depiction or splitting of reality, will seem to yield poems of little worth—to those who have

---

[23] [Our use of rhyme here is meant to correspond, however feebly, to Yakamochi's repetition of sounds: "ima . . . imo . . . ime" and "Kokoro . . . koi . . . kamo." We fiddle with the translation of the next poem for similar reasons.—Ed.]

a single standard of value. Of course I do not regard them as great poems, either. All the same, the spirit of latitude in these poems can only testify to the refined tastes of those who lived in the capital. As a literary phenomenon, this emergence, for the first time in Japan, of "the poetry of those in the capital" is an event of profound significance.

CHAPTER 11

Setsuwa Composition

FROM SETSUWA TO MONOGATARI

In the Archaic Age and in the earlier stage of the Ancient Age, Yamato literature was more or less involved in a homogeneous conception of life. Those earlier people merged the spiritual with the human, and it seems that a literature meant merely to interest and delight did not exist. Even if the poems of those times look to modern readers like ordinary lyrics or descriptions, in fact, it was expected that the kotodama would work in them. And if there were stories (hanashi) abounding in interest, in truth their function was to provide authority for one's clan or ancestors. There was no room to compose poems for pleasure alone or to relate stories to meet some standard of interest. But about the time that waka shifts to play (asobi), there appear setsuwa in which the interesting (omoshirosa) has become the chief concern.

Of course in the Archaic Age the old style of legends was stoutly maintained and most of its setsuwa were rooted in experience. We must inquire therefore of the origin of the movement to break with the old style of tale, even if but partially. As we have had occasion to see, the central feature of setsuwa was that they were oral, and because written transmission was exceptional, the majority of oral setsuwa have simply been lost leaving it difficult for us today to apprehend their actual nature. But if we limit ourselves to setsuwa transmitted by writing, those with interest as their standard seem to have had foreign stories as their guides.

Stories handed down from one's predecessors passed on an important awareness of one's people and land. They could not turn on a taste for the interesting alone. Because various kinds of foreign stories did not, by contrast, carry the responsibilities of indigenous setsuwa, they could be appreciated in relaxed enjoyment. One example is the Urashima setsuwa.[1] The story that my mother told me when I was a child was set forth long ago in the *Nihon Shoki* (in the chapter on Yūryaku Tennō, twenty-second year of his reign, Seventh Month; p. 388), more minutely in a fragment surviving from the *Tango Topography* (475-77); and its waka version appears, as we have seen, in the *Man'yōshū* (9:1740). The version in the *Nihon Shoki* goes as follows.

---

[1] [The author is referring to prose versions, although he will later mention again the poetic version included in the *Man'yōshū*.—Ed.]

A man of Tsutsugawa in the Yosa District of Tamba Province, the son of Urashima of Mizunoe, boarded a boat to fish. By accident he caught a great turtle, who suddenly turned into a woman. The Son of Urashima took a great fancy to her and accompanied her down into the sea. They went to the Land of Eternity where they met an immortal. The story is in another chapter.

We know nothing about that other chapter. In the *Tango Topography* fragment, we read, "This does not disagree at all with the version recorded by Lord Mikotomochi Umakai. The reason is that it is an abbreviation." It is evident that Umakai's version was transmitted in writing, although that does not prove it is the same as that in "another chapter" of the *Nihon Shoki*. Whatever else we think, it cannot be doubted that there existed a written version of the Urashima story prior to the compilation of the *Nihon Shoki* in 720. And whatever the version, the foundation of the story is Taoist wizard lore. The prevailing opinion is that the story was taken up by someone like Iyobe Umakai (658?-702?) who was well versed in Chinese literature and who could add rhetorical coloring from wizard lore. There is a theory that setsuwa like this naturally develop among primitive peoples, and that when popularly disseminated ones are on occasion picked up by intellectuals, they are altered into a kind of narrative that is better suited to writing. This is the "lowborn, upward-moving" model, a pattern tantamount to the axiomatic and founded on self-evident premises. But there also exists what may be termed a "highborn, downward-moving" model.

The area of China south of the Yangtze River produced many stories about visits to the world of the immortals and marriages to dragon maidens. [In Chinese lore, dragons are commonly benign.] One such story from the Tung-ting Lake area of Hunan bears an astonishing resemblance to the Urashima story (Kimishima, 1972, 1-6).

A certain fisherman materially assisted a young woman at Tung-ting Lake. Transforming herself into a dragon, the young woman took the fisherman to the Dragon Palace. The fisherman married her, but longing for his mother in the terrestial world above, he returned. When he left her, the dragon woman gave him a small box: "When you wish me beside you," she said, "please face the box and call my name. But never open it." The fisherman arrived in his native place but found it utterly transformed, without a single soul whom he knew. Each day that he had been in the Dragon Palace counted as fifteen terrestial years. Totally done in, the fisherman thoughtlessly raised the lid of the little box. Smoke poured out and the fisherman who had remained so young till then became in an instant a white-haired old man.

Because the story corresponds, even in minute details, with that of Urashima, there can be no doubt that some popular Chinese tale was transmitted to Japan and evolved into the Urashima setsuwa. The problem lies with the manner of transmission. Because the details agree so very well, it is not simply a matter of a basic motif being transmitted. So that rather than having been taken to Yamato in the Yayoi period and transmitted orally from memory, it would have been transmitted in complete, written form, and the probability must be thought very high that the version received in Japan already incorporated the Taoist magic. That is because in China Taoist wizardry flourished among common people from antiquity.

Presuming that the Urashima story was transmitted as a written text, the language of transmission could only have been Chinese. And no one apart from the intellectuals could have read it. In other words, whatever the transmission of the story in China, within Yamato at least the story was first disseminated among the intellectuals and thereafter spread by oral relation among the populace. The process followed the highborn, downward-moving model. Those accustomed to the lowborn, upward-moving of Yanagida Kunio [the great Japanese folklorist] may find it strange that stories could begin with what was known to the intellectuals and thereafter be handed to the common people.

Another good example is the Tanabata story.[2] Originating in some remote past in central Asia, the story was transmitted to China where, by the Six Dynasties, it had evolved into a festival. There were poems as well as tales about the Herdboy and Weaver Maiden. The poems were brought from China and became subject matter for poetry by the Japanese nobility. Among many examples, there is that in Chinese verse by Fujiwara Fuhito (659-720), whose poem appears in the *Kaifūsō* (33), and in waka there is that by Yamanoe Okura, whose poem appears in the *Man'yōshū* (8:1518).[3]

Yet another illustration of the highborn, downward-moving mode is the Hagoromo story.[4] The oldest extant version in Japan is that transmitted by a fragment of the *Tango Topography* (468-69). But in its larger

[2] [Tanabata: for the Seventh Night Story, see Chapter 4, n. 14. The popularity of the story over the centuries has led to various customs and versions.—Ed.]

[3] Doi, 1960, 37-42. A note to a Tanabata poem from the *Hitomaro Kashū* (*Collected Poems of Hitomaro*; MYS, 10:2033) dates the poem with a zodiac-element designation in the sexagenary cycle that points to either 680 or 740. This involves possible altering of the presumed date for first composition of Tanabata poems. But neither dating would change the fact that the Tanabata story first circulated in court circles.

[4] [In its most famous Japanese version, the nō *Hagoromo*, the story involves a heavenly maiden who descends to earth and removes her feathered cloak (hagoromo) and looks about the terrestial realm. A man happening by picks up the robe, without which she cannot return to the heavens. On her entreaty, the man promises to return the robe if she will dance for him, as she does. Again there are variants.—Ed.]

guise as the White Bird Maiden motif, it is a story spread throughout the world. It is impossible to claim it as a Japanese production. In fact it was no doubt brought directly from China. In a Chinese collection, the *Sou Shen Chi* (*Quests for Mysterious Events*; 1:28), believed to have been compiled in the fourth century, there is the story of Tung Yung's wife that, in basic motifs, shares the essential points of the Japanese story. But in later China there are many stories corresponding yet more closely, so that we may presume that an ancestral model was brought to Japan about the eighth century. The story is found in modern China in areas from Hainan Island to Yunnan, Tibet, Shantung, Szechwan, Kweichow, Hunan, Kwangsi, Chekiang, and Kiangsu; and it is found among such Chinese peoples as the Miao, Yao, Thai, Chuang, Li, Lee, Yü, Duar, and many others (Kimishima, 1965, 17-20).[5] It is not known which text of the Hagoromo story was brought directly to Japan, but just as with the other two stories mentioned, it must have been those intellectuals in Japan who understood Chinese who were responsible for disseminating the story.

The Taketori setsuwa provides an example of a Japanese story that had already been given shape in China and that was transmitted in its original form with extraordinary fidelity. The present *Taketori Monogatari* (*The Bamboo Cutter*) is thought to have been written in the early tenth century. But a Taketori setsuwa must have existed prior to that as a story transmitted from China. In a collection of folk tales from the northeastern area of Szechwan (the Autonomous Republic of Tibet), there is a story from the Kam called "The Spotted-Bamboo Maiden."[6] Since this agrees even in details with our present *Taketori Monogatari*, some archetypical version of the folk tale must have been brought to Japan. Here is a summary of the story.

1. There was a poor mother and son (named Lang-pa) who made their living gathering bamboo. The greedy lord of the area bought it from them at a depressed price.
2. Once when a retainer of the lord came to purchase bamboo, Lang-pa cut a trunk of bamboo he particularly prized, and to hide it, threw it in the river.
3. From that bamboo was born a beautiful girl, who was named the Spotted-Bamboo Maiden.

[5] [The author's purpose in this gazeteer of locations of the motif is to drive home the point that this very "Japanese" story is international in provenance, reached Japan in writing, and is highborn, downward-moving.—Ed.]

[6] This was collected in 1954. It is translated by T'ien Hai-yen and appears in *Chin-yü Feng-huang*, vol. 1 (Shanghai: Shao-nien Erh–ting Chu-pan-she, 1959), the first printing (Itō–Momota, 1972, 35-42).

4. When Lang-pa and the maiden reached a suitable age, the mother asked the maiden to marry her son. She promised to do so three years later.

5. Five young men of consequence wished to marry the Spotted-Bamboo Maiden. She assigned a separate ordeal to each of them. She would become the wife of the one who could bring, as assigned: (a) A gold temple bell that would not break though heavily struck, (b) a jade branch that would not break though hard struck, (c) the unburnable leather robe of the Volcano Rat, (d) the water-dividing jewel from the head of a sea dragon, (e) a gold egg from a swallow's nest.

6. When each of the five failed the maiden was happily married to Lang-pa.

In presenting this folk tale to Japanese scholars, Itō Seiji showed that it agrees with *The Bamboo Cutter* not only in details mentioned but even in such fine points as the ways the five suitors fail (1973, 154-75). The story of the child born from bamboo is found in numerous countries and among South Asian peoples who cultivate bamboo. The regions include Malaya, Sumatra, the Philippines, Borneo, Mindanao, Micronesia, Taiwan, etc., as also peoples like the Mantra, Negrito, Thai Lü, Batak, Sulu, Tagalog, Samar, Magin, Danao, and various tribal groups of Taiwan (Matsumoto, 1951, 163-73). During the time required for the basic motif to reach a remote part of Szechwan, the other motif of ordeals for suitors had been added, and the tale of the Spotted-Bamboo Maiden became complete. If, at the end of the Szechwan version, we add the motif of the heavenly maiden of the Hagoromo story, then we have a plot closely corresponding to the *The Bamboo Cutter*.

It is not clear when the plot of the Spotted-Bamboo Maiden became the Taketori setsuwa. But the fact that a story transmitted from China should take root in Japan ought to lead us to consider two things. The first is the acceptance of fictionality in popular literature. For the setsuwa handed down from the Archaic Age, the contents were taken as unquestioned truth, no matter how unnatural they were. In contrast to those native setsuwa, stories of foreign origin could be recognized as fictional and the appeal (omoshirosa) held by the fiction could be enjoyed. And this is what may be thought the ground from which arose the tsukurimonogatari [stories with prose narrative dominant] of the Middle Ages.[7] The other thing is that there were two coexisting modes of transmission—both the lowborn, upward-moving kind and the highborn,

---

[7] [Monogatari are distinguished into various kinds today. The basic distinction relevant to this chapter is that between utamonogatari, in which poems play a central role, e.g., the *Ise Monogatari* (*Tales of Ise*); and tsukurimonogatari, in which prose is central, e.g., *Taketori Monogatari* (*The Bamboo Cutter*).—Ed.]

downward-moving kind. That coexistence testifies to the lack of class opposition in Japanese literature postulated in the General Introduction. It is a very important characteristic of Japanese literature that, from so many points of view, such opposition cannot be observed. Certainly its absence must be inferred from the fact that stories told by common people were turned into written products by the nobility, and from the reciprocal process in which stories fashioned by the nobility spread among common people.

There were numerous setsuwa in the Ancient Age besides those mentioned. Because by their very character they were transmitted orally, it is unclear today what textual versions they may have had. Their plots, however, can often be understood from waka and from forenotes to waka. In one version of this form of presentation, the poem is used to relate the story. In the other, the story is related in the forenote, and the ensuing poem(s) offer situational details or the subjective responses of characters in the work. The poem on Urashima mentioned earlier (*MYS*, 9:1740) is of the former kind, whereas the poems on the Old Bamboo Cutter (*MYS*, 16:3791-3802) appear to be of a middle kind between the two basic types of presentation. Because the Old Bamboo Cutter appears as a character in these poems, it is necessary from time to time to refer to *The Bamboo Cutter* in a discussion of origins. But in motifs, the poems differ starkly from that monogatari. Or perhaps one should say instead that the origin is "The Visit to the Immortals' Dwelling," which also provided the model for Tabito's "Excursion to the Matsura River" (*MYS*, 5:853-60). In Tabito's work ten fictional characters exchange poems, so producing what can be called a dramatic mode for the poems.

When the number of characters is reduced, we may get something like this.

> Once there was a man. He had recently been married. Shortly thereafter he became a mounted courier and was sent to a remote region. Since this commission came as an edict, he had no further time to spend intimately with his wife. On his departure she became distraught with grief and sank deeply into illness. After many years had passed, the husband came back and completed his greetings. That is, he came up to her and looked at her. He felt wretched to see how her face had been wasted with agony, and the words he wished to utter stuck in his throat. The pangs of grief led him to sigh and weep streaming tears. He composed lines of verse that he murmured. This was his poem:

Kaku nomi ni	That you should be so,
Arikeru mono o	Considering what then you were—
Inagawa no	My tears of yearning

Oki o fukamete	Will deepen the Ina River
Aga moerikeri.	As it floods the very sea.

The woman heard the poem as she lay on her bed. Raising her head from her pillow, she responded in a quavering voice with her own poem:

Nubatama no	*Black as lily seeds,*
Kurogami nurete	My dark hair has been wetted
Awayuki no	With white flakes of snow,
Furu ni ya kimasu	And now you come to see them fallen
Kokoda koureba.	Since I have longed for you so much.

(*MYS*, 16:3804-5)

There are other examples where just two persons appear. When the handling involves in this fashion only two poems or so, the description of the scene and the depiction of characters are heightened in meaning by the prose, which is not at all something tacked on but writing that shares responsibility with the poems to form a single expressive world. This may seem of a piece with the utamonogatari of the Middle Ages. Yet the characteristic structure of utamonogatari involves the story's moving toward a point of climax, at which point a poem is composed—a poem or poems that afford the opportunity to resolve the issues happily or to break them in a fall. The poems with prose we have just seen do not show such an inclination. Consequently, rather than saying that the later Ancient Age produced something resembling the utamonogatari, it is better to hold that it opened the way for that form.

Another noteworthy feature of our example is its foundation in ordinary human life. In every country, ancient literature deals with divinities or heroes as chief characters, and it is normal for the events depicted to be extraordinary. But in our example, the newly married couple who appear are downright common, and the circumstances use the unextraordinary event of a lengthy posting to a distant province. For all that, it becomes an impressive *story* [hanashi]. As a literary phenomenon, there is great significance in the fact that by around the eighth century readers already accepted ordinary life as the basis of stories [hanashi]. Before that prose stories had relied for their emotional effect on the expressive power of waka. The art of storytelling did not then skillfully support the evocation of feeling. As a result, at this later stage of the age, it is with the utamonogatari as with tsukurimonogatari—neither truly makes an appearance. But one cannot deny that by the late eighth century the groundwork has been prepared for both kinds.

REALITY AND UNREALITY IN SETSUWA

It is in the nature of popular stories that they seldom concern common, humdrum events. So, in setsuwa, the usual appeal lay in uncommon events or their traces. The uncommon always appears in setsuwa of the earlier Ancient Age, which were highly valued for their authority as genuine accounts bequeathed by ancestors, and which were therefore not to be taken with partial enjoyment as unusual stories. A man born with a tail pushes aside a boulder in order that he can emerge (*KJK, Jimmuki,* 58); large and small fish gently bear a boat on their backs, enabling it to cross the sea (*KJK, Jingūki,* 154). These unusual matters are not taken as amusement but as undeniable facts. Yet as we have seen, by the eighth century there appear setsuwa in which the focus of attention is on the story as story, and no doubt that tendency strengthened amain during the ninth century. It seems likely that it was sometime between 785 and 822 that there was assembled the *Nihonkoku Gempō Zen'aku Ryōiki* (*Miraculous Stories of Karmic Retribution of Good and Evil in Japan*)—or, in its usual shortened title, *Nihon Ryōiki* (also *Reiiki; Miraculous Stories of Japan*). The stories included there demonstrate the new inclination.

This first Japanese collection of setsuwa seems to have established the pattern of collecting setsuwa into the High Middle Ages, and its obvious, central aim is to disseminate Buddhism. That implication is clear enough from part of the title, *Gempō Zen'aku* (*Karmic Retribution of Good and Evil*), which is the fundamental Buddhist principle that good causes have good effects and bad ones bad ones. In the preface by the compiler, Keikai, we read:

> If the karmic nature of good and evil were not made known to us, how could we rectify wickedness and establish righteousness? And if karmic causation were not demonstrated to us, by what means could we lead people to amend their wicked minds and follow the path of virtue? Long ago in China, the *Ming-pao Chi* was written, as was the *Pan-jo Yen-chi* during the great T'ang. Whatever else, we respect the writings of other countries, and should we not stand in awe of strange events in our own land? (*Ryōiki,* 54).

The emphasis is clear. We should pay particular attention, however, to the *Ryōiki* (*Miracles*) of the title and the "kiji" (strange events) of the preface. Of course the compiler's aim is the pious one of making known the principle of karmic causation and of working for good, and it is in order to realize that aim that he offers us details making a strong impression. Those details include so many extraordinary marvels that if, for the moment, we put the Buddhist aim of propagating the teaching into secularizing brackets, and take our pleasure solely in the "miraculous" or "strange," the result is clearly "A Collection of Miracles Heard and Strange Things Told."

The compiler himself seems to have been aware of this. The evidence comes out plainly in his comments: "There was a strange event in Japan" (74); "There was a strange, miraculous matter" (96); "At this juncture we come to a strange, miraculous matter" (156). Of course, given the things dealt with, the comments are natural enough, but we should note that in order to convey the feeling of the miraculous and strange it was necessary to use narrative and descriptive techniques thitherto unknown. That is, the narrative is not confined to the world of traditional telling, but instead enlarges the sphere of actuality. When Keikai is relating events or traditions, he does his best to write concretely of times, places, and names. Here, in summary, is one example.

> Fujiwara Ieyori fell ill. He had a priest come to offer prayers for his recovery, but they seemed unable to take effect. When the priest addressed the Buddha, saying "I shall offer my life in exchange for that of this sick man—please save him from his ills," the spirit of a dead person entered Ieyori, speaking through his mouth. "I am your father Nagata. While alive, I had the banners of the temple Hokkedō struck down and interfered with the construction of the temple Sai-daiji. For these sins I have borne anguishing punishment. But because of the efficaciousness of the prayers, King Yama [or Emma] has returned me to this world. I have, however, lost my body and there is no place where my soul can rest; and it is condemned to drift about."
>
> Ieyori regained his health (Ryōiki, 3:424-26).

In his detailed version of this uncanny event, Keikai begins by telling that Fujiwara Nagata was of the senior first rank of the nobility and prime minister during the reign of Kōnin (r. 770-81). Keikai adds that the event he is about to relate occurred in 782, when Ieyori held the junior fourth rank, upper grade.[8] In brief, he narrates the circumstances of actual events experienced by historical persons a few decades earlier, presenting people whose world of time and space and natural occurrences was the same as that in which he and his contemporaries now lived.

The feeling of actuality gains strength particularly when Keikai himself takes over as narrator in the thirty-eighth story of the third part (Ryōiki, 430-46).

---

[8] This is historically inaccurate. Nagata died in 771, and had been Minister of the Left (sadaijin) rather than prime minister (Shokuki, 31:389). [The title erroneously given him, dajō daijin or prime minister, would have been the office deserving the highest court rank of senior first attributed to him.—Ed.]

In the summer of 796, a fox came to my room during the Fourth and Fifth Months, barking night after night. The fox also dug a hole in the wall that I had made around its lair. Through that it managed to enter the hall, where it soiled the area of the dais of the Buddha; it would face the entry, barking during the day. When some 220 days passed—on the seventeenth of the Twelfth Month—my son died.[9]

This is obviously an example of the view that, for good occurrences or bad, there is always a premonition that evolves into its appropriate result. That is the kind of superstitious fare offered. Yet at the same time Keikai is not laconic about personal experience. From all this the reader is expected to assume that such uncanny events can take place in his own world as well. Many stories and legends related in the *Miraculous Stories of Japan* derive from times long before Keikai—from the reigns of Yūryaku (legendary reign 456-79) or Kimmei (historical reign 539-71). Yet because these and other stories are set forth with the maximum sense of reality, the whole work gives the sense that its happenings can only be those of our world, too.

We may term all this "strange things heard and miracles that occurred in the real world," and remark that setsuwa drawing their materials in this fashion date from the latter half of the eighth century into the earlier part of the ninth. This is unlikely to be an autonomous Japanese development but one owed to the importation of numerous Chinese collections of stories. The evidence lies in Keikai's citing in his preface the Chinese works *Ming-pao Chi* and *Pan-jo Yen-chi*, both of which share the property of setting forth strange things heard and miracles that occurred in the real world.[10] Other evidence for Chinese origin will be found in Yamanoe Okura's "Essay Lamenting His Own Long Illness" (following *MYS*, 5:896), a composition of the same kind as Keikai's.

The *Chih-kuai Chi* states: "Hsü Hsüan-fang of Pei-hai, former governor of Kuang-p'ing, had a daughter who died at the age of eighteen. Her ghost appeared to Feng Ma-tzu and said, 'I estimate my allotted lifespan to have been more than eighty years.' Because she told this to Feng Ma-tzu, she was able to return to life."[11]

[9] [In this passage, Keikai speaks of himself by name; perhaps "I, Keikai" should replace the pronoun in our translation.—Ed.]

[10] The *Ming-pao Chi* was compiled by T'ang Lin. Although it was lost at an early date in China, Kōzan Temple has a T'ang period copy and the Sankeikaku Bunko has a copy dated 1105. The *Pan-jo Yen-chi* was compiled by Meng Hsien-chung. It is properly entitled *Chin-kang Pan-jo Chi-yen Chi*. It dates from 718, and it too does not exist in China. Two copies exist in Japan, including a copy at the temple Ishiyamadera, both dating from the ninth century.

[11] [Translated by Levy, p. 395, very slightly revised. The essay is a medley of Chinese

The *Chih-kuai Chi* was probably the first of this kind of work brought to Japan, but several other Chinese works of the same nature must have been available to intellectuals of that time.

The *Chih-kuai Chi* has been lost. But from its very title (meaning *A Work Accounting for Marvels*), its chief constituents would seem to belong to that class of strange things and miracles, those stories classified by the Chinese as hsiao-shuo. From the Han Dynasty through the Six Dynasties, the label "hsiao-shuo" was put on stories deemed low in quality and short in length. Certainly this kind is not to be taken as if its name could be translated as "novel" or "roman."[12] In its Han origins, the hsiao-shuo amounted to no more than idle tales of the streets. Because their written versions were not taken seriously, all earlier examples have been lost. The esteem given hsiao-shuo appears to have risen somewhat by the Six Dynasties, and some copied down for collections. According to Lu Hsün, those among them which dealt with the strange and marvelous were classified as chih-kuai hsiao-shuo and were the most numerous of the kind. As I have had occasion to observe before, the people of the Han had an extremely practical outlook and, especially under the guiding rationalism of Confucianism, severely criticized the mystic and supernatural. Against this official attitude, the common people appear to have had a considerable fancy for the supernatural and mysterious, and so the chih-kuai hsiao-shuo came into being.

The popularity of this kind greatly benefited from the advance of Taoism. After the Han Dynasty, those adepts who mediated between the realm of the immortals and the human world increased their activity, and by the Six Dynasties such pursuits were regarded positively. It is said that in the section on literature in the *History of the Former Han* there is an entry for writers of hsiao-shuo that gives the names of a number of Taoist adepts. We should also not ignore the influence of Buddhism, which was making such rapid strides from the beginning of the Six Dynasties. The Buddhist sutras are rich in parables or stories applying features of the supernatural to actual human life, and all are by nature fictional. The inclusion of so many fictional stories in the sutras—which is to say in the most revered sacred writings—very plausibly contributed to the higher valuation of hsiao-shuo.

Only some eight of those Six Dynasties tales of the marvelous are extant, and there can be no certainty that we possess versions close to

---

lore, including prose and poetic sources, with a Buddhist emphasis characteristic of Okura.—Ed.]

[12] [The author distinguishes between two kinds of writing that are designated by the same Chinese characters. One is the old Chinese hsiao-shuo, discussed here; the other is the modern Japanese shōsetsu, using the same characters. Different languages, dates, assumptions, subjects, and length are involved.—Ed.]

the originals—in fact some have survived only in fragments. Some do survive in reliable versions. These include, among others: Kan Pao's *Quests for Mysterious Events*, Ko Hung's *Shen-hsien Chuan*, Tai Tsu's *Chen-i Chi*, T'ao Yüan-ming's *Sou-shen Hou-chi*, Liu I-ch'ing's *Yu-ming Lu*, Liu Ching-shu's *I Yüan*, Jen Fang's *Shu-i Chi*, and Yen Chih-t'ui's *Huan-yüan Chi*. These stories all vary in their compilers and age of compilation, so that there is no unity of narrative method. But they do share the properties of being fictional and of narrating subject matter that is not separated from the actual human world. In his preface to *Quests*, Kan Pao comments as follows:

> If, among the things recorded here, there are matters from former times containing errors, that is not my personal responsibility. If however for matters from present times, investigation and documentation should reveal the least in the way of falsehood or mistake, I wish to receive the same censure as that accorded to the wise people of the past and scholars of earlier ages concerning points of great difficulty in grasping exact truth from what has been observed. Whatever else that would do for my work, it would at least give proof of the existence of supernatural events.

In other words, although what is available to us from people of the past does not ordinarily consist solely of perfect truth, the recorder of the stories aims to transmit matters that actually occurred in this world. Even if those matters delivered include marvels and miracles at odds with daily experience, as compiler he takes responsibility, even if he is not the author of the stories. It seems, then, that Keikai's relating strange tales and miracles in the guise of matters that occurred in the real world results from his inheriting in full awareness basic attitudes that existed from the time of the Six Dynasties.

The Japanese absorption of those elements in hsiao-shuo which dealt with the marvelous had another result that must be mentioned. There was no development of lengthy prose narratives. It seems likely that the character of the Han people could have led to lengthy works. Fu of considerable length have come down to us, and among shih there is a narrative that runs to 357 lines: "Composed for the Wife of Chiao Chung-ch'ing" (*Gyokudai*, 1:475-79) with many others of length. Why then did Chinese writers fail to produce long prose narratives? We must await the considerably later Ming Dynasty before we have narrative works bringing together a large number of stories into a story on a grand scale: *The Journey to the West* and the *Shui-hu Chuan* (*The Water Margin*), for example. It seems to derive from an awareness related to the practical temper of Confucianism imbued in people who essayed prose fiction. Fictional prose narrative was resisted as something inferior. As a result, fictional writing low in quality was thought best kept slight in length. Japanese writers, who had a predisposition for short works all along (see the General Introduction), must have felt when they encountered short Chinese stories that, truly, a tale (hanashi) ought to be brief. For such reasons, then, in Japan from the eighth to the tenth century we cannot discover the phenomenon observable in Icelandic literature: the emergence of long works made up from materials of oral songs and stories. Among so much else we discover, there was no *Egil's Saga* or *Njál's Saga* in ancient Japan.

CHRONOLOGICAL TABLE

The table given here has five columns. The first or leftmost column specifies dates (commonly approximate in this early period). The second deals with Japanese literary and related matters in the Archaic and Ancient Ages. The third specifies Chinese dynasties, for which information is comparatively secure. The fourth gives Korean dynasties, for which information is less certain. The fifth and last or rightmost column gives events treated in this volume, or implied by it, in non-Japanese areas, particularly in China and Korea. Non-Chinese events are indicated, for example, by mention that Queen Himiko is of Wa (an obscure part of Japan but designated simply "Japan") or (for Korea) that a person or event is of Koguryŏ, Silla, etc. P'o-hai, a northeastern area of China, constituted itself as a national state at one point, and so also figures in the last column.

Christian Era	Japan	China	Korea	China, Korea, P'o-hai
A.D. 57		Han	Three Kingdoms (Koguryŏ, Paekche, Silla)	Wa (Japan) sends tributes to Han; Han gives a gold seal to Wa, recognizing her status. Wa tributes to Han.
107	[In traditional accounts, the Age of the Gods ends in 660 B.C., when Jimmu Tennō becomes first sovereign of Japan. For Sujin, traditional 10th tennō, supposed reign 97-30 B.C., see below, 258.]			
147				Civil war rages in Japan to 188.
192		Six Dynasties (222-589) Wei		Ts'ao Chih born.
239				Himiko, Queen of Wa, sends her first mission to Wei with tribute.
240				Wei mission visits Wa to give an imperial edict and seal to signify Chinese recognition.

Christian Era	Japan	China	Korea	China, Korea, P'o-hai
243		Wei	Three Kingdoms	Himiko sends her second mission to Wei.
248				Himiko dies.
249				Shih Ch'ung born.
250				Around this year, civil war occurs in Wa. [History of Wei mentions funeral ceremonies in 3rd century Wa.]
258	Sujin Tennō dies.			
261				Lu Chi born.
262		——— Western Chin		Lu Yün born.
266				Toyo, Queen of Wa, sends her tributary mission to Chin.
300	Keikō Tennō accedes about this time.			Shih Ch'ung dies.
305				Wang I-chih born around this year.
		——— Eastern Chin 317-419		*Sou-shen Chi* written ca. early 4th century.
353				Poetic garden party at Tan-t'ing held.
363	Ōjin Tennō accedes.			Wang I-chih dies about this time.
365				T'ao Ch'ien born.
372				In Koguryŏ a national school is established.
384				Yen Yen-chih born.
385				Hsieh Ling-yün born.
391				The epitaph of Hot'ae (or Kwanggaet'o) records invasion by Wa.
395	Nintoku Tennō accedes.			

Christian Era	Japan	China	Korea	China, Korea, P'o-hai
		Liu Sung from 400	Three Kingdoms	
414				A monument with inscription for Hot'ae (Kwanggaet'o) is built in Koguryŏ.
421				King Tsan of Wa [Nintoku Tennō] sends his mission to Liu Sung.
427	Nintoku Tennō dies.			T'ao Ch'ien dies.
433				Hsieh Ling-yün dies.
441				Ch'en Yüeh born.
456				Yen Yen-chih dies.
460				Hsiao Tze-liang born.
464				Hsieh T'iao born.
467				Wang Jung born.
468	Fuhitobe set up.			
478				King Wu of Wa [Yūryaku Tennō] sends a mission to Liu Sung.
485		Southern Ch'i 479-501		Chou Yung dies.
487				From this year through ca. 492 the Yung-ming style, a new poetic, emerges at Hsiao Tze-liang's salon.
493				Hsiao Tze-liang dies. Wang Jung dies.
	About the beginning of the 6th century Kenzō Tennō accedes.			
501				Hsiao T'ung born.
		Liang 502-557		

Christian Era	Japan	China	Korea	China, Korea, P'o-hai
503		Liang	Three Kingdoms	Hsiao Kang born.
513				Yü Hsin born. Ch'en Yüeh dies.
518				Ho Sun dies.
530	Around this year sardonic songs addressed to Kena no Omi.			
531				Hsiao T'ung dies.
547				Between this year and 549 *Yü-t'ai Hsin-yung* compiled.
	In late 6th century the tumulus of Himezuka built.			
551				Hsiao Kang dies.
579		Ch'en 557-581		Ca. this year and 631 "Hyesŏngga" (Song of the Comet) composed in Silla.
581		Sui 581-617		Yü Hsin dies.
592				Hsü Ching-tsung born.
596	"The Inscription at Dōgo Hot Springs in Iyo Province" composed.			
604	*The Constitution in Seventeen Articles* proclaimed.			
607	The "Inscription on the Halo of Medicine King at Horyūji Temple" composed.			
612	A celebration song composed by Soga no Umako.			Ŭlchi Mundŏk of Koguryŏ sends his poem to Yü Chung-wen of Sui.
615	Hyeja returns to Koguryŏ.			
618		T'ang		Wang T'ung dies.

Christian Era	Japan	China	Korea	China, Korea, P'o-hai
620	Tennōki, Kokuki, and Hongi compiled.	T'ang	Three Kingdoms	
624	Suiko Tennō dies. The historical account of Kojiki ends with this year.			
637				Lu Chao-lin born.
640	Prince Arima born.			Around this year Lo Pin-wang born.
643	Sardonic songs composed.			
645				Li Chiao born.
648	Prince Ōtomo [Kōbun Tennō] born.			
650				Wang Po born.
658	Prince Arima dies. Around this year Iyobe Umakai born.			
659	Fujiwara Fuhito born.			
660	Sardonic song about Tsumori Kutsuma composed.			Around this year Chang Wen-ch'eng born.
661	Prince Kadono born.			Ch'en Tze-ang born.
663				Paekche destroyed.
665	Ōtomo Tabito born. Prince Ōtsu born.			
668			Silla	Koguryŏ destroyed; unification of Korea under Silla begins.
670	The 6th mission to the T'ang departs.			
672	Jinshin Civil War. Prince Ōtomo (Kōbun Tennō) dies.			Hsü Ching-tsung dies.
676				Wang Po dies. Sŏl Ch'ong of Silla enters the height of his literary activity from this year.
680	From about this time to 700, Kakinomoto Hitomaro seems to have flourished,			

Christian Era	Japan	China	Korea	China, Korea, P'o-hai
	although an earlier date is also likely as a beginning point.	T'ang	Silla	
682				Silla first establishes a national school.
683	A documentary account about kataribe first appears.			
684				Lo Pin-wang dies.
686	Prince Ōtsu dies.			
692				Kangsu of Silla dies.
695	Fujiwara Maro born.			
702	Accounts of kataribe appear in census registration records. The 7th mission to T'ang departs. Around this year Iyobe Umakai dies.			Ch'en Tze-ang dies. Kim Dae-mun of Silla at the height of his literary activity from this year through about 736.
704	The 7th mission to T'ang returns, bringing "The Visit to the Immortals' Dwelling," etc. In this year or in 707 Yamanoe Okura returns.			Around the beginning of the 8th century the lü-t'i (or lü-shih, regulated verse) form of Chinese poetry is established.
705	Prince Kadono dies.			
712	Kojiki compiled.			Sung Chih-men dies.
713	Compilation of fudoki ordered by Gemmei Tennō.			State of P'o-hai founded. Around this year Ch'en Ch'üan-ch'i dies.
714				Li Chiao dies.
718				Chin-kang Pan-jo Chi-yen-chi compiled.
720	Fujiwara Fuhito dies. Nihon Shoki compiled.			
721	Prince Nagaya appointed Minister of the Right.			
724	Waka with the date of composition first seen. Around this year onward Yamanoe Okura attends poetry parties held by Prince Nagaya.			

Christian Era	Japan	China	Korea	China, Korea, P'o-hai
728	Monjōdō, department of letters, established anew at court school.	T'ang	Silla	P'o-hai begins trade with Japan.
729	Prince Nagaya dies.			
730	A plum-blossom poetry party held at Ōtomo Tabito's residence.			
731	Ōtomo Tabito dies.			
737	Fujiwara Maro dies.			
739	Accounts of kataribe appear in census registration records. Isonokami Otomaro exiled to Tosa.			
740				Chang Wen-ch'eng dies.
746	Ōtomo Yakamochi goes to Etchū as governor.			
750	Prince Kadono dies.			
751	Preface of *Kaifūsō* composed.			
753	Yakamochi composes such famous waka as "Haru no no ni . . ." (*MYS*, 4290).			
755				An Lu-shan rebellion begins. Around this year Wang Ch'ang-ling dies.
756				A Chinese poem, surviving from this year, is composed by Kim Chi-jang of Silla while he had been in T'ang.
759	The last datable waka in *Man'yōshū* composed.			Wang Wei dies.
776				Po Chü-i born.
785	Between this year and 822 *Nihon Ryōiki* compiled.			
807	*Kogo Shūi* compiled.			
838	The 17th mission to T'ang arrives in China.			
839	The 17th mission to T'ang returns.			

Christian Era	Japan	China	Korea	China, Korea, P'o-hai
846		T'ang	Silla	Po Chü-i dies.
857				Ch'oe Ch'i-wŏn of Silla born.
888				*Samdaemok* compiled in Silla.

BIBLIOGRAPHY

Three sections follow. The first includes editions and collections referred to in the main text of this volume. The second includes studies published in Japanese, and the third, in languages other than Japanese. In each instance, the entry here is by the abbreviated form used in the text. Tokyo is the place of publication unless otherwise specified.

A title preceded by an asterisk designates a work that, in the text, is cited by literary unit (uta, shi, etc.) rather than by page.

An "equals" sign indicates that the first element of the "equation" is an abbreviated version of the second or an equivalent—for example, a romanizing of the Chinese rather than the Japanese pronunciation of a Chinese work.

The citation under an author's name of, for example, "1951b" without a preceding "1951a" implies the existence of another work published in 1951 that will be cited as "1951a" in a subsequent volume.

Abbreviations are used for two important series: *NKBT* designates *Nihon Koten Bungaku Taikei* (Iwanami Shoten); and *SZKT* designates *Shintei Zōho Kokushi Taikei* (Yoshikawa Kōbunkan), ed. Kuroita Katsumi.

Also *KKS* = *Kokinshū* = *Kokinwakashū, MYS* = *Man'yōshū*.

A. Editions

Ankōki. See *Kojiki* (a).

Bungei Ruisan. Bungei Ruisan (Ministry of Education, 1878), 8 vols.

Bunkyō Onko Hikō. Kariya Ekisai Zenshū, vol. 8; in *Nihon Koten Zenshū* (Nihon Koten Zenshū Kankōkai, 1928). Republished by Gendai Shichōsha, 1978.

Buretsuki. See *Nihon Shoki* (a).

Chisato Shū = *Ōe no Chisato Shū.* See *Senzaikaku.*

Chōyō = *Chōsen Min'yō Sen.* Kim So-un (tr.), *Chōsen Min'yō Sen; Iwanami Bunko* (Iwanami Shoten, 1933, 1972). 1972 edition used.

Ch'üan T'ang Shih. (Peking: Chung-hua Shu-chü, 1960).

Eika Taigai = *Eika no Taigai.* Hisamatsu Sen'ichi, ed., *Karon Shū; NKBT,* 65 (1961).

Engi Shiki. Engi Shiki; SZKT, 26 (Yoshikawa Kōbunkan, 1937).

*Fudo = Fudoki Kayō. See *Kodai Kayō Shū.*

Fudoki. Akimoto Yoshio, ed., *Fudoki; NKBT,* 2 (1958), including: *Harima no Kuni Fudoki, Hitachi no Kuni Fudoki, Ise no Kuni Fudoki, Iyo no Kuni Fudoki, Izumo no Kuni Fudoki, Tango no Kuni Fudoki.*

Fukurozōshi. Ozawa Masao, Gotō Shigeo, Shimazu Tadao, and Higuchi Yoshimaro, eds., *Fukurozōshi Chūkai* (Hanawa Shobō, 1974-76), 2 vols.

Gishi Wajinden = *San-kuo Chih: Wei Chih,* "Tung-i Chuan, Wo-jen": Wada Kiyoshi and Ishihara Michihiro, eds., *Gishi Wajinden, Gokanjo Waden, Sōjo Wakokuden, Zuisho Wakokuden; Iwanami Bunko* (Iwanami Shoten, 1951).

Gogumaiki, ms., National Diet Library.

Gokanjo Waden = *Hou Han Shu,* "Tung-i Chuan, Wo." See *Gishi Wajinden.*

Gyokudai = *Gyokudai Shin'ei* = *Yü-t'ai Hsin-yung. Gyokudai Shin'ei; Kanshi Taikan,* 1. See *Kanshi Taikan.*

Haku Kōzan Shishū = *Po Hsiang-shan Shih-chi; Kanshi Taikan,* 4. See *Kanshi Taikan.*

Hakushi = *Haku Kōzan Shishū* = *Po Hsiang-shan Shih-chi*. See *Haku Kōzan Shishū*.

Harima no Kuni Fudoki. See *Fudoki*.

Historia = MATSUDAIRA 1967, in Section B.

Hitachi no Kuni Fudoki. See *Fudoki*.

Hou Han Shu. See *Gokanjo Waden* and *Gishi Wajinden*.

Hokke Gisho. Hanayama Shinshō, ed., *Shōtoku Taishi Gyosei Hokke Gisho; Iwanami Bunko* (Iwanami Shoten, 1931-33), 2 vols.

Hokkekyō (*Lotus Sūtra*), ed. Sakamoto Yukio and Iwamoto Yutaka, 3 vols., *Iwanami Bunko* (Iwanami Shoten, 1962-67).

Honjishi = *Pen-shih-shih; Tseng-pu Chin-tai Pi-shu*, 7 (Kyoto: Chūbun Shuppansha, 1980).

Hōō Teisetsu = *Jōgū Shōtoku Hōō Teisetsu*. Ienaga Saburō and Tsukishima Hiroshi, eds., *Shōtoku Taishi Shū; Nihon Shisō Taikei*, 2 (Iwanami Shoten, 1975).

Horyūji Meibun Shūsei. Takada Ryōshin, ed., *Horyūji Meibun Shūsei* (Kokusho Kankōkai, 1977).

Iji = *Sangoku Iji* = *Samguk Yusa*. Imanishi Ryū, ed., *Sangoku Iji* (Seoul: Chōsen Shigaku-kai, 1928); republished (rev.) by Kokusho Kankōkai, 1971.

Ingyōki. See *Kojiki* (a).

Ise no Kuni Fudoki. See *Fudoki*.

Isho Shūsei. Yasui Kōzan, Nakamura Kusuhachi, eds., *Isho Shūsei* (Tokyo University of Education, Kangibunka Kenkyūkai, 1959-64), 8 vols.

Iyo no Kuni Fudoki. See *Fudoki*.

Izumo no Kuni Fudoki. See *Fudoki*.

JDK = *Jindaiki*. See *Kojiki* (a) and *Nihon Shoki* (a).

Jimmuki. See *Kojiki* (a).

Jindaiki. See *Kojiki* (a) and *Nihon Shoki* (a).

Kaden = *Fūshi Kaden*. See *Zeami, Zenchiku*.

*Kagura = *Kagurauta*. See *Kodai Kayō Shū*.

Kaifū = *Kaifūsō*. Kojima Noriyuki, ed., *Kaifūsō; NKBT*, 69 (Iwanami Shoten, 1964).

Kakyō. See *Zeami, Zenchiku*.

Kanshi Taikan. Saku Takashi, ed., *Kanshi Taikan* (Seki Shoin, 1936-39), 8 vols. (Reprinted by Ōtori Shuppan, 1974).

Keikōki. See *Kojiki* (a).

Kenzōki. See *Nihon Shoki* (a).

Kiden = *Nihon Shoki Den; Suzuki Shigetane Zenshū* (Suzuki Shigetane Sensei Gakutoku Ken'yōkai, 1937).

*Kinka = *Kinkafu*. See *Kodai Kayō Shū*.

KJK = *Kojiki*. See *Kojiki* (a).

KJK, Song = *Kojiki, Song*. See *Kodai Kayō Shū*.

Kodai Kayō Shū. Konishi Jin'ichi and Tsuchihashi Yutaka, eds., *Kodai Kayō Shū; NKBT*, 3 (1957).

Kogo Shūi. Yasuda Naomichi, ed., *Kogo Shūi; Takahashi Ujibumi* (Gendai Shichōsha, 1976).

Kōgyokuki. See *Nihon Shoki* (a).

Kojiki
  (a) [Narrative portions] Kanda Hideo, Ōta Yoshimaro, eds., *Kojiki; Nihon Koten Zensho* (Asahi Shimbunsha, 1962-63), 2 vols., including: *Ankōki; Ingyōki; Jimmuki; Jindaiki*; also *Nihon Shoki* (a); *Keikōki; Nintokuki;*

Ōjinki, also *Nihon Shoki* (a); *Seineiki; Sujinki; Yūryakuki*, also *Nihon Shoki* (a).

(b) *Song*. See *Kodai Kayō Shū*.

*KKS = *Kokinshū* = *Kokinwakashū*. Saeki Umetomo, ed., *Kokinwakashū; Iwanami Bunko* (Iwanami Shoten, 1981).

Kōtokuki. See *Nihon Shoki* (a).

Kyorai Shō. Ebara Taizō, ed., *Kyorai Shō, Sanzōshi, Tabine Ron; Iwanami Bunko* (Iwanami Shoten, 1939).

Kyū Tōjo = *Chiu T'ang-shu*, "Wo-kuo," *Jih=pen Chuan*, ed. Ishikawa Michihiro (Iwanami Shoten, 1976).

Lun-yü. See *Rongo*.

*MYS = *Man'yōshū*. Satake Akihiro, Kinoshita Masatoshi, Kojima Noriyuki, eds., *Man'yōshū: Yakubun Hen* (Hanawa Shobō, 1972).

Mao Shih. See *Shih Ching*.

Nan'yō-Amami. Tabata Hidekatsu, Kamei Katsunobu, Hokama Shuzen, eds., *Nantō Kayō Taisei: Amami Hen* (Kadokawa Shoten, 1979).

Nan'yō-Myāku. Hokama Shuzen, Niizato Kōshō, eds., *Nantō Kayō Taisei: Miyako Hen* (Kadokawa Shoten, 1978).

Nan'yō-Okinawa. Hokama Shuzen, Tamashiro Masami, eds., *Nantō Kayō Taisei: Okinawa Hen*, vol. 1 (Kadokawa Shoten, 1980); vol. 2, Hokama Shuzen, Hika Minoru, Nakahodo Shotoku, eds. (ibid., 1981).

Nan'yō-Yaima. Hokama Shuzen, Miyanaga Yasuhiko, eds., *Nantō Kayō Taisei: Yaeyama Hen* (Kadokawa Shoten, 1979).

Nihon Shoki.

(a) [Narrative portions] Kuroita Katsumi, ed., *Nihon Shoki; SZKT*, 1 (Yoshikawa Kōbunkan, 1951), including: *Buretsuki; Jindaiki*, also *Kojiki* (a); *Kenzōki; Kōgyokuki; Kōtokuki; Ōjinki*, also *Kojiki* (a); *Saimeiki; Suikoki; Temmuki; Yōmeiki; Yūryakuki*, also *Kojiki* (a).

(b) *Song*. See *Kodai Kayō Shū*.

Nintokuki. See *Kojiki* (a).

Norito. Takeda Yūkichi, ed., *Norito; NKBT*, 1 (Iwanami Shoten, 1958).

NSK = *Nihon Shoki*. See *Nihon Shoki* (a).

NSK, Song = *Nihon Shoki, Song*. See *Kodai Kayō Shū*.

Ō I = *Wang Wei* = *Ō Yūjō Shū* = *Wang Yu-ch'eng Chi*. *Ō Yūjō Shū*; see *Kanshi Taikan*, 3.

Ōjinki. See *Kojiki* (a) and *Nihon Shoki* (a).

Pei Shih (Peking: Chung-hua Shu-chü, 1974).

Pen-shih-shi. See *Honjishi*.

Rishi = *Ri Taihaku Shishū* = *Li T'ai-po Shih-chi*. *Ri Taihaku Shishū; Kanshi Taikan*, 2.

Rongo = *Lun-yü*. Kanaya Osamu, ed., *Rongo; Iwanami Bunko* (Iwanami Shoten, 1963).

**Roppyakuban Utaawase*. Konishi Jin'ichi, ed., *Shinkō Roppyakuban Utaawase* (Yūseidō, 1976).

Ryōiki = *Nihonkoku Gempō Zen'aku Ryōiki* [also *Reiiki*]. Endō Yoshimoto, ed., *Nihon Ryōiki; NKBT*, 70 (Iwanami Shoten, 1967).

*Ryūka. Shimabukuro Seibin, Okinaga Toshio, eds., *Hyōon Hyōshaku Ryūka Zenshū* (Musashino Shoin, 1968).

*Saibara. See *Kodai Kayō Shū*.

Saimeiki. See *Nihon Shoki* (a).

Samguk Sagi. See *Sangoku Shiki*.

Samguk Yusa. See *Iji.*

Sangoku Shiki = *Samguk Sagi.* Imanishi Ryū, ed., *Sangoku Shiki* (Seoul: Chikazawa Shoten, 1928). Revised by Suematsu Yasukazu in the third edition, 1941; reprinted by Kokusho Kankōkai, 1971. 1971 edition used.

Sanzōshi. See *Kyorai Shō.*

Seineiki. See *Kojiki* (a).

Senzaikaku = *Heian Jidai Bungaku to Hakushi Monjū: Kudai Waka, Senzaikaku Kenkyūhen,* ed. Kaneko Hikojirō (Baifūkan, 1943, rev. ed., 1955; rpt. Geirinsha, 1977). 1955 edition used.

Shih Ching = *Mao Shih. Mao Shih; Shih-san-ching Chu-su,* 2 vols. (Taipei: I-wen Yin-shu-kuan, 1976).

Shin'yō. Ainu Jojishi Shin'yō Seiden no Kenkyū = KUBODERA 1977 in Section B.

Shokuki = *Shoku Nihongi; SZKT,* 2 (Yoshikawa Kōbunkan, 1935).

Shōseki = *Koshi Shōseki* = *Ku-shih Shang-hsi. Koshi Shōseki;* see *Kanshi Taikan,* 1.

Shūgyoku = *Shūgyokushū.* Taga Munehaya, ed., *Kōhon Shūgyokushū* (Yoshikawa Kōbunkan, 1971).

Shūi Gusō. Reizei Tameomi, ed., *Fujiwara Teika Zenkashū* (Bummeisha, 1940). Reprinted by Kokusho Kankōkai, 1974.

Sōjo Wakokuden. See *Gishi Wajinden.*

Sou-shen Chi. Chin-t'ai Pi-shu, 11 (Shanghai: Po-ku-chai, 1922)

Suga Zenshū = *Suga Masatomo Zenshū* (Kokusho Kankōkai, 1907).

Sui Shu (Peking: Chung-hua Shu-chü, 1973).

Suikoki. See *Nihon Shoki* (a).

Sujinki. See *Kojiki* (a).

Taedong Sisŏn. (Seoul: Cho Lyong-sŭng, 1978).

Taiheiki. Gotō Tanji, Kamata Kisaburō, Okami Masao, eds., *Taiheiki; NKBT,* 34-36 (Iwanami Shoten, 1960-62), 3 vols.

Tango no Kuni Fudoki. See *Fudoki.*

Temmuki. See *Nihon Shoki* (a).

Theogony = HIROKAWA 1975 in Section B.

Toshi = *To Shōryō Shishū* = *Tu Shao-ling Shih-chi. To Shōryō Shishū.* See *Kanshi Taikan,* 3.

Tōshi = *Tō Emmei Shishū* = *T'ao Yüan-ming Shih-chi. Tō Emmei Shishū.* See *Kanshi Taikan,* 1.

*Umuru = *Umuru Suosi* = *Omoro Sōshi.* Hokama Shuzen, ed., *Omoro Sōshi; Nihon Shisō Taikei,* 18 (Iwanami Shoten, 1972).

Wei Chih. See *Gishi Wajinden.*

Wen Hsüan. (Hong Kong: Hong Kong Branch of Shang-wu Yin-shu-kuan, 1936, 1978). 1978 edition used.

Yōmeiki. See *Nihon Shoki* (a)

"Yu Hsien-k'u." See "Yūsenkutsu."

Yūkara = *Yūkara Shū.* Kindaichi Kyōsuke, ed., *Ainu Jojishi Yūkara Shū* (Sanseidō, 1959-75), 9 vols.

Yūryakuki. See *Kojiki* (a) and *Nihon Shoki* (a).

"Yūsenkutsu" = "Yu Hsien-k'u." Ogaeri Yoshio, ed., *Kan'yaku Yūsenkutsu* (Soku Shobō, 1948).

Yü-t'ai Hsin-yung. See *Gyokudai.*

Zeami, Zenchiku. Omote Akira, ed., *Zeami, Zenchiku; Nihon Shisō Taikei,* 24 (Iwanami Shoten, 1974).

Zuimonki = *Shōbō Genzō Zuimonki.* Nishio Minoru, Kagamijima Genryū,

Sakai Tokugen, Mizuno Yaoko, eds., *Shōbō Genzō, Shōbō Genzō Zuimonki;* *NKBT*, 81 (Iwanami Shoten, 1965).

B. STUDIES PUBLISHED IN JAPANESE

AMI Yūji
1960   *Chūgoku Chūsei Bungaku Kenkyū: Nansei Eimei-Jidai o Chūshin to Shite* (Shinjusha, 1960).
ANDŌ Masatsugu
1939   "*Kojiki* no Buntaironteki Kōsatsu," *Hompō Shigakushi Ronsō*, I (Fuzambō, 1939). Republished in *Andō Masatsugu Chosakushū*, vol. 4 (Yūzankaku, 1974). 1974 edition used.
AOKI Masaru
1935a   "Shina no Shizenkan," *Iwanami Kōza: Tōyō Shisō* (Iwanami Shoten, 1935). Republished as "Shinajin no Shizenkan," *Shina Bungaku Geijitsu Kō* (Kyoto: Kōbundō, 1942); republished in *Aoki Masaru Zenshū*, vol. 2 (Shunjūsha, 1970). 1970 edition used.
1935b   "Shina Shisō: Bungaku Shisō," *Iwanami Kōza: Tōyō Shisō* (Iwanami Shoten, 1935-36). Republished as *Shina Bungaku Shisōshi*, part one (Iwanami Shoten, 1943); republished in *Aoki Masaru Zenshū*, vol. 1 (Shunjūsha, 1969). 1969 edition used.
CHIRI Mashiho
1953   "Ainu no Shin'yō," *Kenkyū Hōkoku*, 9 (Sapporo: Hoppō Bunka Kenkyūjo, 1953). Republished in *Chiri Mashiho Chosakushū*, vol. 1 (Heibonsha, 1973). 1973 edition used.
1955   *Ainu Bungaku* (Gengensha, 1955).
1960   "Ainu ni Denshō Sareru Kabu Ongyoku ni Kansuru Chōsa Kenkyū," *Bunkazai Itaku Kenkyū Hōkoku*, vol. 2 (Ministry of Education, 1960). Republished in *Chiri Mashiho Chosakushū*, vol. 2 (Heibonsha, 1973). 1973 edition used.
CHIRI Yukie
1923   *Ainu Shin'yō Shū* (Kyōdo Kenkyūsha, 1923). Republished in *Iwanami Bunko* with an introduction by Chiri Mashiho (Iwanami Shoten, 1978). 1978 edition used.
DOI Kōchi
1927   "Genshi Jidai no Bungaku," *Bungaku Josetsu* (Iwanami Shoten, 1927, 1978). Republished in *Doi Kōchi Chosakushū*, vol. 5 (Iwanami Shoten, 1977). 1978 edition used.
1960   *Kodai Densetsu to Bungaku* (Iwanami Shoten, 1960). Republished in *Doi Kōchi Chosakushū*, vol. 2 (Iwanami Shoten, 1977). 1960 edition used.
FUJII Kiyoshi
1966   *Man'yō Ikoku Fūbutsushi* (Bunri Shoin, 1966).
FUJII Nobuo
1944   "*Kojiki* ni Okeru Shishō no Chūki ni Tsuite," *Kokugo to Kokubungaku*, vol. 21, no. 1, 1944.
FUJII Shigetoshi
1976a   "Suiko Chō Ibun no Kana to Chōsen Kanjion," *Bungakuka Ronshū* (Kagoshima University), no. 11, 1976.
1976b   "Man'yōgana to Chōsen Kanjion," *Jōdai Bungaku* (Jōdai Bungaku Kai), no. 38, 1976.

1977   "*Man'yōshū* no Ongana to Chōsen Kanjion," *Bungakuka Ronshū* (Kagoshima University), no. 12, 1977.

GOTŌ Moriichi
1947   *Nihon Kodaishi no Kōkogakuteki Kentō* (Yamaoka Shoten, 1947).

HANAYAMA Shinshō
1933   *Shōtoku Taishi Gyosei Hokke Gisho no Kenkyū; Tōyō Bunko Ronsō*, 18, 1-2 (Tōyō Bunko, 1933); reprinted by Sankibō Busshorin, 1978.

HASEGAWA Nyozekan
1933   "*Man'yōshū* ni Okeru Shizenshugi: Kakumeiki ni Okeru Seiji Keitai to no Kankei," *Kaizō*, vol. 15, no. 1, 1933.

HATTORI Shirō
1959   *Nihongo no Keitō* (Iwanami Shoten, 1959).
1968   "Nihongo no Ryūkyū Hōgen ni Tsuite," *Bungaku*, vol. 36, no. 1, 1968.

HAYASHI Kokei
1944   *Kaifūsō Shinchū* (Meiji Shoin, 1958). Ready for issue in 1944, wartime conditions led to posthumous publication in 1958.

HAYASHIYA Tatsusaburō
1960   *Chūsei Geinōshi no Kenkyū: Kodai kara no Keishō to Sōzō* (Iwanami Shoten, 1960).
1971   *Nihon no Kodai Bunka* (Iwanami Shoten, 1971).

HIROKAWA Yōichi
1975   *Heshiodosu [Hesiod] Kenkyū Josetsu* (Miraisha, 1975).

HOKAMA Shuzen
1976   *Nantō Bungaku; Kanshō Nihon Koten Bungaku*, vol. 25 (Kadokawa Shoten, 1976).
1979   *Okinawa Bungaku no Sekai* (Kadokawa Shoten, 1979).

HOKAMA-NIIZATO = Hokama Shuzen and Niizato Kōshō
1972   *Miyakojima no Shinga* (San'ichi Shobō, 1972).

IDE Itaru
1973   "Kachōka no Genryū," *Man'yōshū Kenkyū*, 2 (Hanawa Shobō, 1973).

IKEDA Genta
1956   *Rekishi no Shigen to Kōshōdenshō* (Sōgeisha, 1956).

IKEMIYA Masaji
1976   "Hondo Bungei no Juyō," Supplement of *Nantō Bungaku*. See HOKAMA, 1976.

INOUE Mitsusada
1980   "*Kojiki* to Inariyama Tekken," *Bungaku*, vol. 48, no. 4, 1980.

INOUE Tatsuo
1979   *Kodai Ōken to Kataribe* (Kyōikusha, 1979).

ISHIDA Yoshisada
1969   "*Meigetsuki* to Fujiwara Shunzei no Shi," *Gakuen* (Shōwa Women's College), no. 359, 1969.

ITŌ Haku *Kodai Wakashi Kenkyū* (Hanawa Shobō, 1974-76), 6 vols.
1975a   Vol. 3 (1975)
1975b   Vol. 4 (1975)
1976c   Vol. 5 (1976)

ITŌ Seiji
1970   "Nihon Shinwa to Chūgoku," *Gekkan Dentō to Gendai* (Dentō to Gendai Sha), vol. 1, no. 1, 1970. Republished as *Nihon Shinwa to Chūgoku Shinwa* (Gakuseisha, 1979). 1979 edition used.

1973   *Kaguya Hime no Tanjō: Kodai Setsuwa no Kigen*; Gendai Shinsho, 306 (Kōdansha, 1973).

ITŌ-MOMOTA = Itō Seiji and Momota Yaeko

1971-72   "*Taketori Monogatari* Genryūkō," *Chūgoku Tairiku Kobunka Kenkyū* (Chūgoku Tairiku Kobunka Kenkyūkai), nos. 5 and 6, 1971-72.

KAKIMURA Shigematsu

1947   *Jōdai Nihon Kambungakushi*, ed. Yamagishi Tokuhei (Nihon Shoin, 1947).

KANDA Hideo

1937   "Onsūritsu no Kaku o Nasu Sosūkeiretsu no Sonzai ni Tsuite," *Kokugo to Kokubungaku*, vol. 14, no. 2, 1937.

1950a   "*Kojiki* no Buntai ni Kansuru Ichishiron," *Kokugo to Kokubungaku*, vol. 27, no. 6, 1950.

1950b   "*Kojiki* no Buntai ni Kansuru Ichishiron Hosetsu," *Kokugo to Kokubungaku*, vol. 27, no. 8, 1950.

1951   " '*Kojiki* no Buntai' ni Tsuite," *Kokugo Kokubun*, vol. 20, no. 5, 1951.

1959   *Kojiki no Kōzō* (Meiji Shoin, 1959).

1972   "Kasō ni Yoru Banka no Suitai ni Tsuite," *Man'yōshū Kenkyū*, vol. 1 (Hanawa Shobō, 1972).

KATŌ Shūichi

1975-80   *Nihon Bungakushi Josetsu* (Chikuma Shobō, 1975-80), 2 vols.

KAWARA-KOJIMA = Kawara Hiroshi and Kojima Noriyuki

1937   "*Hitachi Fudoki* no Seiritsu ni Kansuru Ichikōsatsu," *Kokugo Kokubun*, vol. 7, no. 8, 1937.

KIM Sa-yŏp

1973   *Chōsen Bungakushi* (Kanazawa Bunko, 1973).

KIM So-un

1933   "Chōsen Kōden Min'yō Ron," in *Chōsen Min'yō Sen; Iwanami Bunko* (Iwanami Shoten, 1933, 1972). 1972 edition used.

KIM Tong-uk

1974   *Chōsen Bungakushi* (Nihon Hōsō Shuppan Kyōkai, 1974).

KIMISHIMA Hisako

1965   "Chūgoku no Hagoromo Densetsu," *Chūgoku Tairiku Kobunka Kenkyū*, no. 1, 1965.

1972   "Dōteiko no Ryūjo Setsuwa," *Chūgoku Tairiku Kobunka Kenkyū*, no. 6, 1972.

KINDAICHI Kyōsuke

1923   *Ainu Seiten; Sekai Seiten Zenshū Koshū*, 23 (Sekai Bunko Kankōkai, 1923).

1931   *Ainu Jojishi Yūkara no Kenkyū* (Tōyō Bunko, 1931), 2 vols.

KISHABA Eijun

1937   "Paifuta Funtaka Yungutu: Kurushima no Jushi," *Nantō Ronsō* (Okinawa Nipposha, 1937).

1970   *Yaima Koyō* (Okinawa Taimuzusha, 1970), 2 vols.

KOBAYASHI Hideo

1942   "*Heike Monogatari*," *Bungakukai*, vol. 9, no. 7, 1942. Republished in *Mujō to Yū Koto* (Sōgensha, 1946); republished in *Shintei Kobayashi Hideo Zenshū*, 8 vols. (Shinchōsha, 1978). 1978 edition used.

KOBAYASHI Shigemi
1967   "Kōsaka, Oshikuma Ōkimi Monogatari: Kuma no Geinō to Kazuku
            Tori no Geiyō," *Nihon Kayō Kenkyū*, no. 5, 1967.
KOBAYASHI-IKEDA-KADOKAWA = Kobayashi Yukio, Ikeda Yasaburō, and
Kadokawa Gen'yoshi
1967   *Kami to Kami o Matsuru Mono; Nihon Bungaku no Rekishi*, 1
            (Kadokawa Shoten, 1967).
KOJIMA Noriyuki
1951   "*Kojiki* no Buntai," *Kokugo Kokubun*, vol. 20, no. 3, 1951.
1952   "Okura no 'Kōkyo Kōrai,' " *Man'yō*, no. 5, 1952.
1954   "Ushinawareta *Tsuminoe Den*: Densetsu no Hyōgen," *Jimbun Kenkyū*
            (Osaka City University), vol. 5, no. 4, 1954.
1962-65   *Jōdai Nihon Bungaku to Chūgoku Bungaku* (Hanawa Shobō, 1962-
            65), 3 vols.
1968-79   *Kokufū Ankoku Jidai no Bungaku* (Hanawa Shobō, 1968-79).
KONDŌ Haruo
1936   "*Yūsenkutsu* to *Man'yōshū* Maki-5 'Matsuragawa ni Asobu Jo,' "
            Gakuen, vol. 3, no. 7, 1936.
KONISHI Jin'ichi
1948-53d   *Bunkyō Hifuron Kō* (Ōyashima Shuppan & Kōdansha, 1948-53), 3
            vols.
1951d   *Tosa Nikki Hyōkai* (Yūseidō, 1951).
1953a   "Chūseijin no Bi," *Kokugo to Kokubungaku*, 13(1953).
1953c   "Chūsei ni Okeru Hyōgensha to Kyōjusha," *Bungaku*, vol. 21, no.
            5, 1953.
1953f   "Chūseibi no Hi-Nihonteki Seikaku," *Bungaku*, vol. 21, no. 9, 1953.
1953i   *Nihon Bungakushi; Atene Shinsho*, vol. 57 (Kyoto: Kōbundō, 1953).
1975   *Michi: Chūsei no Rinen; Gendai Shinsho*, 393 (Kōdansha, 1975).
1978   "Jo to Makurakotoba no Setsu," *Jōdai Bungaku Kōkyū* (Hanawa
            Shobō, 1978).
KUBODERA Itsuhiko
1956   "Ainu Bungaku Josetsu," *Tōkyō Gakugei Daigaku Kenkyū Hōkoku*,
            7. Republished as *Ainu no Bungaku; Iwanami Shinsho*, 989 (Iwa-
            nami Shoten, 1977). 1977 edition used.
1977   *Ainu Jojishi Shin'yō Seiden no Kenkyū* (Iwanami Shoten, 1977).
KUME Tsunetami
1979   *Man'yō Kayō Ron* (Kadokawa Shoten, 1979).
KURE Shigeichi
1964   "Sukui o Motomeru Onnatachi," *Aisukyurosu, Sopokuresu* [*Aes-
            chylus, Sophocles*]; *Sekai Koten Bungaku Zenshū*, vol. 8 (Chikuma
            Shobō, 1964).
MACHIDA Kōichi
1977   *Jōdai Chōkokushi no Kenkyū* (Yoshikawa Kōbunkan, 1977).
MASUDA Katsumi
1972   *Kiki Kayō; Nihon Shijin Sen*, vol. 1 (Chikuma Shobō, 1972).
1980   "Bungakushi Jō no *Kojiki*," *Bungaku*, vol. 48, no. 5, 1980.
MASUDA Seiichi
1976   *Haniwa no Kodaishi* (Shinchōsha, 1976).
MATSUDAIRA Chiaki
1967   Herodotus, *Historia*, tr. by Matsudaira in *Sekai Koten Bungaku
            Zenshū* (Chikuma Shobō, 1967), vol. 10.

MATSUMOTO Nobuhiro
1931   *Nihon Shinwa no Kenkyū* (Dōbunkan, 1931). Republished by Heibonsha (1971). 1971 edition used.
1951   "Chikuchū Seitandan no Genryū," *Shigaku*, vol. 25, no. 2, 1951. Republished in *Toā Minzoku Bunka Ronkō* (Seibundō Shinkōsha, 1968). 1968 edition used.

MATSUMURA Takeo
1954-58 *Nihon Shinwa no Kenkyū* (Baifūkan, 1954-58), 4 vols.

MISATO Chōkei
1966   *Ryūka no Kenkyū* (Naha: Ryūkyū Bunkyō Tosho, 1966).

MISHINA Akihide
1970   *Nihon Shinwaron; Mishina Akihide Rombunshū*, vol. 1 (Heibonsha, 1970).
1974   *Shiragi Karō no Kenkyū; Mishina Akihide Rombunshū*, vol. 6 (Heibonsha, 1974).

MITANI Eiichi
1952   *Monogatari Bungakushiron* (Yūseidō, 1952).

MIZUTANI Teijirō
1977   *Kō Taiō Hi Kō* (Kaimei Shoin, 1977).

MURAYAMA-KOKUBU = Murayama Shichirō and Kokubu Naoichi
1979   *Genshi Nihongo to Minzoku Bunka* (San'ichi Shobō, 1979).

NAKANISHI Susumu
1963   *Man'yōshū no Hikakubungakuteki Kenkyū* (Nan'undō Ōfūsha, 1963).
1973   "*Man'yōshū* no Rengo Hyōgen," *Man'yōshū Kenkyū*, vol. 2 (Hanawa Shobō, 1973).

NAKAYAMA Kyūshirō
1930   *Sekai Insatsu Tsūshi* (Sanshūsha, 1930), 2 vols.

NOGAMI Toyoichirō
1930   *Nō: Kenkyū to Hakken* (Iwanami Shoten, 1930).

NOSE Asaji
1948   *Bashō no Hairon; Haibungaku Sōkan*, vol. 8 (Osaka: Ōyashima Shuppan, 1948).

ŌBAYASHI Taryō
1961   *Nihon Shinwa no Kigen* (Kadokawa Shoten, 1961, 1973). 1973 edition used.

OBI Kōichi
1962   *Chūgoku Bungaku ni Arawareta Shizen to Shizenkan* (Iwanami Shoten, 1962).

OGI Mitsuo
1977   *Nihon Kodai Ongakushiron* (Yoshikawa Kōbunkan, 1977).

OGURA Shimpei
1929   *Kyōka Oyobi Rito no Kenkyū; Keijō Teikoku Daigaku Hōbun Gakubu Kiyō*, 1 (Keijō Teikoku Daigaku, 1929). Reprinted in *Ogura Shimpei Hakushi Chosakushū*, vol. 1 (Kokubun Gakkai, Kyoto University, 1974).

OKADA Masayuki
1929a   *Ōmi Nara Chō no Kambungaku; Tōyō Bunko Ronsō*, vol. 10 (Tōyō Bunko, 1929). Republished by Yōtokusha, Tenri City, 1946). 1946 edition used.

1929b   *Nihon Kambungakushi* (Kyōritsusha, 1929). Revised, enlarged edition by Yamagishi Tokuhei and Nagasawa Kikuya (Yoshikawa Kōbunkan, 1954). 1954 edition used.

OKAZAKI Yoshie

1947-48   *Fūryū no Shisō; Nihon Geijitsu Shichō* (Iwanami Shoten, 1947-48), 2 vols.

OMODAKA Hisataka

1937   "Makurakotoba o Tōshite Mitaru Hitomaro no Dokusōsei," *Kokugo Kokubun*, vol. 7, nos. 1-2, 1937. Republished in *Man'yō no Sakuhin to Jidai* (Iwanami Shoten, 1941). 1941 edition used.

ŌNISHI Yoshinori

1943   *Man'yōshū no Shizenkanjō* (Iwanami Shoten, 1943).

1960   *Kotenteki to Romanteki; Atene Bunko,* 301 (Kyoto: Kōbundō, 1960).

ONO Jūrō

1977a   *Nantō Kayō; NHK Books,* 275 (Nihon Hōsō Kyōkai, 1977).

1977b   *Nantō no Kokayō; Shin Minzoku Bunka Sōsho,* 2 vols. (Japan Publishers, 1977).

ŌNO Susumu

1965   "*Kiki* no Sōsei Shinwa no Kōsei," *Bungaku,* vol. 33, no. 8, 1965. Republished in *Nihon Shinwa,* vol. 1; *Nihon Bungaku Kenkyū Shiryō Sōsho* (Yūseidō, 1970). 1970 edition used.

ORIGUCHI Shinobu

1924   "Kokubungaku no Hassei: Jugen to Jojishi to," *Nikkō,* vol. 1, no. 1, 1924. Republished in *Kodai Kenkyū: Kokubungaku Hen; Origuchi Shinobu Zenshū,* vol. 1, *Chūkō Bunko* (Chūō Kōronsha, 1975). 1975 edition used.

ŌTA Yoshimaro

1961-66   *Kodai Nihon Bungaku Shichōron* (Ōfūsha, 1961-66), 4 vols.

REKISHIGAKU KENKYŪKAI

1953   *Minzoku no Bunka ni Tsuite*: Report of Annual Conference by Rekishigaku Kenkyūkai in 1952 (Iwanami Shoten, 1953).

SAEKI Arikiyo

1973   "Kōkuri Kōkaido Ō no Hibun to Nihon," *Kodaishi no Nazo o Saguru* (Yomiuri Shimbunsha, 1973). Republished in *Kodai no Nihon to Chōsen* (Gakuseisha, 1974). 1973 edition used.

1974   *Kenkyūshi Kōkaido Ō Hi* (Yoshikawa Kōbunkan, 1974).

SAEKI Tomi

1970a   "Higashi Ajia Sekai no Tenkai: I," *Iwanami Kōza: Sekai Rekishi, Chūsei,* vol. 3 (Iwanami Shoten, 1970).

1970b   "Sōchō Shūken Kanryōsei no Seiritsu" (Ibid.).

SAIGŌ Nobutsuna

1951   *Nihon Kodai Bungakushi; Iwanami Zensho,* 149 (Iwanami Shoten, 1951; revised in 1963). Both editions used.

SASAKI Nobutsuna

1948   *Man'yōshū Ruika Ruiku Kō; Man'yōshū no Kenkyū,* vol. 3 (Iwanami Shoten, 1948).

SEKINE Masao

1978-80   *Kyūyaku Seisho Bungakushi; Iwanami Zensho,* 304 & 321 (Iwanami Shoten, 1978-80).

SHIBA Rokurō

1958   *Chūgoku Bungaku ni Okeru Kodokukan* (Iwanami Shoten, 1958).

SHIMODE Seikyo
1975   *Dōkyō to Nihonjin; Gendai Shinsho*, 411 (Kōdansha, 1975).

SHIRAISHI Mitsukuni
1941   *Norito no Kenkyū* (Shibundō, 1941).

SHIRAKAWA Shizuka
1979   *Shoki Man'yōron* (Chūō Kōronsha, 1979).

SUGIMOTO Yukio
1943   *Kaifūsō* (Kyoto: Kōbundō, 1943).

SUZUKI Torao
1927   *Shina Shironshi* (Kyoto: Kōbundō, 1927).
1928   "Shin Kyūbun [Ch'en Hsiu-wen] Nempu," *Shina Bungaku Ronsō* (Kyoto: Kōbundō, 1928). Republished in *Gyōkan Roku* (Kyoto: Kōbundō, 1929). 1929 edition used.
1936   *Fushi Taiyō* (Fuzambō, 1936).

TAKAGI Ichinosuke
1941   *Yoshino no Ayu: Kiki Man'yō Zakkō* (Iwanami Shoten, 1941).
1974   *Hinkyūmondōka no Ron* (Iwanami Shoten, 1974).

TAKAGI Toshio
1925   *Nihon Shinwa Densetsu no Kenkyū* (Oka Shoin, 1925). Revised, enlarged edition by Ōbayashi Taryō in *Tōyō Bunko* (Heibonsha, 1973-74), 2 vols. Heibonsha edition used.

TAKEDA Yūkichi
1927   *"Tsuminoeden," Nara Bunka* (Chikuhakukai, Nara Branch), no. 10, 1927.
1944.   *Teiki Kō; Kojiki Kenkyū*, vol. 1 (Seijisha, 1944). Republished in *Takeda Yūkichi Chosakushū*, vol. 2 (Kadokawa Shoten, 1973). 1944 edition used.

TAKEUCHI Rizō
1952   "Daiō Tennō Kō," *Nihon Rekishi*, no. 51 (1952).

TANIGUCHI Yukio
1973   *Edda-Hoknō Kayōshū* (Shinchōsha, 1973).

TOKUMITSU Hisaya
1966   *Kojiki no Hihyōteki Kenkyū: Eiyū Jidai to Eiyū Monogatari* (Hokkai Shuppan, 1966).

TSUCHIDA Tomoo
1962   "*Kiki* Kayō no Makurakotoba no Shizenkan," *Kokugakuin Zasshi*, vol. 63, no. 9, 1962.

TSUCHIHASHI Yutaka
1960   *Kodai Kayō Ron* (San'ichi Shobō, 1960).
1965   *Kodai Kayō to Girei no Kenkyū* (Iwanami Shoten, 1965).
1968   *Kodai Kayō no Sekai; Hanawa Sensho*, 65 (Hanawa Shobō, 1968).
1972-76 *Kodai Kayō Zenchūshaku* (Kadokawa Shoten, 1972-76), 2 vols.

TSUCHIYA Bummei
1932   *Man'yōshū Nempyō* (Iwanami Shoten, 1932; 1980). 1980 edition used.
1951   "Kakinomoto Hitomaro," *Nihon Bungaku Kōza*, vol. 1 (Kawade Shobō, 1951).

TSUDA Saukichi [or Sōkichi]
1916-65 *Bungaku ni Arawaretaru Waga Kokumin Shisō no Kenkyū* (Rakuyōdō, 1916-21), 4 vols. Revised as *Bungaku ni Arawaretaru Kokumin Shisō no Kenkyū* (Iwanami Shoten, 1951-55). Vol. 5 was added

in *Tsuda Saukichi Zenshū*, 5 (Iwanami Shoten, 1965). Iwanami edition used.

1920   "Tennō Kō," *Tōyō Gakuhō*, vol. 10, no. 3, 1920. Republished in *Nihon Jōdaishi no Kenkyū* (Iwanami Shoten, 1947); republished in *Tsuda Saukichi Zenshū*, vol. 3, 1963. 1963 edition used.

1923   *Jindaishi no Kenkyū* (Iwanami Shoten, 1923). Republished in *Tsuda Saukichi Zenshū*, vol. 1, 1963. 1963 edition used.

1930   "Ōjinki Igo no Kiki no Kisai," *Nihon Jōdaishi Kenkyū*: Part One (Iwanami Shoten, 1930). Republished in *Tsuda Saukichi Zenshū*, vol. 2, 1963. 1963 edition used.

1933a   "Shoki no Kakikata Oyobi Yomikata," *Jōdai Nihon no Shakai Oyobi Shisō*: Part One (Iwanami Shoten, 1933). Republished in *Tsuda Saukichi Zenshū*, vol. 2, 1963. 1963 edition used.

1933b   "Taika Kaishin no Kenkyū," *Jōdai Nihon no Shakai Oyobi Shisō*: Part Three. Republished in *Tsuda Saukichi Zenshū*, vol. 3, 1963. 1963 edition used.

1947   "Sekai Bungaku to Shite no Nihon Bungaku," *Bungaku*, vol. 15, no. 1, 1947. Republished in *Tsuda Saukichi Zenshū*, vol. 10, 1964. 1964 edition used.

UESEDO Tōru
1979   *Taketomijima Shi: Kayō Geinō Hen* (Hōsei University Press, 1979).

UMEHARA Kaoru
1970   "Ō Anseki [Wang An-shih] no Shimpō," *Iwanami Kōza: Sekai Rekishi, Chūsei*, vol. 3 (Iwanami Shoten, 1970).

WADA-ISHIHARA
1951   See *Gishi Wajinden*, Biblio., Pt. A.

YAMADA Yoshio
1935   *Kojiki Jobun Kōgi* (Shiogama, Miyagi: Shibahiko Shrine and Shiogama Shrine, 1935, 1938). 1938 edition used.

YAMAGUCHI Tadashi
1964   *Man'yō Shūji no Kenkyū* (Musashino Shoin, 1964).

YAMAMOTO Kenkichi
1962   *Kakinomoto Hitomaro* (Shinchōsha, 1962).

1971   *Ōtomo Yakamochi; Nihon Shijin Sen*, vol. 5 (Chikuma Shobō, 1971).

YI Chin-hŭi
1972   *Kōkaido Ōryō Hi no Kenkyū* (Yoshikawa Kōbunkan, 1972).

YOSHII Iwao
1958   "Yamato Takeru no Mikoto Monogatari to Juka: Sono Sōka ni Tsuite no Ichikasetsu," *Kokugo Kokubun*, vol. 27, no. 10, 1958.

YOSHIKAWA Kōjirō
1941   "Kinsei Shina no Rinri Shisō," *Iwanami Kōza: Rinrigaku*, vol. 12 (Iwanami Shoten, 1941). Republished in *Yoshikawa Kōjirō Zenshū*, vol. 13 (Chikuma Shobō, 1969). 1969 edition used.

1942   "Zoku no Rekishi," *Tōhō Gakuhō: Kyoto*, vol. 12, no. 4, 1942. Republished in *Yoshikawa Kōjirō Zenshū*, vol. 2, 1973. 1973 edition used.

1944   *Shinajin no Koten to Sono Seikatsu* (Iwanami Shoten, 1944). Republished in *Yoshikawa Kōjirō Zenshū*, vol. 2, 1973. 1973 edition used.

1948   *Genkyoku: Kokukantei* (Iwanami Shoten, 1948). Republished in *Yoshikawa Kōjirō Zenshū*, vol. 15, 1974. 1974 edition used.

1950   *To Ho [Tu Fu] Shiki*, vol. 1 (Chikuma Shobō, 1950). Republished in *Yoshikawa Kōjirō Zenshū*, vol. 12, 1974. 1974 edition used.
1952   "Kōchakugo no Bungaku," *Kokugo Kokubun*, vol. 21, no. 1, 1952. Republished in *Yoshikawa Kōjirō Zenshū*, vol. 18, 1975. 1975 edition used.
1959   "Nihon Bummei ni Okeru Juyō to Nōdō," *Nihon Bunka Kenkyū*, vol. 7 (Shinchōsha, 1959). Republished in *Yoshikawa Kōjirō Zenshū*, vol. 17, 1975. 1975 edition used.
1960   "Kunshin Fushi," *The Asahi Shimbun*, January 1, 1960. Republished in *Yoshikawa Kōjirō Zenshū*, vol. 17, 1975. 1975 edition used.
1962   *Sōshi Gaisetsu; Chūgoku Shijin Senshū*, 21 (Iwanami Shoten, 1962). Republished in *Yoshikawa Kōjirō Zenshū*, vol. 13, 1974. 1962 edition used.

C. STUDIES NOT PUBLISHED IN JAPANESE.

AUERBACH, Erich
1946   *Mimesis: Dargestellte Wirklichkeit in der abendländischen Literatur* (Bern: A. Francke, 1946). Willard Trask (tr.), *Mimesis: The Representation of Reality in Western Literature* (Princeton: Princeton University Press, 1953).
BARTHES, Roland
1957   *Mythologies* (Paris: Editions du Seuil, 1957). Annette Lavers (tr.), *Mythologies* (London: J. Cape, 1972).
BEATLE, Bruce A.
1964   "Oral-traditional Composition in the Spanish *Romancero* of the Sixteenth Century," *Journal of the Folklore Institute*, vol. 1, nos. 1-2 (The Hague, 1964).
BECKWITH, Martha Warren
1918   *The Hawaiian Romance of Laieikawai* (Washington: Government Printing Office, 1918).
1938   "Kepelino's Tradition of Hawaii," *B. P. Bishop Museum Bulletin*, no. 9, 5: appendix, pp. 180-82 (Honolulu, 1938).
BERNDT, Catherine H.
1963   "Art and Aesthetic Expression," *Australian Aboriginal Studies: A Symposium of Papers Presented at the 1961 Research Conference* (Melbourne: Australian Institute of Aboriginal Studies, 1963); ed. W.E.H. Stanner and Helen Sheilis.
BLEEK, Dorothea F., ed.
1923   *The Mantis and His Friends: Bushman Folklore* (Cape Town: T. Mashew Miller, 1923).
1928   *The Narons: A Bushman Tribe of the Central Kalahari* (Cambridge: Cambridge University Press, 1928).
BLEEK-LLOYD = W.H.I. Bleek and L. C. Lloyd
1911   *Specimens of Bushman Folklore* (London: George Allen, 1911).
BOWRA, C. M.
1952   *Heroic Poetry* (London: Macmillan, 1952).
1962   *Primitive Song* (London: Weidenfeld and Nicolson, 1962). Republished as a Mentor Book (New York: New American Library of World Literature, 1963). 1963 edition used.

1972   *Homer: Classical Life and Letters* (London: Gerald Duckworth, 1972); ed. by Hugh Lloyd-Jones.

BROWER-MINER = Robert H. Brower and Earl Miner

1961   *Japanese Court Poetry* (Stanford: Stanford University Press, 1961).

CASALIS, Eugène A.

1859   *Les Bassoutos: ou Vingt-trois années de séjour et d'observation au sud de l'Afrique* (Paris: C. Meyrueis, 1859). Translated by the author, *The Basutos: or Twenty-three Years in South Africa* (London: Nisbet, 1861); reprinted in Cape Town by C. Struik in 1965. 1965 edition used.

CASSIRER, Ernst

1923-31   *Philosophie der symbolischen Formen* (Berlin: Bruno Cassirer Verlag, 1 [1923], 2 [1925], 3 [1929], 4 [1931], 2nd ed., Darmstadt: Wissenschaftliche Buchgesellschaft, 1964). Ralph Mannheim (tr.), *The Philosophy of Symbolic Forms* (New Haven & London: Yale University Press, 1955), 3 vols. 1964 edition used.

1925a   *Das mythische Denken = Philosophie der symbolischen Formen*, vol. 2.

1925b   *Sprache und Mythos: Ein Beitrag zum Problem der Götternamen*; Fritz Saxl, ed., *Studien der Bibliothek Warburg*, 6 (Leipzig & Berlin: B. G. Teuner, 1925). Susanne K. Langer (tr.), *Language and Myth* (New York: Harper & Brothers, 1946). 1946 edition used.

FOKKEMA-KUNNE = D. W. Fokkema and Elrud Kunne-Ibsch

1977   *Theories of Literature in the Twentieth Century: Structuralism, Marxism, Aesthetics of Reception, Semiotics* (London: C. Hurst, 1977).

GUISINDE, Martine

1975   *Folk Literature of the Selknam Indians*, Johannes Wilbert, ed., *UCLA Latin American Center Publications* (Berkeley and Los Angeles: University of California Press, 1975).

1977   *Folk Literature of the Yamana Indians*, Johannes Wilbert, ed., ibid. (Ibid., 1977).

HOWITT, A. W.

1904   *The Native Tribes of South-East Australia* (London: Macmillan, 1904).

KEESING, Felix M.

1966   *Cultural Anthropology: The Science of Custom* (New York: Holt, Rinehart & Winston, 1966).

KIRBY, Percival R.

1937   "The Musical Practices of the Auni and Khomani Bushmen," J. D. Rheinallt and C. M. Doke, eds., *Bushmen of the Southern Kalahari* (Johannesburg: The University of Witwaterland Press, 1937).

KONISHI, Jin'ichi

1962   "*Fūryū*: An Ideal of Japanese Esthetic Life," Earl Miner (tr.), *Orient/West*, vol. 7, no. 7 (1962). Republished in Maurice Schneps and Alvin D. Coox, ed., *The Japanese Image* (Tokyo & Philadelphia: Orient/West Inc., 1965). 1965 edition used.

KUO, Shao-yü

1934-47   *Chung-kuo Wen-hsüeh P'i-p'ing-shih* (Shanghai: Shang-wu Yin-shu-kuan: vol. 1, 1934; vol. 2, 1947). Reprinted in Taipei by Taiwan Shang-wu Yin-shu-kuan, 1970. 1970 edition used.

KURTZ, Benjamin P.
1922   "Twelve Andamanese Songs," *University of California Publications in Modern Philology*, vol. 11 (Berkeley: University of California Press, 1922).
LESSA, William
1961   "Tales from Ulithi Atoll: A Comparative Study in Oceanic Folklore," *University of California Publications, Folklore Studies*, vol. 13 (Berkeley & Los Angeles: University of California Press, 1961).
LESTRADE, G. P.
1937   "Traditional Literature," Isaac Schapera, ed., *The Bantu-speaking Tribes of South Africa* (London: Routledge, 1937).
LEVY, Ian Hideo
1981   *The Ten Thousand Leaves* [tr., *Man'yōshū*, 1-5] (Princeton: Princeton University Press, 1981).
LIU, Ling-sheng
1936   *Chung-kuo P'ien-wen-shih* (Shanghai: Shang-wu Yin-shu-kuan, 1936).
LIVINGSTONE, David
1857   *Missionary Travels and Researches in South Africa* (London: Murray, 1857).
LOEB, Edwin M.
1935   "Sumatra: Its History and People," *Wiener Beiträge zur Kulturgeschichte und Linguistik*, vol. 3 (Wien: Verlag des Instituts für Volkskunde des Universität Wien, 1935).
LORD, Albert B.
1960   *The Singer of Tales; Harvard Studies in Comparative Literature*, 24 (Cambridge, Mass.: Harvard University Press, 1960). Republished in New York by Atheneum, 1965. 1965 edition used.
MALINOWSKI, Bronislaw Kasper
1926   *Myth in Primitive Psychology* (London: Paul, Trench, Trubner, 1926).
MANDEL, Oscar
1961   *A Definition of Tragedy* (New York: New York University Press, 1961).
MARETT, Robert R.
1909   *The Threshold of Religion* (London: Methuen, 1909). Republished (rev. and enl.) in New York by AMS, 1979. 1979 edition used.
MINER, Earl
1958   *The Japanese Tradition in British and American Literature* (Princeton: Princeton University Press, 1958).
1973   "Towards a New Conception of Classical Japanese Poetics," *Studies on Japanese Culture* (Tokyo: The Japan P.E.N. Club, 1973), vol. 1.
1978-79   "On the Genesis and Development of Literary Systems," *Critical Inquiry*, 5(1978-79).
MITCHELL, Roger
1972   "Micronesian Folklore and Culture Change," *Journal of the Folklore Institute*, vol. 9 (Bloomington: Indiana University, 1972).
MURRAY, Gilbert
1897   *A History of Ancient Greek Literature* (New York: D. Appleton, 1897). Republished in New York by Frederick Ungar, 1966. 1966 edition used.

PAK, Pyŏng-ch'ae
1971   *Kodae Kugŏ ŭi Yŏngu* (Seoul: Korea University Press, 1971, 1973).
            1973 edition used.
PARRY, Milman
1930   "Studies in the Epic Techniques of Oral Verse-making, I: Homer
            and Homeric Style," *Harvard Studies in Classical Philology*, vol. 41
            (Cambridge, Mass.: Harvard University Press, 1930).
1971   *The Making of Homeric Verse: The Collected Papers of Milman
            Parry*, ed. Adam Parry (Oxford: Clarendon Press, 1971), with pref-
            atory and bibliographical material.
PHILIPPI, Donald L. (tr.)
1968   *Kojiki* (University of Tokyo Press, 1968).
RIGHTER, William
1975   *Myth and Literature: Concepts of Literature* (London & Boston:
            Routledge & Kegan Paul, 1975).
SCHAPERA, Isaac
1965   *Praise-poems of Tswana Chiefs* (Oxford: Clarendon Press, 1965).
SCHEBESTA, Paul
1957   *Die Negrito Asiens: Religion und Mythologie; Studia Institute An-
            thropos*, vol. 13, 2, 2nd Halbband (Wien Mödling: St. Gabriel Ver-
            lag, 1957).
STRICH, Fritz
1924   *Deutsche Klassik und Romantik: oder Vollendung und Unend-
            lichkeit* (München: Meyer und Jessen, 1924). 2nd ed. (München:
            C. H. Beck, 1928). 1928 edition used.
THILENIUS, Georg,
1913-38   *Ergebniss der Südsee-Expedition 1908-10; Hamburgische Wissen-
            schaftliche Stiftung und Notgemeinschaft der deutschen Wissenschaft*
            (Hamburg: Friederschen, De Gruyter, 1913-38), 16 vols.
TILLYARD, E.M.W
1954   *The English Epic and Its Background* (New York: Oxford University
            Press, 1954).
TRILLES, R. P.
1931   *Les Pygmées de la Forêt* (Paris: Librairie Bloud & Gay, 1931).
TYLOR, Sir Edward Burnett
1865   *Primitive Culture: Researches into the Development of Mythology,
            Philosophy, Religion, Art and Custom*; 3rd American, from the 2nd
            English ed. (New York: Gordon Press, 1977), 2 vols.
USENER, Hermann K.
1896   *Götternamen: Versuch einer Lehre von der religiösen Begriffsbildung*
            (Bonn: F. Cohen, 1896).
WALEY, Arthur (tr.)
1925-33   *The Tale of Genji* (London: Allen and Unwin, 1973; 2 vols. in 1).
WANG, Kuo-wei
1915   *Sung-Yüan Hsi-ch'ü-chih* (Shanghai: Shang-wu Yin-shu-kuan, 1915).
            Republished in *Kuo-hsüeh Hsiao-ts'ung-shu* (Shang-wu Yin-shu-kuan,
            1933). 1933 edition used.
WELLEK, René
1965   *Confrontations: Studies in the Intellectual and Literary Relations
            Between Germany, England, and the United States During the Nine-
            teenth Century* (Princeton: Princeton University Press, 1965).

WELLEK-WARREN = René Wellek and Austin Warren
1949   *Theory of Literature* (New York: Harcourt, Brace & World, 1949, 1954; London: Penguin Books, 1963). 1963 edition used.
WU, Ch'u
1955   "Jih-pen Chih Han-shih," *Chung-Jih Wen-hua Lun-chi* (Taipei: Chung-kuo Wen-hua Ch'u-pan Shih-yeh Hsieh-hui, 1955).
YI, Ka-wŏn
1961   *Hanguk Hanmunhaksa* (Seoul: Minjung Sŏgwan, 1961).
YI, Sung-nyŏng
1955   "Silla Sidae ŭi P'yogipŏp Ch'egye e Kwanhan Siron," *Sŏul Taehakkyo Nonmunjip, Inmun Sahoe Kwahak*, vol. 2 (Seoul National University, 1955).

FINDING LIST FOR
JAPANESE POEMS

Works of verse-prose are also included here. Important quotations from Japanese prose as well as Chinese, Korean, and other non-Japanese works are signalled in the following Index by "quoted."

The words given for each citation here are those of the first line quoted by the author. With very few exceptions, that line is also the first of the poem.

This finding list is keyed to the author's Bibliography. For poems apart from those in the *Man'yōshū*, familiarity with the Bibliography will be required. Numbers after the lines designate pages in this volume.

36. Yasumishishi, 338-39, 353
37. Miredo akanu, 339
43. Wa ga seko wa, 231
61. Masurao ga, 209

2.85. Kimi ga yuki, 335
126. Miyabio to, 222
127. Miyabio ni, 222
129. Furinishi, 240
131. Iwami no umi, 343-44
133. Sasa no ha wa, 359
141. Iwashiro no, 329
142. Ie ni areba, 329
147. Ama no hara, 327
167. Ame tsuchi no, 206-07
194. Tamamo nasu, 362
196. Iwahashi ni, 354-55
199. Ōmimi ni, 352, 355, 357-58
210. Utsusemi to, 246
213. Utsusemi to, 246
217. Tsuyu koso ba, 354
223. Kamoyama no, 360
224. Kyō kyō to, 360
225. Tada ni awaba, 360
230. Azusayumi, 210

3.235. Ōkimi wa, 349
236. Ina to iedo, 169
237. Ina to iedo, 170
239. Yasumishishi, 275-76
250. Tamamo karu, 208
271. Sakurada e, 274
323. Momoshiki no, 290
328. Aoniyoshi, 406
340. Inishie no, 220
342. Iwan sube, 220
343. Nakanaka ni, 220
348. Kono yo ni shi, 219
349. Ikeru mono, 219
382. Kamiyo yori, 238
385. Arare furi, 284

4.471. Ime no ai wa, 407-408
472. Hitoe nomi, 408
488. Kimi matsu to, 328
502. Natsuno yuku, 347
589. Koromode o, 209
705. Hanekazura, 416
706. Hanekazura, 416
707. Omoiyaru, 242-43
721. Ashihiki no, 223
785. Waga yado no, 405
791. Okuyama no, 405

5.793. Yo no naka wa, 221, 399
802. Uri hameba, 399-400
803. Shirokane mo, 400
822. Waga sono ni, 403
823. Ume no hana, 410
858. Wakayu tsuru, 404

894. Kamiyo yori, 103, 203

6.919. Waka no ura ni, 249, 274
972. Chiyorozu no, 104
978. Onoko ya mo, 228
993. Tsuki tachite, 408
994. Furisakete, 408
1016. Unhara no, 224
1019. Isonokami, 400-401
1020. Ōkimi no, 401
1021. Chichigimi ni, 401
1022. Ōsaki no, 402
1027. Tachibana no, 248

7.1088. Ashihiki no, 382

8.1441. Uchikirashi, 410
1518. Amanogawa, 238-39, 250
1662. Awayuki no, 211-12

9.1666. Asagiri ni, 231
1681. Okure ite, 231
1730. Yamashina no, 231

10.1832. Uchinabiku, 411
1834. Ume no hana, 411
1848. Yama no ki ni, 411
1893. Idete miru, 346
2095. Yū sareba, 382

11.2456. Nubatama no, 346

12.3098. Onore yue, 250
3192. Kusakage no, 231
3193. Tamakatsuma, 232
3194. Iki no o ni, 232

13.3222. Mimoro wa, 269
3250. Akizushima, 105
3253. Ashihara no, 104, 203
3254. Shikishima no, 103, 203
3310. Komoriku no, 281-82
3311. Komoriku no, 282
3314. Tsuginefu, 285
3315. Izumikawa, 285
3331. Komoriku no, 267

15.3606. Tamamo karu, 246
3728. Aoniyoshi, 406

16.3804. Kaku nomi ni, 423-24
3805. Nubatama no, 424
3837. Hisakata no, 227
3840. Teradera no, 415
3841. Hotoke tsukuru, 415
3856. Baramani no, 414
3858. Kono koro no, 414-15

17.3927. Kusamakura, 393

18.4065. Asabiraki, 242
4120. Mimaku hori, 232
4121. Mairi no, 233
4124. Aga horishi, 105

19.4139. Haru no sono, 409

INDEX

Japanese poems are entered in the preceding Finding List. Other important passages given and discussed in this volume are signalled here by "quoted."

As the Bibliography shows, when the author mentions a work in both the *Kojiki* and *Nihon Shoki*, without differentiation, the entry is under *Chronicles*, but usually there are separate entries for both. There are always separate entries when the author cites a part unique to one or the other: e.g., *Keitōki* references are entered under *Kojiki*, and those for *Kenzōki* under *Nihon Shoki*.

Names offer a special problem, and the entries for them are commonly given redundantly: "Nukada no Ōkimi (Princess)" designates the person by the Japanese name with the parenthesis giving her usual designation in this volume. Names are also normalized to modern Japanese: "Kakinomoto Hitomaro" rather than "Kakinomoto no Asomi (no) Fitomaro." And there are cross-references: e.g., from "Hitomaro" to "Kakinomoto Hitomaro." Some of these matters are dealt with in the Editor's Foreword.

Titles are given as entries in their original (transliterated) form, with Japanese versions and translations of Chinese and Korean works where those are widely known. For example, the entry for the Chinese *Hsi-yu Chi* offers parenthetically *Saiyūki* and *Journey to the West*. Most Korean, Ainu, and Ryukyuan titles are given in the original.

When an entry includes "defined," the reference is to a page where some manner of description or explanation is offered.

Barthes, Roland, 187
Beatle, Bruce A., 228, 246
Beckworth, Martha Warren, 167
beholding the country (kunimi), 237, 269
bembun. *See* p'ien-wen
benreibun. *See* p'ien-wen
Benshō, 379, 396, 397
bentai. *See* p'ien-wen
Beowulf, 17
Berndt, Catherine H., 372
Bible, quoted, 165-66, 299
Bleek, Dorothea F., 372
Bleek, W.H.I., 84, 372
Book of Songs, The. See Shih Ching
Bowra, C. M., 30, 83-94, 99, 113, 125, 140, 195-200
Brown, Norman O., 371
Buddhism, 27, 31, 32, 69, 72, 214-22, 317, 372, 387-88, 395, 399-400; *see also* Mahāyāna, Tendai, Zen
bungaku, defined, 6; *see also* literature
bungakushi, 6
bungei (literature). *See* literature
Buretsu Tennō, 133
Bushman song, quoted, 84, 85, 99

Caesar, Julius, *Gallic Wars* of, quoted, 167
capital school of waka poets, 405-14
Casalis, Eugène A., 260
Cassirer, Ernst, 177-80, 182, 184, 187
Ch'an. *See* Zen Buddhism
ch'ang. *See* luan
Chang Jung, 216
Chang Lai, 28
Chang Wen-ch'eng, 384
Chanson de Roland, 195
Ch'an-yü, King, 363
Chao K'uang-yin, Emperor, 350
Ch'ao Pu-chih, 28
Ch'en, Emperor of, quoted, 318-19
Ch'en Shih-tao, 28
Ch'en Tzu-ang, 379
Ch'eng I, 213
Ch'ens of Lin-an, 165
Chia I, 71
Chiao-jan, 319
Chien-wen, Emperor, 65
Chih-kuai Chi, 427-28
chih-kuai hsiao-shuo, 428
chih-shih. *See* shitsujitsu
Ch'ih-shih Ching, 399
Chi K'ang, 221
ch'i-li. *See* kirei
Ch'in Kuan, 28
China, southern, produces fantastic stories, 423

Chinese literature: drama late in, 134; features of, 20-34; parallels with Japanese literature, 65-67; periodizing of, 69-77
Chinese poems, posting of, 241-42
Chinese poetry: composed by Japanese, 315-23, 324-26, 379-84; intentionality in, 30, 383; parallelism in, 23; prefaces to, 384-85; tone of, 29-31
Chinese presence in waka, 407-10
Chinese prose, composed by Japanese, 309-15
Chinsŏn, King, 336
Chin-yü Feng-huan, 421
Chiri Mashiho, 36, 42, 88
Chiu T'ang-shu (J. *Kyūtōjo*), 396
Chizō, quoted, 326
cho (the rough), 63
Ch'oe Ch'i-wŏn, 68, 72
Ch'oe Kwang-yu, 72
Ch'oe Sin-ji, 72
chōka, 10, 104, 109, 117, 332-64, 388; defined, 23; emergence of, 146-48
chōka-hanka, debt of, to Korean hyangga-hugu, 322-26
Chong, poem by, 383-84
Chou Yung, 216
Chronicles, 87, 91, 92, 101, 104, 106, 113-56, 156-200, 251-65, 336, 342, 361; criteria for dating songs in, 137-38; old and new strata in, 125-36; quoted, 101, 102, 251-65, 266-86; *see also Kojiki, Nihon Shoki*
Chu Hsi, 31, 73, 124, 213
Ch'u Tz'u (The Songs of the South), 25-26
Chūai Tennō, 367
Ch'üan T'ang Shih (J. *Zentōshi; Complete T'ang Poems*), 392
Chuang Tzu, 32, 212-13, 221, 225
chüeh-chü, defined, 20
Ch'un Ch'iu (J. *Shunjū; Spring and Autumn Annals*), quoted, 349
ch'ung. *See* luan
chungin, defined, 73
Ch'ungnŏl, King, 336
Ch'unhyang Chŏn (The Song of Spring Fragrance), 74
Confucianism, 26, 62, 63, 212-14, 215-22, 225, 317, 348, 429-30
Confucius, 31; *Hsi-tz'u* by, 213
Constitution in Seventeen Articles, The. See Jūshichijō Kempō
Cooper, Lane, 6
court song, 278, 285; defined, 268
creation setsuwa, 172-79; South Pacific analogues for, 172; Sumatran analogues for, 173

joshi. *See* jokotoba
Journey to the West, The. See Hsi-yu Chi
Jūbutsu, 5
Jūshichijō Kempō (The Constitution in Seventeen Articles), 61, 310-14; *see also* Shōtoku Taishi

kabuki, 18, 356, 359; defined, 13
Kadokawa Gen'yoshi, 98, 104
Kadono no Ōkimi (Prince), 325-26
Kagekiyo, 18
kagura, 87, 268; quoted, 44, 272, 273
Kaifūsō, 317, 341, 377-78, 385-89, 400, 402, 420; preface to, quoted, 315-16; quoted, 318, 321-22
kakekotoba (pivot-words), 211
Kakimura Shigematsu, 311, 353
Kakinomoto Hitomaro, 11, 23, 40, 61, 203, 206-207, 208, 235-36, 239, 244, 245-47, 277, 291, 327, 371, 373, 393, 394, 402, 403-404; chōka of, 351-60; differing evaluations of, 337; influence of shih on, 354-56; issue of audience of, 359-61; kotodama and ga coexistent in poetry of, 337; poetry of, discussed, 337-64; quoted, 246, 275-76; varieties of parallelism used by, 352-56, 358-59; vitality of kotodama in poetry of, 337-64; *see also Kitomaro Kashū*
Kakinomoto Hitomaro Kashū. See Hitomaro Kashū
Kakka, 313
kami (god), defined, 82
Kamita Sōei, 47
Kamo no Chōmei, 70
Kamo no Mabuchi, 292-93, 335, 402
kamtutsi, 75
Kamu Yamato Iwarebiko. *See* Jimmu Tennō
kamugatariuta, 124, 148-49; defined, 132
kamui-yukar, 98; *see also* yukar
Kan Pao, quoted, 429
Kanda Hideo, 142, 153-54, 161, 191-92, 215, 252, 260, 342, 361-62, 372
Kang Su, 72
Kannami, 135
karazae, defined, 61
Kariya Mochiyuki, 311
Karu, of Kinashi, Taishi (Crown Prince), 260, 278
Karu no Ōiratsume (Princess), 278
Karu no Sakaibara no Miya (Prince), 361
kasa (Korean poetic kind), 74; defined, 27
Kasa no Iratsume (Lady), 209
Kasa no Kanamura, 210, 294; *Kasa no Kanamura Shū (Collection of)*, 394

Kataribe (Reciters), 168-70, 254, 256-60, 264, 265, 280; defined, 11
katarigoto (narrations), 61
katauta (partial poems), 153
Katō Shūichi, 68
Kawahigashi Hekigodō, 67
Kawara Hiroshi, 367
Kawara Maro, quoted, 330-32
Kawashima no Miko (Prince), 362
Kawatake Mokuami, 181
kayō (song), 11, 13
Kazuraki no Omi (Lord), 314
Keesing, Felix M., 107
Keichō Chokuhan (Royal Printer), 65
Keichū, 408
Keikai, 425-27
Keikō Tennō, 155, 209
Keitai Tennō, 87
Kena no Ōmi, 135-36
Kenzō Tennō, 154-55, 190, 262, 356
Ki no Tomonori, 27
Ki no Tsurayuki, 16, 268, 287, 317-18
kikō (travel accounts), 5
kikoe ōigimi (Ryukyuan great high priestess), 93
Kil T'aesong, 323
Kim Chi-jang, Prince, Chinese poem by, 392
Kim Hwang-wŏn, 73
Kim Man-jung, 32
Kim Pu-sik, 68, 73
Kim Sa-yŏp, 26, 27, 73, 310, 336
Kim Tae-mun, 72
Kim Tong-uk, 22, 27, 31, 74, 135
Kimishima Hisako, 419, 421
Kimmei Tennō, 87, 155, 427
Kindaichi Kyōsuke, 40, 44, 51, 98, 121
kinka, defined, 273
Kinkafu, 141, 269, 287; melodies in, 266-67; quoted, 269-70, 273, 278, 280
Kirby, Percival R., 99
kirei (Ch. ch'i-li; ornate beauty), 317
Kishaba Eijun, 39, 47
Kobayashi Hideo, 19
Kobayashi Shigemi, 119
Kobayashi Yukio, 98, 104
Kōbun Tennō, 189, 318; *see also* Ōtomo no Ōji
Kogo Shūi, 87-88, 102, 168; quoted, 166
Kōgyoku Tennō (later reigned as Saimei Tennō, q.v.), 140, 329
Kojiki, 4, 7, 11, 13, 16, 35, 46, 53, 82, 83, 102, 113-56, 156-200, 238, 251-65, 345, 365, 369-73, 385, 425; creation of, 369-73; melodic terms used in, 260; preface to, 161-62; quality of, 164; quoted, 105, 106, 125, 132, 133, 134,

Nakanoōe no Ōji (Prince), 329, 330-31

Nakatomi Kamako. *See* Fujiwara Kamatari

Nakatomi Ōshima, 163, 380

Nakatomi Shii, 169-70

Nakayama Kyūshirō, 65

Namiki Shōzō, 362

Nara designed like Ch'ang-an, 406

narrative, archaic, 156-200

nature poetry: developed from praise of
places, 274; emergence of, in Japan and
China, 380-83; relative lack of, in
Chinese, 25-27

nēli, 39

Neoconfucianism, 213; Korean, 73

*New Songs from the Jade Terrace. See Yü-
t'ai Hsin-yung*

Nibelungenlied, 195

nigaifutsi, 75

Nihon Reiiki. See Niho Ryōiki

Nihon Ryōiki (i.e., *Nihonkoku Gempō
Zen'aku Ryōiki; Miraculous Stories of
Karmic Retribution of Good and Evil in
Japan*), 341; quoted, 425-27

Nihon Shoki, 4, 11, 13, 35, 46-47, 53,
82-83, 100, 113-56, 156-200, 251-65,
311, 312, 329, 395, 418-19; quoted,
100, 102, 107, 130, 132, 133, 266-68,
338; *see also Chronicles*

Nihongi. See Nihon Shoki

Niizato Kōshō, 75

Nijō In Sanuki, 28

nikki ("diaries"; present-tense accounts—
see Vol. 2, forthcoming), 27, 251; defined, 5

Ninigi (Hohoninigi) no Mikoto (god),
100, 133, 140, 158-59, 185-86

ninjō, defined, 63

Nintoku Tennō, 121, 189, 190, 193, 238,
258, 260, 261, 262, 275, 279-80, 283-
84, 344-45

Nishiharu Akata, 39

Nitushi, Ainu poem from, 121-22

Njál's Saga, 430

nō, 11, 12, 18-20, 24, 108, 135, 420; *see
also* Zeami

Nogami Toyoichirō, 12

Nonomiya, 19

non-Yamato-line literature, 34-52

Norito (sacred verse-prose works), 207-
208, 301-306, 356; quoted, 301-303

Nose Asaji, 59

novelty in waka, 410

Nü-hsien Wai-shih, 31

Nukada no Ōkimi (Princess), 330; quoted,
324-26, 327-28, 353-54

Nunakawahime (Princess), 127, 282

Nuribe, Dame of (an immortal), 340-41

Ō no Yasumaro, 161-62, 258; achievements of, 369-73; quoted, 252-53, 256

Ōama no Ōji. *See* Temmu Tennō

Obasute, 19

Ōbayashi Taryō, 171-72

Obi Kōichi, 26

Ochi o Hirose, 225

Odohime, Kasuga no (Princess), 280

Odyssey, 11, 17, 57, 195, 234, 333

Ōhara Takayasu, 245

"Ōharae" ("Great Purification"), 301

oina, 98

Ōjin Tennō, 119, 193, 194, 238

Okada Masayuki, 310, 318, 379

Okazaki Yoshie, 223

Oke no Ōkimi (Prince; later Ninken
Tennō), 261-64, 295-98

Okime, 154-55, 356

ōkimi (Ch. ta-wang), 364; as title for
tennō, 349

Okina, 108

Okinawan literature. *See* Ryukyuan literature

Ōkuninushi no Mikoto (or Yachihoko no
Ōkuninushi, God of Eight Thousand
Halberds), 100, 127-29, 147-49, 158,
281-84, 356, 361; aliases of, 179

Ōkura. *See* Yamanoe Okura

Ōmiwa Okimori Ason (Lord), 415

Ōmodaka Hisataka, 235, 255, 291

Ōnishi Yoshimori, 13, 50

Ono Jūrō, 38, 40, 93-94

Ōno Susumu, 174-76, 179, 334

Origuchi Shinobu draws parallels between
Ryukyuan and Japanese literature, 95-
98

Osakabe no Miko (Prince), 361-62

Ōshikōchi Mitsune, 27

Oshikuma no Miko (Prince), 118-19

Oshiwa no Ōkimi (Prince), 260-64, 297

Ōta Nampo, 5

Ōta Shigemichi, 371

Ōta Yoshimaro, 145, 163, 189, 204

otogizōshi, defined, 5

Ōtomo Fumimochi, 398

Ōtomo Ikenushi, 241

Ōtomo Momoyo, quoted, 410-11

Ōtomo no Ōji (Crown Prince, later Kōbun Tennō, q.v.), 61, 318-22

Ōtomo Sakanoe no Iratsume (Lady), 223,
407-408; quoted, 393

Ōtomo Tabito, 61, 65, 218-21, 225, 226,
250-51, 384, 405-406, 407, 410, 423;
ornate Chinese prose by, 390-91; Plum
Blossom Banquet of, 397-98; quoted,

Library of Congress Cataloging in Publication Data

Konishi, Jin'ichi, 1915-
A history of Japanese literature.

Includes bibliographies and index.
Contents: 1. The archaic and ancient ages.
1. Japanese literature—History and criticism—
Collected works. I. Miner, Earl Roy. II. Title.
PL717.K6213   1984   895.6'09   83-43082
ISBN 0-691-06592-6   ISBN 0-691-10146-9 (pbk.)

This book has been composed and printed by
Princeton University Press
Designed by Jan Lilly
Typography: Linotron Sabon and Zapf Chancery
Paper: Warren's 1854

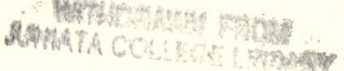